CONTENTS

Quick Reference Specifications For Your Vehicle

Fill in this chart with the most commonly used specifications for your vehicle. Specifications can be found in Chapters 1 through 3 or on the tune-up decal under the hood of the vehicle.

 ## Tune-Up

Firing Order_____

Spark Plugs:

    Type_____

    Gap (in.)_____

Point Gap (in.)_____

Dwell Angle (°)_____

Ignition Timing (°)_____

    Vacuum (Connected/Disconnected)_____

Valve Clearance (in.)

    Intake_____   **Exhaust**_____

 ## Capacities

Engine Oil (qts)

    With Filter Change_____

    Without Filter Change_____

Cooling System (qts)_____

Manual Transmission (pts)_____

    Type_____

Automatic Transmission (pts)_____

    Type_____

Front Differential (pts)_____

    Type_____

Rear Differential (pts)_____

    Type_____

Transfer Case (pts)_____

    Type_____

FREQUENTLY REPLACED PARTS

Use these spaces to record the part numbers of frequently replaced parts.

PCV VALVE	**OIL FILTER**	**AIR FILTER**
Manufacturer_____	Manufacturer_____	Manufacturer_____
Part No._____	Part No._____	Part No._____

CHILTON'S
REPAIR & TUNE-UP GUIDE

FORD
MERCURY
MID-SIZE
1971-82

**Torino 1971-76 • Ranchero 1971-78 • Gran Torino 1972-76
Elite 1974-76 • LTD II 1977-79 • Thunderbird 1977-82
Montego 1971-76 • Cougar 1972-82 • XR-7 1980-82 • Continental 1982**

Managing Editor KERRY A. FREEMAN, S.A.E.
Senior Editor RICHARD J. RIVELE, S.A.E.

President WILLIAM A. BARBOUR
Executive Vice President JAMES A. MIADES
Vice President and General Manager JOHN P. KUSHNERICK

CHILTON BOOK COMPANY
Radnor, Pennsylvania

SAFETY NOTICE

Proper service and repair procedures are vital to the safe, reliable operation of all motor vehicles, as well as the personal safety of those performing repairs. This book outlines procedures for servicing and repairing vehicles using safe, effective methods. The procedures contain many NOTES, CAUTIONS and WARNINGS which should be followed along with standard safety procedures to eliminate the possibility of personal injury or improper service which could damage the vehicle or compromise its safety.

It is important to note that repair procedures and techniques, tools and parts for servicing motor vehicles, as well as the skill and experience of the individual performing the work vary widely. It is not possible to anticipate all of the conceivable ways or conditions under which vehicles may be serviced, or to provide cautions as to all of the possible hazards that may result. Standard and accepted safety precautions and equipment should be used when handling toxic or flammable fluids, and safety goggles or other protection should be used during cutting, grinding, chiseling, prying, or any other process that can cause material removal or projectiles.

Some procedures require the use of tools specially designed for a specific purpose. Before substituting another tool or procedures, you must be completely satisfied that neither your personal safety, nor the performance of the vehicle will be endangered.

Although the information in this guide is based on industry sources and is as complete as possible at the time of publication, the possibility exists that the manufacturer made later changes which could not be included here. While striving for total accuracy, Chilton Book Company cannot assume responsibility for any errors, changes, or omissions that may occur in the compilation of this data.

PART NUMBERS

Part numbers listed in this reference are not recommendations by Chilton for any product by brand name. They are references that can be used with interchange manuals and aftermarket supplier catalogs to locate each brand supplier's discrete part number.

ACKNOWLEDGMENTS

The Chilton Book Company expresses its appreciation to the Ford Motor Company for the technical information and illustrations contained within this manual.

Copyright © 1982 by Chilton Book Company
All Rights Reserved
Published in Radnor, Pa., by Chilton Book Company
and simultaneously in Canada
by VNR Publishers, 1410 Birchmount Road,
Scarborough, Ontario M1P 2E7

Manufactured in the United States of America
1234567890   1098765432

Chilton's Repair & Tune-Up Guide: Ford and Mercury Mid-Size 1971–82
ISBN 0-8019-7194-2 pbk.
Library of Congress Catalog Card No. 81-70239

General Information and Maintenance

HOW TO USE THIS BOOK

This book is designed to enable you, the automotive do-it-yourselfer, to perform all sorts of maintenance, troubleshooting and repair operations. Included are procedures with varying levels of difficulty, from simple fluid checks to complex engine rebuilding techniques. But, regardless of how complicated a particular job may be and regardless of how difficult it may seem, each procedure has been presented with the average do-it-yourselfer in mind. Thus, by following the step-by-step outline, you will be able to perform successfully every operation in this book even if you have never done it before.

Of course, there is no substitute for experience, and for this reason it is suggested that you thoroughly familiarize yourself with all the necessary steps before beginning work. Nothing is more frustrating than to get halfway through a job only to find that you are in need of a certain tool to finish.

Also, safety is an important factor in any service operation. Areas of special hazard are noted in the text, but always use common sense. Here are some general safety rules:

1. When working around gasoline or its vapors, don't smoke, and remember to be careful about sparks which could ignite it.

2. Always support the car securely with jackstands (not milk crates!) if it is necessary to raise it. Don't rely on a tire changing jack as the only means of support. Be sure that the jackstands have a rated load capacity adequate for your car.

3. Block the wheels of the car which remain on the ground, if only one end is being raised. If the front end is being raised, set the parking brake as well.

4. If a car equipped with an automatic transmission must be operated with the engine running and the transmission in gear, always set the parking brake and block the *front* wheels.

5. If the engine is running, watch out for the cooling fan blades. Be sure that clothing, hair, tools, etc., can't get caught in them.

6. If you are using metal tools around or if you are working near the battery terminals, it is a good idea to disconnect it.

7. If you want to crank the engine, but don't want it to start, remove the high-tension lead which runs from the coil to the distributor.

TOOLS AND EQUIPMENT

In order to use this book effectively you must have certain basic tools. A set comprised of the items listed below should be adequate to perform most of the maintenance and light repair operations found in this book:

- Sliding T-bar handle or ratchet wrench;
- ⅜ in. drive socket wrench set (with 12 in. breaker bar);
- Universal adapter for socket wrench set;
- Flat blade and phillips head screwdrivers;
- Pliers;
- Adjustable wrench;
- Locking pliers;
- Open-end wrench set;
- Feeler gauge set;
- Oil filter strap wrench;
- Brake adjusting spoon;
- Drift pin;
- Torque wrench;
- Hammer.

Along with the above mentioned tools, the following equipment should be on hand:

- Scissors jack or hydraulic jack of sufficient capacity;
- Jackstands of sufficient capacity;
- Wheel blocks;
- Grease gun (hand-operated type);
- Drip pan (low and wide);
- Drop light;
- Tire pressure gauge;
- Penetrating oil (spray lubricant);
- Waterless hand cleaner.

In addition, the following items will prove to be well worth their dollar investment in terms of performance and fuel economy:

- 12-volt test light;
- Compression gauge;
- Manifold vacuum gauge;
- Power timing light;
- Dwell-techometer.

Special Tools

Some repair procedures in this book call for the use of special factory tools. Although every effort is made to explain the repair job using your regular set of tools, sometimes the use of a special tool cannot be avoided. These tools are obtainable from your local Ford dealer or can be ordered directly through the Owatonna Tool Company, Owatonna, Minnesota, 55060.

SERVICING YOUR VEHICLE SAFELY

It is virtually impossible to anticipate all of the hazards involved with automotive main-tenance and service but care and common sense will prevent most accidents.

The rules of safety for mechanics range from "don't smoke around gasoline," to "use the proper tool for the job." The trick to avoiding injuries is to develop safe work habits and take every possible precaution.

Do's

- Do keep a fire extinguisher and first aid kit within easy reach.
- Do wear safety glasses or goggles when cutting, drilling, grinding or prying. If you wear glasses for the sake of vision, then they should be made of hardened glass that can serve also as safety glasses, or wear safety goggles over your regular glasses.
- Do shield your eyes whenever you work around the battery. Batteries contain sulphuric acid; in case of contact with the eyes or skin, flush the area with water or a mixture of water and baking soda and get medical attention immediately.
- Do use safety stands for any under-car service. Jacks are for raising vehicles; safety stands are for making sure the vehicle stays raised until you want it to come down. Whenever the vehicle is raised, block the wheels remaining on the ground and set the parking brake.
- Do use adequate ventilation when working with any chemicals. Asbestos dust resulting from brake lining wear can cause cancer.
- Do disconnect the negative battery cable when working on the electrical system. The primary ignition system can contain up to 40,000 volts.
- Do follow manufacturer's directions whenever working with potentially hazardous materials. Both brake fluid and antifreeze are poisonous if taken internally.
- Do properly maintain your tools. Loose hammerheads, mushroomed punches and chisels, frayed or poorly grounded electrical cords, excessively worn screwdrivers, spread wrenches (open end), cracked sockets, slipping ratchets, or faulty droplight sockets can cause accidents.
- Do use the proper size and type of tool for the job being done.
- Do when possible, pull on a wrench handle rather than push on it, and adjust your stance to prevent a fall.
- Do be sure that adjustable wrenches are tightly adjusted on the nut or bolt and pulled so that the face is on the side of the fixed jaw.

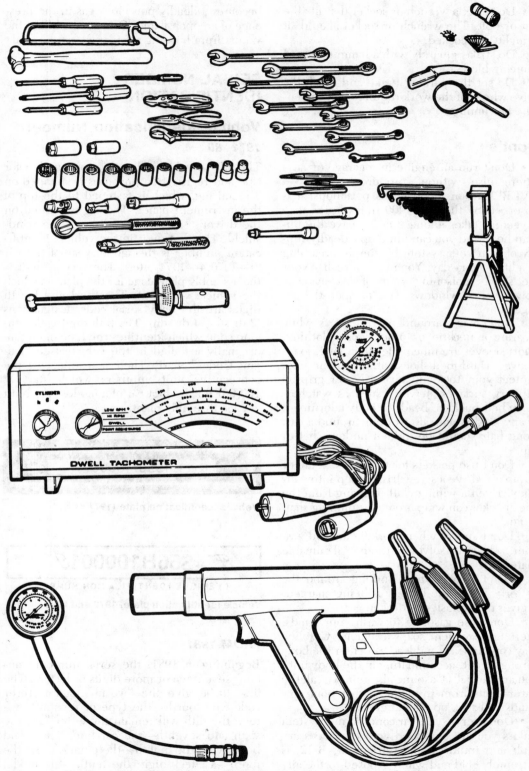

You need this basic assortment of tools for most maintenance and repair jobs

• Do select a wrench or socket that fits the nut or bolt. The wrench or socket should sit straight, not cocked.

• Do strike squarely with a hammer; avoid glancing blows.

• Do set the parking brake and block the drive wheels if the work requires that the engine be running.

Dont's

• Don't run an engine in a garage or anywhere else without proper ventilation—EVER! Carbon monoxide is poisonous; it is absorbed by the body 400 times faster than oxygen; it takes a long time to leave the human body and you can build up a deadly supply of it in your system by simply breathing in a little every day. You may not realize your are slowly poisoning yourself. Always use power vents, windows, fans or open the garage doors.

• Don't work around moving parts while wearing a necktie or other loose clothing. Short sleeves are much safer than long, loose sleeves. Hard-toed shoes with neoprene soles protect your toes and give a better grip on slippery surfaces. Jewelry such as watches, fancy belt buckles, beads or body adornment of any kind is not safe working around a car. Long hair should be hidden under a hat or cap.

• Don't use pockets for toolboxes. A fall or bump can drive a screwdriver deep into your body. Even a wiping cloth hanging from the back pocket can wrap around a spinning shaft or fan.

• Don't smoke when working around gasoline, cleaning solvent or other flammable material.

• Don't smoke when working around the battery. When the battery is being charged, it gives off explosive hydrogen gas.

• Don't use gasoline to wash your hands; there are excellent soaps available. Gasoline may contain lead, and lead can enter the body through a cut, accumulating in the body until you are very ill. Gasoline also removes all the natural oils from the skin so that bone dry hands will suck up oil and grease.

• Don't service the air conditioning system unless you are equipped with the necessary tools and training. The refrigerant, R-12, is extremely cold and when exposed to the air, will instantly freeze any surface it comes in contact with, including your eyes. Although the refrigerant is normally non-toxic, R-12

becomes a deadly poisonous gas in the presence of an open flame. One good whiff of the vapors from burning refrigerant can be fatal.

SERIAL NUMBER IDENTIFICATION

Vehicle Identification Number

1971–80

The official vehicle identification number for title and registration purposes is stamped on a metal tag, which is fastened to the top of the instrument panel. The tag is located on the driver's side, visible through the windshield. The first digit in the vehicle identification number is the model year of the car (0—1970, 4—1974, etc.). The second digit is the assembly plant code for the plant in which the vehicle was built. The third and fourth digits are the body serial code designations (2-dr sdn, 4-dr sdn). The fifth digit is the engine code which identifies the type of engine originally installed in the vehicle (see "Engine Codes" chart). The last six digits are the consecutive unit numbers which start at 100,001 for the first car of a model year built at each assembly plant.

Vehicle identification plate (1971 only)

F **4S56H100001** *F*

(VEHICLE IDENTIFICATION NUMBER)

Vehicle identification plate, 1972 and later

FROM 1981

Beginning in 1981, the serial number contains seventeen or more digits or letters. The first three give the "world" manufacturer code; the fourth—the type of restraint system; the fifth will remain the letter "P"; the sixth and seventh—the car line, series and body type; the eighth—the engine type; the ninth—a check digit; the tenth—the model year; the eleventh—the assembly plant; the remaining numbers are the production sequence.

Vehicle Certification Label

The vehicle certification label is attached to the left door lock pillar on 2-door models and on the rear face of the driver's door on 4-door models. The top half of the label contains the name of the vehicle manufacturer, date of manufacture and the manufacturer's certification statement. On 1973 and later models, the top half of the label also contains the gross vehicle weight rating and the front and rear gross vehicle axle ratings. The gross vehicle weight rating is useful in determining the load carrying capacity of your car. Merely subtract the curb weight from the posted gross weight and what is left over is how much you can haul around. The bottom half of the vehicle certification label contains the vehicle identification number (as previously described), the body type code, the exterior paint color code, the interior trim color and material code, the rear axle code (see "Rear Axle Codes" chart), the transmission code (see Transmission Codes" chart) and the district and special order codes.

The vehicle certification label is constructed of special material to guard against its alteration. If it is tampered with or removed, it will be destroyed or the word "VOID" will appear.

NOTE: *Windsor and Cleveland versions of the 351 2 bbl engine were used interchangeably through 1974. Starting 1975,*

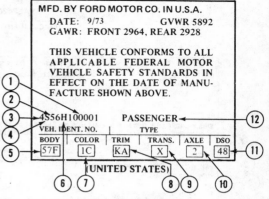

① CONSECUTIVE UNIT NO.
② BODY SERIAL CODE
③ MODEL YEAR CODE
④ ASSEMBLY PLANT CODE
⑤ ENGINE CODE
⑥ BODY TYPE CODE
⑦ COLOR CODE
⑧ VEHICLE TYPE
⑨ DISTRICT—SPECIAL EQUIPMENT
⑩ REAR AXLE CODE
⑪ TRANSMISSION CODE
⑫ TRIM CODE

Vehicle certification label, 1973–80

Windsor and Modified Cleveland engines were used. A quick visual means of identification is the location of the thermostat housing/water outlet; Windsor engines have it mounted to the front face of the intake manifold, Cleveland and Modified Cleveland engines have it on top of the engine block.

ROUTINE MAINTENANCE

Air Cleaner

At the recommended intervals of the maintenance chart, the air filter element must be replaced. If the vehicle is operated under severely dusty conditions, the element should be changed sooner. On all six and 8 cylinder models, the air filter cover is retained with a single wing nut on top of and in the center of the cover. To replace the element, unscrew the wing nut, lift off the cover and discard the old element.

While the air cleaner is removed, check the choke plate and external linkage for freedom of movement. Brush away all dirt and spray the plate corners and linkage with a small amount of penetrating cleaner/lubricant such as CRC®.

Wipe the air filter housing clean with a sol-

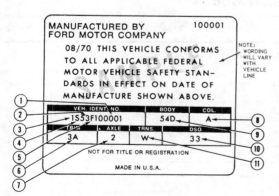

① CONSECUTIVE UNIT NO.
② BODY SERIAL CODE
③ MODEL YEAR CODE
④ ASSEMBLY PLANT CODE
⑤ ENGINE CODE
⑥ TRIM CODE
⑦ REAR AXLE CODE
⑧ COLOR CODE
⑨ BODY TYPE CODE
⑩ DISTRICT—SPECIAL EQUIPMENT CODE
⑪ TRANSMISSION CODE

Vehicle certification label (1971–72)

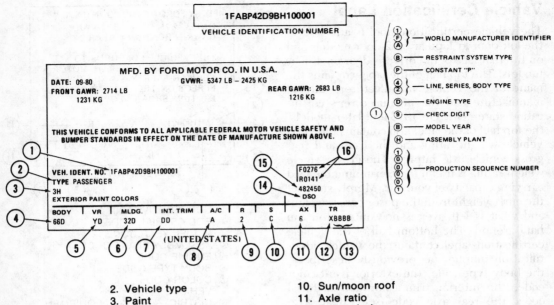

2. Vehicle type
3. Paint
4. Body type code
5. Vinyl roof
6. Body side moulding
7. Trim code—(First code letter = fabric and seat type. Second code = color)
8. Air conditioning
9. Radio
10. Sun/moon roof
11. Axle ratio
12. Transmission
13. Springs—Front l. and r., rear l. and r. (4 codes)
14. District sales office
15. PTO/SPL order number
16. Accessory reserve load

1981–82 vehicle identification

Transmission Codes

Type	'71	'72	'73	'74	'75	'76	'77	'78	'79	'80	'81	'82
3-speed manual	1	1	1	1	—	—	—	—	—	—	—	—
4-speed manual	6	6	6	—	—	—	—	—	—	4	4	4
C4 automatic	W	W	W	W	—	—	—	W	W	W	—	—
C5 automatic	—	—	—	—	—	—	—	—	—	—	—	C
AOD*	—	—	—	—	—	—	—	—	—	T	T	T
FMX automatic	X	X	X	X	X	X	X	X	X	X	—	—
CW automatic	—	—	—	Y	Y	—	—	—	—	—	—	—
C6 automatic	U	U	U	U	U	U	U	U	U	U	—	—
C6 automatic special (towing)	Z	Z	Z	Z	Z	Z	Z	Z	Z	—	—	—

*Automatic overdrive

Engine Identification Code

The engine code designation through 1980 is the 5th digit of the vehicle identification number. 1981 and later models use the 8th digit for the engine code. The VIN is stamped on a plate located on the left side of the instrument panel, visible through the windshield.

Engine	Carb.	'71	'72	'73	'74	'75	'76	'77	'78	'79	'80	'81	'82
4-140	2-bbl											A	A
6-200	1-bbl											B	B
6-232	2-bbl												3
6-250	1-bbl	L	L	L	L								
8-255	2-bbl										D	D	D
8-302	2-bbl	F	F	F	F			F	F	F	F	F	F
8-351C	2-bbl	H	H	H	H								
8-351C	4-bbl	M											
8-351CJ	4-bbl		Q	Q	Q								
8-351M	2-bbl					Q	Q	Q	Q	Q			
8-351W	2-bbl			H	H	H	H	H	H	H			
8-400	2-bbl		S	S	S	S	S	S	S				
8-429CJ	4-bbl	C											
8-429	4-bbl		N	N									
8-429CJ-RA	4-bbl	J											
8-460PI	4-bbl				C	C	C	C					
8-460	4-bbl					A	A						

C: Cleveland   CJ: Cobra Jet
M: Modified Cleveland   RA: Ram Air
W: Windsor   PI: Police Interceptor

vent-moistened rag and install the new element with the word "FRONT" facing the front of the car. Install the cover and wing nut finger-tight.

Crankcase Ventilation Filter (*In Air Cleaner*) Replacement

At the recommended intervals in the maintenance chart, or sooner (if the car is operated in dusty areas, at low rpm, for trailer towing, or if the car is used for short runs preventing the engine from reaching operating temperature), the crankcase ventilation filter in the air cleaner must be replaced. Do not attempt to clean this filter.

To replace the filter, simply remove the air filter cover and pull the old crankcase filter out of its housing. Push a new crankcase filter into the housing and install the air filter cover.

Rear Axle Ratio Codes

Ratio	'71	'72	'73	'74	'75	'76	'77	'78	'79	'80	'81	'82
2.26:1	—	—	—	—	—	—	—	—	G	G	—	—
2.47:1	—	—	—	—	—	—	—	B	—	—	—	B(C)
2.50:1	—	—	—	—	—	—	—	1(J)	—	—	—	—
2.73:1	—	—	—	—	—	—	—	—	8(H)	8	8(M)	8(M)
2.75:1	2(K)	2(K)	2(K)	2(K)	2(K)	2(K)	2(K)	2(K)	—	—	—	—
2.80:1	—	—	—	—	—	—	—	—	—	—	—	—
3.00:1	6(O)	6(O)	6(O)	6(O)	6(O)	6(O)	6(O)	6(O)	—	—	—	—
3.07:1	B	—	—	5(E)	5(E)	—	—	—	—	—	—	—
3.08:1	—	—	—	—	—	—	—	—	Y	Y(Z)	Y(Z)	Y(Z)
3.10:1	—	—	—	—	—	—	—	—	—	—	—	—
3.25:1	9(R)	9(R)	9(R)	9(R)	9(R)	9(R)	9(R)	—	—	—	—	—
3.42:1	—	—	—	—	—	—	—	—	—	—	—	4(D)
3.45:1	—	—	—	—	—	—	—	—	—	—	—	F(R)
3.50:1	—	—	—	—	—	—	—	—	—	—	—	—

NOTE: *Figures in Parentheses indicate locking differential.*

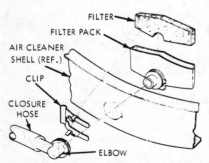

Crankcase ventilation hose and filter pack assembly

PCV Valve

All models use a closed ventilation system with a sealed breather cap connected to the air cleaner by a rubber hose. The PCV valve is mounted in the valve cover and connected to the intake manifold by a rubber hose. Its task is to regulate the amount of crankcase (blow-by) gases which are recycled.

Since the PCV valve works under severe load it is very important that it be replaced at the interval specified in the maintenance chart. Replacement involves removing the valve from the grommet in the rocker arm

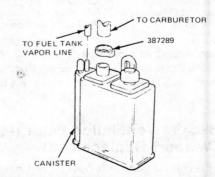

Typical carbon canister

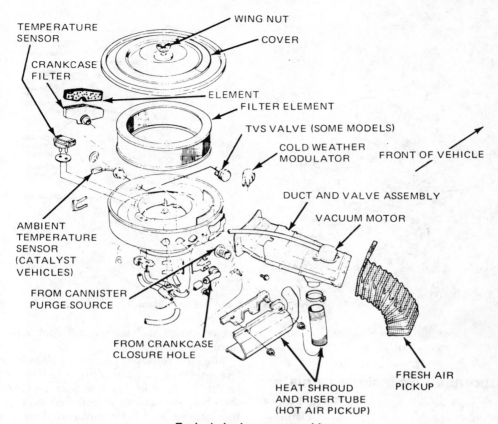

Typical air cleaner assembly

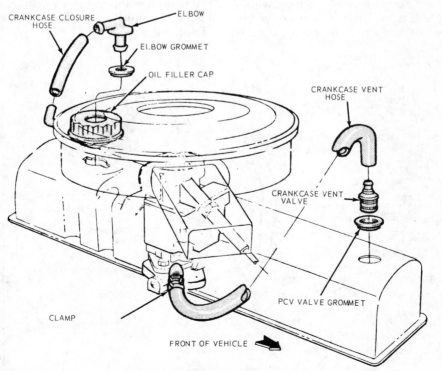

PCV valve installation—6 cylinder

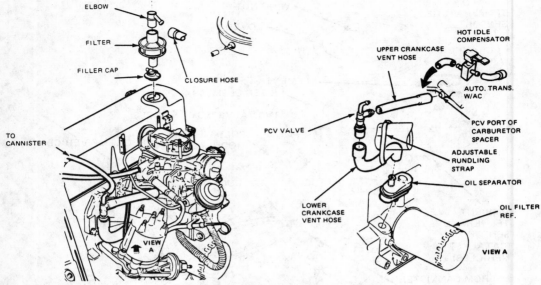

4-140 positive crankcase ventilation system

cover and installing a new valve. Do not attempt to clean a used valve.

Evaporative Emissions Canister

The canister functions to cycle the fuel vapor from the fuel tank into the intake manifold and eventually into the cylinders for combustion. The activated charcoal element within the canister acts as a storage device for the fuel vapor at times when the engine operat-

ing condition will not permit fuel vapor to burn efficiently.

The only required service for the evaporative emissions canister is inspection at the interval specified in the maintenance chart. If the charcoal element is gummed up the entire canister should be replaced. Disconnect the canister purge hose from the air cleaner fitting; loosen the canister retaining bracket; lift out the canister. Installation is the reverse of removal.

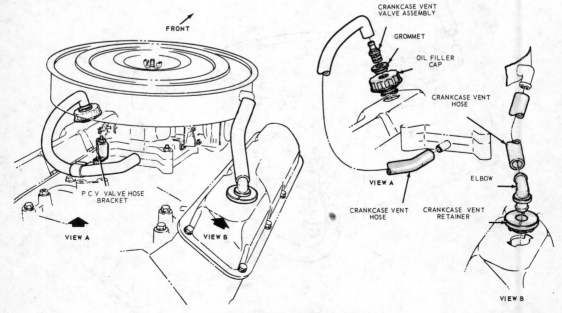

PCV valve installation—302 V8

Drive Belt Adjustment

Once a year or at 12,000 mile intervals, the tension (and condition) of the alternator, power steering (if so equipped), air conditioning (if so equipped), and Thermactor air pump drive belts should be checked, and, if necessary, adjusted. Loose accessory drive belts can lead to poor engine cooling and diminish alternator, power steering pump, air conditioning compressor or Thermactor air pump output. A belt that is too tight places a severe strain on the water pump, alternator, power steering pump, compressor or air pump bearings.

Replace any belt that is so glazed, worn or stretched that it cannot be tightened sufficiently. On vehicles with matched belts, replace both belts. New belts are to be adjusted to a tension of 140 lbs ($\frac{1}{2}$ in., $\frac{3}{8}$ in., and $\frac{15}{32}$ in. wide belts) or 80 lbs ($\frac{1}{4}$ in. wide belts) measured on a belt tension gauge. Any belt that has been operating for a mimimum of 10 minutes is considered a used belt. In the first 10 minutes, the belt should stretch to its maximum extent. After 10 minutes, stop the engine and recheck the belt tension. Belt tension for a used belt should be maintained at 110 lbs (all except $\frac{1}{4}$ in. wide belts) or 60 lbs ($\frac{1}{4}$ in. wide belts). If a belt tension gauge is not available, the following procedures may be used.

ALTERNATOR (FAN DRIVE) BELT

All Except "Serpentine" (Single) Belt

1. Position a ruler perpendicular to the drive belt at its longest run. Test the tightness of the belt by pressing it firmly with your

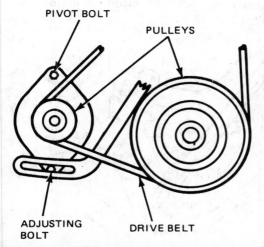

Alternator belt adjustment

PIVOT BOLT

PULLEYS

ADJUSTING BOLT

DRIVE BELT

thumb. The deflection should not exceed $\frac{1}{4}$ in.

2. If the deflection exceeds $\frac{1}{4}$ in., loosen the alternator mounting and adjusting arm bolts.

3a. On 1971–72 V8 and 6 cylinder models, use a pry bar or broom handle to move the alternator toward or away from the engine until the proper tension is reached.

CAUTION: *Apply tension to the front of the alternator only. Positioning the pry bar against the rear end housing will damage the alternator.*

3b. On 1973–82 V8 models, place a 1 in. open-end or adjustable wrench on the adjusting arm bolt and pull on the wrench until the proper tension is achieved.

4. Holding the alternator in place to maintain tension, tighten the adjusting arm bolt. Recheck the belt tension. When the belt is properly tensioned, tighten the alternator mounting bolt.

POWER STEERING DRIVE BELT

All Six-Cylinder and 1971–72 V8 Models

1. Holding a ruler perpendicular to the drive belt at its longest run, test the tightness of the belt by pressing it firmly with your thumb. The deflection should not exceed $\frac{1}{4}$ in.

2. To adjust the belt tension, loosen the adjusting and mounting bolts on the front face of the steering pump cover plate (hub side).

3. Using a pry bar or broom handle on the pump hub, move the power steering pump toward or away from the engine until the proper tension is reached. Do not pry against the reservoir as it is relatively soft and easily deformed.

4. Holding the pump in place, tighten the adjusting arm bolt and then recheck the belt tension. When the belt is properly tensioned tighten the mounting bolts.

1973–82 V8 Models (Except Single Drive Belt)

1. Position a ruler perpendicular to the drive belt at its longest run. Test the tightness of the belt by pressing it firmly with your thumb. The deflection should be about $\frac{1}{4}$ in.

2. To adjust the belt tension, loosen the three bolts in the three elongated adjusting slots at the power steering pump attaching bracket.

3. Turn the steering pump drive belt adjusting nut as required until the proper de-

flection is obtained. Turning the adjusting nut clockwise will increase tension and decrease deflection; counterclockwise will decrease tension and increase deflection.

4. Without disturbing the pump, tighten the three attaching bolts.

AIR CONDITIONING COMPRESSOR DRIVE BELT

1. Position a ruler perpendicular to the drive belt at its longest run. Test the tightness of the belt by pressing it firmly with your thumb. The deflection should not exceed ¼ in.

2. If the engine is equipped with an idler pulley, loosen the idler pulley adjusting bolt, insert a pry bar between the pulley and the engine (or in the idler pulley adjusting slot), and adjust the tension accordingly. If the engine is not equipped with an idler pulley, the alternator must be moved to accomplish this adjustment, as outlined under "Alternator (Fan Drive) Belt."

3. When the proper tension is reached, tighten the idler pulley adjusting bolt (if so equipped) or the alternator adjusting and mounting bolts.

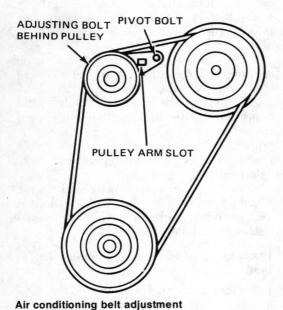

Air conditioning belt adjustment

THERMACTOR AIR PUMP DRIVE BELT

1. Position a ruler perpendicular to the drive belt at its longest run. Test the tightness of the belt by pressing it firmly with your thumb. The deflection should be about ¼ in.

2. To adjust the belt tension, loosen the

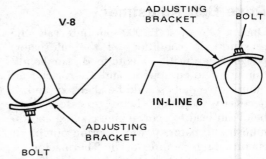

Air pump adjustment points

adjusting arm bolt slightly. If necessary, also loosen the mounting belt slightly.

3. Using a pry bar or broom handle, pry against the pump rear cover to move the pump toward or away from the engine as necessary.

CAUTION: *Do not pry against the pump housing itself, as damage to the housing may result.*

4. Holding the pump in place, tighten the adjusting arm bolt and recheck the tension. When the belt is properly tensioned, tighten the mounting bolt.

SINGLE DRIVE BELT—V8 MODELS
(Serpentine Drive Belt)

Some late models (starting in 1979) feature a single, wide, ribbed V-belt that drives the water pump, alternator and power steering. To install a new belt, simply retract the belt tensioner with a pry bar and slide the old belt off of the pulleys. Slip on a new belt and release the tensioner. The spring powered tensioner eliminates the need for periodic adjustments.

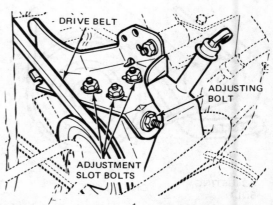

Power steering belt adjustment (slider type)

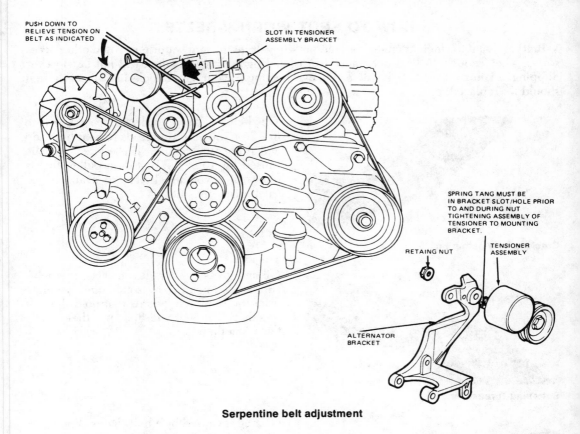

PUSH DOWN TO RELIEVE TENSION ON BELT AS INDICATED

SLOT IN TENSIONER ASSEMBLY BRACKET

SPRING TANG MUST BE IN BRACKET SLOT/HOLE PRIOR TO AND DURING NUT TIGHTENING ASSEMBLY OF TENSIONER TO MOUNTING BRACKET.

RETAING NUT

TENSIONER ASSEMBLY

ALTERNATOR BRACKET

Serpentine belt adjustment

Air Conditioning

CHECKING REFRIGERANT LEVEL

Sight Glass Equipped (1971–74)

First, wipe the sight glass clean with a cloth wrapped around the eraser end of a pencil. Connect a tachometer to the engine with the positive line connected to the distributor side of the ignition coil and the negative line connected to a good ground, such as the steering box. Have a friend operate the air conditioner controls while you look at the sight glass. Have your friend set the dash panel control to maximum cooling. Start the engine and idle at 1,500 rpm. While looking at the sight glass, signal your friend to turn the blower switch to the High position. If a few bubbles appear immediately after the blower is turned on and then disappear, the system is sufficiently charged with refrigerant. If, on the other hand, a large amount of bubbles, foam or froth continue after the blower has operated for a few seconds, then the system is in need of additional refrigerant.

If no bubbles appear at all, then there is either sufficient refrigerant in the system or it is bone dry. To make a determination fol-low the procedure given below for models without a sight glass.

Models Without a Sight Glass

To determine if the refrigerant is at the proper level of charge, turn on the engine and run the air conditioner for a few minutes. Feel the temperature of the hose running from the receiver/dryer and of the hose running to the condensor. They should both be cold and approximately the same temperature. If they are both warm the system probably has no refrigerant. If they are different temperatures there is a malfunction in the system.

CAUTION: *Do not attempt to work on the air conditioning system yourself. Consult a professional garage with the proper testing equipment.*

Fluid Level Checks

ENGINE OIL

The engine oil level should be checked frequently; for instance, at each refueling stop. Be sure that the vehicle is parked on a level surface with the engine off. Also, allow a few minutes after turning off the engine for the

HOW TO SPOT WORN V-BELTS

V-Belts are vital to efficient engine operation—they drive the fan, water pump and other accessories. They require little maintenance (occasional tightening) but they will not last forever. Slipping or failure of the V-belt will lead to overheating. If your V-belt looks like any of these, it should be replaced.

This belt has deep cracks, which cause it to flex. Too much flexing leads to heat build-up and premature failure. These cracks can be caused by using the belt on a pulley that is too small. Notched belts are available for small diameter pulleys.

Cracking or weathering

Oil and grease on a belt can cause the belt's rubber compounds to soften and separate from the reinforcing cords that hold the belt together. The belt will first slip, then finally fail altogether.

Softening (grease and oil)

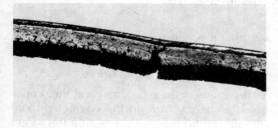

Glazing is caused by a belt that is slipping. A slipping belt can cause a run-down battery, erratic power steering, overheating or poor accessory performance. The more the belt slips, the more glazing will be built up on the surface of the belt. The more the belt is glazed, the more it will slip. If the glazing is light, tighten the belt.

Glazing

The cover of this belt is worn off and is peeling away. The reinforcing cords will begin to wear and the belt will shortly break. When the belt cover wears in spots or has a rough jagged appearance, check the pulley grooves for roughness.

Worn cover

This belt is on the verge of breaking and leaving you stranded. The layers of the belt are separating and the reinforcing cords are exposed. It's just a matter of time before it breaks completely.

Separation

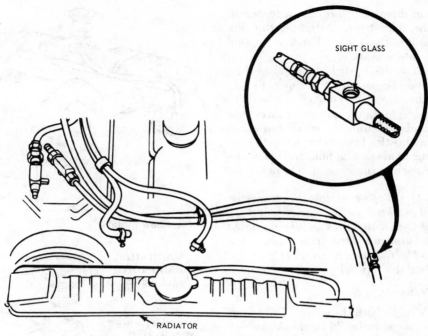

SIGHT GLASS

RADIATOR

Typical air conditioning sight glass location

oil to drain into the pan or an inaccurate reading will result.

1. Open the hood and remove the engine oil dipstick.

2. Wipe the dipstick with a clean, lint-free rag and reinsert it. Be sure to insert it all the way.

3. Pull out the dipstick and note the oil level. It should be between the SAFE (MAX) mark and the ADD (MIN) mark.

4. If the level is below the lower mark, replace the dipstick and add fresh oil to bring the level within the proper range. Do not overfill.

5. Recheck the oil level and close the hood.

NOTE: *Use a multi-grade oil with API classification SE, or SF*

TRANSMISSION FLUID
Automatic Transmission

It is very important to maintain the proper fluid level in an automatic transmission. If the level is either too high or too low, poor shifting operation and internal damage are likely to occur. For this reason a regular check of the fluid level is essential.

1. Drive the vehicle for 15–20 minutes to allow the transmission to reach operating temperature.

2. Park the car on a level surface, apply the parking brake and leave the engine idling. Shift the transmission and engage each gear, then place the gear selector in P (PARK).

3. Wipe away any dirt in the area of the

ADD 2 | ADD 1 → SAFE ← WARRANTY

ADD → SAFE ← WARRANTY

ADD ← SAFE → ← MAX. OVERFILL

(Note lubricant level should be within the safe range) typical engine oil dipstick

° ° ADD)← → DON'T ADD IF BETWEEN ARROWS   CHECK WHEN HOT & IDLING IN PARK

Typical automatic transmission dipstick

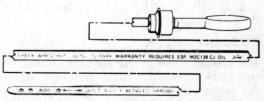

CHECK WHEN HOT   IDLE IN PARK   WARRANTY REQUIRES ESP M2C138 CJ OIL

° ° ADD °← →   ADD IF BETWEEN ARROWS

C-6 automatic transmission dipstick (note the special fluid designation)

transmission dipstick to prevent it from falling into the filler tube. Withdraw the dipstick, wipe it with a clean, lint-free rag and reinsert it until it seats.

4. Withdraw the dipstick and note the fluid level. It should be between the upper (FULL) mark and the lower (ADD) mark.

5. If the level is below the lower mark, use a funnel and add fluid in small quantities through the dipstick filler neck. Keep the engine running while adding fluid and check the level after each small amount. Do not overfill.

NOTE: *Use Type-F automatic transmission fluid in all transmission except the 1977 and later C-6, which uses an oil designated CJ. All Automatic Overdrive models use type CJ. The C-5 uses Dexron® II.*

6. Replace the dipstick.

Manual Transmission

The fluid level in both three-speed and four-speed transmissions should be checked every 6 months/6,000 miles, whichever comes first. All manual transmissions use SAE 90-weight oil.

1. Park the car on a level surface, turn off the engine, apply the parking brake and block the wheels.

2. Remove the filler plug from the side of the transmission case with an adjustable wrench. The fluid level should be even with the bottom of the filler hole.

3. If additional fluid is necessary, add it through the filler hole using a syphon pump.

4. Replace the filler plug; do not overtighten.

BRAKE MASTER CYLINDER

The brake fluid should be checked every 6 months/6,000 miles.

1. Park the car on a level surface and open the hood.

2. Pry the retaining bar on the master cylinder to one side using a screwdriver. Remove the cover and gasket.

3. Fill the reservoir to within ¼ inch of the top, if necessary. Use DOT-3 brake fluid.

4. Install the gasket and cap, and position the retaining bar.

COOLANT CHECK

The coolant level in the radiator should be checked on a monthly basis, preferably when the engine is cold. On a cold engine, the coolant level should be maintained at one inch below the filler neck on vertical flow radia-

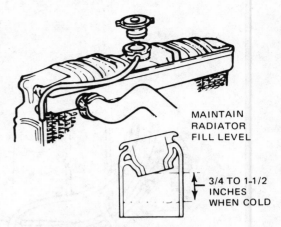

MAINTAIN RADIATOR FILL LEVEL

3/4 TO 1-1/2 INCHES WHEN COLD

Vertical flow radiator

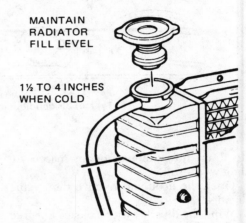

MAINTAIN RADIATOR FILL LEVEL

1½ TO 4 INCHES WHEN COLD

Crossflow radiator

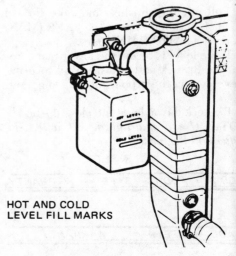

HOT AND COLD LEVEL FILL MARKS

Coolant recovery system

tors, and 2½ in. below the filler neck at the "COLD FILL" mark on crossflow radiators. On cars equipped with the Coolant Recovery System, the level is maintained at the "COLD

HOW TO SPOT BAD HOSES

Both the upper and lower radiator hoses are called upon to perform difficult jobs in an inhospitable environment. They are subject to nearly 18 psi at under hood temperatures often over 280°F., and must circulate nearly 7500 gallons of coolant an hour—3 good reasons to have good hoses.

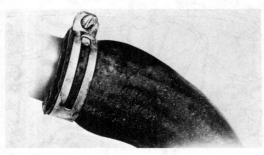

A good test for any hose is to feel it for soft or spongy spots. Frequently these will appear as swollen areas of the hose. The most likely cause is oil soaking. This hose could burst at any time, when hot or under pressure.

Swollen hose

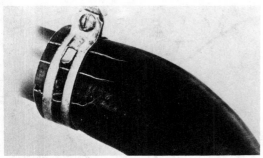

Cracked hoses can usually be seen but feel the hoses to be sure they have not hardened; a prime cause of cracking. This hose has cracked down to the reinforcing cords and could split at any of the cracks.

Cracked hose

Weakened clamps frequently are the cause of hose and cooling system failure. The connection between the pipe and hose has deteriorated enough to allow coolant to escape when the engine is hot.

Frayed hose end (due to weak clamp)

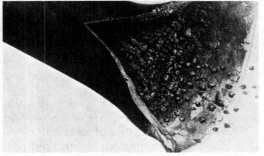

Debris, rust and scale in the cooling system can cause the inside of a hose to weaken. This can usually be felt on the outside of the hose as soft or thinner areas.

Debris in cooling system

LEVEL" mark in the translucent plastic expansion bottle. Top up as necessary with a mixture of 50% water and 50% ethylene glycol antifreeze, to ensure proper rust, freezing and boiling protection. If you have to add coolant more often than once a month or if you have to add more than one quart at a time, check the cooling system for leaks. Also check for water in the crankcase oil, indicating a blown cylinder head gasket.

CAUTION: Exercise extreme care when removing the cap from a hot radiator. Wait a *few minutes until the engine has time to cool somewhat, then wrap a thick towel around the radiator cap and slowly turn it counterclockwise to the first stop. Step back and allow the pressure to release from the cooling system. Then, when the steam has stopped venting, press down on the cap, turn it one more stop counterclockwise and remove the cap.*

Check the Radiator Cap

While you are checking the coolant level, check the radiator cap for a worn or cracked gasket. If the cap doesn't seal properly, fluid will be lost and the engine will overheat.

Worn caps should be replaced with a new one.

Clean Radiator of Debris

Periodically clean any debris—leaves, paper, insects, etc.—from the radiator fins. Pick the large piece off by hand. The smaller pieces can be washed away with water pressure from a hose.

Carefully straighten any bent radiator fins with a pair of needle nose pliers. Be careful—the fins are very soft. Don't wiggle the fins back and forth too much. Straighten them once and try not to move them again.

Drain and Refill the Cooling System

Completely draining and refilling the cooling system every two years at least will remove accumulated rust, scale and other deposits. Coolant in late model vans is a 50–50 mixture of ethylene glycol and water for year round use. Use a good quality antifreeze with water pump lubricants, rust inhibitors and other corrosion inhibitors along with acid neutralizers.

1. Drain the existing antifreeze and coolant. Open the radiator and engine drain petcocks, or disconnect the bottom radiator hose, at the radiator outlet.

NOTE: *Before opening the radiator pet-*

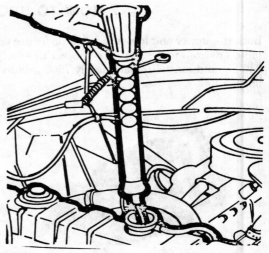

Testing coolant condition with a tester

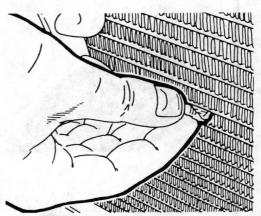

Clean debris from the radiator fins

cock, *spray it with some penetrating lubricant.*

2. Close the petcock or re-connect the lower hose and fill the system with water.

3. Add a can of quality radiator flush.

4. Idle the engine until the upper radiator hose gets hot.

5. Drain the system again.

6. Repeat this process until the drained water is clear and free of scale.

7. Close all petcocks and connect all the hoses.

8. If equipped with a coolant recovery system, flush the reservoir with water and leave empty.

9. Determine the capacity of your cooling system (see capacities specifications). Add a 50/50 mix of quality antifreeze (ethylene glycol) and water to provide the desired protection.

Capacities

Year	Engine No. Cyl Displacement (cu in.)	Engine Crankcase (Add 1 qt for new filter)	Transmission (pts to refill after draining)			Drive Axle (pts)	Gasoline Tank (gals)	Cooling System (qts)	
			Manual		Automatic			W/heater	W A/C
			3 spd	4 spd					
'71	6-250	3.5	3.5	—	18	4	20[3]	11	11
	8-302	4	3.5	—	18	4	20[3]	15	15.5
	8-351	4	3.5	4	22	5	20[3]	15.5	16.5
	8-429	6[2]	—	4	26	5	20[3]	19.5	19.5
'72–'73	6-250	3.5	3.5	—	18	4	22.5[3]	11.5	11.5
	8-302	4	3.5	—	18	4	22.5[3]	15	15
	8-351	4	—	4	20.5[4]	4	22.5[3]	15.5	16
	8-400	4	—	—	26	4	22.5[3]	17.5	17.5
	8-429	4	—	—	26	5	22.5	19	19
'74	6-250	4	—	—	[5]	4	26.5[6]	11.5	—
	8-302	4	3.5	—	[5]	4	26.5[6]	15.7	15.7
	8-351	4	—	—	[7]	4	26.5[6]	[8]	[8]
	8-400	4	—	—	25	5	26.5[6]	17.7	18.3
	8-460	6	—	—	25	5	26.5[6]	18.9	19.5
'75	8-351	3½[11]	—	—	[9]	4	26.5[6]	[10]	[10]
	8-400	3½[11]	—	—	[9]	5	26.5[6]	17.1	17.5
	8-460	4	—	—	[9]	5	26.5[6]	19.2	19.2
'76	8-351	4	—	—	[9]	5	26.5[6]	[10]	[10]
	8-400	4	—	—	[9]	5	26.5[6]	17.1	17.5[13]
	8-460	4[1]	—	—	24.4	5	26.5[6]	19.2	19.2[14]
'77–'78	8-302	4	—	—	22	4	26.0[6]	14.8	15.1
	8-351	4	—	—	[17]	5	26.0[6][12]	[15]	[15]
	8-400	4	—	—	[18]	5	26.0[6]	17.0[16]	17.0[16]
'79	8-302	4	—	—	[19]	5	[20]	14.6	14.6

Capacities (cont.)

Year	Engine No. Cyl Displacement (cu in.)	Engine Crankcase (Add 1 qt for new filter)	Transmission (pts to refill after draining) Manual 3 spd	4 spd	Automatic	Drive Axle (pts)	Gasoline Tank (gals)	Cooling System (qts) W/heater	W A/C
'79	8-351W	4	—	—	⑲	5	⑳	15.7	15.7
	8-351M	4	—	—	⑲	5	⑳	16.5	16.5
'80–'81	4-140	4	—	2.8	16	3.5	14.7	8.6	8.6
	6-200	4	—	—	16	3.5	㉒	㉓	㉓
	8-255	4	—	—	20㉑	3.5	㉒	13.2	13.3
	8-302	4	—	—	20㉑	3.5	17.5	12.7	12.8
'82	4-140	4	—	—	16	㉕	16.0㉖	10.2	10.2
	6-200	4	—	—	22	3.25	21.0㉗	8.4	8.4
	6-231	4	—	—	24㉔	3.25	㉘	8.3	8.3
	8-255	4	—	—	24	3.25	21.0	14.9	15.0
	8-302	4	—	—	24	3.25	22.6	13.3	13.4

① 460 police is 4
② 429 4 bbl—4 qts
  429 CJ, SCJ—6 qts
  add 1 qt if equipped with oil cooler
③ Less 2 gals—station wagon, Ranchero
④ 26 pts for 351 CJ
⑤ C4—18 or 20 pts; FMX—22 pts
⑥ Station wagon—21.2 gallons
⑦ 351 2V with C4—20 pts; 351 2V with FMX—22 pts;
  351 2V with C6—25 pts; 351 4V with C6—21 pts
⑧ 351W 2v—16.4 qts w/heater; 16.8 w/AC
  351C 2v—15.9 qts w/heater; 16.5 w/AC
  351C 4v—15.9 qts w/heater; 16.9 w/AC
⑨ C4—20 pts; FMX—22 pts; C6—25 pts
⑩ 351 Windsor—15.9 qts w/heater; 16.2 w/AC
  351 Modified—17.1 qts w/heater; 17.5 w/AC; 18.0 police
⑪ Add only ½ qt of oil for new service filter
⑫ T-bird w/351 for Calif.—22.0
⑬ Police or heavy trailer tow—18.0
⑭ Police or heavy trailer tow—19.7
⑮ 351W—15.9 w/heater; 16.2 w/AC
  351M—17.0 w/heater or w/AC; 17.5 police and taxi

⑯ 17.5 police
⑰ 351W with C4—20½; with FMX—22
  351M with C6—24½; with FMX—22
⑱ With C6—24½; with FMX—22
— Not applicable
⑲ All except Versailles: C4—21; C6—25; FMX—22
  Versailles: 20
⑳ All except Versailles: 21.0
  Versailles: 19.2
  Optional tank: 27.5
㉑ Automatic Overdrive: 24
㉒ XR-7 and Thunderbird: 17.5
  Cougar: 16.0
㉓ XR-7 and Thunderbird: 13.0
  Cougar: 8.1
㉔ Cougar: 22
㉕ 6.75" axle: 2.5
  7.5" axle: 3.5
㉖ Optional tank: 20.0
㉗ Cougar: 16.0 with opt. 20.0
㉘ All exc. Cougar & Continental: 21.0
  Cougar: 16.0 with opt. 20.0
  Continental: 20.0 with opt. 22.6

10. Run the engine to operating temperature.

11. Stop the engine and check the coolant level.

12. Check the level of protection with an anti-freeze tester, replace the cap and check for leaks.

REAR AXLE FLUID CHECK

The fluid level in the rear axle should be checked at six-month or 6,000 mile intervals. It is not necessary to periodically drain the fluid. The factory fill should remain in the housing for the life of the vehicle, except when repairs are made. When adding to or replacing rear axle fluid SAE 90 hypoid gear lubricant. Limited-slip differentials require special fluid and locking differential additive.

1. Park the car on a level surface, turn off the engine, set the parking brake and block the wheels.

2. Remove the filler plug from the rear axle housing. The fluid level should be wihin ¼ inch of the filler plug hole.

3. If necessary, add fluid with a syphon pump.

4. Reinstall the filler plug.

MANUAL STEERING GEAR LUBRICANT CHECK

If there is binding in the steering gear or if the wheels do not return to a straight-ahead position after a turn, the lubricant level of the steering gear should be checked. Remove the filler plug using a $^{11}/_{16}$ in. open-end wrench and remove the lower cover bolt using a $^{9}/_{16}$ in. wrench, to expose both holes. Slowly turn the steering wheel to the left until it stops. At this point, lubricant should be rising in the lower cover bolt hole. Then slowly turn the steering wheel to the right until it stops. At this point, lubricant should be rising in the filler plug hole. If the lubricant does not rise when the wheel is turned, add a small amount of SAE 90 steering gear lubricant until it does. Replace the cover bolt and the filler plug when finished.

POWER STEERING RESERVOIR FLUID CHECK

The level of the fluid in the power steering reservoir should be checked every six months or 6,000 miles. Run the engine until the fluid is at normal operating temperature. Turn the steering wheel from lock to lock several times and turn off the engine. Remove the filler cap and wipe clean the small dipstick attached to it. Reinsert the dipstick by tightening the cap, and then remove it again and check the level. The fluid should show on the dipstick at any point below the FULL mark. Add automatic transmission fluid if necessary. Do not overfill.

Battery

FLUID LEVEL (EXCEPT "MAINTENANCE FREE" BATTERIES)

Check the battery electrolyte level at least once a month, or more often in hot weather or during periods of extended car operation. The level can be checked through the case on translucent polypropylene batteries; the cell caps must be removed on other models. The electrolyte level in each cell should be kept filled to the split ring inside, or the line marked on the outside of the case.

If the level is low, add only distilled water, or colorless, odorless drinking water, through the opening until the level is correct. Each cell is completely separate from the others, so each must be checked and filled individually.

If water is added in freezing weather, the car should be driven several miles to allow

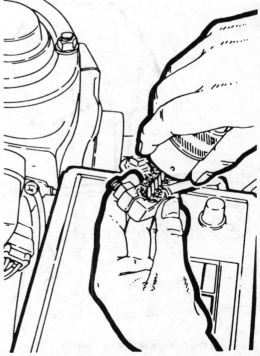

Clean the battery cable clamps with a wire brush

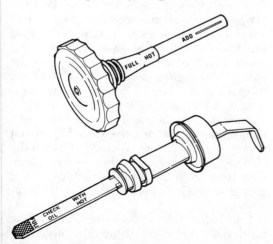

Typical power steering pump reservoir dipsticks

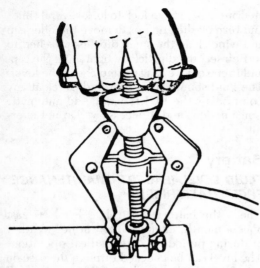

Use a puller to remove the battery cable

the water to mix with the electrolyte. Otherwise, the battery could freeze.

SPECIFIC GRAVITY (EXCEPT "MAINTENANCE FREE" BATTERIES)

At least once a year, check the specific gravity of the battery. It should be between 1.20 and 1.26 at room temperature.

The specific gravity can be checked with the use of an hydrometer, an inexpensive instrument available from many sources, in-

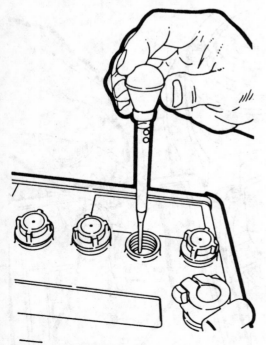

Checking the battery with a hydrometer

cluding auto parts stores. The hydrometer has a squeeze bulb at one end and a nozzle at the other. Battery electrolyte is sucked into the hydrometer until the float is lifted from its seat. The specific gravity is then read by noting the position of the float. Generally, if after charging, the specific gravity between any two cells varies more than 50 points (.50), the battery is bad and should be replaced.

It is not possible to check the specific gravity in this manner on sealed ("maintenance free") batteries. Instead, the indicator built into the top of the case must be relied on to display any signs of battery deterioration. If the indicator is dark, the battery can be assumed to be OK. If the indicator is light, the specific gravity is low, and the battery should be charged or replaced.

CABLES AND CLAMPS

Once a year, the battery terminals and the cable clamps should be cleaned. Loosen the clamps and remove the cables, negative cable first. On batteries with posts on top, the use of a puller specially made for the purpose is recommended. These are inexpensive, and available in auto parts stores. Side terminal battery cables are secured with a bolt.

Clean the cable clamps and the battery terminal with a wire brush, until all corrosion, grease, etc. is removed and the metal is shiny. It is especially important to clean the inside of the clamp thoroughly, since a small deposit of foreign material or oxidation there will prevent a sound electrical connection and inhibit either starting or charging. Special tools are available for cleaning these parts, one type for conventional batteries and another type for side terminal batteries.

Before installing the cables, loosen the battery hold-down clamp or strap, remove the battery and check the battery tray. Clear it of any debris, and check it for soundness. Rust should be wire brushed away, and the metal given a coat of anti-rust paint. Replace the battery and tighten the hold-down clamp or strap securely, but be careful not to overtighten, which will crack the battery case.

After the clamps and terminals are clean, reinstall the cables, negative cable last; do not hammer on the clamps to install. Tighten the clamps securely, but do not distort them. Give the clamps and terminals a thin external coat of grease after installation, to retard corrosion.

Check the cables at the same time that the terminals are cleaned. If the cable insulation is cracked or broken, or if the ends are frayed, the cable should be replaced with a new cable of the same length and gauge.

NOTE: *Keep flame or sparks away from the battery; it gives off explosive hydrogen gas. Battery electrolyte contains sulphuric acid. If you should splash any on your skin or in your eyes, flush the affected area with plenty of clear weater; if it lands in your eyes, get medical help immediately.*

Tires and Wheels

Inspect the tires regularly for wear and damage. Remove stones or other foreign particles which may be lodged in the tread. If tread wear is excessive or irregular it could be a sign of front end problems, or simply improper inflation.

The inflation should be checked at least once per month and adjusted if necessary. The tires must be cold (driven less than one mile) or an inaccurate reading will result. Do not forget to check the spare.

The correct inflation pressure for your vehicle can be found on a decal mounted to the car. Depending upon model and year, the decal can be located at the driver's door, the passenger's door or the glove box. If you cannot find the decal a local automobile tire dealer can furnish you with the information.

TIRE ROTATION

Tires should be rotated periodically to get the maximum tread life available. A good time to do this is when changing over from regular tires to snow tires, or about once per year. If front end problems are suspected have them corrected before rotating the tires. Torque the lug nuts to 70–115 ft. lbs.

Fuel Filter

All engines use an in-line disposable type fuel filter, located at the carburetor fuel inlet. Replace the fuel filter according to the schedule found in the maintenance chart.

1. Remove the air cleaner and place a rag directly below the fuel filter.

2. Loosen the retaining clamps securing the fuel inlet hose to the fuel filter.

3. Unscrew the fuel filter from the carburetor and discard the gasket, if so equipped. Disconnect the fuel filter from the inlet hose and discard the retaining clamps.

4. Install a new clamp on the inlet hose and reconnect the hose to the new filter. Screw the new filter into the carburetor inlet port and tighten it.

5. Position the fuel line hose clamps and crimp the clamps securely.

6. Start the engine and check for fuel leaks.

7. Install the air cleaner.

LUBRICATION

Engine Oil and Filter Change

At the recommended intervals in the maintenance schedule, the oil and filter are changed. After the engine has reached oper-

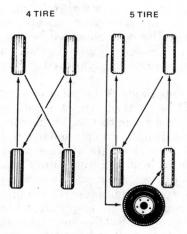

BIAS AND BIAS BELTED TIRES

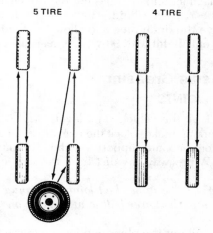

RADIAL PLY TIRES

Tire rotation diagram

ating temperature, shut it off, firmly apply the parking brake, block the wheels, place a drip pan beneath the oil pan and remove the drain plug. Allow the engine to drain thoroughly before replacing the drain plug. Place the drip pan beneath the oil filter. To remove the filter, turn it counterclockwise using a strap wrench. Wipe the contact surface of the new filter clean of all dirt and coat the rubber gasket with clean engine oil. Clean the mating surface of the adapter on the block. To install, hand turn the new filter clockwise until the gasket just contacts the cylinder block. Do not use a strap wrench to install. Then hand-turn the filter ½ additional turn. Unscrew the filter cap on the valve cover and fill the crankcase to the proper level on the dipstick with the recommended grade of oil. Install the cap, start the engine and operate at fast idle. Check the oil filter contact area and the drain plug for leaks.

Transmission Fluid (and Filter) Change

Both the manual and automatic transmissions require no fluid or filter change as a part of normal maintenance. The only time it will be necessary to change the fluid is if the transmission is being disassembled.

On Manual transmissions, remove the drain plug and allow the oil to drain out. Refill with 90-weight gear oil. For automatic transmission servicing refer to Chapter 6.

Rear Axle Fluid Change

Normal maintenance does not require changing the rear axle fluid. However, to do so, remove the drain plug and allow the fluid to drain out. Refill with 90-weight gear oil.

Chassis Greasing

BALL JOINTS

1. Park the vehicle on a level surface, set the parking brake, block the rear wheels, raise the front end and support it with jack stands.
2. Wipe away any dirt from the ball joint lubrication plugs.
NOTE: *The upper ball joint has a plug on the top; the lower ball joint has one on the bottom.*
3. Pull out the plugs and install grease fittings.
4. Using a hand-operated grease gun con-

taining multi-purpose grease, force lubricant into the joint until the joint boot swells.
5. Remove the grease fitting and push in the lubrication plug.
6. Lower the vehicle.

STEERING ARM STOPS

The steering arm stops are attached to the lower control arm. They are located between each steering arm and the upturned end of the front suspension strut.

1. Park the vehicle on a level surface, set the parking brake, block the rear wheels, raise the front end and support it with jack stands.
2. Clean the friction points and apply multi-purpose grease.
3. Lower the vehicle.

Body Lubrication

Lubricate lock cylinders with graphite grease. Use a light grease on the hood and door hinges, and motor oil on the hood and door latches. Silicone spray lubricant can be used on seat tracks and noisy door glass weatherstripping.

Front Wheel Bearings

These should be repacked with grease whenever performing a brake job. Refer to Chapter 9, "Brakes" for procedure.

Heat Riser

Some models are equipped with exhaust control (heat riser) valves located near the head pipe connection in the exhaust manifold. These valves aid initial warmup in cold weather by restricting exhaust gas flow slightly. The heat generated by this restriction is transferred to the intake manifold where it results in improved fuel vaporization.

The operation of the exhaust control valve should be checked every 6 months or 6,000 miles. Make sure that the thermostatic spring is hooked on the stop pin and that the tension holds the valve shut. Rotate the counterweight by hand and make sure that it moves freely through about 90° of rotation. A valve which is operating properly will open when light finger pressure is applied (cold engine). Lubricate the shaft bushings with a mixture of penetrating oil and graphite. Operate the valve manually a few times to work in the lubricant.

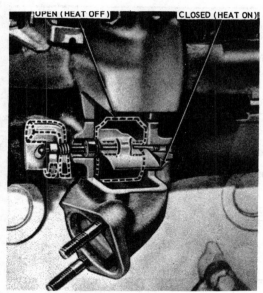

Six cylinder heat riser

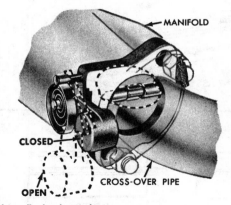

Eight cylinder heat riser

Windshield Wipers

For maximum effectiveness and longest element life, the windshield and wiper blades should be kept clean. Dirt, tree sap, road tar and so on will cause streaking, smearing and blade deterioration if left on the glass. It is advisable to wash the windshield carefully with a commercial glass cleaner at least once a month. Wipe off the rubber blades with the wet rag afterwards. Do not attempt to move the wipers by hand; damage to the motor and drive mechanism will result.

If the blades are found to be cracked, broken or torn, they should be replaced immediately. Replacement intervals will vary with usage, although ozone deterioration usually limits blade life to about one year. If the wiper pattern is smeared or streaked, or if the blade

chatters across the glass, the elements should be replaced. It is easiest and most sensible to replace the elements in pairs.

There are basically three different types of refills, which differ in their method of replacement. One type has two release buttons, approximately one-third of the way up from the ends of the blade frame. Pushing the buttons down releases a lock and allows the rubber filler to be removed from the frame. The new filler slides back into the frame and locks in place.

The second type of refill has two metal tabs which are unlocked by squeezing them together. The rubber filler can then be withdrawn from the frame jaws. A new refill is installed by inserting the refill into the front frame jaws and sliding it rearward to engage the remaining frame jaws. There are usually four jaws; be certain when installing that the refill is engaged in all of them. At the end of its travel, the tabs will lock into place on the front jaws of the wiper blade frame.

The third type is a refill made from polycarbonate. The refill has a simple locking device at one end which flexes downward out of the groove into which the jaws of the holder fit, allowing easy release. By sliding the new refill through all the jaws and pushing through the slight resistance when it reaches the end of its travel, the refill will lock into position.

Regardless of the type of refill used, make sure that all of the frame jaws are engaged as the refill is pushed into place and locked. The metal blade holder and frame will scratch the glass if allowed to touch it.

ARM AND BLADE REPLACEMENT

A detailed description and procedures for replacing the wiper arm and blade is found in Chapter five.

PUSHING AND TOWING

When using jumper cables to jump start a car, a few precautions must be taken to avoid both charging system damage and damage to yourself should the battery explode. The old "positive to positive and negative to negative" jumper cable rule of thumb has been scrapped for a new revised procedure (see the special "jump starting" page at the end of this chapter). Here it is. First, remove all the battery cell covers and cover the cell openings with a clean, dry cloth. Then, connect the positive cable of the assist battery to the positive pole

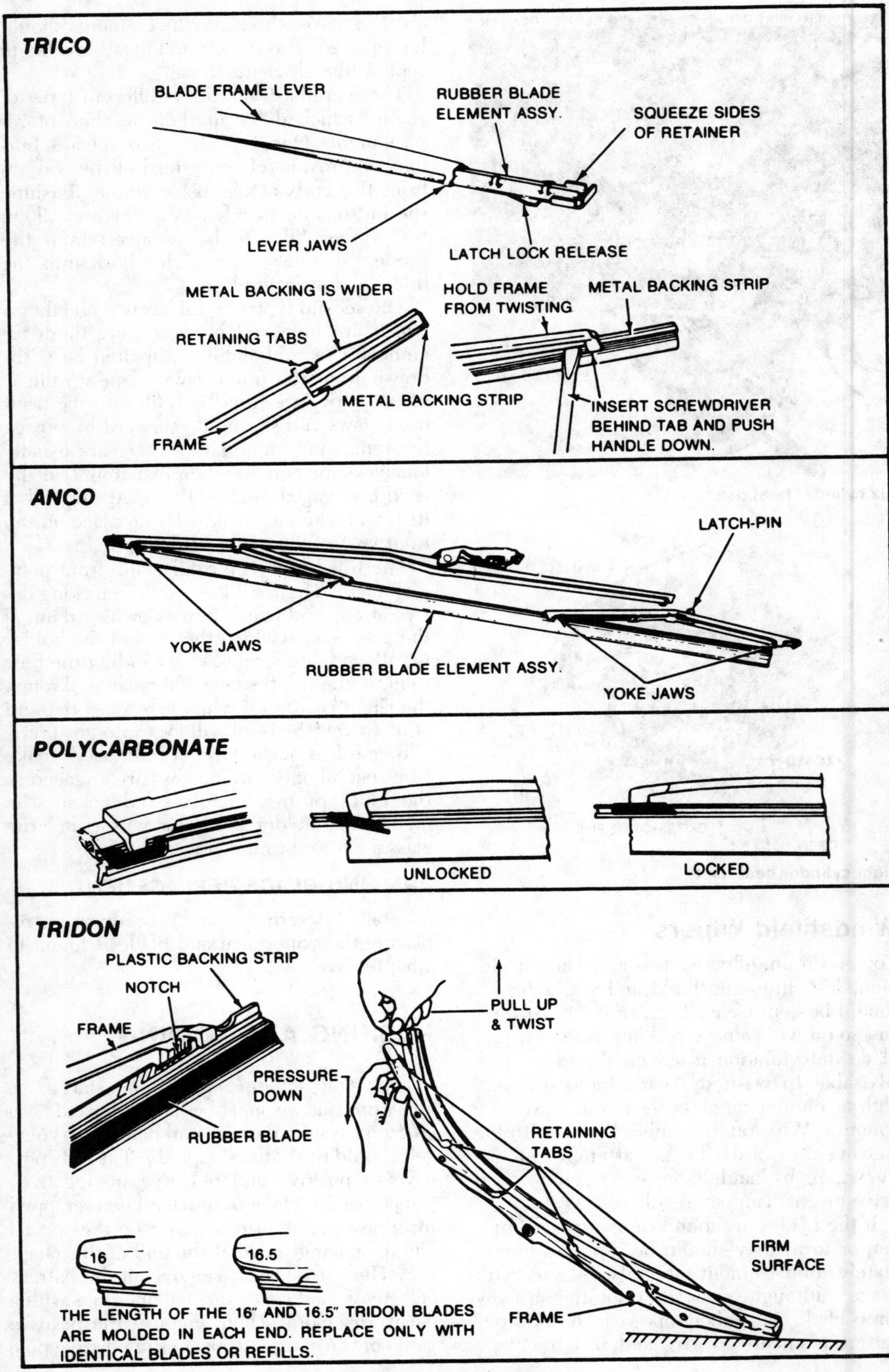

TRICO

BLADE FRAME LEVER

RUBBER BLADE ELEMENT ASSY.

SQUEEZE SIDES OF RETAINER

LEVER JAWS

LATCH LOCK RELEASE

METAL BACKING IS WIDER

HOLD FRAME FROM TWISTING

METAL BACKING STRIP

RETAINING TABS

METAL BACKING STRIP

FRAME

INSERT SCREWDRIVER BEHIND TAB AND PUSH HANDLE DOWN.

ANCO

LATCH-PIN

YOKE JAWS

RUBBER BLADE ELEMENT ASSY.

YOKE JAWS

POLYCARBONATE

UNLOCKED

LOCKED

TRIDON

PLASTIC BACKING STRIP

NOTCH

FRAME

PULL UP & TWIST

PRESSURE DOWN

RUBBER BLADE

RETAINING TABS

FIRM SURFACE

16

16.5

FRAME

THE LENGTH OF THE 16" AND 16.5" TRIDON BLADES ARE MOLDED IN EACH END. REPLACE ONLY WITH IDENTICAL BLADES OR REFILLS.

Wiper insert replacement

of your battery to the engine block of your car. This will prevent the possibility of a spark from the negative assist cable igniting the highly explosive hydrogen and oxygen battery fumes. Once your car is started, allow the engine to return to idle speed before disconnecting the jumper cables, and don't cross the cables. Replace the cell covers and discard the cloth. Now if your car fails to start by jump starting and it is equipped with manual transmission, it may be push started. Cars equipped with automatic transmission cannot be push started. If the bumper of the car pushing you and your car's bumper do not match perfectly, it is wise to tie an old tire either on the back of your car or on the front of the pushing car. This will avoid unnecessary trips to the body shop. To push start the car, switch the ignition to the "ON" position (not the "START" position) and depress the clutch pedal. Place the transmission in Third gear and hold the accelerator pedal about halfway down. When the car speed reaches about 10 mph, gradually release the clutch pedal and the engine should start.

If all else fails and the car must be towed to a garage, there are a few precautions that must be observed. If the transmission and rear axle are in proper working order, the car can be towed with the rear wheels on the ground for distances under 15 miles at speeds no greater than 30 mph. If the transmission or rear is known to be damaged or if the car has to be towed over 15 miles or over 30 mph, the car must be towed with the rear wheels raised and the steering wheel locked so that the front wheels remain in the straight-ahead position.

NOTE: *IF the ignition key is not available to unlock the steering and transmission lock system, it will be necessary to dolly the car under the rear wheels with the front wheels raised.*

JACKING AND HOISTING

When it becomes necessary to raise the car for service, proper safety precautions must be taken. Fords and Mercurys are equipped with bumper jacks. These jacks are fine for changing a tire, but never crawl under the car when it is supported only by the bumper jack. If the jack should slip or tip over, as jacks sometimes do, you would be pinned under 2 tons of automobile.

When raising the car with the bumper jack to change a tire, follow these precautions: Fully apply the parking brake, block the wheel diagonally opposite the wheel to be raised, stop the engine, place the gear lever in Park (automatic) or 1st or Reverse gear (manual), and make sure that the jack is firmly planted on a level, solid surface. Notches are provided in the bumpers to insert the jack hook.

If you are going to work beneath the car, always install jackstands beneath an adjacent frame member. When using a floor jack, the car may be raised at a frame rail, front crossmember, or at either front lower arm strut connection.

The best way to raise a car for service is to use a garage hoist. There are several different types of garage hoists, each having their own special precautions. Types you most often will encounter are the drive-on (ramp type), the frame contact and the twin post or rail type. On all types of hoists, avoid contact with the steering linkage as damage may result. When using a drive-on type, make sure that there is enough clearance between the upright flanges of the hoist rails and the underbody. When using a frame contact hoist, make sure that all four of the adapter pads are positioned squarely on a frame rail. When using a twin post or rail type, make sure that the front adapters are positioned squarely beneath the lower control arms and the rear adapters positioned carefully beneath the rear axle housing at points no further outboard than one inch from the circumference welds near the differential housing (to prevent shock absorber damage). Always raise the car slowly, observing the security of the hoist adapters as it is raised.

NOTE: *If it is desired to unload the front suspension ball joints for purposes of inspection, position the jack beneath the lower control arm of the subject ball joints.*

JUMP STARTING A DEAD BATTERY

The chemical reaction in a battery produces explosive hydrogen gas. This is the safe way to jump start a dead battery, reducing the chances of an accidental spark that could cause an explosion.

Jump Starting Precautions

1. Be sure both batteries are of the same voltage.
2. Be sure both batteries are of the same polarity (have the same grounded terminal).
3. Be sure the vehicles are not touching.
4. Be sure the vent cap holes are not obstructed.
5. Do not smoke or allow sparks around the battery.
6. In cold weather, check for frozen electrolyte in the battery.
7. Do not allow electrolyte on your skin or clothing.
8. Be sure the electrolyte is not frozen.

Jump Starting Procedure

1. Determine voltages of the two batteries; they must be the same.
2. Bring the starting vehicle close (they must not touch) so that the batteries can be reached easily.
3. Turn off all accessories and both engines. Put both cars in Neutral or Park and set the handbrake.
4. Cover the cell caps with a rag—do not cover terminals.
5. If the terminals on the run-down battery are heavily corroded, clean them.
6. Identify the positive and negative posts on both batteries and connect the cables in the order shown.
7. Start the engine of the starting vehicle and run it at fast idle. Try to start the car with the dead battery. Crank it for no more than 10 seconds at a time and let it cool off for 20 seconds in between tries.
8. If it doesn't start in 3 tries, there is something else wrong.
9. Disconnect the cables in the reverse order.
10. Replace the cell covers and dispose of the rags.

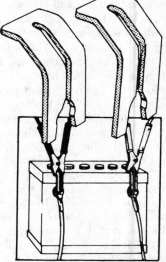

Side terminal batteries occasionally pose a problem when connecting jumper cables. There frequently isn't enough room to clamp the cables without touching sheet metal. Side terminal adaptors are available to alleviate this problem and should be removed after use.

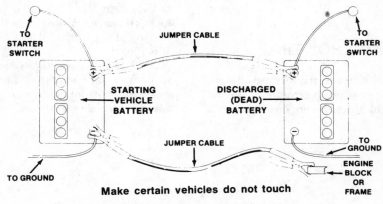

TO STARTER SWITCH   JUMPER CABLE   TO STARTER SWITCH

STARTING VEHICLE BATTERY   DISCHARGED (DEAD) BATTERY

JUMPER CABLE   TO GROUND

TO GROUND   ENGINE BLOCK OR FRAME

Make certain vehicles do not touch

This hook-up for negative ground cars only

Maintenance Interval Chart

Operation	'71	'72	'73	'74	'75	'76	'77–'79	'80	'81–82	See Chapter
ENGINE										
Air cleaner replacement—6 cyl	12	12	—	—	—	—	—	—	—	1
Air cleaner replacement—V8	24	12	12	24	20	20	30	30	30	1
Air intake temperature control system check	12	12	12	12	15	15	20	22.5	22.5	4
Carburetor idle speed and mixture, fast idle, throttle solenoid adj	12	12	12	24	15	15	22.5	30	30	2
Cooling system check	12	12	12	12	15	15	12	12	12	1
Coolant replacement; system draining and flushing	24	24	24	24	40	40	45	52.5	52.5	1
Crankcase breather cap cleaning	6	6	12	12	20	20	30	52.5	52.5	1
Crankcase breather filter replacement (in air cleaner)	6	6	8	24	20	20	30	52.5	52.5	1
Distributor breaker points inspection	12	12	12	6	—	—	—	—	—	2
Distributor breaker points replacement	12	12	24	24	—	—	—	—	—	2
Distributor cap and rotor inspection	12	12	24	①	15	15	22.5	22.5	22.5	2
Drive belts adjustment	12	12	12	12	15	15	22.5	30	30	1
Evaporative control system check; inspect carbon canister	12	12	12	24	20	20	30	52.5	52.5	1
Exhaust control valve (heat riser) lubrication and inspection	6	6	8	6	15	15	15	15	15	1
Exhaust gas recirculation system (EGR) check	—	—	12	12	15	15	15	15	15	4
Fuel filter replacement	12	12	12	6	15	10	10	12	12	1
Ignition timing adjustment	12	12	12	②	⑤	⑤	⑤	⑤	⑤	2
Intake manifold bolt torque check (V8 only)	12	12	24	12	15	15	15	15	15	3
Oil change	6	6	4	6	5	5	7.5	7.5	7.5	1
Oil filter replacement	6	6	8	12	10	10	15	15	15	1
PCV system valve replacement, system cleaning	12	12	12	24	20	20	22.5	52.5	52.5	4
Spark plug replacement; plug wire check	12	12	12	③	15	15	22.5	30	30	2
Thermactor air injection system check	—	—	—	24	15	15	22.5	22.5	22.5	4

Maintenance Interval Chart (cont.)

Operation	'71	'72	'73	'74	'75	'76	'77– '79	'80	'81– 82	See Chapter
CHASSIS										
Automatic transmission band adjustment	④	④	④	④	④	④	④	④	④	6
Automatic transmission fluid level check	6	6	8	12	15	15	15	15	15	1
Brake system inspection, lining replacement	30	30	24	24	25	30	30	30	30	9
Brake master cylinder reservoir fluid level check	6	6	8	12	15	30	30	30	30	1
Clutch pedal free-play adjustment	6	—	—	—	—	—	—	—	—	6
Front suspension ball joints and steering linkage lubrication	36	36	36	36	30	30	30	30	30	1
Front wheel bearings cleaning, adjusting and repacking	30	30	24	24	25	30	30	30	30	9
Manual transmission fluid level check	6	—	—	—	—	—	—	—	—	1
Power steering pump reservoir fluid level check	6	6	4	6	15	15	15	15	15	1
Rear axle fluid level check	6	6	8	12	15	15	15	15	15	1
Steering arm stop lubrication; steering linkage inspection	12	12	12	12	15	15	15	15	15	1

① Conventional ignition— 24; electronic ignition— 18
② Conventional ignition— 12; electronic ignition— 18
③ Conventional ignition— 12; electronic ignition— 18
④ Normal service— 12,000 mi. only; severe (fleet) service— 6,000/18,000/30,000 mi. intervals
⑤ Periodic adjustment unnecessary

Tune-Up

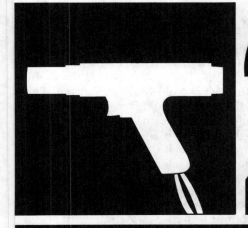

TUNE-UP PROCEDURES

Spark Plugs

A typical spark plug consists of a metal shell surrounding a ceramic insulator A metal electrode extends downward through the center of the insulator and protrudes a small distance. Located at the end of the plug and attached to the side of the outer metal shell is the side electrode. The side electrode bends in at a 90° angle so that its tip is even with, and parallel to, the tip of the center electrode. The distance between these two electrodes (measured in thousandths of an inch) is called the spark plug gap. The spark plug in no way produces a spark but merely provides a gap across which the current can arc. The coil produces anywhere from 20,000 to 40,000 volts which travels to the distributor where it is distributed through the spark plug wires to the spark plugs. The current passes along the center electrode and jumps the gap to the side electrode, and, in so doing, ignites the air/fuel mixture in the combustion chamber.

SPARK PLUG HEAT RANGE

Spark plug heat range is the ability of the plug to dissipate heat. The longer the insulator (or the farther it extends into the engine), the hotter the plug will operate; the shorter the insulator the cooler it will operate. A plug that absorbs little heat and remains too cool will quickly accumulate deposits of oil and carbon since it is not hot enough to burn them off. This leads to plug fouling and consequently to misfiring. A plug that absorbs too much heat will have no deposits, but, due to the excessive heat, the electrodes will burn away quickly and in some instances, preignition may result. Preignition takes place when plug tips get so hot that they glow sufficiently to ignite the fuel/air mixture before the actual

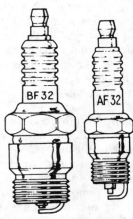

Typical spark plugs—left is $13/16$ in. (18 mm); right is $5/8$ in. (14 mm)

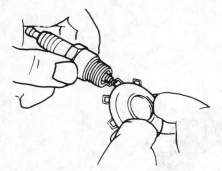

Checking spark plug gap

spark occurs. This early ignition will usually cause a pinging during low speeds and heavy loads.

The general rule of thumb for choosing the correct heat range when picking a spark plug is: if most of your driving is long distance, high speed travel, use a colder plug; if most of your driving is stop and go, use a hotter plug. Original equipment plugs are compromise plugs, but most people never have occasion to change their plugs from the factory-recommended heat range.

REPLACING SPARK PLUGS

A set of spark plugs usually requires replacement after about 10,000 miles on cars with conventional ignition systems and after about 20,000 to 30,000 miles on cars with electronic ignition, depending on your style of driving. In normal operation, plug gap increases about 0.001 in. for every 1,000–2,500 miles. As the gap increases, the plug's voltage requirement also increases. It requires a greater voltage to jump the wider gap and about two to three times as much voltage to fire a plug at high speeds than at idle.

When you're removing spark plugs, you should work on one at a time. Don't start by removing the plug wires all at once, because unless you number them, they may become mixed up. Take a minute before you begin and number the wires with tape. The best location for numbering is near where the wires come out of the cap.

1. Twist the spark plug boot and remove the boot and wire from the plug. Do not pull on the wire itself as this will ruin the wire.

2. If possible, use a brush or rag to clean the area around the spark plug. Make sure that all the dirt is removed so that none will enter the cylinder after the plug is removed.

3. Remove the spark plug using the proper size socket. A $^{13}/_{16}$" size socket may be used on all models from 1971–72. 1974 and later

models use either a $^5/_8$" or $^{13}/_{16}$" size socket depending on the engine. Turn the socket counterclockwise to remove the plug. Be sure to hold the socket straight on the plug to avoid breaking the plug, or rounding off the hex on the plug.

4. Once the plug is out, check it against the plugs shown in the "Color" section of chapter four to determine engine condition. This is crucial since plug readings are vital signs of engine condition.

5. Use a round wire feeler gauge to check the plug gap. The correct size gauge should pass through the electrode gap with a slight drag. If you're in doubt, try one size smaller and one larger. The smaller gauge should go through easily while the larger one shouldn't go through at all. If the gap is incorrect, use the electrode bending tool on the end of the gauge to adjust the gap. When adjusting the gap, always bend the side electrode. The center electrode is non-adjustable.

6. Squirt a drop of penetrating oil on the threads of the new plug and install it. Don't oil the threads too heavily. Turn the plug in clockwise by hand until it is snug.

7. When the plug is finger tight, tighten it with a wrench. If you don't have a torque wrench, tighten the plug as shown.

8. Install the plug boot firmly over the plug. Proceed to the next plug.

CHECKING AND REPLACING SPARK PLUG CABLES

Visually inspect the spark plug cables for burns, cuts, or breaks in the insulation. Check the spark plug boots and the nipples on the distributor cap and coil. Replace any damaged wiring. If no physical damage is obvious, the wires can be checked with an ohmmeter for excessive resistance. (See the tune-up and troubleshooting section.)

When installing a new set of spark plug cables, replace the cables one at a time so there will be no mixup. Start by replacing the longest cable first. Install the boot firmly over the spark plug. Route the wire exactly the same as the original. Insert the nipple firmly into the tower on the distributor cap. Repeat the process for each cable.

Breaker Points and Condenser

NOTE: *Some 1974 and all 1975 and later models are equipped with a breakerless, solidstate ignition system. The breakerless system eliminates the points and condenser completely.*

CONDITION	CAUSED BY
BURNED	ANY DISCOLORATION OTHER THAN A FROSTED SLATE GREY SHALL BE CONSIDERED AS BURNED POINTS.
EXCESSIVE METAL TRANSFER OR PITTING	INCORRECT ALIGNMENT. INCORRECT VOLTAGE REGULATOR SETTING. RADIO CONDENSER INSTALLED TO THE DISTRIBUTOR SIDE OF THE COIL. IGNITION CONDENSER OF IMPROPER CAPACITY. EXTENDED OPERATION OF THE ENGINE AT SPEEDS OTHER THAN NORMAL.

Breaker points diagnosis

The points function as a circuit breaker for the primary circuit of the ignition system. The ignition coil must boost the 12 volts of electrical pressure supplied by the battery to as much as 25,000 volts in order to fire the spark plugs. To do this, the coil depends on the points and the condenser to make a clean break in the primary circuit.

The coil has both primary and secondary circuits. When the ignition is turned on, the battery supplies voltage through the coil and on to the points. The points are connected to ground, completing the primary circuit. As the current passes through the coil, a magnetic field is created in the iron center core of the coil. As the cam in the distributor turns, the points open and the primary circuit is interrupted. The magnetic field in the primary circuit of the coil collapses and cuts through the secondary circuit windings around the iron core. Because of the scientific phenomenon called "electromagnetic induction," the battery voltage is at this point increased to a level sufficient to fire the spark plugs.

When the points open, the electrical charge in the primary circuit jumps the gap created between the two open contacts of the points. If this electrical charge were not transferred elsewhere, the metal contacts of the points would melt and the gap between the points would start to change rapidly. If this gap is not maintained, the points will not break the primary circuit. If the primary circuit is not broken, the secondary circuit will not have enough voltage to fire the spark plugs.

The function of the condenser is to absorb excessive voltage from the points when they open and thus prevent the points from becoming pitted or burned.

The cycle must be completed by the ignition system every time a spark fires. In a V8 engine, all of the spark plugs fire once for every two revolutions of the crankshaft. That means that in one revolution, four spark plugs fire. So, when the engine is at an idle speed of 800 rpm, the points are opening and closing 3,200 times a minute.

There are two ways to check the breaker point gap: It can be done with a feeler gauge or a dwell meter. Either way you set the points, you are basically adjusting the amount of time that the points remain open. The time is measured in degrees of distributor rotation. When you measure the gap between the breaker points with a feeler gauge, you are setting the maximum amount the points will open when the rubbing block on the points is on a high point of the distributor cam. When you adjust the points with a dwell meter, you are adjusting the number of degrees that the points will remain closed before they start to open as a high point of the distributor cam approaches the rubbing block of the points.

When you replace a set of points, always replace the condenser at the same time.

When you change the point gap or dwell, you will also have changed the ignition timing. So, if the point gap or dwell is changed, the ignition timing must be adjusted also. Changing the ignition timing, however, does not affect the dwell.

INSPECTION OF THE POINTS

1. Disconnect the high-tension wire from the top of the distributor and the coil.

2. Remove the distributor cap by prying off the spring clips on the side of the cap.

3. Remove the rotor from the distributor

shaft by pulling it straight up. Examine the condition of the rotor. If it is cracked or the metal tip is excessively worn or burned, it should be replaced.

4. Pry open the contacts of the points with a screwdriver and check the condition of the contacts. If they are excessively worn, burned or pitted, they should be replaced.

5. If the points are in good condition, adjust them, and replace the rotor and the distributor cap. If the points need to be replaced, follow the replacement procedure given below.

REPLACEMENT OF THE BREAKER POINTS AND CONDENSER

1. Remove the coil high-tension wire from top of the distributor cap. Remove the distributor cap from the distributor and place it out of the way. Remove the rotor from the distributor shaft.

2. Loosen the screw which holds the condenser lead to the body of the breaker points and remove the condenser lead from the points.

3. Remove the screw which holds and grounds the condenser to the distributor body. Remove the condenser from the distributor and discard it.

4. Remove the points assembly attaching screws and adjustment lockscrews. A screwdriver with a holding mechanism will come in handy here so that you don't drop a screw into the distributor and have to remove the entire distributor to retrieve it.

5. Remove the points by lifting them straight up and off the locating dowel on the plate. Wipe off the cam and apply new cam lubricant. Discard the old set of points.

6. Slip the new set of points onto the locating dowel and install the screws that hold

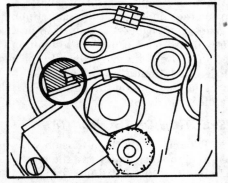

Checking point face alignment

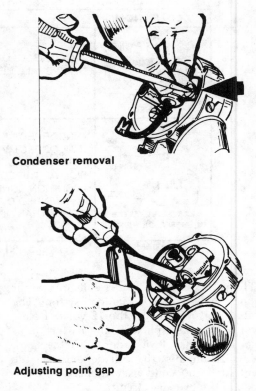

Condenser removal

Adjusting point gap

the assembly onto the plate. Do not tighten them all the way.

7. Attach the new condenser to the plate with the ground screw.

8. Attach the condenser lead to the points at the proper place.

9. Apply a small amount of cam lubricant to the shaft where the rubbing block of the points touches.

ADJUSTMENT OF THE BREAKER POINTS WITH A FEELER GAUGE

1. If the contact points of the assembly are not parallel, bend the stationary contact so that they make contact across the entire surface of the contacts. Bend only the stationary bracket part of the point assembly; not the moveable contact.

2. Turn the engine until the rubbing block of the point is on one of the high points of the distributor cam. You can do this by either turning the ignition switch to the start position and releasing it quickly ("bumping" the engine) or by using a wrench on the bolt which holds the crankshaft pulley to the crankshaft.

3. Place the correct size feeler gauge between the contacts. Make sure that it is parallel with the contact surfaces.

4. With your free hand, insert a screw-

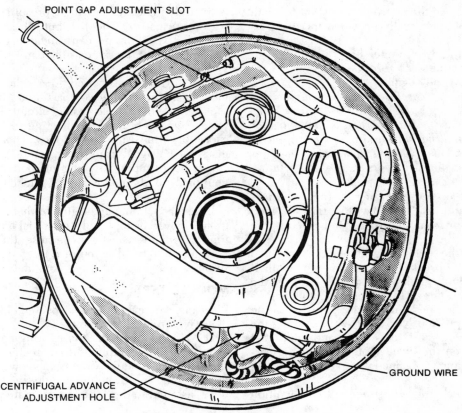

POINT GAP ADJUSTMENT SLOT

CENTRIFUGAL ADVANCE
ADJUSTMENT HOLE

GROUND WIRE

Dual point set used on Super Cobrajet engines

driver into the notch provided for adjustment or into the eccentric adjusting screw, then twist the screwdriver to either increase or decrease the gap to the proper setting.

5. Tighten the adjustment lockscrew and recheck the contact gap to make sure that it didn't change when the lockscrew was tightened.

6. Replace the rotor and distributor cap, and the high-tension wire that connects the top of the distributor and the coil. Make sure that the rotor is firmly seated all the way onto the distributor shaft and that the tab of the rotor is aligned with the notch in the shaft. Align the tab in the base of the distributor cap with the notch in the distributor body. Make sure that the cap is firmly seated on the distributor and that the retainer clips are in place. Make sure that the end of the high-tension wire is firmly placed in the top of the distributor and the coil.

NOTE: *1972–73 351V & CJ engines with manual transmissions have distributors equipped with dual points. On these models, set each gap to .020 in., then take a combined dwell reading.*

ADJUSTMENT OF THE BREAKER POINTS WITH A DWELL METER

1. Adjust the points with a feeler gauge as described earlier.

2. Connect the dwell meter to the ignition circuit according to the manufacturer's instructions. One lead of the meter is connected to a ground and the other lead is to be

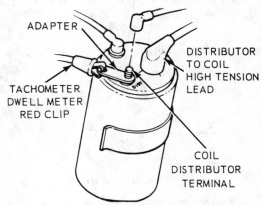

ADAPTER

DISTRIBUTOR
TO COIL
HIGH TENSION
LEAD

TACHOMETER
DWELL METER
RED CLIP

COIL
DISTRIBUTOR
TERMINAL

Attaching dwell/tachometer, with adaptor, on ignition coil (1971–74 models)

connected to the distributor post on the coil. An adapter is usually provided for this purpose.

3. If the dwell meter has a set line on it, adjust the meter to zero the indicator.

4. Start the engine.

NOTE: *Be careful when working on any vehicle while the engine is running. Make sure that the transmission is in Neutral or Park and that the parking brake is applied. Keep hands, clothing, tools, and the wires of the test instruments clear of the rotating fan blades.*

5. Observe the reading on the dwell meter. If the reading is within the specified range, turn off the engine and remove the dwell meter.

6. If the reading is above the specified range, the breaker point gap is too small. If the reading is below the specified range, the gap is too large. In either case, the engine must be stopped and the gap adjusted in the manner previously covered. After making the adjustment, start the engine and check the reading on the dwell meter. When the correct reading is obtained, disconnect the dwell meter.

7. Check the adjustment of the ignition timing.

Breakerless Distributor (Solid State)

Some 1974 and all 1975 and later engines are equipped with the breakerless electronic ignition system. The conventional contact breaker points and condenser in the distributor are replaced by a permanent magnet low-voltage generator. The generator consists of an armature with four or six teeth mounted on the top of the distributor shaft, and a permanent magnet inside a small coil. The coil

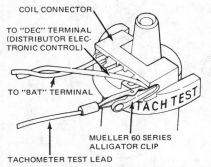

COIL CONNECTOR

TO "DEC" TERMINAL (DISTRIBUTOR ELECTRONIC CONTROL)

TO "BAT" TERMINAL

TACH TEST

MUELLER 60 SERIES ALLIGATOR CLIP

TACHOMETER TEST LEAD

Attaching dwell/tachometer lead to coil connector (electronic ignition)

is riveted in place to provide a preset air gap with the armature. The distributor base, cap, rotor and vacuum and centrifugal spark advance are about the same as the conventional system.

The distributor is wired to a solid state module in the engine compartment. Inside the module is an electronic circuit board which consists of inner connecting resistors, capacitors, transistors and diodes. The module senses a signal from the magnetic generator to perform the switching function of conventional points and it senses and controls dwell.

Unless a malfunction occurs, or the distributor is moved or replaced, the initial ignition timing remains constant. Because the low voltage coil in the distributor is riveted in position, gap adjustment is not possible.

MODULE TEST

If the electronic module is suspected of being defective, proceed as follows.

1. Without removing the existing module from the vehicle, unplug the connectors from the electronic module. Connect a known good module. The substitute module does not have to be fastened to the vehicle to operate properly.

2. Attempt to start the engine. If the engine starts and accelerates properly, proceed to step three. If the engine will still not start, the fault is in the wiring or other vehicle systems. Inspect and repair as necessary.

3. Reconnect the original module. Again attempt to start and run the engine. If the engine once again will not start, remove the original module and replace with a new one. If, however, the engine will now start and run on the original module, the module is not defective.

4. With the engine operating, check all connections in the primary wiring of the ignition system for such faults as poor wire crimp to terminal or improper engagement. The faulty connection will be observed when the engine misfires or stops. Correct as necessary.

TACHOMETER-TO-COIL CONNECTION—ELECTRONIC IGNITION

The new solid state ignition coil connector allows a tachometer test lead with an alligator-type clip to be connected to the DEC (Distributor Electronic Control) terminal without removing the connector.

When engine rpm must be checked, install

the tachometer alligator clip into the "TACH TEST" cavity as shown. If the coil connector must be removed, grasp the wires and pull horizontally until it disconnects from the terminals.

Ignition Timing

Ignition timing is the measurement, in degrees of crankshaft rotation, of the point at which the spark plugs fire in each of the cylinders. It is measured in degrees before or after Top Dead Center (TDC) of the compression stroke. Ignition timing is controlled by turning the distributor body in the engine.

Ideally, the air/fuel mixture in the cylinder will be ignited by the spark plug just as the piston passes TDC of the compression stroke. If this happens, the piston will be beginning the power stroke just as the compressed and ignited air/fuel mixture starts to expand. The expansion of the air/fuel mixture then forces the piston down on the power stroke and turns the crankshaft.

Because it takes a fraction of a second for the spark plug to ignite the mixture in the cylinder, the spark plug must fire a little before the piston reaches TDC. Otherwise, the mixture will not be completely ignited as the piston passes TDC and the full power of the explosion will not be used by the engine.

The timing measurement is given in degrees of crankshaft rotation before the piston reaches TDC (BTDC). If the setting for the ignition timing is 5° BTDC, each spark plug must fire 5° before each piston reaches TDC. This only holds true, however, when the engine is at idle speed.

As the engine speed increases, the pistons go faster. The spark plugs have to ignite the fuel even sooner if it is to be completely ignited when the piston reaches TDC. To do this, the distributor has a means to advance the timing of the spark as the engine speed increases. This is accomplished by centifugal weights within the distributor and a vacuum diaphragm mounted on the side of the distributor. It is necessary to disconnect the vacuum lines from the diaphragm when the ignition timing is being set.

If the ignition is set too far advanced (BTDC), the ignition and expansion of the fuel in the cylinder will occur too soon and tend to force the piston down while it is still traveling up. This causes engine ping. If the ignition spark is set too far retarded after TDC

(ATDC), the piston will have already passed TDC and started on its way down when the fuel is ignited. This will cause the piston to be forced down for only a portion of its travel. This will result in poor engine performance and lack of power.

The timing is best checked with a timing light. This device is connected in series with the No. 1 spark plug. The current that fires the spark plug also causes the timing light to flash.

There is a notch on the crankshaft pulley on all 6 cyl. engines. A scale of degrees of crankshaft rotation is attached to the engine block in such a position that the notch will pass close by the scale. On the V8 engines, the scale is located on the crankshaft pulley and a pointer is attached to the engine block so that the scale will pass close by. When the engine is running, the timing light is aimed at the mark on the crankshaft pulley and the scale.

IGNITION TIMING ADJUSTMENT

1. Locate the timing marks on the crankshaft pulley and the front of the engine.

2. Clean the timing marks so that you can see them.

3. Mark the timing marks with a piece of chalk or with paint. Color the mark on the scale that will indicate the correct timing when it is aligned with the mark on the pulley or the pointer. It is also helpful to mark the notch in the pulley or the tip of the pointer with a small dab of color.

4. Attach a tachometer to the engine.

5. Attach a timing light according to the manufacturer's instructions. If the timing light has three wires, one is attached to the No. 1 spark plug with an adapter. The other wires are connected to the battery. The red wire goes to the positive side of the battery and the black wire is connected to the negative terminal of the battery.

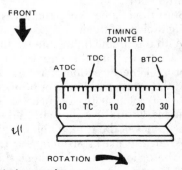

4-140 timing marks

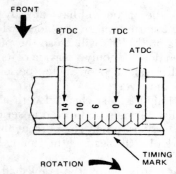

6-200, 250 timing marks

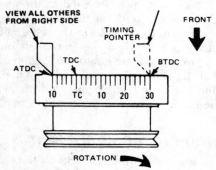

V6 and V8 timing marks

6. Disconnect the vacuum line to the distributor at the distributor and plug the vacuum line. A golf tee does a fine job.

7. Check to make sure that all of the wires clear the fan and then start the engine.

8. Adjust the idle to the correct setting.

9. Aim the timing light at the timing marks. If the marks that you put on the flywheel or pulley and the engine are aligned when the light flashes, the timing is correct. Turn off the engine and remove the tachometer and the timing light. If the marks are not in alignment, proceed with the following steps.

10. Turn off the engine.

11. Loosen the distributor lockbolt just enough so that the distributor can be turned with a little effort.

12. Start the engine. Keep the wires of the timing light clear of the fan.

13. With the timing light aimed at the pulley and the marks on the engine, turn the distributor in the direction of rotor rotation to retard the spark, and in the opposite direction of rotor rotation to advance the spark. Align the marks on the pulley and the engine with the flashes of the timing light.

14. When the marks are aligned, tighten the distributor lockbolt and recheck the timing with the timing light to make sure that

the distributor did not move when you tightened the lockbolt.

15. Turn off the engine and remove the timing light.

Valve Clearance Adjustment
429 SCJ ONLY

NOTE: *Only engines with solid (mechanical) lifters require valve adjustments. All Ford engines covered in this book, except the 429 SCJ, have hydraulic lifters.*

1. Run the engine to operating temperature.

2. Turn off the engine and remove both valve covers.

3. Insert a feeler gauge with a thickness of 0.019″ between the rocker arm and the top of the valve. Adjustment is accomplished by loosening the jam nut, or locking nut (the top nut on the rocker arm stud), and moving the adjusting nut (the lower nut) up or down as needed. When the proper adjustment has been attained, tighten the jam nut against the adjusting nut while holding the adjusting nut in position with a separate wrench. Check the clearance to make sure that the tightening of the jam nut against the adjusting nut did not alter the adjustment.

5. When all valves have been adjusted in this manner, stop the engine and reinstall the rocker covers.

Carburetor Adjustments

This section contains only carburetor adjustments as they normally apply to engine tune-up. Descriptions of the carburetor and complete adjustment procedures can be found in Chapter 4, under "Fuel System."

IDLE SPEED AND MIXTURE ADJUSTMENTS

NOTE: *Since the design of the 2700 VV and 7200 VV carburetor is different from all other Motorcraft carburetors in many respects, the adjusting procedures are necessarily different as well. Although the idle speed adjustment alone is identical, there is further information you will need to know in order to adjust the 2700 VV and 7200 VV properly. Refer to Chapter 4 for an explanation.*

NOTE: *In order to limit exhaust emissions, plastic caps have been installed on the idle*

Tune-Up Specifications

Year	Engine No. Cyl Displacement (cu. in.)	hp	Spark Plugs Orig. Type	Gap (in.)	Distributor Point Dwell* (deg)	Point Gap (in.)	Ignition Timing (deg)▲ Man Trans	Auto Trans	Intake Valve Opens ■(deg)	Fuel Pump Pressure (psi)	Idle Speed (rpm)▲● Man Trans	Auto Trans
'71	6-250	145	BRF-82	.034	36	.027/.025	6B	6B	10	4-6	750	600
	8-302	210	BRF-42	.034	27	.021	6B	6B	16	4-6	800/500	575 (600/500)
	8-351C	240	ARF-42	.034	27	.021	6B	6B	12	5-7	700/500	600
	8-351W	240	BRF-42	.034	27	.021	6B	6B	12	5-7	700/500	575 (600/500)
	8-351C	285	AFR-32	.034	27/29	.021/.017	6B	6B	18	5-7	800/500	600
	8-429	360	BRF-42	.034	27/29	.021/.017	4B	4B	16	5-7	700	600 (600/500)
	8-429CJ	370	ARF-42	.034	25	.020	10B	10B	32	4½-6½	700	650 (650/500)
	8-429SCJ	385	ARF-42	.034	28	.020	10B	10B	40½	4½-6½	650/500	700/500
'72	6-250	95	BRF-82	.034	37	.027	6B	6B	10(16)	4½-6½	750/500	600/500
	8-302	140	BRF-42	.034	28	.017	6B	6B	16	5½-6½	800/500	575 (600/500)
	8-351C	165	ARF-42	.034	28	.017	6B	6B	12	5½-6½	800/500	575/500 (625/500)

Tune-Up Specifications (cont.)

Year	Engine No. Cyl Displacement (cu. in.)	hp	Spark Plugs Orig. Type	Gap (in.)	Distributor Point Dwell* (deg)	Point Gap (in.)	Ignition Timing (deg)▲ Man Trans	Auto Trans	Intake Valve Opens ■(deg)	Fuel Pump Pressure (psi)	Idle Speed (rpm)▲● Man Trans	Auto Trans
'72	8-351W	165	BRF-42	.034	28	.017	—	6B	12	5½-6½	—	575 (600/500)
	8-400	168	ARF-42	.034	28	.017	—	6B	17	4½-5½	—	625/500
	8-429	205	ARF-42	.034	28	.017	—	10B	8	5½-6½	—	600/500
'73	6-250	95	BRF-82	.034	37	.027/.025	6B	6B	16	4½-6½	750/500	600/500
	8-302	140	BRF-42	.034	28	.017	6B	6B	16	5½-6½	800/500	575 (600/500)
	8-351C	165	ARF-42	.034	28	.017	—	6B	12	5½-6½	—	625/500
	8-351W	165	BRF-42	.034	28	.017	—	6B	12	5½-6½	—	575 (600/500)
	8-400	168	ARF-42	.034	28	.017	—	6B	17	5½-6½	—	625/500
	8-429	205	ARF-42	.034	28	.017	—	10B	8	5½-6½	—	600/500
	8-460PI	269	ARF-42	.035	28	.017	—	10B	18	5½-7½	—	600
'74	6-250	91	BRF-82	.044	37⑩	.027	6B	6B	26	5½-6½	800/500	625/500
	8-302	140	BRF-42	.044	28⑩	.017	10B	6B	16⑦	5½-6½	800/500	625/500
	8-351W	162	BRF-42	.044	28⑩	.017	—	6B	15	5½-6½	—	600/500

Year	Engine	No.	Spark Plug	Gap	Dwell	Point Gap	Timing				RPM
'74	8-351C	163	ARF-42	.044	28 ⑩	.017	14B	11.5	5½–6½	—	600/500
	8-400	170	ARF-42	.044	Electronic	—	12B ⑥	17	5½–6½	—	625/500
	8-460	195,220 260	ARF-42	.054	Electronic	—	14B	8	5½–6½	—	650/500
'75	8-351W	153, 154	ARF-42	.044	Electronic	—	6B	15	5½–6½	—	600/500
	8-351M	148, 150	ARF-42	.044	Electronic	—	6B	19½	5½–6½	—	700/500
	8-400	144, 158	ARF-42	.044	Electronic	—	6B	17	5½–6½	—	625/500
	8-460	216, 217	ARF-52	.044	Electronic	—	14B	8	5½–6½	—	650/500
	8-460PI	226	ARF-52	.044	Electronic	—	14B	18	5½–7	—	700/500
'76	8-351W	All	ARF-42/52 ⑧	.054	Electronic	—	⑧	15	5½–6½	—	650
	8-351M	All	ARF-42/52 ⑧	.044	Electronic	—	⑧	19½	5½–6½	—	650 (650/675 ⑧)
	8-400	All	ARF-42/52 ⑧	.044	Electronic	—	⑧	17	5½–6½	—	650(625)
	8-460	All	ARF-52	.044	Electronic	—	8/14B ⑧ ⑨ @ 650	8	5½–6½	—	650
	8-460PI	226	ARF-52	.044	Electronic	—	14B ⑨ @ 650	18	5½–7	—	650
'77	8-302	All	ARF-52 ④	.050	Electronic	—	8B ⑬	16	5½–6½	—	650
	8-351W	All	ARF-52 ④	.050	Electronic	—	4B	23	4–6	—	650

Tune-Up Specifications (cont.)

Year	Engine No. Cyl Displacement (cu. in.)	hp	Spark Plugs Orig. Type	Gap (in.)	Distributor Point Dwell* (deg)	Point Gap (in.)	Ignition Timing (deg)▲ Man Trans	Auto Trans	Intake Valve Opens ■(deg)	Fuel Pump Pressure (psi)	Idle Speed (rpm)▲● Man Trans	Auto Trans
'77	8-351M	All	ARF-52④	.050	Electronic		—	8B⑭	19½	6½–7½	—	650
	8-400	All	ARF-54④	.050	Electronic		—	8B	17	7–8	—	650
'78	8-302	All	ARF-52⑮	.050	Electronic		—	14B	16	5½–6½	—	650
	8-351M	All	ARF-52⑮	.050	Electronic		—	14B	23	4–6	—	650
	8-351W	All	ARF-52⑮	.050	Electronic		—	14B⑯	19½	6½–7½	—	650
	8-400	All	ARF-5⑯	.050	Electronic		—	13B⑯	17	6½–7½	—	650
'79	8-302	All	ASF-52	.050	Electronic		—	8B	16	5½–6½	—	600
	8-351M	All	ASF-52	.050	Electronic		—	12B⑪	17⑫	7–8	—	600
	8-351W	All	ASF-52	.050	Electronic		—	15B	23	6½–8	—	600
'80	8-255	All	ASF-42	.050	Electronic		—	8B	16	5½–6	—	550
	8-255 Calif.	All	ASF-42	.050	Electronic		—	EEC	16	5½–6½	—	EEC
	8-302	All	ASF-52	.050	Electronic		—	8B	16	5½–6½	—	550
	8-302 Calif.	All	ASF-52	.050	Electronic		—	EEC	16	5½–6½	—	EEC
'81	4-140	All	AWSF-42	.034	Electronic		6B	6B	22	5½–6½	700	700

Year	Engine		Spark Plug	Gap	Distributor			Dwell			
'81	6-200	All	BSF-92	.050	Electronic	10B	10B	20	6-8	900	900
	8-255	All	ASF-52	.050	Electronic	—	10B	16	6-8	—	800
	8-302	All	ASF-52	.050	Electronic	—	8B	16	6-8	—	800
'82	4-140	All	AWSF-42	.034	Electronic	—	⑧	22	6-8	850	750
	6-200	All	BSF-92	.050	Electronic	—	⑧	20	6-8	—	700
	6-232	All	AGSP-52	.044	Electronic	—	⑧	13	6-8	—	500⑰
	8-255	All	ASF-52	.050	Electronic	—	⑧	16	6-8	—	700
	8-302	All	ASF-52	.050	Electronic	—	⑧	16	6-8	—	500

NOTE: The underhood specifications sticker often reflects tune-up specification changes made in production. Sticker figures must be used if they disagree with those in this chart.

* Where two dwell or point gap figures are separated by a slash, the first figure is for engines equipped with dual diaphragm distributors and the second figure is for engines equipped with single diaphragm distributors

▲ See text for procedure

● In all cases where two idle speed figures are separated by a slash, the first is for idle speed with solenoid energized and automatic transmission in Drive, while the second is for idle speed with solenoid disconnected and automaticc transmission in Neutral. Figures in parentheses are for California

■ All figures are in degrees Before Top Dead Center

① For air conditioned vehicles, adjust idle speed to 600 rpm with A/C on
② For air conditioned vehicles, adjust idle speed to 800 rpm with A/C on
③ Figure is .020 for manual transmission with dual point distributor
④ ARF-52-6 for Calif. engines, gap is .060 in.
⑤ Figure is 32°–35° on manual transmission model with dual point distributor with both point sets combined
⑥ At 500 rpm
⑦ 20° BTC for 302 automatic
⑧ Depends on emission equipment; check underhood specifications sticker
⑨ In Drive
⑩ Electronic ignition used on all engines assembled after May, 1974
⑪ 14B in Calif.
⑫ Calif. 19.5
⑬ Versailles: 12B
⑭ California: 9B
⑮ California: ARF-52-6; gap .060
⑯ California: 16B
⑰ California: T'bird & XR-7—700 w/TSP on
    Cougar—650 w/TSP off
    Continental—700 w/TSP on

B Before Top Dead Center
C Cleveland
M Modified Cleveland
CJ Cobra Jet
HO High Output
N.A. Not available
SCJ Super Cobra Jet
W Windsor
EEC: Electrical Engine Control; Adjustment is not possible.
— Not applicable

Mechanical Valve Lifter Clearance

Engine	Intake (Hot) in.	Exhaust (Hot) in.
429 SCJ	.019	.019

fuel mixture screw(s), which prevent the carburetor from being adjusted to an overly rich idle fuel mixture. Under no circumstances should these limiters be modified or removed. A satisfactory idle should be obtained within the range of the limiter(s).

1. Start the engine and run it at idle until it reaches operating temperature (about 10–20 minutes, depending on outside temperatures). Stop the engine.

2. Check the ignition timing as outlined earlier in this chapter.

3. Remove the air cleaner, taking note of the hose locations, and check that the choke plate is in the open position (plate in vertical position). Check the accompanying illustrations to see where the carburetor adjustment locations are. If you cannot reach them with the air cleaner installed, leave it off temporarily. Otherwise, reinstall the air cleaner assembly including all the hose connections.

NOTE: *Leaving the air cleaner removed will*

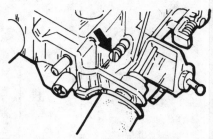

Location of idle speed adjustment—Rochester "Quadrajet" 4MV 4-V

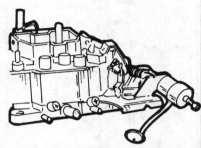

Location of idle speed adjustment—Carter "Thermoquad" 4-V

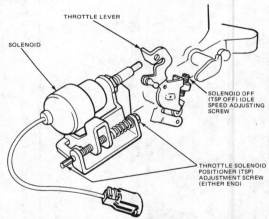

Location of idle speed adjustment—Motorcraft 2100, 2150, 4300, 4350 (all with TSP)

Location of idle speed adjustment—Carter RBS 1-V

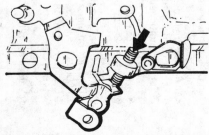

Location of idle speed adjustment—Motorcraft 4300 4-V

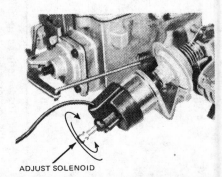

Location of idle speed adjustment—Motorcraft 2150 with solenoid dashpot TSP

affect the idle speed; therefore, adjust the curb idle speed to a setting 50–100 rpm higher than specified, if the air cleaner is off. When the air cleaner is reinstalled the idle speed should be to specifications.

4. Attach a tachometer to the engine, with the positive wire connected to the distributor side of the ignition coil, and the negative wire connected to a good ground, such as an engine bolt.

NOTE: *In order to attach an alligator clip to the distributor side (terminal) of the coil (primary connection), it will be necessary to lift off the connector and slide a female loop type connector (commercially available) down over the terminal threads. Then push down the rubber connector over the loop connector and connect the alligator clip of your tachometer.*

5. All idle speed adjustments are made with the headlights off (unless otherwise specified on the engine decal), with the air conditioning off (if so equipped), with all vacuum hoses connected, with the throttle solenoid positioner activated (connected, if so equipped), and with the air cleaner on. (See note after step 3.) Finally, all idle speed adjustments are made in Neutral on cars with manual transmission, and in Drive on cars equipped with automatic transmission.

CAUTION: *Whenever performing these adjustments, block all four wheels and set the parking brake.*

6a. On cars not equipped with a throttle solenoid positioner, the idle speed is adjusted with the curb idle speed adjusting screw. Start the engine. Turn the curb idle speed adjusting screw inward or outward until the correct idle speed (see "Tune-Up Specifications" chart) is reached, remembering to make the 50–100 rpm allowance if the air cleaner is removed.

6b. On cars equipped with a throttle sole-noid positioner, the idle speed is adjusted with solenoid adjusting screw (nut), in two stages. Start the engine. The higher speed is adjusted with the solenoid connected. Turn the solenoid adjusting screw (nut) on 1 or 4 barrel carburetors, or the entire bracket on 2 barrel carburetors inward or outward until the correct higher idle speed (see "Tune-Up Specifications" chart) is reached, remembering to make the 50–100 rpm allowance if the air cleaner is removed. After making this adjustment on cars equipped with 2 barrel carburetors, tighten the solenoid adjusting locknut. The lower idle speed is adjusted with the solenoid lead wire disconnected near the harness (not at the carburetor). Place automatic transmission equipped cars in Neutral for this adjustment. Using the curb idle speed adjusting screw on the carburetor, turn the idle speed adjusting screw inward or outward until the correct lower idle speed (see "Tune-Up Specifications" chart) is reached, remembering again to make the 50–100 rpm allowance if the air cleaner is removed. Finally, reconnect the solenoid, slightly depress the throttle lever and allow the solenoid plunger to fully extend.

7. If removed, install the air cleaner. Recheck the idle speed. If it is not correct, Step 6 will have to be repeated and the approximate corrections made.

8. To adjust the idle mixture, turn the idle mixture screw(s) inward to obtain the smoothest idle possible within the range of the limiter(s).

9. Turn off the engine and disconnect the tachometer.

NOTE: *If any doubt exists as to the proper idle mixture setting for your car, have the exhaust emission level checked at a diagnostic center or garage with an exhaust (HC/CO) analyzer or an air/fuel ratio meter.*

Engine and Engine Rebuilding

ENGINE ELECTRICAL

Point-type Distributor

All 1971–74 models covered in this book are equipped with a dual advance distributor. The centrifugal advance unit governs ignition timing according to engine rpm, the vacuum advance unit controls the timing according to engine load. Centrifugal advance is controlled by spring-mounted weights contained in the distributor, located under the breaker point mounting plate on conventional systems and under the fixed base plate on breakerless systems. As engine speed increases, centrifugal force moves the weights outward from the distributor shaft advancing the position of the distributor cam, thereby advancing the ignition timing. Vacuum advance is controlled by a vacuum diaphragm which is mounted on the side of the distributor and attached to the breaker point mounting plate via the vacuum advance link. Under light acceleration, the engine is operating under a low-load condition, causing the carburetor vacuum to act on the distributor vacuum diaphragm, moving the breaker point mounting plate (conventional) or pickup coil assembly (breakerless) opposite the direction of distributor shaft rotation, thereby advancing the ignition timing.

The distributors on many models also incorporate a vacuum retard mechanism. The retard mechanism is contained in the rear part of the vacuum diaphragm chamber. When the engine is operating under high-vacuum conditions (deceleration or idle), intake manifold vacuum is applied to the retard mechanism. The retard mechanism moves the breaker point mounting plate in the direction of distributor rotation, thereby retarding the ignition timing. Ignition retard, under these conditions, reduces exhaust emissions of hydrocarbons, although it does reduce engine efficiency somewhat.

In 1972–73, some models equipped with a

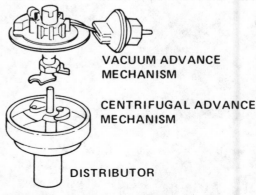

VACUUM ADVANCE MECHANISM

CENTRIFUGAL ADVANCE MECHANISM

DISTRIBUTOR

Dual advance distributor (typical)

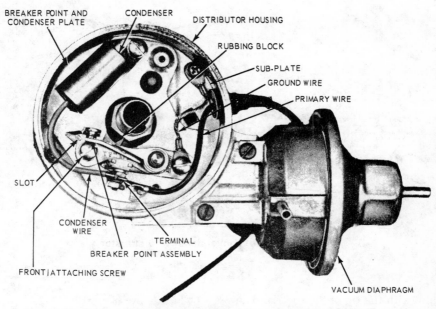

Conventional 6 cylinder distributor (cap and rotor removed)

"Cobra Jet" engine used a dual point, dual advance distributor.

REMOVAL AND INSTALLATION

1. On V8 engines only, in order to gain access to the distributor, remove the air cleaner assembly and take note of the hose locations.

2. On all models equipped with a conventional ignition system, disconnect the primary wire at the coil.

3. Noting the position of the vacuum line(s) on the distributor diaphragm, disconnect the lines at the diaphragm. Unsnap the two distributor cap retaining clamps and remove the cap. Position the cap and ignition wires to one side.

4. Using chalk or paint, carefully mark the position of the distributor roto in relation to the distributor housing and mark the position of the distributor housing in relation to the engine block. When this is done, you should have a line on the distributor housing di-

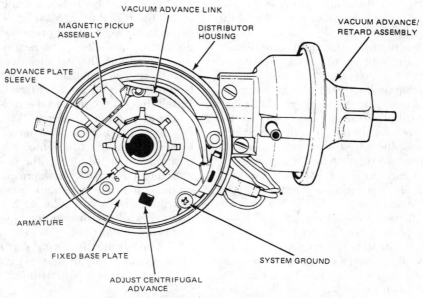

Breakerless V8 distributor (cap and rotor removed)

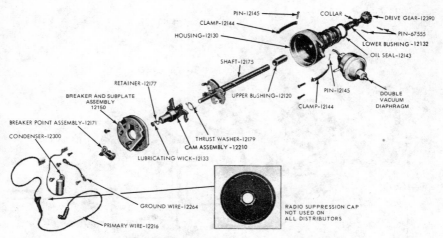

Exploded view of conventional V8 distributor

rectly in line with the tip of the rotor and another line on the engine block directly in line with the mark on the distributor housing. This is very important because the distributor must be reinstalled in the exact same location from which it was removed, if correct ignition timing is to be maintained.

5. Remove the distributor hold-down bolt and clamp. Remove the distributor from the engine.

NOTE: *Do not disturb the engine while the distributor is removed. If you attempt to start the engine with the distributor removed, you will have to retime the engine.*

6a. If the distributor was cranked (disturbed) with the distributor removed, it will now be necessary to retime the engine. If the distributor has been installed incorrectly and the engine will not start, remove the distributor from the engine and start over again. Hold the distributor close to the engine and install the cap on the distributor in its normal position. Locate the No. 1 spark plug tower on the distributor cap. Scribe a mark on the body of the distributor directly below the No. 1 spark plug wire tower on the distributor cap. Remove the distributor cap from the distributor and move the distributor and cap to one side. Remove the No. 1 spark plug and crank the engine over until the No. 1 cylinder is on its compression stroke. To accomplish this, place a wrench on the lower engine pulley and turn the engine slowly in a clockwise (6 cylinder) or counterclockwise (V8) direction until the TDC mark on the crankshaft damper aligns with the timing pointer. If you place your finger in the No. 1

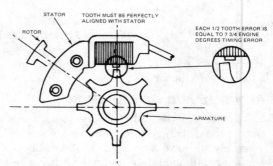

Breakerless distributor static timing position

spark plug hole, you will feel air escaping as the piston rises in the combustion chamber. The rotor must be at No. 1 firing position to install the distributor. Make sure that the oil pump intermediate shaft properly engages the distributor shaft. It may be necessary to crank the engine with the starter, after the distributor drive gear is partially engaged, in order to engage the oil pump intermediate shaft. Install, but do not tighten the retaining clamp and bolt. Tighten the clamp.

6b. If the engine was not cranked (disturbed) when the distributor was removed, position the distributor in the block with the rotor aligned with the mark previously scribed on the distributor body and the marks on the distributor body and cylinder block in alignment. Install the distributor hold-down bolt and clamp fingertight.

7. Install the distributor cap and wires.

8. Connect the primary wire at the coil.

9. Check the ignition timing as outlined in Chapter 2.

10. Install the air cleaner, if removed.

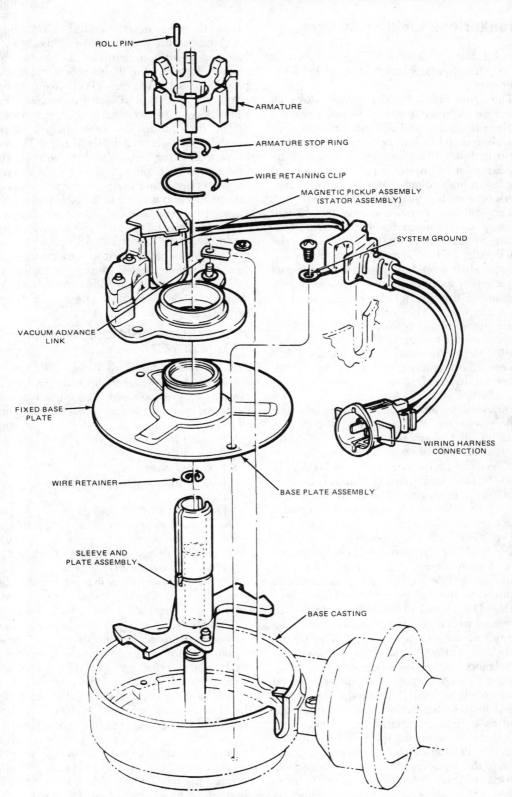

ROLL PIN

ARMATURE

ARMATURE STOP RING

WIRE RETAINING CLIP

MAGNETIC PICKUP ASSEMBLY
(STATOR ASSEMBLY)

SYSTEM GROUND

VACUUM ADVANCE
LINK

FIXED BASE
PLATE

WIRING HARNESS
CONNECTION

WIRE RETAINER

BASE PLATE ASSEMBLY

SLEEVE AND
PLATE ASSEMBLY

BASE CASTING

Exploded view of breakerless V8 distributor

Breakerless Ignition System

A solid state (breakerless) ignition system called Dura-Spark is standard on all 1975 and later cars.

The Dura-Spark ignition system uses an armature and magnetic pickup coil assembly in the distributor and a solid state amplifer module located in line between the coil and the distributor. The distributor is driven by the camshaft at one-half crankshaft rpm and employs a high voltage rotor, distributor cap, spark plug wiring, and an oil filled coil.

The ignition system converts the 12 volt primary voltage from the battery, into secondary voltage (up to 42,000 volts) to fire the spark plugs. In the Dura-Spark system, a distributor shaft mounted armature rotates past a magnetic pickup coil assembly causing fluctuations in the magnetic field generated by the pickup coil. These fluctuations in turn, cause the amplifier module to turn the ignition coil current on and off, creating the high tension to fire the spark plugs. The amplifier module electronically controls the dwell, hence no dwell adjustment is possible or required.

Different verions of the Dura-Spark ignition system are used. The Dura-Spark I is used on all California models in 1978 and 1979, while the 49 states and Canadian versions use the Dura-Spark II through 1979. In 1980–82 the Dura-Spark II system is used on all models, except the California version of the 4.2 liter V8 which uses the Dura-Spark III System.

The basic difference between the Dura-Spark I, II and III is the coil charging current. A higher current is necessary for California cars to fire the leaner fuel/air mixtures required by the stricter emission laws.

The Dura-Spark I and II systems are equipped with dual advance distributors. The vacuum advance unit governs ignition timing according to engine load, while the centrifugal advance unit governs ignition timing according to engine rpm. Centrifugal advance is controlled by spring-mounted weights contained in the distributor, located under the fixed base plate. As engine speed increases, centrifugal force moves the weights outward from the distributor shaft advancing the position of the armature, thereby advancing the ignition timing. Vacuum advance is controlled by a vacuum diaphragm which is mounted on the side of the distributor and attached to the magnetic pickup coil assembly via the vacuum advance link. Under light acceleration, the engine is operating under a low-load condition, causing the carburetor vacuum to act on the distributor vacuum diaphragm, moving the pickup coil assembly opposite the direction of distributor shaft rotation, thereby advancing the ignition timing.

The distributors on some models incorporate a vacuum retard mechanism. The retard mechanism is contained in the rear part of the vacuum diaphragm chamber. When the engine is operating under high-vacuum conditions (deceleration or idle), intake manifold vacuum is applied to the retard mechanism. The retard mechanism moves the pickup coil assembly in the direction of distributor rotation, thereby retarding the ignition timing. Ignition retard, under these conditions, reduces exhaust emissions of hydrocarbons, although it does reduce engine efficiency somewhat.

TROUBLESHOOTING DURA-SPARK I & II IGNITION

The symptoms of a defective component within the Dura-Spark system are exactly the same as those you would encounter in a conventional ignition system. Some of the symptoms are:

• Hard or no starting
• Rough idle
• Poor fuel economy
• Engine misses while under load or while accelerating.

NOTE: *Due to the sensitive nature of the Dura-Spark system and the complexity of the test procedures, it is recommended that you refer to your dealer if you suspect a problem in your electronic ignition system. The system can, of course, be tested by substituting known good components (module, stator, etc.).*

CAUTION: *If you wish to do your own troubleshooting read the next pages carefully, be sure you understand the charts and procedures before you attempt any ignition system tests.*

Wire color-coding is critical to servicing the Dura-Spark Ignition. Battery current reaches the electronic module through either the *white* or *red* wire, depending on whether the engine is cranking or running. When the engine is cranking, battery current is flowing through the *white* wire. When the engine is running, battery current flows through the *red* wire. All distributor signals flow through the *orange* and *purple* wires. The *green* wire carries primary current from the coil to the module. The *black* wire is a ground between the distributor and the module.

The orange and purple wires which run from the stator to the module must *always* be connected to the same color wire at the module. If these connections are crossed, polarity will be reversed and the system will be thrown out of phase. Some replacement wiring harnesses were sold with the wiring crossed, which complicates the problem considerably. As previously noted, the black wire is the ground wire. The screw which grounds the black wire also, of course, grounds the entire primary circuit. If this screw is loose, dirty, or corroded, a seemingly incomprehensible ignition problem will develop.

NOTE: *The Dura Spark II amplifier and module are ON when the ignition system is ON. Because of this, it is possible to generate a spark when the ignition is turned to the OFF position. Certain other service procedures such as removing the distributor cap with the ignition switch ON can also cause the system to fire. The ignition switch should remain OFF during underhood operations unless you wish to perform a specific test that requires the ignition switch to be ON.*

To properly diagnose the ignition system remember the following notes and cautions.

• Your car is equipped with a catalytic converter; any test that requires removal of a spark plug wire while the engine is running should be kept to a thirty second maximum. Any longer than thirty seconds may damage the converter. A list of converter precautions is included in Chapter 2. Read them before you attempt any troubleshooting.

• Do not pierce any spark plug wires with a probe while testing spark plug wires. Test the wires at their terminals only.

• If for any reason a high tension wire is disconnected, the interior of the terminal boot must be greased with silicone grease (Fort Part Number D7AZ19A331AA or the equivalent) before reconnection. Apply a thin layer of silicone grease (use a clean screwdriver) to the boot interior from the terminal to the end of the boot.

When removing the two piece distributor cap, the top must be removed first, followed by the rotor and then the bottom portion of the cap.

Unless otherwise specified, all high voltage tests are to be made with a clamp-on type

high voltage probe connected to the coil high tension wire.

Never pull a spark plug wire from the plug. Always twist the spark plug boot carefully to loosen its seal on the plug insulator.

Do not remove spark plug wires from the distributor cap except for replacement purposes.

All distributor rotor brass tips have a coating of silicone grease. Do not attempt to remove the grease from the rotor tip or the cap inserts to which some of the grease may have been transferred. As the grease ages it may appear to be contaminated. This is normal. If the rotor does not have a coating of silicone grease, coat the surface.

If you suspect a problem in your ignition system, first perform a spark intensity test to pinpoint the problem. Using insulated pliers, hold the end of one of the spark plug leads about ½ in. away from the engine block or other good ground, and crank the engine. If you have a nice, fat spark, then your problem is not in the ignition system. If you have no spark or a very weak spark, then proceed to the following tests.

NOTE: *Equipment necessary for the following tests; A voltmeter and an ohmmeter. Several jumper wires with both blade ends and alligator clips and a modified spark plug (side electrode clipped off).*

Stator Test

To test the stator (also known as the magnetic pickup assembly), you will need an ohmmeter. Run the engine until it reaches operating temperature, then turn the ignition switch to the "off" position. Disconnect the wire harness from the distributor. Connect the ohmmeter between the orange and purple wires. Resistance should be between 400 and 800 ohms. Next, connect the ohmmeter between the black wire and a good ground on the engine. Operate the vacuum advance either by hand or with an external vacuum source. Resistance should be zero ohms. Finally, connect the ohmmeter between the orange wire and ground, and then the purple wire and ground. Resistance should be over 70,000 ohms in both cases. If any of your ohmmeter readings differ from the above specifications, then the stator is defective and must be replaced as a unit.

If the stator is good, then either the electronic module or the wiring connections must be checked next. Because of its complicated electronic nature, the module itself cannot be checked, except by substition. If you have access to a module which you know to be good, then perform a substitution test at this time. If this cures the problem, then the original module is faulty and must be replaced. If it does not cure the problem or if you cannot locate a known-good module, then disconnect the two wiring harnesses from the module, and, using a voltmeter, check the following circuits.

NOTE: *Make no tests at the module side of the connectors.*

1. Starting circuit—Connect the voltmeter leads to ground and to the corresponding female socket of the white male lead from the module (you will need a jumper wire with a blade end). Crank the engine over. The voltage should be between 8 and 12 volts.

2. Running circuit—Turn the ignition switch to the "on" position. Connect the voltmeter leads to ground and the corresponding female socket of the red male lead from the module. Voltage should be battery voltage plus or minus 0.1 volts.

3. Coil circuit—Leave the ignition switch "on." Connect the voltmeter leads to ground and to the corresponding female socket of the green male lead from the module. Voltage should be battery voltage plus or minus 0.1 volts.

If any of the preceeding readings are incorrect, inspect and repair any loose, broken, frayed or dirty connections. If this doesn't solve the problem, perform a battery source test.

Battery Source Test

To make this test, *do not* disconnect the coil. Connect the voltmeter leads to the BAT terminal at the coil and a good ground. Connect a jumper wire from the DEC terminal at the coil to a good ground. Make sure all lights and accessories are off. Turn the ignition to the "on" position. Check the voltage. If the voltage is below 4.9 volts (11 volts for Dura Spark I), then check the primary wiring for broken strands, cracked or frayed wires, or loose or dirty terminals. Repair or replace any defects. If, however, the voltage is above 7.9 volts (14 volts for Dura-Spark I), then you have a problem in the resistance wiring and it must be replaced.

It should be noted here that if you do have a problem in your electronic ignition system, most of the time it will be a case of loose, dirty or frayed wires. The electronic module, being completely solid-state, is not ordinarily subject to failure. It is possible for the unit to fail, of course, but as a general rule, the source of an ignition system problem will be somewhere else in the circuit.

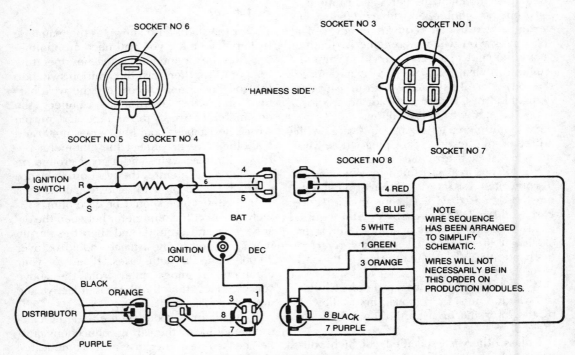

1975 solid state ignition testing

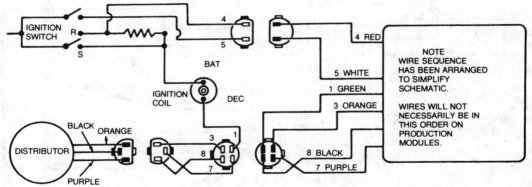

1976 electronic ignition schematic

Spark Plug Wire Resistance Test

To test the spark plug wire resistance; label all plug wires to identify their location and remove the wires from the spark plugs. Remember to twist the plug wire boot to loosen the seal on the plug insulator, do not pull on the wire to remove it. Disconnect the wire seperators from the valve covers and remove the distributor cap top with the plug wires attached. Check the resistance of each wire by connecting an ohmmeter between the plug terminal and the corresponding distributor cap insert. The resistance should measure 5k ohms per inch of cable max. Replace any wires that are not within specs. Check the spark plug boot for possible damage from heat and handling. Replace as required. Grease the rotor with silicone grease (if necessary) and replace the distributor cap. Reconnect the plug wire seperators. Grease the plug wire terminal boots and reinstall the wires on the spark plugs.

Suggestions for Intermittent Operation

If the ignition system becomes operative while performing any tests and you have not made any repairs, it is likely a connection or ignition component has become functional. With the engine running, attempt to recreate the problem by wiggling the wires at the coil, module, distributor and other harness connectors. Start with the connectors you may have already disturbed. Also check the ground connection in the distributor. Disconnecting and reconnecting the different wire connectors may also be helpful in locating the trouble spot.

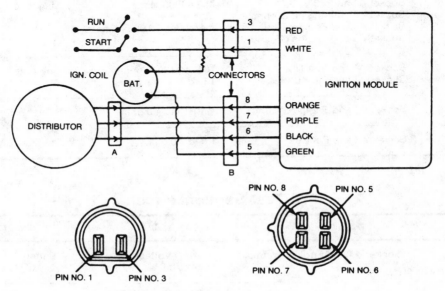

ELECTRONIC MODULE CONNECTORS – HARNESS SIDE

1977 Dura Spark II schematic

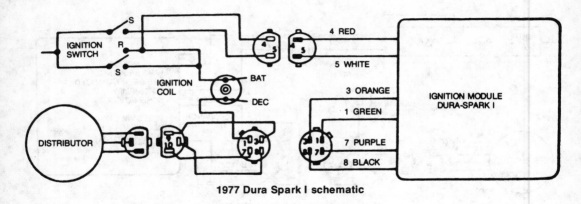

1977 Dura Spark I schematic

1975 Test Sequence

	Test Voltage Between	Should Be	If Not, Conduct
Key On	Socket #4 and Engine Ground	Battery Voltage ± 0.1 Volt	Module Bias Test
	Socket #1 and Engine Ground	Battery Voltage ± 0.1 Volt	Battery Source Test
Cranking	Socket #5 and Engine Ground	8 to 12 volts	Cranking Test
	Jumper #1 to #8 Read #6	more than 6 volts	Starting Circuit Test
	Pin #7 and Pin #8	½ volt minimum AC or any DC volt wiggle	Distributor Hardware Test
	Test Voltage Between	Should Be	If Not, Conduct
Key Off	Socket #7 and #3 Socket #8 and Engine Ground Socket #7 and Engine Ground Socket #3 and Engine Ground	400 to 800 ohms 0 ohms more than 70,000 ohms	Magnetic Pick-up (Stator) Test
	Socket #4 and Coil Tower Socket #1 and Pin #6	7000 to 13000 ohms 1.0 to 2.0 ohms	Coil Test
	Socket #1 and Engine Ground	more than 4.0 ohms	Short Test
	Socket #4 and Pin #6	1.0 to 2.0 ohms	Resistance Wire Test

1976 Test Sequence (cont.)

	Test Voltage Between	Should Be	If Not, Conduct
Key On	Socket #4 and Engine Ground	Battery Voltage ± 0.1 Volt	Battery Source Test
	Socket #1 and Engine Ground	Battery Voltage ± 0.1 Volt	Battery Source Test

1976 Test Sequence (cont.)

	Test Voltage Between	Should Be	If Not, Conduct
Cranking	Socket #5 and Engine Ground	8 to 12 volts	Check Supply Circuit (starting) through Ignition Switch
	Jumper #1 to #8 Read #6	more than 6 volts	Starting Circuit Test
	Pin #3 and Pin #8	½ volt minimum AC or any DC volt wiggle	Distributor Hardware Test
	Test Voltage Between	Should Be	If Not, Conduct
Key Off	Socket #8 and #3 Socket #7 and Engine Ground Socket #8 and Engine Ground Socket #3 and Engine Ground	400 to 800 ohms 0 ohms more than 70,000 ohms more than 70,000 ohms	Magnetic Pick-up (Stator) Test
	Socket #4 and Coil Tower	7000 to 13,000 ohms	Coil Test
	Socket #1 and Engine Ground	more than 4.0 ohms	Short Test

1977 Test Sequence (cont.)

	Test Voltage Between	Should Be	If Not, Conduct
Key On	Socket #4 and Engine Ground	Battery Voltage ± 0.1 volts	Module Bias Test
	Socket #1 and Engine Ground	Battery Voltage ± 0.1 volts	Battery Source Test
Cranking	Socket #5 and Engine Ground	8 to 12 volts	Cranking Test
	Jumper #1 to #8—Read Coil "Bat" Term. & Engine Ground	more than 6 volts	Starting Circuit Test
	Sockets #7 and #3	½ volt minimum wiggle	Distributor Hardware Test
	Test Resistance Between	Should Be	If Not, Conduct
Key Off	Sockets #7 and #3 Socket #8 and Engine Ground Socket #7 and Engine Ground Socket #3 and Engine Ground	400 to 800 ohms 0 ohms more than 70,000 ohms more than 70,000 ohms	Magnetic Pick-up (Stator) Test
	Socket #4 and Coil Tower	7000 to 13,000 ohms	Coil Test
	Socket #1 and Coil "Bat" Term.	1.0 to 2.0 ohms Breakerless & Dura-Spark II	

1976 Test Sequence (cont.)

	Test Voltage Between	Should Be	If Not, Conduct
Key Off		0.5 to 1.5 ohms Dura-Spark I	
	Socket #1 and Engine Ground	more than 4 ohms	Short Test
	Socket #4 and Coil "Bat" Term. (Except Dura-Spark I)	1.0 to 2.0 ohms Breakerless	Resistance Wire Test
		0.7 to 1.7 ohms Dura-Spark II	

1978–82 Test Sequence Dura-Spark I & II

	Test Voltage Between	Should Be	If Not, Conduct
Key On	Socket #4 and Engine Ground	Battery Voltage ±0.1 Volt	Module Bias Test
	Socket #1 and Engine Ground	Battery Voltage ±0.1 Volt	Battery Source Test
Cranking	Socket #5 and Engine Ground	8 to 12 volts	Cranking Test
	Jumper #1 to #8—Read Coil "Bat" Term & Engine Ground	more than 6 volts	Starting Circuit Test
	Sockets #7 and #3	½ volt minimum wiggle	Distributor Hardware Test
Key Off	Sockets #7 and #3 Socket #8 and Engine Ground Socket #7 and Engine Ground Socket #3 and Engine Ground	400 to 800 ohms 0 ohms more than 70,000 ohms more than 70,000 ohms	Magnetic Pick-up (Stator) Test
	Socket #4 and Coil Tower	7000 to 13,000 ohms	Coil Test
	Socket #1 and Coil "Bat" Term	1.0 to 2.0 ohms Breakerless & Dura Spark II	
		0.5 to 1.5 ohms Dura-Spark I	
	Socket #1 and Engine Ground	more than 4.0 ohms	Short Test
	Socket #4 and Coil "Bat" Term (Except Dura-Spark I)	1.0 to 2.0 ohms Breakerless	Resistance Wire Test
		0.7 to 1.7 ohms Dura Spark II	

IGNITION SYSTEM
II. Primary (Low Voltage) Portion—A. Dura Spark II

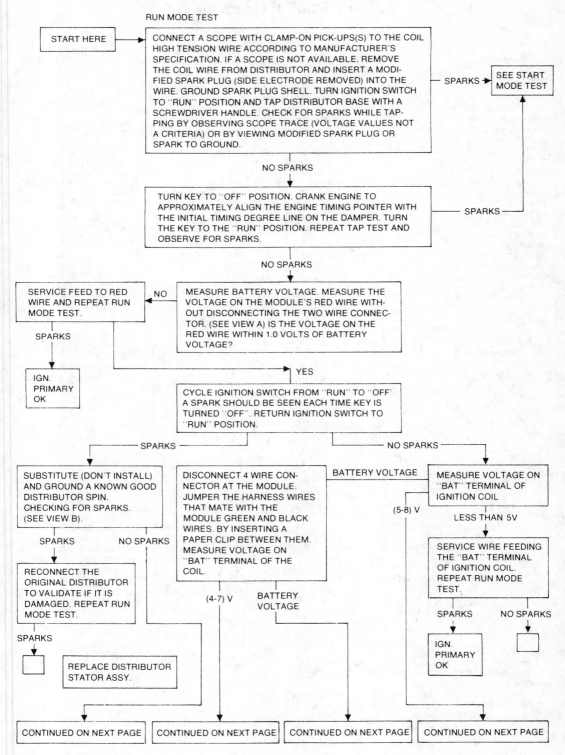

RUN MODE TEST

START HERE

CONNECT A SCOPE WITH CLAMP-ON PICK-UPS(S) TO THE COIL HIGH TENSION WIRE ACCORDING TO MANUFACTURER'S SPECIFICATION. IF A SCOPE IS NOT AVAILABLE, REMOVE THE COIL WIRE FROM DISTRIBUTOR AND INSERT A MODIFIED SPARK PLUG (SIDE ELECTRODE REMOVED) INTO THE WIRE. GROUND SPARK PLUG SHELL. TURN IGNITION SWITCH TO "RUN" POSITION AND TAP DISTRIBUTOR BASE WITH A SCREWDRIVER HANDLE. CHECK FOR SPARKS WHILE TAPPING BY OBSERVING SCOPE TRACE (VOLTAGE VALUES NOT A CRITERIA) OR BY VIEWING MODIFIED SPARK PLUG OR SPARK TO GROUND.

SPARKS → SEE START MODE TEST

NO SPARKS

TURN KEY TO "OFF" POSITION. CRANK ENGINE TO APPROXIMATELY ALIGN THE ENGINE TIMING POINTER WITH THE INITIAL TIMING DEGREE LINE ON THE DAMPER. TURN THE KEY TO THE "RUN" POSITION. REPEAT TAP TEST AND OBSERVE FOR SPARKS.

SPARKS

NO SPARKS

SERVICE FEED TO RED WIRE AND REPEAT RUN MODE TEST.

NO ← MEASURE BATTERY VOLTAGE. MEASURE THE VOLTAGE ON THE MODULE'S RED WIRE WITHOUT DISCONNECTING THE TWO WIRE CONNECTOR. (SEE VIEW A) IS THE VOLTAGE ON THE RED WIRE WITHIN 1.0 VOLTS OF BATTERY VOLTAGE?

SPARKS

IGN. PRIMARY OK

YES

CYCLE IGNITION SWITCH FROM "RUN" TO "OFF" A SPARK SHOULD BE SEEN EACH TIME KEY IS TURNED "OFF". RETURN IGNITION SWITCH TO "RUN" POSITION.

SPARKS

NO SPARKS

SUBSTITUTE (DON'T INSTALL) AND GROUND A KNOWN GOOD DISTRIBUTOR SPIN. CHECKING FOR SPARKS. (SEE VIEW B).

DISCONNECT 4 WIRE CONNECTOR AT THE MODULE. JUMPER THE HARNESS WIRES THAT MATE WITH THE MODULE GREEN AND BLACK WIRES. BY INSERTING A PAPER CLIP BETWEEN THEM. MEASURE VOLTAGE ON "BAT" TERMINAL OF THE COIL.

BATTERY VOLTAGE

MEASURE VOLTAGE ON "BAT" TERMINAL OF IGNITION COIL

(5-8) V

LESS THAN 5V

SPARKS   NO SPARKS

RECONNECT THE ORIGINAL DISTRIBUTOR TO VALIDATE IF IT IS DAMAGED. REPEAT RUN MODE TEST.

(4-7) V   BATTERY VOLTAGE

SERVICE WIRE FEEDING THE "BAT" TERMINAL OF IGNITION COIL. REPEAT RUN MODE TEST.

SPARKS   NO SPARKS

SPARKS

REPLACE DISTRIBUTOR STATOR ASSY.

IGN. PRIMARY OK

CONTINUED ON NEXT PAGE   CONTINUED ON NEXT PAGE   CONTINUED ON NEXT PAGE   CONTINUED ON NEXT PAGE

IGNITION SYSTEM (CONTINUED)
II. Primary (Low Voltage) Portion (continued)
A. Dura Spark II (continued)

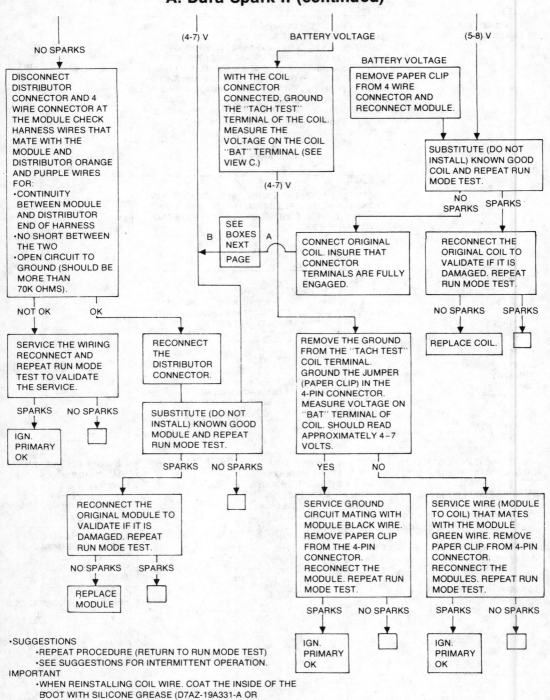

NO SPARKS

(4-7) V

BATTERY VOLTAGE

(5-8) V

BATTERY VOLTAGE

DISCONNECT DISTRIBUTOR CONNECTOR AND 4 WIRE CONNECTOR AT THE MODULE CHECK HARNESS WIRES THAT MATE WITH THE MODULE AND DISTRIBUTOR ORANGE AND PURPLE WIRES FOR:
• CONTINUITY BETWEEN MODULE AND DISTRIBUTOR END OF HARNESS
• NO SHORT BETWEEN THE TWO
• OPEN CIRCUIT TO GROUND (SHOULD BE MORE THAN 70K OHMS).

WITH THE COIL CONNECTOR CONNECTED, GROUND THE "TACH TEST" TERMINAL OF THE COIL. MEASURE THE VOLTAGE ON THE COIL "BAT" TERMINAL (SEE VIEW C.)

REMOVE PAPER CLIP FROM 4 WIRE CONNECTOR AND RECONNECT MODULE.

SUBSTITUTE (DO NOT INSTALL) KNOWN GOOD COIL AND REPEAT RUN MODE TEST.

(4-7) V

B SEE BOXES NEXT PAGE A

CONNECT ORIGINAL COIL. INSURE THAT CONNECTOR TERMINALS ARE FULLY ENGAGED.

NO SPARKS   SPARKS

RECONNECT THE ORIGINAL COIL TO VALIDATE IF IT IS DAMAGED. REPEAT RUN MODE TEST.

NOT OK   OK

NO SPARKS   SPARKS

SERVICE THE WIRING RECONNECT AND REPEAT RUN MODE TEST TO VALIDATE THE SERVICE.

RECONNECT THE DISTRIBUTOR CONNECTOR.

REMOVE THE GROUND FROM THE "TACH TEST" COIL TERMINAL. GROUND THE JUMPER (PAPER CLIP) IN THE 4-PIN CONNECTOR. MEASURE VOLTAGE ON "BAT" TERMINAL OF COIL. SHOULD READ APPROXIMATELY 4–7 VOLTS.

REPLACE COIL.

SPARKS   NO SPARKS

IGN. PRIMARY OK

SUBSTITUTE (DO NOT INSTALL) KNOWN GOOD MODULE AND REPEAT RUN MODE TEST.

SPARKS   NO SPARKS

YES   NO

RECONNECT THE ORIGINAL MODULE TO VALIDATE IF IT IS DAMAGED. REPEAT RUN MODE TEST.

SERVICE GROUND CIRCUIT MATING WITH MODULE BLACK WIRE. REMOVE PAPER CLIP FROM THE 4-PIN CONNECTOR. RECONNECT THE MODULE. REPEAT RUN MODE TEST.

SERVICE WIRE (MODULE TO COIL) THAT MATES WITH THE MODULE GREEN WIRE. REMOVE PAPER CLIP FROM 4-PIN CONNECTOR. RECONNECT THE MODULES. REPEAT RUN MODE TEST.

NO SPARKS   SPARKS

REPLACE MODULE

SPARKS   NO SPARKS

IGN. PRIMARY OK

SPARKS   NO SPARKS

IGN. PRIMARY OK

• SUGGESTIONS
    • REPEAT PROCEDURE (RETURN TO RUN MODE TEST)
    • SEE SUGGESTIONS FOR INTERMITTENT OPERATION.
IMPORTANT
    • WHEN REINSTALLING COIL WIRE. COAT THE INSIDE OF THE BOOT WITH SILICONE GREASE (D7AZ-19A331-A OR EQUIVALENT) USING SMALL, CLEAN SCREWDRIVER BLADE.

IGNITION SYSTEM (CONTINUED)
II. Primary (Low Voltage) Portion (Continued)
A. Dura Spark II (continued)

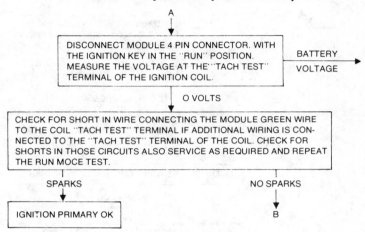

Breakerless Distributor

CAUTION: *1980 California models with the 4.2 liter (255 cu. in.) V8 engine use EEC III ignition system. The distributor is locked into place and adjustment is never required because all timing control is handled by the EEC III module. Rotor alignment is critical with this system and any servicing should be done only by qualified mechanics.*

REMOVAL

1. Remove the air cleaner on the V8 engines.

2. On the 4-cylinder and 6-cylinder in-line engines, remove one thermactor pump mounting bolt, and the drive belt; then swing the pump to one side to allow access to the distributor. If necessary disconnect the thermactor air filter and lines.

3. Disconnect the distributor wiring connector from the vehicle wiring harness.

4. Disconnect the vacuum lines from the distributor.

5. Remove the distributor cap and wires and lay to one side. Remove the rotor and adapter then reinstall the rotor.

6. Scribe a mark on the distributor body and the cylinder block indicating the position of the rotor in the distributor and the distributor in the block. These marks will be used as guides during installation of the distributor.

7. Remove the distributor hold down bolt and clamp and lift the distributor out of the block.

NOTE: *Do not rotate the engine while the distributor is out of the block, or it will be necessary to time the engine.*

INSTALLATION

1a. If the engine was cranked (disturbed) with the distributor removed, it will now be necessary to retime the engine. If the distributor has been installed incorrectly and the engine will not start, remove the distributor from the engine and start over again. Hold the distributor close to the engine and install the cap on the distributor in its normal position. Locate the No. 1 spark plug tower on the distributor cap. Scribe a mark on the body of the distributor directly below the No. 1 spark plug wire tower on the distributor cap. Remove the distributor cap from the distributor and move the distributor and cap to one side. Remove the No. 1 spark plug and crank the engine over until the No. 1 cylinder is on its compression stroke. To accomplish this, place a wrench on the lower engine pulley and turn the engine slowly in a clockwise (4 & 6 cylinder) or counterclockwise (V8) direction until the TDC mark on the crankshaft damper aligns with the timing pointer. If you place your finger in the No. 1 spark plug hole, you will feel air escaping as the piston rises in the combustion chamber. One of the ar-

IGNITION SYSTEM (CONTINUED)
II. Primary (Low Voltage) Portion (continued)
A. Dura Spark II (continued)

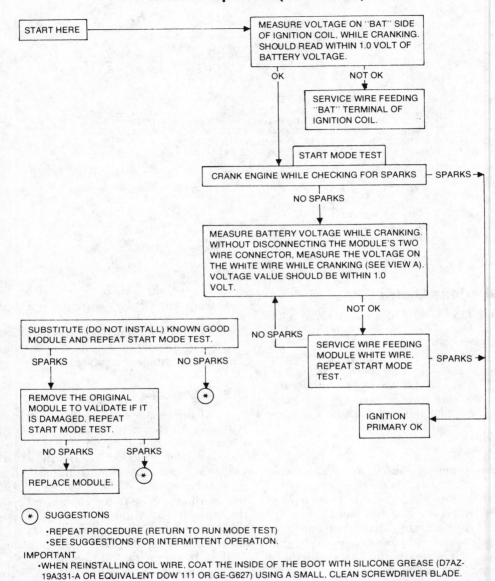

START HERE → MEASURE VOLTAGE ON "BAT" SIDE OF IGNITION COIL, WHILE CRANKING. SHOULD READ WITHIN 1.0 VOLT OF BATTERY VOLTAGE.

OK — NOT OK

NOT OK → SERVICE WIRE FEEDING "BAT" TERMINAL OF IGNITION COIL.

START MODE TEST

CRANK ENGINE WHILE CHECKING FOR SPARKS — SPARKS →

NO SPARKS

MEASURE BATTERY VOLTAGE WHILE CRANKING. WITHOUT DISCONNECTING THE MODULE'S TWO WIRE CONNECTOR, MEASURE THE VOLTAGE ON THE WHITE WIRE WHILE CRANKING (SEE VIEW A). VOLTAGE VALUE SHOULD BE WITHIN 1.0 VOLT.

NOT OK

NO SPARKS

SUBSTITUTE (DO NOT INSTALL) KNOWN GOOD MODULE AND REPEAT START MODE TEST.

SPARKS — NO SPARKS

SERVICE WIRE FEEDING MODULE WHITE WIRE. REPEAT START MODE TEST. — SPARKS →

REMOVE THE ORIGINAL MODULE TO VALIDATE IF IT IS DAMAGED. REPEAT START MODE TEST.

(*)

NO SPARKS — SPARKS

IGNITION PRIMARY OK

REPLACE MODULE.

(*)

(*) SUGGESTIONS
- REPEAT PROCEDURE (RETURN TO RUN MODE TEST)
- SEE SUGGESTIONS FOR INTERMITTENT OPERATION.

IMPORTANT
- WHEN REINSTALLING COIL WIRE, COAT THE INSIDE OF THE BOOT WITH SILICONE GREASE (D7AZ-19A331-A OR EQUIVALENT DOW 111 OR GE-G627) USING A SMALL, CLEAN SCREWDRIVER BLADE.

mature segments must be aligned with the stator as shown in the accompanying illustration to install the distributor. Make sure that the oil pump intermediate shaft properly engages the distributor shaft. It may be necessary to crank the engine with the starter, after the distributor drive gear is partially engaged, in order to engage the oil pump intermediate shaft. Install, but do not tighten the retaining clamp and bolt. Rotate the distributor to advance the timing to a point where the armature tooth is aligned properly. Tighten the clamp.

1b. If the engine was not cranked (disturbed) when the distributor was removed, position the distributor in the block with the rotor aligned with the mark previously scribed on the distributor body and the marks on the

RUN MODE TEST

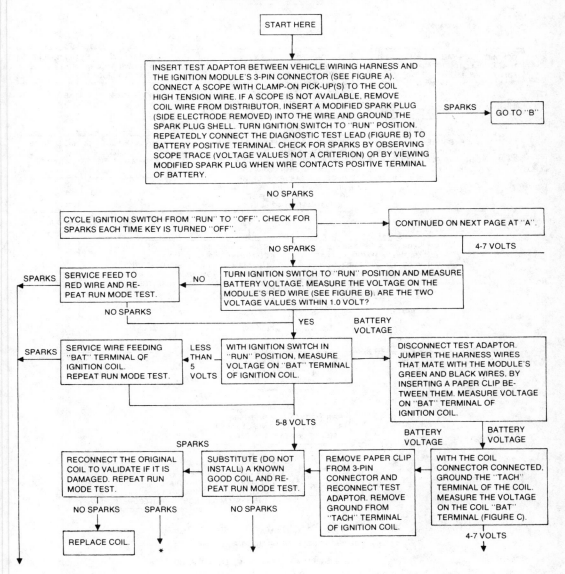

START HERE

INSERT TEST ADAPTOR BETWEEN VEHICLE WIRING HARNESS AND THE IGNITION MODULE'S 3-PIN CONNECTOR (SEE FIGURE A). CONNECT A SCOPE WITH CLAMP-ON PICK-UP(S) TO THE COIL HIGH TENSION WIRE. IF A SCOPE IS NOT AVAILABLE, REMOVE COIL WIRE FROM DISTRIBUTOR, INSERT A MODIFIED SPARK PLUG (SIDE ELECTRODE REMOVED) INTO THE WIRE AND GROUND THE SPARK PLUG SHELL. TURN IGNITION SWITCH TO "RUN" POSITION. REPEATEDLY CONNECT THE DIAGNOSTIC TEST LEAD (FIGURE B) TO BATTERY POSITIVE TERMINAL. CHECK FOR SPARKS BY OBSERVING SCOPE TRACE (VOLTAGE VALUES NOT A CRITERION) OR BY VIEWING MODIFIED SPARK PLUG WHEN WIRE CONTACTS POSITIVE TERMINAL OF BATTERY.

SPARKS → GO TO "B"

NO SPARKS

CYCLE IGNITION SWITCH FROM "RUN" TO "OFF". CHECK FOR SPARKS EACH TIME KEY IS TURNED "OFF".

CONTINUED ON NEXT PAGE AT "A".

4-7 VOLTS

NO SPARKS

SERVICE FEED TO RED WIRE AND REPEAT RUN MODE TEST.

SPARKS

NO

TURN IGNITION SWITCH TO "RUN" POSITION AND MEASURE BATTERY VOLTAGE. MEASURE THE VOLTAGE ON THE MODULE'S RED WIRE (SEE FIGURE B). ARE THE TWO VOLTAGE VALUES WITHIN 1.0 VOLT?

NO SPARKS

YES

BATTERY VOLTAGE

SERVICE WIRE FEEDING "BAT" TERMINAL OF IGNITION COIL. REPEAT RUN MODE TEST.

SPARKS

LESS THAN 5 VOLTS

WITH IGNITION SWITCH IN "RUN" POSITION, MEASURE VOLTAGE ON "BAT" TERMINAL OF IGNITION COIL.

DISCONNECT TEST ADAPTOR. JUMPER THE HARNESS WIRES THAT MATE WITH THE MODULE'S GREEN AND BLACK WIRES, BY INSERTING A PAPER CLIP BETWEEN THEM. MEASURE VOLTAGE ON "BAT" TERMINAL OF IGNITION COIL.

5-8 VOLTS

BATTERY VOLTAGE

BATTERY VOLTAGE

SPARKS

RECONNECT THE ORIGINAL COIL TO VALIDATE IF IT IS DAMAGED. REPEAT RUN MODE TEST.

SUBSTITUTE (DO NOT INSTALL) A KNOWN GOOD COIL AND REPEAT RUN MODE TEST.

REMOVE PAPER CLIP FROM 3-PIN CONNECTOR AND RECONNECT TEST ADAPTOR. REMOVE GROUND FROM "TACH" TERMINAL OF IGNITION COIL.

WITH THE COIL CONNECTOR CONNECTED, GROUND THE "TACH" TERMINAL OF THE COIL. MEASURE THE VOLTAGE ON THE COIL "BAT" TERMINAL (FIGURE C).

NO SPARKS   SPARKS

NO SPARKS

4-7 VOLTS

REPLACE COIL.

*

*SUGGESTIONS:

•REPEAT PROCEDURE (START AT RUN MODE TEST)

•SEE SUGGESTIONS FOR INTERMITTENT OPERATION

distributor body and cylinder block in alignment. Install the distributor hold-down bolt and clamp fingertight.

2. Install the vacuum hoses and connect the ignition wire to the wiring harness.

3. Install the rotor adapter and distributor cap.

4. Install the thermactor pump and belt on the four and in-line six cylinder engines. Adjust the belt tension so that there is a ¼ inch deflection at its longest point.

5. Connect the thermactor hoses and the filter.

6. Install the air cleaner if removed and check the ignition timing.

Alternator

The alternator charging system consists of the alternator, voltage regulator, warning light, battery, and fuse link wire.

A failure of any component of the charging

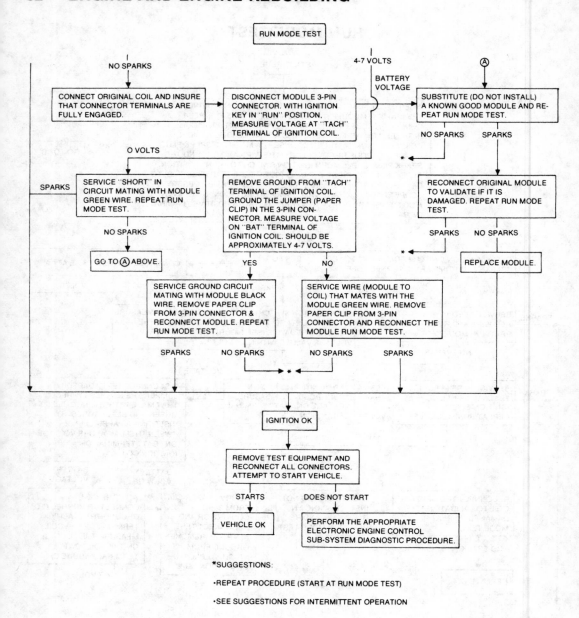

RUN MODE TEST

NO SPARKS

4-7 VOLTS

BATTERY VOLTAGE

Ⓐ

CONNECT ORIGINAL COIL AND INSURE THAT CONNECTOR TERMINALS ARE FULLY ENGAGED.

DISCONNECT MODULE 3-PIN CONNECTOR. WITH IGNITION KEY IN "RUN" POSITION, MEASURE VOLTAGE AT "TACH" TERMINAL OF IGNITION COIL.

SUBSTITUTE (DO NOT INSTALL) A KNOWN GOOD MODULE AND RE-PEAT RUN MODE TEST.

O VOLTS

NO SPARKS   SPARKS

SPARKS

SERVICE "SHORT" IN CIRCUIT MATING WITH MODULE GREEN WIRE. REPEAT RUN MODE TEST.

REMOVE GROUND FROM "TACH" TERMINAL OF IGNITION COIL. GROUND THE JUMPER (PAPER CLIP) IN THE 3-PIN CON-NECTOR. MEASURE VOLTAGE ON "BAT" TERMINAL OF IGNITION COIL. SHOULD BE APPROXIMATELY 4-7 VOLTS.

RECONNECT ORIGINAL MODULE TO VALIDATE IF IT IS DAMAGED. REPEAT RUN MODE TEST.

NO SPARKS

*

GO TO Ⓐ ABOVE.

YES   NO

SPARKS   NO SPARKS

*

REPLACE MODULE.

SERVICE GROUND CIRCUIT MATING WITH MODULE BLACK WIRE. REMOVE PAPER CLIP FROM 3-PIN CONNECTOR & RECONNECT MODULE. REPEAT RUN MODE TEST.

SERVICE WIRE (MODULE TO COIL) THAT MATES WITH THE MODULE GREEN WIRE. REMOVE PAPER CLIP FROM 3-PIN CONNECTOR AND RECONNECT THE MODULE RUN MODE TEST.

SPARKS   NO SPARKS   NO SPARKS   SPARKS

*

IGNITION OK

REMOVE TEST EQUIPMENT AND RECONNECT ALL CONNECTORS. ATTEMPT TO START VEHICLE.

STARTS   DOES NOT START

VEHICLE OK

PERFORM THE APPROPRIATE ELECTRONIC ENGINE CONTROL SUB-SYSTEM DIAGNOSTIC PROCEDURE.

*SUGGESTIONS:

•REPEAT PROCEDURE (START AT RUN MODE TEST)

•SEE SUGGESTIONS FOR INTERMITTENT OPERATION

system can cause the entire system to stop functioning. Because of this, the charging system can be very difficult to troubleshoot when problems occur.

When the ignition key is turned on, current flows from the battery, through the charging system indicator light on the instrument panel, to the voltage regulator, and to the alternator. Since the alternator is not producing any current, the alternator warning light comes on. When the engine is started, the alternator begins to produce current and turns the alternator light off. As the alternator turns and produces current, the current

is divided in two ways: part to the battery to charge the battery and power the electrical components of the vehicle, and part is returned to the alternator to enable it to increase its output. In this situation, the alternator is receiving current from the battery and from itself. A voltage regulator is wired into the current supply to the alternator to prevent it from receiving too much current which would cause it to put out too much current. Conversely, if the voltage regulator does not allow the alternator to receive enough current, the battery will not be fully charged and will eventually go dead.

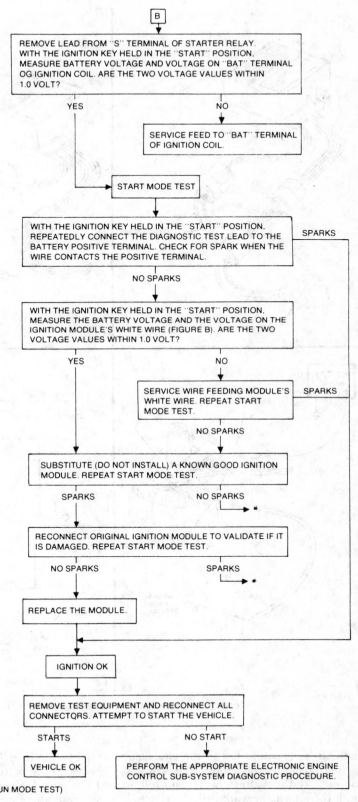

B

REMOVE LEAD FROM "S" TERMINAL OF STARTER RELAY. WITH THE IGNITION KEY HELD IN THE "START" POSITION, MEASURE BATTERY VOLTAGE AND VOLTAGE ON "BAT" TERMINAL OG IGNITION COIL. ARE THE TWO VOLTAGE VALUES WITHIN 1.0 VOLT?

YES   NO

SERVICE FEED TO "BAT" TERMINAL OF IGNITION COIL.

START MODE TEST

WITH THE IGNITION KEY HELD IN THE "START" POSITION, REPEATEDLY CONNECT THE DIAGNOSTIC TEST LEAD TO THE BATTERY POSITIVE TERMINAL. CHECK FOR SPARK WHEN THE WIRE CONTACTS THE POSITIVE TERMINAL.   SPARKS

NO SPARKS

WITH THE IGNITION KEY HELD IN THE "START" POSITION, MEASURE THE BATTERY VOLTAGE AND THE VOLTAGE ON THE IGNITION MODULE'S WHITE WIRE (FIGURE B). ARE THE TWO VOLTAGE VALUES WITHIN 1.0 VOLT?

YES   NO

SERVICE WIRE FEEDING MODULE'S WHITE WIRE. REPEAT START MODE TEST.   SPARKS

NO SPARKS

SUBSTITUTE (DO NOT INSTALL) A KNOWN GOOD IGNITION MODULE. REPEAT START MODE TEST.

SPARKS   NO SPARKS
                                    → *

RECONNECT ORIGINAL IGNITION MODULE TO VALIDATE IF IT IS DAMAGED. REPEAT START MODE TEST.

NO SPARKS   SPARKS
                                → *

REPLACE THE MODULE.

IGNITION OK

REMOVE TEST EQUIPMENT AND RECONNECT ALL CONNECTQRS. ATTEMPT TO START THE VEHICLE.

STARTS   NO START

VEHICLE OK   PERFORM THE APPROPRIATE ELECTRONIC ENGINE CONTROL SUB-SYSTEM DIAGNOSTIC PROCEDURE.

*SUGGESTIONS:

•REPEAT PROCEDURE (START AT RUN MODE TEST)

•SEE SUGGESTIONS FOR INTERMITTENT OPERATION

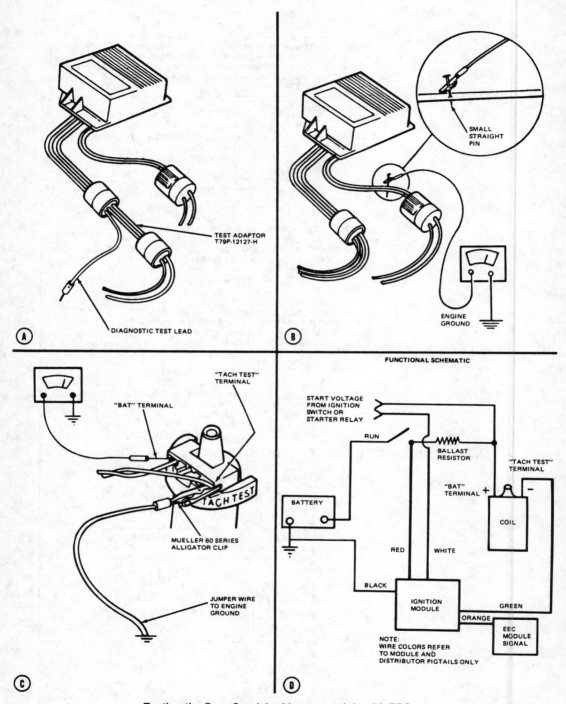

A — TEST ADAPTOR T79P-12127-H

DIAGNOSTIC TEST LEAD

B — SMALL STRAIGHT PIN

ENGINE GROUND

C — "TACH TEST" TERMINAL

"BAT" TERMINAL

TACH TEST

MUELLER 60 SERIES ALLIGATOR CLIP

JUMPER WIRE TO ENGINE GROUND

D — FUNCTIONAL SCHEMATIC

START VOLTAGE FROM IGNITION SWITCH OR STARTER RELAY

RUN

BALLAST RESISTOR

"TACH TEST" TERMINAL

"BAT" TERMINAL

COIL

BATTERY

RED   WHITE

BLACK

IGNITION MODULE

GREEN

ORANGE

EEC MODULE SIGNAL

NOTE: WIRE COLORS REFER TO MODULE AND DISTRIBUTOR PIGTAILS ONLY

Testing the Dura Spark ignition on models with EEC

The battery is connected to the alternator at all times, whether the ignition key is turned on or not. If the battery were shorted to ground, the alternator would also be shorted. This would damage the alternator. To pre-vent this, a fuse link is installed in the wiring between the battery and the alternator on all 1970 and later models. If the battery is shorted, the fuse link is melted, protecting the alternator.

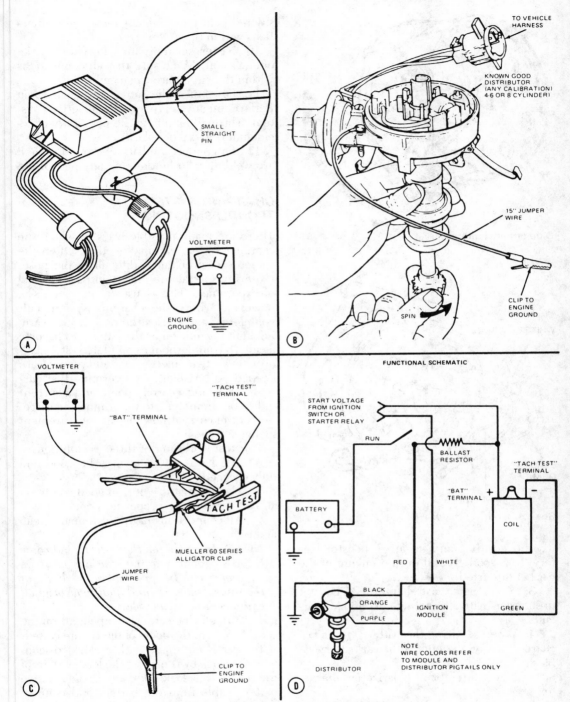

A

SMALL STRAIGHT PIN

VOLTMETER

ENGINE GROUND

B

TO VEHICLE HARNESS

KNOWN GOOD DISTRIBUTOR (ANY CALIBRATION) 4-6 OR 8 CYLINDER)

15" JUMPER WIRE

CLIP TO ENGINE GROUND

SPIN

C

VOLTMETER

"TACH TEST" TERMINAL

"BAT" TERMINAL

MUELLER 60 SERIES ALLIGATOR CLIP

JUMPER WIRE

CLIP TO ENGINE GROUND

D

FUNCTIONAL SCHEMATIC

START VOLTAGE FROM IGNITION SWITCH OR STARTER RELAY

RUN

BALLAST RESISTOR

"TACH TEST" TERMINAL

"BAT" TERMINAL

COIL

BATTERY

RED   WHITE

BLACK
ORANGE
PURPLE

IGNITION MODULE

GREEN

DISTRIBUTOR

NOTE
WIRE COLORS REFER TO MODULE AND DISTRIBUTOR PIGTAILS ONLY

Testing the Dura Spark ignition on models without EEC

ALTERNATOR PRECAUTIONS

Several precautions must be observed with alternator equipped vehicles to avoid damaging the unit. They are as follows:

1. If the battery is removed for any reason, make sure that it is reconnected with the correct polarity. Reversing the battery connections may result in damage to the one-way rectifiers.

2. When utilizing a booster battery as a starting aid, always connect it as follows: pos-

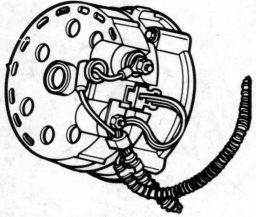

Side terminal alternator

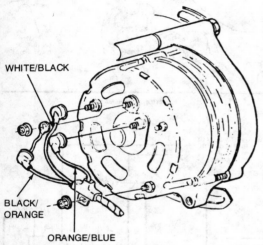

WHITE/BLACK

BLACK/ ORANGE

ORANGE/BLUE

Rear terminal alternator

itive to positive, and negative (booster battery) to a good ground on the engine of the car being started.

3. Never use a fast charger as a booster to start cars with alternating-current (AC) circuits.

4. When servicing the battery with a fast charger, always disconnect the car battery cables.

5. Never attempt to polarize an alternator.

6. Avoid long soldering times when replacing diodes or transistors. Prolonged heat is damaging to alternators.

7. Do not use test lamps of more than 12 volts (V) for checking diode continuity.

8. Do not short across or ground any of the terminals on the alternator.

9. The polarity of the battery, alternator, and regulator must be matched and considered before making any electrical connections within the system.

10. Never separate the alternator on an open circuit. Make sure that all connections within the circuit are clean and tight.

11. Disconnect the battery terminals when performing any service on the electrical system. This will eliminate the possibility of accidental reversal of polarity.

12. Disconnect the battery ground cable if arc welding is to be done on any part of the car.

CHARGING SYSTEM TROUBLESHOOTING

There are many possible ways in which the charging system can malfunction. Often the source of a problem is difficult to diagnose, requiring special equipment and a good deal of experience. This is usually not the case, however, where the charging system fails completely and causes the dash board warning light to come on or the battery to become dead. To troubleshoot a complete system failure only two pieces of equipment are needed—a test light, to determine that current is reaching a certain point; and a current indicator (ammeter), to determine the direction of the current flow and its measurement in amps.

This test works under three assumptions:

A. The battery is known to be good and fully charged;

B. The alternator belt is in good condition and adjusted to the proper tension;

C. All connections in the system are clean and tight.

NOTE: *In order for the current indicator to give a valid reading, the car must be equipped with battery cables which are of the same gauge size and quality as original equipment battery cables.*

1. Turn off all electrical components on the car. Make sure the doors of the car are closed. If the car is equipped with a clock, disconnect the clock by removing the lead wire from the rear of the clock. Disconnect the positive battery cable from the battery and connect the ground wire on a test light to the disconnected positive battery cable. Touch the probe end of the test light to the positive battery post. The test light should not light. If the test light does light, there is a short or open circuit on the car.

2. Disconnect the voltage regulator wiring harness connector at the voltage regulator. Turn on the ignition key. Connect the wire

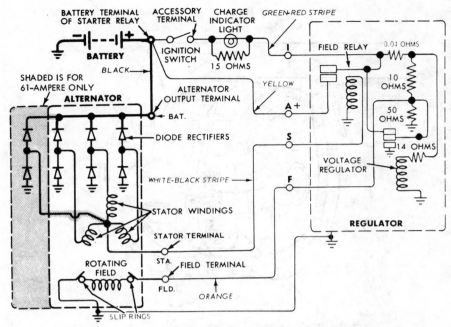

Alternator charging circuit w/indicator light—rear terminal type

on a test light to a good ground (engine bolt). Touch the probe end of a test light to the ignition wire connector into the voltage regulator wiring connector. This wire corresponds to the "I" terminal on the regulator. If the test light goes on, the charging system warning light circuit is complete. If the test light does not come on and the warning light on the instrument panel is on, either the resistor wire, which is parallel with the warning

light, or the wiring to the voltage regulator, is defective. If the test light does not come on and the warning light is not on, either the bulb is defective or the power supply wire from the battery through the ignition switch to the bulb has an open circuit. Connect the wiring harness to the regulator.

3. Examine the fuse link wire in the wiring harness from the starter relay to the alternator. If the insulation on the wire is cracked

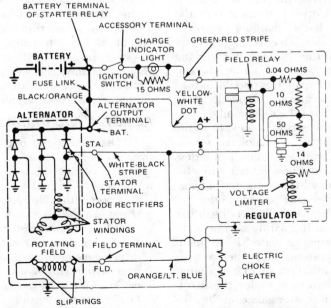

Alternator charging circuit w/indicator light—side terminal type

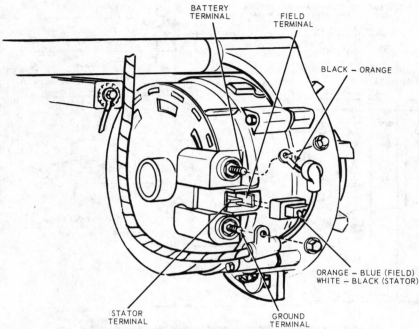

BATTERY
TERMINAL

FIELD
TERMINAL

BLACK – ORANGE

ORANGE – BLUE (FIELD)
WHITE – BLACK (STATOR)

STATOR
TERMINAL

GROUND
TERMINAL

Alternator terminal locations—side terminal type

or split, the fuse link may be melted. Connect a test light to the fuse link by attaching the ground wire on the test light to an engine bolt and touching the probe end of the light to the bottom of the fuse link wire where it splices into the alternator output wire. If the bulb in the test light does not light, the fuse link is melted.

4. Start the engine and place a current indicator on the positive battery cable. Turn off all electrical accessories and make sure the doors are closed. If the charging system is working properly, the gauge will show a draw of about 5 amps. If the system is not working properly, the gauge will show a draw of about 5 amps. A charge moves the needle toward the battery, a draw moves the needle away from the battery. Turn the engine off.

5. Disconnect the wiring harness from the voltage regulator at the regulator connector. Connect a male spade terminal (solderless connector) to each end of a jumper wire. Insert one end of the wire into the wiring harness connector which corresponds to the "A" terminal on the regulator. Insert the other end of the wire into the wiring harness connector which corresponds to the "F" terminal on the regulator. Position the connector with the jumper wire installed so that it cannot contact any metal survace under the hood. Position a current indicator gauge on the positive battery cable. Have an assistant start the

engine. Observe the reading on the current indicator. Have your assistant slowly raise the speed of the engine to about 2,000 rpm or until the current indicator needle stops moving, whichever comes first. Do not run the engine for more than a short period of time in this condition. If the wiring harness connector or jumper wire becomes excessively hot during this test, turn off the engine and check for a grounded wire in the regulator wiring harness. If the current indicator shows a charge of about three amps less than the output of the alternator, the alternator is working properly. If the previous tests showed a draw, the voltage regulator is defective. If the gauge does not show the proper charging rate, the alternator is defective.

REMOVAL AND INSTALLATION

1. Disconnect the negative battery cable from the battery.

2. Disconnect the wires from the alternator or generator.

3. Loosen the alternator mounting bolts and remove the drive belt.

NOTE: *1981 and later Thunderbird and XR-7 cars equipped with automatic overdrive transmissions and air conditioning have a five rib, K-section belt and automatic tensioner. A special tool must be made to remove the tension from the tensioner arm. Loosen the idler pulley pivot and ad-*

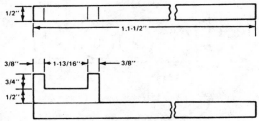

Fabricated absorber arm deflection tool

juster bolts before using the tool. See the accompanying illustration for tool details.

4. Remove the alternator mounting bolts and spacer (if equipped), and remove the alternator.

5. To install, position the alternator on its brackets and install the attaching bolts and spacer (if so equipped).

6. Connect the wires to the alternator.

7. Position the drive belt on the alternator pulley. Adjust the belt tension as outlined in Chapter 1.

8. Connect the negative battery cable.

Firing Order

To avoid confusion, replace spark plug wires one at a time.

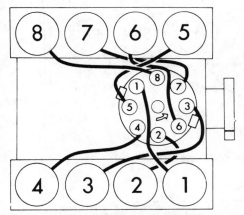

FORD MOTOR CO. 302, 429, 460 V8 (through 1974)
Engine firing order: 1-5-4-2-6-3-7-8
Distributor rotation: counterclockwise

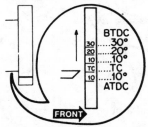

1971 timing mark
(except 429 Hi-Perf.)

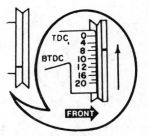

1971 429 V8 Hi-Perf.

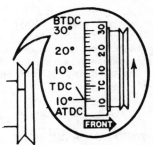

Timing mark through
1974 and 1971
429 Hi-Perf.

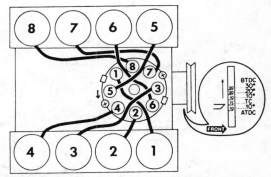

Ford Motor Co. 255, 302, 460 V8 (1975 and later)
Engine firing order: 1-5-4-2-6-3-7-8 Distributor rotation: counterclockwise (Squares are positions of latches on 1975–76 models; circles are positions of latches on 1977 and later models)

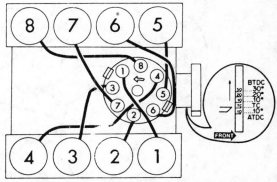

FORD MOTOR CO. 351, 400 V8 (through 1974)
Engine firing order: 1-3-7-2-6-5-4-8
Distributor rotation: counterclockwise

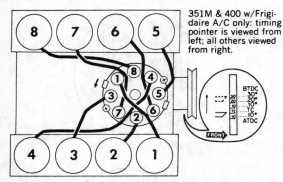

351M & 400 w/Frigidaire A/C only; timing pointer is viewed from left; all others viewed from right.

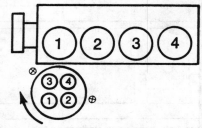

FORD MOTOR CO. 4-140 (2300cc)
Engine firing order: 1-3-4-2
Distributor rotation: clockwise

FORD MOTOR CO. 351, 400 V8 (1975 and later)
Engine firing order: 1-3-7-2-6-5-4-8
Distributor rotation: counterclockwise
(Squares are position of latches on 1975–76 models; circles are position of latches on 1977 and later models.)

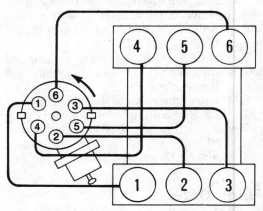

FORD MOTOR CO. V6-232
Engine firing order: 1-4-2-5-3-6
Distributor rotation: counterclockwise

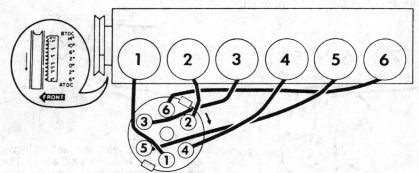

FORD MOTOR CO. 200, 250 6-cyl. (1977 and later)
Engine firing order: 1-5-3-6-2-4
Distributor rotation: clockwise

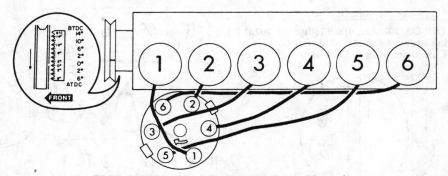

FORD MOTOR CO. 170, 200, 250 6-cyl. (through 1976)
Engine firing order: 1-5-3-6-2-4
Distributor rotation: clockwise

Voltage Regulator

From 1971–73, all models were equipped with a nonadjustable electromechanical voltage regulator. In 1974, an adjustable transistorized unit was introduced, and all models through 1977 were supplied with either type. A simple inspection will determine which regulator is on your vehicle. The cover of the electromechanical regulator is held in place by rivets, the transistorized unit uses screws. Beginning in 1978, a completely solid-state regulator is used.

REMOVAL AND INSTALLATION

1. Remove the battery ground cable. On models with the regulator mounted behind the battery, it is necessary to remove the battery hold-down, and to move the battery.
2. Remove the regulator mounting screws.
3. Disconnect the regulator from the wiring harness.
4. Connect the new regulator to the wiring harness.
5. Mount the regulator to the regulator mounting plate. The radio suppression condenser mounts under one mounting screw; the ground lead under the other mounting screw. Tighten the mounting screws.
6. If the battery was moved to gain access to the regulator, position the battery and install the hold-down. Connect the battery

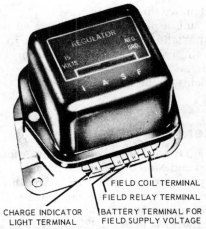

FIELD COIL TERMINAL
FIELD RELAY TERMINAL
CHARGE INDICATOR
LIGHT TERMINAL
BATTERY TERMINAL FOR
FIELD SUPPLY VOLTAGE

Electromechanical voltage regulator

ground cable, and test the system for proper voltage regulation.

VOLTAGE LIMITER ADJUSTMENT

Transistorized Regulator Only

NOTE: *The only reason for making this adjustment is if the alternator field current voltage is too high or too low. The test to determine this information should be performed at a garage with professional testing equipment.*

1. Run the engine to normal operating temperature and then shut it off.

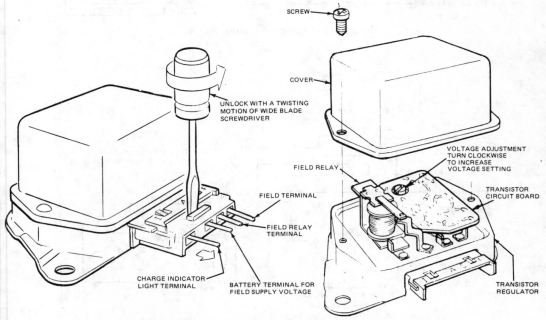

SCREW

COVER

UNLOCK WITH A TWISTING
MOTION OF WIDE BLADE
SCREWDRIVER

FIELD RELAY

FIELD TERMINAL

FIELD RELAY
TERMINAL

VOLTAGE ADJUSTMENT
TURN CLOCKWISE
TO INCREASE
VOLTAGE SETTING

TRANSISTOR
CIRCUIT BOARD

CHARGE INDICATOR
LIGHT TERMINAL

BATTERY TERMINAL FOR
FIELD SUPPLY VOLTAGE

TRANSISTOR
REGULATOR

Voltage limiter adjustment—transistorized regulator only

2. Remove the regulator cover.

3. Using a plastic strip as a screwdriver, turn the adjusting screw clockwise to increase the voltage setting, counterclockwise to decrease the setting.

4. Reinstall the regulator cover.

Starter

There are two different types of starter found on Ford and Mercury mid-size models; their use depends upon engine size. All 6 cylinder engines and most V8's are equipped with a positive engagement starter. A solenoid actuated starter is used on 429 and 460 V8 engines only. Since a greater amount of starting power is required by the 429 and 460 engines, the solenoid actuated starter is constructed with more coil and armature windings to deliver the necessary current. The presence of a solenoid mechanism is incidental and does not affect starting power.

The positive engagement starter system employs a starter relay, usually mounted inside the engine compartment on a fender wall, to transfer battery current to the starter. The relay is activated by the ignition switch and, when engaged, it creates a direct current from the battery to the starter windings. Simultaneously, the armature begins to turn and the starter drive is pushed out to engage the flywheel.

In the solenoid actuated starter system, battery current is first directed to a solenoid assembly which is mounted on the starter case. The current closes the solenoid contacts, which engages the drive pinion and directs current to the coil windings, causing the armature to rotate. While this system does not need a starter relay, some models were nevertheless equipped with one in order to simplify assembly procedures. These vehicles also have a connector link attached to the solenoid, which provides a hook up for the relay wire.

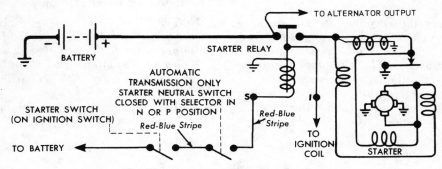

Positive engagement starter circuit

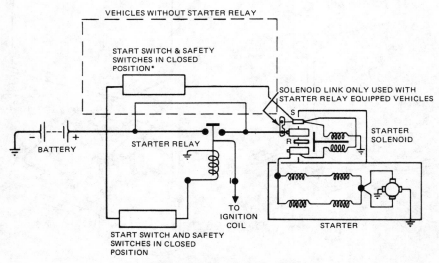

Solenoid actuated starter circuit

REMOVAL AND INSTALLATION

1. Disconnect the negative battery cable.

2. Raise the front of the car and install jackstands beneath the frame. Firmly apply the parking brake and place blocks in back of the rear wheels.

3. Disconnect the heavy starter cable at the starter. On solenoid actuated starters (429 and 460 V8 only), label and disconnect the wires from the solenoid.

4. Turn the front wheels fully to the right. On some later models it will be necessary to remove the frame brace. On many models, it will be necessary to remove the two bolts retaining the steering idler arm to the frame to gain access to the starter.

5. Remove the starter mounting bolts and remove the starter.

6. Reverse the above procedure to install. Torque the mounting bolts to 12–15 ft. lbs. on starters with 3 mounting bolts and 15–20 ft. lbs. on starters with 2 mounting bolts. Torque the idler arm retaining bolts to 28–35 ft. lbs. (if removed). Make sure that the nut securing the heavy cable to the starter is snugged down tightly.

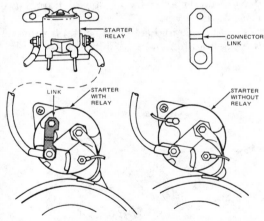

Solenoid connector link for use with starter relay

OVERHAUL

Brush Replacement

1. Remove starter from engine as previously outlined.

2. On positive engagement starters, remove the starter drive plunger lever cover and gasket.

3. On solenoid actuated starters, disconnect the copper strap from the starter terminal on the solenoid. Remove the retaining screws and detach the solenoid assembly from the starter housing.

4. Loosen and remove the brush cover band and remove the brushes from their holders.

5. Remove the two through bolts from the starter frame.

6. Separate the drive-end housing, starter frame and brush end plate assemblies.

7. On positive engagement starters, remove the starter drive plunger lever and pivot pin, and remove the armature.

8. On solenoid actuated starters:

  a. Remove the solenoid plunger and shift fork assembly. (If either the plunger or the fork is to be replaced, they can be separated by removing the roll pin.)

  b. Remove the armature and drive assembly from the frame.

9. Remove the ground brush retaining screws from the frame and remove the brushes.

10. Cut the insulated brush leads from the field coils, as close to the field connection point as possible.

11. Clean and inspect the starter motor.

12. Replace the brush end plate if the insulator between the field brush holder and the end plate is cracked or broken.

13. Position the new insulated field brushes lead on the field coil connection. Position and crimp the clip provided with the brushes to hold the brush lead to the connection. Solder the lead, clip, and connection together using resin core solder. Use a 300-watt soldering iron.

14. Install the ground brush leads to the frame with the retaining screws.

15. Reassemble in reverse order.

17. Torque the through bolts to 55–75 in. lbs.

18. If possible, connect the starter to a battery and check its operation before reinstalling it in the vehicle.

Drive Replacement

1. Remove the starter as outlined previously.

2. On positive engagement starters, remove the starter drive plunger lever and gasket and the brush cover band.

3. On solenoid actuated starters, disconnect the copper strap from the starter terminal on the solenoid. Remove the retaining screws and detach the solenoid assembly from the starter housing.

4. Remove the two through-bolts from the starter frame.

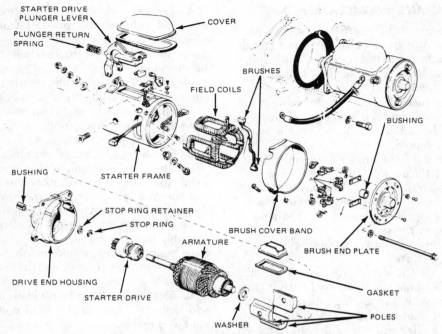

Exploded view of positive engagement starter

5. Separate the drive end housing from the starter frame.

NOTE: *On positive engagement starters, the starter drive plunger lever return spring may fall out after detaching the drive end housing. If not, remove it.*

6. On positive engagement starters, remove the pivot pin which attaches the starter drive plunger lever to the starter frame and remove the lever.

7. On solenoid actuated starters, remove the solenoid plunger and shift fork assembly.

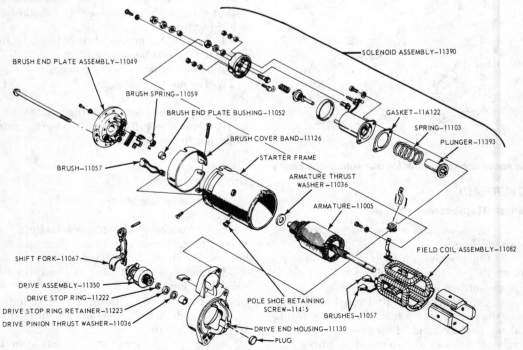

Exploded view of solenoid actuated starter

(If either the plunger or the fork is to be replaced, they can be separated by removing the roll pin.)

8. Remove the stop ring retainer and stop ring from the armature shaft.

9. Slide the starter drive off the armature shaft.

10. Examine the wear pattern on the starter drive teeth. There should be evidence of full contact between the starter drive teeth and the flywheel ring gear teeth. If there is evidence of irregular wear, examine the flywheel ring gear for damage and replace if necessary.

11. Reassemble in reverse order.

12. Apply a thin coat of white grease to the armature shaft before installing the drive gear. Place a small amount of grease in the drive end housing bearing.

13. Tighten the starter through bolts to 55–75 in. lbs.

14. If possible, connect the starter to a battery and check its operation before installing it in the vehicle.

ENGINE MECHANICAL

Design

4 CYLINDER 140 CU. IN. ENGINE

The 4 cylinder 140 cu. in. engine is an overhead cam engine of lightweight iron construction. The crankshaft is supported on five main bearings and the camshaft by four. Main, connecting rod, camshaft and auxiliary shaft bearings are all replaceable.

The camshaft is driven from the crankshaft by a cogged belt, which also operates the auxiliary shaft, and through this shaft, the oil pump, fuel pump and distributor.

The water pump and fan are separately driven from the crankshaft by a conventional V-belt, which also drives the alternator.

Hydraulic valve lash adjusters are used in the valve train. Their action is similar to the hydraulic tappets used in push rod engines and they are constructed and serviced in the same manner. The cylinder head has drilled oil passages to provide engine oil pressure to the lash adjusters. A set of metric wrenches is required to service this engine.

6 CYLINDER 200, AND 250 CU. IN. ENGINE

The 200 cu. in. engines are an overhead valve design of lightweight cast iron construction. Hydraulic valve tappets are used.

V6 AND V8

The remaining engines used on these models are a V6 of 232 cu. in. and 6 V8s with 6 different cubic inch displacements: 255, 302, 351, 400, 429, 460. Moreover, these five engine sizes represent three different engine families. The 232, 255, 302 and 351 Windsor are in the first engine family, the small blocks. They are characterized by wedge-shaped combustion chambers, individual stud-mounted rocker arms and trapezoidal-shaped valve covers.

The second family is based on the small block design, but has larger valves and semi-hemispherical combustion chambers. The engines in this category are the 351 Cleveland, the 351 Modified and the 400. The 351C was used in 1971–74 models, sometimes appearing in its Cobra Jet variation. The 351M, which is a modified Cleveland design, was first available in 1975. And, the 400 cubic inch V8 engine is used on 1972 and later models.

The final group of engines is comprised of the 429 and 460. The 429 was installed in 1971–73 models and was available in several high performance variations. The 460 engine first became available in these models in 1973 and was discontinued after 1976, when it was reserved for full-size models. This family of V8's is also based on the small block design and can be easily identified by their tunnel-port shaped intake manifold.

Precise engine identification is possible by means of the engine code letter in the serial number. Refer to Chapter 1 for the necessary information.

Engine Removal

CAUTION: *Be extremely careful when disconnecting A/C lines. Contact with refrigerant can cause severe injury or blindness.*
NOTE: *Be Sure to familiarize yourself with all the steps before beginning work.*

1. Scribe the hood hinge outline on the under-hood, disconnect the hood, and remove it.

2. Drain the entire cooling system and crankcase.

3. Remove the air cleaner and disconnect the battery at the cylinder head. On cars with automatic transmissions, disconnect the oil cooler lines at the radiator.

4. Remove the upper and lower radiator hoses and the radiator. If the car is equipped with air conditioning, unbolt the compressor and position the compressor out of the way

General Engine Specifications

Year	Engine No. Cyl Displacement (cu. in.)	Carb Type	Advertised Horsepower (@ rpm)	Advertised Torque @ rpm (ft. lbs.)	Bore and Stroke (in.)	Advertised Compression Ratio	Oil Pressure (psi) (@ 2000 rpm)
'71	6-250	1 bbl	145 @ 4000	232 @ 1600	3.682 x 3.910	9.0 : 1	35–60
	8-302	2 bbl	210 @ 4600	296 @ 2600	4.000 x 3.000	9.0 : 1	35–60
	8-351 C	2 bbl	240 @ 4600	355 @ 2600	4.000 x 3.500	9.5 : 1	35–60
	8-351 C	4 bbl	285 @ 5400	370 @ 3400	4.000 x 3.500	10.7 : 1	35–60
	8-429	4 bbl	360 @ 4600	480 @ 2800	4.362 x 3.590	10.5 : 1	35–75
	8-429 CJ	4 bbl	370 @ 5400	450 @ 3400	4.362 x 3.590	11.3 : 1	35–75
	8-429 SCJ	4 bbl	375 @ 5600	450 @ 3400	4.362 x 3.590	11.3 : 1	35–75
'72	6-250	1 bbl	99 @ 3600	184 @ 1600	3.680 x 3.910	8.0 : 1	35–60
	8-302	2 bbl	141 @ 4000	242 @ 2000	4.000 x 3.000	8.5 : 1	35–60
	8-351	2 bbl	164 @ 4000	276 @ 2000	4.000 x 3.500	8.6 : 1	35–85
	8-351 CJ	4 bbl	248 @ 5400	290 @ 3800	4.000 x 3.500	8.6 : 1	35–85
	8-400	2 bbl	168 @ 4200	297 @ 2200	4.000 x 4.000	8.4 : 1	35–85
	8-429	4 bbl	205 @ 4400	322 @ 2600	4.326 x 3.590	8.5 : 1	35–75
'73	6-250	1 bbl	92 @ 3200	197 @ 1600	3.680 x 3.910	8.0 : 1	35–60
	8-302	2 bbl	135 @ 4200 137	228 @ 2200 230	4.000 x 3.000	8.0 : 1	35–60
	8-351 W	2 bbl	156 @ 3800	260 @ 2400	4.000 x 3.500	8.0 : 1	50–70
	8-351 W	2 bbl	154 @ 4000 159	246 @ 2400 250	4.000 x 3.500	8.0 : 1	50–70
	8-351 CJ	4 bbl	246 @ 5400	312 @ 3600	4.000 x 3.500	8.0 : 1	50–70
	8-400	2 bbl	163 @ 3800 168	300 @ 2000 310	4.000 x 4.000	8.0 : 1	50–70
	8-429	4 bbl	197 @ 4400 201	320 @ 2600 322	4.362 x 3.590	8.0 : 1	35–75
	8-460 PI	4 bbl	274 @ 4600	392 @ 2800	4.362 x 3.850	8.8 : 1	50–75
'74	6-250	1 bbl	91 @ 3200	190 @ 1600	3.680 x 3.190	8.0 : 1	35–65
	8-302	2 bbl	140 @ 3800	230 @ 2600	4.000 x 3.000	8.0 : 1	35–55

General Engine Specifications (cont.)

Year	Engine No. Cyl Displacement (cu. in.)	Carb Type	▪ Advertised Horsepower (@ rpm)	▪ Advertised Torque @ rpm (ft. lbs.)	Bore and Stroke (in.)	Advertised Compression Ratio	Oil Pressure (psi) (@ 2000 rpm)
'74	8-351 W	2 bbl	162 @ 4000	275 @ 2200	4.000 x 3.500	8.0 : 1	50 – 70
	8-351 C	2 bbl	163 @ 4200	278 @ 2000	4.000 x 3.500	8.0 :	50 – 70
	8-351 CJ	4 bbl	255 @ 5600	290 @ 3400	4.000 x 3.500	7.9 : 1	50 – 70
	8-400	2 bbl	170 @ 3400	330 @ 2000	4.000 x 4.000	8.0 : 1	50 – 70
	8-460	4 bbl	195 @ 3800	355 @ 2600	4.362 x 3.850	8.0 : 1	35 – 75
	8-460	4 bbl	220 @ 4000	355 @ 2600	4.362 x 3.850	8.0 : 1	35 – 75
	8-460 PI	4 bbl	260 @ 4400	380 @ 2700	4.362 x 3.850	8.8 : 1	50 – 75
'75 – '76	8-351 W 49	2 bbl	154 @ 3800	268 @ 2200	4.000 x 3.500	8.2 : 1	40 – 65
	8-351 W Cal.	2 bbl	153 @ 3400	270 @ 2400	4.000 x 3.500	8.2 : 1	40 – 65
	8-351 M 49	2 bbl	148 @ 3800	243 @ 2400	4.000 x 3.500	8.0 : 1	50 – 75
	8-351 M Cal.	2 bbl	150 @ 3800	244 @ 2800	4.000 x 3.500	8.0 : 1	50 – 75
	8-400 49	2 bbl	158 @ 3800	276 @ 2000	4.000 x 4.000	8.0 : 1	50 – 75
	8-400 Cal.	2 bbl	144 @ 3600	255 @ 2200	4.000 x 4.000	8.0 : 1	50 – 75
	8-460 49	4 bbl	216 @ 4000	366 @ 2600	4.362 x 3.850	8.0 : 1	40 – 65
	8-460 Cal.	4 bbl	217 @ 4000	365 @ 2600	4.362 x 3.850	8.0 : 1	40 – 65
	8-460 PI	4 bbl	266 @ 4000	374 @ 2600	4.263 x 3.850	8.0 : 1	40 – 65
'77 – '78	8-302	2 bbl	130 @ 2400	243 @ 1800	3.000 x 3.000	8.4 : 1	40 – 60
	8-351 W	2 bbl	149 @ 3200	291 @ 1600	4.000 x 3.500	8.3 : 1	40 – 60
	8-351 M	2 bbl	161 @ 3600	285 @ 1800	4.000 x 3.500	8.0 : 1	50 – 75
	8-400	2 bbl	173 @ 3800	326 @ 1600	4.000 x 4.000	8.0 : 1	50 – 75
'79	8-302	2 bbl	140 @ 3600	250 @ 1800	4.000 x 3.000	8.4 : 1	40 – 65
	8-302 Cal.	vv	134 @ 3600	243 @ 2300	4.000 x 3.000	8.1 : 1	40 – 65
	8-351 M	2 bbl	152 @ 3600	270 @ 2200	4.000 x 3.500	8.0 : 1	51 – 75
	8-351 W	2 bbl	135 @ 3200	286 @ 1400	4.000 x 3.500	8.3 : 1	40 – 65

General Engine Specifications (cont.)

Year	Engine No. Cyl Displacement (cu. in.)	Carb Type	■ Advertised Horsepower (@ rpm)	■ Advertised Torque @ rpm (ft. lbs.)	Bore and Stroke (in.)	Advertised Compression Ratio	Oil Pressure (psi) (@ 2000 rpm)
'80	8-255	2 bbl	119 @ 3800	194 @ 2200	3.680 x 3.000	8.8 : 1	40 – 60
	8-255 Cal.	vv	119 @ 3800	194 @ 2200	3.680 x 3.000	8.8 : 1	40 – 60
	8-302	2 bbl	134 @ 3600	232 @ 1600	4.000 x 3.000	8.4 : 1	40 – 60
	8-302	vv	131 @ 3600	231 @ 1400	4.000 x 3.000	8.4 : 1	40 – 60
'81 – '82	4-140	2 bbl	88 @ 4600	118 @ 2600	3.781 x 3.126	9.0 : 1	40 – 60
	6-200	1 bbl	88 @ 3200	154 @ 1400	3.683 x 3.126	8.6 : 1	30 – 50
	6-232	2 bbl	112 @ 4000	175 @ 2600	3.814 x 3.388	8.8 : 1	40 – 60
	8-255	2 bbl	115 @ 3400	205 @ 2200	3.680 x 3.000	8.2 : 1	40 – 60
	8-255	vv	120 @ 3400	205 @ 2600	3.680 x 3.000	8.2 : 1	40 – 60
	8-302	2 bbl	160 @ 4200	247 @ 2400	4.000 x 3.000	8.4 : 1	40 – 60
	8-302	vv	130 @ 3400	235 @ 1800	4.000 x 3.000	8.4 : 1	40 – 50

■ Beginning 1972 horsepower and torque are SAE net figures. They are measured at the rear of the transmission with all accessories installed and operating.
W: Windsor
C: Cleveland
M: Modified Cleveland
PI: Police Interceptor
49: 49 states only
Cal.: California only
VV: Variable Venturi

Valve Specifications

Year	Engine No. Cyl. Displacement (cu. in.)	Seat Angle (deg)	Face Angle (deg)	Spring Test Pressure (lbs @ in.)	Spring Installed Height (in.)	Stem to Guide Clearance (in.) Intake	Stem to Guide Clearance (in.) Exhaust	Stem Diameter (in.) Intake	Stem Diameter (in.) Exhaust
'71	6-250	45	44	150 @ 1.22	$1^{19}/_{32}$	.0008 – .0025	.0010 – .0027	.3104	.3102
	8-302	45	44	180 @ 1.23	$1^{21}/_{32}$	.0010 – .0027	.0015 – .0032	.3420	.3415
	8-351 ①	45	44	215 @ 1.34	$1^{25}/_{32}$	.0010 – .0027	.0015 – .0032	.3420	.3415
	8-351 ②	45	44	210 @ 1.42	$1^{13}/_{16}$	.0010 – .0027	.0015 – .0032	.3420	.3415
	8-351 ③	45	44	285 @ 1.31	$1^{13}/_{16}$	.0010 – .0027	.0015 – .0032	.3420	.3415
	8-429	45	45	229 @ 1.33	$1^{13}/_{16}$	.0010 – .0027	.0010 – .0027	.3420	.3420

Valve Specifications (cont.)

Year	Engine No. Cyl. Displacement (cu. in.)	Seat Angle (deg)	Face Angle (deg)	Spring Test Pressure (lbs @ in.)	Spring Installed Height (in.)	Stem to Guide Clearance (in.)		Stem Diameter (in.)	
						Intake	Exhaust	Intake	Exhaust
'72–'76	6-250	45	44	150 @ 1.22	$1^{19}/_{32}$	.0008–.0025	.0010–.0027	.3104	.3102
	8-302	45	44	200 @ 1.23	$1^{11}/_{16}$	.0010–.0027	.0015–.0032	.3420	.3415
	8-351 ①	45	44	200 @ 1.34	$1^{25}/_{32}$	.0010–0027	.0015–0032	.3420	.3415
	8-351 ②	45	44	210 @ 1.42	$1^{13}/_{16}$	.0010–.0027	.0015–.0032	.3420	.3415
	8-351 ③	45	44	285 @ 1.23	$1^{13}/_{16}$	.0010–.0027	.0015–.0032	.3420	.3415
	8-400	45	44	226 @ 1.39	$1^{13}/_{16}$	.0010–.0027	.0015–.0032	.3420	.3515
	8-429	45	45	229 @ 1.33	$1^{13}/_{16}$	.0010–.0027	.0010–.0027	.3420	.3420
'77–'78	6-250	45	44	150 @ 1.22	$1^{19}/_{32}$	.0008–.0025	.0010–.0027	.3104	.3102
	8-302	45	44	200 @ 1.22	$1^9/_{16}$	.0010–.0027	.0015–.0032	.3420	.3415
	8-351 ①	45	44	200 @ 1.34	$1^{25}/_{32}$	.0010–.0027	.0015–.0032	.3420	3415
	8-351 ②	45	44	282 @ 1.32	$1^{13}/_{16}$	.0010–.0027	.0015–.0032	.3420	.3415
	8-351 ③	45	44	285 @ 1.32	$1^{13}/_{16}$	.0010–.0027	.0015–.0032	.3420	.3415
	8-400	45	44	226 @ 1.39	$1^{13}/_{16}$	.0010–.0027	.0015–.0032	.3420	.3415
	8-460	45	44	253 @ 1.33	$1^{13}/_{16}$	.0010–.0027	.0010–.0027	.3420	.3420
'79	8-302	45	44	④	⑤	.0010–.0027	.0015–.0032	.3420	.3415
	8-351 M	45	44	228 @ 1.39	$1^{13}/_{16}$	.0010–.0027	.0015–.0032	.3420	.3415
	8-351 W	45	44	⑥	⑦	.0010–.0027	.0015–.0032	.3420	.3415
'80	8-255	45	44	⑦	⑧	.0010–.0027	.0015–.0032	.3420	.3415
	8-302	45	44	⑦	⑧	.0010–.0027	.0015–.0032	.3420	.3415
'81	4.140	45	44	⑨	$1^9/_{16}$	.0010–.0027	.0015–.0032	.3420	.3415
	6-200	45	44	55 @ 1.59	$1^{19}/_{32}$	.0008–.0025	.0010–.0027	.3104	.3102
	8-255	45	44	⑦	⑧	.0010–.0027	.0015–.0032	.3420	.3415
	8-302	45	44	⑦	⑧	.0010–.0027	.0015–.0032	.3420	.3415

Valve Specifications (cont.)

Year	Engine No. Cyl. Displacement (cu. in.)	Seat Angle (deg)	Face Angle (deg)	Spring Test Pressure (lbs @ in.)	Spring Installed Height (in.)	Stem to Guide Clearance (in.)		Stem Diameter (in.)	
						Intake	Exhaust	Intake	Exhaust
'82	4-140	45	44	⑨	1⁹/₁₆	.0010–.0027	.0015–.0032	.3420	.3415
	6-200	45	44	55 @ 1.59	1¹⁹/₃₂	.0008–.0025	.0010–.0027	.3104	.3102
	6-232	⑩	⑪	202 @ 1.27	⑧	.0010–.0027	.0015–.0032	.3420	.3415
	8-255	⑩	⑪	⑫	⑧	.0010–.0027	.0015–.0032	.3420	.3415
	8-302	45	45	⑦	⑧	.0010–.0027	.0015–.0032	.3420	.3415

① Windsor heads
② Cleveland or modified Cleveland 2 bbl
③ Cleveland or modified Cleveland 4 bbl
④ Int.: 200 @ 1.31
　 Exh.: 200 @ 1.20
⑤ Int.: 1¹¹/₁₆
　 Exh.: 1⅝
⑥ Int.: 200 @ 1.34
　 Exh.: 200 @ 1.20
⑦ Int.: 204 @ 1.36
　 Exh.: 200 @ 1.20

⑧ Int.: 1¹¹/₁₆
　 Exh.: 1¹⁹/₃₂
⑨ Int.: 75 @ 1.56
　 Exh.: 167 @ 1.16
⑩ 44°30′–45°
⑪ 45°30′–45°45′
⑫ Int.: 192 @ 1.40
　 Exh.: 191 @ 1.23

Ring Gap (Inches)

Year	Engine	Top Compression	Bottom Compression	Oil Control
1971–73	250	.010–.020	.010–.020	.015–.055
1974–82	200, 250	.008–.016	.008–.016	.015–.055
1971	302, 351	.010–.020	.010–.020	.015–.069
1971	429	.010–.020	.010–.020	.010–.035
1972–78	400	.010–.020	.010–.020	.015–.069
1972–82	140, 232, 255, 429, 460	.010–.020	.010–.020	.015–.055 ①

① 1972–73 351C is .015–.069

Ring Side Clearance (Inches)

Year	Engine	Top Compression	Bottom Compression	Oil Control
1971–82	All engines	.002–.004	.002–.004	Snug

Crankshaft and Connecting Rod Specifications

All measurements are given in inches

Year	Engine No. Cyl. Displacement (cu. in.)	Crankshaft				Connecting Rod		
		Main Brg. Journal Dia	Main Brg. Oil Clearance	Shaft End-Play	Thrust on No.	Journal Diameter	Oil Clearance	Side Clearance
'81–'82	4-140	2.3982–2.3990	.0008–.0015 ⑧	.004–.008	3	2.0464–2.0472	.0008–.0015 ⑨	.0035–.0105
'81–'82	6-200	2.2482–2.2490	.0008–.0015 ⑧	.004–.008	5	2.1232–2.1240	.0008–.0015 ⑨	.0035–.0105
'82	6-232	2.5185–2.5195	.0005–.0023⑩	.004–.008	3	2.1228–2.1236	.0008–.0026	.010–.020
'71–'77	6-250	2.3982–2.3990	.0005–.0022	.004–.008	5	2.1232–2.1240	.0008–.00024	.003–.010
'81–'82	8-255	2.2482–2.2490	.0005–.0015 ③ ⑪	.004–.008	3	2.1228–2.1236	.0008–.0015⑫	.010–.020
'71–'82	8-302	2.2482–2.2490	.0005–.0024⑤ ④	.004–.008	3	2.1228–2.1236	.0008–.0026	.010–.020
'73–'79	8-351W	2.9994–3.0002	.0013–.0030 ②	.004–.008	3	2.3103–2.3111	.0008–.0026 ⑦ ①	.010–.020
'71–'79	8-351C or M	2.7484–2.7492 ⑥	.0009–.0026 ⑦	.004–.008	3	2.3103–2.3111	.0008–.0026 ⑦ ①	.010–.020
'72–'78	8-400	2.9994–3.0002	.0011–.0028	.004–.008	3	2.3103–2.3111	.0011–.0026①	.010–.020
'71–'76	8-429, 460	2.9994–3.0002	.0010–.0020③	.004–.008	3	2.4992–2.5000	.0008–.0028	.010–.020

① .008–.0015 in. in 1974–77
② .008–.0025 in. in 1974–77
③ No. 1: .0010–.0015
④ .0005–.0015 in. in 1974–77
⑤ 302: .0001–.0005 No. 1 bearing only
⑥ 8-351C given; 8-351M: 2.9994–3.0002
⑦ 351C or M 4-bbl: .0011–.0015
⑧ 1982: .0008–.0026
⑨ 1982: .0008–.0024
⑩ Horiz.: .0009–.0027
⑪ 1982: .0005–.0024
⑫ 1982: .0007–.0020

Piston Clearance (Inches)

Year	Engine	Piston-to-Bore Clearance
1971–82	200, 250	0.0013–0.0021
1971–82	255, 302, 351W	0.0018–0.0026
1971–82	140, 351C, 351M, 400 429, 460	0.0014–0.0022
1971	429 CJ and SCJ	0.0042–0.0050
1981–82	232	.0014–.0028

with the refrigerant lines intact. Unbolt and lay the refrigerant condenser forward without disconnecting the refrigerant lines.

5. Remove the fan, fan belt and upper pulley. If the vehicle is equipped with a thermactor air pump system, disconnect any parts that might interfere with engine removal.

6. Disconnect the heater hoses at the water pump and the carburetor spacer.

7. Disconnect the alternator wires at the alternator, the starter cable at the starter and the accelerator rod at the carburetor. On cars equipped with power brakes, disconnect the brake vacuum line from the intake manifold.

8. Disconnect the fuel tank line at the fuel pump and plug the line.

9. Disconnect the coil primary wire at the coil. Disconnect the wires at the oil-pressure and water-temperature sending units.

10. Remove the starter and dust seal.

11. On a car equipped with a manual transmission, remove the clutch retracting spring. Disconnect the clutch equalizer shaft and arm bracket at the underbody rail and remove the arm bracket and equalizer shaft.

12. Raise the car. Remove the flywheel or converter housing upper retaining bolts through the access holes in the floor pan.

13. Disconnect the exhaust pipe(s) at the exhaust manifold. Disconnect the right and left motor mounts at the underbody bracket. Remove the flywheel or converter housing cover.

14. On a car with manual shift, remove the flywheel housing lower retaining bolts.

15. On a car with an automatic transmission, disconnect the throttle valve vacuum line at the intake manifold, then disconnect the converter from the flywheel. Remove the converter housing lower retaining bolts. On a car with power steering, disconnect the

power steering pump from the cylinder head. Put the drive belt and wire the steering pump out of the way.

16. Lower the car. Support the transmission and flywheel or converter housing with a jack.

17. Inspect the engine compartment making sure that everything attached to the engine assembly is not attached to something else.

18. Attach an engine lifting hook. Lift the engine up and out of the compartment and onto an adequate workstand.

Engine Installation

1. Place a new gasket over the studs of the exhaust manifold(s).

2. Attach an engine sling and lifting device. Lift the engine from the workstand.

3. Lower the engine into the engine compartment. Be sure the exhaust manifold(s) is in proper alignment with the muffler inlet pipe(s), and the dowels in the block engage the holes in the flywheel housing. On a car with an automatic transmission, start the converter pilot into the crankshaft. On a car with a manual transmission, start the transmission main drive gear into the clutch disc. If the engine hangs up after the shaft enters, rotate the crankshaft slowly (with the transmission in gear) until the shaft and clutch disc splines mesh. Rotate the 4-cyl. engine clockwise only when viewed from the front.

4. Install the flywheel or converter housing upper bolts.

5. Install the engine support insulator-to-bracket retaining nuts. Disconnect the engine lifting sling and remove the lifting brackets.

Torque Specifications
(All Readings in ft. lbs.)

Year	Engine No. Cyl Displacement (cu in.)	Cylinder Head Bolts *	Rod Bearing Bolts	Main Bearing Bolts	Crankshaft Pulley Bolt	Flywheel-to-Crankshaft Bolts	Manifold	
							Intake	Exhaust
'71–'73	6-250	70–75	21–26	60–70	85–100	75–85	—	13–18
	8-302	65–72	19–24	60–70	70–90	75–85	23–25	12–16
	8-351	95–100	40–45	95–105 ②	70–90	75–85	23–25 (5/16) 28–32 (3/8) 6–9 (1/4)	12–22
	8-400	95–105 ③	40–45	④	70–90	75–85	21–25 (5/16) 27–33 (3/8) 6–9 (1/4)	12–16
	8-429, 460	130–140	40–45	95–105 ①	70–90	75–85	25–30	28–33
'74–'79	6-250	70–75	21–26	60–70	85–100	75–85	—	13–18
	8-302	65–72	19–24	60–70	35–50	75–85	19–27	12–16
	8-351W	105–112	40–45	95–105	35–50	75–85	19–27	18–24
	8-351C or M	95–105 ③	40–45	④	70–90	75–85	⑤	12–22
	8-400	95–105 ③	40–45	④	70–90	75–85	⑤	12–16
	8-460	130–140	40–45	95–105	35–50	75–85	22–32	28–33
'80–'82	4-140	80–90	30–36	80–90	100–120	54–64	14–21	16–23
	6-200	70–75	21–26	60–70	85–100	75–85	—	18–24
	6-232	65–81 ⑥	30–36 ⑥	62–81 ⑥	85–100	75–85	17–19	15–22
	8-255	65–75	19–24	60–70	70–90	75–85	18–20 ⑦	18–24
	8-302	65–75	19–24	60–70	70–90	75–85	23–25 ⑦	18–24

① 7/16 in. bolts—70–80 ft. lbs.
② 3/8 in. bolts—34–45 ft. lbs.
③ Three steps—55, 75, then maximum figure
④ 1/2 in.—13 bolts, 95–105, 3/8 in.—16 bolts, 35–45
⑤ 5/16 in. bolt, 21–25, 3/8 in. bolt, 22–32; 1/4 in. bolt, 6–9
⑥ Tighten to listed torque, loosen 2 complete turns, retighten to listed torque. Fasteners must be oil-coated
⑦ Torque cold, then retorque hot
* Tighten cylinder head bolts in three steps

6. Raise the front of the car. Connect the exhaust line(s) and tighten the attachments.

7. Position the dust seal and install the starter.

8. On cars with manual transmissions, install the remaining flywheel housing-to-engine bolts. Connect the clutch release rod. Position the clutch equalizer bar and bracket, and install the retaining bolts. Install the clutch pedal retracting spring.

9. On cars with automatic transmissions, remove the retainer holding the converter in the housing. Attach the converter to the fly-wheel. Install the converter housing inspection cover and the remaining converter housing retaining bolts.

10. Remove the support from the transmission and lower the car.

11. Connect the engine ground strap and the coil primary wire.

12. Connect the water temperature gauge wire and the heater hose at the coolant outlet housing. Connect the accelerator rod at the bellcrank.

13. On cars with automatic transmissions, connect the transmission filler tube bracket. Connect the throttle valve vacuum line.

14. On cars with power steering, install the drive belt and power steering pump bracket. Install the bracket retaining bolts. Adjust the drive belt to the proper tension.

15. Remove the plug from the fuel tank line. Connect the flexible fuel line and the oil-pressure sending-unit wire.

16. Install the pulley, spacer, fan and fan belt. On thermactor equipped cars, connect any parts of that system which may have been disconnected. Adjust belt tension.

17. Tighten the alternator adjusting bolts. Connect the alternator wires and the battery ground cable. On the 4-cyl., install the exhaust manifold heat shroud.

18. Install the radiator. Connect the radiator hoses. On air-conditioned cars, install the compressor and refrigerant radiator.

19. On cars with automatic transmissions, connect the oil cooler lines.

20. Install the oil filter. Connect the heater hose at the water pump, after bleeding the system. Connect the 4-cyl. choke heater hose.

21. Bring the crankcase to level with the correct grade of oil. Run the engine at fast idle and check for leaks. Install the air cleaner and make the final engine adjustments.

22. Install and adjust the hood.

23. Road-test the car.

Cylinder Head

REMOVAL AND INSTALLATION

4 Cylinder 140 Engine

1. Drain the cooling system.

2. Remove the air cleaner.

3. Remove the valve cover. Note the location of the valve cover attaching screws that have rubber grommets.

4. Remove the intake and exhaust mani-

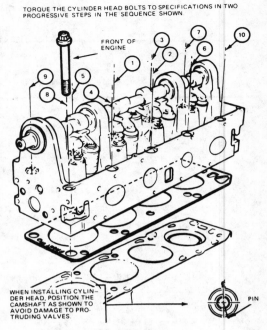

TORQUE THE CYLINDER HEAD BOLTS TO SPECIFICATIONS IN TWO PROGRESSIVE STEPS IN THE SEQUENCE SHOWN

FRONT OF ENGINE

WHEN INSTALLING CYLINDER HEAD, POSITION THE CAMSHAFT AS SHOWN TO AVOID DAMAGE TO PROTRUDING VALVES.

PIN

4-140 cylinder head installation

folds from the head. See the procedures for intake manifold and exhaust manifold removal.

5. Remove the camshaft drive belt cover. Note the location of the belt cover attaching screws that have rubber grommets.

6. Loosen the drive belt tensioner and remove the belt.

7. Remove the water outlet elbow from the cylinder head with the hose attached.

8. Remove the cylinder head attaching bolts.

9. Remove the cylinder head from the engine.

10. Clean all gasket material and carbon from the top of the cylinder block and pistons and from the bottom of the cylinder head.

11. Position a new cylinder head gasket on the engine and place the head on the engine. NOTE: *If you encounter difficulty in positioning the cylinder head on the engine block, it may be necessary to install guide studs in the block to correctly align the head and the block. To fabricate guide studs, obtain two new cylinder head bolts and cut their heads off with a hack saw. Install the bolts in the holes in the engine block which correspond with cylinder head bolt holes nos. 3 and 4, as identified in the cylinder head bolt tightening sequence illustration. Then, install the head gasket and head over the bolts. Install the cylinder head attach-*

ing bolts, *replacing the studs with the original head bolts.*

12. Using a torque wrench, tighten the head bolts in the sequence shown in the illustration.

13. Install the camshaft drive belt. See "Camshaft Drive Belt Installation."

14. Install the camshaft drive belt cover and its attaching bolts. Make sure the rubber grommets are installed on the bolts. Tighten the bolts to 6–13 ft. lbs.

15. Install the water outlet elbow and a new gasket on the engine and tighten the attaching bolts to 12–15 ft. lbs.

16. Install the intake and exhaust manifolds. See the procedures for intake and exhaust manifold installation.

17. Adjust valve clearance. See chapter 2, "Valve Adjustment."

18. Install the air cleaner and the valve cover.

19. Fill the cooling system.

6-200, 250

NOTE: *The six cylinder engine used on these models has an intake manifold which is cast integrally with the cylinder head. The two cannot be separated.*

1. Drain the cooling system, remove the air cleaner, and disconnect the battery cable at the cylinder head.

2. Disconnect the exhaust pipe at the manifold end, spring the exhaust pipe down, and remove the flange gasket.

3. Disconnect the fuel and vacuum lines from the carburetor. Disconnect the intake manifold line at the intake manifold.

4. Disconnect the accelerator and retracting spring at the carburetor.

5. Disconnect the carburetor spacer outlet line at the spacer. Disconnect the radiator upper hose and the heater hose at the water outlet elbow. Disconnect the radiator lower hose and the heater hose at the water pump.

6. Disconnect the distributor vacuum control line at the distributor. Disconnect the

Cylinder head torque sequence for 6-200, 250

gas filter line on the inlet side of the filter and the vacuum line at the fuel pump. Remove these three lines as an assembly, then remove the windshield wiper line at the vacuum pump (if so equipped).

7. Disconnect the spark plug wires and remove the plugs.

8. Remove the rocker arm cover.

9. Back off all of the tappet adjusting screws to relieve tension from the rocker shaft. Loosen the rocker arm shaft attaching bolts and remove the rocker arm and shaft assembly. Remove the valve pushrods, in order, and keep them that way.

10. Remove one cylinder head bolt from each end of the head (at opposite corners) and install the cylinder head guide studs. Remove the remaining cylinder head bolts and lift them off the cylinder head.

To held in removal and installation of the cylinder head, two 6 in. x $^{7}/_{16}$—14 bolts with the heads cut off and the head end slightly tapered and slotted for installation and removal, with a screwdriver, will reduce the possibility of damage during head replacement. These guide studs make a handy tool during head removal and gasket and head replacement.

11. Prior to installation, clean the cylinder head and block surfaces. Be sure of flatness and no surface damage.

12. Apply cylinder head gasket sealer to both sides of the new gasket and slide the gasket down over the two guide studs in the cylinder block.

NOTE: *Apply gasket sealer only to steel shim head gaskets. Steel/asbestos composite head gaskets are to be installed without any sealer.*

13. Carefully lower the cylinder head over the guide studs. Place the exhaust pipe flange on the manifold studs (new gasket).

14. Coat the threads of the end bolts for the right side of the cylinder head with a small amount of water-resistant sealer. Install, but do not tighten, two head bolts at opposite ends to hold the head gasket in place. Remove the guide studs and install the remaining bolts.

15. The cylinder head should be torqued

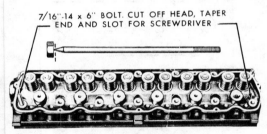

7/16"-14 x 6" BOLT. CUT OFF HEAD, TAPER END AND SLOT FOR SCREWDRIVER

Cylinder head guide stud fabrication

in three steps and in prescribed order. Tighten to 55 ft. lbs., then give them a second tightening to 65 ft. lbs. The final step is to 75 ft. lbs., at which they should remain undisturbed.

16. Lubricate both ends of the pushrods and install them in their original locations.

17. Apply a petroleum jelly lubricant to the rocker arm pads and the valve stem tips, and position the rocker arm shaft assembly on the head. Be sure the oil holes in the shaft are in a down position.

18. Tighten all the rocker shaft retaining bolts to 30–35 ft. lbs. and do a preliminary valve adjustment (make sure there are no tight valve adjustments). Refer to the procedures for "Preliminary Valve Lash Adjustment" at the end of the "Rocker Shafts" section of this chapter.

19. Hook up the exhaust pipe.

20. Reconnect the heater and radiator hoses.

21. Reposition the distributor vacuum line, the carburetor gas line, and the intake manifold vacuum line on the engine. Hook them up to their respective connections and reconnect the battery cable to the cylinder head.

22. Connect the accelerator rod and retracting spring. Connect the choke control cable and adjust the choke.

23. Reconnect the vacuum line at the distributor. Connect the fuel inlet line at the fuel filter and the intake manifold vacuum line at the vacuum pump. Connect the windshield wiper vacuum line to the other side of the vacuum pump.

24. Lightly lubricate the spark plug threads, install them, and torque them to 25 ft. lbs. Connect the spark plug wires and be sure the wires are all the way down in their sockets.

25. Fill the cooling system and bleed it. Run the engine for about ½ hour at a fast idle to stabilize all engine parts temperatures.

26. Adjust the engine idle speed and the idle fuel-air adjustment.

27. Coat one side of a new rocker cover gasket with oil-resistant sealer. Lay the treated side of the gasket on the cover and install the cover. Be sure the gasket seals evenly all around the cylinder head.

V6

1. Drain the cooling system.
2. Disconnect the cable from the battery negative terminal.

3. Remove the air cleaner assembly including air intake duct and heat tube.

4. Loosen the accessory drive belt idler. Remove the drive belt.

5. If the left cylinder head is being removed:

  a. If equipped with power steering, remove the pump mounting brackets' attaching bolts, leaving the hoses connected, place the pump/bracket assembly aside in a position to prevent the fluid from leaking out.

  b. If equipped with air conditioning, remove the mounting brackets' attaching bolts, leaving the hoses connected, position the compressor aside.

6. If the right cylinder head is being removed:

  a. Disconnect the thermactor diverter valve and hose assembly at the by-pass valve and downstream air tube.

  b. Remove the assembly.

  c. Remove the accessory drive idler.

  d. Remove the alternator.

  e. Remove the thermactor pump pulley. Remove the thermactor pump.

  f. Remove the alternator bracket.

  g. Remove the PCV valve.

7. Remove the intake manifold.

8. Remove the valve rocker arm cover attaching screws. Loosen the silicone rubber gasketing material by inserting a putty knife under the cover flange. Work the cover loose and remove. The plastic rocker arm covers will break if excessive prying is applied.

9. Remove the exhaust manifold(s).

10. Loose the rocker arm fulcrum attaching bolts enough to allow the rocker arm to be lifted off the pushrod and rotated to one side.

11. Remove the pushrods. The position of each rod should be installed in the original position during assembly.

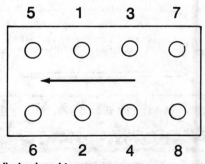

V6 cylinder head torque sequence

12. Remove the cylinder head attaching bolts. Remove the cylinder head(s).

13. Remove and discard the old cylinder head gasket(s). Discard the cylinder head bolts.

14. Lightly oil all bolt and stud bolt threads before installation except those specifying special sealant.

15. Clean the cylinder head, intake manifold, valve rocker arm cover and cylinder head gasket surfaces. If the cylinder head was removed for a cylinder head gasket replacement, check the flatness of the cylinder head and block gasket surfaces.

16. Position new head gasket(s) on the cylinder block using the dowels for alignment.

17. Position the cylinder heads to the block.

18. Apply a thin coating of pipe sealant or equivalent to the threads of the short cylinder head bolts (nearest to the exhaust manifold). Do not apply sealant to the long bolts. Lightly oil the cylinder head bolt flat washers. Install the flat washers and cylinder head bolts (Eight each side).

CAUTION: *Always use new cylinder head bolts to assure a leak tight assembly. Torque retention with used bolts can vary, which may result in coolant or compression leakage at the cylinder head mating surface area.*

19. Tighten the attaching bolts in sequence. Back-off the attaching bolts 2-3 turns. Repeat tightening sequence.

NOTE: *When the cylinder head attaching bolts have been tightened using the above sequential procedure, it is not necessary to retighten the bolts after extended engine operation. However, the bolts can be checked for tightness if desired.*

20. Dip each pushrod end in heavy engine oil. Install the push rods in their original position. For each valve rotate the crankshaft until the tappet rests on the heel (base circle) of the camshaft lobe.

21. Position the rocker arms over the push rods, install the fulcrums, and tighten the fulcrum attaching bolts to 61–132 in. lbs.

CAUTION: *Fulcrums must be fully seated in cylinder head and pushrods must be seated in rocker arm sockets prior to final tightening.*

22. Lubricate all rocker arm assemblies with heavy engine oil. Finally tighten the fulcrum bolts to 19–25 ft. lbs. For final tightening, the camshaft may be in any position.

NOTE: *If the original valve train compo-*

nents are being installed, a valve clearance check is not required. If a component has been replaced, perform a valve clearance check.

23. Install the exhaust manifold(s).

24. Apply a 1/8–3/16 inch bead of RTV silicone sealant to the rocker arm cover flange. Make sure the sealer fills the channel in the cover flange. The rocker arm cover must be installed within 15 minutes after the silicone sealer application. After this time, the sealer may start to set-up, and its sealing effectiveness may be reduced.

25. Position the cover on the cylinder head and install the attaching bolts. Note the location of the wiring harness routing clips and spark plug wire routing clip stud bolts. Tighten the attaching bolts to 36–60 in. lbs. torque.

26. Install the intake manifold.

27. Install the spark plugs, if necessary.

28. Connect the secondary wires to the spark plugs.

29. Install the oil fill cap. If equipped with air conditioning, install the compressor mounting and support brackets.

30. On the right cylinder head:

   a. Install the PCV valve.

   b. Install the alternator bracket. Tighten attaching nuts to 30–40 ft. lbs.

   c. Install the thermactor pump and pump pulley.

   d. Install the alternator.

   e. Install the accessory drive idler.

   f. Install the thermactor diverter valve and hose assembly. Tighten the clamps securely.

31. Install the accessory drive belt and tighten to the specified tension.

32. Connect the cable to the battery negative terminal.

33. Fill the cooling system with the specified coolant.

CAUTION: *This engine has an aluminum cylinder head and requires a special unique corrosion inhibited coolant formulation to avoid radiator damage.*

34. Start the engine and check for coolant, fuel, and oil leaks.

35. Check and, if necessary, adjust the curb idle speed.

36. Install the air cleaner assembly including the air intake duct and heat tube.

V8 Engines

1. Drain the cooling system.

2. Remove the intake manifold and the

carburetor as an assembly, following the procedures under "Intake Manifold Removal."

3. Disconnect the spark plug wires, marking them as to placement. Position them out of the way of the cylinder head. Remove the spark plugs.

4. Disconnect the resonator or muffler inlet pipe(s) at the exhaust manifold(s).

NOTE: *On some 351 and 400 engines, it may be necessary to remove the exhaust manifolds from the cylinder heads to gain access to the lower head bolts.*

5. Disconnect the battery ground cable at the cylinder head (if applicable).

6. Remove the rocker arm covers.

7. On cars with air conditioning, remove the mounting bolts and the drive belt, and position the compressor out of the way of the cylinder head. Remove the compressor upper mounting bracket from the cylinder head.

CAUTION: *If the compressor refrigerant lines do not have enough slack to permit repositioning of the compressor without first disconnecting the refrigerant lines, the air conditioning system will have to be evacuated by a trained air conditioning serviceman. Under no circumstances should an untrained person attempt to disconnect the air conditioning refrigerant lines.*

8. In order to remove the left cylinder head, on cars equipped with power steering, it may be necessary to remove the steering pump and bracket, remove the drive belt, and wire or tie the pump out of the way, but in such a way as to prevent the loss of its fluid.

9. In order to remove the right head it may be necessary to remove the alternator mounting bracket bolt and spacer, the ignition coil, and the air cleaner inlet duct from the right cylinder head.

10. In order to remove the left cylinder head on a car equipped with a Thermactor exhaust emission control system, disconnect the hose from the air manifold on the left cylinder head.

11. If the right cylinder head is to be removed on a car equipped with a Thermactor exhaust emission control system, remove the Thermactor air pump and its mounting bracket. Disconnect the hose from the air manifold on the right cylinder head.

12. Loosen the rocker arm stud nuts enough to rotate the rocker to one side in order to facilitate removal of the pushrods. Remove the pushrods and mark them or keep them in order, so that they can be installed in their original positions. On those engines equipped with exhaust valve stem caps, remove the caps.

13. Remove the cylinder head attaching bolts, making a note each bolt's location. Using a hoist, lift the cylinder head and exhaust manifold assembly off the block. Remove and discard the old cylinder head gasket.

14. Prior to installation, clean all surfaces where gaskets are to be installed. These include the cylinder head, intake manifold, rocker arm (valve) cover, and the cylinder block contact surfaces. If water in the crankcase indicates that the head was removed because of a blown head gasket, check the flatness of the cylinder head and engine block surfaces. The method for this checking is outlined in the "Engine Rebuilding" section under "Cylinder Head Reconditioning."

15. Position the new cylinder head gasket over the cylinder dowels on the block. Coat the head bolts with water-resistant sealer. Position new gaskets on the muffler inlet pipes at the exhaust manifold flange.

16. Position the cylinder head to the block, and install the head bolts, each in its original position. On all engines on which the exhaust manifold has been removed from the head to facilitate removal, it is necessary to properly guide the exhaust manifold studs into the muffler inlet pipe flange when installing the head.

NOTE: *On 429 and 460 engines, the longer bolts belong in the lower row of bolt holes.*

17. Following the cylinder head torque sequence diagrams, step-torque the cylinder head bolts in three stages. First, torque the bolts to 20 ft. lbs. less than the maximum figure listed in the "Torque Specifications" chart. Second, torque the bolts to 10 ft. lbs. less than the maximum figure. Finally, torque the bolts to the maximum figure in the chart. At this point, tighten the exhaust manifold-to-cylinder head attaching bolts to specifications.

18. Tighten the nuts on the exhaust manifold studs at the muffler inlet flanges to 18 ft. lbs.

19. Clean and inspect the pushrods one at a time. Clean the oil passage within each

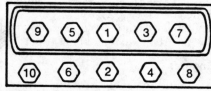

V8 cylinder head torque sequence

pushrod with a suitable solvent and blow the passage out with compressed air. Check the ends of the pushrods for nicks, grooves, roughness, or excessive wear. Visually inspect the pushrods for straightness, and replace any bent ones. Do not attempt to straighten pushrods.

20. Install the pushrods in their original positions. Apply lubriplate or a similar product to the valve stem tips and to the pushrod guides in the cylinder head. Install the exhaust valve stem caps.

21. Lubricate the rocker arm tips and return them to their proper positions. Tighten the stud nuts just enough to hold the rocker arms in position. Make sure that the lower ends of the pushrods have remained properly seated in the valve lifters.

22. Perform a preliminary valve adjustment as outlined at the end of the "Rocker Shafts" section of this chapter.

23. Apply a coat of oil-resistant sealer to the upper side of the new valve cover gasket. Position the gasket with the cemented side to the valve cover.

24. Install the valve covers and torque the bolts to 3–5 ft. lbs.

25. Install the intake manifold (and carburetor) as outlined below, under "Intake Manifold".

26. Refer to Steps 7–11 (inclusive) of the "Removal" procedure and reverse the procedure if applicable to your car.

27. Refer to the "Belt Tension Adjustment" procedure in Chapter 1 and adjust all drive belts which were removed.

28. Refill the cooling system.

29. Connect the battery ground cable at the cylinder head (if applicable).

30. Install the spark plugs and connect the spark plug wires.

31. Start the engine and check for leaks.

32. With the engine running, check and adjust the carburetor idle speed and mixture as explained in Chapter 2.

33. With the engine running, listen for abnormal valve noises or irregular idle and correct them.

OVERHAUL

Procedures for the overhaul of cylinder heads are explained in the "Engine Rebuilding" section, at the end of this chapter.

VALVE GUIDES

All engines used in these models have integral valve guides. That is, they are part of the

casting of the cylinder head and cannot be removed. If the valve stem-to-guide clearance exceeds specifications (see "Valve Specifications" chart), the valve guide can be reamed to accommodate a valve with an oversized stem.

Before reaming, check with a Ford dealer for the diameter of the oversized valves which are available. The valve guide should be reamed to the minimum available oversize which corrects the wear. If wear is considerable, ream the guide in graduated steps to maintain the concentricity of the guide bore with the valve seat. Always resurface the valve seat after the valve guide has been reamed, and use a suitable scraper to break the sharp edge at the top of the valve guide (inner diameter). Refer to the engine rebuilding section for valve seat resurfacing procedures.

Rocker Shafts
6-200,250

All in-line six cylinder engines utilize shaft mounted rocker arm assemblies. Removal and installation procedures for these rocker arm assemblies are included under the "Cylinder Head Removal and Installation" procedure. Remember that the oil holes must always face downward and that the large rocker shaft retaining bolt is always the second from the front of the engine. In all cases, the torque sequence for the rocker shaft retaining bolts is from the front to the rear of the engine, two turns at a time. Torque the retaining bolts to 30–35 ft. lbs.

Rocker Arms
V6 AND V8

These engines are equipped with individually mounted rocker arms. Use the following procedure to remove the rocker arms:

1. Disconnect the choke heat chamber air hose, the air cleaner and inlet duct assembly, the choke heat tube, PCV valve and hose, and the EGR hoses (if so equipped).

2. On modesl so equipped, disconnect the Thermactor by-pass valve and air supply hoses.

3. Label and disconnect the spark plug wires at the plugs. Remove the plug wires from the looms.

4. Remove the valve cover attaching bolts and remove the cover(s).

5. Remove the valve rocker arm stud nut,

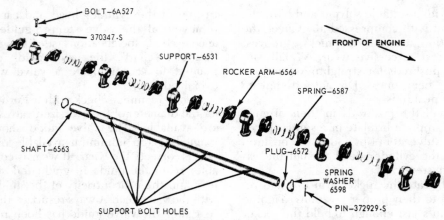

BOLT–6A527

370347-S

SUPPORT–6531

ROCKER ARM–6564

FRONT OF ENGINE

SPRING–6587

SHAFT–6563

PLUG–6572

SPRING
WASHER
6598

SUPPORT BOLT HOLES

PIN–372929-S

Rocker arm shaft assembly on the 6-200, 250

or fulcrum bolt, fulcrum seat, and then the rocker arm.

6. Reverse the above procedure to install, taking care to adjust the valve lash as outlined under "Preliminary Valve Adjustment."

PRELIMINARY VALVE ADJUSTMENT
V6 and V8 Engines Only

This adjustment is actually part of the installation procedure for the individually mounted rocker arms found on the V8 engines, and is necessary to achieve an accurate torque value for each rocker arm nut.

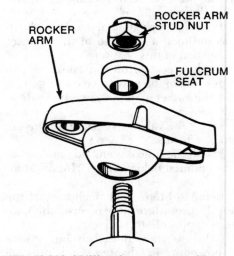

ROCKER ARM
STUD NUT

ROCKER
ARM

FULCRUM
SEAT

1971–78 302, 351W rocker arm assembly

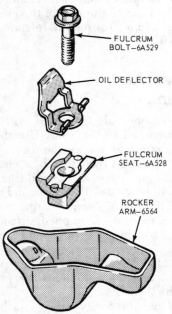

FULCRUM
BOLT–6A529

OIL DEFLECTOR

FULCRUM
SEAT–6A528

ROCKER
ARM–6564

Rocker arm and related parts—351C, 351M, 400, 460 and 1972–73 429 V8

By its nature, an hydraulic valve lifter will expand when it is not under load. Thus, when the rocker arms are removed and the pressure via the pushrod is taken off the lifter, the lifter expands to its maximum. If the lifter happens to be at the top of the camshaft lobe when the rocker arm is being reinstalled, a large amount of torque would be necessary when tightening the rocker arm nut just to overcome the pressure of the expanded lifter. This makes it very difficult to get an accurate torque setting with individually mounted rocker arms. For this reason, the rocker arms are installed in a certain sequence which corresponds to the low points of the camshaft lobes.

1. Crank the engine until no. 1 cylinder is at TDC of the compression stroke and the timing pointer is aligned with the mark on the crankshaft damper.

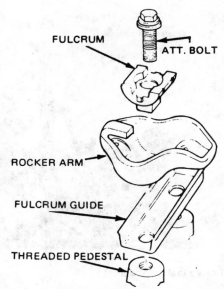

FULCRUM

ATT. BOLT

ROCKER ARM

FULCRUM GUIDE

THREADED PEDESTAL

1978—82 255, 302, 351W rocker arm assembly

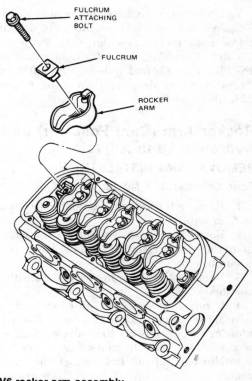

FULCRUM ATTACHING BOLT

FULCRUM

ROCKER ARM

V6 rocker arm assembly

2. Scribe a mark on the damper at this point.

3. Scribe two additional marks on the damper (see illustration).

4. With the timing pointer aligned with mark 1 on the damper, tighten the following valves to the specified torque:

• V6-232 No. 1 intake and exhaust; no. 3 intake and exhaust; no. 4 exhaust and no. 6 intake.

• *255, 302, 429, and 460* No. 1, 7 and 8 Intake; No. 1, 5, and 4 Exhaust

• *351 and 400* No. 1, 4 and 8 Intake; No. 1, 3 and 7 Exhaust.

5. Rotate the crankshaft 180° to point 2 and tighten the following valves:

• V6-232 No. 2 intake; No. 3 exhaust; No.

4 intake; No. 5 intake and exhaust; No. 6 exhaust.

• *255, 302, 429, and 460* No. 5 and 4 Intake; No. 2 and 6 Exhaust

• *351 and 400* No. 3 and 7 Intake; No. 2 and 6 Exhaust

6. Rotate the crankshaft 270° to point 3 and tighten the following valves:

• *302, 429, and 460* No. 2, 3, and 6 Intake; No. 7, 3 and 8 Exhaust

• *351 and 400* No. 2, 5 and 6 Intake; No. 4, 5 and 8 Exhaust

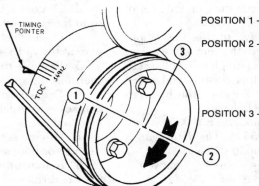

WITH NO. 1 AT TDC AT END OF COMPRESSION STROKE MAKE A CHALK MARK AT POINTS 2 AND 3 APPROXIMATELY 90 DEGREES APART.

TIMING POINTER

POSITION 1 — NO. 1 AT TDC AT END OF COMPRESSION STROKE.

POSITION 2 — ROTATE THE CRANKSHAFT 180 DEGREES (ONE HALF REVOLUTION) CLOCKWISE FROM POSITION 1.

POSITION 3 — ROTATE THE CRANKSHAFT 270 DEGREES (THREE QUARTER REVOLUTION) CLOCKWISE FROM POSITION 2.

Position of crankshaft for preliminary valve adjustment—all V8

7. Rocker arm tighten specifications are: 232, 255, 302 and 351W—tighten nut until it contacts the rocker shoulder, then torque to 18–20 ft. lbs.; 351C and 400—tighten bolt to 18–25 ft. lbs.; 429 and 460—tighten nut until it contacts rocker shoulder, then torque to 18–22 ft. lbs.

Rocker Arm (Cam Follower) and Hydraulic Lash Adjuster

REMOVAL AND INSTALLATION

Four Cylinder 140 Cu In. Engine

1. Remove the valve cover and associated parts as required.
2. Rotate the camshaft so that the base circle of the cam is against the cam follower you intend to remove.
3. Remove the retaining spring from the cam follower, if so equipped.
4. Using special tool T74P-6565-B or a valve spring compressor tool, collapse the lash adjuster and/or depress the valve spring, as necessary, and slide the cam follower over the lash adjuster and out from under the camshaft.
5. Install the cam follower in the reverse order of removal. Make sure that the lash adjuster is collapsed and released before rotating the cam shaft.

VALVE CLEARANCE—HYDRAULIC VALVE LASH ADJUSTERS

Four Cylinder 140 Cu In. Engine

Hydraulic valve lash adjusters are used in the valve train. These units are placed at the fulcrum point of the cam followers (or rocker arms). Their action is similar to the hydraulic tappets used in push rod engines.

1. Position the camshaft so that the base circle of the lobe is facing the cam follower of the valve to be checked.
2. Using a tool shown in the illustration, slowly apply pressure to the cam follower until the lash adjuster is completely collapsed. Hold the follower in this position and insert 0.045 in. feeler gauge between the base circle of the cam and the follower.

NOTE: *The minimum gap is 0.035 in. and the maximum is 0.055 in. The desire gap is between 0.040 in. and 0.050 in.*

3. If the clearance is excessive, remove the cam follower and inspect it for damage.
4. If the cam follower seems OK measure the valve spring assembled height to be sure

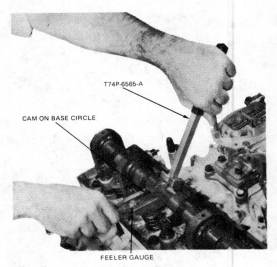

T74P-6565-A

CAM ON BASE CIRCLE

FEELER GAUGE

4-140 valve lash adjustment

the valve is not sticking. See the Valve Specifications chart in this chapter.

5. If the valve spring assembled height is OK check the dimensions of the camshaft.
6. If the camshaft dimensions are OK the lash adjuster should be cleaned and tested.
7. Replace any worn parts as necessary.

NOTE: *For any repair that includes removal of the camshaft follower (rocker arm), each affected hydraulic lash adjuster must be collapsed after reinstallation of the camshaft follower, and then released. This step must be taken prior to any rotation of the camshaft.*

Intake Manifold

REMOVAL AND INSTALLTION

Four Cylinder 140 Cu In. Engine

1. Drain the cooling system.
2. Remove the air cleaner and disconnect the throttle linkage from the carburetor.
3. Disconnect the fuel and vacuum lines from the carburetor.
4. Disconnect the carburetor solenoid wire at the quick-disconnect.
5. Remove the choke water housing and thermostatic spring from the carburetor.
6. Disconnect the water outlet and crankcase ventilation hoses from the intake manifold.
7. Disconnect the deceleration valve-to-carburetor hose at the carburetor.
8. Remove the intake manifold attaching bolts and remove the manifold.
9. Clean all old gasket material from the manifold and cylinder head.

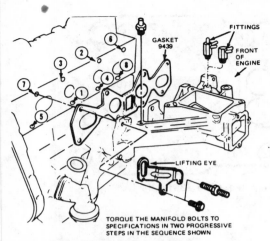

TORQUE THE MANIFOLD BOLTS TO SPECIFICATIONS IN TWO PROGRESSIVE STEPS IN THE SEQUENCE SHOWN

4-140 intake manifold installation

10. If the intake manifold is to be replaced by a new one, transfer all necessary components to the new manifold. Loosen the union fitting on the manifold and remove the deceleration valve from the intake manifold. Remove the deceleration valve adapter from the manifold by inserting a large allen wrench into the adapter and turning the adapter out of the manifold.

11. Apply water-resistant sealer to the intake manifold gasket and position it on the cylinder head.

12. Install the intake manifold attaching nuts. Follow the sequence given in the illustrations.

13. Connect the water and crankcase ventilation hoses to the intake manifold.

14. Connect the deceleration valve-to-carburetor hose to the carburetor.

15. Position the choke water housing and thermostatic spring on the carburetor and engage the end of the spring coil in the slot and the choke adjusting lever. Align the tab on the spring housing. Tighten the choke water housing attaching screws.

16. Connect the carburetor solenoid wire.

17. Connect the fuel and vacuum lines to the carburetor.

18. Connect the throttle linkage to the carburetor.

19. Install the air cleaner and fill the cooling system.

6-200, 250

The six cylinder engine has an intake manifold which is cast as an integral part of the cylinder head. Obviously, this type of intake manifold cannot be separated from the cylin-

der head. See the earlier section under cylinder head removal for the procedure.

V6, V8

1. Drain the cooling system.

2. Disconnect the upper radiator hose and water pump by-pass hose from the thermostat housing. Disconnect the water temperature sending unit wire. Remove the heater hose from the automatic choke housing and disconnect the hose from the intake manifold.

3. Remove the air cleaner. Disconnect the automatic choke heat chamber air inlet hose at the inlet tube near the right valve cover. Remove the crankcase ventilation hose and intake duct assembly. On all models so equipped, disconnect the Thermactor air hose from the check valve at the rear of the intake manifold and loosen the hose clamp at the bracket. Remove the air hose and Thermactor air by-pass valve from the bracket and position it to one side.

4. Remove all carburetor linkage and automatic transmission kick-down linkage that attaches to the manifold. Disconnect the fuel line, choke heat tube, and any vacuum lines

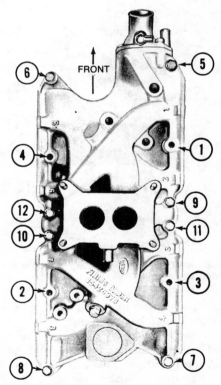

Intake manifold bolt torque sequence on the 8-255 and 302

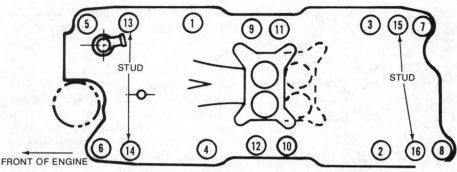

Intake manifold bolt tightening sequence—351W V8

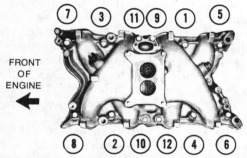

Intake manifold bolt tightening sequence—351C, 351M, 400 V8

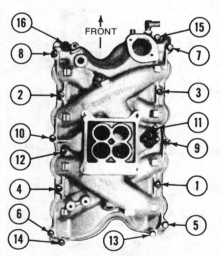

Intake manifold bolt tightening sequence—429 and 460 V8

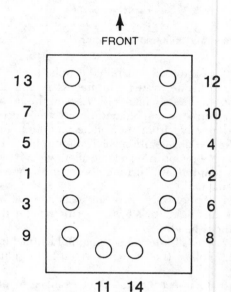

V6 intake manifold torque sequence

from the carburetor or intake manifold, marking them for installation.

5. Disconnect the distributor vacuum hoses from the distributor. Remove the distributor cap and mark the relative position of the rotor on the distributor housing. Disconnect the spark plug wires at the spark plugs and the primary and secondary wires from the coil. Remove the distributor hold-down bolt and remove the distributor.

6. If equipped with air conditioning, remove the brackets retaining the compressor to the intake manifold.

7. Remove the manifold attaching bolts. Lift off the intake manifold and carburetor as an assembly.

NOTE: *If it is necessary to pry the manifold to loosen it from the engine, be careful not to damage any gasket sealing surfaces. Always discard all old gaskets and attaching bolt sealing washers.*

8. Clean all gasket surfaces and firmly cement new gaskets in place, using non-hardening sealer. Make sure that the gaskets interlock with the seal tabs, and that the gasket holes align with those in the cylinder heads.

9. Reverse the above procedure to install, taking care to run a finger around the seal

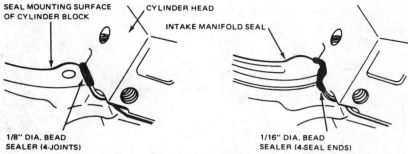

SEAL MOUNTING SURFACE
OF CYLINDER BLOCK

CYLINDER HEAD

INTAKE MANIFOLD SEAL

1/8" DIA. BEAD
SEALER (4-JOINTS)

1/16" DIA. BEAD
SEALER (4-SEAL ENDS)

Sealer application area for intake manifold installation on all V8s except the 460

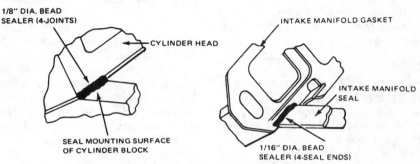

1/8" DIA. BEAD
SEALER (4-JOINTS)

CYLINDER HEAD

SEAL MOUNTING SURFACE
OF CYLINDER BLOCK

INTAKE MANIFOLD GASKET

INTAKE MANIFOLD
SEAL

1/16" DIA. BEAD
SEALER (4-SEAL ENDS)

Sealer application area for intake manifold installation on the 8-460

area on the installed manifold to make sure that the seals did not slip out during intallation. Finally, torque the intake manifold bolts in the proper sequence, and recheck the torque after the engine is warm.

Exhaust Manifold

REMOVAL AND INSTALLATION

Four Cylinder 140 Cu In. Engine

1. Remove the air cleaner.
2. Remove the heat shroud from the exhaust manifold.
3. Place a block of wood under the exhaust pipe and disconnect the exhaust pipe from the exhaust manifold.
4. Remove the exhaust manifold attaching nuts and remove the manifold.
5. Install a light coat of graphite grease on the exhaust manifold mating surface and position the manifold on the cylinder head. This engine does not use an exhaust manifold-to-cylinder head gasket.
6. Install the exhaust manifold attaching nuts and tighten them in the sequence shown in the illustration to 12–15 ft. lbs.
7. Connect the exhaust pipe to the exhaust manifold and remove the wood support from under the pipe.
8. Install the air cleaner.

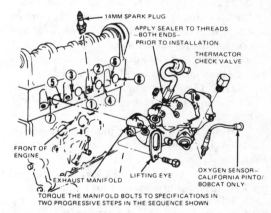

14MM SPARK PLUG

APPLY SEALER TO THREADS
–BOTH ENDS–
PRIOR TO INSTALLATION

THERMACTOR
CHECK VALVE

FRONT OF
ENGINE

EXHAUST MANIFOLD

LIFTING EYE

OXYGEN SENSOR–
CALIFORNIA PINTO/
BOBCAT ONLY

TORQUE THE MANIFOLD BOLTS TO SPECIFICATIONS IN
TWO PROGRESSIVE STEPS IN THE SEQUENCE SHOWN

4-140 exhaust manifold torque sequence

6–200, 250

1. Remove the air cleaner and related parts. Remove the automatic choke tube and any other emissions related devices which may interfere with removal of the manifold.
2. Disconnect the muffler inlet pipe and remove the choke hot air tube from the manifold.
3. Bend the exhaust manifold attaching bolt locktabs back, and remove the bolts and the manifold.
4. Clean all manifold mating surfaces and place a new gasket on the muffler inlet pipe.

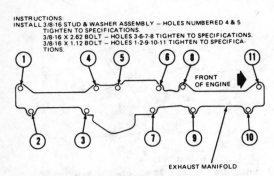

INSTRUCTIONS:
INSTALL 3/8-16 STUD & WASHER ASSEMBLY – HOLES NUMBERED 4 & 5
TIGHTEN TO SPECIFICATIONS.
3/8-16 X 2.62 BOLT – HOLES 3-6-7-8 TIGHTEN TO SPECIFICATIONS.
3/8-16 X 1.12 BOLT – HOLES 1-2-9-10-11 TIGHTEN TO SPECIFICATIONS.

FRONT OF ENGINE

EXHAUST MANIFOLD

6-200, 250 exhaust manifold torque sequence

TOOL — T64T-6316-A

TOOL — T58P-6316-B OR -A

Using a puller to remove the damper on the 6-200, 250

5. Reinstall the manifold by reversing the above procedure, torque the attaching bolts in sequence as shown.

V6, V8 Engines

1. If removing the right side exhaust manifold, remove the air cleaner and related parts and the heat stove, if so equipped.

2. On 351M and 400 engines: if the left exhaust manifold is being removed, first drain the engine oil and remove the oil filter.

3. Disconnect the exhaust manifold(s) from the muffler (or converter) inlet pipe(s).

NOTE: *On certain vehicles with automatic transmission and column shift it may be necessary to disconnect the selector lever cross shaft for clearance.*

4. Disconnect the spark plug wires and remove the spark plugs and heat shields.

NOTE: *On some engines the spark plug wire heat shields are removed with the manifold.*

5. Remove the exhaust manifold attaching bolts and washers, and remove the manifold(s).

6. Inspect the manifold(s) for damaged gasket surfaces, cracks, or other defects.

7. Clean the mating surfaces of the manifold(s), cylinder head and muffler inlet pipe(s).

8. Install the manifold(s) in reverse order of removal. Torque the mounting bolts to the value listed in the "Torque Specifications" chart. Start with the centermost bolt and work outward in both directions.

Timing Gear Cover

REMOVAL AND INSTALLATION

6-200, 250

1. Drain the cooling system and crankcase.

2. Disconnect the upper radiator hose from the intake manifold and the lower hose from the water pump. On cars with automatic transmissions, disconnect the cooler lines from the radiator.

3. Remove the radiator, fan, pulley, and engine drive belts. On models with air conditioning, remove the condenser retaining bolts and position the condenser forward. Do not disconnect the refrigerant lines.

4. Using a puller, remove the vibration damper.

5. Unbolt and lower the engine oil pan and gasket.

6. Remove the timing gear cover bolts and gently pry off the cover.

7. Scrape off all traces of the old gasket. Apply oil-resistant sealer to one side of a new timing gear cover gasket, and position that side of the gasket on the timing cover. Apply sealer to the exposed side of the gasket, and position the cover and gasket on the engine. Tighten the timing gear cover mounting bolts.

8. Install the fan, pulley, and belts. Adjust belt tension.

9. Install the radiator, and connect the radiator hoses and transmission cooling lines. If equipped with air conditioning, install the condenser.

10. Fill the crankcase and cooling system. Start the engine and check for leaks.

V6 and V8

1. Drain the cooling system, remove the air cleaner, and disconnect the battery.

2. Disconnect the radiator hoses and remove the radiator.

3. Disconnect the heater hose at the water pump. Slide the water pump by-pass hose clamp toward the pump.

4. Loosen the generator mounting bolts at the generator. Remove the generator support bolt at the water pump.

5. Remove the fan, spacer, pulley, and drive belt.

Using a puller to remove the vibration damper on the V6 and V8

6. Remove the pulley from the crankshaft pulley adaptor. Remove the cap screw and washer from the front end of the crankshaft. Remove the crankshaft pulley adaptor with a puller.

7. Disconnect the fuel pump outlet line at the pump. Remove the fuel pump retaining bolts and lay the pump to the side.

8. Remove the front cover attaching bolts. On the 351C, 351M and 400 engine, it is necessary to remove the oil pan before the front cover can be removed.

9. Clean the front cover and mating surfaces of old gasket material.

10. Coat a new cover gasket with sealer and position it on the block.

NOTE: *On all except 351C, 351M and 400 engines, trim away the exposed portion of the oil pan gasket flush with the cylinder block. Cut and position the required portion of a new gasket to the oil pan, applying sealer to both sides of it. On 351C, 351M and 400 engines, after installing the cylinder front cover, install the oil pan using a new gasket.*

11. Install the front cover, using a crankshaft-to-cover alignment tool. Torque the attaching bolts to 12–15 ft. lbs.

12. Install the fuel pump, torque the attaching bolts to 23–28 ft. lbs. and connect the fuel pump outlet tube.

13. Install the crankshaft pulley adaptor and torque the attaching bolt to 70–90 ft. lbs. Install the crankshaft pulley.

14. Install the water pump pulley, drive belt, spacer, and fan.

15. Install a generator support bolt at the water pump. Tighten the generator mounting bolts. Adjust the drive belt tension.

16. Install the radiator and connect all coolant and heater hoses. Connect the battery cables.

17. Refill and bleed the cooling system.

18. Start the engine and operate at fast idle to operating temperature.

19. Check for leaks and install air cleaner. Adjust the ignition timing and make all final adjustments.

TIMING GEAR COVER OIL SEAL REPLACEMENT

All Engines except 4–140

It is a recommended practice to replace the cover seal any time the front cover is removed.

1. With the cover removed from the car, drive the old seal from the rear of the cover with a pin-punch. Clean out the recess in the cover.

2. Coat the new seal with grease and drive it into the cover until it is fully seated. Check the seal after installation to be sure the spring is properly positioned in the seal.

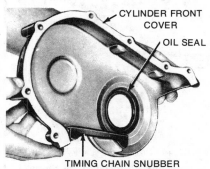

Timing gear cover on the 6-200, 250

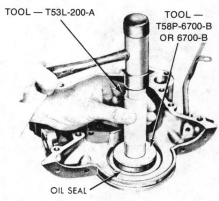

Installing timing gear cover oil seal

Timing Chain and Timing Gear

REMOVAL AND INSTALLATION

All Engines except 4–140

1. Remove the timing gear cover, as outlined earlier in this chapter.

2. Remove the crankshaft oil slinger (V8 engine, so equipped).

3. Measure the timing chain deflection:

   a. Rotate the crankshaft in a counterclockwise direction (as viewed from the front) to take up the slack on the left side of the chain.

   b. Place a mark on the surface of the block with a felt tip marker and measure from this point to the chain.

   c. Rotate the crankshaft in a clockwise

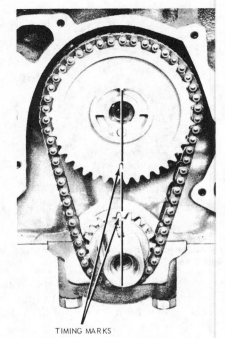

TIMING MARKS

V6 and V8 timing mark alignment

   d. If the deflection exceeds ½ inch, replace the timing chain and sprockets.

4. Rotate the engine until the sprocket timing marks are aligned.

5. Remove the camshaft bolt, washer(s) and fuel pump eccentric (if so equipped).

REFERENCE POINT

Measuring timing chain deflection—typical

direction to take up the slack on the right side of the chain. Force the left side of the chain out with your fingers and measure the distance between the reference point and the chain. The deflection is the difference between the two measurements.

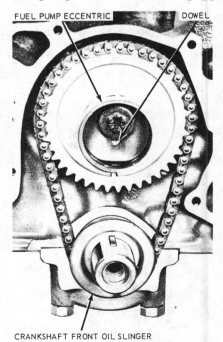

FUEL PUMP ECCENTRIC   DOWEL

CRANKSHAFT FRONT OIL SLINGER

Fuel pump eccentric and front oil slinger installed on the 8-255, 302, 351W

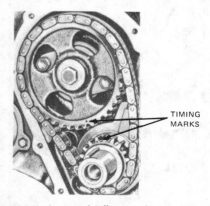

TIMING MARKS

6-200, 250 timing mark alignment

Slide both sprockets and chain forward and off as an assembly.

6. Position the sprockets and chain on the engine, making sure that the timing marks are aligned. Install the fuel pump eccentric (if applicable), the washer(s) and the camshaft bolt. Torque the bolt to 30–35 ft. lbs. on six cylinder engines; 40–45 ft. lbs. on V8 engines.

7. Follow the installation procedure for the timing gear cover, as outlined earlier in this chapter.

Camshaft Drive Belt and Cover

Four Cylinder 140 cu. in. Engine

The correct installation and adjustment of the camshaft drive belt is mandatory if the engine is to run properly. The camshaft controls the opening of the camshaft and the crankshaft. When any given piston is on the intake stroke the corresponding intake valve must be open to admit air/fuel mixture into the cylinder. When the same piston is on the compression and power strokes, both valves in that cylinder must be closed. When the piston is on the exhaust stroke, the exhaust valve for that cylinder must be open. If the opening and closing of the valves is not coordinated with the movements of the pistons, the engine will run very poorly, if at all.

The camshaft drive belt also turns the engine auxiliary shaft. The distributor is driven by the engine auxiliary shaft. Since the distributor controls ignition timing, the auxiliary shaft must be coordinated with the camshaft and the crankshaft, since both valves in any given cylinder must be closed and the piston in that cylinder near the top of the compression stroke when the spark plug fires.

Due to this complex interrelationship between the camshaft, the crankshaft and the auxiliary shaft, the cogged pulleys on each component must be aligned when the camshaft drive belt is installed.

TROUBLESHOOTING

Should the camshaft drive belt jump timing by a tooth or two, the engine could still run; but very poorly. To visually check for correct timing of the crankshaft, auxiliary shaft, and the camshaft follow this procedure:

NOTE: *There is an access plug provided in the cam drive belt cover so that the camshaft timing can be checked without moving the drive belt cover.*

1. Remove the access plug.
2. Turn the crankshaft until the timing marks on the crankshaft indicate TDC.
3. Make sure that the timing mark on the camshaft drive sprocket is aligned with the pointer on the inner belt cover. Also, the rotor of the distributor must align with the No. 1 cylinder firing position.

NOTE: *Never turn the crankshaft of any of the overhead cam engines in the opposite direction of normal rotation. Backward rotation of the crankshaft may cause the timing belt to slip and alter the timing.*

REMOVAL AND INSTALLATION

1. Set the engine to TDC as described in the troubleshooting section. The crankshaft and camshaft timing marks should align with their respective pointers and the distributor rotor should point to the No. 1 plug tower.

2. Loosen the adjustment bolts on the alternator and accessories and remove the drive belts. To provide clearance for removing the camshaft belt, remove the fan and pulley.

3. Remove the belt outer cover.

4. Remove the distributor cap from the distributor and position it out of the way.

5. Loosen the belt tension adjustment and pivot bolts. Lever the tensioner away from the belt and retighten the adjustment bolt to hold it away.

6. Remove the crankshaft bolt and pulley. Remove the belt guide behind the pulley.

7. Remove the camshaft drive belt.

8. Install the new belt over the crank-

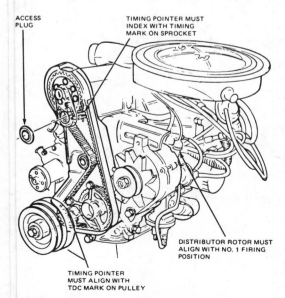

ACCESS PLUG

TIMING POINTER MUST INDEX WITH TIMING MARK ON SPROCKET

DISTRIBUTOR ROTOR MUST ALIGN WITH NO. 1 FIRING POSITION

TIMING POINTER MUST ALIGN WITH TDC MARK ON PULLEY

4-140 camshaft drive train installation

shaft pulley first, then counter-clockwise over the auxiliary shaft sprocket and the camshaft sprocket. Adjust the belt fore and aft so that it is centered on the sprockets.

9. Loosen the tensioner adjustment bolt, allowing it to spring back against the belt.

10. Rotate the crankshaft two complete turns in the normal rotation direction to remove any belt slack. Turn the crankshaft until the timing check marks are lined up. If the timing has slipped, remove the belt and repeat the procedure.

11. Tighten the tensioner adjutment bolt to 14–21 ft. lbs., and the pivot bolt to 28–40 ft. lbs.

12. Replace the belt guide and crankshaft

pulley, distributor cap, belt outer cover, fan and pulley, drive belts and accessories. Adjust the accessory drive belt tension. Start the engine and check the ignition timing.

Camshaft

REMOVAL AND INSTALLATION

Four Cylinder 140 cu in. Engine

1. Remove the cylinder head. Refer to the procedure given earlier in the chapter.

2. Remove the rocker arms.

3. Remove the camshaft drive gear attaching bolt and washer, and remove the gear and belt drive plate.

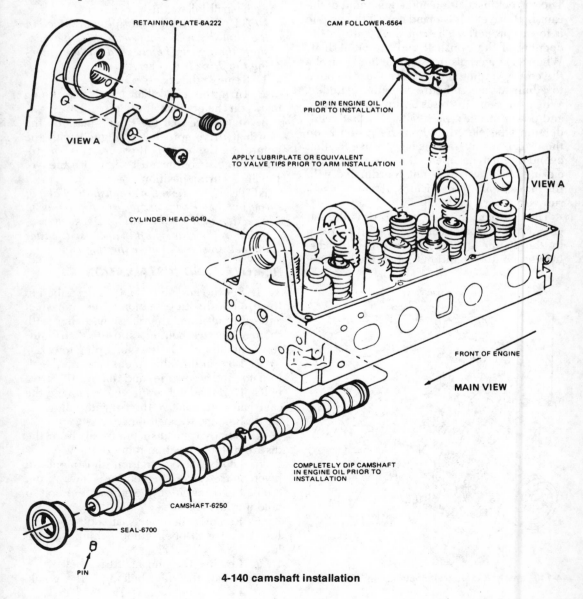

4-140 camshaft installation

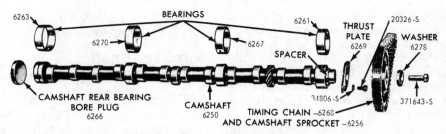

6-200, 250 camshaft and related parts

4. Remove the front cam bearing seal and cylinder head.

5. Reverse the removal procedure to install the camshaft and cylinder head.

NOTE: *Coat the camshaft with oil before sliding it into the cylinder head. Apply a coat of sealer or teflon tape to the cam drive gear bolt before installation.*

NOTE: *After any procedure requiring removal of the rocker arms, each lash adjuster must be fully collapsed after assembly, then released. This must be done before the camshaft is turned. This procedure is given earlier in the chapter. See Valve Clearance-Hydraulic Valve Lash Adjusters.*

6-200, 250

1. Remove the cylinder head, as outlined previously in this chapter.

2. Remove the timing gear cover, timing chain and sprockets, as outlined in the appropriate sections of this chapter.

3. Disconnect and remove the grille. Remove the gravel deflector.

4. Using a magnet, remove the valve liters and keep them in order so that they can be installed in their original positions. (See illustration.)

5. Remove the camshaft thrust plate and remove the camshaft by pulling it from the front of the engine. Use care not to damage the camshaft lobes or journals while removing the cam from the engine.

6. Before installing the camshaft, coat the lobes with Lubriplate, and the journals and all valve parts with heavy oil.

7. Reverse the above procedure to install, following the recommended torque settings and tightening sequences.

V6 and V8

1. Remove the intake manifold as outlined previously.

2. Remove the cylinder front cover, timing chain, and sprockets as directed previously.

3. Remove the grille, and, on models with air conditioning, remove the condenser retaining bolts and position it out of the way. Do not disconnect refrigerant lines.

4. Remove the rocker arm covers.

5. Loosen the rocker arm stud nuts and rotate the rocker arms to the side.

6. Remove the pushrods and lifters and keep them in order so that they can be installed in their original positions.

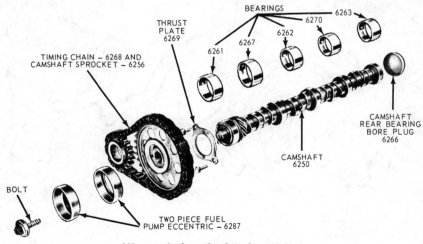

V8 camshaft and related parts

7. Remove the camshaft thrust plate and washer if so equipped. Remove the camshaft from the front of the engine. Use care not to damage the camshaft lobes or journals while rmoving the cam from the engine.

8. Before installing the camshaft, coat the lobes with Lubriplate and the journals and valve parts with heavy oil.

9. Reverse the above procedure for installation.

NOTE: *On engines with individually mounted rocker arms, it is necessary to* perform a preliminary valve adjustment before starting the engine.

Auxiliary Shaft
REMOVAL AND INSTALLATION
Four Cylinder 140 cu in. Engine

1. Remove the camshaft drive belt cover.
2. Remove the drive belt. Remove the auxiliary shaft sprocket. A puller may be necessary to remove the sprocket.
3. Remove the distributor and fuel pump.

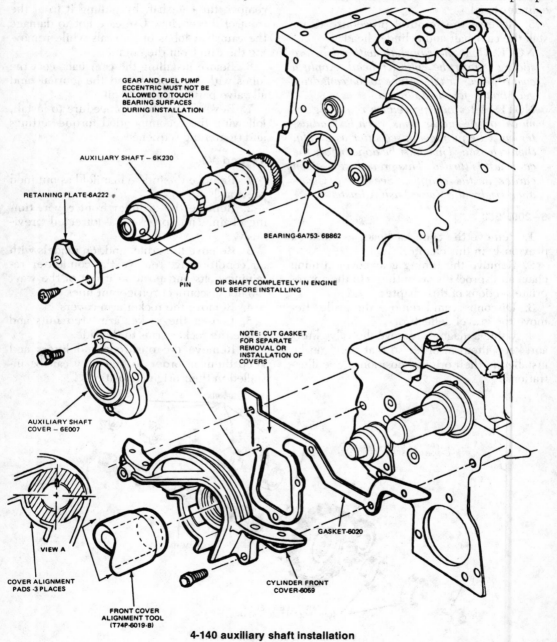

GEAR AND FUEL PUMP ECCENTRIC MUST NOT BE ALLOWED TO TOUCH BEARING SURFACES DURING INSTALLATION

AUXILIARY SHAFT – 6K230

RETAINING PLATE-6A222

PIN

BEARING-6A753- 6B862

DIP SHAFT COMPLETELY IN ENGINE OIL BEFORE INSTALLING

NOTE: CUT GASKET FOR SEPARATE REMOVAL OR INSTALLATION OF COVERS

AUXILIARY SHAFT COVER – 6E007

GASKET-6020

VIEW A

COVER ALIGNMENT PADS -3 PLACES

CYLINDER FRONT COVER-6059

FRONT COVER ALIGNMENT TOOL (T74P-6019-B)

4-140 auxiliary shaft installation

4. Remove the auxiliary shaft cover and thrust plate.

5. Withdraw the auxiliary shaft from the block.

NOTE: *The distributor drive gear and the fuel pump eccentric on the auxiliary shaft must not be allowed to touch the auxiliary shaft bearings during removal and installation. Completely coat the shaft with oil before sliding it into place.*

6. Slide the auxiliary shaft into the housing and insert the thrust plate to hold the shaft.

7. Install a new gasket and auxiliary shaft cover.

NOTE: *The auxiliary shaft cover and cylinder front cover share a gasket. Cut off the old gasket around the cylinder cover and use half of the new gasket on the auxiliary shaft cover.*

8. Fit a new gasket into the fuel pump and install the pump.

9. Insert the distributor and install the auxiliary shaft sprocket.

10. Align the timing marks and install the drive belt.

11. Install the drive belt cover.

12. Check the ignition timing.

Pistons and Connecting Rods

See the "Engine Rebuilding" section which follows later in this chapter.

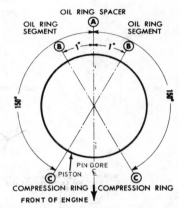

Piston ring spacing (all engines)

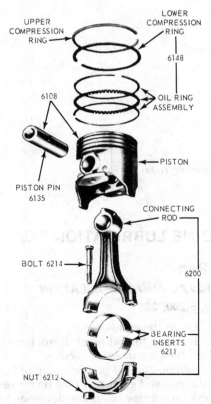

Typical piston and connecting rod assembly

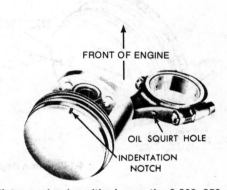

Piston and rod positioning on the 6-200, 250

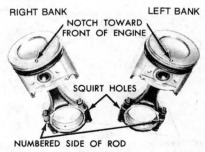

Piston and rod positioning on the V6-232, V8-255, 302, 351W, 429 and 460

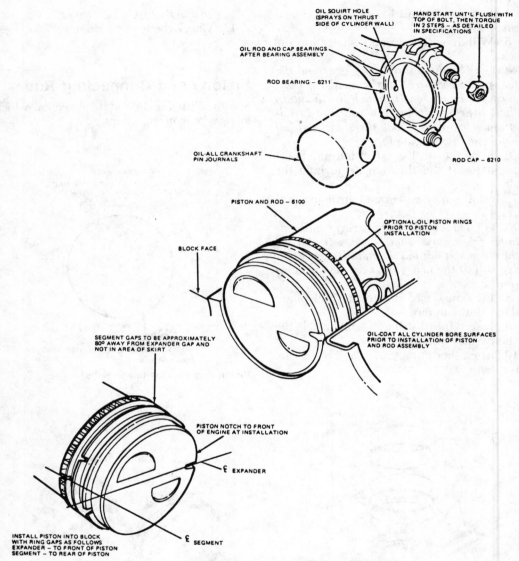

OIL SQUIRT HOLE
(SPRAYS ON THRUST
SIDE OF CYLINDER WALL)

HAND START UNTIL FLUSH WITH
TOP OF BOLT, THEN TORQUE
IN 2 STEPS – AS DETAILED
IN SPECIFICATIONS

OIL ROD AND CAP BEARINGS
AFTER BEARING ASSEMBLY

ROD BEARING – 6211

ROD CAP – 6210

OIL-ALL CRANKSHAFT
PIN JOURNALS

PISTON AND ROD – 6100

OPTIONAL-OIL PISTON RINGS
PRIOR TO PISTON
INSTALLATION

BLOCK FACE

OIL-COAT ALL CYLINDER BORE SURFACES
PRIOR TO INSTALLATION OF PISTON
AND ROD ASSEMBLY

SEGMENT GAPS TO BE APPROXIMATELY
80° AWAY FROM EXPANDER GAP AND
NOT IN AREA OF SKIRT

PISTON NOTCH TO FRONT
OF ENGINE AT INSTALLATION

EXPANDER

INSTALL PISTON INTO BLOCK
WITH RING GAPS AS FOLLOWS
EXPANDER – TO FRONT OF PISTON
SEGMENT – TO REAR OF PISTON

SEGMENT

4-140 piston rings and connecting rods

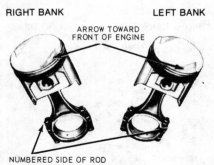

RIGHT BANK

LEFT BANK

ARROW TOWARD
FRONT OF ENGINE

NUMBERED SIDE OF ROD

Correct position of piston and rod—351C, 351M and 400 V8

ENGINE LUBRICATION

Oil Pan

REMOVAL AND INSTALLATION

4-140, 6-200, 250

1. Drain the crankcase.

2. Remove the oil level dipstick and the flywheel housing inspection cover.

3. Remove the oil pan retaining nuts, and drop the pan and gasket. It may be necessary to crank the engine to obtain clearance to remove the pan.

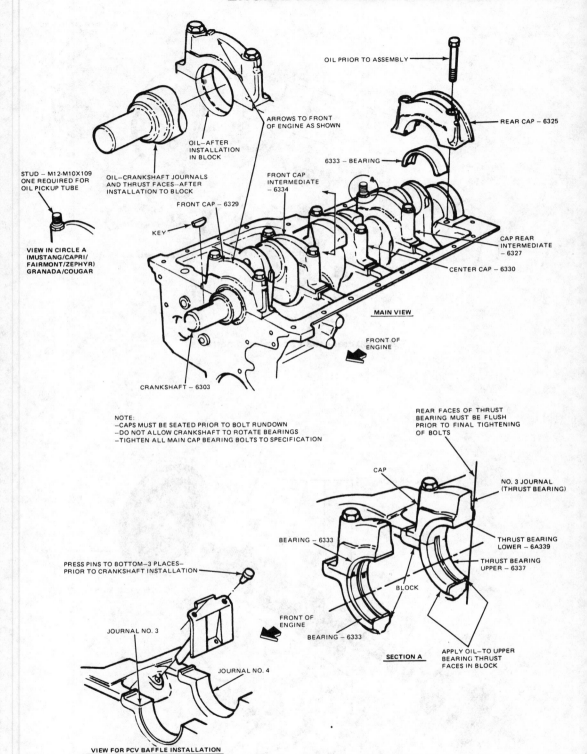

OIL PRIOR TO ASSEMBLY

REAR CAP – 6325

6333 – BEARING

ARROWS TO FRONT
OF ENGINE AS SHOWN

OIL–AFTER
INSTALLATION
IN BLOCK

FRONT CAP
INTERMEDIATE
– 6334

STUD – M12-M10X109
ONE REQUIRED FOR
OIL PICKUP TUBE

OIL–CRANKSHAFT JOURNALS
AND THRUST FACES--AFTER
INSTALLATION TO BLOCK

FRONT CAP – 6329

KEY

CAP REAR
INTERMEDIATE
– 6327

CENTER CAP – 6330

VIEW IN CIRCLE A
(MUSTANG/CAPRI/
FAIRMONT/ZEPHYR)
GRANADA/COUGAR

MAIN VIEW

FRONT OF
ENGINE

CRANKSHAFT – 6303

NOTE:
–CAPS MUST BE SEATED PRIOR TO BOLT RUNDOWN
–DO NOT ALLOW CRANKSHAFT TO ROTATE BEARINGS
–TIGHTEN ALL MAIN CAP BEARING BOLTS TO SPECIFICATION

REAR FACES OF THRUST
BEARING MUST BE FLUSH
PRIOR TO FINAL TIGHTENING
OF BOLTS

CAP

NO. 3 JOURNAL
(THRUST BEARING)

BEARING – 6333

THRUST BEARING
LOWER – 6A339

THRUST BEARING
UPPER – 6337

BLOCK

PRESS PINS TO BOTTOM–3 PLACES–
PRIOR TO CRANKSHAFT INSTALLATION

FRONT OF
ENGINE

BEARING – 6333

JOURNAL NO. 3

SECTION A

APPLY OIL–TO UPPER
BEARING THRUST
FACES IN BLOCK

JOURNAL NO. 4

VIEW FOR PCV BAFFLE INSTALLATION

4-140 crankshaft and main bearing installation

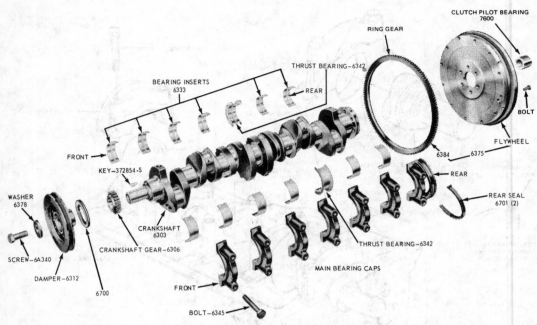

6-200, 250 crankshaft and related parts

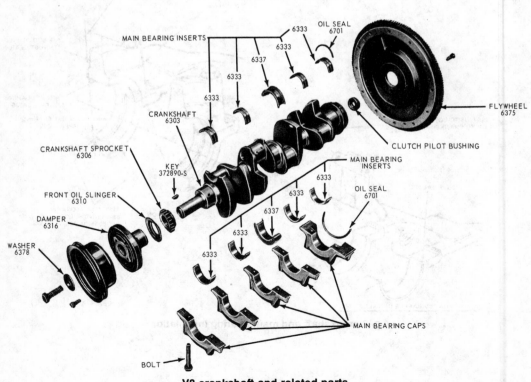

V8 crankshaft and related parts

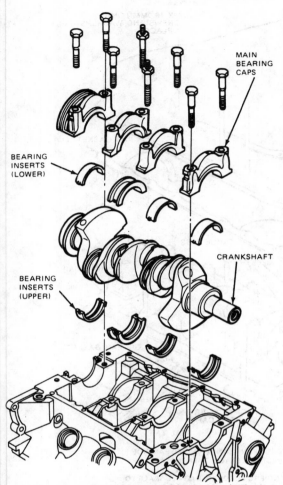

V6 crankshaft and main bearing installation

4. Remove the oil pump screen and inlet tube assembly.

5. Clean and install the oil pump inlet tube and screen assembly.

6. Clean the gasket surfaces of the block and oil pan. Be sure to clean the seal retainer grooves in the cylinder block and oil pan. The oil pan has a two-piece gasket. Coat the block surface and the oil pan gasket surface with oil-resistant sealer. Position the oil pan gaskets on the cylinder block.

7. Position the oil pan front seal on the cylinder front cover. Be sure the tabs on the seal are over the oil pan gasket.

8. Position the oil pan rear seal on the rear main bearing cap. Be sure the tabs on the seal are over the oil pan gasket.

9. Hold the oil pan in place against the block and install a bolt, finger-tight, on each side of the oil pan. Install the remaining bolts. Torque the bolts from the center outward in each direction to specifications.

10. Install the dipstick. Fill the crankcase with the proper grade and quantity of oil, and check for leaks.

Note: *Some engines have been built using RTV silicone gasket material in place of gaskets. To assemble a part using the gasket material, run a ⅛ inch bead of gasket material around the pan sealing surface, enclosing all bolt holes. This material starts to cure in 10–15 minutes, so don't take too long to position and attach the pan.*

All V6 and V8 Engines

1. Remove the oil level dipstick. Remove the bolts attaching the fan shroud to the radiator. Position the shroud over the fan.

2. Raise the vehicle and install safety stands.

3. Drain the crankcase.

4. Remove the stabilizer bar from the chassis.

5. Remove the engine front support thrubolts.

6. Raise the engine and place wood blocks between the engine front supports and chassis brackets.

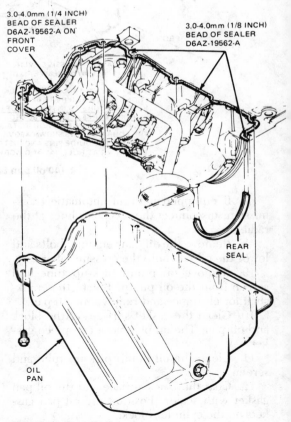

V6 oil pan installation

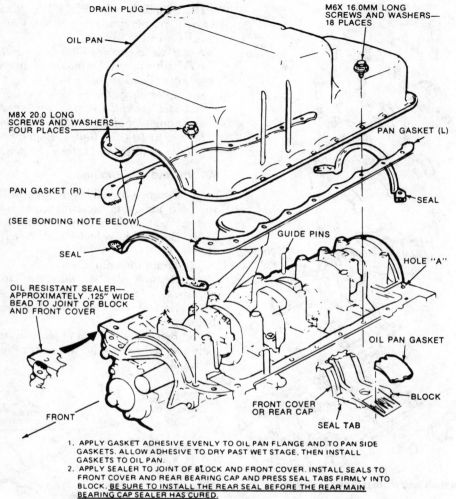

DRAIN PLUG

M6X 16.0MM LONG
SCREWS AND WASHERS—
18 PLACES

OIL PAN

M8X 20.0 LONG
SCREWS AND WASHERS—
FOUR PLACES

PAN GASKET (L)

PAN GASKET (R)

SEAL

(SEE BONDING NOTE BELOW)

SEAL

GUIDE PINS

HOLE "A"

OIL RESISTANT SEALER—
APPROXIMATELY .125" WIDE
BEAD TO JOINT OF BLOCK
AND FRONT COVER

OIL PAN GASKET

FRONT

FRONT COVER
OR REAR CAP

BLOCK

SEAL TAB

1. APPLY GASKET ADHESIVE EVENLY TO OIL PAN FLANGE AND TO PAN SIDE
   GASKETS. ALLOW ADHESIVE TO DRY PAST WET STAGE, THEN INSTALL
   GASKETS TO OIL PAN.
2. APPLY SEALER TO JOINT OF BLOCK AND FRONT COVER. INSTALL SEALS TO
   FRONT COVER AND REAR BEARING CAP AND PRESS SEAL TABS FIRMLY INTO
   BLOCK. BE SURE TO INSTALL THE REAR SEAL BEFORE THE REAR MAIN
   BEARING CAP SEALER HAS CURED.
3. POSITION 2 GUIDE PINS AND INSTALL THE OIL PAN. SECURE THE PAN WITH
   THE FOUR M8 BOLTS SHOWN ABOVE.
4. REMOVE THE GUIDE PINS AND INSTALL AND TORQUE THE EIGHTEEN M6 BOLTS,
   BEGINNING AT HOLE "A" AND WORKING CLOCKWISE AROUND THE PAN.

4-140 oil pan bolt installation

7. If equipped with an automatic transmission, disconnect the oil cooler lines at the radiator.

8. Remove the oil pan retaining bolts and lower the oil pan onto the crossmember.

9. Remove oil pump pick-up tube and screen from the oil pump. Rotate the crankshaft for clearance and remove the oil pan.

10. Clean the gasket surfaces of the block and oil pan. The oil pan has a two-piece gasket.

11. Clean the oil pump pick-up tube and screen.

12. Coat the block surface and the oil pan gasket with sealer. Position the oil pan gaskets on the cylinder block.

13. Position the oil pan front seal on the

cylinder front cover. Be sure the tabs on the seal are over the oil pan gasket.

14. Position the oil pan rear seal on the rear main bearing cap. Be sure the tabs on the seal are over the oil pan gasket.

15. Position the oil pan on the crossmember. Install a new gasket on the oil pump and install the oil pump pick-up tube.

16. Position the oil pan against the block and install a bolt, finger-tight, on each side of the block. Install the remaining bolts. Tighten the bolts from the center outward in each direction to specifications.

17. If equipped with an automatic transmission, connect the oil cooler lines at the radiator.

18. Raise the engine and remove the wood

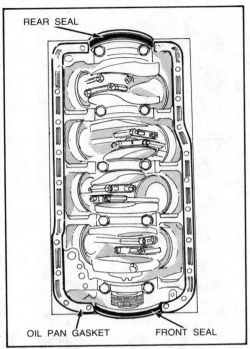

Typical oil pan gasket and seal installation

blocks from between the engine supports and the chassis brackets. Lower the engine and install the engine support thru-bolts. Tighten the bolts to specifications.

19. Install the stabilizer bar to the chassis.

20. Lower the vehicle.

21. Install the fan shroud.

22. Install the oil level dipstick. Fill the crankcase with the proper grade and quantity of engine oil. Start the engine and check for oil leaks.

Rear Main Oil Seal

REMOVAL AND INSTALLATION

All Engines

NOTE: *The rear oil seal installed in these engines is a rubber type seal.*

1. Remove the oil pan, and, if required, the oil pump.

2. Loosen all main bearing caps allowing the crankshaft to lower slightly.

NOTE: *The crankshaft should not be allowed to drop more than $1/32$ in.*

3. Remove the rear main bearing cap and remove the seal from the cap and block. Be

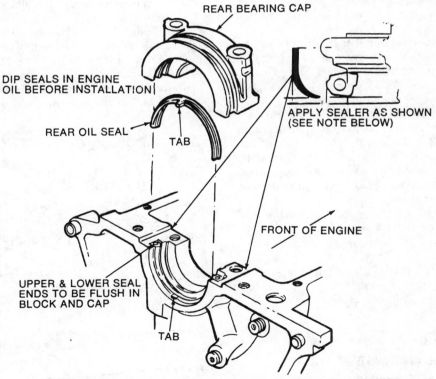

NOTE: CLEAN THE AREA WHERE SEALER IS TO BE APPLIED BEFORE INSTALLING THE SEALS. AFTER THE SEALS ARE IN PLACE, APPLY A 1/16 INCH BEAD OF SEALER AS SHOWN. *SEALER MUST NOT TOUCH SEALS*

4-140 rear main oil seal replacement

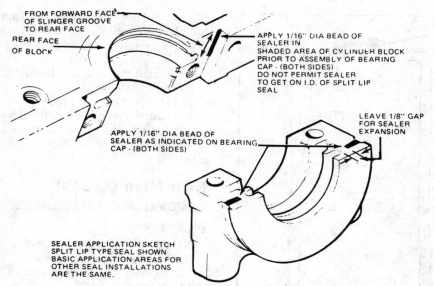

FROM FORWARD FACE
OF SLINGER GROOVE
TO REAR FACE

REAR FACE
OF BLOCK

APPLY 1/16" DIA BEAD OF
SEALER IN
SHADED AREA OF CYLINDER BLOCK
PRIOR TO ASSEMBLY OF BEARING
CAP. (BOTH SIDES)
DO NOT PERMIT SEALER
TO GET ON I.D. OF SPLIT LIP
SEAL

APPLY 1/16" DIA BEAD OF
SEALER AS INDICATED ON BEARING
CAP. (BOTH SIDES)

LEAVE 1/8" GAP
FOR SEALER
EXPANSION

SEALER APPLICATION SKETCH
SPLIT LIP TYPE SEAL SHOWN
BASIC APPLICATION AREAS FOR
OTHER SEAL INSTALLATIONS
ARE THE SAME.

rear main oil seal installation on all except 4-140

very careful not to scratch the sealing surface. Remove the old seal retaining pin from the cap, if equipped. It is not used with the replacement seal.

4. Carefully clean the seal grooves in the cap and block with solvent.

5. Soak the new seal halves in clean engine oil.

6. Install the upper half of the seal in the block with the undercut side of the seal toward the front of the engine. Slide the seal around the crankshaft journal until ⅜ in. protrudes beyond the base of the block.

7. Tighten all the main bearing caps (except the rear main bearing) to specifications.

8. Install the lower seal into the rear cap, with the undercut side facing the front of the engine. Allow ⅜ in. of the seal to protrude above the surface, at the opposite end from the block seal.

9. Squeeze a ¹⁄₁₆ in. bead of silicone sealant onto the areas shown.

10. Install the rear cap and torque to specifications.

11. Install the oil pump and pan. Fill the crankcase with oil, start the engine, and check for leaks.

Oil Pump

REMOVAL AND INSTALLATION

All Engines Except V6

1. Remove the oil pan as outlined previously in this chapter.

2. On 302 and 351W V8 engines, remove

and clean the oil pump inlet tube and screen assembly.

3. Remove the oil pump attaching bolts. Lower the oil pump, gasket and intermediate driveshaft from the crankcase.

4. On all engines except the 302 and 351W V8's, remove the inlet tube and screen assembly. Reinstall after cleaning.

5. Install the oil pump assembly:

a. Prime the pump by filling it with engine oil and rotating the pump shaft to distribute the oil within the pump body.

b. Position the intermediate driveshaft

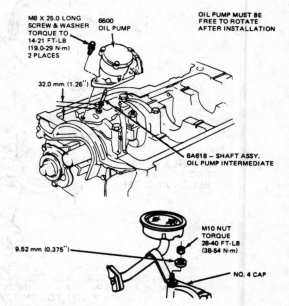

M8 X 25.0 LONG
SCREW & WASHER
TORQUE TO
14-21 FT-LB
(19.0-29 N·m)
2 PLACES

6600
OIL PUMP

OIL PUMP MUST BE
FREE TO ROTATE
AFTER INSTALLATION

32.0 mm (1.26")

6A618 – SHAFT ASSY.
OIL PUMP INTERMEDIATE

M10 NUT
TORQUE
28-40 FT-LB
(38-54 N·m)

9.52 mm (0.375")

NO. 4 CAP

4-140 oil pump installation

into the distributor socket. With the shaft firmly seated in the socket, the stop on the shaft should contact the roof of the crankcase. Remove the shaft and position the stop as necessary.

c. Insert the intermediate driveshaft into the oil pump. Using a new gasket, install the pump and shaft as an assembly.

NOTE: *Do not attempt to force the pump into position if it will not seat readily. If necessary, rotate the intermediate driveshaft hex into a new position so that it will mesh with the distributor shaft.*

6. Torque the oil pump attaching bolts to the following specifications:
- 6-cyl. engines—12–15 ft. lbs.;
- 302 and 351 W—22–32 ft. lbs.;
- 351C, 351M and 400—25–35 ft. lbs.;
- 429 and 460—20–25 ft. lbs.

7. On 302 and 351W engines, install the inlet tube and screen assembly.

8. Install the oil pan as outlined previously.

V6

1. If necessary remove the oil filter.
2. Remove the oil pump cover attaching bolts and remove the cover.
3. Lift the pump gears of the pocket in the front cover.
4. Remove the cover gasket. Discard the gasket.
5. If necessary, remove the pump gears from the cover.
6. Pack the gear pocket with petroleum jelly. DO NOT USE CHASSIS LUBRICANTS.

7. Install the gears in the cover pocket making sure the petroleum jelly fills all voids between the gears and the pocket.

CAUTION: *Failure to properly pack the oil pump gears with petroleum jelly may result in failure of the pump to prime when the engine is started.*

8. Position the cover gasket and install the pump cover.

9. Tighten the pump cover attaching bolts to 18–22 ft. lbs.

ENGINE COOLING

Radiator

REMOVAL AND INSTALLATION

1. Drain the cooling system.
2. Disconnect the upper and lower hoses at the radiator.
3. On cars with automatic transmissions, disconnect the oil cooler lines at the radiator.
4. On vehicles with a fan shroud, remove the shroud retaining screws and position the shroud out of the way.
5. Remove the radiator attaching bolts and lift out the radiator.
6. If a new radiator is to be installed, transfer the petcock from the old radiator to the new one. On cars with automatic transmissions, transfer the oil cooler line fittings from the old radiator to the new one.
7. Position the radiator and install, but do not tighten, the radiator support bolts. On cars with automatic transmissions, connect the oil cooler lines. Then tighten the radiator support bolts.
8. On vehicles with a fan shroud, reinstall the shroud.
9. Connect the radiator hoses. Close the

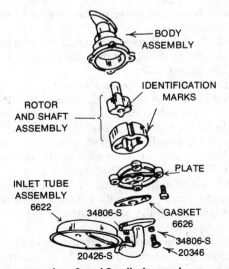

Oil pump used on 6 and 8 cylinder engines

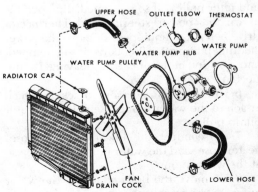

Typical cooling system and related parts—V8 with downflow radiator shown

radiator petcock. Then fill the cooling system.

10. Start the engine and bring to operating temperature. Check for leaks.

11. On cars with automatic transmissions, check the cooler lines for leaks and interference. Check the transmission fluid level.

Water Pump

REMOVAL AND INSTALLATION

Four Cylinder 140 cu in. Engine

1. Drain the cooling system.

2. Disconnect the lower radiator hose and heater hose from the water pump.

3. Loosen the alternator retaining and adjusting bolt, and remove the drive belt.

4. Remove the fan shroud, fan and water pump pulley. On 2300 cc engines, remove the camshaft drive belt cover first. It is not necessary to remove the cam belt or inner cover.

5. Remove the water pump retaining bolts and remove the pump from the engine.

6. Clean all mating surfaces and install the pump with a new gasket coated with sealer. If a new pump is being installed, transfer the heater hose fitting from the old pump.

7. Reverse the removal steps to install the pump. Refill the cooling system.

All except 4-140

1. Drain the cooling system.

2. On 351C, 351M, and 400 V8 engines, disconnect the negative battery cable.

3. If equipped with a fan shroud, remove the shroud attaching bolts and position the shroud over the fan.

4. Remove the fan and spacer from the water pump shaft. Remove the shroud, if so equipped.

5. Remove the air conditioning drive belt and idler pulley, if so equipped. Remove the alternator, power steering and Thermactor drive belts, if so equipped. Remove the power steering pump attaching bolts, if so equipped, and position it to one side (leaving it connected).

6. Remove all accessory brackets which attach to the water pump. Remove the water pump pulley.

7. Disconnect the lower radiator hose, heater hose, and the water pump by-pass hose at the water pump.

8. Remove the bolts attaching the water pump to the front cover. Remove the pump and gasket. Discard the old gasket.

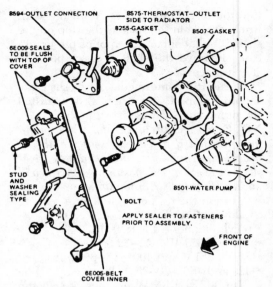

4-140 water pump, thermostat and inner timing bolt installation

9. Clean all gasket surfaces. On the 429 and 460 V8, remove the water pump backing plate and replace the gasket.

NOTE: *The 250 six-cylinder engine originally had a one-piece gasket for the cylinder front cover and the water pump. Trim away the old gasket at the edge of the cylinder cover and replace with a service gasket.*

10. Coat both sides of a new gasket with water-resistant sealer and place it on the front cover. Install the water pump and tighten the attaching bolts diagonally, in rotation, to 15 ft. lbs.

11. Connect the lower radiator hose, heater hose, and water pump by-pass hose at the water pump.

12. Install all accessory brackets attaching to the water pump. Install the pump pulley on the pump shaft.

13. Install the power steering pump and drive belt, if so equipped. Install the alternator, air conditioning, and Thermactor drive belts, if so equipped. Install the air conditioner idler pulley bracket, if so equipped. Adjust the drive belt tension of all accessory drive belts as outlined in Chapter 1.

14. Position the fan shroud, if so equipped, over the water pump pulley. Install the spacer and fan. Install the shroud attaching bolts, if so equipped.

15. Fill the cooling system. Operate the engine until normal running temperature is reached. Check for leaks.

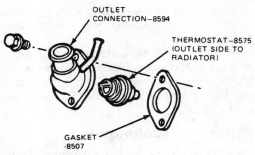

4-140 thermostat

Installing thermostat—typical

Thermostat

REMOVAL AND INSTALLATION

1. Open the drain cock and drain the radiator so that the coolant level is below the coolant outlet elbow which houses the thermostat.

2. Remove the outlet elbow retaining bolts and position the elbow clear of the intake manifold or cylinder head sufficiently to provide access to the thermostat.

3. Remove the thermostat and old gasket. The thermostat must be rotated counterclockwise for removal.

4. Clean the mating surfaces of the outlet elbow and the engine to remove all old gasket material and sealer. Coat the new gasket with water-resistant sealer and install it on the engine. Install the thermostat in the outlet elbow. The thermostat must be rotated clockwise to lock it in position.

5. Install the outlet elbow and retaining bolts on the engine. Torque the bolts to 12–15 ft. lbs.

6. Refill the radiator. Run the engine at operating temperature and check for leaks. Recheck the coolant level.

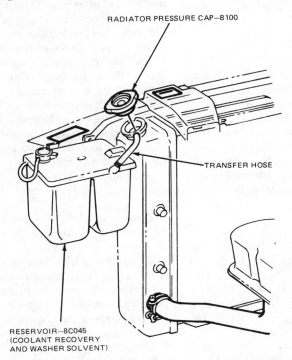

Coolant Recovery System—Typical

ENGINE REBUILDING

Most procedures involved in rebuilding an engine are fairly standard, regardless of the type of engine involved. This section is a guide to accepted rebuilding procedures. Examples of standard rebuilding practices are illustrated and should be used along with specific details concerning your particular engine, found earlier in this chapter.

The procedures given here are those used by any competent rebuilder. Obviously some of the procedures cannot be performed by the do-it-yourself mechanic, but are provided so that you will be familiar with the services that should be offered by rebuilding or machine shops. As an example, in most instances, it is more profitable for the home mechanic to remove the cylinder heads, buy the necessary parts (new valves, seals, keepers, keys, etc.) and deliver these to a machine shop for the necessary work. In this way you will save the money to remove and install the cylinder head and the mark-up on parts.

On the other hand, most of the work involved in rebuilding the lower end is well within the scope of the do-it-yourself mechanic. Only work such as hot-tanking, actually boring the block or Magnafluxing (invisible crack detection) need be sent to a machine shop.

Tools

The tools required for basic engine rebuilding should, with a few exceptions, be those included in a mechanic's tool kit. An accurate torque wrench, and a dial indicator (reading in thousandths) mounted on a universal base should be available. Special tools, where required, are available from the major tool suppliers. The services of a competent automotive machine shop must also be readily available.

Precautions

Aluminum has become increasingly popular for use in engines, due to its low weight and excellent heat transfer characteristics. The following precautions must be observed when handling aluminum (or any other) engine parts:

—Never hot-tank aluminum parts.

—Remove all aluminum parts (identification tags, etc.) from engine parts before hot-tanking (otherwise they will be removed during the process).

—Always coat threads lightly with engine oil or anti-seize compounds before installation, to prevent seizure.

—Never over-torque bolts or spark plugs in aluminum threads. Should stripping occur, threads can be restored using any of a number of thread repair kits available (see next section).

Inspection Techniques

Magnaflux and Zyglo are inspection techniques used to locate material flaws, such as stress cracks. Magnaflux is a magnetic process, applicable only to ferrous materials. The Zyglo process coats the matrial with a fluorescent dye penetrant, and any material may be tested using Zyglo. Specific checks of suspected surface cracks may be made at lower cost and more readily using spot check dye. The dye is sprayed onto the suspected area, wiped off, and the area is then sprayed with a developer. Cracks then will show up brightly.

Overhaul

The section is divided into two parts. The first, Cylinder Head Reconditioning, assumes that the cylinder head is removed from the engine, all manifolds are removed, and the cylinder head is on a workbench. The camshaft should be removed from overhead cam cylinder heads. The second section, Cylinder Block Reconditioning, covers the block, pistons, connecting rods and crankshaft. It is assumed that the engine is mounted on a work stand, and the cylinder head and all accessories are removed.

Procedures are identified as follows:

Unmarked—Basic procedures that must be performed in order to successfully complete the rebuilding process.

Starred (*)—Procedures that should be performed to ensure maximum performance and engine life.

Double starred (**)—Procedures that may be performed to increase engine performance and reliability.

When assembling the engine, any parts that will be in frictional contact must be pre-lubricated, to provide protection on initial start-up. Any product specifically formulated for this purpose may be used. NOTE: *Do not use engine oil. Where semi-permanent* (locked but removable) installation of bolts or nuts is desired, threads should be cleaned and located with Loctite ® or a similar product (non-hardening).

Repairing Damaged Threads

Several methods of repairing damaged threads are available. Heli-Coil® (shown here), Keenserts® and Microdot® are among the most widely used. All involve basically the same principle—drilling out stripped threads, tapping the hole and installing a pre-wound insert—making welding, plugging and oversize fasteners unnecessary.

Two types of thread repair inserts are usually supplied—a standard type for most Inch Coarse, Inch Fine, Metric Coarse and Metric Fine thread sizes and a spark plug type to fit most spark plug port sizes. Consult the individual manufacturer's catalog to determine exact applications. Typical thread repair kits will contain a selection of pre-wound threaded inserts, a tap (corresponding to the outside diameter threads of the insert) and an installation tool. Spark plug inserts usually differ because they require a tap equipped with pilot threads and a combined reamer/tap section. Most manufacturers also supply blister-packed thread repair inserts separately in addition to a master kit containing a variety of taps and inserts plus installation tools.

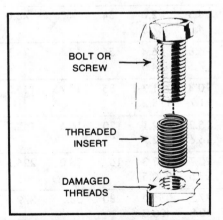

Damaged bolt holes can be repaired with thread repair inserts

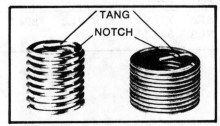

Standard thread repair insert (left) and spark plug thread insert (right)

Before effecting a repair to a threaded hole, remove any snapped, broken or damaged bolts or studs. Penetrating oil can be used to free frozen threads; the offending item can be removed with locking pliers or with a screw or stud extractor. After the hole is clear, the thread can be repaired, as follows:

Drill out the damaged threads with specified drill. Drill completely through the hole or to the bottom of a blind hole

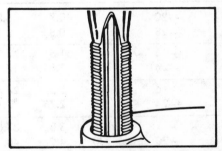

With the tap supplied, tap the hole to receive the thread insert. Keep the tap well oiled and back it out frequently to avoid clogging the threads

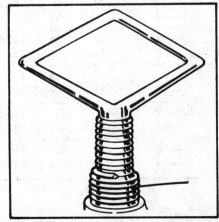

Screw the threaded insert onto the installation tool until the tang engages the slot. Screw the insert into the tapped hole until it is ¼–½ turn below the top surface. After installation break off the tang with a hammer and punch

Standard Torque Specifications and Fastener Markings

The Newton-metre has been designated the world standard for measuring torque and will gradually replace the foot-pound and kilogram-meter. In the absence of specific torques, the following chart can be used as a guide to the maximum safe torque of a particular size/grade of fastener.

- There is no torque difference for fine or coarse threads.
- Torque values are based on clean, dry threads. Reduce the value by 10% if threads are oiled prior to assembly.
- The torque required for aluminum components or fasteners is considerably less.

U. S. BOLTS

SAE Grade Number	1 or 2			5			6 or 7		

Bolt Markings

Manufacturer's marks may vary—number of lines always 2 less than the grade number.

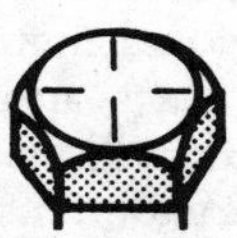

Usage	Frequent			Frequent			Infrequent		
Bolt Size (inches)—(Thread)	Maximum Torque			Maximum Torque			Maximum Torque		
	Ft-Lb	kgm	Nm	Ft-Lb	kgm	Nm	Ft-Lb	kgm	Nm
¼—20	5	0.7	6.8	8	1.1	10.8	10	1.4	13.5
—28	6	0.8	8.1	10	1.4	13.6			
5/16—18	11	1.5	14.9	17	2.3	23.0	19	2.6	25.8
—24	13	1.8	17.6	19	2.6	25.7			
⅜—16	18	2.5	24.4	31	4.3	42.0	34	4.7	46.0
—24	20	2.75	27.1	35	4.8	47.5			
7/16—14	28	3.8	37.0	49	6.8	66.4	55	7.6	74.5
—20	30	4.2	40.7	55	7.6	74.5			
½—13	39	5.4	52.8	75	10.4	101.7	85	11.75	115.2
—20	41	5.7	55.6	85	11.7	115.2			
9/16—12	51	7.0	69.2	110	15.2	149.1	120	16.6	162.7
—18	55	7.6	74.5	120	16.6	162.7			
⅝—11	83	11.5	112.5	150	20.7	203.3	167	23.0	226.5
—18	95	13.1	128.8	170	23.5	230.5			
¾—10	105	14.5	142.3	270	37.3	366.0	280	38.7	379.6
—16	115	15.9	155.9	295	40.8	400.0			
⅞— 9	160	22.1	216.9	395	54.6	535.5	440	60.9	596.5
—14	175	24.2	237.2	435	60.1	589.7			
1— 8	236	32.5	318.6	590	81.6	799.9	660	91.3	894.8
—14	250	34.6	338.9	660	91.3	849.8			

METRIC BOLTS

NOTE: *Metric bolts are marked with a number indicating the relative strength of the bolt. These numbers have nothing to do with size.*

Description	Torque ft-lbs (Nm)			
Thread size x pitch (mm)	Head mark—4		Head mark—7	
6 x 1.0	2.2–2.9	(3.0–3.9)	3.6–5.8	(4.9–7.8)
8 x 1.25	5.8–8.7	(7.9–12)	9.4–14	(13–19)
10 x 1.25	12–17	(16–23)	20–29	(27–39)
12 x 1.25	21–32	(29–43)	35–53	(47–72)
14 x 1.5	35–52	(48–70)	57–85	(77–110)
16 x 1.5	51–77	(67–100)	90–120	(130–160)
18 x 1.5	74–110	(100–150)	130–170	(180–230)
20 x 1.5	110–140	(150–190)	190–240	(160–320)
22 x 1.5	150–190	(200–260)	250–320	(340–430)
24 x 1.5	190–240	(260–320)	310–410	(420–550)

NOTE: *This engine rebuilding section is a guide to accepted rebuilding procedures. Typical examples of standard rebuilding procedures are illustrated. Use these procedures along with the detailed instructions earlier in this chapter, concerning your particular engine.*

Cylinder Head Reconditioning

Procedure	Method
Remove the cylinder head:	See the engine service procedures earlier in this chapter for details concerning specific engines.
Identify the valves:	Invert the cylinder head, and number the valve faces front to rear, using a permanent felt-tip marker.
Remove the rocker arms (OHV engines only):	Remove the rocker arms with shaft(s) or balls and nuts. Wire the sets of rockers, balls and nuts together, and identify according to the corresponding valve.
Remove the camshaft (OHC engines only):	See the engine service procedures earlier in this chapter for details concerning specific engines.
Remove the valves and springs:	Using an appropriate valve spring compressor (depending on the configuration of the cylinder head), compress the valve springs. Lift out the keepers with needlenose pliers, release the compressor, and remove the valve, spring, and spring retainer. See the engine service procedures earlier in this chapter for details concerning specific engines.

Cylinder Head Reconditioning

Procedure	Method

Check the valve stem-to-guide clearance:

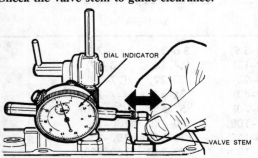

Check the valve stem-to-guide clearance

Clean the valve stem with lacquer thinner or a similar solvent to remove all gum and varnish. Clean the valve guides using solvent and an expanding wire-type valve guide cleaner. Mount a dial indicator so that the stem is at 90° to the valve stem, as close to the valve guide as possible. Move the valve off its seat, and measure the valve guide-to-stem clearance by rocking the stem back and forth to actuate the dial indicator. Measure the valve stems using a micrometer, and compare to specifications, to determine whether stem or guide wear is responsible for excessive clearance.
NOTE: *Consult the Specifications tables earlier in this chapter.*

De-carbon the cylinder head and valves:

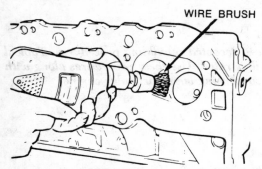

Remove the carbon from the cylinder head with a wire brush and electric drill

Chip carbon away from the valve heads, combustion chambers, and ports, using a chisel made of hardwood. Remove the remaining deposits with a stiff wire brush.
NOTE: *Be sure that the deposits are actually removed, rather than burnished.*

Hot-tank the cylinder head (cast iron heads only):
CAUTION: *Do not hot-tank aluminum parts.*

Have the cylinder head hot-tanked to remove grease, corrosion, and scale from the water passages.
NOTE: *In the case of overhead cam cylinder heads, consult the operator to determine whether the camshaft bearings will be damaged by the caustic solution.*

Degrease the remaining cylinder head parts:

Clean the remaining cylinder head parts in an engine cleaning solvent. Do not remove the protective coating from the springs.

Check the cylinder head for warpage:

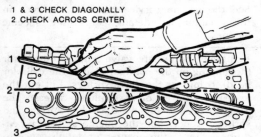

Check the cylinder head for warpage

Place a straight-edge across the gasket surface of the cylinder head. Using feeler gauges, determine the clearance at the center of the straight-edge. If warpage exceeds .003″ in a 6″ span, or .006″ over the total length, the cylinder head must be resurfaced.
NOTE: *If warpage exceeds the manufacturer's maximum tolerance for material removal, the cylinder head must be replaced.* When milling the cylinder heads of V-type engines, the intake manifold mounting position is altered, and must be corrected by milling the manifold flange a proportionate amount.

Cylinder Head Reconditioning

Procedure	Method

*Knurl the valve guides:

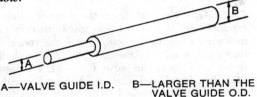

Cut-away view of a knurled valve guide

*Valve guides which are not excessively worn or distorted may, in some cases, be knurled rather than replaced. Knurling is a process in which metal is displaced and raised, thereby reducing clearance. Knurling also provides excellent oil control. The possibility of knurling rather than replacing valve guides should be discussed with a machinist.

Replace the valve guides:
NOTE: *Valve guides should only be replaced if damaged or if an oversize valve stem is not available.*

A—VALVE GUIDE I.D.   B—LARGER THAN THE VALVE GUIDE O.D.

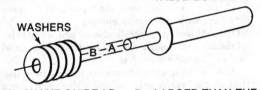

WASHERS

A—VALVE GUIDE I.D.   B—LARGER THAN THE VALVE GUIDE O.D.

Valve guide installation tool using washers for installation

See the engine service procedures earlier in this chapter for details concerning specific engines. Depending on the type of cylinder head, valve guides may be pressed, hammered, or shrunk in. In cases where the guides are shrunk into the head, replacement should be left to an equipped machine shop. In other cases, the guides are replaced using a stepped drift (see illustration). Determine the height above the boss that the guide must extend, and obtain a stack of washers, their I.D. similar to the guide's O.D., of that height. Place the stack of washers on the guide, and insert the guide into the boss.
NOTE: *Valve guides are often tapered or beveled for installation.* Using the stepped installation tool (see illustration), press or tap the guides into position. Ream the guides according to the size of the valve stem.

Replace valve seat inserts:

Replacement of valve seat inserts which are worn beyond resurfacing or broken, if feasible, must be done by a machine shop.

Resurface (grind) the valve face:

FOR DIMENSIONS, REFER TO SPECIFICATIONS

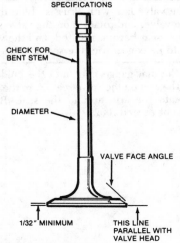

CHECK FOR BENT STEM

DIAMETER

VALVE FACE ANGLE

1/32" MINIMUM   THIS LINE PARALLEL WITH VALVE HEAD

Critical valve dimensions

Using a valve grinder, resurface the valves according to specifications given earlier in this chapter.
CAUTION: *Valve face angle is not always identical to valve seat angle.* A minimum margin of

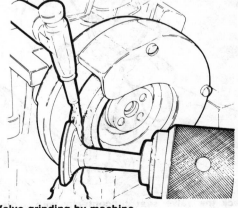

Valve grinding by machine

Cylinder Head Reconditioning

Procedure	Method
	$^1/_{32}''$ should remain after grinding the valve. The valve stem top should also be squared and resurfaced, by placing the stem in the V-block of the grinder, and turning it while pressing lightly against the grinding wheel. NOTE: *Do not grind sodium filled exhaust valves on a machine. These should be hand lapped.*
Resurface the valve seats using reamers or grinder: 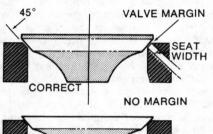 **Valve seat width and centering**  **Reaming the valve seat with a hand reamer**	Select a reamer of the correct seat angle, slightly larger than the diameter of the valve seat, and assemble it with a pilot of the correct size. Install the pilot into the valve guide, and using steady pressure, turn the reamer clockwise. CAUTION: *Do not turn the reamer counterclockwise.* Remove only as much material as necessary to clean the seat. Check the concentricity of the seat (following). If the dye method is not used, coat the valve face with Prussian blue dye, install and rotate it on the valve seat. Using the dye marked area as a centering guide, center and narrow the valve seat to specifications with correction cutters. NOTE: *When no specifications are available, minimum seat width for exhaust valves should be $^5/_{64}''$, intake valves $^1/_{16}''$.* After making correction cuts, check the position of the valve seat on the valve face using Prussian blue dye.
	To resurface the seat with a power grinder, select a pilot of the correct size and coarse stone of the proper angle. Lubricate the pilot and move the stone on and off the valve seat at 2 cycles per second, until all flaws are gone. Finish the seat with a fine stone. If necessary the seat can be corrected or narrowed using correction stones.
Check the valve seat concentricity: 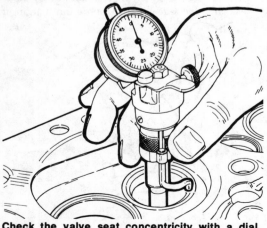 **Check the valve seat concentricity with a dial gauge**	Coat the valve face with Prussian blue dye, install the valve, and rotate it on the valve seat. If the entire seat becomes coated, and the valve is known to be concentric, the seat is concentric.
	*Install the dial gauge pilot into the guide, and rest of the arm on the valve seat. Zero the gauge, and rotate the arm around the seat. Run-out should not exceed .002''.

Cylinder Head Reconditioning

Procedure	Method

*Lap the valves:
NOTE: *Valve lapping is done to ensure efficient sealing of resurfaced valves and seats.*

Lapping the valves by hand

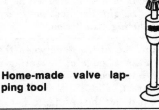

HAND DRILL

Home-made valve lapping tool

ROD

SUCTION CUP

* Invert the cylinder head, lightly lubricate the valve stems, and install the valves in the head as numbered. Coat valve seats with fine grinding compound, and attach the lapping tool suction cup to a valve head.
NOTE: *Moisten the suction cup.* Rotate the tool between the palms, changing position and lifting the tool often to prevent grooving. Lap the valve until a smooth, polished seat is evident. Remove the valve and tool, and rinse away all traces of grinding compound.

** Fasten a suction cup to a piece of drill rod, and mount the rod in a hand drill. Proceed as above, using the hand drill as a lapping tool.
CAUTION: *Due to the higher speeds involved when using the hand drill, care must be exercised to avoid grooving the seat.* Lift the tool and change direction of rotation often.

Check the valve springs:

NOT MORE THAN 5/64"

CLOSED COIL END DOWNWARD

Check the valve spring free length and squareness

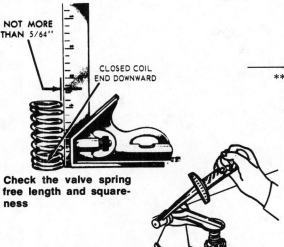

Check the valve spring test pressure

Place the spring on a flat surface next to a square. Measure the height of the spring, and rotate it against the edge of the square to measure distortion. If spring height varies (by comparison) by more than $1/16''$ or if distortion exceeds $1/16''$, replace the spring.

** In addition to evaluating the spring as above, test the spring pressure at the installed and compressed (installed height minus valve lift) height using a valve spring tester. Springs used on small displacement engines (up to 3 liters) should be ∓ 1 lb of all other springs in either position. A tolerance of ∓ 5 lbs is permissible on larger engines.

Cylinder Head Reconditioning

Procedure	Method

*Install valve stem seals:

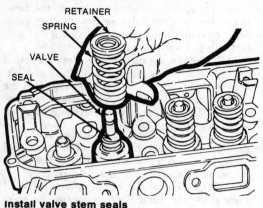

Install valve stem seals

* Due to the pressure differential that exists at the ends of the intake valve guides (atmospheric pressure above, manifold vacuum below), oil is drawn through the valve guides into the intake port. This has been alleviated somewhat since the addition of positive crankcase ventilation, which lowers the pressure above the guides. Several types of valve stem seals are available to rocker arms and balls, and install them on the the stem and guide boss, while others require that the boss be machined. Recently, Teflon guide seals have become popular. Consult a parts supplier or machinist concerning availability and suggested usages.

NOTE: *When installing seals, ensure that a small amount of oil is able to pass the seal to lubricate the valve guides; otherwise, excessive wear may result.*

Install the valves:

See the engine service procedures earlier in this chapter for details concerning specific engines.

Lubricate the valve stems, and install the valves in the cylinder head as numbered. Lubricate and position the seals (if used) and the valve springs. Install the spring retainers, compress the springs, and insert the keys using needle-nose pliers or a tool designed for this purpose.

NOTE: *Retain the keys with wheel bearing grease during installation.*

Check valve spring installed height:

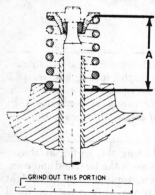

Measure the valve spring installed height (A) with a modified steel rule

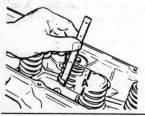

Valve spring installed height (A)

Measure the distance between the spring pad and the lower edge of the spring retainer, and compare to specifications. If the installed height is incorrect, add shim washers between the spring pad and the spring.

CAUTION: *Use only washers designed for this purpose.*

Install the camshaft (OHC engines only) and check end-play:

See the engine service procedures earlier in this chapter for details concerning specific engines.

Cylinder Head Reconditioning

Procedure	Method
Inspect the rocker arms, balls, studs, and nuts (OHV engines only): 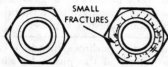 **Stress cracks in the rocker nuts**	Visually inspect the rocker arms, balls, studs, and nuts for cracks, galling, burning, scoring, or wear. If all parts are intact, liberally lubricate the rocker arms and balls, and install them on the cylinder head. If wear is noted on a rocker arm at the point of valve contact, grind it smooth and square, removing as little material as possible. Replace the rocker arm if excessively worn. If a rocker stud shows signs of wear, it must be replaced (see below). If a rocker nut shows stress cracks, replace it. If an exhaust ball is galled or burned, substitute the intake ball from the same cylinder (if it is intact), and install a new intake ball. **NOTE:** *Avoid using new rocker balls on exhaust valves.*
Replacing rocker studs (OHV engines only): 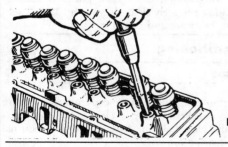 **Extracting a pressed-in rocker stud** 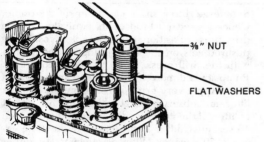 **Ream the stud bore for oversize rocker studs**	In order to remove a threaded stud, lock two nuts on the stud, and unscrew the stud using the lower nut. Coat the lower threads of the new stud with Loctite, and install. 　　Two alternative methods are available for replacing pressed in studs. Remove the damaged stud using a stack of washers and a nut (see illustration). In the first, the boss is reamed .005–.006″ oversize, and an oversize stud pressed in. Control the stud extension over the boss using washers, in the same manner as valve guides. Before installing the stud, coat it with white lead and grease. To retain the stud more positively drill a hole through the stud and boss, and install a roll pin. In the second method, the boss is tapped, and a threaded stud installed.
Inspect the rocker shaft(s) and rocker arms (OHV engines only) 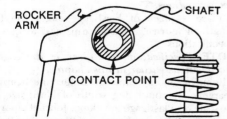 **Check the rocker arm-to-rocker shaft contact area**	Remove rocker arms, springs and washers from rocker shaft. **NOTE:** *Lay out parts in the order as they are removed.* Inspect rocker arms for pitting or wear on the valve contact point, or excessive bushing wear. Bushings need only be replaced if wear is excessive, because the rocker arm normally contacts the shaft at one point only. Grind the valve contact point of rocker arm smooth if necessary, removing as little material as possible. If excessive material must be removed to smooth and square the arm, it should be replaced. Clean out all oil holes and passages in rocker shaft. If shaft is grooved or worn, replace it. Lubricate and assemble the rocker shaft.

Cylinder Head Reconditioning

Procedure	Method
Inspect the pushrods (OHV engines only):	Remove the pushrods, and, if hollow, clean out the oil passages using fine wire. Roll each pushrod over a piece of clean glass. If a distinct clicking sound is heard as the pushrod rolls, the rod is bent, and must be replaced.
	*The length of all pushrods must be equal. Measure the length of the pushrods, compare to specifications, and replace as necessary.
Inspect the valve lifters (OHV engines only): CHECK FOR CONCAVE WEAR ON FACE OF TAPPET USING TAPPET FOR STRAIGHT EDGE **Check the lifter face for squareness**	Remove lifters from their bores, and remove gum and varnish, using solvent. Clean walls of lifter bores. Check lifters for concave wear as illustrated. If face is worn concave, replace lifter, and carefully inspect the camshaft. Lightly lubricate lifter and insert it into its bore. If play is excessive, an oversize lifter must be installed (where possible). Consult a machinist concerning feasibility. If play is satisfactory, remove, lubricate, and reinstall the lifter.
***Testing hydraulic lifter leak down (OHV engines only):**	Submerge lifter in a container of kerosene. Chuck a used pushrod or its equivalent into a drill press. Position container of kerosene so pushrod acts on the lifter plunger. Pump lifter with the drill press, until resistance increases. Pump several more times to bleed any air out of lifter. Apply very firm, constant pressure to the lifter, and observe rate at which fluid bleeds out of lifter. If the fluid bleeds very quickly (less than 15 seconds), lifter is defective. If the time exceeds 60 seconds, lifter is sticking. In either case, recondition or replace lifter. If lifter is operating properly (leak down time 15–60 seconds), lubricate and install it.

Cylinder Block Reconditioning

Procedure	Method
Checking the main bearing clearance: 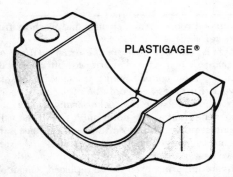 PLASTIGAGE® **Plastigage® installed on the lower bearing shell**	Invert engine, and remove cap from the bearing to be checked. Using a clean, dry rag, thoroughly clean all oil from crankshaft journal and bearing insert. NOTE: *Plastigage® is soluble in oil; therefore, oil on the journal or bearing could result in erroneous readings.* Place a piece of Plastigage along the full length of journal, reinstall cap, and torque to specifications. NOTE: *Specifications are given in the engine specifications earlier in this chapter.* Remove bearing cap, and determine bearing clearance by comparing width of Plastigage to the scale on Plastigage envelope. Journal taper is determined by comparing width of the Plastigage strip near its ends. Rotate crankshaft 90° and retest, to determine journal eccentricity. NOTE: *Do not rotate crankshaft with Plastigage*

Cylinder Block Reconditioning

Procedure	Method

Procedure

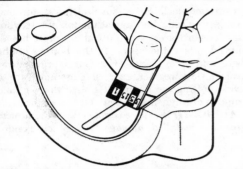

Measure Plastigage® to determine main bearing clearance

Method

installed. If bearing insert and journal appear intact, and are within tolerances, no further main bearing service is required. If bearing or journal appear defective, cause of failure should be determined before replacement.

*Remove crankshaft from block (see below). Measure the main bearing journals at each end tiwce (90° apart) using a micrometer, to determine diameter, journal taper and eccentricity. If journals are within tolerances, reinstall bearing caps at their specified torque. Using a telescope gauge and micrometer, measure bearing I.D. parallel to piston axis and at 30° on each side of piston axis. Subtract journal O.D. from bearing I.D. to determine oil clearance. If crankshaft journals appear defective, or do not meet tolerances, there is no need to measure bearings; for the crankshaft will require grinding and/or undersize bearings will be required. If bearing appears defective, cause for failure should be determined prior to replacement.

Check the connecting rod bearing clearance:

Connecting rod bearing clearance is checked in the same manner as main bearing clearance, using Plastigage. Before removing the crankshaft, connecting rod side clearance also should be measured and recorded.

*Checking connecting rod bearing clearance, using a micrometer, is identical to checking main bearing clearance. If no other service is required, the piston and rod assemblies need not be removed.

Remove the crankshaft:

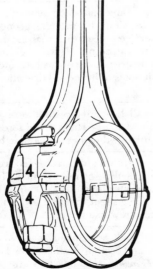

Match the connecting rod to the cylinder with a number stamp

Using a punch, mark the corresponding main bearing caps and saddles according to position (i.e., one punch on the front main cap and saddle, two on the second, three on the third, etc.). Using number stamps, identify the corresponding connecting rods and caps, according to cylinder (if no numbers are present). Remove the main and connecting rod caps, and place sleeves of plastic tubing or vacuum hose over the connecting rod bolts, to protect the journals as the crankshaft is removed. Lift the crankshaft out of the block.

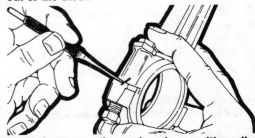

Match the connecting rod and cap with scribe marks

Cylinder Block Reconditioning

Procedure	Method
Remove the ridge from the top of the cylinder: 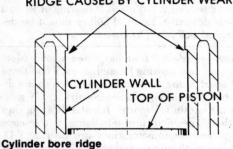 **Cylinder bore ridge**	In order to facilitate removal of the piston and connecting rod, the ridge at the top of the cylinder (unworn area; see illustration) must be removed. Place the piston at the bottom of the bore, and cover it with a rag. Cut the ridge away using a ridge reamer, exercising extreme care to avoid cutting too deeply. Remove the rag, and remove cuttings that remain on the piston. **CAUTION:** *If the ridge is not removed, and new rings are installed, damage to rings will result.*
Remove the piston and connecting rod: 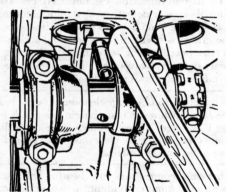 **Push the piston out with a hammer handle**	Invert the engine, and push the pistons and connecting rods out of the cylinders. If necessary, tap the connecting rod boss with a wooden hammer handle, to force the piston out. **CAUTION:** *Do not attempt to force the piston past the cylinder ridge* (see above).
Service the crankshaft:	Ensure that all oil holes and passages in the crankshaft are open and free of sludge. If necessary, have the crankshaft ground to the largest possible undersize.
	** Have the crankshaft Magnafluxed, to locate stress cracks. Consult a machinist concerning additional service procedures, such as surface hardening (e.g., nitriding, Tuftriding) to improve wear characteristics, cross drilling and chamfering the oil holes to improve lubrication, and balancing.
Removing freeze plugs:	Drill a small hole in the middle of the freeze plugs. Thread a large sheet metal screw into the hole and remove the plug with a slide hammer.
Remove the oil gallery plugs:	Threaded plugs should be removed using an appropriate (usually square) wrench. To remove soft, pressed in plugs, drill a hole in the plug, and thread in a sheet metal screw. Pull the plug out by the screw using pliers.
Hot-tank the block: **NOTE:** *Do not hot-tank aluminum parts.*	Have the block hot-tanked to remove grease, corrosion, and scale from the water jackets. **NOTE:** *Consult the operator to determine whether the camshaft bearings will be damaged during the hot-tank process.*

The ridge illustration is labeled: RIDGE CAUSED BY CYLINDER WEAR, CYLINDER WALL, TOP OF PISTON

Cylinder Block Reconditioning

Procedure	Method

Check the block for cracks:	Visually inspect the block for cracks or chips. The most common locations are as follows:
	    Adjacent to freeze plugs.
	    Between the cylinders and water jackets.
	    Adjacent to the main bearing saddles.
	    At the extreme bottom of the cylinders.
	Check only suspected cracks using spot check dye (see introduction). If a crack is located, consult a machinist concerning possible repairs.

	** Magnaflux the block to locate hidden cracks. If cracks are located, consult a machinist about feasibility of repair.
Install the oil gallery plugs and freeze plugs:	Coat freeze plugs with sealer and tap into position using a piece of pipe, slightly smaller than the plug, as a driver. To ensure retention, stake the edges of the plugs. Coat threaded oil gallery plugs with sealer and install. Drive replacement soft plugs into block using a large drift as driver.
	* Rather than reinstalling lead plugs, drill and tap the holes, and install threaded plugs.
Check the bore diameter and surface:  **Measure the cylinder bore with a dial gauge**	Visually inspect the cylinder bores for roughness, scoring, or scuffing. If evident, the cylinder bore must be bored or honed oversize to eliminate imperfections, and the smallest possible oversize piston used. The new pistons should be given to the machinist with the block, so that the cylinders can be bored or honed exactly to the piston size (plus clearance). If no flaws are evident, measure the bore diameter using a telescope gauge and micrometer, or dial gauge, parallel and perpendicular to the engine centerline, at the top (below the ridge) and bottom of the bore. Subtract the bottom measurements from the top to determine taper, and the parallel to the centerline measurements from the perpendicular measurements to determine eccentricity. If the measurements are not within specifications, the cylinder must be bored or honed, and an oversize piston installed. If the measurements are within specifications the cylinder may be used as is, with only finish honing (see below).

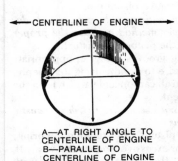

←CENTERLINE OF ENGINE→

A—AT RIGHT ANGLE TO CENTERLINE OF ENGINE
B—PARALLEL TO CENTERLINE OF ENGINE

Cylinder bore measuring points

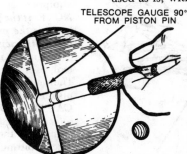

TELESCOPE GAUGE 90° FROM PISTON PIN

Measure the cylinder bore with a telescope gauge

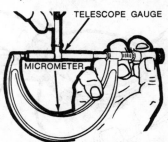

TELESCOPE GAUGE

MICROMETER

Measure the telescope gauge with a micrometer to determine the cylinder bore

Cylinder Block Reconditioning

Procedure	Method
	NOTE: *Prior to submitting the block for boring, perform the following operation(s).*
Check the cylinder block bearing alignment: **Check the main bearing saddle alignment**	Remove the upper bearing inserts. Place a straightedge in the bearing saddles along the centerline of the crankshaft. If clearance exists between the straightedge and the center saddle, the block must be alignbored.
*Check the deck height:	The deck height is the distance from the crankshaft centerline to the block deck. To measure, invert the engine, and install the crankshaft, retaining it with the center main cap. Measure the distance from the crankshaft journal to the block deck, parallel to the cylinder centerline. Measure the diameter of the end (front and rear) main journals, parallel to the centerline of the cylinders, divide the diameter in half, and subtract it from the previous measurement. The results of the front and rear measurements should be identical. If the difference exceeds .005″, the deck height should be corrected. NOTE: *Block deck height and warpage should be corrected at the same time.*
Check the block deck for warpage:	Using a straightedge and feeler gauges, check the block deck for warpage in the same manner that the cylinder head is checked (see Cylinder Head Reconditioning). If warpage exceeds specifications, have the deck resurfaced. NOTE: *In certain cases a specification for total material removal (Cylinder head and block deck) is provided. This specification must not be exceeded.*

Clean and inspect the pistons and connecting rods:
 	
RING EXPANDER
Remove the piston rings
	Using a ring expander, remove the rings from the piston. Remove the retaining rings (if so equipped) and remove piston pin.
	NOTE: *If the piston pin must be pressed out, determine the proper method and use the proper tools; otherwise the piston will distort.*
	    Clean the ring grooves using an appropriate tool, exercising care to avoid cutting too deeply. Thoroughly clean all carbon and varnish from the piston with solvent.
	CAUTION: *Do not use a wire brush or caustic solvent on pistons.*
	    Inspect the pistons for scuffing, scoring, cracks, pitting, or excessive ring groove wear. If wear is evident, the piston must be replaced. Check the connecting rod length by measuring the rod from the inside of the large end to the

Cylinder Block Reconditioning

Procedure	Method

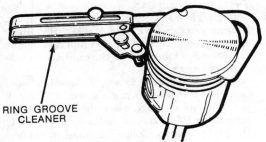

RING GROOVE CLEANER

Clean the piston ring grooves

inside of the small end using calipers (see illustration). All connecting rods should be equal length. Replace any rod that differs from the others in the engine.

* Have the connecting rod alignment checked in an alignment fixture by a machinist. Replace any twisted or bent rods.

* Magnaflux the connecting rods to locate stress cracks. If cracks are found, replace the connecting rod.

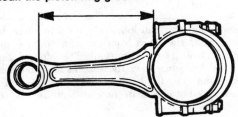

Check the connecting rod length (arrow)

Fit the pistons to the cylinders:

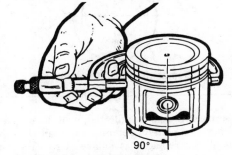

90°

Measure the piston prior to fitting

Using a telescope gauge and micrometer, or a dial gauge, measure the cylinder bore diameter perpendicular to the piston pin, 2½″ below the deck. Measure the piston perpendicular to its pin on the skirt. The difference between the two measurements is the piston clearance. If the clearance is within specifications or slightly below (after boring or honing), finish honing is all that is required. If the clearance is excessive, try to obtain a slightly larger piston to bring clearance within specifications. Where this is not possible, obtain the first oversize piston, and hone (or if necessary, bore) the cylinder to size.

Assemble the pistons and connecting rods:

Install the piston pin lock-rings (if used)

Inspect piston pin, connecting rod small end bushing, and piston bore for galling, scoring, or excessive wear. If evident, replace defective part(s). Measure the I.D. of the piston boss and connecting rod small end, and the O.D. of the piston pin. If within specifications, assemble piston pin and rod.

CAUTION: *If piston pin must be pressed in, determine the proper method and use the proper tools; otherwise the piston will distort.*

Install the lock rings; ensure that they seat properly. If the parts are not within specifications, determine the service method for the type of engine. In some cases, piston and pin are serviced as an assembly when either is defective. Others specify reaming the piston and connecting rods for an oversize pin. If the connecting rod bushing is worn, it may in many cases be replaced. Reaming the piston and replacing the rod bushing are machine shop operations.

Cylinder Block Reconditioning

Procedure	Method

Clean and inspect the camshaft:

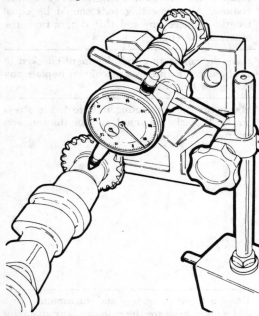

Check the camshaft for straightness

Degrease the camshaft, using solvent, and clean out all oil holes. Visually inspect cam lobes and bearing journals for excessive wear. If a lobe is questionable, check all lobes as indicated below. If a journal or lobe is worn, the camshaft must be reground or replaced.

NOTE: *If a journal is worn, there is a good chance that the bushings are worn.* If lobes and journals appear intact, place the front and rear journals in V-blocks, and rest a dial indicator on the center journal. Rotate the camshaft to check straightness. If deviation exceeds .001″, replace the camshaft.

---

*Check the camshaft lobes with a micrometer, by measuring the lobes from the nose to base and again at 90° (see illustration). The lift is determined by subtracting the second measurement from the first. If all exhaust lobes and all intake lobes are not identical, the camshaft must be reground or replaced.

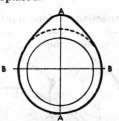

Camshaft lobe measurement

Replace the camshaft bearings (OHV engines only):

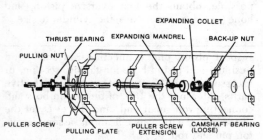

Camshaft bearing removal and installation tool (OHV engines only)

If excessive wear is indicated, or if the engine is being completely rebuilt, camshaft bearings should be replaced as follows: Drive the camshaft rear plug from the block. Assemble the removal puller with its shoulder on the bearing to be removed. Gradually tighten the puller nut until bearing is removed. Remove remaining bearings, leaving the front and rear for last. To remove front and rear bearings, reverse position of the tool, so as to pull the bearings in toward the center of the block. Leave the tool in this position, pilot the new front and rear bearings on the installer, and pull them into position: Return the tool to its original position and pull remaining bearings into position.

NOTE: *Ensure that oil holes align when installing bearings.* Replace camshaft rear plug, and stake it into position to aid retention.

Finish hone the cylinders:

Chuck a flexible drive hone into a power drill, and insert it into the cylinder. Start the hone, and move it up and down in the cylinder at a rate which will produce approximately a 60° cross-hatch pattern.

NOTE: *Do not extend the hone below the cylin-*

Cylinder Block Reconditioning

Procedure	Method

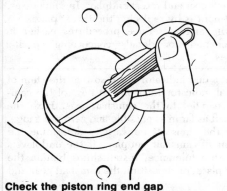

CROSS HATCH PATTERN

50°-60°

Cylinder bore after honing

der bore. After developing the pattern, remove the hone and recheck piston fit. Wash the cylinders with a detergent and water solution to remove abrasive dust, dry, and wipe several times with a rag soaked in engine oil.

Check piston ring end-gap:

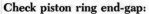

Check the piston ring end gap

Compress the piston rings to be used in a cylinder, one at a time, into that cylinder, and press them approximately 1″ below the deck with an inverted piston. Using feeler gauges, measure the ring end-gap, and compare to specifications. Pull the ring out of the cylinder and file the ends with a fine file to obtain proper clearance.
CAUTION: *If inadequate ring end-gap is utilized, ring breakage will result.*

Install the piston rings:

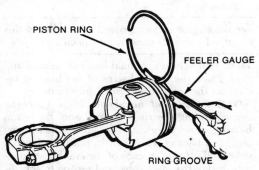

PISTON RING

FEELER GAUGE

RING GROOVE

Check the piston ring side clearance

Inspect the ring grooves in the piston for excessive wear or taper. If necessary, recut the grooves(s) for use with an overwidth ring or a standard ring and spacer. If the groove is worn uniformly, overwidth rings, or standard rings and spacers may be installed without recutting. Roll the outside of the ring around the groove to check for burrs or deposits. If any are found, remove with a fine file. Hold the ring in the groove, and measure side clearance. If necessary, correct as indicated above.
NOTE: *Always install any additional spacers above the piston ring.*

The ring groove must be deep enough to allow the ring to seat below the lands (see illustration). In many cases, a "go-no-go" depth gauge will be provided with the piston rings. Shallow grooves may be corrected by recutting, while deep grooves require some type of filler or expander behind the piston. Consult the piston ring sup-

Cylinder Block Reconditioning

Procedure	Method
	plier concerning the suggested method. Install the rings on the piston, lowest ring first, using a ring expander. **NOTE:** *Position the ring as specified by the manufacturer.* Consult the engine service procedures earlier in this chapter for details concerning specific engines.
Install the camshaft (OHV engines only):	Liberally lubricate the camshaft lobes and journals, and install the camshaft. **CAUTION:** *Exercise extreme care to avoid damaging the bearings when inserting the camshaft.* Install and tighten the camshaft thrust plate retaining bolts. See the engine service procedures earlier in this chapter for details concerning specific engines.
Check camshaft end-play (OHV engines only): **Check the camshaft end-play with a feeler gauge** DIAL INDICATOR CAMSHAFT **Check the camshaft end-play with a dial indicator**	Using feeler gauges, determine whether the clearance between the camshaft boss (or gear) and backing plate is within specifications. Install shims behind the thrust plate, or reposition the camshaft gear and retest endplay. In some cases, adjustment is by replacing the thrust plate. See the engine service procedures earlier in this chapter for details concerning specific engines. * Mount a dial indicator stand so that the stem of the dial indicator rests on the nose of the camshaft, parallel to the camshaft axis. Push the camshaft as far in as possible and zero the gauge. Move the camshaft outward to determine the amount of camshaft endplay. If the endplay is not within tolerance, install shims behind the thrust plate, or reposition the camshaft gear and retest. See the engine service procedures earlier in this chapter for details concerning specific engines.
Install the rear main seal:	See the engine service procedures earlier in this chapter for details concerning specific engines.
Install the crankshaft: 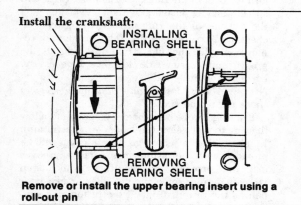 INSTALLING BEARING SHELL REMOVING BEARING SHELL **Remove or install the upper bearing insert using a roll-out pin**	Thoroughly clean the main bearing saddles and caps. Place the upper halves of the bearing inserts on the saddles and press into position. **NOTE:** *Ensure that the oil holes align.* Press the corresponding bearing inserts into the main bearing caps. Lubricate the upper main bearings, and lay the crankshaft in position. Place a strip of Plastigage on each of the crankshaft journals, install the main caps, and torque to specifications. Remove the main caps, and compare the Plastigage to the scale on the Plastigage envelope. If clearances are within tolerances, remove the Plastigage, turn the crankshaft 90°, wipe off all oil and retest. If all clearances are correct, re-

Cylinder Block Reconditioning

Procedure	Method

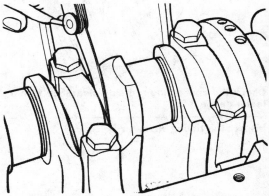

60°

$$\frac{5''}{8}$$

Home-made bearing roll-out pin

move all Plastigage, thoroughly lubricate the main caps and bearing journals, and install the main caps. If clearances are not within tolerance, the upper bearing inserts may be removed, without removing the crankshaft, using a bearing roll out pin (see illustration). Roll in a bearing that will provide proper clearance, and retest. Torque all main caps, excluding the thrust bearing cap, to specifications. Tighten the thrust bearing cap finger tight. To properly align the thrust bearing, pry the crankshaft the extent of its axial travel several times, the last movement held toward the front of the engine, and torque the thrust bearing cap to specifications. Determine the crankshaft end-play (see below), and bring within tolerance with thrust washers.

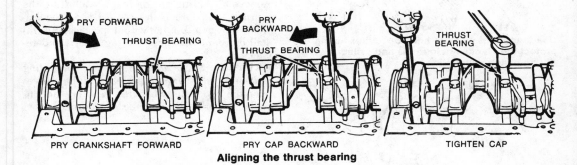

PRY FORWARD

THRUST BEARING

PRY BACKWARD

THRUST BEARING

THRUST BEARING

PRY CRANKSHAFT FORWARD   PRY CAP BACKWARD   TIGHTEN CAP

Aligning the thrust bearing

Measure crankshaft end-play:

Mount a dial indicator stand on the front of the block, with the dial indicator stem resting on the nose of the crankshaft, parallel to the crankshaft axis. Pry the crankshaft the extent of its travel rearward, and zero the indicator. Pry the crankshaft forward and record crankshaft end-play.
NOTE: *Crankshaft end-play also may be measured at the thrust bearing, using feeler gauges (see illustration).*

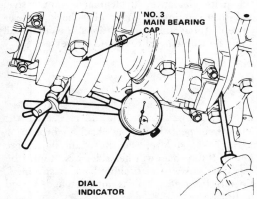

NO. 3 MAIN BEARING CAP

DIAL INDICATOR

Check the crankshaft end-play with a dial indicator

Check the crankshaft end-play with a feeler gauge

Cylinder Block Reconditioning

Procedure	Method

Install the pistons:

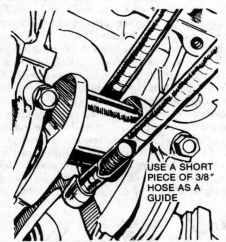

USE A SHORT PIECE OF 3/8" HOSE AS A GUIDE

Use lengths of vacuum hose or rubber tubing to protect the crankshaft journals and cylinder walls during piston installation

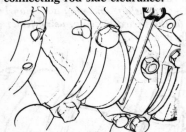

RING COMPRESSOR

Install the piston using a ring compressor

Press the upper connecting rod bearing halves into the connecting rods, and the lower halves into the connecting rod caps. Position the piston ring gaps according to specifications (see car section), and lubricate the pistons. Install a ring compresser on a piston, and press two long (8") pieces of plastic tubing over the rod bolts. Using the tubes as a guide, press the pistons into the bores and onto the crankshaft with a wooden hammer handle. After seating the rod on the crankshaft journal, remove the tubes and install the cap finger tight. Install the remaining pistons in the same manner. Invert the engine and check the bearing clearance at two points (90° apart) on each journal with Plastigage.

NOTE: *Do not turn the crankshaft with Plastigage installed.* If clearance is within tolerances, remove *all* Plastigage, thoroughly lubricate the journals, and torque the rod caps to specifications. If clearance is not within specifications, install different thickness bearing inserts and recheck.

CAUTION: *Never shim or file the connecting rods or caps.* Always install plastic tube sleeves over the rod bolts when the caps are not installed, to protect the crankshaft journals.

Check connecting rod side clearance:

Check the connecting rod side clearance with a feeler gauge

Determine the clearance between the sides of the connecting rods and the crankshaft, using feeler gauges. If clearance is below the minimum tolerance, the rod may be machined to provide adequate clearance. If clearance is excessive, substitute an unworn rod, and recheck. If clearance is still outside specifications, the crankshaft must be welded and reground, or replaced.

Inspect the timing chain (or belt):

Visually inspect the timing chain for broken or loose links, and replace the chain if any are found. If the chain will flex sideways, it must be replaced. Install the timing chain as specified. Be sure the timing belt is not stretched, frayed or broken.

NOTE: *If the original timing chain is to be reused, install it in its original position.*

Cylinder Block Reconditioning

Procedure	Method
Check timing gear backlash and runout (OHV engines):	Mount a dial indicator with its stem resting on a tooth of the camshaft gear (as illustrated). Rotate the gear until all slack is removed, and zero the indicator. Rotate the gear in the opposite direction until slack is removed, and record gear backlash. Mount the indicator with its stem resting on the edge of the camshaft gear, parallel to the axis of the camshaft. Zero the indicator, and turn the camshaft gear one full turn, recording the runout. If either backlash or runout exceed specifications, replace the worn gear(s).

Check the camshaft gear backlash

Check the camshaft gear run-out

Completing the Rebuilding Process

Following the above procedures, complete the rebuilding process as follows:

Fill the oil pump with oil, to prevent cavitating (sucking air) on initial engine start up. Install the oil pump and the pickup tube on the engine. Coat the oil pan gasket as necessary, and install the gasket and the oil pan. Mount the flywheel and the crankshaft vibration damper or pulley on the crankshaft. NOTE: *Always use new bolts when installing the flywheel.* Inspect the clutch shaft pilot bushing in the crankshaft. If the bushing is excessively worn, remove it with an expanding puller and a slide hammer, and tap a new bushing into place.

Position the engine, cylinder head side up. Lubricate the lifters, and install them into their bores. Install the cylinder head, and torque it as specified. Insert the pushrods (where applicable), and install the rocker shaft(s) (if so equipped) or position the rocker arms on the pushrods. Adjust the valves.

Install the intake and exhaust manifolds, the carburetor(s), the distributor and spark plugs. Adjust the point gap and the static ignition timing. Mount all accessories and install the engine in the car. Fill the radiator with coolant, and the crankcase with high quality engine oil.

Break-in Procedure

Start the engine, and allow it to run at low speed for a few minutes, while checking for leaks. Stop the engine, check the oil level, and fill as necessary. Restart the engine, and fill the cooling system to capacity. Check the point dwell angle and adjust the ignition timing and the valves. Run the engine at low to medium speed (800–2500 rpm) for approximately ½ hour, and retorque the cylinder head bolts. Road test the car, and check again for leaks.

Follow the manufacturer's recommended engine break-in procedure and maintenance schedule for new engines.

Emission Controls and Fuel System

EMISSION CONTROLS

There are three basic sources of automotive pollution in the modern internal combustion engine. They are the crankcase with its accompanying blow-by vapors, the fuel system with its evaporation of unburned gasoline, and the combustion chambers with their resulting exhaust emissions. Pollution arising from the incomplete combustion of fuel generally falls into three categories; hydrocarbons (HC), carbon monoxide (CO), and oxides of nitrogen (NO_x).

Positive Crankcase Ventilation System

All models covered in this book are equipped with a positive crankcase ventilation (PCV) system to control crankcase blow-by vapors. The system consists of a PCV valve and oil separator mounted on top of the valve cover, a non-ventilated oil filler cap, and a pair of hoses supplying filtered intake air to the valve cover and delivering the crankcase vapors from the valve cover to the intake manifold (six-cylinder) or carburetor (V8).

The system functions as follows:

When the engine is running, a small portion of the gases which are formed in the combustion chamber leak by the piston rings and enter the crankcase. Since these gases are under pressure, they tend to escape from the crankcase and enter the atmosphere. If these gases are allowed to remain in the crankcase for any period of time, they contaminate the engine oil and cause sludge to build up in the crankcase. If the gases are allowed to escape into the atmosphere, they pollute the air, with unburned hydrocarbons. The job of the crankcase emission control equipment is to recycle these gases back into the engine combustion chamber where they are reburned.

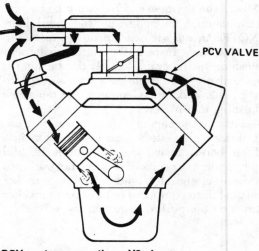

PCV VALVE

PCV system operation—V8 shown

REMOVAL AND INSTALLATION

Since the PCV valve works under severe load it is very important that it be replaced at the interval specified in the maintenance chart (see Chapter 1). Replacement involves removing the valve from the grommet in the rocker arm cover and installing a new valve. Do not attempt to clean a used valve.

Fuel Evaporative Control System

This system, which is found on all Ford and Mercury vehicles, is designed to prevent the evaporation of unburned gasoline. The system consists of a vacuum/pressure relief fuel filler cap, an expansion area at the top of the fuel tank, a foam-filled vapor separator mounted on top of the fuel tank, a carbon canister which stores fuel vapors and a number of hoses which connect the various components. The system functions as follows:

Changes in atmospheric temperature cause the gasoline in fuel tanks to expand or contract. If this expansion and consequent vaporization takes place in a conventional fuel tank, the fuel vapors escape through the filler cap or vent hose and pollute the atmosphere. The fuel evaporative emission control system prevents this by routing the gasoline vapors to the engine where they are burned.

As the gasoline in the fuel tank of a parked car begins to expand due to heat, the vapor that forms moves to the top of the fuel tank.

The fuel tanks are enlarged so that there exists an area representing 10–20% of the total fuel tank volume above the level of the fuel tank filler tube where these gases may collect. The vapors then travel upward into the vapor separator which prevents liquid gasoline from escaping from the fuel tank. The fuel vapor is then drawn through the vapor separator outlet hose, then to the charcoal canister in the engine compartment. The vapor enters the canister, passes through a charcoal filter, and then exits through the canister's grated bottom. As the vapor passes through the charcoal, it is cleansed of hydrocarbons, so that the air that passes out of the bottom of the canister is free of pollutants.

When the engine is started, vacuum from the carburetor draws fresh air into the canister. As the entering air passes through the charcoal in the canister, it picks up the hydrocarbons that were deposited there by the

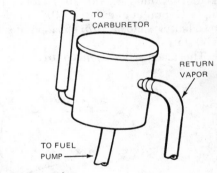

Vapor separator

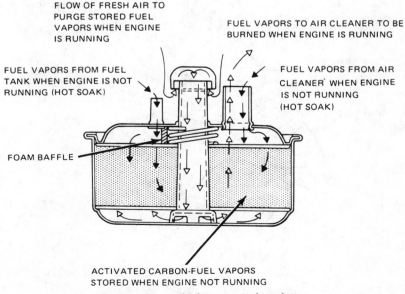

Evaporative emissions control canister

fuel vapors. This mixture of hydrocarbons and fresh air is then carried through a hose to the air cleaner. In the carburetor, it combines with the incoming air/fuel mixture and enters the combustion chambers of the engine where it is burned.

SERVICE

The only required service for the evaporative emissions control system is inspection of the various components at the interval specified in the maintenance chart (see Chapter 1). If the charcoal element in the canister is gummed up the entire canister should be replaced. Disconnect the canister purge hose from the air cleaner fitting, loosen the canister retaining bracket, lift out the canister. Installation is the reverse of removal.

Thermactor System

This sytem is found on the 1971 Cobra Jet and Super Cobra Jet engines, all 1974 models sold in California, and all 1975–82 models sold in the 50 states.

The Thermactor emission control system makes use of a belt-driven air pump to inject fresh air into the hot exhaust stream through the engine exhaust ports. The result is the extended burning of those fumes which were not completely ignited in the combustion chamber, and the subsequent reduction of some of the hydrocarbon and carbon monoxide content of the exhaust emissions into harmless carbon dioxide and water.

The Thermactor system is composed of the following components:

1. Air supply pump (belt-driven)
2. Air by-pass valve
3. Check valves
4. Air manifolds (internal or external)
5. Air supply tubes (on external manifolds only).

Air for the Thermactor system is cleaned by means of a centrifugal filter fan mounted on the air pump driveshaft. The air filter does not require a replaceable element.

To prevent excessive pressure, the air pump is equipped with a pressure relief valve which uses a replaceable plastic plug to control the pressure setting.

The Thermactor air pump has sealed bear-

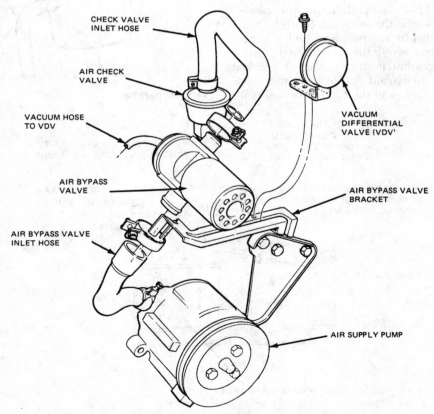

Typical thermactor system components—catalytic equipped

CHECK VALVE INLET HOSE

AIR CHECK VALVE

VACUUM HOSE TO VDV

AIR BYPASS VALVE

AIR BYPASS VALVE INLET HOSE

VACUUM DIFFERENTIAL VALVE (VDV'

AIR BYPASS VALVE BRACKET

AIR SUPPLY PUMP

ings which are lubricated for the life of the unit, and pre-set rotor vane and bearing clearances, which do not require any periodic adjustments.

The air supply from the pump is controlled by the air by-pass valve, sometimes called a dump valve. During deceleration, the air by-pass valve opens, momentarily diverting the air supply through a silencer and into the atmosphere, thus preventing backfires within the exhaust system.

A check valve is incorporated in the air inlet side of the air manifolds. Its purpose is to prevent exhaust gases from backing up into the Thermactor system. This valve is especially important in the event of drive belt failure, and during deceleration, when the air by-pass valve is dumping the air supply.

The air manifolds and air supply tubes channel the air from the Thermactor air pump into the exhaust ports of each cylinder, thus completing the cycle of the Thermactor system.

SERVICE

The entire Thermactor system should be checked periodically according to the maintenance chart in Chapter 1. Use the following procedure to determine if the system is functioning properly.

NOTE: *See Chapter 1 for belt adjustment and replacement procedures.*

1. Remove air cleaner, if necessary.

2. Inspect all components of the thermactor system for any loose connections or other abnormal conditions—repair or replace as necessary.

3. Inspect the air pump drive belt for wear and tension—adjust or replace as necessary.

4. With the transmission in neutral or park and the parking brake on, start engine and bring to normal operating temperature.

5. Stop the engine. Connect a tachometer to the engine. Remove the air supply hose at the check valve. If the engine has two check valves, remove both air supply hoses at the check valves and plug off one hose. Position the open hose so that the air blast emitted is harmlessly dissipated.

6. Start the engine and accelerate to 1500 RPM. Place hand over the open hose. Air flow should be heard and felt. If no air flow is noted, the air bypass valve is defective and should be replaced. The procedure is outlined later in this section.

7. Let the engine speed return to normal idle. Pinch off and remove the vacuum hose from the bypass valve. Accelerate the engine to 1500 RPM. With hand held over the open end of the check valve hose (same as step 6), virtually no air flow should be felt or heard.

If air flow is noted, the bypass valve is defective and is to be replaced.

8. Let the engine speed return to normal idle and reinstall the vacuum hose on the bypass valve vacuum hose nipple. Check hose routing to be sure it is not pinched or restricting normal vacuum signal flow.

9. With hand held over the open end of the check valve hose (same as Step 6), rapidly increase the engine speed to approximately 2500 RPM. Immediately release the throttle for the engine to return to normal idle. Air flow should be felt and/or heard to momentarily diminish or go to zero during the deceleration. If the air flow does not momentarily diminish or go to zero repeat the above using an engine speed of 3000–3200 RPM.

If air flow does not momentarily diminish or stop during the deceleration from 3000–3200 RPM, the vacuum differential control valve should be replaced. Omit this step if the system is not equipped with a differential vacuum valve.

10. Accelerate the engine to 1500 RPM and check for any exhaust gas leakage at the check valve. There should be virtually no pressure felt or heard when hand is held over the open end of the check valve for approximately 15 seconds. If excessive leakage is noted, replace the check valve(s).

CAUTION: *The check valve may be hot and capable of causing a burn if the hands are not protected.*

11. If the engine is equipped with two check valves, repeat step 10 on the second valve.

12. Stop the engine and remove all the test equipment. Reconnect all the related components. Reinstall the air cleaner, if removed.

REMOVAL AND INSTALLATION

Thermactor Air Pump

1. Disconnect the air outlet hose at the air pump.

2. Loosen the pump belt tension adjuster.

3. Disengage the drive belt.

4. Remove the mounting bolt and air pump.

5. To install, position the air pump on the

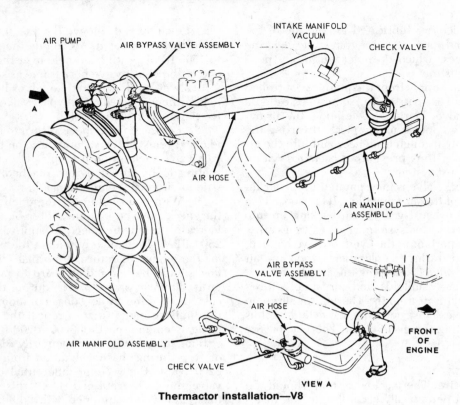

Thermactor installation—V8

mounting bracket and install the mounting bolt.

6. Place drive belt in pulleys and attach the adjusting arm to the air pump.

7. Adjust the drive belt tension to specifications and tighten the adjusting arm and mounting bolts.

8. Connect the air outlet hose to the air pump.

Thermactor Air Pump Filter Fan

1. Loosen the air pump adjusting arm bolt and mounting bracket bolt to relieve drive belt tension.

2. Remove drive pulley attaching bolts and pull drive pulley off the air pump shaft.

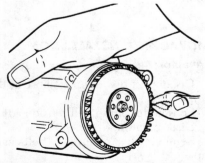

Thermactor air pump filter fan removal

3. Pry the outer disc loose; then, pull off the centrifugal filter fan with slip-joint pliers. CAUTION: *Do not attempt to remove the metal drive hub.*

4. Install a new filter fan by drawing it into position, using the pulley and bolts as an installer. Draw the fan evenly by alternately tightening the bolts, making certain that the outer edge of the fan slips into the housing.

NOTE: *A slight interference with the housing bore is normal. After a new fan is installed, it may squeal upon initial operation, until its outer diameter sealing lip has worn in, which may require 20 to 30 miles of operation.*

Thermactor Check Valve

1. Disconnect the air supply hose at the valve. (Use a 1¼ in. crowfoot wrench, the valve has a standard, right-hand pipe thread.)

2. Clean the threads on the air manifold adaptor (air supply tube on 302 V8 engine) with a wire brush. Do not blow compressed air through the check valve in either direction.

3. Install the check valve and tighten.

4. Connect the air supply hose.

Thermactor Air By-Pass Valve

1. Disconnect the air and vacuum hoses at the air by-pass valve body.
2. Position the air by-pass valve, and connect the respective hoses.

Vacuum Differential Control Valve

1. Remove the hose connections.
2. Unbolt the valve at its mounting bracket.
3. Install in reverse order.

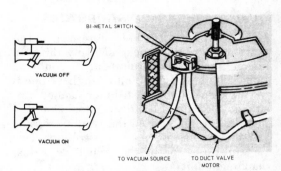

Vacuum-operated duct and valve assembly

Improved Combustion System (IMCO)

All models (except the 1971 429CJ and SCJ are equipped with the Improved Combustion (IMCO) System. The IMCO system controls emissions arising from the incomplete combustion of the air/fuel mixture in the cylinders. The IMCO system incorporates a number of modifications to the distributor spark control system, the fuel system, and the internal design of the engine.

Internal engine modifications include the following: elimination of surface irregularities and crevices as well as a low surface area-to-volume ratio in the combustion chambers, a high-velocity intake manifold combined with short exhaust ports, selective valve timing and a higher temperature and capacity cooling system.

Modifications to the fuel system include the following: recalibrated carburetors to achieve a leaner air/fuel mixture, more precise calibration of the choke mechanism, the installation of idle mixture limiter caps and a heated air intake system.

Modifications to the distributor spark control system include the following: a modified centrifugal advance curve, the use of dual diaphragm distributors in most applications, a ported vacuum switch, a deceleration valve and a spark delay valve.

IMCO System Description
HEATED AIR INTAKE SYSTEM

The heated air intake portion of the air cleaner consists of a thermostat (all 1971–72 models except the 351C and 400 V8), or bimetal switch and vacuum motor (all 1973–75 and all 351C and 400 V8), and a spring-loaded temperature control door in the snorkel of the air cleaner. The temperature control door is located between the end of the air cleaner snorkel which draws in air from the engine compartment and the duct that carries heated air up from the exhaust manifold. When underhood temperature is below 90°F, the temperature control door blocks off underhood air from entering the air cleaner and allows only heated air from the exhaust manifold to be drawn into the air cleaner. When underhood temperature rises above 130°F, the temperature control door blocks off heated air from the exhaust manifold and allows only underhood air to be drawn into the air cleaner.

By controlling the temperature of the engine intake air this way, exhaust emissions are lowered and fuel economy is improved. In addition, throttle plate icing is reduced, and cold weather driveability is improved from the necessary leaner mixtures.

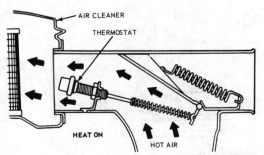

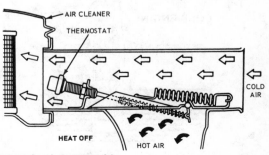

Temperature-operated duct and valve assembly

DUAL DIAPHRAGM DISTRIBUTORS

Dual diaphragm distributors are installed in most models and appear in many different engine/transmission/equipment combinations. The best way to tell if you have one is to take a look at your distributor vacuum capsule on the side of the distributor. One vacuum hose running from the vacuum capsule indicates a single diaphragm distributor. Two vacuum hoses means that you have a dual diaphragm unit.

The dual distributor diaphragm is a two-chambered housing which is mounted on the side of the distributor. The outer side of the housing is a distributor vacuum advance mechanism, connected to the carburetor by a vacuum hose. The purpose of the vacuum advance is to advance ignition timing according to the conditions under which the engine is operating. This device has been used on automobiles for many years now and its chief advantage is economical engine operation. The second side of the dual diaphragm is the side that has been added to help control engine exhaust emissions at idle and during deceleration.

The inner side of the dual diaphragm is connected by a vacuum hose to the intake manifold. When the engine is idling or decelerating, intake manifold vacuum is high and carburetor vacuum is low. Under these conditions, intake manifold vacuum, applied to the inner side of the dual diaphragm, retards ignition timing to promote more complete combustion of the air fuel mixture in the engine combustion chambers.

PORTED VACUUM SWITCH (DISTRIBUTOR VACUUM CONTROL VALVE)

The distributor vacuum control valve is a temperature-sensitive valve which screws into the water jacket of the engine. Three vacuum lines are attached to the vacuum control valve: one which runs from the carburetor to the control valve, one which runs from the control valve to the distributor vacuum advance (outer) chamber, and one which runs from the intake manifold to the distributor vacuum control valve.

During normal engine operation, vacuum from the carburetor passes through the top nipple on the distributor control valve, through the valve to the second nipple on the valve, and out the second nipple on the valve to the distributor vacuum advance chamber. When the engine is idling however, carburetor vacuum is very low, so that there is little, if any, vacuum in the passageways described above.

If the engine should begin to overheat while idling, a check ball inside the distributor vacuum control which normally blocks off the third nipple of the valve (intake manifold vacuum) moves upward to block off the first nipple (carburetor vacuum). This applies intake manifold vacuum (third nipple) to the distributor vacuum advance chamber (second nip-

3-PORT PVS OPERATION

- **EGR/CSC** – switches EGR vacuum from EGR system to distributor advance with cold engine.
- **Cold Start Spark Advance (CSSA)** – supplies manifold vacuum to distributor below 125° F. coolant temperature.
- **Coolant Spark Control (CSC)** – cuts off distributor advance below hot engine temperature.
- **Cooling PVS** – switches advance vacuum from spark port to manifold vacuum if engine overheats.

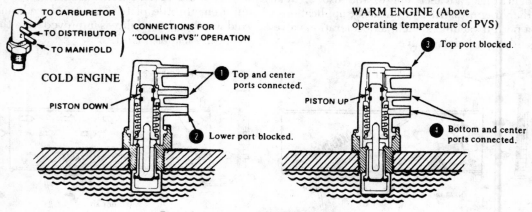

Ported vacuum switch (PVS) operation

ple). Since intake manifold vacuum is very high while the engine is idling, ignition timing is advanced by the application of intake manifold vacuum to the distributor vacuum advance chamber. This raises the engine idle speed and helps to cool the engine.

DECELERATION VALVE

Some IMCO-equipped 1971–72 engines are equipped with a distributor vacuum advance control valve (deceleration valve) which is used with dual-diaphragm distributors to further aid in controlling ignition timing. The deceleration valve is in the vacuum line which runs from the outer (advance) diaphragm to the carburetor—the normal vacuum supply for the distributor. During deceleration, the intake manifold vacuum rises causing the deceleration valve to close off the carburetor vacuum source and connect the intake manifold vacuum source to the distributor advance diaphragm. The increase in vacuum provides maximum ignition timing advance, thus providing more complete fuel combustion, and decreasing exhaust system backfiring.

SPARK DELAY VALVE

The spark delay valve is a plastic, spring-loaded, color-coded valve which is installed in the vacuum line to the distributor advance diaphragm on many models. Under heavy throttle applications, the valve will close, blocking normal carburetor vacuum to the distributor. After the designated period of closed time, the valve opens, restoring the carburetor vacuum to the distributor.

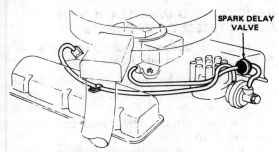

SPARK DELAY VALVE

Spark delay valve installation

Testing IMCO System Components

HEATED AIR INTAKE SYSTEM

Duct and Valve Assembly Test

1. Either start with a cold engine or remove the air cleaner from the engine for at least half an hour. While cooling the air cleaner, leave the engine compartment hood open.

2. Tape a thermometer, of known accuracy, to the inside of the air cleaner so that it is near the temperature sensor unit. Install the air cleaner on the engine but do not fasten its securing nut.

3. Start the engine. With the engine cold and the outside temperature less than 90°F, the door should be in the "heat on" position (closed to outside air).

4. Operate the throttle lever rapidly to one-half to three-quarters of its opening and release it. The air door should open to allow outside air to enter and then close again.

5. Allow the engine to warm up to normal temperature. Watch the door. When it opens to the outside air, remove the cover from the air cleaner. The temperature should be over 90°F and no more than 130°F; 105°F is about normal. If the door does not work within these temperature ranges, or fails to work at all, check for linkage or door binding.

If binding is not present and the air door is not working, proceed with the vacuum tests given below. If these indicate no faults in the vacuum motor and the door is not working, the temperature sensor is defective and must be replaced.

Vacuum Motor Test

NOTE: *Be sure that the vacuum hose that runs between the temperature switch and the vacuum motor is not pinched by the retaining clip under the air cleaner. This could prevent the air door from closing.*

1. Check all the vacuum lines and fittings for leaks. Correct any leaks. If none are found, proceed with the test.

2. Remove the hose which runs from the sensor to the vacuum motor. Run a hose directly from the manifold vacuum source to the vacuum motor.

3. If the motor closes the air door, it is functioning properly and the temperature sensor is defective.

4. If the motor does *not* close the door and no binding is present in its operation, the vacuum motor is defective and must be replaced.

NOTE: *If an alternate vacuum source is applied to the motor, insert a vacuum gauge in the line by using a T-fitting. Apply at least 9 in. Hg of vacuum in order to operate the motor.*

DUAL DIAPHRAGM DISTRIBUTOR ADVANCE AND RETARD MECHANISMS TEST

1. Connect a timing light to the engine. Check the ignition timing.

NOTE: *Before proceeding with the tests, disconnect any spark control devices, distributor vacuum valves, etc. If these are left connected, inaccurate results may be obtained.*

2. Remove the retard hose from the distributor and plug it. Increase the engine speed. The timing should advance. If it fails to do so, then the vacuum unit is faulty and must be replaced.

3. Check the timing with the engine at normal idle speed. Unplug the retard hose and connect it to the vacuum unit. The timing should instantly be retarded from 4°–10°. If this does not occur, the retard diaphragm has a leak and the vacuum unit must be replaced.

PORTED VACUUM SWITCH (DISTRIBUTOR VACUUM CONTROL VALVE) TEST

1. Check the routing and connection of all vacuum hoses.

2. Attach a tachometer to the engine.

3. Bring the engine up to the normal operating temperature. The engine must not be overheated.

4. Note the engine rpm, with the transmission in neutral, and the throttle in the curb idle position.

5. Disconnect the vacuum hose from the intake manifold at the temperature-sensing valve. Plug or clamp the hose.

6. Note the idle rpm with the hose disconnected. If there is no change in rpm, the valve is good. If there is a drop of 100 or more rpm, the valve should be replaced. Replace the vacuum line.

7. Check to make sure that the all-season cooling mixture meets specifications, and that the correct radiator cap is in place and functioning.

8. Block the radiator air flow to induce a higher-than-normal temperature condition.

9. Continue to operate until the engine temperature or heat indicator shows above normal.

If engine speed by this time has increased 100 or more rpm, the temperature-sensing valve is satisfactory. If not, it should be replaced.

SPARK DELAY VALVE TEST

NOTE: *If the distributor vacuum line contains a cut-off solenoid, it must be open during this test.*

1. Detach the vacuum line from the distributor at the spark delay valve end. Connect a vacuum gauge to the valve, in its place.

2. Connect a tachometer to the engine. Start the engine and rapidly increase its speed to 2,000 rpm with the transmission in neutral.

3. As soon as the engine speed is increased, the vacuum gauge reading should drop to zero.

4. Hold the engine speed at a steady 2,000 rpm. It should take longer than two seconds for the gauge to register 6 in. Hg. If it takes less than two seconds, the valve is defective and must be replaced.

5. If it takes longer than the number of seconds specified in the application chart for the gauge to reach 6 in. Hg, disconnect the vacuum gauge from the spark delay valve. Disconnect the hose which runs from the spark delay valve to the carburetor at the valve end. Connect the vacuum gauge to this hose.

6. Start the engine and increase its speed to 2,000 rpm. The gauge should indicate 10–16 in. Hg. If it does not, there is a blockage in the carburetor vacuum port or else the hose itself is plugged or broken. If the gauge reading is within specification, the valve is defective.

7. Reconnect all vacuum lines and remove the tachometer, once testing is completed.

REMOVAL AND INSTALLATION OF IMCO SYSTEM COMPONENTS

Temperature Operated Duct and Valve Assembly (Heated Air Intake System)

1. Remove the hex-head cap screws which secure the air intake duct and valve assembly to the air cleaner.

2. Remove the air intake duct and valve assembly from the engine.

3. If inspection reveals that the valve plate is sticking or the thermostat is malfunctioning, remove the thermostat and valve plates as follows:

   a. Detach the valve plate tension spring from the valve plate using long-nose pliers. Loosen the thermostat locknut and unscrew the thermostat from the mounting bracket. Grasp the valve plate and withdraw it from the cut.

4. Install the air intake duct and valve assembly on the shroud tube.

5. Connect the air intake duct and valve assembly to the air cleaner and tighten the hex-head retaining cap screws.

6. If it was necessary to disassemble the thermostat and air duct and valve, assemble the unit as follows: Install the locknut on the thermostat, and screw the thermostat into the mounting bracket. Install the valve plate tension spring on the valve plate and duct.

7. Install the vacuum override motor (if applicable) and check for proper operation.

Vacuum Operated Duct and Valve Assembly (Heated Air Intake System)

1. Disconnect the vacuum hose at the vacuum motor.

2. Remove the hex cap screws which secure the air intake duct and valve assembly to the air cleaner.

3. Remove the duct and valve assembly from the engine.

4. Position the duct and valve assembly to the air cleaner and heat stove tube. Install the attaching cap screws.

5. Connect the vacuum line at the vacuum motor.

Ported Vacuum Switch (Distributor Vacuum Control Valve)

1. Drain about one gallon of coolant out of the radiator.

2. Tag the vacuum hoses that attach to the control valve and disconnect them.

3. Unscrew and remove the control valve.

4. Install the new control valve.

5. Connect the vacuum hoses.

6. Fill the cooling system.

Spark Delay Valve

1. Locate the spark delay valve in the distributor vacuum line and disconnect it from the line.

2 Install a new spark delay valve in the line, making sure that the black end of the valve is connected to the line from the carburetor and the color coded end is connected to the line from the spark delay valve to the distributor.

Distributor Modulator
DIST-O-VAC SYSTEM

NOTE: *This system is found on the following models only: 1971 vehicles equipped with automatic transmission and the 250 six cylinder engine or the 429 V8 engine with 4 bbl carburetor.*

The Three components of the Dist-O-Vac system are the speed sensor, the thermal switch, and the electronic control module. The electronic control module consists of two sub-assemblies: the electronic control amplifier and the three-way solenoid valve.

The speed sensor, a small unit mounted in the speedometer cable, contains a rotating magnet and a stationary winding which is insulated from ground. The magnet, which rotates with the speedometer cable, generates a small voltage which increases directly with speed. This voltage is directed to the electronic control amplifier.

The thermal switch consists of a bimetallic-element switch which is mounted in the right door pillar and senses the temperature of the air. The switch is closed at 58°F or lower, and open at temperatures about 58°F. This switch is also connected to the electronic control amplifier.

Within the electronic control module case, there is a printed circuit board and an electronic amplifier. The speed sensor and thermal switch are connected to this assembly. The thermal switch is the dominant circuit. When the temperature of the outside air is 58°F or lower, the circuit is closed, so that regardless of speed, the electronic control amplifier will not trigger the three-way solenoid valve. At temperatures above 58°F, however, the thermal switch circuit is open, allowing the circuit from the speed sensor to take over and control the action of the solenoid valve.

The three-way solenoid valve is located within the electronic control module and below the printed circuit board of the amplifier. It is vented to the atmosphere at the top, and connected at the bottom to the carburetor spark port (small hose) and the primary (advance) side of the dual-diaphragm distributor (large hose). The large hose is also channeled through the temperature-sensing valve. The small hose is equipped with an air bleed to provide a positive airflow in the direction of the carburetor. The air bleed purges the hose of vacuum, thus assuring that raw gasoline will not be drawn through the hose and into the distributor diaphragm.

When the thermal switch is closed (air temperature 58°F or lower), or when it is open and the speed sensor is not sending out a strong enough voltage signal (speeds below approximately 35 mph), the amplifier will not

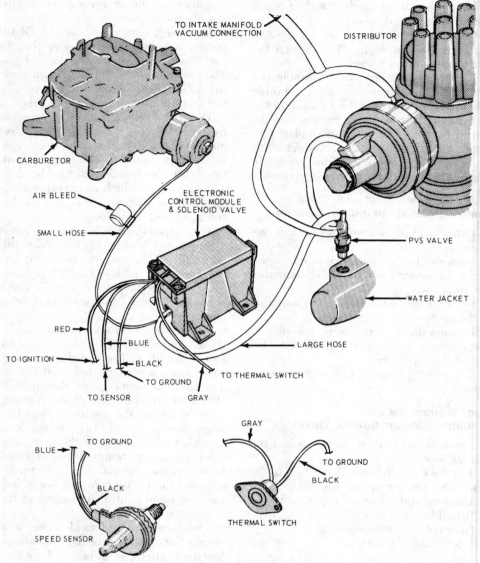

Distributor modulator (Dist-O-Vac) system schematic

activate the solenoid valve and the valve is in the closed position, blocking the passage of air from the small tube through the large tube. With the valve in this position, the larger hose is vented to the atmosphere through the top opening in the three-way valve assembly. Consequently, no vacuum is being supplied to the primary diaphragm on the distributor, and, therefore, no vacuum advance.

When the air temperature is above 85°F and/or the speed of the car is sufficient to generate the required voltage (35 mph or faster), the valve opens, blocking the vent to the atmosphere while opening the vacuum

line from the carburetor spark port to the primary diaphragm of the distributor.

REMOVAL AND INSTALLATION OF DIST-O-VAC SYSTEM COMPONENTS

Dist-O-Vac Temperature Sensor

1. Open the right door and remove the two screws which attach the temperature sensor to the right door pillar.

2. Disconnect the lead wires from the temperature sensor.

3. Connect the lead wires to the new sensor.

4. Position the sensor on the door pillar and install the attaching screws.

Dist-O-Vac Speed Sensor

1. Disconnect the lead wires from the sensor.

2. Disconnect the speed sensor from the speedometer cable.

3. Position the O-rings on both ends of the new speed sensor.

4. Connect both ends of the speedometer cable to the speed sensor.

5. Connect the lead wires to the speed sensor.

Three-way Solenoid Valve

1. Mark each of the vacuum hoses for identification and remove them from the valve.

2. Remove the valve from the engine by turning it counterclockwise, as you would a bolt.

3. Install in reverse order after lightly oiling the threads of the new valve. Be sure to connect the vacuum lines in correct order.

Electronic Control Module

1. Mark each of the vacuum hoses for identification and remove them from the module.

2. Label and remove the two wire harness connectors.

3. Unbolt the module from the fender wall.

4. Installation is the reverse of removal.

Electronic Spark Control

1972 models manufactured for sale in California equipped with a 250 Six, 351C 2 bbl, 351 CJ 4 bbl, or 400 V8 and automatic transmission, as well as all 429 Police Interceptor V8s, use the electronic spark control system.

Electronic Spark Control is a system which blocks off carburetor vacuum to the distributor vacuum advance mechanism under certain temperature and speed conditions. The Electronic Spark Control System consists of four components: a temperature sensor, a speed sensor, an amplifier, and a distributor modulator vacuum valve. The system serves to prevent ignition timing advance (by blocking off carburetor vacuum from the distributor vacuum advance mechanism) until the car reaches a speed of 35 mph when the ambient temperate is over 65°F.

The temperature sensor, which is mounted on the front face of the left door pillar, monitors the outside air temperature and relays this information to the amplifier. The amplifier, which is located under the instrument panel, controls the distributor modulator vacuum valve. The modulator valve, which is attached to the ignition coil mounting bracket, is connected into the carburetor vacuum line to the distributor, and is normally open. If the temperature of the outside air is below 48°F, the contacts in the temperature sensor are open and no signal is sent to the amplifier. Since no signal is sent to the amplifier, the amplifier does not send a signal to the distributor modulator valve, and the vacuum passage from the carburetor to the distributor vacuum advance remains open. When the outside temperature rises to 65°F or above, the contacts in the temperature sensor close, and a signal is sent to the amplifier. The amplifier relays the message to the distributor modulator, which closes to block the vacuum passage to the distributor, preventing ignition timing advance.

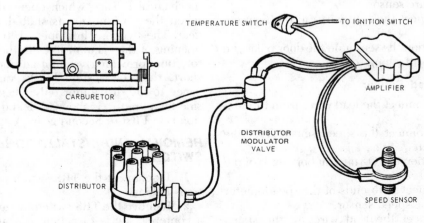

Electronic spark control (ESC) system

When the ambient temperature is 65°F or above, ignition timing advance is prevented until the amplifier receives a signal from the speed sensor that the speed of the vehicle has reached 35 mph, and the distributor modulator vacuum valve can be opened to permit ignition timing advance.

The speed sensor is a miniature generator which is connected to the speedometer cable of the car. As the speedometer cable turns, the inside of the speed sensor turns with the speedometer cable. As the speed of the car increases, a rotating magnet in the speed sensor induces an electronic current in the stationary windings in the speed sensor. This current is sent to the amplifier. As the speed of the vehicle increases, the amount of current sent to the amplifier by the speed sensor increases proportionately. When the car reaches a speed of 35 mph, the amplifier signals the distributor modulator vacuum valve to open, allowing carburetor vacuum to be sent to the distributor vacuum advance chamber. This permits the ignition timing to advance.

It should be noted that this system operates only when the ambient temperature of 65°F or above, and then only when the speed of the car is below 35 mph.

REMOVAL AND INSTALLATION OF ELECTRONIC SPARK CONTROL SYSTEM COMPONENTS

ESC Temperature Sensor

1. Open the right door and remove the two screws which attach the temperature sensor to the right door pillar.
2. Disconnect the lead wires from the temperature sensor.
3. Connect the lead wires to the newsensor.
4. Position the sensor on the door pillar and install the attaching screws.

ESC Speed Sensor

1. Disconnect the lead wires from the sensor.
2. Disconnect the speed sensor from the speedometer cable.
3. Position the O-rings on both ends of the new speed sensor.
4. Connect both ends of the speedometer cable to the speed sensor.
5. Connect the lead wires to the speed sensor.

ESC Amplifier

1. Locate the amplifier under the instrument panel, near the glove compartment.
2. Disconnect the wiring harness from the amplifier.
3. Remove the two amplifier attaching screws and remove the amplifier.
4. Position a new amplifier under the instrument panel and connect the wiring harness to it.
5. Install the two amplifier attaching screws.

ESC Distributor Vacuum Modulator Valve

1. Tag the hoses that attach to the modulator and disconnect them from the amplifier.
2. Disconnect the lead wires from the modulator.
3. Remove the No. 2 left front valve cover bolt (six-cylinder) or the inboard left front valve cover bolt and remove the modulator.
4. Position the new modulator on the valve cover and install the attaching bolt.
5. Connect the wires and hoses to the modulator.

Transmission Regulated Spark System

1972 models equipped with the 250 Six and manual transmission sold in the 49 states, and models equipped with the 351 CJ 4 bbl V8 sold in California use a transmission regulated spark control system.

The transmission regulated spark control system (TRS) differs from the Dist-O-Vac and ESC systems in that the speed sensor and amplifier are replaced by a switch on the transmission. The switch is activated by a mechanical linkage which opens the switch when the transmission is shifted into High gear. The switch, when opened, triggers the opening of the vacuum lines to the distributor, thus providing vacuum advance. So, in short, the TRS system blocks vacuum advance to the distributor only when the outside temperature is above 65°F and transmission is in First or Second gear.

REMOVAL AND INSTALLATION OF TRS SWITCH

1. Disconnect the TRS switch wire at the transmission.
2. Remove the TRS switch by turning it in a conterclockwise direction as you would a bolt.

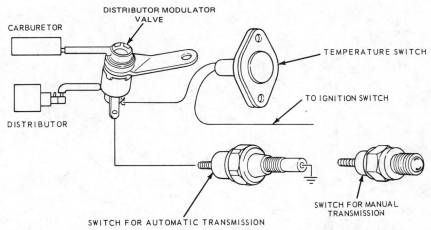

Transmission regulated spark (TRS) system schematic

3. Lightly oil the threads of the new switch and install in reverse order of removal. Torque to 15–20 ft. lbs. on manual transmissions; 4–8 ft. lbs. on automatic transmissions.

Exhaust Gas Recirculation System

All 1973 and later models are equipped with an exhaust gas recirculation (EGR) system to control oxides of nitrogen.

On V8 engines, exhaust gases travel through the exhaust gas crossover passage in the intake manifold. On 6 cylinder engines, an external tube carries exhaust manifold gases to a carburetor spacer. On spacer entry equipped engines, a portion of these gases are diverted into a spacer which is mounted under the carburetor. On floor entry models, a regulated portion of exhaust gases enters the intake manifold through a pair of small holes drilled in the floor of the intake manifold riser. The EGR control valve, which is attached to the rear of the spacer or intake manifold, consists of a vacuum diaphragm with an attached plunger which normally blocks exhaust gases from entering the intake manifold.

On all models, the EGR vale is controlled by a vacuum line from the carburetor which passes through a ported vacuum switch. The EGR ported vacuum switch provides vacuum to the EGR valve at coolant temperatures above 125°F. The vacuum diaphragm then opens the EGR valve permitting exhaust gases to flow through the carburetor spacer and enter the combustion chambers. The exhaust gases are relatively oxygen-free, and tend to dilute the combustion charge. This lowers peak combustion temperature thereby reducing oxides of nitrogen.

On some models equipped with a 351C, 400, 429 or 460 V8, and EGR subsystem, consisting of a speed sensor and control amplifier, prevents exhaust gases from entering the combustion mixture when the car is traveling 65 mph or faster.

The EGR systems on some 1976 and later models employ a backpressure transducer connected to an adapter between the EGR valve and the intake manifold. The transducer modulates EGR flow by varying the EGR valve vacuum signal according to exhaust backpressure. The variations in exhaust backpressure are sensed in the pressure cavity of the transducer spacer.

EGR SYSTEM TEST

1. Allow the engine to warm up, so that the coolant temperature has reached at least 125°F.

2. Disconnect the vacuum hose which runs from the temperature cut-in valve to the EGR valve at the EGR valve end. Connect a vacuum gauge to this hose with a T-fitting.

3. Increase engine speed. The gauge should indicate a vacuum. If no vacuum is present, check the following:

    a. The carburetor—look for a clogged vacuum port.

    b. The vacuum hoses—including the vacuum hoses to the transmission modulator.

    c. The temperature cut-in valve—if no vacuum is present at its outlet with the engine temperature above 125°F and vacuum available from the carburetor, the valve is defective.

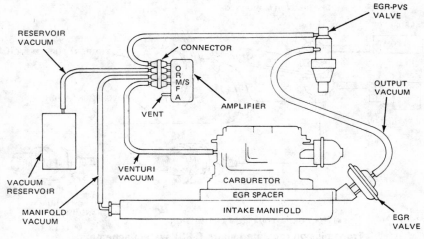

WITH SINGLE CONNECTOR VVA (1974 TYPE)

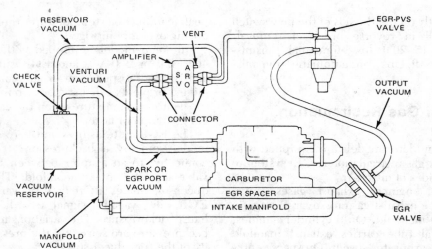

Typical EGR systems with vacuum amplifier—lower diagram is for 1975–78 models

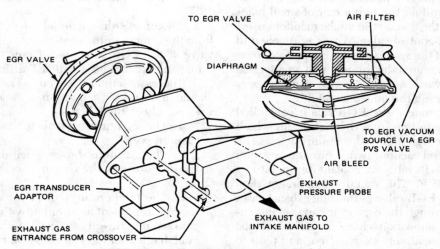

EGR valve exhaust backpressure tranducer

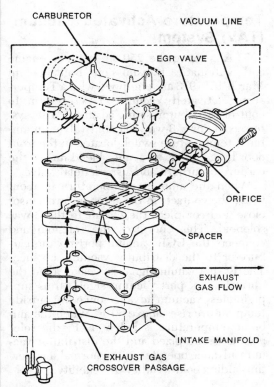

EGR system spacer entry

4. If all the above tests are positive, check the EGR valve itself.

5. Connect an outside vacuum source and a vacuum gauge to the valve.

6. Apply vacuum to the EGR valve. The valve should open at 3–10 in. Hg, the engine idle speed should slow down and the idle quality should become more rough.

7. If this does not happen, i.e., the EGR valve remains closed, the EGR valve is defective and must be replaced.

8. If the valve stem moves but the idle remains the same, the valve orifice is clogged and must be cleaned.

NOTE: *If an outside vacuum source is not available, disconnect the hose which runs between the EGR valve and the temperature cut-in valve and plug the hose connections on the cut-in valve. Connect the EGR valve hose to a source of intake manifold vacuum and watch the idle. The results should be the same as in steps 6–7, above.*

EGR SYSTEM SERVICE

Since the EGR system channels exhaust gases through quite narrow passages, deposits are likely to build up and eventually block the flow of gases. This necessitates servicing of the system at the interval specified in the maintenance chart (see Chapter 1). EGR system service consists of cleaning or replacing the EGR valve and cleaning all the exhaust gas channels.

EGR Valve Cleaning

Remove the EGR valve for cleaning. Do not strike or pry on the valve diaphragm housing or supports, as this may damage the valve operating mechanism and/or change the valve calibration. Check orifice hole in the EGR valve body for deposits. A small hand drill of no more than 0.060 in. diameter may be used to clean the hole if plugged. Extreme care must be taken to avoid enlarging the hole or damaging the surface of the orifice plate.

NOTE: *The remainder of this procedure refers only to EGR valves which can be disassembled. Valves which are riveted or otherwise permanently assembled cannot be cleaned and should be replaced if highly contaminated.*

Separate the diaphragm section from the main mounting body. Clean the valve plates, stem, and the mounting plate, using a small power-driven rotary type wire brush. Take care not to damage the parts. Remove deposits between stem and valve disc by using a steel blade or shim approximately 0.028 in. thick in a sawing motion around the stem shoulder at both sides of the disc.

The poppet must wobble and move axially before reassembly.

Clean the cavity and passages in the main body of the valve with a power-driven rotary wire brush. If the orifice plate has a hole less than 0.050 in. it must be removed for cleaning. Remove all loosened debris using shop compressed air. Reassemble the diaphragm section on the main body using a new gasket between them. Torque the attaching screws to specification. Clean the orifice plate and the counterbore in the valve body. Reinstall the orifice plate using a small amount of con-

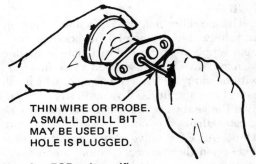

THIN WIRE OR PROBE.
A SMALL DRILL BIT
MAY BE USED IF
HOLE IS PLUGGED.

Cleaning EGR valve orifice

tact cement to retain the plate in place during assembly of the valve to the carburetor spacer. Apply cement only to outer edges of the orifice plate to avoid restriction of the orifice.

EGR Supply Passages and Carburetor Space Cleaning

Remove the carburetor and carburetor spacer on engines so equipped. Clean the supply tube with a small power-driven rotary type wire brush or blast cleaning equipment. Clean the exhaust gas passages in the spacer using a suitable wire brush and/or scraper. The machined holes in the spacer can be cleaned by using a suitable round wire brush. Hard encrusted material should be probed loose first, then brushed out.

EGR Exhaust Gas Channel Cleaning

Clean the exhaust gas channel, where applicable, in the intake manifold, using a suitable carbon scraper. Clean the exhaust gas entry port in the intake manifold by hand passing a suitable drill bit thru the holes to auger out the deposits. Do not use a wire brush. The manifold riser (bore(s)) should be suitably plugged during the above action to prevent any of the residue from entering the induction system.

Venturi Vacuum Amplifier System

Many 1974 and later models use a venturi vacuum amplifier in conjunction with the EGR system. The amplifier is used to boost a relatively weak venturi vacuum signal in the throat of the carburetor into a strong intake manifold vacuum signal to operate the EGR valve. This device improves driveability by more closely matching venturi airflow and EGR flow.

The amplifier features a vacuum reservoir and check valve to maintain an adequate vacuum supply regardless of variations in engine manifold vacuum. Also used in conjunction with the amplifier, is a relief valve, which will cancel the output EGR vacuum signal whenever the venturi vacuum signal is equal to, or greater than, the intake manifold vacuum. Thus, the EGR valve may close at or near wide-open throttle acceleration, when maximum power is needed.

Temperature Activated Vacuum (TAV) System

1973 cars using the 250 six-cylinder engine and automatic transmission built before March 15, 1973 are equipped with a Temperature Activated Vacuum (TAV) system to control distributor spark advance. The system contains a 3-way solenoid valve, an ambient temperature switch located in the front door hinge pillar, a vacuum bleed line to the carburetor airhorn and a spark delay valve.

When the ambient temperature is about 60°F, the contacts in the temperature sensor close and complete the circuit to the 3-way solenoid. This energizes the solenoid and connects the EGR vacuum port on the carburetor to the distributor vacuum advance. The EGR vacuum signal is weaker than the normal spark port vacuum signal, thus supplying less vacuum advance once the outside temperature rises above 60°F. When the ambient temperature is below 49°F, the solenoid is deenergized and the distributor vacuum advance operates in the normal manner, thus aiding cold weather driveability.

Cold Temperature Activated Vacuum (CTAV) System

1973 cars using the 250 six-cylinder engine and automatic transmission built on or after March 15, 1973, as well as all 1974 models using the 250 six and automatic transmission are equipped with a Cold Temperature Activated Vacuum (CTAV) system to control distributor spark advance. This system is basically a refinement of the TAV system with the temperature switch relocated in the air cleaner and a latching relay added to maintain a strong vacuum signal at the distributor, whether it be EGR port or spark port carburetor vacuum, and to keep the system from intermittently switching vacuum signals when the intake air is between 49 and 60°F. When the temperature switch closes at 60°F, the latching relay (normally off) is energized and stays on until the ignition switch is turned off. The latching relay then overrides the temperature switch and forces the solenoid valve to keep the spark port vacuum system closed and open the EGR port vacuum system. This prevents full vacuum advance, once the engine is warmed-up, thereby lowering emissions.

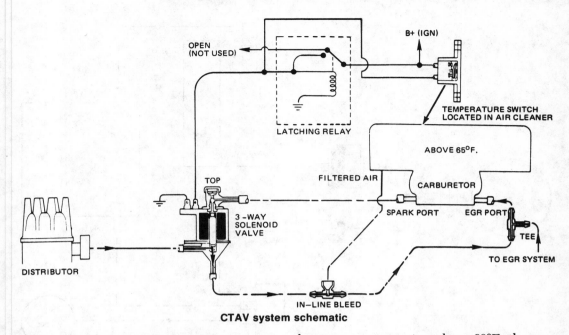

CTAV system schematic

Delay Vacuum By-Pass (DVB) System

All 1973 models equipped with the 351C or 400 V8 manufactured before March 15, 1973 are equipped with the Delay Vacuum By-pass spark control system. This system provides two paths by which carburetor vacuum can reach the distirbutor vacuum advance. The system consists of a spark delay valve, a check valve, a solenoid vacuum valve, and an ambient temperature switch. When the ambient temperature is below 49°F, the temperature switch contacts are open and the vacuum solenoid is open (de-energized). Under these conditions, vacuum will flow from the carburetor, through the open solenoid, and to the distributor. Since the spark delay valve resists the flow of carburetor vacuum, the vacuum will always flow through the vacuum solenoid when it is open, since this is the path of least resistance. When the am-

bient temperature rises above 60°F, the contacts in the temperature switch (which is located in the door post) close. This passes ignition switch current to the solenoid, energizing the solenoid. This blocks one of the two vacuum paths. All distributor vacuum must now flow through the spark delay valve. When carburetor vacuum rises above a certain level on acceleration, a rubber valve in the spark delay valve blocks vacuum from passing through the valve for from 5 to 30 seconds. After this time delay has elapsed, normal vacuum is supplied to the distributor. When the vacuum solenoid is closed, (temperature above 60°), the vacuum line from the solenoid to the distributor is vented to atmosphere. To prevent the vacuum that is passing through the spark delay valve from escaping through the solenoid into the atmosphere, a one-way check valve is installed in the vacuum line from the solenoid to the distributor.

EGR/Coolant Spark Control

CSC SYSTEM

The EGR/CSC system is used on most 1974 and later models. It regulates both distributor spark advance and the EGR valve operation according to coolant temperature by sequentially switching vacuum signals.

The major EGR/CSC system components are:
1. 95°F EGR-PVS valve;
2. Spark Delay Valve (SDV);
3. Vacuum check valve.

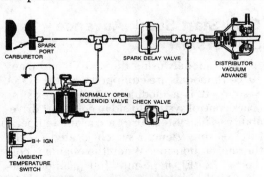

DELAY VACUUM BY-PASS SYSTEM SCHEMATIC

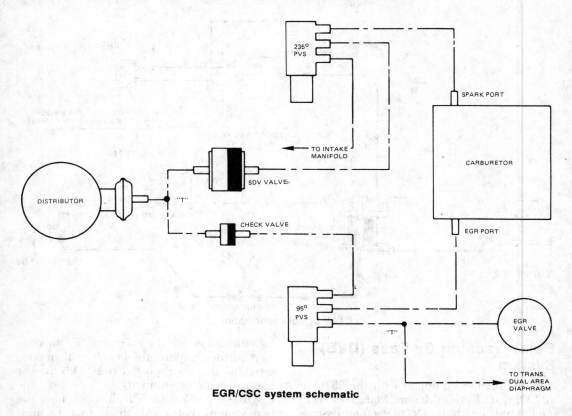

EGR/CSC system schematic

When the engine coolant temperature is below 82°F, the EGR-PVS valve admits carburetor EGR port vacuum (occurring at about 2,500 rpm) directly to the distributor advance diaphragm, through the one-way check valve.

At the same time, the EGR-PVS valve shuts off carburetor EGR vacuum to the EGR valve and transmission diaphragm.

When engine coolant temperature is 95°F and above, the EGR-PVS valve is actuated and directs carburetor EGR vacuum to the EGR valve and transmission instead of the distributor. At temperatures between 82–95°F, the EGR-PVS valve may be opened, closed, or in mid-position.

The SDV valve delays carburetor spark vacuum to the distributor advance diaphragm by restricting the vacuum signal through the SDV valve for a predetermined time. During normal acceleration, little or no vacuum is admitted to the distributor advance diaphragm until acceleration is completed, because of (1) the time delay of the SDV valve and (2) the rerouting of EGR port vacuum if the engine coolant temperature is 95°F or higher.

The check valve blocks off vacuum signal from the SDV to the EGR-PVS so that car-

buretor spark vacuum will not be dissipated when the EGR-PVS is actuated above 95°F.

The 235°F PVS is not part of the EGR/CSC system, but is connected to the distributor vacuum advance to prevent engine overheating while idling (as on previous models). At idle speed, no vacuum is generated at either the carburetor spark port or EGR port and engine timing is fully retarded. When engine coolant temperature reaches 235°F, however, the valve is actuated to admit intake manifold vacuum to the distributor advance diaphragm. This advances the engine timing and speeds up the engine. The increase in coolant flow and fan speed lowers engine temperature.

Cold Start Spark Advance
CSSA SYSTEM

All 1975 models using the 460 V8 and many 1976–78 models are equipped with the CSSA System. It is a modification of the existing spark control system to aid in cold start driveability. The system uses a coolant temperature sensing vacuum switch located on the thermostat housing. When the engine is cold (below 125°F), it permits full manifold vacuum to the distributor advance diaphragm.

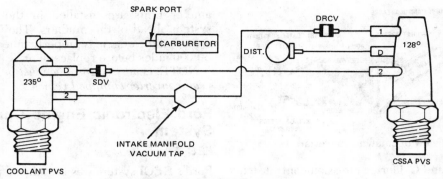

CSSA system schematic

After the engine warms up, normal spark control (retard) resumes.

Vacuum Operated Heat Control Valve (VOHV)

To further aid cold start driveability during engine warmup, most 1975 and later engines use a VOHV located between the exhaust manifold and the exhaust inlet (header) pipe.

When the engine is first started, the valve is closed, blocking exhaust gases from exiting from one bank of cylinders. These gases are then diverted back through the intake manifold crossover passage under the carburetor. The result is quick heat to the carburetor and choke.

The VOHV is controlled by a ported vacuum switch which uses manifold vacuum to keep the vacuum motor on the valve closed until the coolant reaches a predetermined "warm-up" value. When the engine is warmed-up, the PVS shuts off vacuum to the VOHV, and a strong return spring opens the VOHV butterfly.

Dual Signal Spark Advance (DSSA) System

The DSSA system is used on many 1975 and later model engines. It incorporates a spark delay valve (SDV) and a one-way check valve to provide improved spark and EGR function during mild acceleration.

The check valve prevents spark port vacuum from reaching the EGR valve and causing excessive EGR valve flow. It also prevents EGR port vacuum from diluting spark port vacuum, which could result in improper spark advance due to weakened signal. The SDV permits application of full EGR vacuum to the distributor vacuum advance diaphragm during mild acceleration. During steady speed or cruise conditions, EGR port vacuum is applied to the EGR valve and spark port vacuum is applied to the distributor vacuum advance diaphragm.

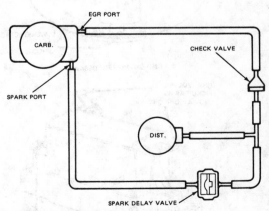

DSSA system schematic

Catalytic Reactor (*Converter*) System

Starting in 1975, all models are equipped with a catalytic converter system to meet 1975

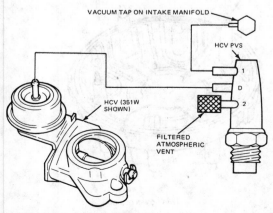

VHV system schematic

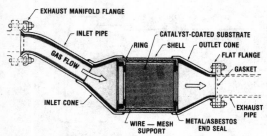

Sectional view of catalytic converter

Federal and California emission control standards. California models are equipped with two converters, while models sold in the other 49 states have only one unit.

Catalytic converters convert noxious emissions of hydrocarbons (HC) and carbon monoxide (CO) into harmless carbon dioxide and water. The reaction takes place inside the reactor(s) at great heat using platinum or palladium metals as the catalyst. The 5 in. di-

ameter units are installed in the exhaust system ahead of the mufflers. They are designed, if the engine is properly tuned, to last 50,000 miles before replacement.

NOTE: *Lead-free gasoline must be used on all converter equipped vehicles.*

Ford Electronic Engine Control System

EEC 1

Ford's EECI system was introduced in 1978, on the Lincoln Versailles. Designed to precisely control ignition timing, EGR and Thermactor (air pump) flow, the system consists of an Electronic Control Assembly (ECA), seven monitoring sensors, a Dura Spark II ignition module and coil, a special distributor assembly, and an EGR system designed to operate on air pressure.

The ECA is a solid state micro computer,

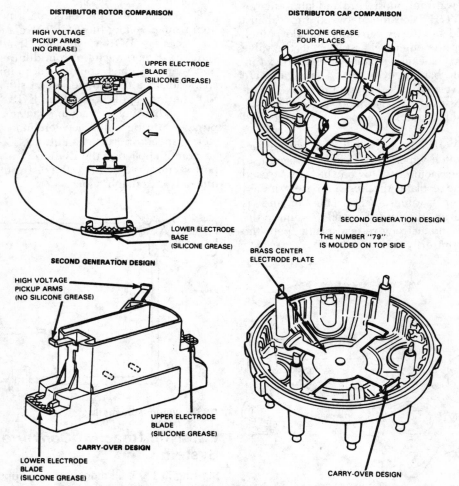

Comparison of early and later model EEC distributor caps

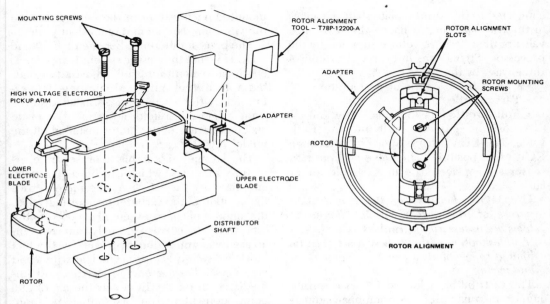

EEC rotor alignment through mid-1979

consisting of a processor assembly and a calibration assembly. The processor continuously receives inputs from the seven sensors, which it converts to usable information for the calculating section of the computer. It also performs ignition timing, Thermactor and EGR flow calculations, processes the information and sends out signals to the ignition module and control solenoids to adjust the timing and flow of the systems accordingly. The calibration assembly contains the memory and programming for the processor.

Processor inputs come from sensors monitoring manifold pressure, barometric pressure, engine coolant temperature, inlet air temperature, crankshaft position, throttle position, and EGR valve position.

The manifold absolute pressure sensor determines changes in intake manifold pressure (barometric pressure minus manifold vacuum) which result from changes in engine load and speed, or in atmospheric pressure. Its signal is used by the ECA to set part throttle spark advance and EGR flow rate.

Barometric pressure is monitored by a sensor mounted on the firewall. Measurements taken are converted into a useable electrical signal. The ECA uses this reference for altitude-dependent EGR flow requirements.

Engine coolant temperature is measured at the rear of the intake manifold by a sensor consisting of a brass housing containing a thermistor (resistance decreases as temperature rises). When reference voltage (about 9 volts, supplied by the processor to all sensors) is applied to the sensor, the resistance can be measured by the resulting voltage drop. Resistance is then interpreted as coolant temperature by the ECA. This sensor replaces both the PVS and EGR PVS in conventional systems. EGR flow is cut off by the ECA when a predetermined temperature value is reached. The ECA will also advance initial ignition timing to increase idle speed if the coolant overheats due to prolonged idle. A faster idle speed increases coolant and radiator air flow.

Inlet air temperature is measured by a sensor mounted in the air cleaner. It functions in the same way as the coolant sensor. The ECA uses its signal for proper spark advance and Thermactor flow. At high inlet temperatures (above 90°F) the ECA modifies timing advance to prevent spark knock.

The crankshaft is fitted with a four-lobed powdered metal pulse ring, positioned 10° BTDC. Its position is constantly monitored by the crankshaft position sensor. Signals are sent to the ECA describing both the position of the crankshaft at any given moment, and the frequency of the pulses (engine rpm). These signals are used to determine optimum ignition timing advance. If either the sensor or wiring is broken, the ECA will not receive a signal, and thus be unable to send any signal to the ignition module. This will prevent the engine from starting.

The throttle position sensor is a rheostat

connected to the throttle plate shaft. Changes in throttle plate angle change the resistance value of the reference voltage supplied by the processor. Signals are interpreted in one of three ways by the ECA:

- Closed throttle (idle or deceleration)
- Part throttle (cruise)
- Full throttle (maximum acceleration)

A position sensor is built into the EGR valve. The ECA uses its signal to determine EGR valve position. The valve and position sensor are replaced as a unit, should either fail.

CAUTION: *Because of the complicated nature of this system, special diagnostic tools are necessary for troubleshooting. Any troubleshooting without these tools must be limited to mechanical checks of connectors and wiring.*

The distributor is locked in place during engine manufacture; no rotational adjustment is possible for initial ignition timing, since all timing is controlled by the ECA. There are no mechanical advance mechanisms or adjustments under the rotor, thus there is no need to remove it except for replacement.

EEC II

The second generation EEC II system was introduced in 1979 on full size Fords and Mercurys. It is based on the EEC I system used on the Versailles, but some changes have been made to reduce complexity and cost, increase the number of controlled functions, and improve reliability and performance.

In general, the EEC II system operates in the same manner as EEC I. An Electronic Control Assembly (ECA) monitors reports from six sensors, and adjusts the EGR flow, ignition timing, Thermactor (air pump) air flow, and carburetor air/fuel mixture in response to the incoming signals. Although there are only six sensors, seven conditions are monitored. The sensors are: (1) Engine Coolant Temperature, (2) Throttle Position, (3) Crankshaft Position, (4) Exhaust Gas Oxygen, (5) Barometric and Manifold Absolute Pressure, and (6) EGR Valve Position. These sensors function in the same manner as the EEC I sensors, and are described in the EEC I section. Note that inlet air temperature is not monitored in the EEC II system, and that the barometric and manifold pressure sensors have been combined into one unit. One more change from the previous system is in the location of the crankshaft sensor: it is mounted on the front of the engine, behind the vibration damper and crankshaft pulley.

The biggest difference between EEC I and EEC II is that the newer system is capable of continually monitoring and adjusting the carburetor air/fuel ratio. Monitoring is performed by the oxygen sensor installed in the right exhaust manifold; adjustment is made via an electric stepper motor installed on the model 7200 VV carburetor.

The stepper motor has four separate armature windings, which can be sequentially energized by the ECA. As the motor varies the position of the carburetor metering valve, the amount of control vacuum exposed to the fuel bowl is correspondingly altered. Increased vacuum reduces pressure in the fuel bowl, causing a leaner air/fuel mixture, and vice versa. During engine starting and immediately after, the ECA sets the motor at a point dependent on its initial position. Thereafter, the motor position is changed in response to the ECA calculations of the six input signals.

EEC II is also capable of controlling purging of vapors from the evaporative emission control storage canister. A canister purge solenoid, a combination solenoid and valve, is located in the line between the intake manifold purge fitting and the carbon canister. It controls the flow of vapors from the canister to the intake manifold, opening and closing in response to signals from the ECA.

CAUTION: *As is the case with EEC I, diagnosis and repair of the system requires special tools and equipment.*

The distributor is locked in place during engine manufacture; no rotational adjustment is possible for initial ignition timing, since all timing is controlled by the ECA. There are no mechanical advance mechanisms or adjustments under the ignition rotor, and thus there is no need to remove it except for replacement.

Air/fuel mixture is entirely controlled by the ECA; no adjustments are possible.

EEC III

EEC III was introduced in 1980. It is a third generation system developed entirely from EEC II. The only real differences between EEC II and III are contained within the Electronic Control Assembly (ECA) and the Dura-Spark ignition module. The EEC III system uses a separate program module which plugs into the main ECA module. This change allows various programming calibrations for specific applications to be made to the program module, while allowing the main ECA module to be standardized. Additionally, EEC III uses a Dura-Spark III ignition module, which contains fewer electronic functions than the Dura-Spark II module; the functions have been incorporated into the main ECA module. There is no interchangeability between the Dura-Spark II and III modules.

NOTE: *Since late 1979 emission controls and air/fuel mixtures have been controlled by various electronic methods. An electronically controlled feedback carburetor is used to precisely calibrate fuel metering, many vacuum check valves, solenoids and regulators have been added and the electronic control boxes (ECU and MCU) can be calibrated and programmed in order to be used by different engines and under different conditions.*

NOTE: *Because of the complicated nature of the Ford system, special tools and procedures are necessary for testing and troubleshooting.*

The following emission control devices described can be tested and maintained, any not mentioned should be serviced by qualified mechanics using the required equipment.

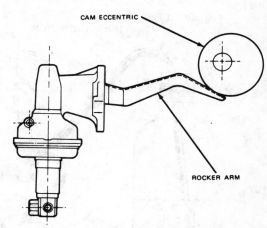

Typical mechanical fuel pump installation

FUEL SYSTEM

Fuel Pump

A single-action, diaphragm-type, mechanical fuel pump, driven by the camshaft, is used on all models except the 1973–75 460 Police Interceptor V8. The mechanical fuel pump is located at the lower left-side of the engine block on six-cylinder models, at the lower left-side of the cylinder front cover on V8 models. The 1973–75 Police Interceptor engines use an electrical fuel pump located in the fuel tank beneath the vapor separator. The tank must be removed for electrical fuel pump service.

Mechanical Fuel Pump
TESTING AND ADJUSTMENT

No adjustments may be made to the fuel pump. Before removing and replacing the old fuel pump, the following test may be made while the pump is still installed on the engine.

1. If a fuel pressure gauge is available, connect the gauge to the engine and operate

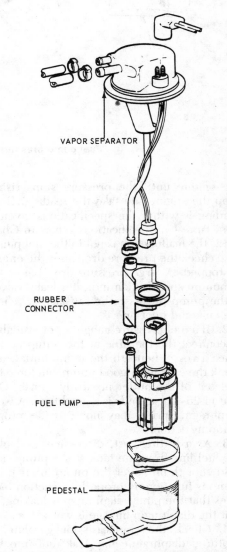

Electric fuel pump assembly—1973–75 460 PI V8

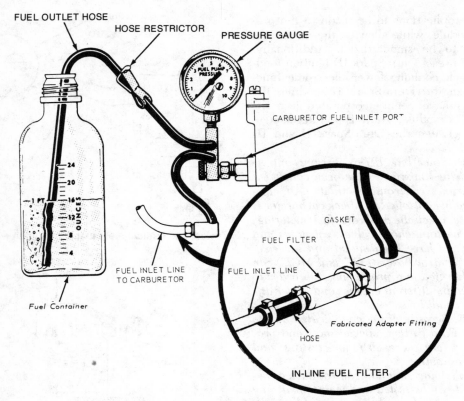

FUEL OUTLET HOSE
HOSE RESTRICTOR
PRESSURE GAUGE
CARBURETOR FUEL INLET PORT
GASKET
FUEL FILTER
FUEL INLET LINE
FUEL INLET LINE TO CARBURETOR
Fabricated Adapter Fitting
Fuel Container
HOSE
IN-LINE FUEL FILTER

Fuel pump pressure and capacity test equipment

the engine until the pressure stops rising. Stop the engine and take the reading. If the reading is within the specifications given in the "Tune-Up Specifications" chart in Chapter 2, the malfunction is not in the fuel pump. Also check the pressure drop after the engine is stopped. A large pressure drop below the minimum specification indicates leaky valves. If the pump proves to be satisfactory, check the tank and inlet line.

2. If a fuel pressure gauge is not available, disconnect the fuel line at the pump outlet, place a vessel beneath the pump outlet, and crank the engine. A good pump will force the fuel out of the outlet in steady spurts. One pint in 25–30 seconds is a good flow. A worn diaphragm spring may not provide proper pumping action.

3. As a further test, disconnect and plug the fuel line from the tank at the pump, and hold your thumb over the pump inlet. If the pump is functioning properly, a suction indicates that the pump diaphragm is leaking, or that the diaphragm linkage is worn.

4. Check the crankcase for gasoline. A ruptured diaphragm may leak fuel into the engine.

REMOVAL AND INSTALLATION

1. Disconnect the plug and inlet and outlet lines from the fuel pump.

2. Remove the fuel pump retaining bolts and carefully pull the pump and old gasket away from the block.

3. Discard the old gasket. Clean the mating surfaces on the block and position a new gasket on the block, using oil-resistant sealer.

4. Mount the fuel pump and gasket to the engine block, being careful to insert the pump lever (rocker arm) in the engine block, aligning it correctly above the camshaft lobe.

NOTE: *If resistance is felt while positioning the fuel pump on the block, the camshaft lobe is probably on the high position. To ease installation, connect a remote engine starter switch to the engine and "tap" the switch until resistance fades.*

5. While holding the pump securely against the block, install the retaining bolts. On six-cylinder engines, torque the bolts to 12–15 ft. lbs., and on V8s, 20–24 ft. lbs.

6. Unplug and reconnect the fuel lines at the pump.

7. Start the engine and check for fuel leaks.

Also check for oil leaks where the fuel pump attaches to the block.

Electric Choke

Starting in 1973, all Fords use an electrically-assisted choke to reduce exhaust emissions of carbon monoxide during warmup. The system consists of a choke cap, a thermostatic spring, a bimetal sensing disc (switch) and a ceramic positive temperature coefficient (PTC) heater.

The choke is powered from the center tap of the alternator, so that current is constantly applied to the temperature sensing disc. The system is grounded through the carburetor body. At temperatures below approximately 60°F, the switch is open and no current is supplied to the ceramic heater, thereby resulting in normal unassisted thermostatic spring choking action. When the temperature rises above about 60°F, the temperature sensing disc closes and current is supplied to the heater, which in turn, acts on the thermostatic spring. Once the heater starts, it causes the thermostatic spring to pull the choke plate(s) open within 1½ minutes, which is sooner than it would open if non-assisted.

ELECTRIC CHOKE OPERATIONAL TEST

1. Detach the electrical lead from the choke cap.

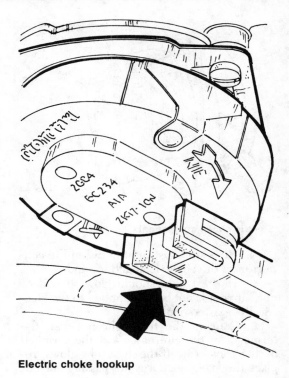

Electric choke hookup

2. Use a jumper lead to connect the terminal on the choke cap and the wire terminal, so that the electrical circuit is still completed.

3. Start the engine.

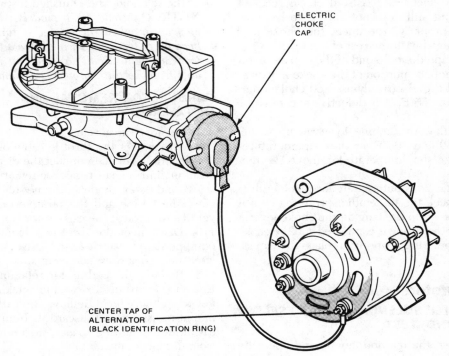

ELECTRIC
CHOKE
CAP

CENTER TAP OF
ALTERNATOR
(BLACK IDENTIFICATION RING)

Electric choke wiring

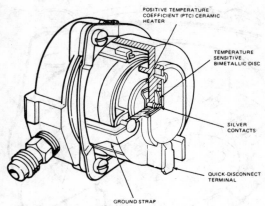

Electric choke components

4. Hook up a test light between the connector on the choke lead and ground.

5. The test light should glow. If it does not, current is not being supplied to the electrically-assisted choke.

6. Connect the test light between the terminal on the alternator and the terminal on the choke cap. If the light now glows, replace the lead, since it is not passing current to the choke assist.

CAUTION: *Do not ground the terminal on the alternator while performing Step 6.*

7. If the light still does not glow, the fault lies somewhere in the electrical system. Check the system out.

If the electrically-assisted choke receives power but still does not appear to be functioning properly, reconnect the choke lead and proceed with the rest of the test.

8. Tape the bulb end of the thermometer to the metallic portion of the choke housing.

9. If the electrically-assisted choke operates below 55°F, it is defective and must be replaced.

10. Allow the engine to warm up to between 80 and 100°F; at these temperatures the choke should operate for about 1½ minutes.

11. If it does not operate for this length of time, check the bimetallic spring to see if it is connected to the tang on the choke lever.

12. If the spring is connected and the choke is not operating properly, replace the cap assembly.

Carburetors

THROTTLE SOLENOID (ANTI-DIESELING SOLENOID) TEST

1. Turn the ignition key on and open the throttle. The solenoid plunger should extend (solenoid energize).

2. Turn the ignition off. The plunger should retract, allowing the throttle to close.

NOTE: *With the antidieseling de-energized, the carburetor idle speed adjusting screw must make contact with the throttle shaft to prevent the throttle plates from jamming in the throttle bore when the engine is turned off.*

3. If the solenoid is functioning properly and the engine is still dieseling, check for one of the following:

a. High idle or engine shut off speed;

b. Engine timing not set to specification;

c. Binding throttle linkage;

d. Too low an octane fuel being used.

Correct any of these problems as necessary.

4. If the solenoid fails to function as outlined in Steps 1–2, disconnect the solenoid leads; the solenoid should de-energize. If it does not, it is jammed and must be replaced.

5. Connect the solenoid to a 12 V power source and to ground. Open the throttle so that the plunger can extend. If it does not, the solenoid is defective.

6. If the solenoid is functioning correctly and no other source of trouble can be found, the fault probably lies in the wiring between the solenoid and the ignition switch or in the ignition switch itself. Remember to reconnect the solenoid when finished testing.

NOTE: *On some 1971 models, dieseling may occur when the engine is turned off because of feedback through the alternator warning light circuit. A diode kit is available from Ford to cure this problem.*

CARBURETOR REMOVAL AND INSTALLATION

1. Remove the air cleaner.

2. Disconnect the throttle cable or rod at the throttle lever. Disconnect the distributor vacuum line, exhaust gas recirculation line (1973 and later models), inline fuel filter, choke heat tube and the positive crankcase ventilation hose at the carburetor.

3. Disconnect the throttle solenoid (if so equipped) and electric choke assist (1973 and later models) at their connectors.

4. Remove the carburetor retaining nuts. Lift off the carburetor carefully, taking care not to spill any fuel. Remove the carburetor mounting gasket and discard it. Remove the carburetor mounting spacer, if so equipped, from the intake manifold.

5. Prior to installation, clean the gasket mounting surfaces of the intake manifold,

spacer (if so equipped), and carburetor. When using a spacer, use two new gaskets, sandwiching the spacer between the gaskets. If a spacer is not used, only one new carburetor mounting gasket is required.

6. Place the new gasket(s) and spacer (if so equipped) on the carburetor mounting studs. Position the carburetor on top of the gasket and hand tighten the retaining nuts. Then tighten the nuts in a crisscross pattern to 10–15 ft. lbs.

7. Connect the throttle linkage, the distributor vacuum line, exhaust gas recirculation line (1973 and later models), inline fuel filter, choke heat tube, positive crankcase ventilation hose, throttle solenoid (if so equipped) and electric-choke assist (1973 and later models).

8. Perform the preliminary adjustments of idle speed and mixture settings as outlined in Chapter 2.

OVERHAUL

All Types Except 2700 VV and 7200 VV

NOTE: *The 2700 VV and 7200 VV are part of the extremely sophisticated EEC system. Do not attempt to overhaul these units.*

Efficient carburetion depends greatly on careful cleaning and inspection during overhaul, since dirt, gum, water, or varnish in or on the carburetor parts are often responsible for poor performance.

Overhaul your carburetor in a clean, dust-free area. Carefully disassemble the carburetor, referring often to the exploded views. Keep all similar and look-alike parts segregated during the disassembly and cleaning to avoid accidental interchange during assembly. Make a note of all jet sizes.

When the carburetor is disassembled, wash all parts (except diaphragms, electric choke units, pump plunger, and any other plastic, leather, fiber, or rubber parts) in clean carburetor solvent. Do not leave parts in the solvent any longer than is necessary to sufficiently loosen the deposits. Excessive cleaning may remove the special finish from the float bowl and choke valve bodies, leaving these parts unfit for service. Rinse all parts in clean solvent and blow them dry with compressed air or allow them to air dry. Wipe clean all cork, plastic, leather, and fiber parts with a clean, lint-free cloth.

Blow out all passages and jets with compressed air and be sure that there are no restrictions or blockages. Never use wire or similar tools to clean jets, fuel passages, or air bleeds. Clean all jets and valves separately to avoid accidental interchange.

Check all parts for wear or damage. If wear or damage is found, replace the defective parts. Especially check the following:

1. Check the float needle and seat for wear. If wear is found, replace the complete assembly.

2. Check the float hinge pin for wear and the float(s) for dents or distortion. Replace the float if fuel has leaked into it.

3. Check the throttle and choke shaft bores for wear or an out-of-round condition. Damage or wear to the throttle arm, shaft, or shaft bore will often require replacement of the throttle body. These parts require a close tolerance of fit; wear may allow air leakage, which could affect starting and idling.

NOTE: *Throttle shafts and bushings are not included in overhaul kits. They can be purchased separately.*

4. Inspect the idle mixture adjusting needles for burrs or grooves. Any such condition requires replacement of the needle, since you will not be able to obtain a satisfactory idle.

5. Test the accelerator pump check valves. They should pass air one way but not the other. Test for proper seating by blowing and sucking on the valve. Replace the valve if necessary. If the valve is satisfactory, wash the valve again to remove breath moisture.

6. Check the bowl cover for warped surfaces with a straightedge.

7. Closely inspect the valves and seats for wear and damage, replacing as necessary.

8. After the carburetor is assembled, check the choke valve for freedom of operation.

Carburetor overhaul kits are recommended for each overhaul. These kits contain all gaskets and new parts to replace those which deteriorate most rapidly. Failure to replace all parts supplied with the kit (especially gaskets) can result in poor performance later.

Some carburetor manufacturers supply overhaul kits of three basic types: minor repair; major repair; and gasket kits. Basically, they contain the following:

Minor Repair Kits:
- All gaskets
- Float needle valve
- Volume control screw
- All diaphragms
- Spring for the pump diaphragm

Major Repair Kits:
- All jets and gaskets
- All diaphragms

- Float needle valve
- Volume control screw
- Pump ball valve
- Float
- Complete intermediate rod
- Intermediate pump lever
- Some cover hold-down screws and washers

Gasket Kits:

- All gaskets

After cleaning and checking all components, reassemble the carburetor, using new parts and referring to the exploded view. When reassembling, make sure that all screws and jets are tight in their seats, but do not overtighten as the tips will be distorted. Tighten all screws gradually, in rotation. Do not tighten needle valves into their seats; uneven jetting will result. Always use new gaskets. Be sure to adjust the float level when reassembling.

Carburetor Adjustments

NOTE: *Adjustments for the 2700 VV, are covered following adjustments for all other carburetors.*

AUTOMATIC CHOKE HOUSING ADJUSTMENT

All Carburetors

By rotating the spring housing of the automatic choke, the reaction of the choke to engine temperature can be controlled. To adjust, remove the air cleaner assembly, loosen the thermostatic spring housing retaining screws and set the spring housing to the specified index mark. The marks are shown in the accompanying illustration. After adjusting the setting, tighten the retaining screws and replace the air cleaner assembly to the carburetor.

CHOKE PLATE PULL-DOWN CLEARANCE ADJUSTMENT

Carter RBS

1. Remove the carburetor air cleaner, and remove the choke thermostatic spring housing.

2. Bend a section of 0.026 in. diameter wire at a 90° angle approximately ⅛ in. from one end.

3. Insert the bent end of the wire gauge between the choke piston slot and the right-hand slot in the choke housing. Rotate the choke piston lever counterclockwise until the gauge is snug in the piston slot.

4. Exert light pressure upon the choke piston lever to hold the gauge in position. Check the specified clearance with a drill of the correct diameter between the lower edge of the choke plate and the carburetor bore.

5. Choke plate pull-down clearance may be adjusted by bending the choke piston lever as required to obtain the desired clearance. It is recommended that the choke piston lever be removed prior to bending, in order to prevent distorting the piston link.

6. Install the choke thermostatic spring housing and gasket, and set the housing to the proper specification.

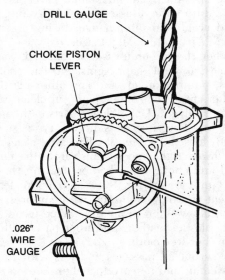

Adjusting choke plate pull-down—Carter RBS

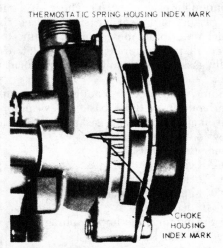

Automatic choke housing adjustment

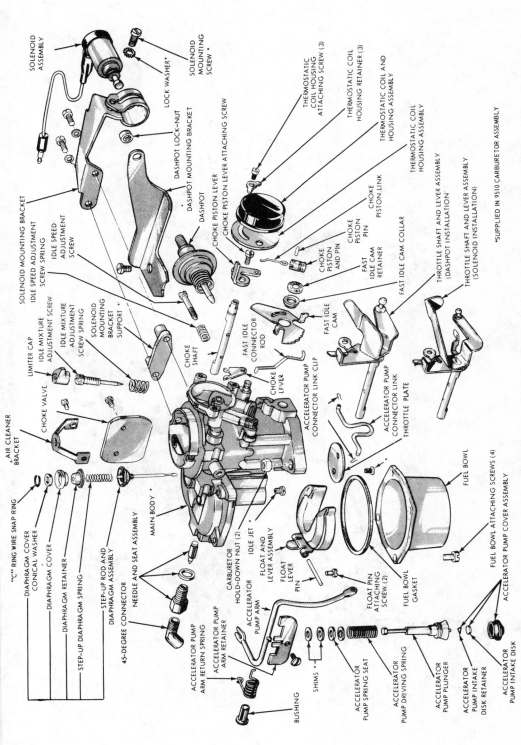

Exploded view—Carter RBS-1V

SOLENOID ASSEMBLY

LOCK WASHER*

SOLENOID MOUNTING SCREW *

DASHPOT LOCK-NUT

DASHPOT MOUNTING BRACKET

CHOKE PISTON LEVER

CHOKE PISTON LEVER ATTACHING SCREW

DASHPOT

THERMOSTATIC COIL HOUSING ATTACHING SCREW (3)

THERMOSTATIC COIL HOUSING RETAINER (3)

THERMOSTATIC COIL AND HOUSING ASSEMBLY

THERMOSTATIC COIL HOUSING ASSEMBLY

CHOKE PISTON LINK

SOLENOID MOUNTING BRACKET

IDLE SPEED ADJUSTMENT SCREW SPRING

IDLE SPEED ADJUSTMENT SCREW

CHOKE PISTON PIN

CHOKE PISTON AND PIN

FAST IDLE CAM RETAINER

FAST IDLE CAM COLLAR

THROTTLE SHAFT AND LEVER ASSEMBLY (DASHPOT INSTALLATION)

THROTTLE SHAFT AND LEVER ASSEMBLY (SOLENOID INSTALLATION)

*SUPPLIED IN 9510 CARBURETOR ASSEMBLY

SOLENOID MOUNTING BRACKET

IDLE MIXTURE ADJUSTMENT SCREW

IDLE MIXTURE ADJUSTMENT SCREW SPRING

SOLENOID MOUNTING BRACKET SUPPORT *

LIMITER CAP

CHOKE SHAFT

FAST IDLE CONNECTOR ROD

FAST IDLE CAM

CHOKE VALVE

CHOKE LEVER

ACCELERATOR PUMP CONNECTOR LINK CLIP

ACCELERATOR PUMP CONNECTOR LINK

THROTTLE PLATE

AIR CLEANER BRACKET

"C" RING WIRE SNAP RING

DIAPHRAGM COVER CONICAL WASHER

DIAPHRAGM COVER

DIAPHRAGM RETAINER

STEP-UP DIAPHRAGM SPRING

STEP-UP ROD AND DIAPHRAGM ASSEMBLY

45-DEGREE CONNECTOR

NEEDLE AND SEAT ASSEMBLY

MAIN BODY

CARBURETOR HOLD-DOWN NUT (2)

IDLE JET *

FLOAT AND LEVER ASSEMBLY

FLOAT LEVER PIN

FLOAT PIN ATTACHING SCREW (2)

FUEL BOWL GASKET

FUEL BOWL

FUEL BOWL ATTACHING SCREWS (4)

ACCELERATOR PUMP ARM RETURN SPRING

ACCELERATOR PUMP ARM RETAINER

ACCELERATOR PUMP ARM

SHIMS *

BUSHING

ACCELERATOR PUMP SPRING SEAT

ACCELERATOR PUMP DRIVING SPRING

ACCELERATOR PUMP PLUNGER

ACCELERATOR PUMP INTAKE DISK RETAINER

ACCELERATOR PUMP INTAKE DISK

ACCELERATOR PUMP COVER ASSEMBLY

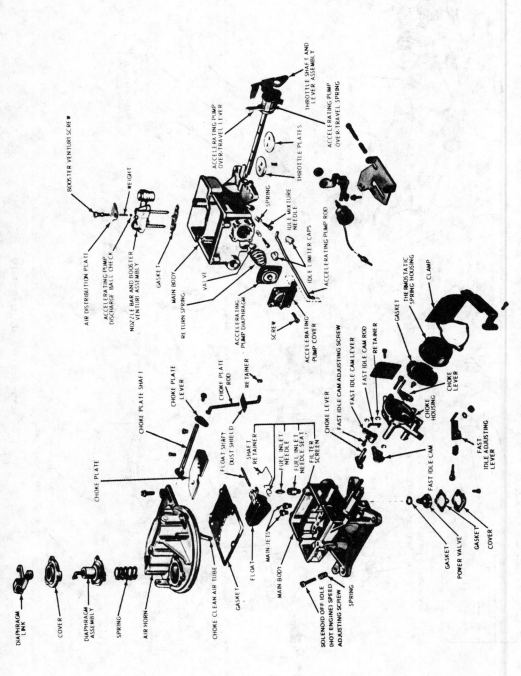

Exploded view—Autolite (Motorcraft) 2100-2V

Autolite (*Motorcraft*) 2100

1970–74

1. Remove the air cleaner.

2. With the engine at its normal operating temperature, loosen the choke thermostatic spring housing retaining screws, and set the housing 90° in the rich direction.

3. Disconnect and remove the choke heat tube from the choke housing.

4. Turn the fast idle adjusting screw outward one full turn.

5. Start the engine. Use a drill of the specified diameter to check the clearance between the lower edge of the choke plate and the air horn wall.

6. To adjust the clearance, turn the diaphragm stopscrew (located on the underside of the choke diaphragm housing). Turning clockwise will decrease the clearance; counterclockwise will increase it.

7. Connect the choke heat tube, and set the choke thermostatic spring housing to the proper specification. Adjust the fast idle speed to specifications.

Motorcraft 2150

1. Remove the air cleaner assembly.

2. Set the throttle on the top step of the fast idle cam.

3. Noting the position of the choke housing cap, loosen the retaining screws and rotate the cap 90 degrees in the rich (closing) direction.

4. Activate the pull-down motor by manually forcing the pull-down control diaphragm link in the direction of applied vacuum or by applying vacuum to the external vacuum tube.

5. Using a drill gauge of the specified diameter, measure the clearance between the choke plate and the center of the air horn wall nearest the fuel bowl.

6. To adjust, reset the diaphragm stop on the end of the choke pull-down diaphragm.

7. After adjusting, reset the choke housing cap to the specified notch. Check and reset fast idle speed, if necessary. Install the air cleaner.

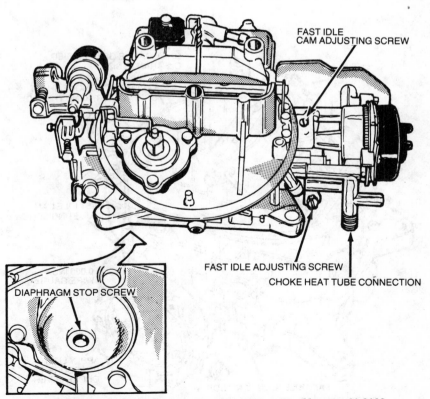

Adjusting choke plate pull down—1971-74 Autolite (Motorcraft) 2100

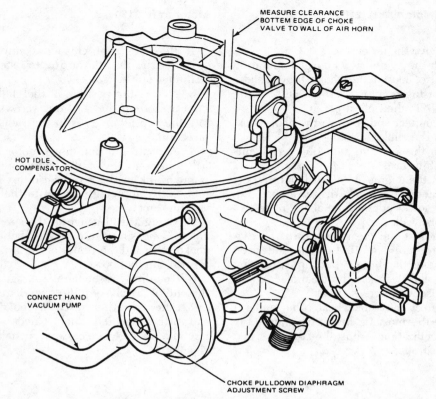

MEASURE CLEARANCE BOTTEM EDGE OF CHOKE VALVE TO WALL OF AIR HORN

HOT IDLE COMPENSATOR

CONNECT HAND VACUUM PUMP

CHOKE PULLDOWN DIAPHRAGM ADJUSTMENT SCREW

Adjusting the choke plate pulldown on the Motorcraft 2150

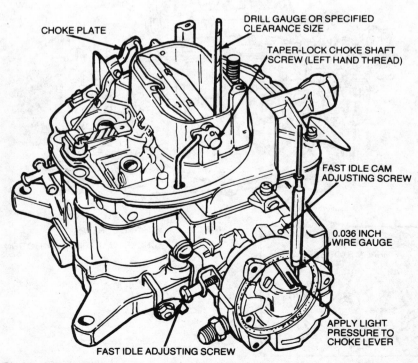

CHOKE PLATE

DRILL GAUGE OR SPECIFIED CLEARANCE SIZE

TAPER-LOCK CHOKE SHAFT SCREW (LEFT HAND THREAD)

FAST IDLE CAM ADJUSTING SCREW

0.036 INCH WIRE GAUGE

APPLY LIGHT PRESSURE TO CHOKE LEVER

FAST IDLE ADJUSTING SCREW

Choke plate pulldown and fast idle cam adjustment on the Motorcraft 4300, 4350

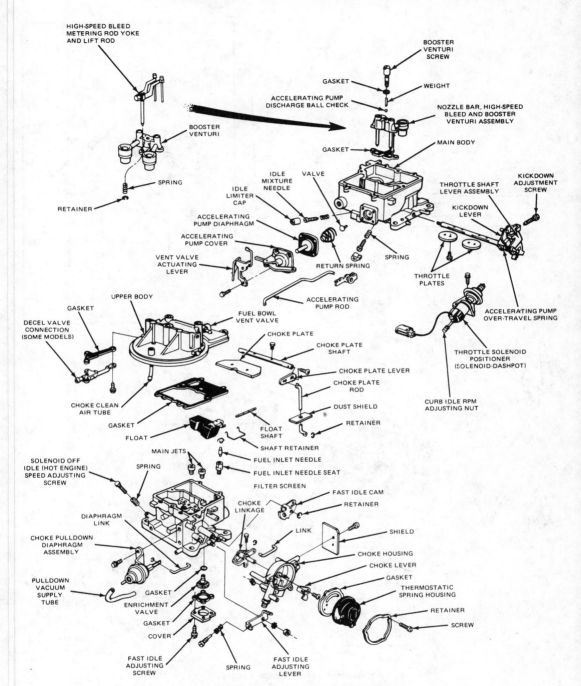

Exploded view—Motorcraft 2150-2V

Autolite (*Motorcraft*) 4300, 4350

1. Follow Steps 1–5 under "Autolite 1101."
2. To adjust, loosen the hex head screw (left-hand thread) on the choke plate shaft and pry the link away from the tapered shaft. Using a drill gauge 0.010 in. thinner than the specified clearance (to allow for tolerances in the linkage), insert the gauge between the lower edge of the choke plate and the air horn wall. Hold the choke plate against the gauge and maintain a light pressure in a counterclockwise direction on the choke lever. Then, with the choke piston snug against the 0.036 in. wire gauge and the choke plate against the 0.010 in. smaller drill gauge, tighten the hex

CHOKE PLATE SHAFT

AIR HORN

SCREW

SCREW

TUBE

CHOKE PLATE

SECONDARY THROTTLE CONTROL
VACUUM PICK-UP TUBE

FLOAT SHAFT

CHOKE PLATE ROD

SECONDARY FLOAT
FLOAT SHAFT

SPRING

PRIMARY
FLOAT

SPRING

WASHER

RETAINER

FUEL INLET
NEEDLE

GASKET

FUEL INLET NEEDLE

WASHER

INLET NEEDLE SEAT

GASKET

INLET NEEDLE
SEAT

GASKET

RETAINER

FILTER SCREEN

FILTER SCREEN

BOOSTER VENTURI SCREW

GASKET

WEIGHT

BOOSTER VENTURI SCREW

ACCELERATING PUMP
CHECK BALL DISCHARGE

SECONDARY NOZZLE BAR
AND BOOSTER VENTURI

PRIMARY NOZZLE BAR
AND BOOSTER VENTURI

DASHPOT

SCREW

GASKETS

HOT ENGINE IDLE
SPEED ADJUSTING
SCREW

NUT

GASKET

SPRING

PRIMARY THROTTLE
SHAFT AND LEVER
ASSEMBLY

BRACKET

ACCELERATING PUMP ROD

LEVER

ACCELERATING
PUMP COVER

ANTI-FRICTION
BEARING

RETAINER

RETAINER

PRIMARY JETS

SCREW

BAFFLES

SECONDARY
JETS

SPRING

ACCELERATING PUMP DIAPHRAGM

RETURN SPRING

PRIMARY
THROTTLE
PLATES

ACCELERATING PUMP
OVER-TRAVEL
LEVER

ELASTOMER VALVE

IDLE MIXTURE NEEDLE AND SPRING

SCREW

FAST IDLE CAM ROD

FAST IDLE CAM

RETAINER

AUTOMATIC CHOKE HOUSING SHAFT AND LEVER

SCREW

FAST IDLE CAM LEVER

GASKET

WASHER

SECONDARY
BALL
CHECK

MAIN BODY

SCREW

CHOKE HOUSING

★ SCREW

SECONDARY THROTTLE
PLATES

SCREW

PIN

CLAMP

RETURN
SPRING

RETAINER

FAST IDLE
ADJUSTING
LEVER

SCREW

COVER

SECONDARY
OPERATING ROD

FAST IDLE
ADJUSTING
SCREW

NUT

CHOKE PISTON
ASSEMBLY

GASKET

POWER VALVE

SECONDARY THROTTLE
SHAFT AND LEVER
ASSEMBLY

SCREW

SCREW

SECONDARY OPERATING
DIAPHRAGM

GASKET

SCREW

GASKET

COVER

CHOKE SHIELD

SCREW

SCREW

THERMOSTATIC SPRING HOUSING ASSY.

Exploded view—Autolite 4100-4V

MANUAL CHOKE LINKAGE

AIR HORN

SCREW

CHOKE PLATE
SHAFT

TUBE

CHOKE PLATE

SPRING

NUT

MAIN BODY

SWIVEL

CHOKE
PLATE ROD

FAST IDLE
CAM

WASHER

SCREW

RETAINER

CHOKE
BRACKET
ASSY.

RETAINER

WASHER

SECONDARY
THROTTLE
PLATES

SCREW

NUT

SECONDARY OPERATING ROD

SECONDARY THROTTLE SHAFT
AND LEVER ASSEMBLY

FAST IDLE
ADJUSTING
LEVER

FAST IDLE ADJUSTING SCREW

head screw (left-hand thread) on the choke plate shaft. After tightening the hex head screw, make a final check using a drill gauge of the specified clearance between the choke plate and air horn.

3. After adjustment, install the choke cover and adjust as outlined under "Automatic Choke Housing Adjustment." Install the air cleaner.

Holley 4150C

1. Remove the choke thermostatic housing cap.

2. Place the choke plate in the fully closed position by opening the throttle lever to about ⅓ throttle and pressing down on the front side of the choke plate. While holding the choke plate closed, release the throttle lever.

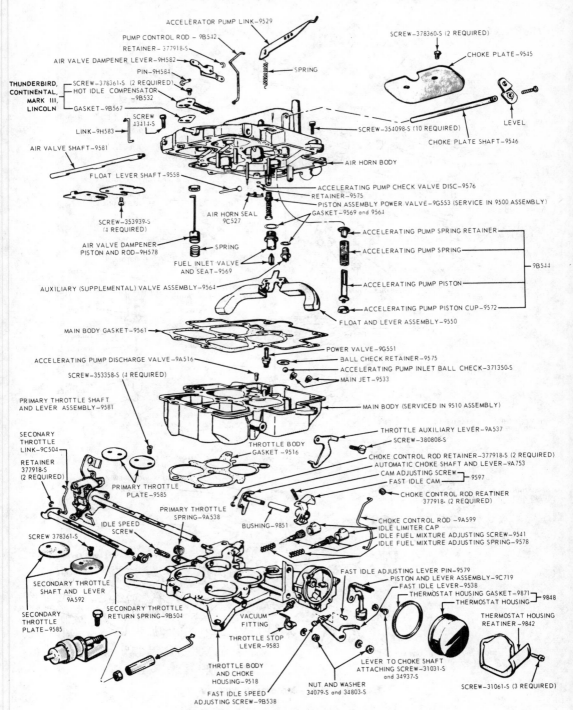

ACCELERATOR PUMP LINK—9529
PUMP CONTROL ROD — 9B542
RETAINER — 377918-S
AIR VALVE DAMPENER LEVER—9H582
PIN—9H584
SCREW—378361-S (2 REQUIRED)
HOT IDLE COMPENSATER —9B532
GASKET—9B567
SCREW 43414-S
LINK—9H583

THUNDERBIRD,
CONTINENTAL,
MARK III,
LINCOLN

SCREW—378360-S (2 REQUIRED)
CHOKE PLATE—9545
SPRING
LEVEL
SCREW—354098-S (10 REQUIRED)
CHOKE PLATE SHAFT—9546

AIR HORN BODY

AIR VALVE SHAFT—9581
FLOAT LEVER SHAFT—9558

ACCELERATING PUMP CHECK VALVE DISC—9576
RETAINER—9575
PISTON ASSEMBLY POWER VALVE—9G553 (SERVICE IN 9500 ASSEMBLY)
GASKET—9569 and 9564

SCREW—353939-S
(4 REQUIRED)

AIR HORN SEAL
9C527

AIR VALVE DAMPENER
PISTON AND ROD—9H578
SPRING
FUEL INLET VALVE
AND SEAT—9569

AUXILIARY (SUPPLEMENTAL) VALVE ASSEMBLY—9564

ACCELERATING PUMP SPRING RETAINER
ACCELERATING PUMP SPRING
9B544
ACCELERATING PUMP PISTON
ACCELERATING PUMP PISTON CUP—9572
FLOAT AND LEVER ASSEMBLY—9550

MAIN BODY GASKET—9561

ACCELERATING PUMP DISCHARGE VALVE—9A516
SCREW—353358-S (4 REQUIRED)

POWER VALVE—9G551
BALL CHECK RETAINER—9575
ACCELERATING PUMP INLET BALL CHECK—371350-S
MAIN JET—9533

PRIMARY THROTTLE SHAFT
AND LEVER ASSEMBLY—9581

MAIN BODY (SERVICED IN 9510 ASSEMBLY)

SECONARY
THROTTLE
LINK—9C504

RETAINER
377918-S
(2 REQUIRED)

PRIMARY THROTTLE
PLATE—9585

PRIMARY THROTTLE
SPRING—9A538

IDLE SPEED
SCREW

THROTTLE BODY
GASKET—9516

BUSHING—9851

THROTTLE AUXILIARY LEVER—9A537
SCREW—380808-S
CHOKE CONTROL ROD RETAINER—377918-S (2 REQUIRED)
AUTOMATIC CHOKE SHAFT AND LEVER—9A753
CAM ADJUSTING SCREW
FAST IDLE CAM
9597
CHOKE CONTROL ROD REATINER
377918- (2 REQUIRED)
CHOKE CONTROL ROD —9A599
IDLE LIMITER CAP
IDLE FUEL MIXTURE ADJUSTING SCREW—9541
IDLE FUEL MIXTURE ADJUSTING SPRING—9578

SCREW 378361-S

SECONDARY THROTTLE
SHAFT AND LEVER
9A592

SECONDARY
THROTTLE
PLATE—9585

SECONDARY THROTTLE
RETURN SPRING—9B504

VACUUM
FITTING

THROTTLE STOP
LEVER—9583

THROTTLE BODY
AND CHOKE
HOUSING—9518

FAST IDLE SPEED
ADJUSTING SCREW—9B538

NUT AND WASHER
34079-S and 34803-S

FAST IDLE ADJUSTING LEVER PIN—9579
PISTON AND LEVER ASSEMBLY—9C719
FAST IDLE LEVER—9538
THERMOSTAT HOUSING GASKET—9871
THERMOSTAT HOUSING
9848

THERMOSTAT HOUSING
REATINER—9842

LEVER TO CHOKE SHAFT
ATTACHING SCREW—31031-S
and 34937-S

SCREW—31061-S (3 REQUIRED)

Exploded view—Autolite (Motorcraft) 4300-4V

3. With the choke plate in the closed position, measure the distance between the flat of the fast idle cam and the choke housing mounting post. If adjustment is required, straighten or bend the choke rod until the desired clearance is obtained.

4. Bend a 0.036 in. wire at a 90° angle at approximately $^1/_{16}$–$^1/_8$ in. from one end. Insert the bent end between the lower edge of the piston slot and the upper edge of the slot in the choke housing. Open the throttle lever to approximately $^1/_3$ throttle and rotate the

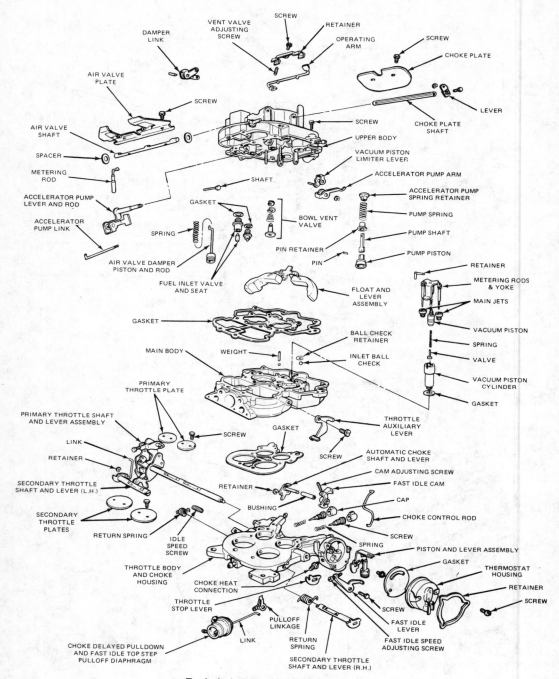

Exploded view—Motorcraft 4350-4V

choke lever counterclockwise so that the bent end of the wire is held in the housing slot by the piston slot with light pressure applied to the choke lever. Measure the distance between the air horn wall and the lower edge of the choke plate. If the clearance does not meet specifications, bend the adjusting tab on the choke lever to obtain the specified clearance.

5. Install the choke thermostatic housing. Be sure that the bimetallic loop is installed around the choke lever. Set the cap notch to specifications.

Holley 1946

NOTE: *On these carburetors, this adjustment is preset at the factory and protected by a tamper-proof plug.*

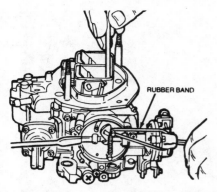

Motorcraft 5200 choke plate pulldown adjustment

Motorcraft 5200

1. Remove the choke thermostatic spring cover.

2. Pull the coolant cover and the thermostatic spring cover assembly, or electric assist assembly out of the way.

3. Set the fast idle cam on the second step.

4. Push the diaphragm stem against its top and insert the specified gauge between the wall and the lower edge of the choke plate.

5. Apply sufficient pressure against the upper edge of the choke plate to take up any slack in the linkage.

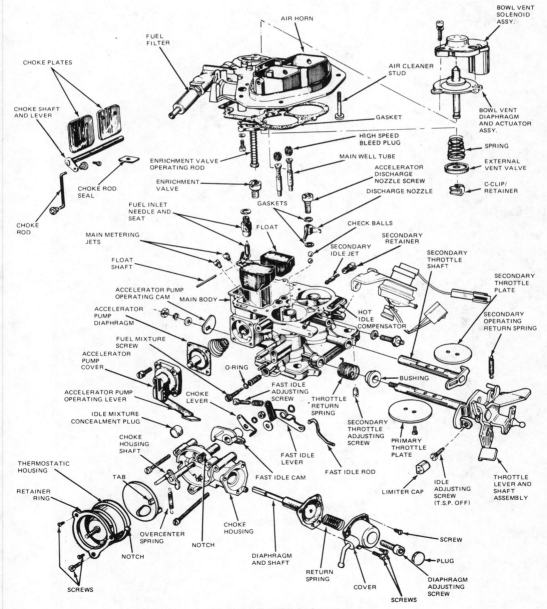

Motorcraft 5200 carburetor

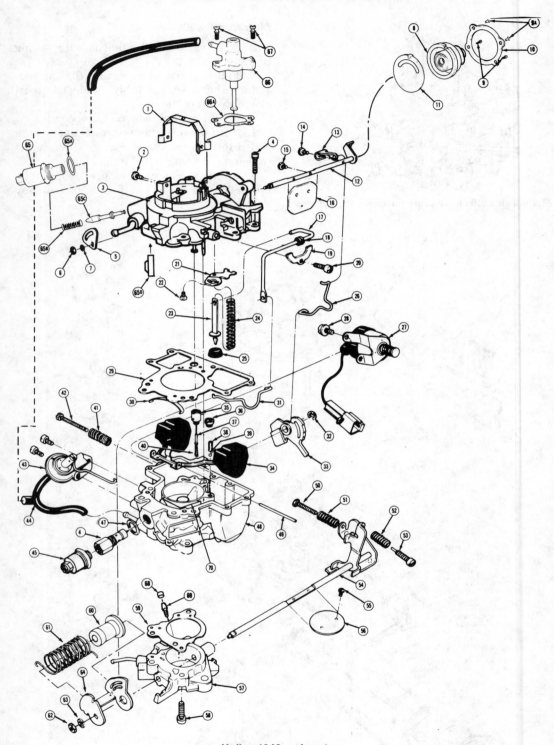

Holley 1946 carburetor

6. Turn the adjusting screw in or out to get the proper clearance.

FLOAT LEVEL ADJUSTMENT

Carter RBS

1. Remove the fuel bowl and its gasket.

2. Invert the main body of the carburetor, so that the float assembly is pressing against the inlet needle and seat. Measure the vertical distance from the main body casting surface for the fuel bowl to the raised tips formed on the outer ends of the float.

3. Measure for the specified setting at both ends of the float. If it is necessary to equalize the measurement, hold the float lever securely with needle-nose pliers at the narrow portion, and twist the float as required. While holding the float lever, adjust the float to the specified setting, while holding the tab of the float lever away from the inlet needle.

4. Replace the gasket and fuel bowl. In-

stall the carburetor if no further adjustments are required.

Autolite (Motorcraft) 2100, 2150

DRY ADJUSTMENT

This preliminary setting of the float level adjustment must be done with the carburetor removed from the engine.

1. Remove the air horn and see that the float is raised and the fuel inlet needle is seated. Check the distance between the top surface of the main body (with the gasket removed) and the top surface of the float. Depress the float tab to seat the fuel inlet needle. Take a measurement near the center of the float, at a point $\frac{1}{8}$ in. from the free end. If you are using a prefabricated float gauge, place the gauge in the corner of the enlarged end section of the fuel bowl. The gauge should touch the float near the end, but not on the end radius.

2. If necessary, bend the tab on the end of

1. Air cleaner bracket (1)
2. Air cleaner bracket screw (2)
3. Air horn
4. Screw and washer (8)
5. Choke pulldown lever
6. Choke shaft nut
7. Lockwasher (1)
8. Choke bimetal assembly
9. Screw (2)
9A. Rivet (2)
10. Choke cover retainer
11. Choke thermostatic housing locating disc
12. Choke shaft and lever assembly
13. Choke control lever
14. Screw (1)
15. Screw (1)
16. Choke plate
17. Accelerator pump operating rod
18. Accelerator pump rod grommet
19. Rod retaining clamp
20. Screw (1)
21. Accelerator pump spring retaining plate
22. Screw (1)
23. Accelerator pump piston stem
24. Accelerator pump spring
25. Accelerator pump piston cup
26. Fast idle cam link
27. Anti-diesel solenoid
28. Screw (2)
29. Air horn gasket
30. Float-hinge retainer
31. Accelerator pump operating link
32. Retaining clip (fast idle cam)
33. Fast idle cam
34. Float assembly
35. Power valve body
36. Main metering jet
37. Power valve pin
38. Accelerator pump weight

39. Accelerator pump check ball
40. Power valve spring
41. Spring
42. Low idle (solenoid off) adjusting screw
43. Choke pulldown diaphragm assembly
44. Choke diaphragm vacuum hose
45. Fuel filter
46. Fuel inlet needle & seat assembly
47. Gasket
48. Main body assembly
49. Float hinge pin
50. Curb idle adjusting screw
51. Spring
52. Spring
53. Fast idle adjusting screw
54. Throttle shaft & Lever assembly
55. Screw (2)
56. Throttle plate
57. Throttle body assembly
58. Throttle body screw (3)
59. Throttle body gasket
60. Throttle return spring bushing
61. Throttle return spring
62. Nut
63. Lock washer
64. Throttle return spring bracket
65. Bowl vent solenoid
65A. Washer
65B. Spring
65C. Pintle
65D. Seal
66. Power valve piston assembly
66A. Gasket
67. Screw (2)
68. Idle mixture
69. Concealment plug
      idle mixture needle
70. Fuel bowl filler

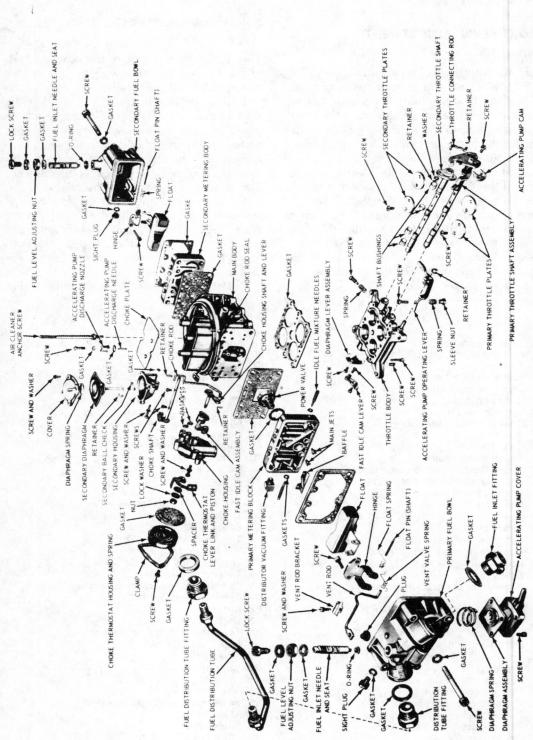

Exploded view—Holley 4150C

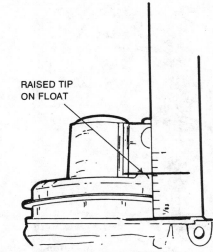

Checking float level—Carter RBS

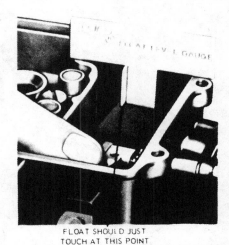

FLOAT SHOULD JUST
TOUCH AT THIS POINT

Dry float level check—Autolite (Motorcraft) 2100, 2150

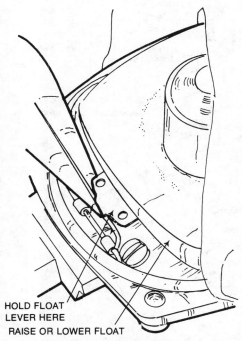

HOLD FLOAT
LEVER HERE

RAISE OR LOWER FLOAT

Adjusting float level—Carter RBS

the float to bring the setting within the specified limits.

WET ADJUSTMENT

1. Bring the engine to its normal operating temperature, park the car on as nearly level a surface as possible, and stop the engine.

2. Remove the air cleaner assembly from the carburetor.

3. Remove the air horn retaining screws and the carburetor identification tag. Leave

the air horn and gasket in position on the carburetor main body. Start the engine, let it idle for several minutes, rotate the air horn out of the way, and remove the gasket to provide access to the float assembly.

4. With the engine idling, use a standard depth scale to measure the vertical distance from the top machined surface of the carburetor main body to the level of the fuel in the fuel bowl. This measurement must be made at least ¼ in. away from any vertical surface in order to assure an accurate reading.

5. Stop the engine before making any adjustment to the float level. Adjustment is accomplished by bending the float tab (with contacts the fuel inlet valve) up or down as required to raise or lower the fuel level. After making an adjustment, start the engine, and allow it to idle for several minutes before repeating the fuel level check. Repeat as necessary until the proper fuel level is attained.

6. Reinstall the air horn with a new gasket and secure it with the screws. Include the installation of the identification tag in its proper location.

7. Check the idle speed, fuel mixture, and dashpot adjustments. Install the air cleaner assembly.

Autolite (Motorcraft) 4300, 4350

1. Refer to the illustration for details of construction of a tool for checking the parallel setting of the dual pontoons.

2. Install the gauge on the carburetor and set it to the specified height.

3. Check the clearance and alignment of the pontoons to the gauge. Both pontoons

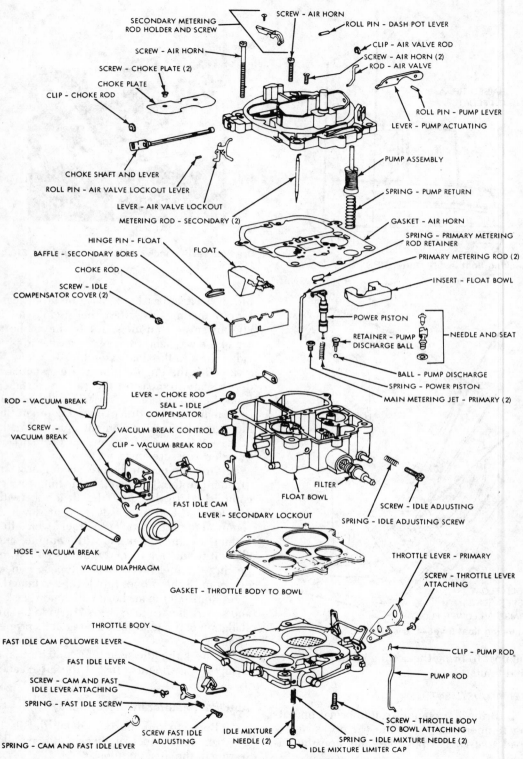

Exploded view—Rochester Quadrajet 4MV-4V

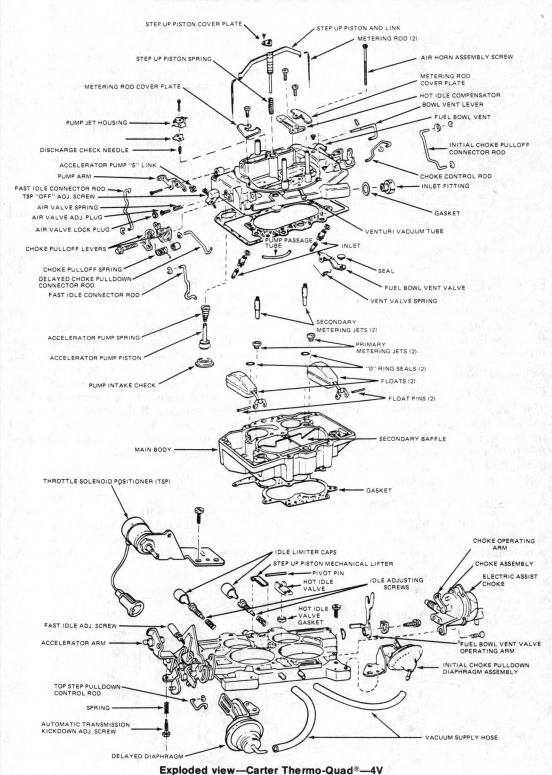

STEP UP PISTON COVER PLATE

STEP UP PISTON AND LINK

METERING ROD (2)

STEP UP PISTON SPRING

AIR HORN ASSEMBLY SCREW

METERING ROD COVER PLATE

METERING ROD COVER PLATE

HOT IDLE COMPENSATOR

BOWL VENT LEVER

FUEL BOWL VENT

PUMP JET HOUSING

INITIAL CHOKE PULLOFF CONNECTOR ROD

DISCHARGE CHECK NEEDLE

CHOKE CONTROL ROD

ACCELERATOR PUMP "S" LINK

PUMP ARM

INLET FITTING

FAST IDLE CONNECTOR ROD

TSP "OFF" ADJ. SCREW

AIR VALVE SPRING

GASKET

AIR VALVE ADJ. PLUG

AIR VALVE LOCK PLUG

VENTURI VACUUM TUBE

CHOKE PULLOFF LEVERS

PUMP PASSAGE TUBE

INLET

CHOKE PULLOFF SPRING

SEAL

DELAYED CHOKE PULLDOWN CONNECTOR ROD

FUEL BOWL VENT VALVE

FAST IDLE CONNECTOR ROD

VENT VALVE SPRING

SECONDARY METERING JETS (2)

ACCELERATOR PUMP SPRING

PRIMARY METERING JETS (2)

ACCELERATOR PUMP PISTON

"O" RING SEALS (2)

FLOATS (2)

PUMP INTAKE CHECK

FLOAT PINS (2)

SECONDARY BAFFLE

MAIN BODY

THROTTLE SOLENOID POSITIONER (TSP)

GASKET

IDLE LIMITER CAPS

CHOKE OPERATING ARM

STEP UP PISTON MECHANICAL LIFTER

CHOKE ASSEMBLY

PIVOT PIN

ELECTRIC ASSIST CHOKE

HOT IDLE VALVE

IDLE ADJUSTING SCREWS

HOT IDLE VALVE GASKET

FAST IDLE ADJ. SCREW

ACCELERATOR ARM

FUEL BOWL VENT VALVE OPERATING ARM

INITIAL CHOKE PULLDOWN DIAPHRAGM ASSEMBLY

TOP STEP PULLDOWN CONTROL ROD

SPRING

AUTOMATIC TRANSMISSION KICKDOWN ADJ. SCREW

DELAYED DIAPHRAGM

VACUUM SUPPLY HOSE

Exploded view—Carter Thermo-Quad®—4V

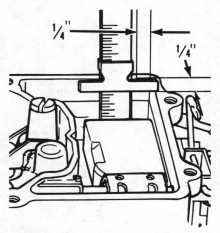

Motorcraft 2100, 2150 wet fuel level adjustment

should just barely touch the gauge for the proper setting. Pontoons may be aligned if necessary by slightly twisting them.

4. To adjust the float level, bend the primary needle tab down to raise the float and up to lower it.

Holley 4150C

FUEL FLOAT LEVEL ADJUSTMENT—DRY

This preliminary adjustment—which is accomplished with the carburetor removed from the car—is performed by simply inverting the fuel bowl and checking to see that the center of the float is an equal distance from the top and bottom of the fuel bowl.

FUEL FLOAT LEVEL ADJUSTMENT—WET

1. Position the vehicle on a level floor, be sure that the fuel pump pressure is within specifications, and operate the engine until

normal operating temperature has been reached.

2. Check the fuel level in each fuel bowl separately. Place a suitable container below the fuel level sight plug to catch any fuel spillover. Remove the fuel level sight plug and gasket, and check the fuel level. The fuel level within the bowl should be at the lower edge of the sight plug opening $1/16$ in.

3. If the fuel level is satisfactory, install the sight plug. Do not install the air cleaner at this time.

4. If the fuel level is too high, stop the engine, install the sight plug, drain the fuel bowl, refill it, and check it again before altering the float setting. This will eliminate the possibility that dirt or foreign matter caused a temporary flooding condition. To drain the fuel bowl, loosen one lower retaining bolt from the fuel bowl and drain the fuel into a suitable container. Install the bolt and the fuel lever sight plug, and start the engine to fill the fuel bowl. After the fuel level has stabilized, stop the engine and check the fuel level.

If the fuel level is too high, it should be first lowered below specifications and then raised until it is just at the lower edge of the sight plug opening. If the level was too low, it is necessary only to raise it to the specified level. If either is necessary, refer to the procedures for either adjustment.

TO LOWER FUEL LEVEL

1. With the engine stopped, loosen the lockscrew on top of the fuel bowl just enough to allow rotation of the adjusting nut underneath. Do not loosen the lockscrew or attempt to adjust the fuel level with the sight

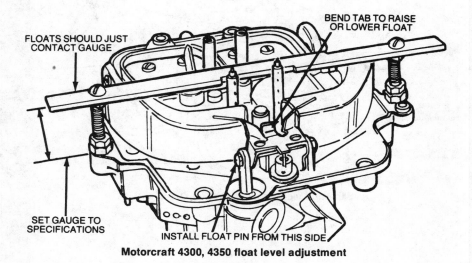

Motorcraft 4300, 4350 float level adjustment

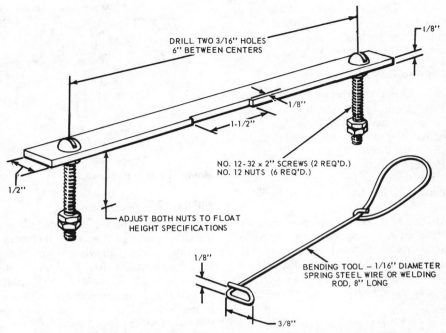

DRILL TWO 3/16" HOLES
6" BETWEEN CENTERS

1/8"

1/8"

1-1/2"

1/2"

NO. 12-32 x 2" SCREWS (2 REQ'D.)
NO. 12 NUTS (6 REQ'D.)

ADJUST BOTH NUTS TO FLOAT
HEIGHT SPECIFICATIONS

1/8"

BENDING TOOL — 1/16" DIAMETER
SPRING STEEL WIRE OR WELDING
ROD, 8" LONG

3/8"

Float gauge and bending tool details—Autolite (Motorcraft) 4300, 4350

plug removed and the engine running because the pressure in the line will spray fuel out and present a fire hazard.

2. Turn the adjusting nut approximately ½ turn in to lower the fuel level below specifications (⅙ turn of the adjusting nut, depending on direction of rotation, will raise or lower the float assembly at the fuel level sight plug opening ³/₆₄ in.).

3. Tighten the lockscrew and reinstall the fuel level sight plug. Start the engine. After the fuel level has stabilized, stop the engine and check the fuel level at the sight plug opening. The fuel level should be below

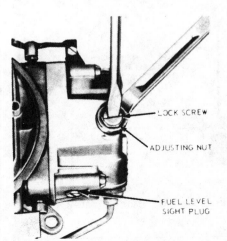

LOCK SCREW

ADJUSTING NUT

FUEL LEVEL
SIGHT PLUG

Wet float level adjustment—Holley 4150C

specified limits. If it is not, repeat the previous steps, turning the adjusting nut an additional amount sufficient to lower the fuel below the specified level.

4. Loosen the lockscrew and turn the adjusting nut out in increments of ⅙ turn or less until the correct fuel level is achieved. After each adjustment, tighten the lockscrew, install the fuel level sight plug, and then start the engine and stabilize the fuel level. Check the fuel level at the sight plug opening. Install the sight plug and gasket.

5. Check the idle fuel mixture and idle speed adjustments. Adjust the carburetor as required.

TO RAISE FUEL LEVEL

Perform Steps 1, 4, and 5 under the procedure "To Lower Fuel Level."

Rochester Quadrajet 4MV

1. Remove the air horn assembly.

2. With an adjustable T-scale, measure the distance from the top of the float bowl surface (gasket removed) to the top of the float at the toe (locate gauging point ¹/₁₆ in. back from the toe on the float surface). Do not gauge on top of part number.

When checking the adjustment, make sure the float hinge pin is firmly seated and the float arm is held down against the float needle so that it is seated.

3. To adjust, bend the float pontoon up or down at the point shown in the illustration.

4. Install a new air horn gasket on the float bowl, then install the air horn.

Carter Thermo-Quad®

1. Taking note of their placement, disconnect all linkages and rods which connect the bowl cover to the carburetor body.

2. Remove the 10 screws retaining the bowl cover to the body.

3. Using legs to protect the throttle valves, remove the bowl cover. Invert the bowl cover, taking care not to lose any of the small parts.

4. With the bowl cover inverted and the floats resting on the seated needle, measure the distance between the bowl cover (new gasket installed) to the bottom side of each float.

5. If not to specifications, bend the float lever to suit.

NOTE: *Never allow the lip of the float to be pressed against the needle when adjusting the float height.*

6. Reverse Steps 1–3 to install. Make sure that the float pin does not protrude past the edge of the bowl cover.

Motorcraft 5200

1. Remove the float bowl cover and hold it upside down.

2. With the float tang resting lightly on the spring loaded fuel inlet needle, measure the clearance between the edge of the float and the bowl cover.

3. To adjust the float, bend the float tang. Make sure that both floats are adjusted equally.

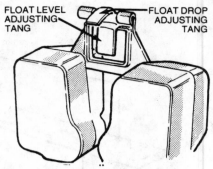

Motorcraft 5200 float adjustment

Holley 1946

1. Remove the air horn and place a finger over the hinge pin retainer and catch the accelerator pump ball when it falls out.

2. Lay a ruler across the housing under the floats. The lowest point of the floats should be just touching the ruler for all except California models. For California models, the ruler should just contact the heel (raised step) of the float.

3. Bend the tang of the float to adjust.

DECHOKE CLEARANCE ADJUSTMENT
Carter RBS

1. Remove the carburetor air cleaner.

2. Hold the throttle plate to the full open position while closing the choke plate as far as possible without forcing it. Use a drill of the proper diameter (see 'Carburetor Specifications" chart) to check the clearance between the choke plate and air horn.

3. Adjust as necessary by bending the tang on the throttle lever.

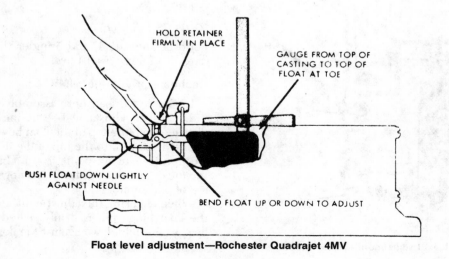

Float level adjustment—Rochester Quadrajet 4MV

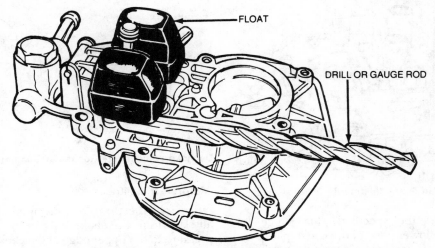

Measuring float clearance on the Motorcraft 5200

FLOAT

DRILL OR GAUGE ROD

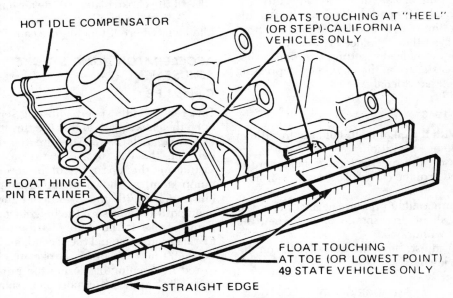

Holley 1946 float clearance adjustment

HOT IDLE COMPENSATOR

FLOATS TOUCHING AT "HEEL" (OR STEP)-CALIFORNIA VEHICLES ONLY

FLOAT HINGE PIN RETAINER

FLOAT TOUCHING AT TOE (OR LOWEST POINT) 49 STATE VEHICLES ONLY

STRAIGHT EDGE

Autolite (Motorcraft) 4300, 4350

1. Remove the air clearner assembly.
2. Remove the automatic choke spring housing from the carburetor.
3. With the throttle plate wide open and the choke plate closed as far as possible without forcing it, insert a drill gauge of the specified diameter between the choke plate and air horn.
4. To adjust, bend the arm on the choke trip lever. Bend downward to increase clearance and upward to decrease clearance. After adjusting, recheck the clearance.
5. Install the automatic choke housing, taking care to engage the thermostatic spring with the tang on the choke lever and shaft assembly.
6. Adjust the automatic choke setting. Install the air cleaner. Adjust the idle speed and dashpot, if so equipped.

Rochester Quadrajet 4MV

1. Hold the choke plate in the closed position. This can be done by attaching a rubber band or spring to the vacuum break lever and a stationary part of the carburetor.
2. Open the primary throttle plates to the wide open position.

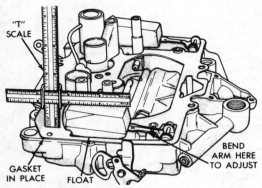

ThermoQuad float adjustment

Dechoke adjustment—Rochester Quadrajet 4MV

3. Insert the specified plug gauge between the lower edge of the choke plates and inside the air horn wall. The choke rod should be in bottom of slot when checking setting.

4. To adjust, bend the tang on the fast idle lever to the rear to increase and to the front to decrease the clearance. It is advisable to recheck the unloader setting after the carburetor is installed on the engine by depressing the accelerator pedal.

Holley 1946

1. With the engine off, hold the throttle in the wide open position.

2. Insert the specified gauge between the upper edge of the choke plate and the air horn wall.

3. With a slight pressure against the choke shaft, a slight drag should be felt when the gauge is withdrawn.

4. To adjust, bend the unloader tab on the throttle lever.

Motorcraft 5200

1. Hold the throttle wide open. Remove all slack from the choke linkage by applying pressure to the upper edge of the choke plate.

2. Measure the distance between the lower edge of the choke plate and the air horn wall.

3. Adjust by bending the tab on the fast idle lever where it touches the cam.

ACCELERATOR PUMP STROKE ADJUSTMENT

Carter RBS

Unscrew the idle speed adjusting screw and open the choke plate so that the throttle plate is seated in its bore. Measure the distance between the flat surface of the main body casting and the top surface of the accelerating pump stem, as shown in the accompanying illustration. With the throttle in the wide-open position, measure the height again. The pump stroke is the difference between the first measurement and the second, and should be 0.400 in. The pump stroke may be adjusted by opening or closing the pump connector link at the offset portion as shown.

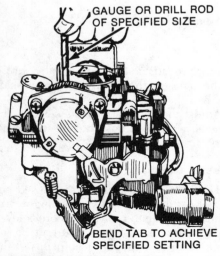

Holley 1946 dechoke adjustment

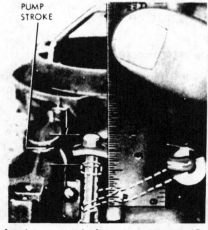

Accelerator pump stroke measurement—Carter RBS

Autolite (*Motorcraft*) 2100, 2150

In order to keep the exhaust emission level of the engine within the specified limits, the accelerating pump stroke has been preset at the factory. The additional holes are provided for differing engine-transmission-body applications only. The primary throttle shaft lever (overtravel lever) has four holes and the accelerating pump link two holes to control the pump stroke. The accelerating pump operating rod should be in the overtravel lever hole number listed in the "Carburetor Specifications" chart, and in the inboard hole (hole closest to the pump plunger) in the accelerating pump link. If the pump stroke has been changed from the specified settings, use the following procedure to correct the stroke.

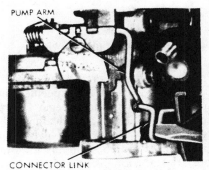

Adjusting accelerator pump stroke—Carter RBS

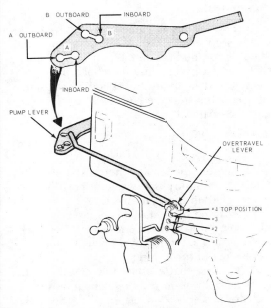

Accelerator pump stroke adjustment—Autolite (Motorcraft) 2100, 2150

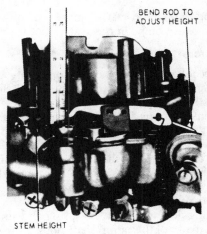

Accelerator pump stroke and piston stem height—Autolite (Motorcraft) 4300

1. Release the operating rod from the retaining clip by pressing the tab end of the clip toward the rod while pressing the rod away from the clip until it disengages.

2. Position the clip over the specified hole (see "Carburetor Specifications" chart) in the overtravel lever. Press the ends of the clip together and insert the operating rod through the clip and the overtravel lever. Release the clip to engage the rod.

Autolite (Motorcraft) 4300

The pump stroke is preset at the factory to limit exhaust emissions. The additional holes in the operating arm are provided for different engine applications. The stroke should not be changed from the specified hole (see "Carburetor Specifications" chart).

The only adjustments possible are the pump stroke and pump stem height. To change the pump stroke, merely remove the pivot pin and reposition it in the specified hole. To adjust the pump stem height, bend

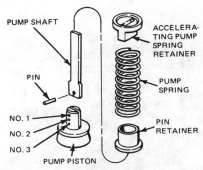

Accelerator pump stroke adjustment—Motorcraft 4350

the operating rod at the angles, taking care not to cause binds in the system.

Motorcraft 4350

The accelerator pump adjustment is preset at the factory for reduced exhaust emissions. Adjustment is provided only for different engine installations. The adjustment is internal, with three piston-to-shaft pin positions in the pump piston.

To check that the shaft pin is located in the specified piston hole, remove the carburetor air horn and invert it. Disconnect the accelerator pump from the operating arm by pressing downward on the spring and sliding the arm out of the pump shaft slot. Disassemble the spring and nylon keeper retaining the adjustment pin. If the pin is not in its specified hole, remove it, reposition the shaft to the correct hole in the piston assembly and reinstall the pin. Then, slide the nylon retainer over the pin and position the spring on the shaft. Finally, compress the spring on the shaft and install the pump on the pump arm.

NOTE: *Under no circumstances should you adjust the stroke of the accelerator pump by turning the vacuum limiter lever adjusting nut. This adjustment is preset at the factory and modification could result in poor cold driveability.*

ANTI-STALL DASHPOT ADJUSTMENT

All Carburetors Except Rochester Quadrajet

Having made sure that the engine idle speed and mixture are correct and that the engine is at normal operating temperature, loosen the anti-stall dashpot locking nut (see accompanying illustration). With the throttle held closed, depress the plunger with a screwdriver blade and measure the clearance be-

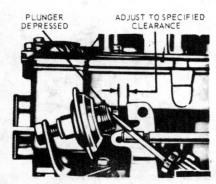

PLUNGER DEPRESSED   ADJUST TO SPECIFIED CLEARANCE

Typical anti-stall dashpot adjustment

DASHPOT ADJUSTING SCREW

ADJUST THROTTLE TO HOT IDLE POSITION PRIOR TO ADJUSTING DASHPOT

Anti-stall dashpot adjustment—Autolite 1100

tween the throttle lever and the plunger tip. If the clearance is not as specified in the "Carburetor Specifications" chart, turn the dashpot until the proper clearance is obtained between the throttle lever and the plunger tip. After tightening the locking nut, recheck the adjustment.

FAST IDLE CAM INDEX SETTING

Carter RBS

1. Position the fast idle screw on the kickdown step of the fast idle cam against the shoulder of the high step.

2. Adjust by bending the choke plate connecting rod to obtain the specified clearance between the lower edge of the choke plate and the carburetor bore.

Autolite 2100

1971–72

1. Loosen the choke thermostatic spring housing retaining screws and position the housing 90° in the rich direction.

2. Position the fast idle speed screw at the kick-down step of the fast idle cam. This kick-down step is identified by a small "V" stamped in the side of the casting.

3. Be sure that the fast idle cam is in the kick-down position while checking or adjusting the fast idle cam clearance. Check the clearance between the lower edge of the choke plate and the wall of the air horn by

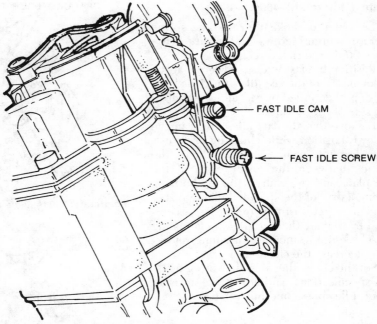

Fast idle cam index setting—Carter RBS

inserting a drill of the specified diameter between them. Adjustment may be accomplished by turning the fast idle cam adjusting screw clockwise to increase or counterclockwise to decrease the clearance.

4. Set the choke thermostatic spring housing to specifications, and adjust the antistall dashpot, idle speed, and fuel mixture.

Motorcraft 2100, 2150

1973–75

1. Loosen the choke thermostatic spring housing retaining screws and rotate the housing 90° in the rich direction.

2. Position the fast idle speed screw or lever on the high step of the cam.

3. Depress the choke pull-down diaphragm against the diaphragm stop screw thereby placing the choke in the pull-down position.

4. While holding the choke pull-down diaphragm depressed, slightly open the throttle and allow the fast idle cam to fall.

5. Close the throttle and check the position of the fast idle cam or lever. When the fast idle cam is adjusted correctly, the screw should contact the "V" mark on the cam. Adjustment is accomplished by rotating the fast idle cam adjusting screw as needed.

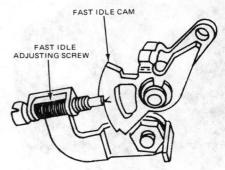

CONVENTIONAL ONE-PIECE FAST IDLE LEVER

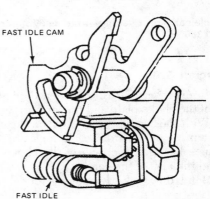

TWO-PIECE FAST IDLE LEVER
FOR 351-C AND 400 ENGINES

Fast idle cam index setting—Autolite (Motorcraft) 2100

Autolite (Motorcraft) 4300, 4350

1. Loosen the choke thermostatic spring housing retaining screws and position the housing 90° in the rich direction.

2. Position the fast idle speed screw at the kick-down step of the fast idle cam. This kick-down step is identified by a small "V" stamped in the side of the casting.

3. Be sure that the fast idle cam is in the kick-down position while checking or adjusting the fast idle cam clearance. Check the clearance between the lower edge of the choke plate and the wall of the air horn by inserting a drill of the specified diameter between them. Adjustment may be accomplished by turning the fast idle cam adjusting screw clockwise to increase or counterclockwise to decrease the clearance.

4. Set the choke thermostatic spring housing to specifications, and adjust the antistall dashpot, idle speed, and fuel mixture.

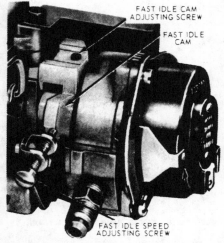

Fast idle cam index setting—Autolite (Motorcraft) 4300, 4350

Motorcraft 5200

1. Insert a $5/32$ in. drill between the lower edge of the choke plate and the air horn wall.

2. With the fast idle screw held on the second step of the fast idle cam, measure the clearance between the tang of the choke lever and the arm of the cam.

3. Bend the choke lever tang for adjustment.

Holley 1946

1. Position the fast idle adjusting screw on the second step of the fast idle cam.

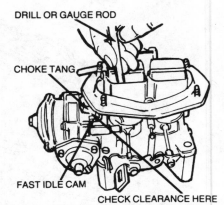

Motorcraft 5200 fast idle cam adjustment

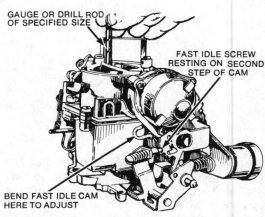

Holley 1946 fast idle cam position adjustment

2. Lightly move the choke plate towards the closed position.

3. Check the fast idle cam setting by placing the specified gauge between the upper edge of the choke plate and the air horn wall.

4. Bend the fast idle cam link to adjust.

AIR VALVE DASHPOT ADJUSTMENT

Rochester Quadrajet 4MV

1. Seat the vacuum break diaphragm, using an outside vacuum source.

2. With the air valve completely closed and the diaphragm seated, measure the clearance between the air valve dashpot rod and the air valve lever.

3. The dimension should be $1/32$ in. If not, bend the rod at the air valve end to adjust.

THROTTLE AND DOWNSHIFT LINKAGE ADJUSTMENT

Manual Transmission

Throttle linkage adjustments are not normally required, unless the carburetor or link-

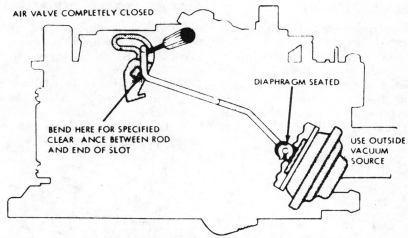

AIR VALVE COMPLETELY CLOSED

DIAPHRAGM SEATED

BEND HERE FOR SPECIFIED
CLEAR ANCE BETWEEN ROD
AND END OF SLOT

USE OUTSIDE
VACUUM
SOURCE

Air valve dashpot adjustment—Rochester Quadrajet 4MV

age have been removed from the car or otherwise disturbed. In all cases, the car is first brought to operating temperature, with the choke open and off the fast idle cam. The idle speed is then set to specifications (see Chapter 2).

Motorcraft 2700 VV and 7200 VV
DESIGN

Since the design of the 2700 VV (variable venturi) carburetor differs considerably from the other carburetors in the Ford lineup, an explanation in the theory and operation is presented here.

In exterior appearance, the variable venturi carburetor is similar to conventional carburetors and, like a conventional carburetor, it uses a normal float and fuel bowl system. However, the similarity ends there. In place of a normal choke plate and fixed area venturis, the 2700 VV carburetor has a pair of small oblong castings in the top of the upper carburetor body where you would normally expect to see the choke plate. These castings slide back and forth across the top of the carburetor in response to fuel-air demands. Their movement is controlled by a spring-loaded diaphragm valve regulated by a vacuum signal taken below the venturis in the throttle bores. As the throttle is opened, the strength of the vacuum signal increases, opening the venturis and allowing more air to enter the carburetor.

Fuel is admitted into the venturi area by means of tapered metering rods that fit into the main jets. These rods are attached to the venturis, and, as the venturis open or close in response to air demand, the fuel needed to maintain the proper mixture increases or decreases as the metering rods slide in the jets. In comparison to a conventional carburetor with fixed venturis and a variable air supply, this system provides much more precise control of the fuel-air supply during all modes of operation. Because of the variable venturi principle, there are fewer fuel metering systems and fuel passages. The only auxiliary fuel metering systems required are an idle trim, accelerator pump (similar to a conventional carburetor), starting enrichment, and cold running enrichment.

NOTE: *Adjustment, assembly and disassembly of this carburetor require special tools for some of the operations. These tools are available (see the Tools and Equipment Section). Do not attempt any operations on this carburetor without first checking to see if you need the special tools for that particular operation. The adjustment and repair procedures given here mention when and if you will need the special tools.*

The Motorcraft model 7200 variable venturi (VV) carburetor shares most of its design features with the model 2700 VV. The major difference between the two is that the 7200 is designed to work with Ford's EEC (electronic engine control) feedback system. The feedback system precisely controls the air/fuel ratio by varying signals to the feedback control monitor located on the carburetor, which opens or closes the metering valve in response. This expands or reduces the amount of control vacuum above the fuel bowl, leaning or richening the mixture accordingly.

FLOAT LEVEL ADJUSTMENT

1. Remove and invert the upper part of the carburetor, with the gasket in place.

2. Measure the vertical distance between the carburetor body, outside the gasket, and the bottom of the float.

3. To adjust, bend the float operating lever that contacts the needle valve. Make sure that the float remains parallel to the gasket surface.

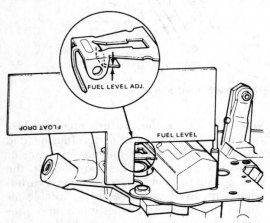

2700VV float adjustment

FLOAT DROP ADJUSTMENT

1. Remove and hold upright the upper part of the carburetor.

2. Measure the vertical distance between the carburetor body, outside the gasket, and the bottom of the float.

3. Adjust by bending the stop tab on the float lever that contacts the hinge pin.

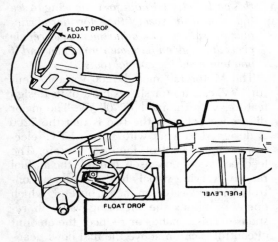

2700 VV float drop adjustment

FAST IDLE SPEED ADJUSTMENT

1. With the engine warmed up and idling, place the fast idle lever on the step of the fast idle cam specified on the engine compartment sticker or in the specifications chart. Disconnect and plug the EGR vacuum line.

2. Make sure the high speed cam positioner lever is disengaged.

3. Turn the fast idle speed screw to adjust to the specified speed.

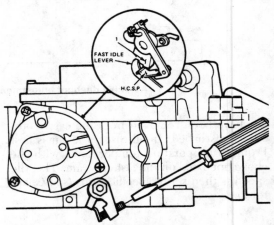

2700 VV fast idle speed adjustment

FAST IDLE CAM ADJUSTMENT

You will need a special tool for this job; Ford calls it a stator cap (#T77L-9848-A). It fits over the choke thermostatic lever when the choke cap is removed.

1. Remove the choke coil cap. On 1980 and later California models, the choke cap is riveted in place. The top rivets will have to be drilled out; the bottom rivet will have to be driven out from the rear. New rivets must be used upon installation.

2. Place the fast idle lever in the corner of the specified step of the fast idle cam (the highest step is first) with the high speed cam positioner retracted.

3. If the adjustment is being made with the carburetor removed, hold the throttle lightly closed with a rubber band.

4. Turn the stator cap clockwise until the lever contacts the fast idle cam adjusting screw.

5. Turn the fast idle cam adjusting screw until the index mark on the cap lines up with the specified mark on the casting.

6. Remove the stator cap. Install the choke coil cap and set to the specified housing mark.

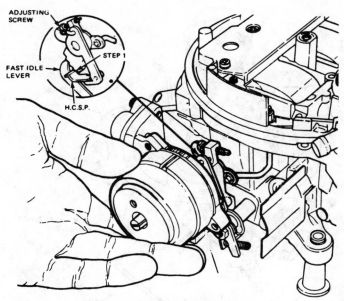

2700 VV fast idle cam adjustment

COLD ENRICHMENT METERING ROD ADJUSTMENT

A dial indicator and the stator cap are required for this adjustment.

1. Remove the choke coil cap. See Step 1 of the "Fast Idle Cam Adjustment."

2. Attach a weight to the choke coil mechanism to seat the cold enrichment rod.

3. Install and zero a dial indicator with the tip on top of the enrichment rod. Raise and release the weight to verify zero on the dial indicator.

4. With the stator cap at the index position, the dial indicator should read the specified dimension. Turn the adjusting nut to correct.

5. Install the choke cap at the correct setting.

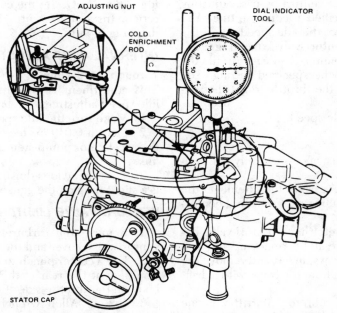

2700 VV cold enrichment metering rod adjustment

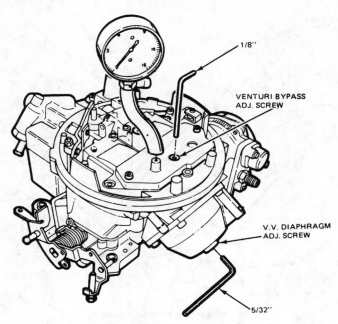

2700 VV control vacuum adjustment

CONTROL VACUUM ADJUSTMENT

1977 Only

1. Make sure the idle speed is correct.
2. Using a $5/32$ in. Allen wrench, turn the venturi valve diaphragm adjusting screw clockwise until the valve is firmly closed.
3. Connect a vacuum gauge to the vacuum tap on the venturi valve cover.
4. Idle the engine and use a $1/8$ in. Allen wrench to turn the venturi by-pass adjusting screw to the specified vacuum setting. You may have to correct the idle speed.
5. Turn the venturi valve diaphragm adjusting screw counter-clockwise until the vacuum drops to the specified setting. You will have to work the throttle to get the vacuum to drop.
6. Reset the idle speed.

1980–82 Only

This adjustment is necessary only on non-feedback systems.

1. Remove the carburetor. Remove the venturi valve diaphragm plug with a center-punch.
2. If the carburetor has a venturi valve by-pass plug, remove it by removing the two cover retaining screws; invert and remove the by-pass screw plug from the cover with a drift. Install the cover.
3. Install the carburetor. Start the engine and allow it to reach normal operating tem-

perature. Connect a vacuum gauge to the venturi valve cover. Set the idle speed to 500 rpm with the transmission in Drive.
4. Push and hold the venturi valve closed. Adjust the bypass screw to obtain a reading of 8 in. H_2O on the vacuum gauge. Make sure the idle speed remains constant. Open and close the throttle and check the idle speed.
5. With the engine idling, adjust the venturi valve diaphragm screw to obtain a reading of 6 in. H_2O. Set the curb idle to specification. Install new venturi valve bypass and diaphragm plugs.

INTERNAL VENT ADJUSTMENT

Through 1978 Only

This adjustment is required whenever the idle speed adjustment is changed.

1. Make sure the idle speed is correct.
2. Place a 0.010 in. feeler gauge between the accelerator pump stem and the operating link.
3. Turn the nylon adjusting nut until there is a slight drag on the gauge.

VENTURI VALVE LIMITER ADJUSTMENT

1. Remove the carburetor. Take off the venturi valve cover and the two rollers.
2. Use a center punch to loosen the expansion plug at the rear of the carburetor main body on the throttle side. Remove it.
3. Use an Allen wrench to remove the venturi valve wide open stop screw.

4. Hold the throttle wide open.

5. Apply a light closing pressure on the venturi valve and check the gap between the valve and the air horn wall. To adjust, move the venturi valve to the wide open position and insert an Allen wrench into the stop screw hole. Turn clockwise to increase the gap. Remove the wrench and check the gap again.

6. Replace the wide open stop screw and turn it clockwise until it contacts the valve.

7. Push the venturi valve wide open and check the gap. Turn the stop screw to bring the gap to specifications.

8. Reassemble the carburetor with a new expansion plug.

CONTROL VACUUM REGULATOR ADJUSTMENT

There are two systems used. The earlier system's C.V.R. rod threads directly through the arm. The revised system, introduced in late 1977, has a ⅜ in. nylon hex adjusting nut on the C.V.R. rod and a flange on the rod.

Early System

1. Make sure that the cold enrichment metering rod adjustment is correct.

2. Rotate the choke coil cap half a turn clockwise from the index mark. Work the throttle to set the fast idle cam.

3. Press down lightly on the regulator rod. If there is no down travel, turn the adjusting screw counter-clockwise until some travel is felt.

4. Turn the regulator rod clockwise with an Allen wrench until the adjusting nut just begins to rise.

5. Press lightly on the regulator rod. If there is any down travel, turn the adjusting screw clockwise in ¼ turn increments until it is eliminated.

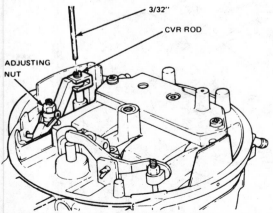

2700 VV control vacuum regulator adjustment

6. Return the choke coil cap to the specified setting.

Revised System

The cold enrichment metering rod adjustment must be checked and set before making this adjustment.

1. After adjusting the cold enrichment metering rod, leave the dial indicator in place but remove the stator cap. Do not re-zero the dial indicator.

2. Press down on the C.V.R. rod until it bottoms on its seat. Measure this amount of travel with the dial indicator.

3. If the adjustment is incorrect, hold the ⅜ in. C.V.R. adjusting nut with a box wrench to prevent it from turning. Use a ³/₃₂ in. Allen wrench to turn the C.V.R. rod; turning counter-clockwise will increase the travel, and vice versa.

HIGH SPEED CAM POSITIONER ADJUSTMENT

Through 1979 Only

1. Place the high speed cam positioner in the corner of the specified cam step, counting the highest step as the first.

2. Place the fast idle lever in the corner of the positioner.

3. Hold the throttle firmly closed.

4. Remove the diaphragm cover. Adjust the diaphragm assembly clockwise until it lightly bottoms. Turn it counter-clockwise ½ to 1½ turns until the vacuum port and diaphragm hole line up.

5. Replace the cover.

IDLE MIXTURE ADJUSTMENT

Through 1977 Only

The results of this adjustment should be checked with an emissions tester, to make sure that emission limits are not exceeded. Idle mixture (idle trim) is not adjustable 1978 and later models.

1. Remove the air cleaner cover only.

2. Use a ³/₃₂ in. Allen wrench to adjust the mixture for each barrel by turning the air adjusting screw. Turn clockwise to richen.

DISASSEMBLY

NOTE: *Special tools are required. If you have any doubts about your ability to successfully complete this procedure, leave it to a professional service person.*

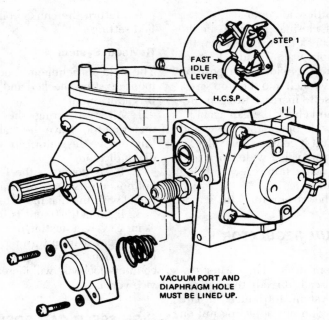

2700 VV high speed cam positioner adjustment

Upper Body

1. Remove the fuel inlet fitting, fuel filter, gasket and spring.

2. Remove the screws retaining the upper body assembly and remove the upper body.

3. Remove the float hinge pin and float assembly.

4. Remove the fuel inlet valve, seat and gasket.

5. Remove the accelerator pump rod and the choke control rod.

6. Remove the accelerator pump link retaining pin and the link.

7. Remove the accelerator pump swivel and the retaining nut.

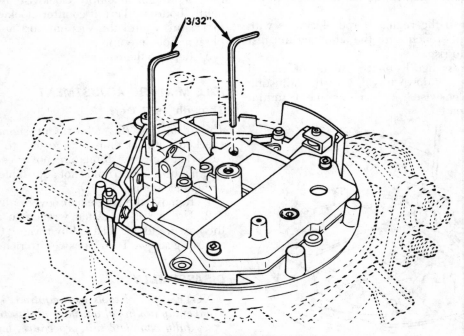

2700 VV idle mixture adjustment

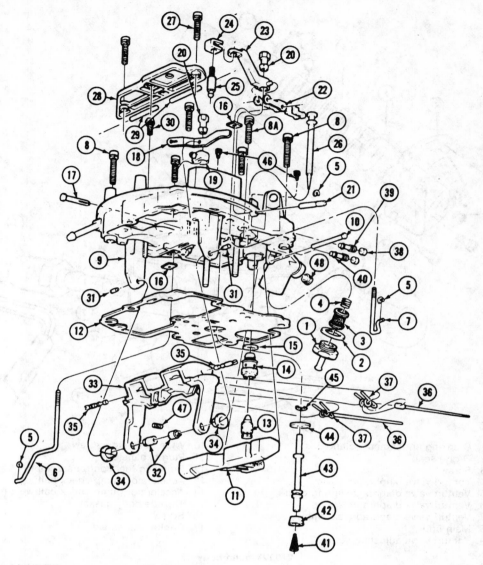

1. Fuel inlet fitting	17. Pin	33. Venturi valve
2. Fuel inlet fitting gasket	18. Accelerator pump link	34. Venturi valve pivot pin bushing
3. Fuel filter	19. Accelerator pump swivel	35. Metering rod pivot pin
4. Fuel filter spring	20. Nut	36. Metering rod
5. Retaining E-ring	21. Choke hinge pin	37. Metering rod spring
6. Accelerator pump rod	22. Cold enrichment rod lever	38. Cup plug
7. Choke control rod	23. Cold enrichment rod swivel	39. Main metering jet assembly
8. Screw	24. Control vacuum regulator	40. O-ring
8A. Screw	adjusting nut	41. Accelerator pump return spring
9. Upper body	25. Control vacuum regulator	42. Accelerator pump cup
10. Float hinge pin	26. Cold enrichment rod	43. Accelerator pump plunger
11. Float assembly	27. Screw	44. Internal vent valve
12. Float bowl gasket	28. Venturi valve cover plate	45. Retaining E-ring
13. Fuel inlet valve	29. Roller bearing	46. Idle trim screw
14. Fuel inlet seat	30. Venturi air bypass screw	47. Venturi valve limiter adjusting
15. Fuel inlet seat gasket	31. Venturi valve pivot plug	screw
16. Dust seal	32. Venturi valve pivot pin	48. Pipe plug

2700VV upper body

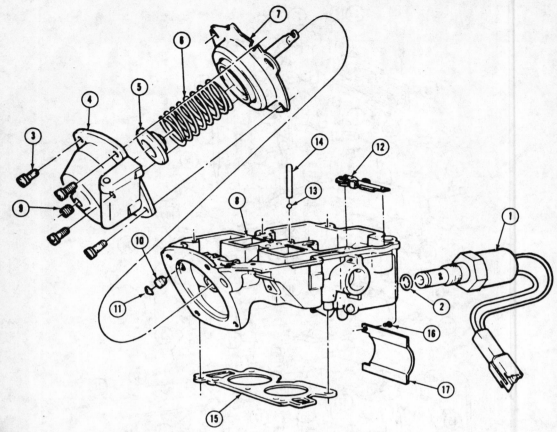

1. Cranking enrichment solenoid
2. O-ring seal
3. Screw
4. Venturi valve diaphragm cover
5. Venturi valve diaphragm spring guide
6. Venturi valve diaphragm spring
7. Venturi valve diaphragm assembly
8. Main body
9. Venturi valve adjusting screw
10. Wide open stop screw
11. Plug expansion
12. Cranking fuel control assembly
13. Accelerator pump check ball
14. Accelerator pump check ball weight
15. Throttle body gasket
16. Screw
17. Choke heat shield

2700VV main body

8. Remove the E-ring on the choke hinge pin and slide the pin out of the casting.

9. Remove the cold enrichment rod adjusting nut, lever and swivel; remove the control vacuum nut and regulator as an assembly.

10. Remove the cold enrichment rod.

11. Remove the venturi valve cover plate and roller bearings. Remove the venturi valve cover plate and roller bearings. Remove the venturi air bypass screw.

12. Using special tool T77P-9928-A, press the tapered plugs out of the venturi valve pivot pins.

13. Remove the venturi valve pivot pins, bushings and the venturi valve.

14. Remove the metering rod pivot pins, springs and metering rods. Be sure to mark the rods so that you know on which side they belong. Also, keep the venturi valve blocked open when working on the jets.

15. Using tool T77L-9533-B, remove the cup plugs.

16. Using tool T77L-9533-A, turn each main metering jet clockwise, counting the number of turns, until they bottom in the casting. You will need to know the number of turns when you reassemble the carbu-

CHILTON'S
FUEL ECONOMY
& TUNE-UP TIPS

Tune-Up • Spark Plug Diagnosis • Emission Controls

Fuel System • Cooling System • Tires and Wheels

General Maintenance

CHILTON'S FUEL ECONOMY & TUNE-UP TIPS

Fuel economy is important to everyone, no matter what kind of vehicle you drive. The maintenance-minded motorist can save both money and fuel using these tips and the periodic maintenance and tune-up procedures in this Repair and Tune-Up Guide.

There are more than 130,000,000 cars and trucks registered for private use in the United States. Each travels an average of 10-12,000 miles per year, and, in total they consume close to 70 billion gallons of fuel each year. This represents nearly ⅔ of the oil imported by the United States each year. The Federal government's goal is to reduce consumption 10% by 1985. A variety of methods are either already in use or under serious consideration, and they all affect your driving and the cars you will drive. In addition to "down-sizing", the auto industry is using or investigating the use of electronic fuel delivery, electronic engine controls and alternative engines for use in smaller and lighter vehicles, among other alternatives to meet the federally mandated Corporate Average Fuel Economy (CAFE) of 27.5 mpg by 1985. The government, for its part, is considering rationing, mandatory driving curtailments and tax increases on motor vehicle fuel in an effort to reduce consumption. The government's goal of a 10% reduction could be realized — and further government regulation avoided — if every private vehicle could use just 1 less gallon of fuel per week.

How Much Can You Save?

Tests have proven that almost anyone can make at least a 10% reduction in fuel consumption through regular maintenance and tune-ups. When a major manufacturer of spark plugs sur-

TUNE-UP

1. Check the cylinder compression to be sure the engine will really benefit from a tune-up and that it is capable of producing good fuel economy. A tune-up will be wasted on an engine in poor mechanical condition.

2. Replace spark plugs regularly. New spark plugs alone can increase fuel economy 3%.

3. Be sure the spark plugs are the correct type (heat range) for your vehicle. See the Tune-Up Specifications.

Heat range refers to the spark plug's ability to conduct heat away from the firing end. It must conduct the heat away in an even pattern to avoid becoming a source of pre-ignition, yet it must also operate hot enough to burn off conductive deposits that could cause misfiring.

The heat range is usually indicated by a number on the spark plug, part of the manufacturer's designation for each individual spark plug. The numbers in bold-face indicate the heat range in each manufacturer's identification system.

Manufacturer	Typical Designation
AC	R **45** TS
Bosch (old)	WA **145** T30
Bosch (new)	HR **8** Y
Champion	RBL **15** Y
Fram/Autolite	**415**
Mopar	P-**62** PR
Motorcraft	BR**F**-42
NGK	BP **5** ES-15
Nippondenso	W **16** EP
Prestolite	14GR **5** 2A

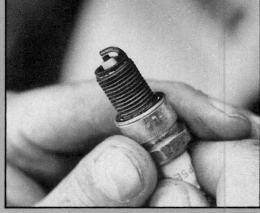

Periodically, check the spark plugs to be sure they are firing efficiently. They are excellent indicators of the internal condition of your engine.

On AC, Bosch (new), Champion, Fram/Autolite, Mopar, Motorcraft and Prestolite, a higher number indicates a hotter plug. On Bosch (old), NGK and Nippondenso, a higher number indicates a colder plug.

4. Make sure the spark plugs are properly gapped. See the Tune-Up Specifications in this book.

5. Be sure the spark plugs are firing efficiently. The illustrations on the next 2 pages show you how to "read" the firing end of the spark plug.

6. Check the ignition timing and set it to specifications. Tests show that almost all cars

veyed over 6,000 cars nationwide, they found that a tune-up, on cars that needed one, increased fuel economy over 11%. Replacing worn plugs alone, accounted for a 3% increase. The same test also revealed that 8 out of every 10 vehicles will have some maintenance deficiency that will directly affect fuel economy, emissions or performance. Most of this mileage-robbing neglect could be prevented with regular maintenance.

Modern engines require that all of the functioning systems operate properly for maximum efficiency. A malfunction anywhere wastes fuel. You can keep your vehicle running as efficiently and economically as possible, by being aware of your vehicles operating and performance characteristics. If your vehicle suddenly develops performance or fuel economy problems it could be due to one or more of the following:

PROBLEM	POSSIBLE CAUSE
Engine Idles Rough	Ignition timing, idle mixture, vacuum leak or something amiss in the emission control system.
Hesitates on Acceleration	Dirty carburetor or fuel filter, improper accelerator pump setting, ignition timing or fouled spark plugs.
Starts Hard or Fails to Start	Worn spark plugs, improperly set automatic choke, ice (or water) in fuel system.
Stalls Frequently	Automatic choke improperly adjusted and possible dirty air filter or fuel filter.
Performs Sluggishly	Worn spark plugs, dirty fuel or air filter, ignition timing or automatic choke out of adjustment.

Check spark plug wires on conventional point type ignition for cracks by bending them in a loop around your finger.

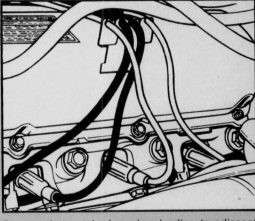

Be sure that spark plug wires leading to adjacent cylinders do not run too close together. (Photo courtesy Champion Spark Plug Co.)

have incorrect ignition timing by more than 2°.

7. If your vehicle does not have electronic ignition, check the points, rotor and cap as specified.

8. Check the spark plug wires (used with conventional point-type ignitions) for cracks and burned or broken insulation by bending them in a loop around your finger. Cracked wires decrease fuel efficiency by failing to deliver full voltage to the spark plugs. One misfiring spark plug can cost you as much as 2 mpg.

9. Check the routing of the plug wires. Misfiring can be the result of spark plug leads to adjacent cylinders running parallel to each other and too close together. One wire tends to pick up voltage from the other causing it to fire "out of time".

10. Check all electrical and ignition circuits for voltage drop and resistance.

11. Check the distributor mechanical and/or vacuum advance mechanisms for proper functioning. The vacuum advance can be checked by twisting the distributor plate in the opposite direction of rotation. It should spring back when released.

12. Check and adjust the valve clearance on engines with mechanical lifters. The clearance should be slightly loose rather than too tight.

SPARK PLUG DIAGNOSIS

Normal

APPEARANCE: This plug is typical of one operating normally. The insulator nose varies from a light tan to grayish color with slight electrode wear. The presence of slight deposits is normal on used plugs and will have no adverse effect on engine performance. The spark plug heat range is correct for the engine and the engine is running normally.

CAUSE: Properly running engine.

RECOMMENDATION: Before reinstalling this plug, the electrodes should be cleaned and filed square. Set the gap to specifications. If the plug has been in service for more than 10-12,000 miles, the entire set should probably be replaced with a fresh set of the same heat range.

Oil Deposits

APPEARANCE: The firing end of the plug is covered with a wet, oily coating.

CAUSE: The problem is poor oil control. On high mileage engines, oil is leaking past the rings or valve guides into the combustion chamber. A common cause is also a plugged PCV valve, and a ruptured fuel pump diaphragm can also cause this condition. Oil fouled plugs such as these are often found in new or recently overhauled engines, before normal oil control is achieved, and can be cleaned and reinstalled.

RECOMMENDATION: A hotter spark plug may temporarily relieve the problem, but the engine is probably in need of work.

Incorrect Heat Range

APPEARANCE: The effects of high temperature on a spark plug are indicated by clean white, often blistered insulator. This can also be accompanied by excessive wear of the electrode, and the absence of deposits.

CAUSE: Check for the correct spark plug heat range. A plug which is too hot for the engine can result in overheating. A car operated mostly at high speeds can require a colder plug. Also check ignition timing, cooling system level, fuel mixture and leaking intake manifold.

RECOMMENDATION: If all ignition and engine adjustments are known to be correct, and no other malfunction exists, install spark plugs one heat range colder.

Photos Courtesy Champion Spark Plug Co.

Carbon Deposits

APPEARANCE: Carbon fouling is easily identified by the presence of dry, soft, black, sooty deposits.

CAUSE: Changing the heat range can often lead to carbon fouling, as can prolonged slow, stop-and-start driving. If the heat range is correct, carbon fouling can be attributed to a rich fuel mixture, sticking choke, clogged air cleaner, worn breaker points, retarded timing or low compression. If only one or two plugs are carbon fouled, check for corroded or cracked wires on the affected plugs. Also look for cracks in the distributor cap between the towers of affected cylinders.

RECOMMENDATION: After the problem is corrected, these plugs can be cleaned and reinstalled if not worn severely.

MMT Fouled

APPEARANCE: Spark plugs fouled by MMT (Methycyclopentadienyl Maganese Tricarbonyl) have reddish, rusty appearance on the insulator and side electrode.

CAUSE: MMT is an anti-knock additive in gasoline used to replace lead. During the combustion process, the MMT leaves a reddish deposit on the insulator and side electrode.

RECOMMENDATION: No engine malfunction is indicated and the deposits will not affect plug performance any more than lead deposits (see Ash Deposits). MMT fouled plugs can be cleaned, regapped and reinstalled.

High Speed Glazing

APPEARANCE: Glazing appears as shiny coating on the plug, either yellow or tan in color.

CAUSE: During hard, fast acceleration, plug temperatures rise suddenly. Deposits from normal combustion have no chance to fluff-off; instead, they melt on the insulator forming an electrically conductive coating which causes misfiring.

RECOMMENDATION: Glazed plugs are not easily cleaned. They should be replaced with a fresh set of plugs of the correct heat range. If the condition recurs, using plugs with a heat range one step colder may cure the problem.

Ash (Lead) Deposits

APPEARANCE: Ash deposits are characterized by light brown or white colored deposits crusted on the side or center electrodes. In some cases it may give the plug a rusty appearance.

CAUSE: Ash deposits are normally derived from oil or fuel additives burned during normal combustion. Normally they are harmless, though excessive amounts can cause misfiring. If deposits are excessive in short mileage, the valve guides may be worn.

RECOMMENDATION: Ash-fouled plugs can be cleaned, gapped and reinstalled.

Detonation

APPEARANCE: Detonation is usually characterized by a broken plug insulator.

CAUSE: A portion of the fuel charge will begin to burn spontaneously, from the increased heat following ignition. The explosion that results applies extreme pressure to engine components, frequently damaging spark plugs and pistons.

Detonation can result by over-advanced ignition timing, inferior gasoline (low octane) lean air/fuel mixture, poor carburetion, engine lugging or an increase in compression ratio due to combustion chamber deposits or engine modification.

RECOMMENDATION: Replace the plugs after correcting the problem.

Photos Courtesy Fram Corporation

EMISSION CONTROLS

13. Be aware of the general condition of the emission control system. It contributes to reduced pollution and should be serviced regularly to maintain efficient engine operation.

14. Check all vacuum lines for dried, cracked or brittle conditions. Something as simple as a leaking vacuum hose can cause poor performance and loss of economy.

15. Avoid tampering with the emission control system. Attempting to improve fuel econ-

---

FUEL SYSTEM

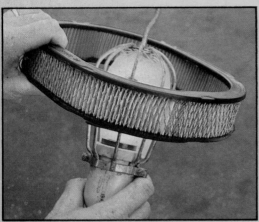

Check the air filter with a light behind it. If you can see light through the filter it can be reused.

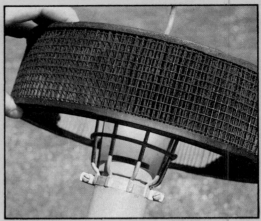

Extremely clogged filters should be discarded and replaced with a new one.

18. Replace the air filter regularly. A dirty air filter richens the air/fuel mixture and can increase fuel consumption as much as 10%. Tests show that 1/3 of all vehicles have air filters in need of replacement.

19. Replace the fuel filter at least as often as recommended.

20. Set the idle speed and carburetor mixture to specifications.

21. Check the automatic choke. A sticking or malfunctioning choke wastes gas.

22. During the summer months, adjust the automatic choke for a leaner mixture which will produce faster engine warm-ups.

COOLING SYSTEM

29. Be sure all accessory drive belts are in good condition. Check for cracks or wear.

30. Adjust all accessory drive belts to proper tension.

31. Check all hoses for swollen areas, worn spots, or loose clamps.

32. Check coolant level in the radiator or expansion tank.

33. Be sure the thermostat is operating properly. A stuck thermostat delays engine warm-up and a cold engine uses nearly twice as much fuel as a warm engine.

34. Drain and replace the engine coolant at least as often as recommended. Rust and scale

---

TIRES & WHEELS

38. Check the tire pressure often with a pencil type gauge. Tests by a major tire manufacturer show that 90% of all vehicles have at least 1 tire improperly inflated. Better mileage can be achieved by over-inflating tires, but never exceed the maximum inflation pressure on the side of the tire.

39. If possible, install radial tires. Radial tires deliver as much as 1/2 mpg more than bias belted tires.

40. Avoid installing super-wide tires. They only create extra rolling resistance and decrease fuel mileage. Stick to the manufacturer's recommendations.

41. Have the wheels properly balanced.

omy by tampering with emission controls is more likely to worsen fuel economy than improve it. Emission control changes on modern engines are not readily reversible.

16. Clean (or replace) the EGR valve and lines as recommended.

17. Be sure that all vacuum lines and hoses are reconnected properly after working under the hood. An unconnected or misrouted vacuum line can wreak havoc with engine performance.

23. Check for fuel leaks at the carburetor, fuel pump, fuel lines and fuel tank. Be sure all lines and connections are tight.

24. Periodically check the tightness of the carburetor and intake manifold attaching nuts and bolts. These are a common place for vacuum leaks to occur.

25. Clean the carburetor periodically and lubricate the linkage.

26. The condition of the tailpipe can be an excellent indicator of proper engine combustion. After a long drive at highway speeds, the inside of the tailpipe should be a light grey in color. Black or soot on the insides indicates an overly rich mixture.

27. Check the fuel pump pressure. The fuel pump may be supplying more fuel than the engine needs.

28. Use the proper grade of gasoline for your engine. Don't try to compensate for knocking or "pinging" by advancing the ignition timing. This practice will only increase plug temperature and the chances of detonation or pre-ignition with relatively little performance gain.

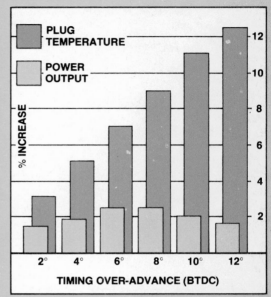

Increasing ignition timing past the specified setting results in a drastic increase in spark plug temperature with increased chance of detonation or preignition. Performance increase is considerably less. (Photo courtesy Champion Spark Plug Co.)

that form in the engine should be flushed out to allow the engine to operate at peak efficiency.

35. Clean the radiator of debris that can decrease cooling efficiency.

36. Install a flex-type or electric cooling fan, if you don't have a clutch type fan. Flex fans use curved plastic blades to push more air at low speeds when more cooling is needed; at high speeds the blades flatten out for less resistance. Electric fans only run when the engine temperature reaches a predetermined level.

37. Check the radiator cap for a worn or cracked gasket. If the cap does not seal properly, the cooling system will not function properly.

42. Be sure the front end is correctly aligned. A misaligned front end actually has wheels going in different directions. The increased drag can reduce fuel economy by .3 mpg.

43. Correctly adjust the wheel bearings. Wheel bearings that are adjusted too tight increase rolling resistance.

Check tire pressures regularly with a reliable pocket type gauge. Be sure to check the pressure on a cold tire.

GENERAL MAINTENANCE

Check the fluid levels (particularly engine oil) on a regular basis. Be sure to check the oil for grit, water or other contamination.

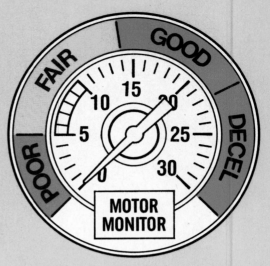

A vacuum gauge is another excellent indicator of internal engine condition and can also be installed in the dash as a mileage indicator.

44. Periodically check the fluid levels in the engine, power steering pump, master cylinder, automatic transmission and drive axle.

45. Change the oil at the recommended interval and change the filter at every oil change. Dirty oil is thick and causes extra friction between moving parts, cutting efficiency and increasing wear. A worn engine requires more frequent tune-ups and gets progressively worse fuel economy. In general, use the lightest viscosity oil for the driving conditions you will encounter.

46. Use the recommended viscosity fluids in the transmission and axle.

47. Be sure the battery is fully charged for fast starts. A slow starting engine wastes fuel.

48. Be sure battery terminals are clean and tight.

49. Check the battery electrolyte level and add distilled water if necessary.

50. Check the exhaust system for crushed pipes, blockages and leaks.

51. Adjust the brakes. Dragging brakes or brakes that are not releasing create increased drag on the engine.

52. Install a vacuum gauge or miles-per-gallon gauge. These gauges visually indicate engine vacuum in the intake manifold. High vacuum = good mileage and low vacuum = poorer mileage. The gauge can also be an excellent indicator of internal engine conditions.

53. Be sure the clutch is properly adjusted. A slipping clutch wastes fuel.

54. Check and periodically lubricate the heat control valve in the exhaust manifold. A sticking or inoperative valve prevents engine warm-up and wastes gas.

55. Keep accurate records to check fuel economy over a period of time. A sudden drop in fuel economy may signal a need for tune-up or other maintenance.

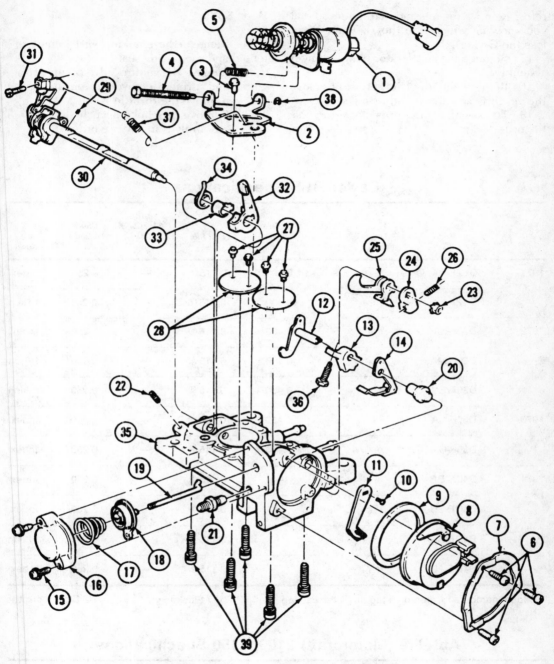

1. Throttle return control device
2. Throttle return control device bracket
3. Mounting screw
4. Adjusting screw
5. Adjusting screw spring
6. Screw
7. Choke thermostatic housing retainer
8. Choke thermostatic housing
9. Choke thermostatic housing gasket
10. Screw
11. Choke thermostatic lever
12. Choke lever and shaft assembly
13. Fast idle cam
14. High cam speed positioner assembly
15. Screw
16. High cam speed positioner diaphragm cover
17. High cam speed positioner diaphragm spring
18. High cam speed positioner diaphragm assembly
19. High cam speed positioner rod
20. Choke housing bushing

2700VV throttle body

retor. Remove the jets and mark them so that you know on which side they belong. Don't lose the O-rings.

17. Remove the accelerator pump plunger assembly.

18. Remove the idle trim screws. Remove the venturi valve limiter adjusting screw.

19. To assemble the upper body, reverse the order.

Main Body

1. Remove the cranking enrichment solenoid and the O-ring seal.

2. Remove the venturi valve cover, spring guide, and spring. Remove the venturi valve.

3. Remove the throttle body.

4. Remove the choke heat shield.

5. Assembly is in reverse order.

Carter RBS Specifications

Year	Model ①	Float Level (in.)	Bowl Vent (in.)	Accelerator Pump (in.)	Fast Idle (rpm)	Fast Idle Throttle Plate (in.)	Choke Unloader (in.)	Choke
1971	D1ZF-HA, LA	9/16	—	0.400 ③	0.115 ②	—	0.250	Index
	D1ZF-NA, KA	9/16	—	0.400 ③	0.115 ②	—	0.250	1 Rich
1972	D20F-LA	9/16	—	0.400 ③	0.115 ②	—	0.250	Index
	D20F-MA	9/16	—	0.400 ③	0.115 ②	—	0.250	1 Rich
	D20F-SA	9/16	—	0.400 ③	0.115 ②	—	0.250	1 Rich
1973	D30F-BA	9/16	—	0.420 ③	0.115 ②	—	0.250	Index
	D30F-CA	9/16	—	0.400 ③	0.115 ②	—	0.250	Index
1974	D4DE-BB	9/16	—	—	0.115 ②	—	0.250	Index
	D4DE-SB	9/16	—	—	0.115 ②	—	0.250	Index
	D4DE-AAA	9/16	—	—	0.115 ②	—	0.250	1 Lean
	D4DE-AB	9/16	—	—	0.115 ②	—	0.250	Index

① Model numbers located on a tag or on the casting   ② At kickdown   ③ Closed throttle

Autolite (Motorcraft) 2100, 2150 Specifications

Year	(9510)* Carburetor Identification	Dry Float Level (in.)	Wet Float Level (in.)	Pump Setting Hole # ①	Choke Plate Pulldown (in.)	Fast Idle Cam Linkage Clearance (in.)	Fast Idle (rpm)	Dechoke (in.)	Choke Setting
1971	D1YF-DA	7/16	13/16	3	0.200	0.160	1500	0.060	Index
	D1MF-JA	7/16	13/16	3	0.190	0.160	1500	0.060	1 Rich
	D1MF-FA	7/16	13/16	3	0.200	0.160	1500	0.060	1 Rich

Autolite (Motorcraft) 2100, 2150 Specifications (cont.)

Year	(9510)* Carburetor Identification	Dry Float Level (in.)	Wet Float Level (in.)	Pump Setting Hole # ①	Choke Plate Pulldown (in.)	Fast Idle Cam Linkage Clearance (in.)	Fast Idle (rpm)	Dechoke (in.)	Choke Setting
1972	D2AF-FB	$7/16$	$13/16$	3	0.140	0.130	1500	0.030	Index
	D2AF-GB	$7/16$	$13/16$	3	0.140	0.130	1500	0.030	Index
	D2AF-HA	$7/16$	$13/16$	2	0.150	0.130	1400	0.060	1 Rich
	D2GF-AA	$7/16$	$13/16$	2	0.150	0.130	1400	0.060	1 Rich
	D2GF-BA	$7/16$	$13/16$	2	0.150	0.130	1400	0.060	1 Rich
	D2MF-FB	$7/16$	$13/16$	4	0.180	0.150	1500	0.060	1 Rich
	D2OF-KA	$7/16$	$13/16$	2	0.150	0.130	1400	0.060	1 Rich
	D2OF-VB	$7/16$	$13/16$	3	0.190	0.160	1400	0.030	2 Rich
	D2WF-CA	$7/16$	$13/16$	3	0.190	0.160	1400	0.030	2 Rich
	D2ZF-FA	$7/16$	$13/16$	2	0.150	0.130	1400	0.060	1 Rich
	D2ZF-LA	$7/16$	$13/16$	3	0.240	0.210	1500	0.030	1 Rich
1973	D3AF-CE	$7/16$	$13/16$	3	②	②	1500	②	1 Rich
	D3AF-DC	$7/16$	$13/16$	3	②	②	1500	②	3 Rich
	D3GF-AF	$7/16$	$13/16$	2	②	②	1400	②	3 Rich
	D3GF-BB	$7/16$	$13/16$	2	②	②	1250	②	3 Rich
	D3ZF-EA	$7/16$	$13/16$	2	②	②	1400	②	1 Rich
	D3AF-KA	$7/16$	$13/16$	3	②	②	1500	②	3 Rich
	D3MF-AE	$7/16$	$13/16$	3	②	②	1500	②	3 Rich
	D3MF-BA	$7/16$	$13/16$	3	②	②	1500	②	3 Rich
1974	D4AE-DA	$7/16$	$13/16$	2	②	②	1500	②	1 Rich
	D4AE-EA	$7/16$	$13/16$	2	②	②	1500	②	3 Rich
	D4AE-FA	$7/16$	$13/16$	3	②	②	1500	②	3 Rich
	D4AE-GA	$7/16$	$13/16$	3	②	②	1500	②	3 Rich
	D4DE-LA	$7/16$	$13/16$	2	②	②	1500	②	3 Rich

Autolite (Motorcraft) 2100, 2150 Specifications (cont.)

Year	(9510)* Carburetor Identification	Dry Float Level (in.)	Wet Float Level (in.)	Pump Setting Hole # ①	Choke Plate Pulldown (in.)	Fast Idle Cam Linkage Clearance (in.)	Fast Idle (rpm)	Dechoke (in.)	Choke Setting
1974	D4DE-RB	$7/16$	$13/16$	2	②	②	1500	②	3 Rich
	D40E-FA	$7/16$	$13/16$	2	②	②	1500	②	3 Rich
	D4AE-HB	$7/16$	$13/16$	3	②	②	1500	②	3 Rich
	D4DE-NB	$7/16$	$13/16$	2	②	②	1500	②	3 Rich
	D4DE-PA	$7/16$	$13/16$	2	②	②	1500	②	3 Rich
	D4OE-CA	$7/16$	$13/16$	2	②	②	1500	②	3 Rich
	D4ME-BA	$7/16$	$13/16$	3	②	②	1500	②	3 Rich
	D4ME-CA	$7/16$	$13/16$	3	②	②	1500	②	3 Rich
1975	D5ZE-AC	$3/8$	$3/4$	2	0.145	②	1500	②	2 Rich
	D5ZE-BC	$3/8$	$3/4$	2	0.145	②	1500	②	2 Rich
	D5ZE-CC	$3/8$	$3/4$	3	0.145	②	1500	②	2 Rich
	D5ZE-DC	$3/8$	$3/4$	2	0.145	②	1500	②	2 Rich
	D5DE-AA	$7/16$	$13/16$	2	0.140	②	1500	②	3 Rich
	D5DE-BA	$7/16$	$13/16$	2	0.140	②	1500	②	3 Rich
	D5DE-JA	$7/16$	$13/16$	2	0.140	②	1500	②	3 Rich
	D5ZE-JA	$7/16$	$13/16$	2	0.140	②	1500	②	3 Rich
	D5OE-AA	$7/16$	$13/16$	2	0.140	②	1500	②	3 Rich
	D5OE-DA	$7/16$	$13/16$	2	0.140	②	1500	②	3 Rich
	D5DE-HA	$7/16$	$13/16$	3	0.140	②	1500	②	3 Rich
	D5DE-UA	$7/16$	$13/16$	2	0.140	②	1500	②	3 Rich
	D5OE-BA	$7/16$	$13/16$	3	0.125	②	1500	②	3 Rich
	D5OE-CA	$7/16$	$13/16$	3	0.125	②	1500	②	3 Rich
	D5OE-GA	$7/16$	$13/16$	2	0.125	②	1500	②	3 Rich
	D5AE-AA	$7/16$	$13/16$	3	0.125	②	1500	②	3 Rich

Autolite (Motorcraft) 2100, 2150 Specifications (cont.)

Year	(9510)* Carburetor Identification	Dry Float Level (in.)	Wet Float Level (in.)	Pump Setting Hole # ①	Choke Plate Pulldown (in.)	Fast Idle Cam Linkage Clearance (in.)	Fast Idle (rpm)	Dechoke (in.)	Choke Setting
1975	D5AE-EA	$7/16$	$13/16$	3	0.125	②	1500	②	3 Rich
	D5ME-BA	$7/16$	$13/16$	2	0.125	②	1500	②	3 Rich
	D5ME-FA	$7/16$	$13/16$	2	0.125	②	1500	②	3 Rich
1976–77	D5ZE-BE	$3/8$	$3/4$	2	0.105	②	1600 ③	②	3 Rich
	D6ZE-AA	$3/8$	$3/4$	2	0.100	②	1600 ③	②	3 Rich
	D6ZE-BA	$3/8$	$3/4$	2	0.100	②	1600 ③	②	3 Rich
	D6ZE-CA	$13/32$	$3/4$	2	0.110	②	1600 ③	②	3 Rich
	D6ZE-DA	$3/8$	$3/4$	3	0.110	②	1600 ③	②	3 Rich
	D5DE-AEA	$7/16$	$13/16$	2	0.160	②	2000 ④	②	3 Rich
	D5DE-AFA	$7/16$	$13/16$	2	0.160	②	2000 ④	②	3 Rich
	D5WE-FA	$7/16$	$13/16$	2	0.160	②	2000 ④	②	3 Rich
	D6ZE-JA	$7/16$	$13/16$	2	0.160	②	2000 ④	②	3 Rich
	D6OE-AA	$7/16$	$13/16$	3	0.160	②	2000 ④	②	3 Rich
	D6OE-BA	$7/16$	$13/16$	3	0.160	②	2000 ④	②	3 Rich
	D6OE-CA	$7/16$	$13/16$	3	0.160	②	2000 ④	②	3 Rich
	D6WE-AA	$7/16$	$13/16$	2	0.160	②	1350 ⑤	②	3 Rich
	D6WE-BA	$7/16$	$13/16$	2	0.160	②	1350 ⑤	②	3 Rich
	D6AE-HA	$7/16$	$13/16$	2	0.160	②	1350 ⑤	②	3 Rich
	D6ME-AA	$7/16$	$13/16$	2	0.160	②	1350 ⑤	②	3 Rich
1978–79	D84E-EA	$7/16$	$13/16$	2	0.110	⑥	⑦	—	3 Rich
	D8AE-JA	$3/8$	$3/4$	3	0.167	⑥	⑦	—	3 Rich
	D8BE-ACA	$7/16$	$3/4$	4	0.155	⑥	⑦	—	2 Rich
	D8BE-ADA	$7/16$	$13/16$	2	0.110	⑥	⑦	—	3 Rich
	D8BE-AEA	$7/16$	$13/16$	2	0.110	⑥	⑦	—	4 Rich

Autolite (Motorcraft) 2100, 2150 Specifications (cont.)

Year	(9510)* Carburetor Identification	Dry Float Level (in.)	Wet Float Level (in.)	Pump Setting Hole # ①	Choke Plate Pulldown (in.)	Fast Idle Cam Linkage Clearance (in.)	Fast Idle (rpm)	Dechoke (in.)	Choke Setting
1978–79	D8BE-AFA	$7/16$	$13/16$	2	0.110	⑥	⑦	—	4 Rich
	D8BE-MB	$3/8$	$13/16$	3	0.122	⑥	⑦	—	Index
	D8DE-HA	$19/32$	$13/16$	3	0.157	⑥	⑦	—	Index
	D8KE-EA	$19/32$	$13/16$	2	0.135	⑥	⑦	—	3 Rich
	D8OE-BA	$3/8$	$3/4$	3	0.167	⑥	⑦	—	3 Rich
	D8OE-EA	$19/32$	$13/16$	2	0.136	⑥	⑦	—	Index
	D8OE-HA	$7/16$	$13/16$	3	0.180	⑥	⑦	—	2 Rich
	D8SE-CA	$19/32$	$13/16$	3	0.150	⑥	⑦	—	2 Rich
	D8ZE-TA	$3/8$	$3/4$	4	0.135	⑥	⑦	—	Index
	D8ZE-UA	$3/8$	$3/4$	4	0.135	⑥	⑦	—	Index
	D8WE-DA	$7/16$	$13/16$	4	0.143	⑥	⑦	—	1 Rich
	D8YE-AB	$3/8$	$13/16$	3	0.122	⑥	⑦	—	Index
	D8SE-DA, EA	$7/16$	$13/16$	3	0.147	⑥	⑦	—	3 Rich
	D8SE-FA, GA	$3/8$	$13/16$	3	0.147	⑥	⑦	—	3 Rich
1980	EO4E-PA, RA	—	$13/16$	2	0.104	⑥	⑦	$1/4$	⑦
	EOBE-AUA	—	$13/16$	3	0.116	⑥	⑦	$1/4$	⑦
	EODE-SA, TA	—	$13/16$	2	0.104	⑥	⑦	$1/4$	⑦
	EOKE-CA, DA	—	$13/16$	3	0.116	⑥	⑦	$1/4$	⑦
	EOKE-GA, HA	—	$13/16$	3	0.116	⑥	⑦	$1/4$	⑦
	EOKE-JA, KA	—	$13/16$	3	0.116	⑥	⑦	$1/4$	⑦
	D84E-TA, UA	—	$13/16$	2	0.125	⑥	⑦	$1/4$	⑦
	EO4E-ADA, AEA	—	$13/16$	2	0.104	⑥	⑦	$1/4$	⑦
	EO4E-CA	—	$13/16$	2	0.104	⑥	⑦	$1/4$	⑦
	EO4E-EA, FA	—	$13/16$	2	0.104	⑥	⑦	$1/4$	⑦

Autolite (Motorcraft) 2100, 2150 Specifications (cont.)

Year	(9510)* Carburetor Identification	Dry Float Level (in.)	Wet Float Level (in.)	Pump Setting Hole # ①	Choke Plate Pulldown (in.)	Fast Idle Cam Linkage Clearance (in.)	Fast Idle (rpm)	Dechoke (in.)	Choke Setting
1980	EO4E-JA, KA	—	13/16	2	0.137	⑥	⑦	1/4	⑦
	EO4E-SA, TA	—	13/16	2	0.104	⑥	⑦	1/4	⑦
	EO4E-VA, YA	—	13/16	2	0.104	⑥	⑦	1/4	⑦
	EODE-TA, VA	—	13/16	2	0.104	⑥	⑦	1/4	⑦
	EOSE-GA, HA	—	13/16	2	0.104	⑥	⑦	1/4	⑦
	EOSE-LA, MA	—	13/16	2	0.104	⑥	⑦	1/4	⑦
	EOSE-NA	—	13/16	2	0.104	⑥	⑦	1/4	⑦
	EOSE-PA	—	13/16	2	0.137	⑥	⑦	1/4	⑦
	EOVE-FA	—	13/16	2	0.104	⑥	⑦	1/4	⑦
	EOWE-BA, CA	—	13/16	2	0.137	⑥	⑦	1/4	⑦
	D9AE-ANA, APA	—	13/16	3	0.129	⑥	⑦	1/4	⑦
	D9AE-AVA, AYA	—	13/16	3	0.129	⑥	⑦	1/4	⑦
	EOAE-AGA	—	13/16	3	0.159	⑥	⑦	1/4	⑦
1981	EIKE-CA	7/16	0.810	3	0.124	⑥	⑦	0.250	⑦
	EIKE-EA	7/16	0.810	3	0.124	⑥	⑦	0.250	⑦
	EIKE-DA	7/16	0.810	3	0.124	⑥	⑦	0.250	⑦
	EIKE-FA	7/16	0.810	3	0.124	⑥	⑦	0.250	⑦
	EIWE-FA	7/16	0.810	2	0.120	⑥	⑦	0.250	⑦
	EIWE-EA	7/16	0.810	2	0.120	⑥	⑦	0.250	⑦
	EIWE-CA	7/16	0.810	2	0.120	⑥	⑦	0.250	⑦
	EIWE-DA	7/16	0.810	2	0.120	⑥	⑦	0.250	⑦
	EIAE-YA	7/16	0.810	3	0.124	⑥	⑦	0.250	⑦
	EIAE-ZA	7/16	0.810	3	0.124	⑥	⑦	0.250	⑦
	EIAE-ADA	7/16	0.810	3	0.124	⑥	⑦	0.250	⑦

Autolite (Motorcraft) 2100, 2150 Specifications (cont.)

Year	(9510)* Carburetor Identification	Dry Float Level (in.)	Wet Float Level (in.)	Pump Setting Hole # ①	Choke Plate Pulldown (in.)	Fast Idle Cam Linkage Clearance (in.)	Fast Idle (rpm)	Dechoke (in.)	Choke Setting
1981	EIAE-AEA	7/16	0.810	3	0.124	⑥	⑦	0.250	⑦
	EIAE-TA	—	0.810	2	0.104	⑥	⑦	0.250	⑦
	EIAE-UA	—	0.810	2	0.104	⑥	⑦	0.250	⑦

* Basic carburetor number for Ford products
① With link in inboard hole of pump lever
② Electric choke; see procedure in text
③ Figure given is for manual transmission; for automatics add 100 RPM.
④ Figure given is for 49 states Granada and Monarch; for Calif. Granada and Monarch and all Torino, Montego and Cougar models, figure is 1400 RPM.
⑤ Figure given is for 49 states model; Calif. specification is 1150 RPM.

Autolite (Motorcraft) 4300, 4350 Specifications

Year	(9510)* Carburetor Identification①	Dry Float Level (in.)	Pump Hole Setting	Choke Plate Pulldown (in.)	Fast Idle Cam Linkage (in.)	Fast Idle (rpm)	Dechoke (in.)	Choke Setting	Dashpot
1971	D1AF-MA	49/64	2	0.220	—	1350	—	Index	1/16
	D1OF-EA	13/16	2	0.180	0.160	1250	—	Index	—
	D1OF-AAA	13/16	2	0.200	0.180	1400	—	Index	—
	D1SF-AA	49/64	2	0.220	—	1350	—	Index	1/16
	D1VF-AA	49/64	2	0.220	0.170	1250	—	1 Rich	0.100
1972	D2AF-AA	49/64	1	0.220	0.200	1350	—	2 Rich	—
	D2AF-LA	49/64	1	0.215	0.190	1900	—	2 Rich	—
	D2SF-AA	49/64	1	0.220	0.200	1350	—	2 Rich	—
	D2SF-BA	49/64	1	0.220	0.200	1350	—	2 Rich	—
	D2VF-AA	49/64	1	0.230	0.200	1250	—	Index	—
	D2VF-BA	49/64	1	0.230	0.200	1250	—	Index	—
	D2ZF-AA	13/16	1	0.200	0.180	1200	—	Index	—
	D2ZF-BB	13/16	1	0.200	0.200	1200	—	Index	—
	D2ZF-DA	13/16	1	0.200	0.200	1200	—	Index	—

Autolite (Motorcraft) 4300, 4350 Specifications (cont.)

Year	(9510)* Carburetor Identification1	Dry Float Level (in.)	Pump Hole Setting	Choke Plate Pulldown (in.)	Fast Idle Cam Linkage (in.)	Fast Idle (rpm)	Dechoke (in.)	Choke Setting	Dashpot
	D2ZF-GA	$13/16$	1	0.200	0.180	1200	—	Index	—
1973	D3VF-DA	0.76	1	0.210	0.190	1350	—	Index	—
	D3ZF-AC	0.82	1	0.180	0.180	1300	—	Index	—
	D3ZF-BC	0.82	1	0.170	0.170	1300	—	INR	—
	D3ZF-DC	0.82	1	0.180	0.180	1300	—	Index	—
	D3AF-HA	0.76	1	0.210	0.200	1350	—	Index	—
	D3AF-EB	0.88	1	0.200	0.200	1900	—	Index	—
1974	D4AE-AA	$3/4$	1	0.230	0.200	1900	—	Index	—
	D4AE-NA, D4VE-AB	$3/4$	1	0.220	0.200	1250	—	Index	—
	D4TE-ATA	$13/16$	1	0.220	0.180	1250	—	Index	—
	D4OE-AA	$13/16$	1	0.180	0.180	1800	—	Index	—
1975	D5VE-AD	$15/16$	1	②	0.160	1600	0.300	2 Rich	—
	D5VE-BA	$15/16$	1	②	0.160	1600	0.300	2 Rich	—
	D5AE-CA	$31/32$	1	②	0.160	1600	0.300	2 Rich	—
	D5AE-DA	$31/32$	1	②	0.160	1600	0.300	2 Rich	—
1976–77	D6AE-CA	1.00	2	0.140③	0.140	1350	0.30	2 Rich	—
	D6AE-FA	1.00	2	0.140③	0.140	1350	0.30	2 Rich	—
	D6AE-DA	1.00	2	0.160④	0.160	1350	0.30	2 Rich	—

* Basic carburetor number for Ford products.
① The identification tag is on the bowl cover.
② Initial—0.160 in.
   Delayed—0.190 in.
③ Initial Figure given; delayed—0.190
④ Initial Figure given; delayed—0.210

Motorcraft Model 2700 VV Specifications

Year	Model	Float Level (in.)	Float Drop (in.)	Fast Idle Cam Setting (notches)	Cold Enrichment Metering Rod (in.)	Control Vacuum (in. H₂O)	Venturi Valve Limiter (in.)	Choke Cap Setting (notches)	Control Vacuum Regulator Setting (in.)
1977–78	All	1³/₆₄	1¹⁵/₃₂	1 Rich/3rd step	.125	5.0	6¹/₆₄	Index	—
1979	D9ZE-LB	1³/₆₄	1¹⁵/₃₂	1 Rich/2nd step	.125	①	②	Index	.230
	D84E-KA	1³/₆₄	1¹⁵/₃₂	1 Rich/3rd step	.125	5.5	6¹/₆₄	Index	—
1980	All	1³/₆₄	1¹⁵/₃₂	1 Rich/4th step	.125	③	④	⑤	.075
1981	EIAE-AAA	1.015–1.065	1.435–1.485	—	—	③	④	⑤	

① Venturi Air Bypass 6.8–7.3
   Venturi Valve Diaphragm 4.6–5.1
② Limiter Setting .38–.42
   Limiter Stop Setting .73–.77

③ See text
④ Opening gap: 0.99–1.01
   Closing gap: 0.94–0.98
⑤ See underhood decal

Rochester Quadrajet Specifications

Year	Carburetor Identification ①	Float Level (in.)	Air Valve Spring	Pump Rod (in.)	Vacuum Break (in.)	Secondary Opening (in.)	Choke Rod (in.)	Choke Unloader (in.)	Fast Idle Speed (rpm)
1971	DOOF-A	¹¹/₃₂	0.030	⁵/₁₆	0.140	—	0.130	0.300	1800②
	DOOF-E	¹¹/₃₂	0.030	⁵/₁₆	0.190	—	0.166	0.300	2000②

① The carburetor identification tag is located at the rear of the carburetor on one of the air horn screws.
② Second step of cam.

Ford, Autolite, Motorcraft Model 5200 Specifications

Year	(9510)* Carburetor Identification ①	Dry Float Level (in.)	Pump Hole Setting	Choke Plate Pulldown (in.)	Fast Idle Cam Linkage (in.)	Fast Idle (rpm)	Dechoke (in.)	Choke Setting
1981	EIZE-YA	.41–.51	2	0.200	.080	②	0.200	②
	EOEE-RB	.41–.51	2	0.200	.080	②	0.200	②
	EIZE-VA	.41–.51	2	0.200	.080	②	0.200	②
	D9EE-ANA	.41–.51	2	0.240	0.720	②	0.200	②
	D9EE-APA	.41–.51	2	0.240	0.120	②	0.200	②

* Basic carburetor number
① Figure given is for all manual transmissions; for automatic trans. the figures are: (49 states) 2000 RPM; (Calif.) 1800 RPM.
② See underhood decal

Carter Thermo-Quad Specifications

Year	Model ①	Float Setting (in.)	Secondary Throttle Linkage (in.)	Secondary Air Valve Opening (in.)	Secondary Air Valve Spring (turns)	Accelerator Pump (in.)	Choke Control Lever (in.)	Choke Unloader (in.)	Vacuum Kick (in.)	Fast Idle Speed (rpm)
1974	6488S	1	②	$1/2$	$1^1/4$	$^{35}/64$	$3^3/8$	.310	21	1800
	6452S	1	②	$1/2$	$1^1/4$	$^{35}/64$	$3^3/8$	.310	4	1900
	6453S	1	②	$1/2$	$1^1/4$	$^{31}/64$	$3^3/8$	.310	21	1900
	6454S	1	②	$1/2$	$1^1/4$	$^{35}/64$	$3^3/8$	.310	4	1900
	6455S	1	②	$1/2$	$1^1/4$	$^{31}/64$	$3^3/8$	.310	21	1900
	6489S	1	②	$1/2$	$1^1/4$	$^{31}/64$	$3^3/8$	.310	21	2000
	6496S	1	②	$1/2$	$1^1/4$	$^{31}/64$	$3^3/8$	.310	21	2000
	6456S	1	②	$1/2$	$1^1/4$	$^{35}/64$	$3^3/8$	.310	4	1700
	6457S	1	②	$1/2$	$1^1/4$	$^{31}/64$	$3^3/8$	.310	21	1800
	6459	1	②	$1/2$	$1^1/4$	$^{31}/64$	$3^3/8$	.310	21	1800
	6460S	1	②	$1/2$	$1^1/4$	$^{31}/64$	$3^3/8$	.310	21	1700
	6461S	1	②	$1/2$	$1^1/4$	$^{31}/64$	$3^3/8$	.310	21	1700
	6462S	1	②	$1/2$	$1^1/4$	$^{31}/64$	$3^3/8$	.310	21	1700
	6463S	1	②	$1/2$	$1^1/4$	$^{31}/64$	$3^3/8$	.310	21	1700

① Model numbers located on the tag or on the casting
② Adjust link so primary and secondary stops both contact at same time
NOTE: All choke settings are fixed

Holley 4150C Specifications

Year	Carb. Part No. ①	Float Level (Dry) (in.)	Accelerator Pump Lever Adjustment (in.)	Choke Setting (in.)	Choke Unloader Clearance (in.)	Fast Idle On Car (rpm)	Choke Vacuum Break (in.)
1971	R4800-A	②	0.015	1.320③	0.350	2200	0.350
	R4801-A	②	0.015	1.320③	0.350	2200	0.350
	R4802-A	②	0.015	1.320③	0.350	2200	0.350
	R4803-A	②	0.015	1.320③	0.350	2200	0.350

① Located on tag attached to carburetor, or on the casting or choke plate
② The fuel level is adjusted to the lower edge of the sight plug hole on the Holley 4150C carburetor.
③ Bottom of throttle body to center of hole in operating lever

Motorcraft Model 7200 VV Specifications

Year	Model	Float Level (in.)	Float Drop (in.)	Fast Idle Cam Setting (notches)	Cold Enrichment Metering Rod (in.)	Control Vacuum (in. H₂O)	Venturi Valve Limiter (in.)	Choke Cap Setting (notches)
1979	D9AE-ACA	1³/₆₄	1¹⁵/₃₂	1 Rich/3rd step	.125	7.5	.73–.77 ①	Index
	D9ME-AA	1³/₆₄	1¹⁵/₃₂	1 Rich/3rd step	.125	7.5	.73–.77 ①	Index
1980	All	1³/₆₄	1¹⁵/₃₂	1 Rich/3rd step	.125	②	③	④
1981	D9AE-AZA	1.015–1.065	1.435–1.485	1 Rich/3rd step	.125	②	⑤	Index
	EIAE-LA	1.015–1.065	1.435–1.485	0.360/2nd step	⑦	②	⑥	INR
	EIAE-SA	1.015–1.065	1.435–1.485	0.360/2nd step	⑦	②	⑥	INR
	EIVE-AA	1.015–1.065	1.435–1.485	0.360/2nd step	⑦	②	③	Index

① Limiter Stop Setting: .99–1.01
② See text
③ Opening gap: 0.99–1.01
   Closing gap: 0.39–0.41
④ See underhood decal
⑤ Maximum opening: .99/1.01
   Wide open on throttle: .94/.98
⑥ Maximum opening: .99/1.01
   Wide open on throttle: .74/.76
⑦ 0°F—0.490 @ starting position
   75°F—0.475 @ starting position

Model 1946

Year	Part Number	Float Level (in.)	Choke Pulldown (in.)	Dechoke (in.)	Fast Idle Cam (in.)	Accelerator Pump Stroke Slot
1981	EIBE-AFA	.69	.113	.150	.082	#2
	EIBE-AKA	.69	.113	.150	.082	#2
	EOBE-CA	.69	.100	.150	.070	#2
	EOBE-AA	.69	.100	.150	.070	#2

Chassis Electrical

HEATER

Non-Air Conditioned Cars

HEATER CORE REMOVAL AND INSTALLATION

Torino, Montego, Elite, LTD II, Cougar and Thunderbird Through 1979

1. Drain coolant.
2. Disconnect both heater hoses at the firewall.
3. Remove the nuts retaining the heater assembly to the firewall.
4. Disconnect temperature and defroster cables at heater.
5. Disconnect wires from resistor, and disconnect blower motor wires and clip retaining heater assembly to defroster nozzle.
6. Remove glove box.
7. Remove bolt and nut connecting the right air duct control to instrument panel. Remove nuts retaining right air duct and remove duct assembly.
8. Remove heater assembly to bench.
9. Open the case and remove the core.
10. Installation is the reverse of removal.

1981–82 Cougar

It is not necessary to remove the heater case for access to the heater core.

1. Drain enough coolant from the radiator to drain the heater core.
2. Loosen the heater hose clamps on the engine side of the firewall and disconnect the heater hoses. Cap the heater core tubes.
3. Remove the glove box liner.
4. Remove the instrument panel-to-cowl brace retaining screws and remove the brace.
5. Move the temperature lever to warm.
6. Remove the heater core cover screws. Remove the cover through the glove box.
7. Loosen the heater case mounting nuts on the engine side of the firewall.
8. Push the heater core tubes and seal toward the interior of the car to loosen the core.
9. Remove the heater core through the glove box opening.

1980 and Later Cougar XR-7 and Thunderbird, 1982 Continental

1. Disconnect the negative battery cable. Remove the steering column cover assembly and the left and right finish panels.
2. Remove the screw at each end of the instrument panel pad and retainer assembly. Remove the four screws which retain the upper finish panel to the instrument panel. Remove the pad and retainer and the upper finish panel as an assembly.
3. Loosen the steering column attachments and lower the column slightly. It needs

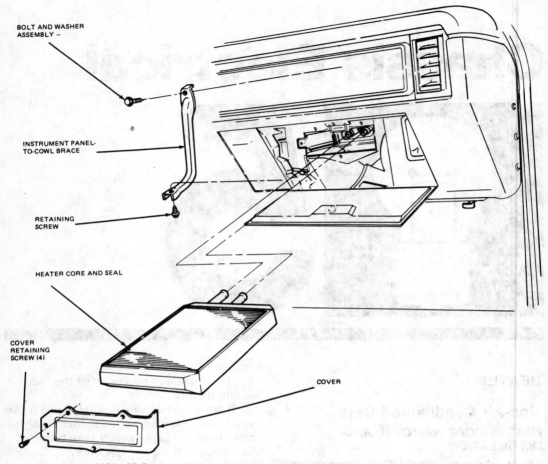

BOLT AND WASHER
ASSEMBLY –

INSTRUMENT PANEL-
TO-COWL BRACE

RETAINING
SCREW

HEATER CORE AND SEAL

COVER
RETAINING
SCREW (4)

COVER

1981–82 Cougar heater core removal on cars without air conditioning

to be dropped only far enough to reach the transmission lever and cable assembly. Be careful not to lower it too far, or damage to the lever and/or the case will result. Reach

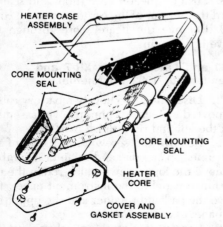

HEATER CASE
ASSEMBLY

CORE MOUNTING
SEAL

CORE MOUNTING
SEAL

HEATER
CORE

COVER AND
GASKET ASSEMBLY

Typical heater core removal on all non-air conditioned cars, except 1981–82 Cougar

between the column and the panel; lift the selector lever cable from the lever. Remove the cable clamp from the steering column tube.

4. Rest the column on the front seat.

5. Remove the instrument panel-to-brake pedal support screw at the column opening.

6. Disconnect the temperature cable from the blend door and evaporator case bracket. Disconnect the vacuum hose connectors from the case. Disconnect the resistor wire and the blower feed wire.

7. Remove the three instrument panel-to-cowl screws. Remove the screws at each end of the instrument panel which secure it to the cowl side panels. Remove the two panel-to-floor screws. Pull the panel back and disconnect the speedometer cable. Disconnect the panel wiring. Lay the panel on the front seat.

8. Drain the coolant. Disconnect and plug the heater hoses at the core tubes.

9. Remove the two nuts inside the en-

gine compartment which retain the evaporator case to the firewall.

10. Inside the car, remove the heater assembly support bracket and air inlet duct support bracket-to-cowl top panel screws.

11. Remove the one nut retaining the left heater assembly bracket to the firewall, and the one nut at the bottom bracket.

12. Pull the assembly away from the firewall for access to the heater core cover. Remove the five core cover screws. Remove the core and seals. Installation is the reverse.

BLOWER MOTOR REMOVAL AND INSTALLATION

The blower motor on all models except the 1980–82 Cougar XR-7, Thunderbird and 1982 Lincoln Continental is located inside the heater assembly. To replace the blower motor on all models except the 1980–82 Cougar XR-7 and Thunderbird, and 1981–82 Cougar, remove the heater assembly from the car. Once the heater assembly is removed, it is a simple operation to remove the motor attaching bolts and remove the motor. On all models except as noted, the motor and cage are removed as an assembly.

1981–82 Cougar

The right side ventilator assembly must be removed for access to the blower motor and wheel.

1. Remove the retaining screw for the right register duct mounting bracket.

2. Remove the screws holding the con-

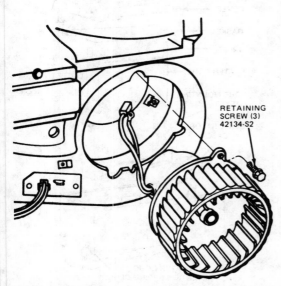

RETAINING
SCREW (3)
42134-S2

Blower motor removal on 1981–82 Cougar without air conditioning

trol cable lever assembly to the instrument panel.

3. Remove the glove box liner.

4. Remove the plastic rivets securing the grille to the floor outlet, and remove the grille.

5. Remove the right register duct and register assembly:

    a. Remove the register duct bracket retaining screw on the lower edge of the instrument panel, and disengage the duct from the opening and remove through the glove box opening.

    b. Insert a thin blade under the retaining tab and pry the tab toward the louvers until retaining tab pivot clears the hole in the register opening. Pull the register assembly end out from the housing only enough to prevent the pivot from going back into the pivot hole. Pry the other retaining tab loose and remove the register assembly from the opening.

6. Remove the retaining screws securing the ventilator assembly to the blower housing. The upper right screw can be reached with a long extension through the register opening; the upper left screw can be reached through the glove box opening. The other two screws are on the bottom of the assembly.

7. Slide the assembly to the right, then down and out from under the instrument panel.

8. Remove the motor lead wire connector from the register and push it back through the hole in the case. Remove the right side cowl trim panel for access, and remove the ground terminal lug retaining screw.

9. Remove the hub clamp spring from the motor shaft and remove the blower wheel.

10. Remove the blower motor bolts from the housing and remove the motor.

1980 and Later Cougar XR-7 and Thunderbird, 1982 Continental

1. Disconnect the negative battery cable. Remove the glove compartment. Disconnect the vacuum hose from the outside/recirc flap vacuum motor.

2. Remove the instrument panel-to-cowl lower right side attaching bolt. Remove the air inlet duct top support brace screw.

3. Disconnect the blower feed wire.

4. Remove the blower housing lower support bracket-to-evaporator case retaining nut.

5. Remove the cowl side trim panel. Remove the blower ground wire screw. Remove the air inlet duct top screw. Move the

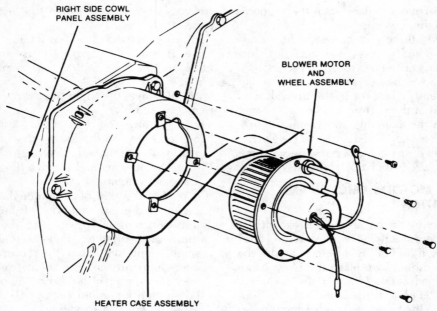

RIGHT SIDE COWL
PANEL ASSEMBLY

BLOWER MOTOR
AND
WHEEL ASSEMBLY

HEATER CASE ASSEMBLY

Typical blower motor removal on non-air conditioned cars, except 1981–82 Cougar

inlet duct and blower housing down and away from the heater case.

6. Remove the four blower motor mounting plate screws. Remove the motor and fan wheel. Do not remove the mounting plate from the motor. Installation is the reverse.

Vehicles with Integral Heater-Air Conditioning

NOTE: *Removal of the heater-air conditioner housing requires evacuation of the air conditioner refrigerant. This operation requires special tools and training. Failure to follow proper safety precautions may cause personal injury. It is recommended that discharging and charging of the A/C system by performed by an experienced professional mechanic.*

HEATER CORE REMOVAL AND INSTALLATION

Torino, Montego, and Elite; Cougar through 1976

1. Drain the cooling system and disconnect the heater hoses at the core.

2. Remove the glove box.

3. Remove the two snap clips and the heater air outlet register from the plenum.

4. Remove the temperature control cable assembly mounting screw, and disconnect the

end of the cable from the blend door crank arm.

5. Remove the blue and red vacuum hoses from the high-low door vacuum motor; the yellow hose from the panel-defrost door motor, and the brown hose from the inline tee connector.

6. Disconnect the wires at the resistor block.

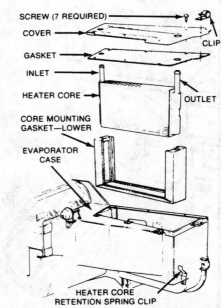

SCREW (7 REQUIRED)

COVER

CLIP

GASKET

INLET

HEATER CORE

OUTLET

CORE MOUNTING
GASKET—LOWER

EVAPORATOR
CASE

HEATER CORE
RETENTION SPRING CLIP

Typical heater core removal on air conditioned cars

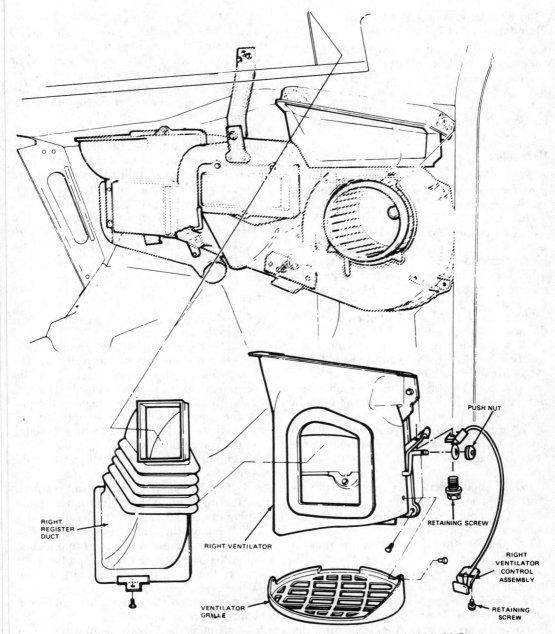

Right ventilator and register duct removal on non-air conditioned 1981–82 Cougar

7. Remove the ten screws and the rear half of the plenum.

8. Remove the mounting nut from the heater core tube support bracket.

9. Reverse the procedure to install, taking care to apply body sealer around the case flanges to insure a positive seal.

LTD II, Thunderbird, 1977–79 Cougar

1. Drain the engine coolant and disconnect the hoses from the core.

2. Remove the heater core cover plate, under the hood.

3. Press down on the core and tilt it toward the front of the vehicle to release it from the seal.

4. Pull the core up and out.

5. To install, press downward on the core and tilt it toward the rear to engage the notch on the seal with the flange on the housing. Replace any deformed sealer. Install all other parts.

1980 and Later Cougar XR-7 and Thunderbird, 1982 Continental

Heater core removal and installation for air conditioned models is the same as the procedure given earlier for non-air conditioned models. It is not necessary to discharge the A/C system; simply pull the evaporator case far enough wway from the firewall to reach the heater core cover screws.

Versailles

NOTE: *The refrigerant system components and charge do not have to be disturbed when removing and installing the heater core.*

1. Drain the coolant and disconnect the battery.

2. Disconnect 2 heater hose clamps at the firewall in the engine compartment. Plug the core tubes to prevent coolant leakage during removal.

3. Remove the heat distribution duct from the instrument panel.

4. On models through 1978, remove the seat belt interlock module and bracket.

5. Remove the glovebox liner.

6. Loosen the right door sill scuff plate, right A pillar trim cover, and remove the right cowl side trim panel.

7. Loosen instrument panel-to-right cowl side bolt and remove the instrument panel brace bolt at the lower rail, below the glove box.

8. On models with ATC, remove the instrument panel crash pad.

9. On models with ATC, remove the radio speaker or panel cowl brace.

10. Remove the 4 nozzle-to-cowl bracket mounting screws.

11. Lift the defroster nozzle upward through the crash pad opening.

12. Disconnect the vacuum hoses from the A/C-Defrost and Heat-Defrost door motors. Remove the screw from the cliph olding the vacuum harness to the plenum.

13. Remove 2 Heat/Defrost door mounting nuts and swing the motor rearward on the door crankarm.

14. Remove 2 screws attaching the plenum to the left mounting bracket. Then remove the screws and clips securing the plenum to the evaporator case.

15. Swing the bottom of the plenum away from the evaporator case to disengage the S-clip on the forward flange of the Plenum. Raise the plenum to clear the tabs on the top of the evaporator case.

16. Move the plenum to the left as far as possible (about 4 inches), pulling rearward on the instrument panel to gain clearance. Take care when pulling back on the instrument panel to avoid cracking the plastic panel.

NOTE: *There is very little clearance between the plenum and the wiper motor assembly.*

17. Pull the heater core to the left using the tab molded into the rear heater core seal. As the rear surface of the heater core clears the evaporator case, pull the core rearward and downward to clear the instrument panel.

18. Reverse the procedure to install.

NOTE: *Before installing the core, make sure that the heater core tube to firewall seal is in place between the evaporator case and the firewall.*

1981–82 Cougar

The instrument panel must be removed for access to the heater core.

1. Disconnect the battery ground cable.

2. Remove the instrument panel pad:

a. Remove the screws attaching the instrument cluster trim panel to the pad.

b. Remove the screw attaching the pad to the panel at each defroster opening.

c. Remove the screws attaching the edge of the pad to the panel.

3. Remove the steering column opening cover.

4. Remove the nuts and bracket retaining the steering column to the instrument panel and lay the column against the seat.

5. Remove the instrument panel to brake pedal support screw at the column opening.

6. Remove the screws attaching the lower brace to the panel below the radio, and below the glove box.

7. Disconnect the temperature cable from the door and case bracket.

8. Unplug the 7-port vacuum hose connectors at the evaporator case.

9. Disconnect the resistor wire connector and the blower feed wire.

10. Remove the screws attaching the top of the panel to the cowl. Support the panel while doing this.

11. Remove the one screw at each end attaching the panel to the cowl side panels.

12. Move the panel rearward and disconnect the speedometer cable and any wires preventing the panel from lying flat on the seat.

13. Drain the coolant and disconnect the

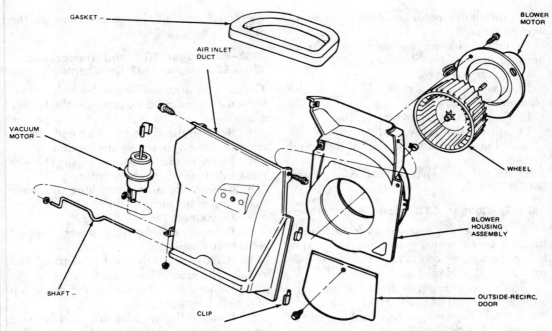

Air inlet duct and blower housing on air conditioned 1981–82 Cougar

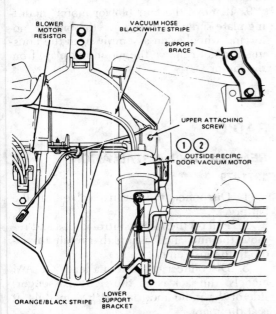

Air inlet and blower system assembled on 1981–82 Cougar

heater hoses from the heater core. Plug the core tubes.

14. Remove the nuts retaining the evaporator case to the firewall in the engine compartment.

15. Remove the case support bracket screws and air inlet duct support bracket.

16. Remove the nut retaining the bracket to the dash panel at the left side of the evap-

orator case, and the nut retaining the bracket below the case to the dash panel.

17. Pull the case assembly away from the panel to get to the screws retaining the heater core cover to the case.

18. Remove the cover screws and the cover.

19. Lift the heater core and seals from the evaporator case.

BLOWER MOTOR REMOVAL AND INSTALLATION

Torino, Montego, Elite; Cougar Through 1976

1. Disconnect the battery and take out the glove box.

2. Remove the recirculating air duct. On 1975 and later models, remove the instrument panel pad and side cowl trim.

3. Remove the screws which attach the blower lower housing to the firewall and bracket.

4. Disconnect the vacuum line from the actuator and move it out of the way.

5. Disconnect the plug from the resistor block and lift out the resistor block.

6. Remove all blower housing flange screws, separate blower housing halves, and unscrew and remove blower assembly.

7. Remove the blower wheel.

8. Install the blower wheel on the motor.

9. Install the motor and shell and ground wire in the case.

10. Install blower assembly into lower housing, and reassemble housing.

11. Connect the wires.

12. Fasten the resistor block to the plenum.

13. Install the recirculating air duct.

14. Install the screws which attach the blower lower housing to the firewall and bracket.

15. Install the glove box and connect the battery. Install the pad and trim.

1977–79 Cougar, LTD II and Thunderbird

1. Remove the two screws from around the instrument cluster opening, the screw above the steering column and the two screws from above the glove box door.

2. Remove the screw from the top right surface of the upper finish panel.

3. Pull the panel pad rearward then up to disengage the clips.

4. Remove the glove box.

5. Remove the side cowl trim panel.

6. Remove the instrument panel attachment on the right side.

7. Remove the blower housing-to-dash attaching nut in the engine compartment and the one in the passenger compartment.

8. Disconnect the outside air recirculating door vacuum hose and the blower motor wiring.

9. Remove the blower assembly and remove the motor and the wheel as an assembly.

10. Reverse to install.

Versailles

1. Disconnect the negative battery cable.

2. Loosen the passenger side door sill scuff plate and the right A pillar trim cover. Remove the right cowl side trim panel.

3. Remove the bolt retaining the lower side of the instrument panel to the cowl. Remove the right cowl side brace bolt.

4. Disconnect the wiring harness connectors at the blower motor.

5. If so equipped, remove the cooling tube from the blower motor.

6. Remove the 4 screws retaining the blower motor and wheel assembly to the scroll. To remove the motor, pull rearward on the lower edge of the instrument panel to provide clearance. Do not remove the mounting plate from the blower motor.

7. Installation is the reverse of removal. If necessary, cement the cooling tube to the blower motor.

1980–82 Cougar XR-7 and Thunderbird 1981–82 Cougar, 1982 Continental

The air inlet duct and blower housing assembly must be removed for access to the blower motor.

1. Remove the glove box liner and disconnect the hose from the vacuum motor.

2. Remove the instrument panel lower right side to cowl attaching bolt.

3. Remove the screw attaching the brace to the top of the air inlet duct.

4. Disconnect the motor wire.

5. Remove the housing lower support bracket to case nut.

6. Remove the side cowl trim panel and remove the ground wire screw.

7. Remove the attaching screw at the top of the air inlet duct.

8. Remove the air inlet duct and housing assembly down and away from the evaporator case.

9. Remove the four blower motor mounting plate screws and remove the blower motor and wheel as an assembly from the housing. Do not remove the mounting plate from the motor.

RADIO

REMOVAL AND INSTALLATION
1971–79

1. Disconnect the negative cable from the battery.

2. Pull off the radio control knobs and remove the nuts and washers that retain the radio to the instrument panel.

3. Disconnect the antenna lead. On AM models, the jack is on the right (passenger) side of the radio and, on AM/FM models, it is at the rear.

4. Disconnect the speaker, power, and dial light leads at their respective quick-disconnects.

5. Remove the radio support bracket(s).

6. Lower the radio from the instrument panel and remove it.

7. To install, position the radio on the floor below its mounting location and attach the antenna, speaker, power, and dial light leads if they will reach. Then place the radio in the instrument panel and install the retain-

ing nuts and washers. Connect all leads not previously connected.

8. Install the radio support bracket(s).

9. Push the radio control knobs onto their shafts.

10. Connect the negative cable to the battery.

11. Adjust the antenna trimmer, if necessary, and check radio operation.

Versailles

1. Disconnect the negative battery cable.

2. Remove the headlight switch from the instrument panel. Remove the heater, air conditioner, windshield wiper/washer knobs, and radio knobs and discs.

3. Remove the six screws which attach the applique to the instrument panel and remove the applique. Disconnect the antenna lead-in cable from the radio.

4. Remove the four screws which attach the radio bezel to the instrument panel. Slide the radio and bezel out of the lower rear support bracket and instrument panel opening toward the interior far enough to disconnect the electrical connections, and remove the radio.

5. Remove the nut attaching the rear support bracket to the radio and remove the bracket. Remove the nuts and washer from the radio control shafts and remove the bezel.

6. To install, attach the rear support bracket to the radio. Install the bezel, washers and nuts.

7. Insert the radio with rear support bracket and bezel through the instrument panel opening far enough to connect the electrical leads and antenna lead-in cable. Install the radio upper rear support bracket into the lower rear support bracket.

8. Center the radio and bezel in the opening and install the four bezel attaching screws.

9. Install the instrument panel applique with its six attaching screws. Install all knobs removed from the instrument panel and radio. Install the headlight switch.

10. Connect the negative battery cable.

1981–82 Cougar

1. Disconnect the negative battery cable.

2. Disconnect the electrical, speaker, and antenna leads from the radio.

3. Remove the knobs, discs, and control shaft nuts and washers from the radio shafts.

4. Remove the ash tray receptacle and bracket.

5. Remove the rear support nut from the radio.

6. Remove the instrument panel lower reinforcement and the heater or air conditioning floor ducts.

7. Remove the radio from the rear support, and drop the radio down and out from behind the instrument panel.

8. To install, reverse the removal procedure.

1980 and Later Thunderbird and Cougar XR-7, 1982 Continental

1. Disconnect the negative battery cable.

2. Remove the radio knobs (pull off). Remove the center trim panel.

3. Remove the radio mounting plate screws. Pull the radio towards the front seat to disengage it from the lower bracket.

4. Disconnect the radio and antenna connections.

5. Remove the radio. Remove the nuts and washers (conventional radios) or mounting plate screws (electronic radios) as necessary.

6. On electronic radios, install the mounting plates before installing the retaining nuts and washers or screws. The rest of installation is the reverse of removal.

WINDSHIELD WIPERS

MOTOR REMOVAL AND INSTALLATION
Torino, Montego, LTD II With Non-Hidden Wipers

1. Disconnect battery and wiper motor connector.

2. Remove cowl top left vent screen by removing four retaining drive pins.

3. Remove wiper link retaining clip from wiper motor arm.

4. Remove three wiper motor retaining bolts, and remove wiper motor and mounting bracket.

5. To install motor, place wiper motor and mounting bracket against firewall and install three retaining bolts.

6. Position wiper link on motor drive arm, and install connecting clip. Be sure to force clip locking flange into locked position.

7. Install cowl top vent screen and secure with four drive pins.

8. Check motor operation and connect wiring plugs.

1977 Versailles

1. Remove instrument cluster.
2. If air conditioned, remove center connector and duct assembly. Remove mounting bracket screw behind center duct, disconnect assembly from plenum chamber and left duct, and pull center connector and duct assembly out through cluster opening.
3. Working through cluster opening, disconnect two pivot shaft links from motor drive arm by removing retaining clip.
4. Disconnect wiring plug at motor, remove three retaining bolts, and remove motor through cluster opening.
5. To install motor, bolt motor to mounting plate with three retaining bolts.
6. Connect right pivot shaft link to motor and then connect left pivot shaft link. Lock clip.
7. On air conditioned vehicles, insert end of center connector and duct assembly near mounting bracket into left duct and opposite end into plenum chamber.
8. Secure assembly with mounting bracket screw.
9. Install instrument cluster, and check operation of wiper motor.

1978–80 Versailles

1. Disconnect the battery ground cable.
2. Remove the instrument panel pad, retained by eight screws.

3. Remove the speaker mounting bracket, disconnect and remove the speaker.
4. Remove the interlock module from the bracket and disconnect the multiple connector.
5. Remove the motor bracket bolts and the drive arm clip. Remove the motor.
6. Install in reverse order.

Torino, Elite, LTD II, Montego; Cougar and Thunderbird Through 1979 (Hidden Wipers)

1. Disconnect the battery ground cable.
2. Remove the wiper arm and blade assemblies from the pivot shafts.
3. Remove the left cowl screen for access through the cowl opening. Disconnect the linkage drive arm from the motor output arm crankpin by removing the retaining clip. From the engine side of the firewall, disconnect the two push-on wire connectors from the motor.
4. Remove the three bolts which retain the motor to the firewall and remove the motor. If the output arm catches on the firewall during removal, hand turn the arm clockwise, so that it will clear the opening in the firewall.
5. Before installing the motor, be sure that the output arm is in the Park position.

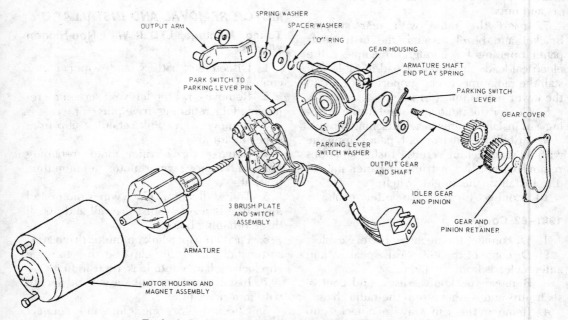

Typical single or two-speed wiper motor disassembled

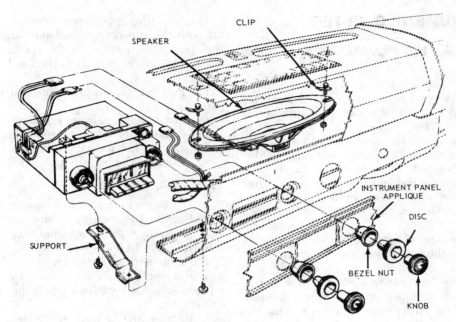

Typical radio installation

1980–82 Thunderbird and Cougar XR-7
1981–82 Cougar, 1982 Continental

1. Disconnect the ground cable.
2. Remove the right hand wiper arm from the pivot shaft and lay it on the top grille.
3. Remove the cowl top grille screws.
4. Reach under the left front corner of the grille to disconnect the linkage drive arm from the motor crank by removing the retaining clip.
5. Disconnect the electrical connector. Remove the motor mounting bolts and remove the motor.
6. Install in reverse order.

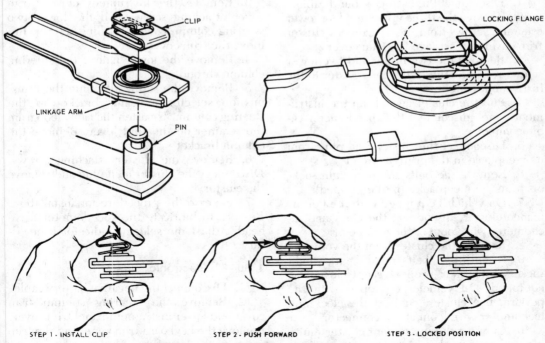

Removing or installing wiper arms connecting clips

INSTRUMENT CLUSTER

REMOVAL AND INSTALLATION

1971

1. Disconnect the battery.
2. Remove one retaining screw from the lower edge of the dash pad at the left of the instrument cluster.
3. Remove the five pad-to-instrument panel screws across the bottom edge of the pad to the right of the cluster.
4. Pull the pad and retainer assembly free from the clips on the instrument panel.
5. Disconnect the speaker and remove the pad.
6. Remove the four screws that retain the cluster to the panel and move the cluster part way out of the panel.
7. Disconnect the speedometer cable, the multiple plug which goes to the printed circuit and the feed plug which services the tachometer or clock, if so equipped.
8. Disengage the three light bulb and socket assemblies from their receptacles.
9. Disconnect the cable and the five vacuum hoses from the heater control, and feed plug to the heater control switch and the connector to the heater control light.
10. Remove the cluster. Reverse the procedure to install.

1972

1. Disconnect the battery ground cable.
2. Remove the three upper and four lower retaining screws from the instrument cluster trim cover and remove the trim cover.
3. Remove the two upper and two lower screws retaining the instrument cluster to the instrument panel.
4. Pull the cluster away from the instrument panel; disconnect the speedometer cable connector.
5. Disconnect the cluster feed plug from its receptacle in the printed circuit.
6. Remove the belts and park light sockets from the receptacles (if so equipped).
7. On vehicles equipped with the performance cluster, disconnect the clock and tachometer wire loom at the connector.
8. Remove the cluster from the vehicle.
9. Install the "belts" and "park" light sockets into their proper receptacles, if so equipped. On vehicles equipped with the performance cluster, connect the clock and tachometer wire loom at the connector.
10. Connect the instrument cluster multiple connector to the printed circuit.

11. Align the speedometer cable connector with the speedometer adaptor and push the speedometer cable on the speedometer with a twisting motion until the catch is engaged.
12. Position the cluster to the instrument panel.
13. Install the four cluster retaining screws.
14. Position the cluster front trim cover and install the seven retaining screws.
15. Connect the battery ground cable.

1973–79

1. Disconnect the negative battery cable.
2. Remove the steering column cover.
3. Disconnect the speedometer cable and the wire plugs to the printed circuit.
4. Remove the cluster trim cover.
5. Remove the screw attaching the transmission selector lever indicator cable to the column.
6. Remove the instrument cluster retaining screws and lift the cluster from the instrument panel.
7. Reverse the above procedure to install, taking care to ensure that the selector pointer is aligned.

1980–82 Non-Electronic Cluster

1. Disconnect the negative battery cable.
2. Disconnect the speedometer cable (refer to the following section for instructions).
3. Remove the instrument cluster trim cover attaching screws and the lower two steering column cover attaching screws. Remove the trim covers.
4. Remove the lower half of the steering column shroud.
5. Remove the screw attaching the transmission selector indicator bracket to the steering column. Unfasten the cable loop from the retainer on the shift lever. Remove the column bracket.
6. Remove the cluster attaching screws. Disconnect the cluster feed plug and remove the cluster.
7. Reverse the procedure for installation. Be sure to lubricate the speedometer drive head. Adjust the selector indicator if necessary.

1980–82 Electronic Cluster

1. Disconnect the negative battery cable.
2. Remove the steering column trim cover and lower instrument panel trim cover. Remove the keyboard trim panel and the trim panel on the left of the column.

3. Remove the instrument cluster trim cover screws and remove the trim panel.

4. Remove the instrument cluster mounting screws and pull the cluster forward. Disconnect the feed plugs and the ground wire from the back of the cluster. Disconnect the speedometer cable (see following section for details).

5. Remove the screw attaching the transmission indicator cable bracket to the steering column. Unfasten the cable loop from the retainer. Remove the bracket.

6. Unfasten the plastic clamp from around the steering column. Remove the cluster.

7. To install the cluster: Apply a small amount of silicone lubricant into the drive hole of the speedometer head.

8. Connect the feed plugs and the ground wire to the cluster. Install the speedometer cable. Attach the instrument cluster to the instrument panel.

9. Install the plastic indicator cable clamp around the steering column and engage the clamp locator pin in the column tube.

10. Place the transmission selector in the "Drive" position. Install the mounting screw into the retainer but do not tighten.

11. Rotate the plastic cable clamp until the indicator flag covers *both* location dots. Tighten the retainer screw.

12. Move the selector through all positions. Readjust if necessary.

13. The rest of the installation is in the reverse order of removal.

Ignition Lock Cylinder
REPLACEMENT

1. Disconnect the negative battery cable.

2. On cars with a fixed steering column, remove the steering wheel trim pad and the steering wheel. Insert a stiff wire into the hole located in the lock cylinder housing. On cars with a tilt steering wheel, this hole is located on the outside of the column near the 4-way flasher button. It is not necessary to remove the wheel. On 1980–82 Thunderbirds and XR-7s, 1981–82 Cougars, and 1982 Continentals, remove the four column shroud screws. The hole in the casting is angled down toward the seat. Insert a ⅛ in. diameter wire.

3. Place the gear shift lever in Reverse on standard shift cars and in Park on cars with automatic transmissions and turn the ignition key to the "on" position.

4. Depress the wire and remove the lock cylinder and wire.

5. Insert a new cylinder into the housing and turn to the "off" position. This will lock the cylinder into position.

6. Reinstall the steering wheel and pad.

7. Connect the negative battery cable.

Ignition Switch
REPLACEMENT

1. Disconnect the negative battery cable.

2. Remove shrouding from the steering column. Detach and lower the steering column from the brake support bracket on all

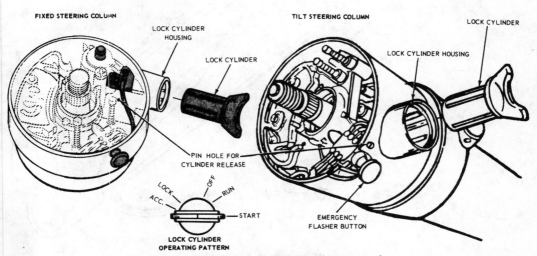

FIXED STEERING COLUMN

LOCK CYLINDER HOUSING

LOCK CYLINDER

PIN HOLE FOR CYLINDER RELEASE

LOCK — OFF — RUN — ACC. — START

LOCK CYLINDER OPERATING PATTERN

TILT STEERING COLUMN

LOCK CYLINDER

LOCK CYLINDER HOUSING

EMERGENCY FLASHER BUTTON

Lock cylinder replacement on locking type column

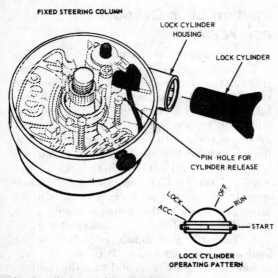

Lock cylinder replacement

models except the 1980–82 Thunderbird and Cougar XR-7, 1981–82 Cougar and 1982 Continental.

3. Disconnect the switch wiring at the multiple plug.

4. Remove the two nuts that retain the switch to steering column. On the models specified in Step 2, the break-off head bolts that attach the switch to the lock cylinder housing must be drilled out with a ⅛ in. drill. Remove the bolts with an Easy-Out extractor. Disengage the ignition switch from the pin.

5. On models with a steering column-mounted gearshift lever, disconnect the ignition switch plunger from the ignition switch actuator rod and remove the ignition switch. On models with a floor mounted gearshift lever, remove the pin that connects the switch plunger to the switch actuator and remove the switch.

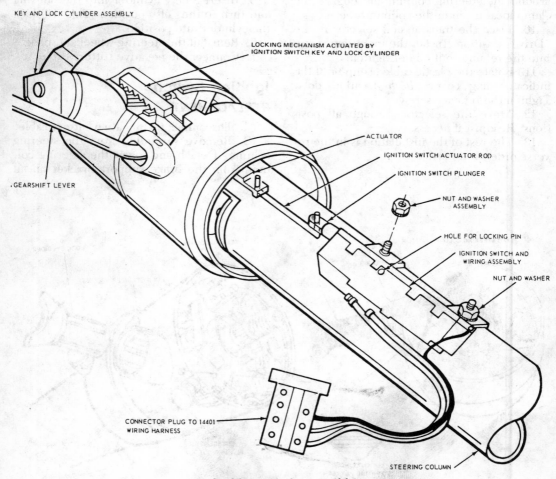

Ignition switch assembly

6. To re-install the switch, place both locking mechanism at top of column and switch itself in lock position for correct adjustment. To hold column in lock position, place automatic shift lever in PARK or manual shift lever in reverse, and turn to LOCK and remove the key. New switches are held in lock by plastic shipping pins. To pin existing switches, pull the switch plunger out as far as it will go and push back in to first detent. Insert 3/32 in. diameter wire into locking hole in the top of the switch.

7. Connect the switch plunger to the switch actuator rod.

8. Position the switch on the column and install the attaching nuts. Be sure the proper break-off head bolts are used on the models mentioned in Step 2. Do not tighten them.

9. Move the switch up and down to locate the mid-position of rod lash, and then tighten the nuts. On the models specified in Step 2, tighten the bolts until the heads break off.

10. Remove the locking pin or wire. Connect the electrical connector. Reconnect the battery cable and check for proper switch operation.

11. Attach the steering column to the brake support bracket and install the shrouding.

Turn Signal Flasher Locations

| 1971 | On fuse board to left of column |
| 1972 and later | On fuse panel |

SEAT-BELT/STARTER INTERLOCK

1974–75 Models

All 1974 and some 1975 Ford and Mercury vehicles are equipped with the Federally-required starter interlock system. The purpose of this system is to force the wearing of seat belts.

The system includes a warning light and buzzer (as in late 1972 and 1973), weight sensors in the front seats, switches in the outboard front seat belt retractors, and an electronic control module. The center front seat is tied into the warning light and buzzer system, but not into the starter interlock.

The electronic control module requires that the driver and right front passenger first sit down, then pull out their seat belts. If this is not done, the starter will not operate, but the light and buzzer will. The sequence must be followed each time the engine is started unless the driver and passenger have remained seated and buckled. If the seat belts have been pulled out and left buckled, the engine will not start. The switches in the retractors must be cycled for each start. If the belts are released after the start, the light and buzzer will operate.

If the system should fail, preventing starting, the interlock by-pass switch under the hood can be used. This switch permits one start without interference from the interlock system. This by-pass switch can also be used for servicing purposes.

TROUBLESHOOTING

If the starter will not crank or the warning buzzer will not shut off, perform the following checks:

Problem: Front seat occupant sits on a pre-buckled seat belt.

Solution: Unbuckle the prebuckled belt, fully retract, extract, and then rebuckle the belt.

Problem: The front seat occupants are buckled, but the starter will not crank.

Solution: The unoccupied seat sensor switch stuck closed before the seat was occupied. Reset the unoccupied seat sensor switches by applying and then releasing 50lbs or more of weight to the seat directly over the seat sensor switches.

Problem: Starter will not crank with a heavy parcel on the front seat.

Solution: Buckle the seat belt around the parcel somewhere else in the car. Unbuckle the seat belt when the parcel is removed from the front seat.

Problem: Starter will not crank due to starter interlock system component failure.

Solution: An emergency starter interlock override switch is located under the hood on the fender apron. Depress the red push button on the switch and release it. This will allow one complete cycle of the ignition key from Off to Start and back to Off. Do not tape the button down as this will result in deactivation of the override feature.

DISCONNECTING SEAT BELT/STARTER INTERLOCK

As of October 29, 1974, it is legal to disconnect the seat belt/starter interlock system. However, the warning light portion of the system must be left operational.

STARTER INTERLOCK DELETION — ALL VEHICLES SO EQUIPPED — 1974–75

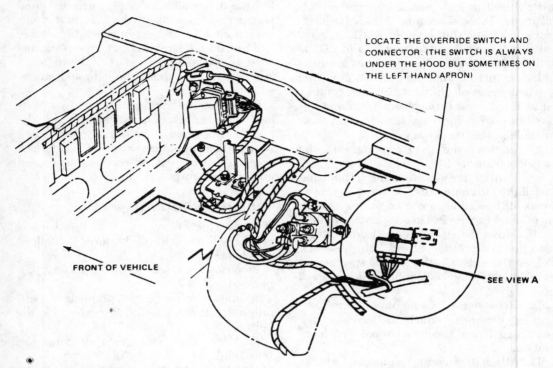

LOCATE THE OVERRIDE SWITCH AND CONNECTOR. (THE SWITCH IS ALWAYS UNDER THE HOOD BUT SOMETIMES ON THE LEFT HAND APRON)

FRONT OF VEHICLE

SEE VIEW A

CAUTION: SET THE PARKING BRAKE AND REMOVE THE IGNITION KEY BEFORE ANY REWORK IS PERFORMED.
(IF THE NO. 640 CIRCUIT IS ACCIDENTALLY SPLICED INTO THE NO. 32 OR NO. 33 CIRCUITS, THE CAR WILL START IN GEAR)

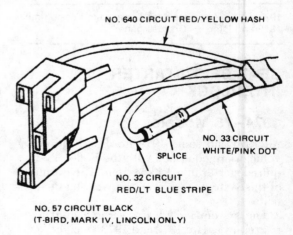

NO. 640 CIRCUIT RED/YELLOW HASH

NO. 33 CIRCUIT WHITE/PINK DOT

SPLICE

NO. 32 CIRCUIT RED/LT BLUE STRIPE

NO. 57 CIRCUIT BLACK (T-BIRD, MARK IV, LINCOLN ONLY)

VIEW A

Seat belt/starter interlock system deletion—all models

1. Apply the parking brake and remove the ignition key.

2. Open the hood and locate the system emergency override switch and connector. Remove the connector.

3. Cut the white wire(s) with the pink dots (#33 circuit) and the red wire(s) with the light blue stripe (#32 circuit).

4. Splice the two (four) wires together and tape the splice. Use a "butt" connector if available.

NOTE: *Do not cut and splice the other connector wires. If the red/yellow hash wire is spliced to any of the other wires the car will start in gear.*

5. Install the connector back on the override switch. Close the hood.

6. Apply the parking brakes, buckle the seat belt, and turn the key to the "ON" position. If the starter cranks in "ON" or any gear selected, the wrong wires have been cut and spliced. Repeat Steps 3–5.

7. Unbuckle the belt and try to start the car. If the car doesn't start, repeat Steps 3–5. If the car starts, everything is OK.

8. To stop the warning buzzer from operating, remove it from its connector and throw it away. Tape the connector to the wiring harness so that it can't rattle.

WIRING DIAGRAMS

Wiring diagrams have been left out of this book. As cars have become more complex, and available with longer and longer option lists, wiring diagrams have grown in size and complexity also. It has become virtually impossible to provide a readable reproduction in a reasonable number of pages. Information on ordering wiring diagrams from the vehicle manufacturer can be found in the owners manual.

Clutch and Transmission

MANUAL TRANSMISSION

A three-speed column-shifted transmission was standard equipment on base Ford models from 1971 to 1974. A four-speed floor-shifted transmission was available from 1971 until 1973. From 1974 through 1980 no manual transmission was offered. In 1981 and 1982 models with the 4 cylinder engine, a German model 82 ET 4-speed was used.

1971–73
REMOVAL

1. On floor-shift models, remove the boot retainer and shift lever. Raise the car, taking proper safety precautions.
2. Disconnect the driveshaft at the rear universal joint and remove the driveshaft.
3. Disconnect the speedometer cable at the transmission extension. On transmission regulated spark equipped cars, disconnect the lead wire at the connector.
4. Disconnect the gearshift rods from the transmission shift levers. If the car is equipped with a four-speed, remove the bolts that secure the shift control bracket to the extension housing.
5. Remove the bolt holding the extension housing to the rear support, and remove the muffler inlet pipe bracket-to-housing bolt.

6. Remove the two rear support bracket insulator nuts from the underside of the cross-member. Remove the cross-member.
NOTE: *On 1972 and later models the no. 3 crossmember's mounting bolts have a plastic locking compound on the threads. To remove the insulator nuts, heat them with a torch.*
7. Place a jack (equipped with a protective piece of wood) under the rear of the engine oil pan. Raise the engine, slightly.
8. Remove the transmission-to-fly-wheel housing bolts. On clutch removal only, install two guide studs into the bottom attaching bolt holes.
NOTE: *On 429 cu in. engines, the upper left-hand transmission attaching bolt is a seal bolt. Carefully note its position so that it may be reinstalled in its original position.*
9. Slide the transmission back and out of the car.

INSTALLATION

1. Start the transmission extension housing up and over the rear support. After moving the transmission back just far enough for the pilot shaft to clear the clutch housing, move it upward into position onto the transmission guide studs.

2. Slide the transmission forward and into place against the flywheel housing.

3. Remove the guide studs and torque the transmission to flywheel bolts to 37–42 ft. lbs.

4. Position the crossmember to the frame and install the attaching bolts. Slowly lower the engine onto the crossmember.

5. Install the insulator-to-cross-member nuts. Torque the nuts to 30–50 ft. lbs.

6. Connect the gear shift rods and the speedometer cable. On cars with transmission-regulated spark, connect the lead wire at the plug connector. On floor-shift models, install the shift lever and boot.

7. Connect the driveshaft.

8. Refill the transmission to the proper level.

1981–82
REMOVAL

1. Place the gear shift lever in Neutral position.

2. Remove the attaching screws at rear of coin tray and lift to release from front hold down notch on boot retainer. Lift it over the gear shift lever boot.

3. Remove the four capscrews attaching the boot to the floor pan and move the boot upward out of the way.

4. Remove the three lever attaching bolts.
NOTE: *The attaching bolts are Metric (M8).*

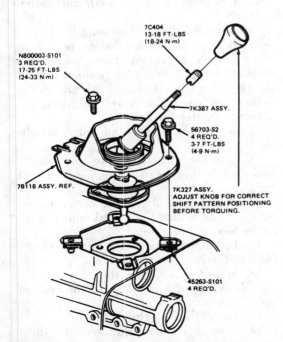

7C404
13-18 FT-LBS
(18-24 N·m)

N800003-S101
3 REQ'D.
17-25 FT-LBS
(24-33 N·m)

7K387 ASSY.

56703-S2
4 REQ'D.
3-7 FT-LBS
(4-9 N·m)

7B118 ASSY. REF.

7K327 ASSY.
ADJUST KNOB FOR CORRECT
SHIFT PATTERN POSITIONING
BEFORE TORQUING.

45263-S101
4 REQ'D.

Shift lever installation on model 82ET 4-speed

Remove the lever and boot assembly from the extension housing.

5. Remove the gear shift knob and locknut and slide the boot off the lever.

6. Working from under the hood, disconnect the negative (ground) cable from the battery. Remove upper bolts (or stud nuts) that attach flywheel housing to engine.

7. Raise the vehicle and support on jackstands.

8. Mark the position of the driveshaft relative to the axle companion flange. Remove the driveshaft and seal the extension housing with a plastic bag or equivalent to prevent lubricant leakage.

9. Remove the clutch release lever dust cover.

10. Disconnect the clutch release cable from the release lever.

11. Remove the starter motor attaching bolts and place the starter to one side.

12. Remove the speedometer cable attaching screw and lift the cable from the extension housing.

13. Support the rear of the engine with a jack and remove the bolts that attach the crossmember to the body.

14. Remove the bolt (or bolts) that attaches crossmember to extension housing, and remove the crossmember.

15. Lower the engine as required to permit removal of bolts that attach the flywheel housing to the engine. Slide the transmission away from the engine and from under the vehicle.
NOTE: *It may be necessary to slide the mounting bracket forward from the catalytic converter heat shield in order to move the transmission rearward far enough to remove it.*

16. Remove the cover attaching bolts and drain the lubricant into a container.

17. Remove the bolts that attach flywheel housing to transmission case and remove the housing.

INSTALLATION, 1981 MODELS

1. Install a new shift rod seal in the flywheel housing (if the old seal is damaged).

2. Position flywheel housing on transmission case, and install and tighten the attaching bolts to specification.

3. Install the clutch release lever and bearing.

4. Make certain that machined surfaces of flywheel housing and engine are free of dirt and foreign material.

5. Apply lubricant to the input shaft bearing retainer. Position the flywheel housing and transmission assembly on the engine block.

NOTE: *It may be necessary to place the transmission in gear and rotate the output shaft to align the input shaft and clutch splines.*

6. Slide the flywheel housing firmly and squarely onto the locating dowels, to be sure of a positive engagement. Then, holding the flywheel housing firmly in position on the dowels, thread the attaching bolts through the hollow portion of the dowels and into the housing. Tighten the bolts to specification.

7. Install and tighten the center attaching bolts.

8. Lower the vehicle and install the two upper attaching bolts or stud nuts. Tighten to specification.

9. Make sure the shift lever insulator is in a straight downward position on the shift rail.

10. Position the shift lever in the extension housing so that the forked ends engage in the insulator properly.

11. Install the three metric attaching bolts (M8) and tighten to specifications.

12. Slide the boot over the lever and install the attaching bolts. Tighten the bolts to specifications.

13. Install the gear shift knob and adjust as shown in the illustrations.

14. Position the coin tray over the shift-lever boot.

15. Secure the tray to front notch on boot retaining ring and attach at rear with screws.

16. Raise the vehicle. Raise the engine until the transmission reaches its normal position. Secure the crossmember to the body with the attaching bolts, and tighten to specification. Install the bolt that attaches crossmember to extension housing, and tighten to specification.

17. Position the catalytic converter heat shield mounting bracket to the transmission mount.

18. Remove the plastic bag, install the speedometer cable and tighten the attaching screw.

19. Position the starter, install the attaching bolts.

20. Apply grease to the ball end of the clutch release cable and connect it to the release lever. Install the clutch release fork dust cover.

21. Install the driveshaft, making sure that it is connected to the pinion flange in its original position.

22. Fill the transmission with the specified lubricant until it appears at the bottom of the filler plug hole. Install the filler plug.

23. Install the backup lamp switch and connect the wire to the switch.

24. Lower the vehicle to the ground. Install and tighten the upper flywheel housing mounting bolts. Connect the negative battery cable.

25. Check the transmission for proper operation.

INSTALLATION, 1982 MODELS

1. Install a new shift rod seal in the flywheel housing (if the old seal is damaged).

2. Position flywheel housing on transmission case, and install and tighten the attaching bolts.

3. Install the clutch release lever and bearing.

4. Make certain that machined surfaces of flywheel housing and engine are free of dirt and foreign material.

5. Apply a film of C4AZ-19584-A lubricant or equivalent to the input shaft bearing retainer. Position the flywheel housing and transmission assembly on the engine block.

NOTE: *It may be necessary to place the transmission in gear and rotate the output shaft to align the input shaft and clutch splines.*

6. Slide the flywheel housing firmly and squarely onto the locating dowels, to be sure of a positive engagement. Then, holding the flywheel housing firmly in position on the dowels, thread the attaching bolts through the hollow portion of the dowels and into the housing. Tighten the bolts.

7. Install and tighten the center attaching bolts.

8. Make sure the shift lever insulator is in a straight downward position on the shift rail.

9. Position the shift lever in the extension housing so that the forked ends engage in the insulator properly.

10. Install the three metric attaching bolts (M8) and tighten to specifications.

11. Slide the boot over the lever and install the attaching bolts. Tighten the bolts to specifications.

13. Install the gear shift knob.

14. Position the coin tray over the shift-lever boot.

15. Secure the tray to front notch on boot retaining ring and attach at rear with screws.

16. Raise the engine until the transmission reaches its normal position. Secure the crossmember to the body with the attaching bolts. Install the bolts that attach crossmember to extension housing, and tighten.

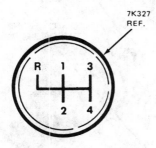

7K327
REF.

WITH LEVER IN NEUTRAL POSITION, INSTALL LOCKING NUT 7C404 UNTIL HAND TIGHT. THEN INSTALL KNOB 7K327 UNTIL HAND TIGHT. BACK KNOB OFF UNTIL SHIFT PATTERN ALIGNS WITH THE ℄ OF DRIVE LINE. TIGHTEN LOCKING NUT 13-18 FT-LBS (18-24 N·m) NO THREADS SHALL BE VISIBLE AFTER NUT HAS BEEN TIGHTENED. SHIFT PATTERN ALIGNMENT MUST BE WITHIN ±15⁰ OF ℄ OF DRIVE LINE.

Shift knob installation on model 82ET 4-speed

LINKAGE ADJUSTMENT

3-Speed Column Shift

If the transmission shifts hard or a gear will not engage, the gear shift rods may need adjustment. Move the selector lever through all shift positions to be certain that the crossover operation is smooth. If not, adjust the gear shift rods.

1. Place the lever in Neutral.
2. Loosen the two gear shift rod adjustment nuts.
3. Insert $^3/_{16}$ in. diameter alignment pin through First and Reverse gear shift lever and Second and Third gear shift lever. Align the levers to insert the pin.
4. Tighten the gear shift rod adjustment nuts and remove the pin.
5. Check the gear lever for smooth crossover.

1971–73 4-Speed Floor and Console Shift

1. Place the hand shifter lever in Neutral, then raise the car on a hoist.
2. Insert a ¼ in. rod into the alignment holes of the shift levers.
3. If the holes are not in exact alignment, check for bent connecting rods or loose lever

AN ALIGNMENT TOOL CAN BE MADE FROM 1/4" DIAMETER DRILL ROD BENT TO AN "L" SHAPE. THE EXTENSIONS SHOULD BE 1 - 1/2" AND 3 - 3/4" FROM THE ELBOW. SHORT END OF ALIGNMENT TOOL SHOULD BE INSERTED INTO CONTROL BRACKET AND LINKAGE HOLES UNTIL IT BOTTOMS.

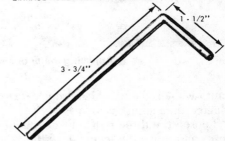

1 - 1/2"

3 - 3/4"

¼ in. alignment rod

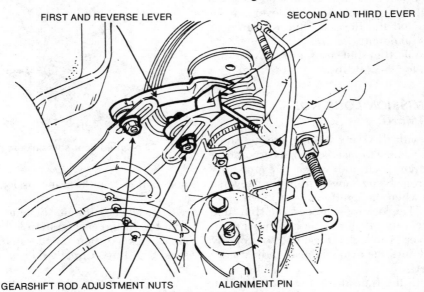

FIRST AND REVERSE LEVER   SECOND AND THIRD LEVER

GEARSHIFT ROD ADJUSTMENT NUTS   ALIGNMENT PIN

Column shift linkage adjustment

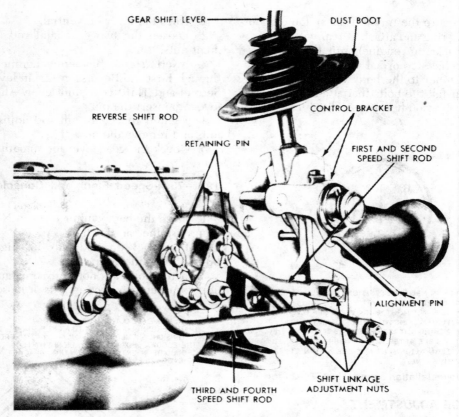

GEAR SHIFT LEVER

DUST BOOT

REVERSE SHIFT ROD

CONTROL BRACKET

RETAINING PIN

FIRST AND SECOND
SPEED SHIFT ROD

ALIGNMENT PIN

THIRD AND FOURTH
SPEED SHIFT ROD

SHIFT LINKAGE
ADJUSTMENT NUTS

Adjusting the floor shift linkage on 1971–73 models

locknuts at the rod ends. Make replacements or repairs, then adjust as follows.

4. Loosen the three rod-to-lever retaining locknuts and move the levers until the ¼ in. gauge rod will enter the alignment holes. Be sure that the transmission shift levers are in Neutral, and the Reverse shifter lever is in the Neutral detent.

5. Install the shift rods and torque the locknuts to 18–23 ft. lbs.

TRANSMISSION LOCK ROD ADJUSTMENT

Models with floor or console-mounted shifters and manual transmissions incorporate a transmission lock rod which prevents the shifter from being moved from the Reverse position when the ignition lock is in the "off" position. The lock rod connects the shift tube in the steering column to the transmission reverse lever. The lock rod cannot be properly adjusted until the manual linkage adjustment is correct.

1. With the transmission selector lever in the Neutral position, loosen the lock rod ad-

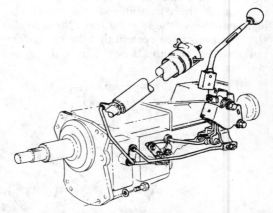

1972–73 4-speed floor shift linkage and lock rod

justment nut on the transmission Reverse lever.

2. Insert a 0.180 in. diameter rod (no. 15 drill bit) in the gauge pin hole located at the six o'clock position on the steering column socket casting, directly below the ignition lock.

3. Manipulate the pin until the casting will not move with the pin inserted.

4. Torque the lock rod adjustment rod to 10–20 ft. lbs.

5. Remove the pin and check the linkage operation.

CLUTCH

1971–73

REMOVAL AND INSTALLATION

1. Disconnect and remove the starter and dust ring. On floor-shift models, remove the boot retainer and shift lever.

2. Raise the car, taking proper safety precautions.

3. Remove the transmission as outlined in the manual transmission removal section.

4. Remove the release lever retracting spring and disconnect the pedal at the equilizer bar.

5. Remove the bolts that secure the engine rear plate to the front lower part of the bellhousing.

6. Remove the bolts that attach the bellhousing to the cylinder block and remove the housing and release lever as a unit.

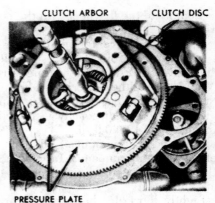

Installing clutch disc

7. Loosen the six pressure plate cover attaching bolts evenly to release spring pressure. Mark the cover and flywheel to facilitate reassembly in the same position.

8. Remove the six attaching bolts while holding the pressure plate cover.

9. Remove the pressure plate and clutch disc.

10. Wash the flywheel surface with alcohol.

11. Attach the clutch disc and pressure

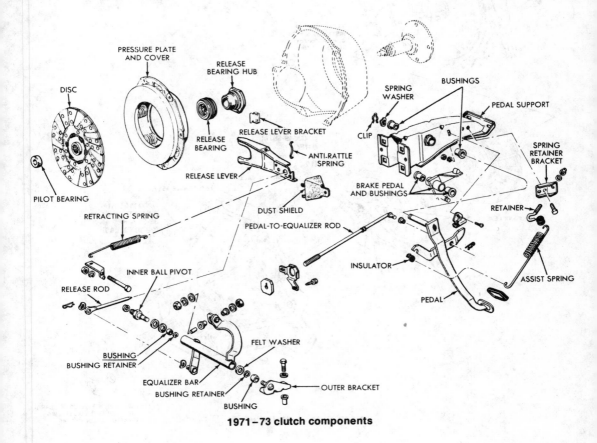

1971–73 clutch components

plate assembly to the flywheel with the bolts finger-tight.

12. Using a clutch centering arbor, or an input shaft out of an old transmission, align the clutch disc with the pilot bearing (bushing). While holding the centering shaft firmly against the pilot bearing, torque the pressure plate retaining bolts, diagonally in rotation, to a final figure of 12–20 ft. lbs.

13. Apply a small amount of lubricant to the release lever fulcrum ends. Install the release lever in the flywheel housing and install the dust shield.

14. Lightly lubricate the release bearing retainer journal. Attach the release bearing and hub on the release lever.

15. Install the flywheel housing. Torque the attaching bolts to 40–50 ft. lbs. Install the dust cover and torque the bolts to 17–20 ft. lbs.

16. Connect the release rod and the retracting spring. Connect the pedal to equalizer rod at the equalizer bar.

17. Install the starter and dust ring.

18. Install the transmission as outlined in the manual transmission installation section.

1981–82
REMOVAL

1. Disconnect negative battery cable from battery. Raise the vehicle and support on jackstands.

2. Remove the dust shield and return spring.

3. Loosen the clutch cable lock and adjusting nut. Remove rubber cable plug and disconnect the cable from the release lever.

4. Remove the retaining clip and remove the clutch cable from the flywheel housing.

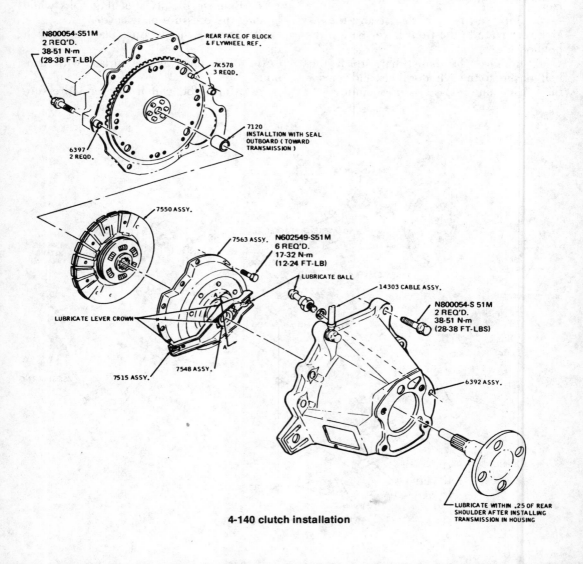

4-140 clutch installation

5. Remove the starter electrical cable and the starter motor from the flywheel housing.

6. Remove the bolts that secure the engine rear plate to the front lower part of the flywheel housing.

7. Remove the transmission (see previous section) flywheel housing.

8. Remove the clutch release lever from the housing by pulling it through the window in the housing until the retainer spring is disengaged from the pivot. Inspect clutch release bearing and replace if required. If original bearing is reused, note orientation, mark, and install in the same position.

9. Loosen the six pressure plate cover attaching bolts evenly to release the spring tension gradually and avoid distorting the cover. If the same pressure plate and cover are to be reinstalled, mark the cover and flywheel so that the pressure plate can be reinstalled in its original position. Remove the pressure plate and clutch disc from the flywheel.

INSTALLATION

1. Install the clutch release lever if it was removed.

2. Position the clutch disc and pressure plate assembly on the flywheel. The three dowel pins on the flywheel must be properly aligned with the pressure plate. Bent, damaged or missing dowels must be replaced. Start the cover attaching bolts but do not tighten them. Avoid touching the clutch disc face, dropping parts or contaminating parts with oil or grease.

3. Align the clutch disc using the proper alignment tool inserted in the pilot bearing. Alternately tighten the cover bolts to specification. Remove the alignment tool.

4. Apply a light film of lithium base grease to (1) the outside diameter of the transmission front bearing retainer, (2) the release lever bearing fork and anti-rattle spring where they contact the release bearing hub, and (3) to the release bearing surface that contacts the pressure plate release fingers. Then, fill the grease groove of the release bearing hub with the same grease. Clean all excess grease from inside the bore of the bearing hub, otherwise, excess grease will be forced onto the spline by the transmission input shaft bearing retainer, and will contaminate the clutch disc.

5. Attach the clutch release bearing to the release lever.

6. Attach the release lever and release bearing to the flywheel housing.

7. Inspect the flywheel housing dowel holes for misalignment and wear.

8. Make certain that the flywheel housing and cylinder block mounting surfaces are clean and that the dowels are in good condition.

9. Install the flywheel housing and/or the transmission.

10. Install the bolts that secure the engine rear plate to the front lower part of the flywheel housing.

11. Connect the clutch cable to the flywheel housing and connect the retaining clip.

12. Install the starter motor and starter electrical cable.

13. Connect the clutch cable and return spring to the release lever and reinstall the dust shield and return spring to the rear crossmember.

14. Adjust the clutch pedal height adjustment or freeplay.

15. Lower car and connect negative battery cable.

CLUTCH PEDAL ADJUSTMENT

The free travel of the clutch pedal should be checked every six months or 6,000 miles and adjusted whenever the clutch does not engage properly or when new clutch parts are installed. Improper adjustment of clutch pedal free travel is one of the most frequent causes of clutch failure and can be a contributing factor in transmission failures.

1981–82 models require no free-play adjustment. A clutch pedal height adjustment is required instead.

1971–1973

1. Disconnect the clutch return spring from the release lever.

2. Loosen the release lever rod locknut and adjusting nut.

3. Move the clutch release lever rearward until the release bearing lightly contacts the pressure plate release fingers.

4. Adjust the length of the rod adaptor until the adaptor seats in the release lever pocket.

5. Insert the specified feeler gauge against the back face of the rod adaptor. Tighten the adjusting nut finger-tight against the gauge. The proper feeler gauge sizes (in in.) and their respective years of application are as follows.

1971 . . . . . . 390, 427, 428, and 429—
                  0.178; all others—0.136
1972–73 . . . . all—0.194

6. Tighten the locknut against the adjusting nut, being careful not to disturb the adjustment. Torque the locknut to 10–15 ft. lbs. and remove the feeler gauge.

7. Install the clutch return spring.

8. Depress and release the clutch pedal a minimum of five times and recheck the freeplay setting with a feeler gauge. Readjust if necessary.

9. With the engine running at 3,000 rpm and the transmission in Neutral, check the pedal free travel. The free travel at this speed must be at least ½ in. Free travel must be exactly to specification. Otherwise, the release fingers may contact the release bearing continuously, resulting in premature bearing and clutch failure.

1981–82

1. Jack up the front of the car and support on jackstands.

2. At the clutch "bell" housing, remove the return spring and the dust shield.

3. Loosen the clutch cable locknut and the adjusting nut.

4. To raise the pedal, turn the adjusting nut clockwise. To lower-turn counterclockwise. Adjust the pedal travel to 5.3 inches. (Total length of travel). Tighten the locknut.

5. Depress and releaser the clutch pedal several times. Recheck the freeplay or pedal travel. Readjust if necessary. To check the proper adjustment you should be able to raise the clutch pedal (from the end of its normal

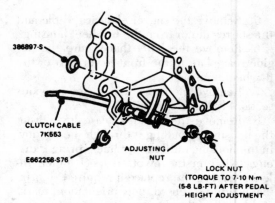

4-140 clutch pedal adjustment

return height to the pedal stop) about 2 and ¾ inches.

6. Reinstall clutch return spring and dust shield. Lower car.

AUTOMATIC TRANSMISSION

Seven different automatic transmissions have been used since 1971. The medium-duty C4 automatic is installed in six-cylinder and small V8 applications. In 1981, the C5 replaced the C4 on the 6-200 and 6-232. The C4 was discontinued in 1980. The C3 was used on most sixes along with the C5 beginning in 1980. The medium-duty FMX automatic is installed in most mid-sized V8's (e.g. 351 and some 400 V8's). A similar CW automatic is

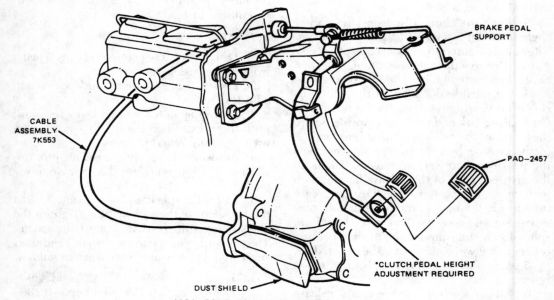

1981–82 clutch pedal and cable assembly

installed in 1974–75 cars equipped with the 2.75:1 rear axle ratio. The heavy-duty C6 automatic is mated to the biggest V8's (429 and 460 V8's). In 1982 an automatic overdrive unit was offered on some models with V6 and V8 engines.

NEUTRAL START SWITCH ADJUSTMENT

Console Shift

1. With the manual linkage properly adjusted and the brakes on, try to engage the starter at each position on the quadrant. The starter should engage only in Neutral and Park positions.

2. Remove the shift handle from the shift lever and the console from the vehicle.

3. Loosen the switch attaching screws and move the shift lever back and forward until the gauge pin .091 in. (no. 43 drill) can be inserted fully.

4. Place the shift lever firmly against the neutral detent stop and slide the switch backward and forward until the switch lever contacts the shift lever.

5. Tighten the switch attaching screws and check starter engagement as in Step 1.

6. Reinstall the console and shift linkage.

Column Shift

1. With the manual linkage properly adjusted and the brakes on, try to engage the starter in each position on the quadrant. The starter should engage only in Neutral or Park.

2. Place the shift lever in the Neutral detent.

3. Disconnect the start switch wires at the plug connector. Disconnect the vacuum hoses, if any. Remove the screws securing the neutral start switch to the steering column and

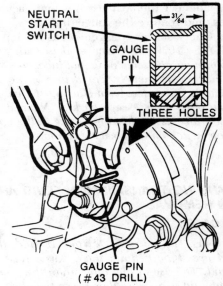

GAUGE PIN
(#43 DRILL)

C4 neutral start switch adjustment

remove the switch. Remove the actuator lever along with the Type III switches.

4. With the switch wires facing up, move the actuator lever fully to the left and insert the gauge pin (no. 43 drill) into gauge pin hole at point A. See the accompanying figure. On a Type III switch, be sure the gauge pin is inserted a full ½ in.

5. With the pin in place, move the actuator lever to the right until the positive stop is engaged.

6. On Type I and Type II switches, remove the gauge pin and insert it at point B. On Type III switches, remove the gauge pin, align two holes in the switch at point A, and reinstall the gauge pin.

7. Reinstall the switch on the steering column. Be sure that the shift lever is engaged in the Neutral detent.

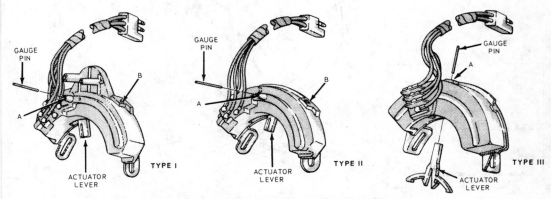

Neutral start switch adjustment—1971 column shift

8. Connect the switch wires and vacuum hoses, and remove the gauge pin.

9. Check starter engagement as in Step 1. NOTE: *1972 and later models with column-mounted selector do not incorporate a Neutral start switch. The driver of the vehicle is prevented from starting the car in any other gear except Park or Neutral by the transmission locking device in the ignition switch on the steering column.*

CHANGING TRANSMISSION FLUID AND PAN REMOVAL

C3, C4, C5

NOTE: *The C3 uses Dexron® II fluid; the C4 uses type F fluid; the C5 uses type H fluid. The use of any other than the specified fluid may cause damage to the unit.*

1. Raise the vehicle so that the transmission oil pan is readily accessible.

2. Disconnect the fluid filler tube from the pan and allow the fluid to drain into an appropriate container.

NOTE: *It is not recommended that the drained fluid be used over again; refill the transmission with new fluid. However, in an emergency situation, the old fluid can be reused. The old fluid should be strained through a #100 screen or a fine mesh cloth before being reinstalled.*

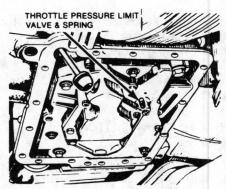

C4 throttle limit valve and spring. They are held in place by the transmission filter. The valve is installed with the large end towards the valve body, the spring fits over the valve stem.

3. Remove the transmission oil pan attaching bolts, pan and gasket.

To install the transmission oil pan:

4. Clean the transmission oil pan and transmission mating surfaces.

5. Install the transmission oil pan in the reverse order of removal, torquing the attaching bolts to 12–16 ft. lbs. and using a new gasket. Fill the transmission with 3 qts of the correct type fluid, check the operation of the transmission and check for leakage.

C6, CW, FMX, and AOD

1. Raise the car on a hoist or jackstands.

2. Place a drain pan under the transmission.

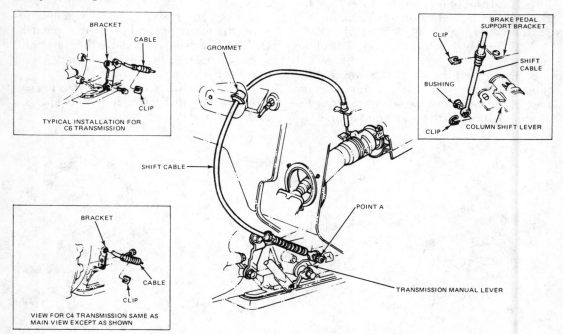

Manual linkage adjustment—column shift

3. Loosen the pan attaching bolts and drain the fluid from the transmission.

4. When the fluid has drained to the level of the pan flange, remove the remaining pan bolts working from the rear and both sides of the pan to allow it to drop and drain slowly.

5. When all of the fluid has drained, remove the pan and clean it thoroughly. Discard the pan gasket.

6. Place a new gasket on the pan, and install the pan on the transmission. Tighten the attaching bolts to 12–16 ft. lbs.

7. Add three quarts of fluid to the transmission through the filler tube.

NOTE: *Use only Type F automatic transmission fluid for 1970–76 models. 1977–82 C6 and AOD models require type CJ fluid or Dexron® II. Do not race the engine after it is started. Move the gearshift selector through all of the gears before moving the car.*

SHIFT LINKAGE ADJUSTMENT

Column Shift

1. With the engine off, place the gear selector in the D (Drive) position, or D (overdrive) position (AOD). Either hang a weight on the shifter or have an assistant sit in the car and hold the selector against the stop.

2. Loosen the adjusting nut or clamp at the shift lever so that the shift rod is free to slide. On models with a shift cable, remove the nut from the transmission lever and disconnect the cable from the transmission.

3. Place the manual shift lever on the transmission in the D (Drive) or D (Overdrive) position. This is the second detent position from the full counterclockwise position.

4. Tighten the adjusting bolt. On cars with a cable, position the cable end on the transmission lever stud, aligning the flats. Tighten the adjusting nut.

5. Check the pointer alignment and transmission operation for all selector positions. If not correct, adjust linkage.

Floor or Console Shift

1. Place the transmission shift lever in D.

2. Raise the vehicle and loosen the manual lever shift rod retaining nut. Move the transmission lever to D_1 or D position. D is the fourth detent from the rear.

3. With the transmission shift lever and transmission manual lever in position, tighten the nut at point A to 10–20 ft. lbs.

4. Check transmission operation for all selector lever detent positions.

NOTE: *All 1971 models with a floor or console-mounted selector lever have incorporated a transmission lockout rod to prevent the transmission selector from being moved out of the Park position when the ignition lock is in the "off" position. The lock rod connects the shift tube in the steering column to the transmission manual lever. The lock rod cannot be properly adjusted until the manual linkage adjustment is correct.*

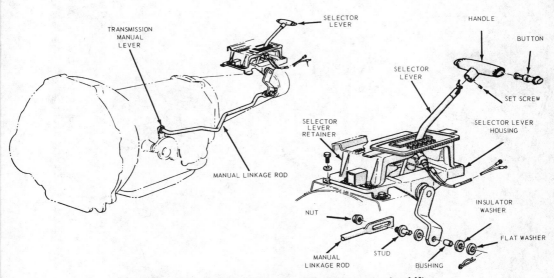

Early type manual linkage adjustment with console shift

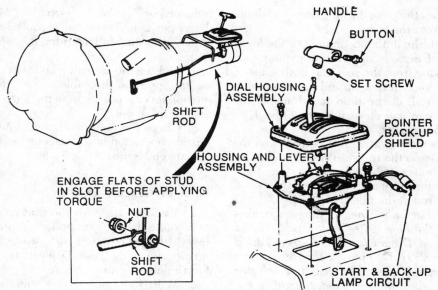

Later type automatic transmission floor shift linkage

DOWNSHIFT (THROTTLE) LINKAGE ADJUSTMENT

All Models Except (AOD) Automatic Overdrive

1. With the engine off, disconnect the throttle and downshift return springs, if equipped.

2. Hold the carburetor throttle lever in the wide open position against the stop.

3. Hold the transmission downshift linkage in the full downshift position against the internal stop.

4. Turn the adjustment screw on the carburetor downshift lever to obtain 0.010–0.080 in. clearance between the screw tip and the throttle shaft lever tab.

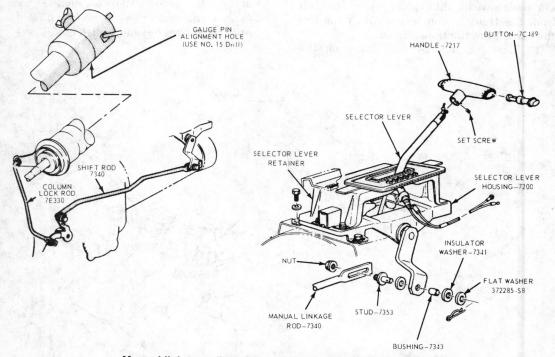

Manual linkage adjustment—1971 console shift with lockrod

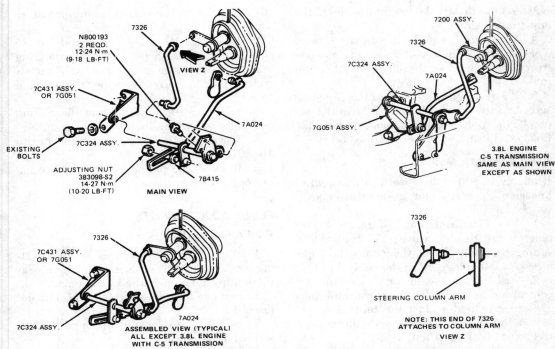

Manual linkage on column shift automatic transmission, 1981–82 Cougar

5. Release the transmission and carburetor to their normal free positions. Install the throttle and downshift return springs, if removed.

AOD

1. With the engine off, remove the air cleaner and make sure the fast idle cam is released—the throttle lever must be at the idle stop.

2. Turn the linkage lever adjusting screw counterclockwise until the end of the screw is flush with the face of the lever.

3. Turn the linkage adjustment screw in until there is a maximum clearance of .005 in.

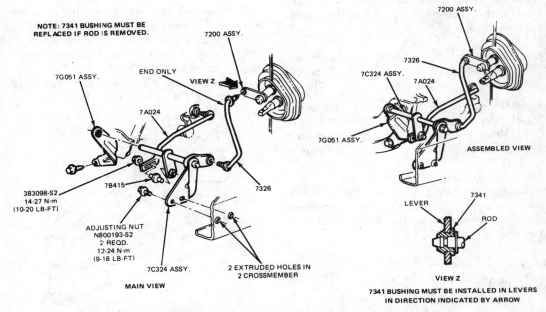

Rod-type column shift linkage on Thunderbird, XR-7, and Continental

between the throttle lever and the end of the adjustment screw.

4. Turn the linkage lever adjusting screw clockwise three full turns. A minimum of one turn is permissible if the screw travel is limited.

5. If it is not possible to turn the adjusting screw at least one full turn or if the initial gap of .005 in. could not be obtained, perform the linkage adjustment at the transmission.

AOD Alternate Method

If unable to adjust the throttle valve control linkage at the carburetor, as described above, proceed as follows.

1. At the transmission, loosen the 8 mm bolt on the throttle valve (TV) control rod sliding trunnion block. Make sure the trunnion block slides freely on the control rod.

2. Push up on the lower end of the TV control rod to insure that the carburetor linkage lever is held against the throttle lever. When the pressure is released, the control rod must stay in position.

3. Force the TV control lever on the transmission against its internal stop. While maintaining pressure tighten the trunnion block bolt. Make sure the throttle lever is at the idle stop.

AOD IDLE SPEED ADJUSTMENT

Whenever it is necessary to adjust the idle speed by more than 50 rpm either above or below the factory specifications, the adjustment screw on the linkage lever at the carburetor should also be adjusted to the following specifications:

Idle Speed Change (rpm)	Adjustment Screw Turns
50–100 increase	1½ turns out
50–100 decrease	1½ turns in
100–150 increase	2½ turns out
100–150 decrease	2½ turns in

After making any idle speed adjustments, make sure the linkage lever and throttlelever are in contact with the throttle lever at its idle stop and verify that the shift lever is in N (neutral).

LOCK ROD ADJUSTMENT
1971 Console Shift

1. With the transmission selector lever in the Drive position, loosen the lock rod ad-

justment nut on the transmission manual lever.

2. Insert a 0.180 in. diameter rod (no. 15 drill bit) in the gauge pin hole in the steering column socket casting. It is located at the six o'clock position directly below the ignition lock.

3. Manipulate the pin so that the casting will not move when the pin is fully inserted.

4. Torque the lock rod adjustment nut to 10–20 ft. lbs.

5. Remove the pin and check the linkage operation.

BAND ADJUSTMENTS
C3 Front Band

1. Wipe clean the area around the adjusting screw on the side of the transmission, near the left front corner of the transmission.

2. Remove the adjusting screw locknut and discard it.

3. Install a new locknut on the adjusting screw but do not tighten it.

4. Tighten the adjusting screw to *exactly 10 ft. lbs.*

5. Back off the adjusting screw *exactly 1½ turns* on models through 1979, and 2 turns on 1980–82 models.

6. Hold the adjusting screw so that it *does not turn* and tighten the adjusting screw locknut to 35–45 ft. lbs.

C4 and C5 Intermediate Band

1. Clean all the dirt from the adjusting screw and remove and discard the locknut.

2. Install a new locknut on the adjusting screw using a torque wrench, tighten the adjusting screw to 10 ft. lbs.

3. Back off the adjusting screw *exactly 1¾ turns* for the C4 and 4¼ turns for the C5.

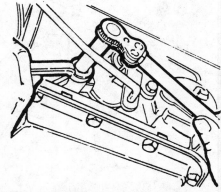

C4, C5 and C6 intermediate band adjustment

4. Hold the adjusting screw steady and tighten the locknut to the proper torque.

C4 Low-Reverse Band

1. Clean all dirt from around the band adjusting screw, and remove and discard the locknut.

2. Install a new locknut of the adjusting screw. Using a torque wrench, tighten the adjusting screw to 10 ft. lbs.

3. Back off the adjusting screw *exactly three full turns*.

4. Hold the adjusting screw steady and tighten the locknut to the proper torque.

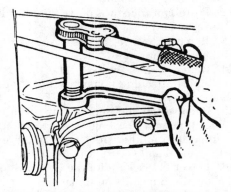

C4, and C5 low-reverse band adjustment

C6 Intermediate Band Adjustment

1. Raise the car on a hoist or place it on jack stands.

2. Clean the threads of the intermediate band adjusting screw.

3. Loosen the adjustment screw locknut.

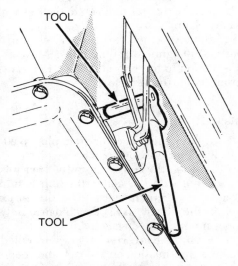

C6 intermediate band adjustment

4. Tighten the adjusting screw to 10 ft. lbs. and back the screw off *exactly 1½ turns*. Tighten the adjusting screw locknut.

FMX, CW Front Band Adjustment

1. Drain the transmission fluid and remove the oil pan, fluid filter screen, and clip.

2. Clean the pan and filter screen and remove the old gasket.

3. Loosen the front servo adjusting screw locknut.

4. Pull back the actuating rod and insert a ¼ in. spacer bar between the adjusting screw and the servo piston stem. Tighten the adjusting screw to 10 in. lbs. torque. Remove the spacer bar and tighten the adjusting screw *an additional ¾ turn*. Hold the adjusting screw fast and tighten the locknut securely (20–25 ft. lbs.).

5. Install the transmission fluid filter screen and clip. Install pan with a new pan gasket.

6. Refill the transmission to the mark on the dipstick. Start the engine, run for a few minutes, shift the selector lever through all positions, and place it in Park. Recheck the fluid level and add fluid if necessary.

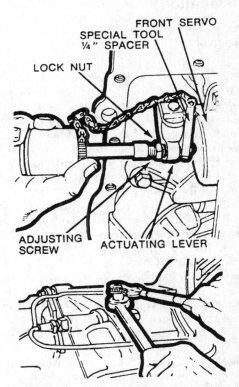

FMX and CW front band (top) and rear band (bottom) adjustments

FMX, CW Rear Band Adjustments

On certain cars with a console floor shift, the entire console shift lever and linkage will have to be removed to gain access to the rear band external adjusting screw.

1. Locate the external rear band adjusting screw on the transmission case, clean all dirt from the threads, and coat the threads with light oil.

NOTE: *The adjusting screw is located on the upper right-side of the transmission case. Access is often through a hole in the front floor to the right of center under the carpet.*

2. Loosen the locknut on the rear band external adjusting screw.

3. Using torque wrench tighten the adjusting screw to 10 ft. lbs. torque. If the adjusting screw is tighter than 10 ft. lbs. torque, loosen the adjusting screw and retighten to the proper torque.

4. Back off the adjusting screw *exactly 1½ turns*. Hold the adjusting screw steady while tightening the locknut to the proper torque (35–40 ft. lbs.).

Transmission Removal and Installation

C3

Removal

1. Raise the vehicle on a hoist.

2. Place a drain pan under the transmission fluid pan. Starting at the rear of the pan and working toward the front, loosen the attaching bolts and allow the fluid to drain. Then remove all of the pan attaching bolts except two at the front, to allow the fluid to further drain. After all the fluid has drained, install two bolts on the rear side of the pan to temporarily hold it in place.

3. Remove the converter drain plug access cover and adapter plate bolts from the lower end of the converter housing.

4. Remove the four flywheel to converter attaching nuts. Crank the engine to turn the converter to gain access to the nuts, using a wrench on the crankshaft pulley attaching bolt. **On belt driven overhead camshaft engines, never turn the engine backwards.**

5. Crank the engine until the converter drain plug is accessible and remove the plug. Place a drain pan under the converter to catch the fluid. After all the fluid has been drained from the converter, reinstall the plug and tighten to specification.

6. Remove the driveshaft and install the extension housing seal replacer tool in the extension housing.

7. Remove the speedometer cable from the extension housing.

8. Disconnect the shift rod at the transmission manual lever. Disconnect the downshift rod at the transmission downshift lever.

9. Remove the starter-to-converter housing attaching bolts and position the starter out of the way.

10. Disconnect the neutral start switch wires from the switch.

11. Remove the vacuum line from the transmission vacuum unit.

12. Position a transmission jack under the transmission and raise it slightly.

13. Remove the engine rear support-to-crossmember nut.

14. Remove the crossmember-to-frame side support attaching bolts and remove the crossmember.

15. Remove the inlet pipe steady rest from the inlet pipe and rear engine support; then disconnect the muffler inlet pipe at the exhaust manifold and secure it.

16. Lower the jack under the transmission and allow the transmission to hang.

17. Position a jack to the front of the engine and raise the engine to gain access to the two upper converter housing-to-engine attaching bolts.

18. Disconnect the oil cooler lines at the transmission. Plug all openings to keep out dirt.

19. Remove the lower converter housing-to-engine attaching bolts.

20. Remove the transmission filler tube.

21. Secure the transmission to the jack with a safety chain.

22. Remove the two upper converter housing-to-engine attaching bolts. Move the transmission to the rear and down to remove it from under the vehicle.

Installation

1. Tighten the converter drain plug to 20–30 ft. lb. if not previously done.

2. Position the converter to the transmission making sure the converter hub is fully engaged in the pump gear. The dimension given in the illustration is for guidance only. It does not indicate engagement.

3. With the converter properly installed, place the transmission on the jack and secure with safety chain.

4. Rotate the converter so the drive studs and drain plug are in alignment with their holes in the flywheel.

5. With the transmission mounted on a transmission jack, move the converter and transmission assembly forward into position being careful not to damage the flywheel and the converter pilot.

During this move, to avoid damage, do not allow the transmission to get into a nosed down position as this will cause the converter to move forward and disengage from the pump gear. The converter must rest squarely against the flywheel. This indicates that the converter pilot is not binding in the engine crankshaft.

6. Install the two upper converter housing-to-engine attaching bolts and tighten to 28–38 ft. lb.

7. Remove the safety chain from the transmission.

8. Insert the filler tube in the stub tube and secure it to the cylinder block with the attaching bolt. Tighten the bolt to 28–38 ft. lb. If the stub tube is loosened or dislodged, it should be replaced.

9. Install the oil cooler lines in the retaining clip at the cylinder block. Connect the lines to the transmission case.

10. Remove the jack supporting the front of the engine.

11. Position the muffler inlet pipe support bracket to the converter housing and install the four lower converter housing-to-engine attaching bolts. Tighten the bolts to 28–38 ft. lb.

12. Raise the transmission. Position the crossmember to the frame side supports and install the attaching bolts. Tighten the bolts to 30–40 ft. lb.

13. Lower the transmission and install the rear engine support-to-crossmember nut. Tighten the nut to 30–40 ft. lb.

14. Remove the transmission jack.

15. Install the vacuum hose on the transmission vacuum unit. Install the vacuum line into the retaining clip.

16. Connect the neutral start switch plug to the switch.

17. Install the starter and tighten the attaching bolts.

18. Install the four flywheel-to-converter attaching nuts.

When assembling the flywheel to the converter, first install the attaching nuts and tighten to 20–34 lb. ft.

19. Install the converter drain plug access cover and adaptor plate bolts. Tighten the bolts to 15–20 ft. lb.

20. Connect the muffler inlet pipe to the exhaust manifold.

21. Connect the transmission shift rod to the manual lever.

22. Connect the downshift rod to the downshift lever.

23. Connect the speedometer cable to the extension housing.

24. Install the driveshaft. Tighten the companion flange U-bolt attaching nuts to 30 ft. lb.

25. Adjust the manual and downshift linkage as required.

26. Lower the vehicle. Fill the transmission to the proper level with Dexron® II.

Pour in five quarts of fluid; then run the engine and add fluid as required.

27. Check the transmission, converter assembly and oil cooler lines for leaks.

C4

Removal

1. Raise the vehicle on a hoist.

2. Place the drain pan under the transmission fluid pan. Remove the fluid filler tube from the pan and drain the transmission fluid. On some models it may be necessary to loosen the pan attaching bolts and allow the fluid to drain. Start loosening the bolts at the rear of the pan and work toward the front. Finally remove all of the pan attaching bolts except two at the front, to allow the fluid to further drain. After the fluid has drained, install two bolts on the rear side of the pan to temporarily hold it in place.

3. Remove the converter drain plug access cover from the lower end of the converter housing.

4. Remove the converter-to-flywheel attaching nuts. Place a wrench on the crankshaft pulley attaching bolt to turn the converter to gain access to the nuts.

5. With the wrench on the crankshaft pulley attaching bolt, turn the converter to gain access to the converter drain plug. Then, remove the plug. Place a drain pan under the converter to catch the fluid. After the fluid has been drained from the converter, reinstall the plug.

6. Remove the drive shaft and install the extension housing seal replacer tool in the extension housing.

7. Remove the vacuum line hose from the transmission vacuum unit. Disconnect the

vacuum line from the retaining clip. Disconnect the transmission regulated spark (T.R.S.) switch wire at the transmission, if so equipped.

8. Remove the engine support to crossmember bolts or nuts.

9. Remove the speedometer cable from the extension housing.

10. Disconnect the oil cooler lines from the transmission case.

11. Disconnect the selector rod or cable at the transmission manual lever. Disconnect the downshift rod at the transmission downshift lever.

12. On console and floor shift vehicles, disconnect the column lock rod at the transmission, if so equipped.

13. Disconnect the starter cable. Remove the starter attaching bolts and remove the starter from the converter housing.

14. Remove the bolt that secures the transmission fluid filler tube to the cylinder head and lift the fluid filler tube from the case.

15. Position the transmission jack to support the transmission and secure the transmission to the jack with a safety chain.

16. Remove the crossmember attaching bolts and lower the crossmember.

17. Remove the five converter housing-to-engine attaching bolts. Lower the transmission and remove it from under the vehicle.

Installation

1. Torque the converter drain plug to 20–30 ft. lb.

2. Position the converter to the transmission making sure the converter drive flats are fully engaged in the pump gear.

3. With the converter properly installed, place the transmission on the jack. Secure the transmission to the jack with the safety chain.

4. Rotate the converter so that the studs and drain plug are in alignment with their holes in the flywheel.

5. With the transmission mounted on a transmission jack, move the converter and transmission assembly forward into position, using care not to damage the flywheel and the converter pilot. The converter must rest squarely against the flywheel. This indicates that the converter pilot is not binding in the engine crankshaft.

6. Install the five converter housing-to-engine attaching bolts. Torque the bolts to 23–28 ft. lb. Remove the safety chain from the transmission.

7. Position the crossmember and install the attaching bolts. Torque the bolts to 40–50 ft. lb.

8. Lower the transmission and install the engine support to crossmember bolts or nuts. Torque the bolts or nuts to 30–40 ft. lb.

9. Install the flywheel to the converter attaching nuts. Torque the nuts to 23–28 ft. lb.

10. Remove the transmission jack. Install the fluid filler tube in the transmission case or pan. Secure the tube to the cylinder head with the attaching bolt. Install the vacuum hose on the transmission vacuum unit. Install the vacuum line retaining clip. Connect the transmission regulated spark (T.R.S.) switch wire to the switch, if so equipped.

12. Connect the fluid cooling lines to the transmission case.

13. Connect the downshift rod to the downshift lever.

14. Connect the selector rod or cable to the transmission manual lever. Connect the column lock rod on console and floor shift vehicles, if so equipped.

15. Connect the speedometer cable to the extension housing.

16. Install the converter housing cover and torque the attaching bolts to 12–16 ft. lb.

18. Install the starter and torque the attaching bolts to 25–30 ft. lb. Connect the starter cable.

19. Install the drive shaft. Torque the companion flange U-bolts attaching nuts to 25–30 ft. lb.

20. Lower the vehicle. Fill the transmission to the proper level with Type F fluid. Adjust the manual and downshift linkage as required.

C5

Removal

1. Open the hood and install protective covers on the fenders.

2. Disconnect the battery negative cable.

3. On Cougar models equipped with a 3.8L engine, remove the air cleaner assembly.

4. Remove the fan shroud attaching bolts and position the shroud back over the fan.

5. On Cougar models equipped with a 3.8L engine, loosen the clamp and disconnect the thermactor air injection hose at the catalytic converter check valve. The check valve is located on the right side of the engine compartment near the dash panel.

6. On Cougar models equipped with a

3.8L engine, remove the two transmission-to-engine attaching bolts located at the top of the transmission bell housing. These bolts are accessible from the engine compartment.

7. Raise the vehicle.

8. Remove the driveshaft.

9. Disconnect the muffler inlet pipe from the catalytic converter outlet pipe. Support the muffler/pipe assembly by wiring it to a convenient underbody bracket.

10. Remove the nuts attaching the exhaust pipe(s) to the exhaust manifold(s).

11. Pull back on the catalytic converters to release the converter hangers from the mounting bracket.

12. Remove the speedometer clamps bolt and pull the speedometer out of the extension housing.

13. Separate the neutral start switch harness connector.

14. Disconnect the kick down rod at the transmission lever.

15. Disconnect the shift linkage at the linkage bellcrank. On vehicles equipped with floor mounted shift, remove the shift cable routing bracket attaching bolts and disconnect the cable at the transmission lever.

16. Remove the converter dust shield.

17. Remove the torque converter to drive plate attaching nuts. To gain access to the converter nuts, turn the crankshaft and drive plate using a ratchet handle and socket on the crankshaft pulley attaching bolt.

18. Remove the starter attaching bolts.

19. Loosen the nuts attaching the rear support to the No. 3 crossmember.

20. Position a transmission jack under the transmission oil pan. Secure the transmission to the jack with a safety chain.

21. Remove the through bolts attaching the No. 3 crossmember to the body brackets.

22. Lower the transmission enough to allow access to the cooler line fittings. Disconnect the cooler lines.

23. On Cougar models, remove the (4) remaining transmission-to-engine attaching bolts (2 each side). On all other models, remove the (6) transmission-to-engine attaching bolts.

24. Pull the transmission back to disengage the converter studs from the drive plate. Lower the transmission out of the vehicle.

Installation

1. Raise the transmission into the vehicle. As the transmission is being slowly raised into position, rotate the torque converter until the studs and drain plug are aligned with the holes in the drive plate.

2. Move the converter/transmission assembly forward against the back of the engine. Make sure the converter studs engage the drive plate and that the transmission dowels on the back of the engine engage the bolt holes in the bell-housing.

3. On Cougar models equipped with a 3.8L engine, install four transmission-to-engine attaching bolts (2 each side). On all other models, install the (6) transmission-to-engine attaching bolts. Tighten the attaching bolts to 40–50 ft. lb.

4. Connect the cooler lines.

5. Raise the transmission and install the No. 3 crossmember through bolts. Tighten the attaching nuts to 20–30 ft. lb.

6. Remove the safety chain and transmission jack.

7. Tighten the rear support attaching nuts to 30–50 ft. lb.

8. Position the starter and install the attaching bolts.

9. Install the torque converter to drive plate attaching nuts. Tighten the attaching nuts to 20–30 ft. lb.

10. Position the dust shield and on vehicles with column mounted shift, position the linkage bellcrank bracket. Install the attaching bolts and tighten to 12–16 ft. lb.

11. Connect the shift linkage to the linkage bellcrank. On vehicles equipped with floor mounted shift, connect the cable to the shift lever and install the routing bracket attaching bolt.

12. Connect the kick down rod to the transmission lever.

13. Connect the neutral start switch harness.

14. Install the speedometer and the clamp bolt. Tighten the clamp bolt to 36–54 in. lb.

15. Install the catalytic converters using new seal(s) at the pipe(s) to exhaust manifold connection(s).

16. Install the pipe(s) to exhaust manifold attaching nuts. Do not tighten the attaching nuts.

17. Remove the wire supporting the muffler/pipe assembly and connect the pipe to the converter outlet. Do not tighten the attaching nuts.

18. Align the exhaust system and tighten the manifold and converter outlet attaching nuts.

19. Install the driveshaft.

20. Check and if necessary, adjust the shift linkage.

21. Lower the vehicle.

22. On Cougar models equipped with a 3.8L engine, install the two transmission-to-engine attaching bolts located at the top of the transmission bell housing.

23. On Cougar models equipped with a 3.8L engine, connect the thermactor air injection hose to the converter check valve.

24. Position the fan shroud and install the attaching bolts.

25. On Cougar models equipped with a 3.8L engine, install the air cleaner assembly.

26. Connect the battery negative cable.

27. Start the engine. Make sure the engine cranks only when the selector lever is positioned in the neutral (N) or Park (P) detent.

28. Fill the transmission with type H fluid.

29. Raise the vehicle and inspect for fluid leaks.

C6

Removal

1. Working from the engine compartment, remove the two bolts retaining the fan shroud to the radiator.

2. Connect a remote control starter button on Torino and Motego vehicles equipped with a 400 CID engine.

3. Raise the vehicle on a hoist or stands.

4. Place the drain pan under the transmission fluid pan. Starting at the rear of the pan and working toward the front, loosen the attaching bolts and allow the fluid to drain. Finally remove all of the pan attaching bolts except two at the front, to allow the fluid to further drain. After the fluid has drained, install two bolts on the rear side of the pan to temporarily hold it in place.

5. Remove the converter drain plug access cover and adapter plate bolts from the lower end of the converter housing.

6. Remove the converter-to-flywheel attaching nuts. On Torino and Montego vehicles equipped with a 400 CID engine, crank the engine until the nuts are accessible.

7. Crank the engine on Torino and Montego vehicles with a 400 CID engine to turn the converter to gain access to the converter drain plug. Then, remove the plug. Place a drain pan under the converter to catch the fluid. After the fluid has been drained from the converter, reinstall the plug.

8. Disconnect the drive shaft from the rear axle and slide the shaft rearward from the transmission. Install a seal installation tool in the extension housing to prevent fluid leakage.

9. Disconnect the speedometer cable from the extension housing.

10. Disconnect the downshift rod from the transmission downshift lever.

11. Disconnect the shift cable from the manual lever at the transmission.

12. Remove the two bolts that secure the shift cable bracket to the converter housing and position the cable and bracket out of the way.

13. Remove the starter motor attaching bolts and position the starter out of the way.

14. Disconnect the rubber hose from the vacuum diaphragm at the rear of the transmission. Remove the vacuum tube from the retaining clip at the transmission. Disconnect the transmission regulated spark (T.R.S.) switch wire at the transmission, if so equipped.

15. Disconnect the muffler inlet pipe at the exhaust manifolds and allow the pipe to hang.

16. Remove the crossmember to frame side support bolts and nuts. Remove the nuts securing the rear engine supports to the crossmember. Position a jack under the transmission and raise it slightly. Remove the bolts securing the rear engine supports to the extension housing and remove the crossmember and rear supports from the vehicle.

17. Loosen the parking brake adjusting nut at the equalizer and remove the cable from the idler hook attached to the floor pan.

18. Lower the transmission, then disconnect the oil cooler lines from the transmission case.

19. Secure the transmission to the jack with a chain.

20. Remove the six bolts that attach the converter housing to the cylinder block.

21. Remove the bolt that secures the transmission filler tube to the cylinder block. Lift the filler tube and dipstick from the transmission.

22. Move the transmission away from the cylinder block.

23. Carefully lower the transmission and remove it from under the vehicle.

24. Remove the converter and mount transmission in a holding fixture.

Installation

1. Torque the converter drain plug to 14–28 ft. lb.

2. Position the converter to the transmission making sure the converter drive flats are fully engaged in the pump gear.

3. With the converter properly installed, place the transmission on the jack. Secure the transmission to the jack with the safety chain.

4. Rotate the converter so that the studs and drain plug are in alignment with their holes in the flywheel.

5. With the transmission mounted on a transmission jack, move the converter and transmission assembly forward into position using care not to damage the flywheel and converter pilot. The converter must rest squarely against the flywheel. This indicates that the converter pilot is not binding in the engine crankshaft.

6. Install a new O-ring on the lower end of the transmission filler tube. Insert the tube in the transmission case and secure the tube to the engine with the attaching bolt.

7. Install the converter housing-to-engine attaching bolts. Torque the bolts to 40–50 ft. lb. Remove the safety chain from the transmission.

8. Connect the oil cooler lines to the transmission case.

9. Raise the transmission.

10. Position the parking brake cable in the idler hook and tighten the adjusting nut at the equalizer.

11. Place the rear engine supports on the crossmember and position the crossmember on the frame side supports.

12. Secure the engine rear supports to the extension housing with the attaching bolts. Torque the bolts to 35–40 ft. lb.

13. Remove the transmission jack from under the vehicle and install the crossmember-to-frame side support bolts and nuts. Torque the bolts and nuts to 35–40 ft. lb.

14. Install and torque the engine rear support-to-crossmember attaching nuts.

15. Connect the muffler inlet pipe to the exhaust manifolds.

16. Connect the vacuum line to the vacuum diaphragm making sure that the metal tube is secured in the retaining clip. Connect the transmission regulated spark (T.R.S.) switch wire to the switch, if so equipped.

17. Position the starter motor to the converter housing and secure it with the attaching bolts.

18. Install the torque converter-to-flywheel attaching nuts and torque them to 20–30 ft. lb.

19. Position the shift cable bracket to the converter housing and install the two attaching bolts.

20. Connect the shift cable to the manual lever at the transmission.

21. Connect the downshift rod to the lever on the transmission.

22. Connect the speedometer cable to the extension housing.

23. Install the drive shaft.

24. Install the converter drain plug access cover and adapter plate bolts. Torque the bolts to 12–16 ft. lb.

25. Adjust the manual and downshift linkage as required.

26. Lower the vehicle.

27. Working from the engine compartment, position the fan shroud to the radiator and secure with the two attaching bolts.

28. Remove the remote starter button on Torino and Montego vehicles equipped with the 400 CID engine.

29. Fill the transmission to the proper level with Type F for 1971–76 models and Dexron® II for 1977 and later.

30. Check the transmission, converter assembly and oil cooler lines for leaks.

CW AND FMX

Removal

1. Drive the vehicle on a hoist, but do not raise at this time.

2. Remove the two upper bolts and lockwashers which attach the converter housing to the engine.

3. Raise the vehicle.

4. Place the drain pan under the transmission fluid pan. Starting at the rear of the pan and working toward the front, loosen the attaching bolts and allow the fluid to drain. Finally remove all of the pan attaching bolts except two at the front, to allow the fluid to further drain. With fluid drained, install two bolts on the rear side of the pan to temporarily hold it in place.

5. Remove the converter drain plug access cover from the lower end of the converter housing.

6. Remove the converter-to-flywheel attaching nuts. Place a wrench on the crankshaft pulley attaching bolt to turn the converter to gain access to the nuts.

7. With the wrench on the crankshaft pulley attaching bolt, turn the converter to gain access to the converter drain plug, and remove the plug. Place a drain pan under the

converter to catch the fluid. After the fluid has been drained, reinstall the plug.

8. Disconnect the driveshaft from the rear companion flange (marking it to assure correct assembly). Slide the shaft rearward from the transmission. Position a seal installation tool in the extension housing to prevent fluid leakage.

9. Disconnect the vacuum hoses from the vacuum diaphragm unit and the tube from the extension housing clip.

10. Install the converter housing front plate to hold the converter in place when the transmission is removed. Under no conditions should the converter be left attached to the engine when the transmission is removed. This could damage the input shaft, converter and pump.

11. Disconnect the starter cables from the starter and remove the starter.

12. Disconnect the oil cooler lines from the transmission.

13. Disconnect the downshift linkage from the transmission.

14. Disconnect the selector rod or cable from the transmission manual lever.

15. Disconnect the speedometer cable from the extension housing. Disconnect the exhaust inlet pipes at the exhaust manifolds (LTD II, Thunderbird and Cougar).

16. Support the transmission on a transmission jack. Secure the transmission to the jack with safety chain. Remove the two engine rear support to transmission bolts. Remove the two crossmember to frame side rail attaching bolts and nuts. Raise the transmission slightly to take the weight off the crossmember. Remove the rear support to crossmember bolt and nut and remove the crossmember.

17. Lower the transmission slightly and disconnect the fluid filler tube.

18. Remove the remaining converter housing to engine attaching bolts. Move the transmission and converter assembly to the rear and down to remove it.

Installation

1. Torque the converter drain plug to 15–28 ft. lb.

2. If the converter has been removed from the converter housing, carefully position the converter to the transmission making sure the converter drive flats are fully engaged in the pump gear.

3. With the converter properly installed, place the transmission on the jack. Secure the transmission to the jack with safety chain.

4. Rotate the converter until the studs and drain plug are in alignment with their holes in the flywheel.

5. With the transmission mounted on a transmission jack, move the converter and transmission assembly forward into position, using care not to damage the flywheel and converter pilot. The converter must rest squarely against the flywheel. This indicates that the converter pilot is not binding in the engine crankshaft.

6. Install the lower converter housing-to-engine bolts. Torque bolts to 40–50 ft. lb. Remove the safety chain from the transmission.

7. Connect the fluid filler tube.

8. Install the crossmember.

9. Lower the transmission until the extension housing rests on the crossmember, and then install the rear support-to-crossmember bolts. Connect the exhaust inlet pipes at the exhaust manifolds (LTD II, Thunderbird and Cougar).

10. Install the converter attaching nuts. Install the access plates.

11. Connect the oil cooler inlet and outlet lines to the transmission case.

12. Coat the front universal joint yoke seal and spline with C1AZ-19590B lubricant (or equivalent), and install the drive shaft. Be sure that the drive shaft markings match those of the companion flange for correct balance.

13. Connect the speedometer cable at the transmission.

14. Connect the manual selector rod or cable to the transmission manual lever.

15. Connect the downshift linkage at the transmission downshift lever.

16. Install the starter motor and connect the starter cables.

17. Connect the vacuum hoses to the vacuum diaphragm unit and the tube to its clip.

18. Lower the transmission and install the upper two converter housing-to-engine bolts. Torque bolts to 40–50 ft. lb.

19. Lower the vehicle and fill the transmission with type F fluid.

20. Check the transmission, converter assembly, and fluid cooler lines for fluid leaks. Adjust the manual and downshift linkages.

AUTOMATIC OVERDRIVE (AOD)
Removal

1. Raise the vehicle on a hoist or stands.

2. Place the drain pan under the transmission fluid pan. Starting at the rear of the pan and working toward the front, loosen the

attaching bolts and allow the fluid to drain. Finally remove all of the pan attaching bolts except two at the front, to allow the fluid to further drain. With fluid drained, install two bolts on the rear side of the pan to temporarily hold it in place.

3. Remove the converter drain plug access cover from the lower end of the converter housing.

4. Remove the converter-to-flywheel attaching nuts. Place a wrench on the crankshaft pulley attaching bolt to turn the converter to gain access to the nuts.

5. Place a drain pan under the converter to catch the fluid. With the wrench on the crankshaft pulley attaching bolt, turn the converter to gain access to the converter drain plug and remove the plug. After the fluid has been drained, reinstall the plug.

6. Disconnect the driveshaft from the rear axle and slide shaft rearward from the transmission. Install a seal installation tool in the extension housing to prevent fluid leakage.

7. Disconnect the cable from the terminal on the starter motor. Remove the three attaching bolts and remove the starter motor. Disconnect the neutral start switch wires at the plug connector.

8. Remove the rear mount-to-crossmember attaching bolts and the two crossmember-to-frame attaching bolts.

9. Remove the two engine rear support-to-extension housing attaching bolts.

10. Disconnect the TV linkage rod from the transmission TV lever. Disconnect the manual rod from the transmission manual lever at the transmission.

11. Remove the two bolts securing the bellcrank bracket to the converter housing.

12. Raise the transmission with a transmission jack to provide clearance to remove the crossmember. Remove the rear mount from the crossmember and remove the crossmember from the side supports.

13. Lower the transmission to gain access to the oil cooler lines.

14. Disconnect each oil line from the fittings on the transmission.

15. Disconnect the speedometer cable from the extension housing.

16. Remove the bolt that secures the transmission fluid filler tube to the cylinder block. Lift the filler tube and the dipstick from the transmission.

17. Secure the transmission to the jack with the chain.

18. Remove the converter housing-to-cylinder block attaching bolts.

19. Carefully move the transmission and converter assembly away from the engine and, at the same time, lower the jack to clear the underside of the vehicle.

20. Remove the converter and mount the transmission in a holding fixture.

Installation

1. Tighten the converter drain plug to 20–28 ft. lb.

2. Position the converter on the transmission, making sure the converter drive flats are fully engaged in the pump gear by rotating the converter.

3. With the converter properly installed, place the transmission on the jack. Secure the transmission to the jack with a chain.

4. Rotate the converter until the studs and drain plug are in alignment with the holes in the flywheel.

IMPORTANT: Lube pilot.

5. Align the yellow balancing marks on converter and flywheel for Continental.

6. Move the converter and transmission assembly forward into position, using care not to damage the flywheel and the converter pilot. The converter must rest squarely against the flywheel. This indicates that the converter pilot is not binding in the engine crankshaft.

7. Install and tighten the converter housing-to-engine attaching bolts to 40–50 ft. lb. Make sure that the vacuum tube retaining clips are properly positioned.

8. Remove the safety chain from around the transmission.

9. Install a new O-ring on the lower end of the transmission filler tube. Insert the tube in the transmission case and secure the tube to the engine with the attaching bolt.

10. Connect the speedometer cable to the extension housing.

11. Connect the oil cooler lines to the right side of transmission case.

12. Position the crossmember on the side supports. Position the rear mount on the crossmember and install the attaching bolt and nut.

13. Secure the engine rear support to the extension housing and tighten the bolts to 35–40 ft. lb.

14. Lower the transmission and remove the jack.

15. Secure the crossmember to the side supports with the attaching bolts and tighten them to 35–40 ft. lb.

16. Position the bellcrank to the converter housing and install the two attaching bolts.

17. Connect the TV linkage rod to the transmission TV lever. Connect the manual linkage rod to the manual lever at the transmission.

18. Secure the converter-to-flywheel attaching nuts and tighten them to 20–30 ft. lb.

19. Install the converter housing access cover and secure it with the attaching bolts.

20. Secure the starter motor in place with the attaching bolts. Connect the cable to the terminal on the starter. Connect the neutral start switch wires at the plug connector.

21. Connect the driveshaft to the rear axle.

22. Adjust the shift linkage as required.

23. Adjust throttle linkage.

24. Lower the vehicle.

25. Fill the transmission to the correct level with Dexron® II. Start the engine and shift the transmission to all ranges, then recheck the fluid level.

Drive Train

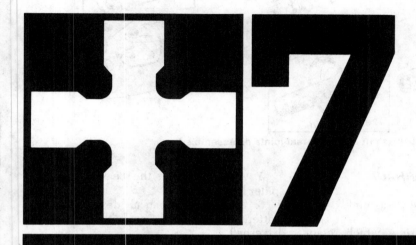

DRIVELINE

Driveshaft and U-Joints

The driveshaft is the means by which the power from the engine and transmission (in the front of the car) is transferred to the differential and rear axles, and finally to the rear wheels.

The driveshaft assembly incorporates two universal joints—one at each end—and a slip yoke at the front end of the assembly, which fits into the back of the transmission.

All driveshafts are balanced when installed in a car. It is therefore imperative that before applying undercoating to the chassis, the driveshaft and universal joint assembly be completely covered to prevent the accidental application of undercoating to the surfaces, and the subsequent loss of balance.

DRIVESHAFT REMOVAL

The procedure for removing the driveshaft assembly—complete with universal joint and slip yoke—is as follows:

1. Mark the relationship of the rear driveshaft yoke and the drive pinion flange of the axle. If the original yellow alignment marks are visible, there is no need for new marks. The purpose of this marking is to facilitate installation of the assembly in its exact original position, thereby maintaining proper balance.

2. Remove the four bolts which hold the rear universal joint to the pinion flange. Wrap tape around the loose bearing caps in order to prevent them from falling off the spider.

3. Pull the driveshaft toward the rear of the vehicle until the slip yoke clears the transmission housing and the seal. Plug the hole at the rear of the transmission housing or place a container under the opening to catch any fluid which might leak.

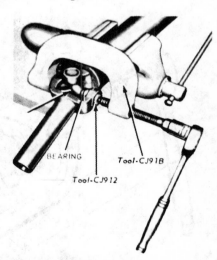

Removing universal joint bearing

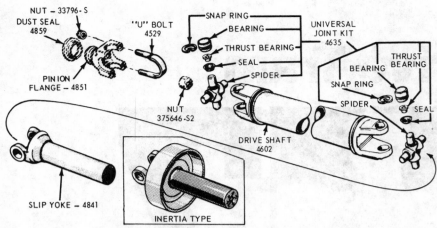

Driveshaft and universal joints disassembled

UNIVERSAL JOINT OVERHAUL

1. Position the driveshaft assembly in a sturdy vise.

2. Remove the snap-rings which retain the bearings in the slip yoke (front only) and in the driveshaft (front and rear).

3. Using a large punch or an arbor press, drive one of the bearings in toward the center of the universal joint, which will force the opposite bearing out.

4. As each bearing is pressed or punched far enough out of the universal joint assembly that it is accessible, grip it with a pair of pliers, and pull it from the driveshaft yoke. Drive or press the spider in the opposite direction in order to make the opposite bearing accessible, and pull it free with a pair of pliers. Use this procedure to remove all bearings from both universal joints.

5. After removing the bearings, lift the spider from the yoke.

6. Thoroughly clean all dirt and foreign matter from the yokes on both ends of the driveshaft.

NOTE: *When installing new bearings in the yokes, it is advisable to use an arbor press. However, if this tool is not available, the bearings should be driven into position with extreme care, as a heavy jolt on the needle bearings can easily damage or misalign them, greatly shortening their life and hampering their efficiency.*

7. Start a new bearing into the yoke at the rear of the driveshaft.

8. Position a new spider in the rear yoke and press (or drive) the new bearing ¼ in. below the outer surface of the yoke.

9. With the bearing in position, install a new snap-ring.

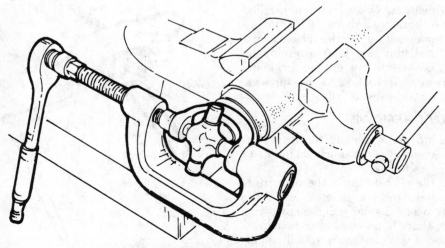

Installing universal joint bearing

10. Start a new bearing into the opposite side of the yoke.

11. Press (or drive) the bearing until the opposite bearing—which you have just installed—contacts the inner surface of the snap-ring.

12. Install a new snap-ring on the second bearing. It may be necessary to grind the surface of this second snap-ring.

13. Reposition the driveshaft in the vise, so that the front universal joint is accessible.

14. Install the new bearings, new spider, and ndw snap-rings in the same manner as you did for the rear universal joint.

15. Position the slip yoke on the spider. Install new bearings, nylon thrust bearings, and snap-rings.

16. Check both reassembled joints for freedom of movement. If misalignment of any part is causing a bind, a sharp rap on the side of the yoke with a brass hammer should seat the bearing needle and provide the desired freedom of movement. Care should be exercised to firmly support the shaft end during this operation, as well as to prevent blows to the bearings themselves. Under no circumstances should a driveshaft be installed in a car if there is any binding in the universal joints.

DRIVESHAFT INSTALLATION

1. Carefully inspect the rubber seal on the output shaft and the seal in end of the transmission extension housing. Replace them if they are damaged.

2. Examine the lugs on the axle pinion flange and replace the flange if the lugs are shaved or distorted.

3. Coat the yoke spline with special-purpose lubricant. The Ford art number for this lubricant is B8A-19589-A.

4. Remove the plug from the rear of the transmission housing.

5. Insert the yoke into the transmission housing and onto the transmission output shaft. Make sure that the yoke assembly does not bottom on the output shaft with excessive force.

6. Locate the marks which you made on the rear driveshaft yoke and the pinion flange prior to removal of the driveshaft assembly. Install the driveshaft assembly with the marks properly aligned.

7. Install the U-bolts and nuts which attach the universal joint to the pinion flange. Torque the U-bolt nuts to 8–15 ft. lbs.

REAR AXLE ASSEMBLY

All cars use the removable carrier assembly type rear axle. As the name implies, this type of axle features a differential carrier which may be removed from the car without removing the axle housings.

AXLE SHAFT AND/OR BEARING REPLACEMENT

NOTE: *Bearings must be pressed on and off the shaft with an arbor press. Unless you have access to one, it is inadvisable to attempt any repair work on the axle shaft and bearing assemblies.*

1. Remove the wheel, tire, and brake drum.

2. Remove the nuts holding the retainer plate to the backing plate. Disconnect the brake line.

3. Remove the retainer and install nuts, finger-tight to prevent the brake backing plate from being dislodged.

4. Pull out the axle shaft and bearing assembly, using a slide hammer.

NOTE: *If end-play is found to be excessive, the bearing should be replaced. Shimming the bearing is not recommended as this ignores end-play of the bearing itself and could result in improper seating of the bearing.*

5. Using a chisel, nick the bearing retainer in three or four places. The retainer does not have to be cut, but merely collapsed sufficiently to allow the bearing retainer to be slid from the shaft.

6. Press off the bearing and install the new one by pressing it into position.

7. Press on the new retainer.

NOTE: *Do not attempt to press the bearing and the retainer on at the same time.*

8. Assemble the shaft and bearing in the housing, being sure that the bearing is seated properly in the housing.

9. Install the retainer, drum, wheel, and tire. Bleed the brakes.

AXLE SHAFT SEAL REPLACEMENT

1. Remove the axle shaft from the rear axle assembly, following the procedures previously discussed.

2. Using a two-fingered seal puller (slide hammer), remove the seal from the axle housing.

3. Thoroughly clean the recess in the rear axle housing from which the seal was removed.

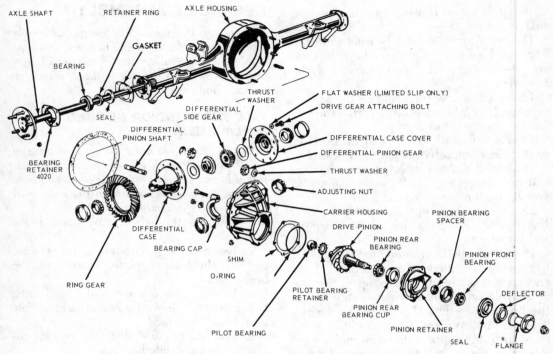

Removable carrier axle assembly

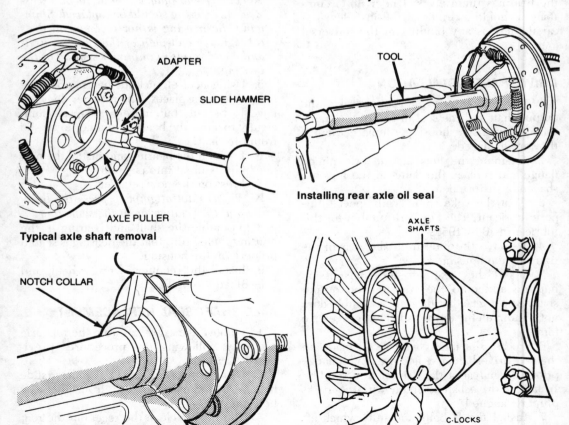

Typical axle shaft removal

Installing rear axle oil seal

Loosening the bearing retaining ring on the 6¾ inch rear axle

Removal and installation of the C-locks on a 7½ inch rear axle

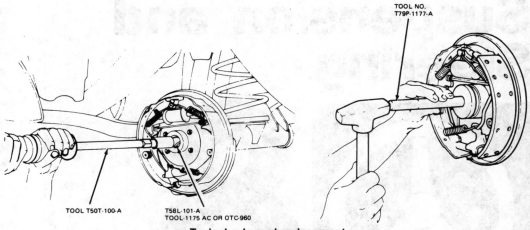

TOOL NO.
T79P-1177-A

TOOL T50T-100-A

T58L-101-A
TOOL-1175 AC OR OTC-960

Typical axle seal replacement

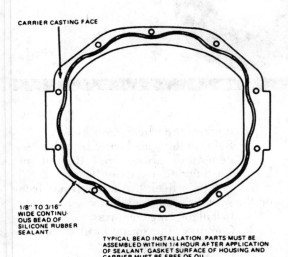

CARRIER CASTING FACE

1/8" TO 3/16"
WIDE CONTINU-
OUS BEAD OF
SILICONE RUBBER
SEALANT

TYPICAL BEAD INSTALLATION. PARTS MUST BE
ASSEMBLED WITHIN 1/4 HOUR AFTER APPLICATION
OF SEALANT. GASKET SURFACE OF HOUSING AND
CARRIER MUST BE FREE OF OIL.

Installing sealer on rear axle housing cover

4. Position a new seal on the housing and drive it into place with a seal installation tool. If this tool is not available, a wood block may be substituted.

NOTE: *Although the right and left-hand seals are identical, there are many different types of seals which have been used on rear axle assemblies. It is advisable to have one of the old seals with you when you are purchasing new ones.*

5. When the seal is properly installed, install the axle shaft.

Differential Overhaul

A differential overhaul is a complex, highly technical, and time-consuming operation—one which requires a great many tools, extensive knowledge of the unit and the way it works, and a high degree of mechanical experience and ability. It is highly advisable that the amateur mechanic not attempt any work on the differential unit.

Improved Traction Differentials

Ford calls their improved traction differential "Traction-Lok". In this assembly, a multiple-disc clutch is employed to control differential action. Repair procedures are the same as for conventional axles (within the scope of this book).

Suspension and Steering

FRONT SUSPENSION

Coil Spring On Upper Arm Suspension

On these models, the front coil springs are mounted on top of the upper control arm to a tower in the sheet metal of the body. This type of mounting provides good stability. The lower arm and stabilizing strut substitute for the conventional A frame and serve to guide the lower part of the spindle through its cycle of up-and-down movement. The rod-type stabilizing strut is mounted between two rubber buffer pads and the front end to cushion fore and aft thrust of the suspension. The effective length of this rod is variable and must be considered in maintenance. Ball joints are of the usual steel construction.

NOTE: *Extreme caution should be exercised when removing or installing coil springs.*

COIL SPRING REMOVAL AND INSTALLATION

1. Raise the hood and remove the shock absorber upper mounting bracket bolts.
2. Raise the front of the vehicle and place safety stands under the end of the lower control arms.
3. Remove the shock absorber lower attaching nuts, washer, and insulators.
4. Remove the wheel cover hub cap.
5. Remove the wheel cover or hub cap.
6. Remove the grease cap, cotter pin, nut lock, adjusting nut, and outer bearing.
7. Pull the wheel, tire and hub and drum off the spindle as an assembly.
8. Install a spring compressor.
9. Compress the spring until all tension is removed from the control arms.
10. Remove the two upper control arm attaching nuts and swing the control arm outboard.
11. Release the spring compressor cautiously and remove it.
12. Remove the spring.
13. place the upper spring insulator on the spring and secure it in place with tape.
14. Position the spring in the spring tower and compress it with the spring compressor.
15. Swing the upper control arm and install the attaching nuts. Torque the nuts to 75–100 ft. lbs.
16. Release the spring pressure and guide spring into the upper arm spring seat. The end of the spring must be not more than ½ in. from the tab on the spring seat.
17. Remove the spring compressor and position the wheel, tire, and hub and drum on spindle.
18. Install bearing, washer, and adjusting nut.

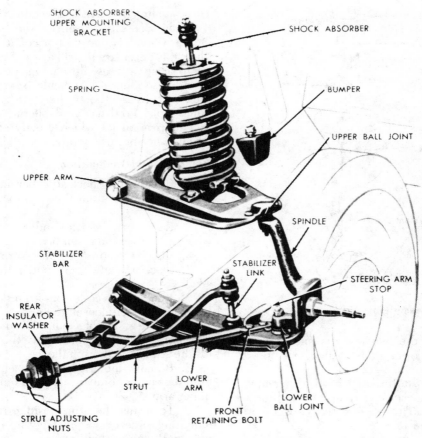

1971 front suspension assembly—coil spring on upper arm type

19. On cars with disc brakes, loosen adjusting nut three turns and rock wheel hub and rotor assembly in and out to push disc brake pads away from rotor.

20. While rotating wheel, hub and drum assembly, torque the adjusting nut to 17–25 ft. lbs. to seat the bearing.

21. With 1⅛ in. box wrench back off the adjusting nut ½ turn, and tighten nut to 10–15 in. lbs. or finger-tight.

22. Position the lock on adjusting nut and install new cotter pin. Bend the ends of the pin around the castellated flange of the nut lock.

23. Check the front wheel rotation and install the grease cap and hub cap.

24. Install shock absorber and upper bracket assembly, making sure shock absorber lower studs have insulators and are in pivot plate holes.

25. Install nuts and washers on the lower studs and torque to 8–21 ft. lbs.

26. Install the nuts on the shock absorber upper bracket and torque to 20–28 ft. lbs.

27. Remove safety stands and lower the vehicle.

SHOCK ABSORBER REMOVAL AND INSTALLATION

1. Raise the hood and remove the three shock absorber-to-spring tower attaching bolts.

2. Raise the front of the vehicle and place jackstands under the lower control arms.

3. Remove the shock absorber lower attaching nuts, washers, and insulators.

4. Lift the shock absorber and upper bracket from the spring tower and remove the bracket from the shock absorber. Remove the insulators from the lower attaching studs.

5. Install the upper mounting bracket on the shock absorber and torque to 20–30 ft. lbs. Install the insulators on the lower attaching studs.

6. Place the shock absorber and upper bracket assembly in the spring tower, making sure that the shock absorber lower studs are in the pivot plate holes.

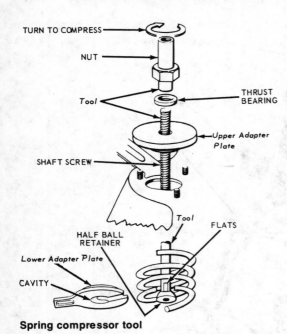

TURN TO COMPRESS

NUT

THRUST BEARING

Tool

Upper Adapter Plate

SHAFT SCREW

Tool

FLATS

HALF BALL RETAINER

Lower Adapter Plate

CAVITY

Spring compressor tool

7. Install the two washers and attaching nuts on the lower studs of the shock absorbers and torque to 8–12 ft. lbs.

8. Install the three shock absorber upper mounting bracket attaching nuts and torque them to 15–25 ft. lbs. Remove the jackstands and lower the vehicle.

UPPER CONTROL ARM

When upper control arm bushings become low on lubrication, they become very noisy.

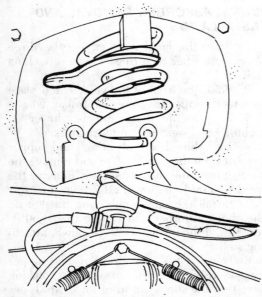

MacPherson strut front suspension

This can often be corrected by lubrication and it is not necessary to replace the bushings. On early models that do not contain grease plugs it is necessary to drill and tap the bushing to accept a grease fitting. On later models with grease plugs it is difficult to remove the plug and grease the bushing with conventional tools. Ford has available an upper A-arm lubrication kit which greatly eases the performance of this operation.

Removal and Installation

1. Remove the shock absorber and upper mounting bracket from the car as an assembly.

2. Raise the vehicle and remove the wheel and tire as an assembly.

3. Install the spring compressor tool.

4. Place a safety stand under the lower arm.

5. Remove the cotter pin from the upper ball joint stud and loosen the nut.

6. Using a suitable tool, loosen the ball joint in the spindle then, remove the nut and lift the stud from the spindle.

7. Remove the upper arm attaching nuts from the engine compartment and remove the upper arm.

8. To install the arm, position it on the mounting bracket and install the attaching nuts on the inner shaft attaching bolts.

NOTE: *The original equipment keystone-type lockwashers must be used with the inner shaft attaching nuts and bolts.*

9. Install the upper ball joint stud in the spindle and tighten the nut to 60–80 ft. lbs. Install a new cotter pin.

10. Remove the spring compressor and position spring on upper arm. Install wheel and check front end alignment.

LOWER BALL JOINT/LOWER CONTROL ARM INSPECTION

On all intermediate size cars the lower ball joint is an integral part of the lower control arm. If the lower ball joint is defective the entire lower control arm must be replaced.

1. Raise the vehicle on a hoist or floor jack so that the front wheel falls to the full down position.

2. Have an assistant grasp the bottom of the tire and move the wheel in and out.

3. As the wheel is being moved, observe the lower control arm where the spindle attaches to it.

4. Any movement between the lower part of the spindle and the lower control arm in-

dicates a bad control arm which must be re-placed.

NOTE: *During this check, the upper ball joint will be unloaded and may move; this is normal and not an indication of a bad ball joint. Also, do not mistake a loose wheel bearing for a worn ball joint.*

LOWER BALL JOINT/CONTROL ARM REMOVAL AND INSTALLATION

1. Position an upper control arm support between the upper arm and side rail.

2. Raise the vehicle, position jackstands, and remove the wheel and tire.

3. Remove the stabilizer bar-to-link attaching nut and disconnect the bar from the link.

4. Remove the link bolt from the lower arm.

5. Remove the strut bar-to-lower attaching nuts and bolts.

6. Remove the lower ball joint cotter pin and back off the nut. Using a suitable tool, loosen the ball joint stud in the spindle.

7. Remove the nut from the arm and lower the arm.

8. Remove the lower arm-to-under-body cam attaching parts and remove the arm.

9. To install, position the lower arm in the underbody and install the ball joint and cam attaching parts loosely.

10. Install the stabilizer and strut and torque the attaching parts to specifications.

11. Torque the lower arm pivot and ball joint stud to specifications.

12. Lower the car and remove the upper arm support.

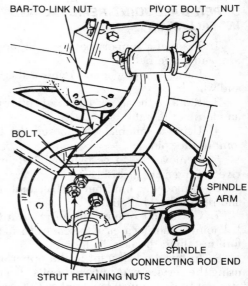

Lower control arm installed

13. Front end alignment must be re-checked.

UPPER BALL JOINT INSPECTION

1. Raise the vehicle on a hoist or floor jack so that the front wheels hang in the full down position.

2. Have an assistant grasp the wheel top and bottom and apply alternate in and out pressure to the top and bottom of the wheel.

3. Radial play of ¼ in. is acceptable measured at the inside of the wheel adjacent to the upper arm.

NOTE: *This radial play measurement is multiplied at the outer circumference of the tire and should not be measured here. Measure only at the inside of the wheel.*

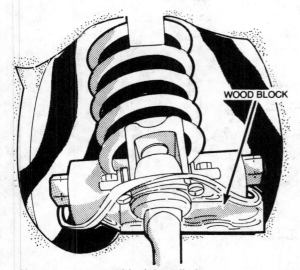

Upper arm support block installed

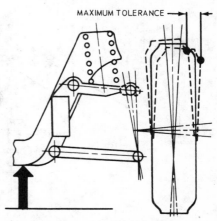

Measuring upper ball joint radial play

UPPER BALL JOINT REMOVAL AND INSTALLATION

1. Position a support between the upper arm and frame rail.

2. Raise the vehicle and remove the tire and wheel.

3. Remove the upper ball joint cotter pin and loosen the nut.

4. Using a suitable tool, loosen the ball joint in the spindle.

5. Remove the three ball joint retaining rivets using a large chisel.

6. Remove the nut from the ball joint stud and remove the ball joint.

7. Clean and remove all burrs from the ball joint mounting area of the control arm before installing the new ball joint.

8. Install the ball joint in the upper arm using the service part nuts and bolts. Do not attempt to rivet a new ball joint to the arm.

9. Install and torque the ball joint stud nut and install the cotter pin.

10. Lubricate the new joint with a hand grease gun only, using an air pressure gun may loosen the ball joint seal.

11. Install the wheel, lower the vehicle, and remove the upper arm support.

12. Check the front end alignment.

Coil Spring on Lower Arm Suspension

Each front wheel rotates on a spindle. The spindle's upper and lower ends attach to the upper and lower ball joints which mount to an upper and lower arm respectively. The upper arm pivots on a bushing and shaft assembly bolted to the frame. The lower arm pivots on the no. 2 crossmember bolt. The coil spring is seated between the lower arm and the top of the spring housing on the underside of the upper arm. A shock absorber is bolted to the lower arm at the bottom and the top of the spring housing.

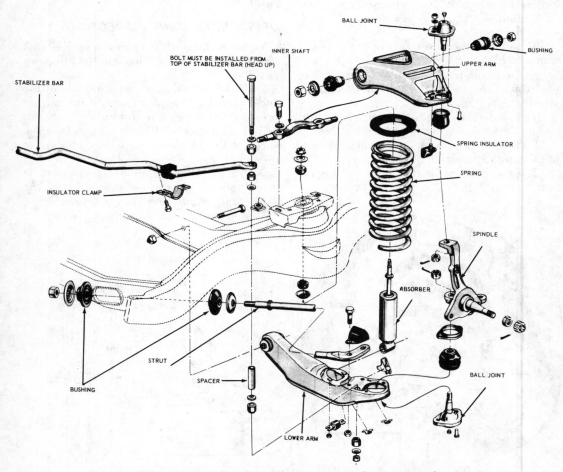

1972 and later coil spring on lower arm type front suspension

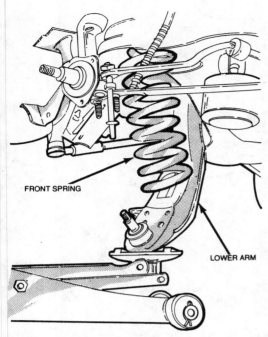

FRONT SPRING

LOWER ARM

Removing front spring

COIL SPRING AND LOWER CONTROL ARM REMOVAL AND INSTALLATION

1. Raise the car and support it with stands placed in back of the lower arms.

2. Remove the wheel from the hub. Remove the two bolts and washers that hold the caliper and brake hose bracket to the spindle. Remove the caliper from the rotor and wire it back out of the way. Remove the hub and rotor from the spindle.

3. Disconnect the lower end of the shock absorber and push it up to the retracted position.

4. Disconnect the stabilizer bar link from the lower arm.

5. Remove the cotter pins from the upper and lower ball joint stud nuts.

6. Remove the two bolts and nuts holding the strut to the lower arm.

7. Loosen the lower ball joint stud nut two turns. Do not remove this nut.

8. Install spreader tool T57P-3006-A between the upper and lower ball joint studs.

9. Expand the tool until the tool exerts considerable pressure on the studs. Tap the spindle near the lower stud with a hammer to loosen the stud with tool pressure only.

10. Position the floor jack under the lower arm and remove the lower ball joint stud nut.

11. Lower the floor jack and remove the spring and insulator.

12. Remove the A-arm-to-crossmember attaching parts and remove the arm from the car.

13. Reverse the above procedure to install. If the lower control arm was replaced because of damage, check front end alignment. Torque lower arm-to-no. 2 crossmember nut to 60–90 ft. lbs. Torque the strut-to-lower arm bolts to 80–115 ft. lbs. The caliper-to-spindle bolts are torqued to 90–120 ft. lbs. Torque the ball joint-to-spindle attaching nut to 60–90 ft. lbs.

SHOCK ABSORBER REMOVAL AND INSTALLATION

1. Remove the nut, washer, and bushing from the upper end of the shock absorber.

2. Raise the vehicle on a hoist and install jackstands under the frame rails.

3. Remove the two bolts securing the shock absorber to the lower arm and remove the shock absorber.

4. Inspect the shock absorber for leaks. Extend and compress the unit several times to check the damping action and remove any trapped air. Replace in pairs if necessary.

5. Install a new bushing and washer on the top of the shock absorber and position the unit inside the front spring. Install the two lower attaching bolts and torque them to 8–15 ft. lbs.

6. Remove the safety stands and lower the vehicle.

7. Place a new bushing and washer on the shock absorber top stud and install the attaching nut. Torque to 22–30 ft. lbs.

UPPER CONTROL ARM REMOVAL AND INSTALLATION

1. Perform Steps 1–11 of the previous "Coil Spring and Lower Control Arm Removal and Installation" procedure.

2. Remove the upper arm inner shaft attaching bolts and remove the arm and shaft from the chassis as an assembly.

3. Reverse above procedure to install. Torque the ball joint-to-spindle attaching nut to 60–90 ft. lbs.

4. Adjust front end alignment.

LOWER BALL JOINT INSPECTION

1. Raise the vehicle by placing a floor jack under the lower arm or, raise the vehicle on a hoist and place a jackstand under the lower arm and lower the vehicle onto it to remove the preload from the lower ball joint.

2. Have an assistant grasp the top and bot-

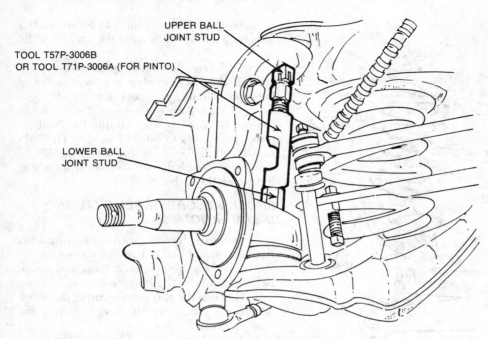

TOOL T57P-3006B
OR TOOL T71P-3006A (FOR PINTO)

UPPER BALL
JOINT STUD

LOWER BALL
JOINT STUD

Loosening lower ball joint stud

tom of the wheel and apply alternate in and out pressure to the top and bottom of the wheel.

3. Radial play of ¼ in. is acceptable measured at the inside of the wheel adjacent to the lower arm.

LOWER BALL JOINT REMOVAL AND INSTALLATION

1. Raise the vehicle on a hoist and allow the front wheels to fall to their full down position.

2. Drill a ⅛ in. hole completely through each ball joint attaching rivet.

3. Use a ⅜ in. drill in the pilot hole to drill off the head of the rivet.

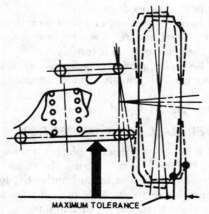

MAXIMUM TOLERANCE

Measuring lower ball joint radial play

4. Drive the rivets from the lower arm.

5. Place a jack under the lower arm and lower the vehicle about 6 in.

6. Remove the lower ball joint stud cotter pin and attaching nut.

7. Using a suitable tool, loosen the ball joint from the spindle and remove the ball joint from the lower arm.

8. Clean all metal burrs from the lower arm and install the new ball joint, using the service part nuts and bolts to attach the ball joint to the lower arm. Do not attempt to rivet the ball joint again once it has been removed.

9. Check front end alignment.

UPPER BALL JOINT INSPECTION

1. Raise the vehicle by placing a floor jack under the lower arm. Do not allow the lower arm to hang freely with the vehicle on a hoist or bumper jack.

2. Have an assistant grasp the top and bottom of the tire and move the wheel in and out.

3. As the wheel is being moved, observe the upper control arm where the spindle attaches to it. Any movement between the upper part of the spindle and the upper ball joint indicates a bad ball joint which must be replaced.

NOTE: *During this check, the lower ball joint will be unloaded and may move; this is normal and not an indication of a bad ball joint. Also, do not mistake a loose wheel bearing for a defective ball joint.*

UPPER BALL JOINT REMOVAL AND INSTALLATION

1. Raise the vehicle on a hoist and allow the front wheels to fall to their full down position.

2. Drill a ⅛ in. hole completely through each ball joint attaching rivet.

3. Using a large chisel, cut off the head of each rivet and drive them from the upper arm.

4. Place a jack under the lower arm and lower the vehicle about 6 in.

5. Remove the cotter pin and attaching nut from the ball joint stud.

6. Using a suitable tool, loosen the ball joint stud from the spindle and remove the ball joint from the upper arm.

7. Clean all metal burrs from the upper arm and install the new ball joint, using the service part nuts and bolts to attach the ball joint to the upper arm. Do not attempt to rivet the ball joint again once it has been removed.

8. Check front end alignment.

MacPherson Strut Suspension

The design utilizes shock struts with coil springs mounted between the lower arm and a spring pocket in the No. 2 crossmember. The shock struts are non-repairable, and must be replaced as a unit. The ball joints lower suspension arm bushings are not separately serviced, and they also must be replaced by replacing the suspension arm assembly. The ball joint seal can be replaced separately.

SPRINGS

NOTE: *Always use extreme caution when working with coil springs. Make sure the vehicle is supported sufficiently.*

Removal

1. Raise the front of the vehicle and place safety stands under both sides of the jack pads just back of the lower arms.

2. Remove the wheel and tire assembly.

3. Disconnect the stabilizer bar link from the lower arm.

4. Remove the steering gear bolts, and move the steering gear out of the way.

5. Disconnect the tie rod from the steering spindle.

6. Using a spring compressor, install one plate with the pivot ball seat down into the

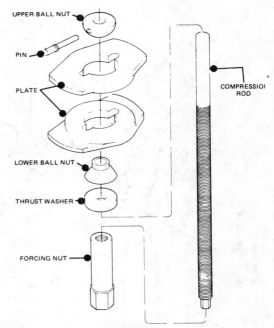

UPPER BALL NUT

PIN

PLATE

COMPRESSION ROD

LOWER BALL NUT

THRUST WASHER

FORCING NUT

Exploded view of a MacPherson strut

coils of the spring. Rotate the plate, so that it is fully seated into the lower suspension arm spring seat.

7. Install the other plate with the pivot ball seat up into the coils of the spring. Insert the ball nut through the coils of the spring, so it rests in the upper plate.

8. Insert the compression rod into the opening in the lower arm through the lower and upper plate. Install the upper ball nut on the rod, and return the securing pin.

NOTE: *This pin can only be inserted one*

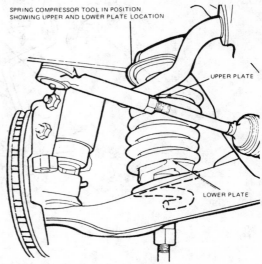

SPRING COMPRESSOR TOOL IN POSITION
SHOWING UPPER AND LOWER PLATE LOCATION

UPPER PLATE

LOWER PLATE

Spring compressor in position

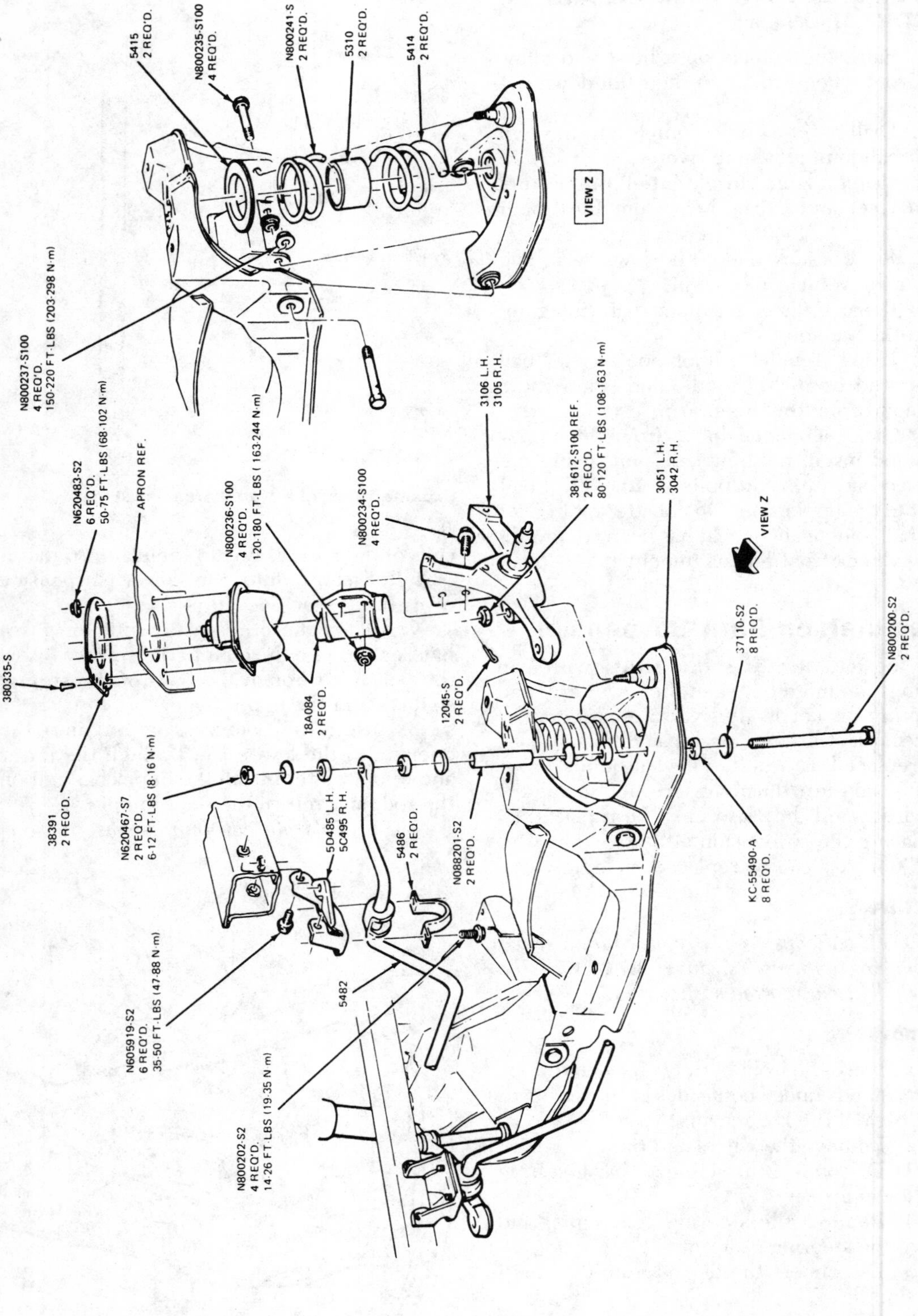

5415
2 REQ'D.

N800235-S100
4 REQ'D.

N800241-S
2 REQ'D.

5310
2 REQ'D.

5414
2 REQ'D.

VIEW Z

N800237-S100
4 REQ'D.
150-220 FT-LBS (203-298 N·m)

N620483-S2
6 REQ'D.
50-75 FT-LBS (68-102 N·m)

APRON REF.

N800236-S100
4 REQ'D.
120-180 FT-LBS (163-244 N·m)

N800234-S100
4 REQ'D.

3106 L.H.
3105 R.H.

381612-S100 REF.
2 REQ'D.
80-120 FT-LBS (108-163 N·m)

3051 L.H.
3042 R.H.

VIEW Z

37110-S2
8 REQ'D.

N800200-S2
2 REQ'D.

380335-S

38391

N620467-S7
2 REQ'D.
6-12 FT-LBS (8-16 N·m)

18A084
2 REQ'D.

12045-S
2 REQ'D.

5D485 L.H.
5C495 R.H.

5486
2 REQ'D.

N088201-S2
2 REQ'D.

KC-55490-A
8 REQ'D.

N605919-S2
6 REQ'D.
35-50 FT-LBS (47-88 N·m)

5482

N800202-S2
4 REQ'D.
14-26 FT-LBS (19-35 N·m)

MacPherson strut front suspension

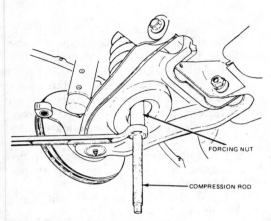

Spring compressed for removal

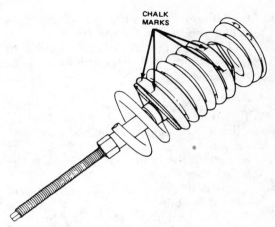

CHALK MARKS

Spring removed from car

way into the upper ball nut because of a stepped hole design.

9. With the upper ball nut secured turn the upper plate, so it walks up the coil until it contacts the upper spring seat.

10. Install the lower ball nut, thrust bearing and forcing nut on the compression rod.

11. Rotate the nut until the spring is compressed enough so that it is free in its seat.

12. Remove the two lower control arm pivot bolts and nuts, and disengage the lower arm from the frame crossmember and remove the spring assembly.

13. If a new spring is to be installed, mark the position of the upper and lower plates on the spring with chalk. Measure the compressed length of the spring as well as the amount of the spring curvature to assist in the compressing and installation of a new spring.

14. Loosen the nut to relieve spring tension, and remove the tools from the spring.

Installation

1. Assemble the spring compressor tool, and locate it in the same position as indicated in step 13 of the removal procedure.

NOTE: *Before compressing the coil spring, be sure the upper ball nut securing pin is inserted properly.*

2. Compress the coil spring until the spring height reaches the dimension in step 13.

3. Position the coil spring assembly into the lower arm.

NOTE: *Make sure that the lower end of the spring is properly positioned between the two holes in the lower arm spring pocket depression.*

4. To finish installing the coil spring reverse the removal procedure.

BALL JOINTS

Ball joints are not replaceable. If the ball joints are found to be defective the lower control arm assembly must be replaced.

Inspection

1. Support the vehicle in normal driving position with both ball joints loaded.

2. Wipe the grease fitting and checking surface, so they are free of dirt and grease. The checking surface is the round boss into which the grease fitting is threaded.

3. The checking surface should project outside the cover. If the checking surface is inside the cover, replace the lower arm assembly.

SHOCK STRUT

Removal

1. Place the ignition key in the unlocked position to permit free movement of the front wheels.

2. Working from the engine compartment remove the nut (16 mm) that attaches the strut to the upper mount. A screwdriver in the slot will hold the rod stationary while removing the nut.

NOTE: *The vehicle should not be driven while the nut is removed so make sure the car is in position for hoisting purposes.*

3. Raise the front of the vehicle by the lower control arms, and place safety stands under the frame jacking pads, rearward of the wheels.

4. Remove the tire and wheel assembly.

5. Remove the brake caliper, rotor assembly, and dust shield.

6. Remove the two lower nuts and bolts attaching the strut to the spindle.

7. Lift the strut up from the spindle to compress the rod, then pull down and remove the strut.

Installation

1. With the rod half extended, place the rod through the upper mount and hand start the mount as soon as possible.

2. Extend the strut and position into the spindle.

3. Install the two lower mounting bolts and hand start the nuts.

4. Tighten the nut that attaches the strut to the upper body mount to 60–75 ft. lbs. This can be done from inside the engine compartment.

NOTE: *Position a screwdriver in the slot to hold the rod stationary while the nut is being tightened.*

5. Remove the suspension load from the lower control arms by lowering the hoist and tighten the lower mounting nuts to 150 ft. lbs.

6. Raise the suspension control arms and install the brake caliper, rotor assembly and dust shield.

7. Install the tire and wheel assembly.

8. Remove the safety stands and lower the vehicle.

LOWER CONTROL ARM

Removal

1. Raise the front of the vehicle and position safety stands under both sides of the jack pads, just to the rear of the lower arms.

2. Remove the wheel and tire assembly.

3. Disconnect the stabilizer bar link from the lower arm.

4. Remove the disc brake caliper, rotor and dust shield.

5. Remove the steering gear bolts and position out of the way.

6. Remove the cotter pin from the ball joint stud nut, and loosen the ball joint nut one or two turns.

7. Tap the spindle sharply to relieve the stud pressure.

8. Remove the tie-rod end from the spindle. Place a floor jack under the lower arm, supporting the arm at both bushings. Remove both lower arm bolts, lower the jack and remove the coil spring as outlined earlier in the chapter.

9. Remove the ball nut and remove the arm assembly.

Installation

1. Place the new arm assembly into the spindle and tighten the ball joint nut to 100 ft. lbs. Install the cotter pin.

2. Position the coil spring in the upper spring pocket. Make sure the insulator is on top of the spring and the lower end is properly positioned between the two holes in the depression of the lower arm.

3. Carefully raise the lower arm with the floor jack until the bushings are properly positioned in the crossmember.

4. Install the lower arm bolts and nuts, finger tight only.

5. Install and tighten the steering gear bolts.

6. Connect the tie-rod end and tighten the nut to 35–47 ft. lbs.

7. Connect the stabilizer link bolt and nut and tighten to 10 ft. lbs.

8. Install the brake dust shield, rotor and caliper.

9. Install the wheel and tire assembly.

10. Remove the safety stands and lower the vehicle. After the vehicle has been lowered to the floor and at curb height, tighten the lower arm nuts to 210 ft. lbs.

Wheel Alignment
EXCEPT MACPHERSON STRUT

NOTE: *The procedure for checking and adjusting front wheel alignment requires specialized equipment and professional skills. The following descriptions and adjustment procedures are for general reference only.*

Front wheel alignment is the position of the front wheels relative to each other and to the vehicle. It is determined, and must be maintained to provide safe, accurate steering with minimum tire wear. Many factors are involved in wheel alignment and adjustments are provided to return those that might change due to normal wear to their original value. The factors which determine wheel alignment are dependent on one another; therefore, when one of the factors is adjusted, the others must be adjusted to compensate.

Descriptions of these factors and their affects on the car are provided below.

NOTE: *Do not attempt to check and adjust the front wheel alignment without first making a thorough inspection of the front suspension components.*

CAMBER

Camber angle is the number of degrees that the centerline of the wheel is inclined from the vertical. Camber reduces loading of the outer wheel bearing and improves the tire contact patch while cornering.

CASTER

Caster angle is the number of degrees that a line drawn through the steering knuckle pivots is inclined from the vertical, toward the front or rear of the car (when viewed from the side of the car). Caster improves the directional stability and decreases susceptibility to crosswinds or road surface deviations.

TOE-IN

Toe-in is the difference of the distance between the centers of the front and rear of the front wheels. It is most commonly measured in inches, but is occasionally referred to as an angle between the wheels. Toe-in is necessary to compensate for the tendency of the wheels to deflect rearward while in motion.

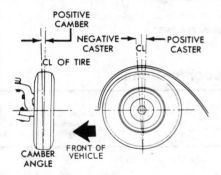

Caster and camber angles

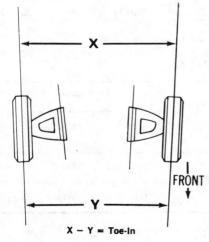

Toe-in

Due to this tendency, the wheels of a vehicle, with properly adjusted toe-in, are traveling straight forward when the vehicle itself is traveling straight forward, resulting in directional stability and minimum tire wear.

Steering wheel spoke misalignment is often an indication of incorrect front end alignment. Care should be exercised when aligning the front end to maintain steering wheel spoke position. When adjusting the tie rod ends, adjust each an equal amount (in the opposite direction) to increase or decrease toe-in. If, following toe-in adjustment, further adjustments are necessary to center the steering wheel spokes, adjust the tie-rod ends an equal amount in the same direction.

ADJUSTMENT PROCEDURES

1971

Caster is adjusted by lengthening or shortening the struts at the frame crossmember. To adjust, turn both nuts an equal number of turns in the same direction. Caster adjustments should be within ¼° of the opposing side of the car.

To adjust camber, loosen the lower control arm pivot bolt and rotate the eccentrics.

Adjust toe-in by loosening the clamp bolts, and turning the adjuster sleeves at the outer ends of the tie-rod. Turn each sleeve an equal amount in the opposite direction, in order to maintain steering wheel spoke alignment.

1972 and Later

Install Ford tool T65P-3000D, or its equivalent, on the frame rail, position the hooks around the upper control arm pivot shaft, and tighten the adjusting nuts slightly. Loosen the pivot shaft retaining bolts to permit adjustment.

To adjust caster, loosen or tighten either the front or rear adjusting nut. After adjusting caster, adjust the camber by loosening or

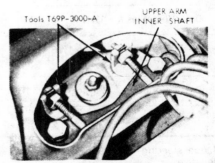

Caster and camber adjustments—1972 and later

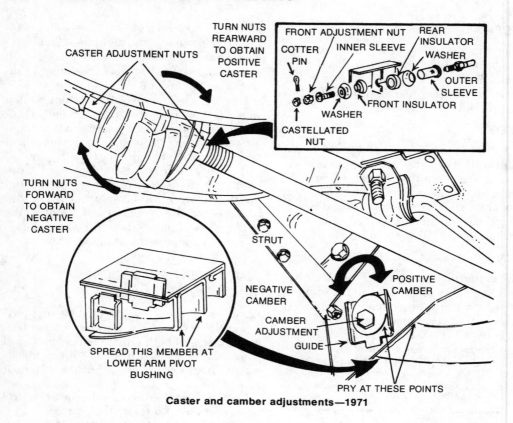

Caster and camber adjustments—1971

Wheel Alignment Specifications

Year	Model	Caster Range (deg)	Pref Setting	Camber Range (deg)	Pref Setting	Toe-in (in.)	Steering Axis Inclination (deg)	Wheel Pivot Ratio (deg) Inner	Outer
'71	All	1¼N to ¼N	¾N	½N to 1P	¼P	⅛ to ⅜	7⅔	20	①
'72–'73	All	1¼N to 2¾P	¾P	¼N to 1¾P	¾P	1/16 to 7/16	7⅔	20	17¾
'74	All	½P to 3½P	2P	Left ⅜N to 1⅝P Right ⅞N to 1⅛P	½P ⅛P	0 to ⅜	9	20	18⁷/₆₄
'75–'79	All	3¼P to 4¾P	4P	Left ¼N to 1¼P Right ½N to 1P	½P ¼P	0 to ⅜	9	20	18¹/₁₀
'78–'80	Versailles	1¼N to ¼P	½N	½N to 1P	¼P	0 to ¼	6¾	20	②
'80–'82	Thunderbird, XR-7	⅛P to 1⅞P	1P	½N to 1¼P	⅖P	1/16 to 5/16	15⅓	20	19.77
'80–'82	Cougar	⅛P to 1⅞P	1P	5/16N to 1³/₁₆P	7/16P	1/16 to 5/16	15¼	20	19.84
'82	Continental	1¾N to 2¼P	1¼P	½N to 1¼P	⅖P	0 to ¼	15¼	20	19.84

① Manual steering—17° 19'; power steering—17° 49'
N Negative
P Positive

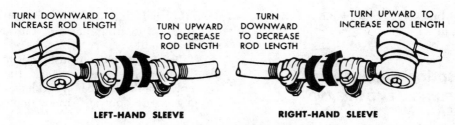

TURN DOWNWARD TO INCREASE ROD LENGTH

TURN UPWARD TO DECREASE ROD LENGTH

TURN DOWNWARD TO DECREASE ROD LENGTH

TURN UPWARD TO INCREASE ROD LENGTH

LEFT-HAND SLEEVE   RIGHT-HAND SLEEVE

Tie-rod (toe-in) adjustments

tightening both nuts an equal amount. Tighten the shaft retaining bolts to specifications, remove the tool, and recheck the adjustments.

Adjust toe-in by loosening the clamp bolts, and turning the adjuster sleeves at the outer ends of the tie-rod. Turn the sleeves an equal amount in the opposite direction, to maintain steering wheel spoke alignment.

Wheel Alignment
MACPHERSON STRUT

The caster and camber are set at the factory and cannot be changed. Only the toe is adjustable.

TOE ADJUSTMENT

Toe is the difference in width (distance), between the front and rear inside edges of the front tires.

1. Turn the steering wheel, from left to right, several times and center.

NOTE: *If car has power steering, start the engine before centering the steering wheel.*

2. Secure the centered steering wheel with a steering wheel holder, or any device that will keep it centered.

3. Release the tie-rod end bellows clamps so the bellows will not twist while adjustment is made. Loosen the jam nuts on the tie-rod ends. Adjust the left and right connector

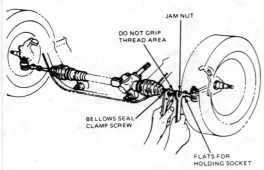

JAM NUT

DO NOT GRIP THREAD AREA

BELLOWS SEAL CLAMP SCREW

FLATS FOR HOLDING SOCKET

Toe adjustment on MacPherson strut front ends

sleeves until each wheel has one-half of the desired toe setting.

4. After the adjustment has been made, tighten the jam nuts and secure the bellows clamps. Release the steering wheel lock and check for steering wheel center. Readjust, if necessary until steering wheel is centered and toe is within specs.

REAR SUSPENSION

1971 Fairlanes Torinos and Montegos utilize a semi-elliptic leaf spring suspension. The axle housing is supported by a pair of leaf springs mounted on spring pads on the axle housing. The housing is secured to the center of the springs by two U-bolts, retaining plates and nuts. Each spring is suspended from the underbody side rail by a hanger at the front and a shackle at the rear. The shock absorbers are mounted between the leaf spring retaining plates and brackets bolted to the crossmember. Some high-performance 1971 models were equipped with staggered rear shock absorbers.

1972 and later models use a four-link coil spring suspension. The axle housing is suspended from the frame by an upper and lower trailing arm and a shock absorber at each side of the vehicle. These arms pivot in the frame members and the rear axle housing brackets. Each coil spring is mounted between a lower seat which is welded to the axle housing and an upper seat which is integral with the frame. The shock absorbers are bolted to the spring upper seats at the top and brackets mounted on the axle housing at the bottom. The upper trailing arms are attached to the frame crossmember brackets at the front and brackets located near the outer ends of the axle housing at the rear. Both lower arms attach similarly to the frame side members and the axle housing brackets. A rear stabilizer bar attached to the frame side rail brackets and the two axle housing brackets is available as optional equipment.

Leaf Spring Suspension
LEAF SPRING REMOVAL AND INSTALLATION

1. Raise the vehicle on a hoist and place supports beneath the underbody and under the axle.

2. Disconnect the lower end of the shock absorber from the spring clip plate and position it out of the way. Remove the supports from under the axle.

3. Remove the spring plate nuts from the U-bolts and remove the clip plate. Raise the rear axle just enough to remove the weight of the housing from the spring.

4. Remove the two rear shackle attaching nuts, the shackle bar, and the two inner bushings.

5. Remove the rear shackle assembly and two outer bushings.

6. Remove the nut from the spring mounting bolt and tap the bolt out of the bushing at the front hanger. Lift out the spring assembly.

7. If the front hanger bushing is to be replaced, it may be necessary to take the spring assembly to a machine shop and have the old bushing pressed out and a new one pressed in.

8. Inspect the rear shackle and hanger assembly, bushings, and studs for wear, damage, cracks, or distortion. Check for broken spring leaves. Inspect the anti-squeak inserts between the leaves. Inspect the spring clips for worn or damaged threads. Check the spring clip plate and insulator retainers for distortion. If the spring center tie bolt requires replacement, clamp the spring in a vise to keep the spring compressed during bolt removal and replacement. Replace all parts found to be defective.

NOTE: *All used attaching components (nuts, bolts, etc.) must be discarded and replaced with new ones prior to reassembly. This is due to the extreme stresses and weather conditions imposed on the attach-*

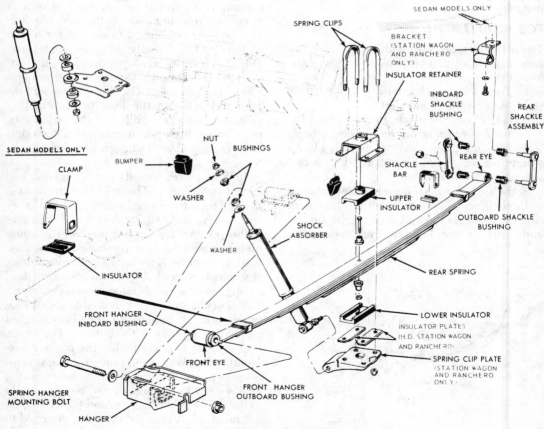

1971 leaf spring rear suspension assembly

ing hardware. If a used component is reinstalled, it may break.

9. Position the leaf spring under the axle housing and insert the shackle assembly into the rear hanger bracket and the rear eye of the spring.

10. Install the shackle inner bushings, the shackle plate, and the locknuts. Hand tighten the locknuts.

11. Position the spring front eye in the front hanger, slip the washer on the front hanger bolt, and, from the inboard side, insert the bolt through the hanger and eye. Install the locknut on the hanger bolt and tighten finger-tight.

12. Lower the rear axle housing so that it rests on the spring. Place the spring plate on the U-bolts. Install the U-bolt nuts and torque to 35–50 ft. lbs.

13. Attach the lower end of the shock absorber to the spring plate using a new nut.

14. Place safety stands under the axle housing, lower the vehicle until the spring is in the approximate curb load position, and then torque the front hanger stud locknut to 90–110 ft. lbs.

15. Torque the locknuts on the rear shackle to 18–29 ft. lbs. Close the hole in the inner rail with a body plug.

16. Remove the safety stands and lower the vehicle.

SHOCK ABSORBER REMOVAL AND INSTALLATION

1. Remove the spare from the trunk. On the Ranchero, remove the attaching screws and lift the forward half of the floor panel from the body; remove the access cover from the opening in the floor pan over the shock absorber. On station wagon models, remove the access cover from the opening in the seat riser over the shock absorber.

2. On all other models, fold back the floor mat in the trunk and remove the shock absorber access cover from the floor pan. Remove the nut, outer washer, and rubber bushing from the top of the shock absorber.

3. Raise the vehicle and remove the attaching nut, outer washer and bushing from the shock absorber at the spring plate. Compress the shock absorber and remove it from the vehicle.

4. If the shock absorber is not in need of replacement but requires new bushings, remove the inner bushings and washers from the shock absorber studs.

NOTE: All standard equipment shock ab-

sorbers are not refillable and cannot be repaired. Wipe off the shock absorber then extend and compress it several times. Severe leakage or weak action requires replacement. As a general rule, shock absorbers should be replaced in pairs (front and rear sets).

5. Position the inner washer and bushing on each shock absorber stud.

6. Expand the shock absorber and place it between the spring plate and the mounting in the floor pan.

7. Connect the lower stud to the spring plate and install the bushing, outer washer, and a new nut on the stud. Make sure that the spring plate is free of burrs. On the Ranchero, torque the stud nut to 15–25 ft. lbs. and install the forward half of the floor panel.

8. From inside the trunk, install the bushing, outer washer, and new attaching nut to the upper mounting stud, and torque to 15–25 ft. lbs. On station wagon models, replace the floor bed panel.

9. Replace and secure the spare in the trunk.

Coil Spring Suspension

COIL SPRING REMOVAL AND INSTALLATION

1. Place a hoist under the rear axle housing of the vehicle. Raise the vehicle and place jackstands under the frame side rails.

2. Disconnect the lower studs of the rear shock absorbers from the mounting brackets on the axle housing.

3. Lower the hoist and axle housing until the coil springs are fully released.

4. Remove the springs and the insulators from the vehicle.

5. Place the insulators in each upper seat and position the springs between the upper and lower seats.

6. With the springs in position, raise the hoist under the axle housing until the lower studs of the rear shock absorbers reach the mounting brackets on the axle housing. Connect the lower studs and install the attaching nuts. Torque to 50–85 ft. lbs.

7. Remove the jackstands and lower the vehicle.

SHOCK ABSORBER REMOVAL AND INSTALLATION

1. Raise the vehicle on a hoist.

2. Remove the shock absorber attaching

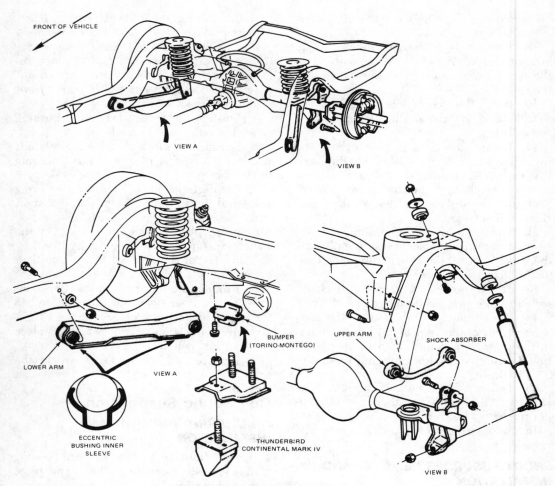

FRONT OF VEHICLE

VIEW A

VIEW B

LOWER ARM

VIEW A

BUMPER
(TORINO-MONTEGO)

ECCENTRIC
BUSHING INNER
SLEEVE

THUNDERBIRD
CONTINENTAL MARK IV

UPPER ARM

SHOCK ABSORBER

VIEW B

Coil spring rear suspension assembly

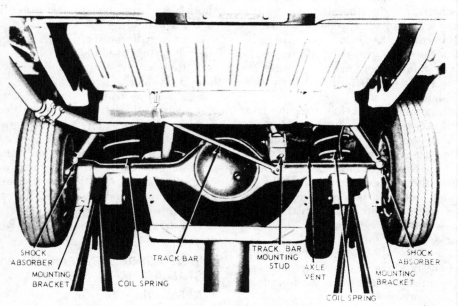

SHOCK
ABSORBER
MOUNTING
BRACKET

COIL SPRING

TRACK BAR

TRACK BAR
MOUNTING
STUD

AXLE
VENT

COIL SPRING

SHOCK
ABSORBER
MOUNTING
BRACKET

Removing rear coil springs

nut, washer, and insulator from the stud at the top side of the spring upper seat. Compress the shock absorber sufficiently to clear the spring seat hole and remove the inner insulator and washer from the upper attaching stud.

3. Remove the locknut and disconnect the shock absorber lower stud at the mounting bracket on the axle housing.

4. Remove the shock absorber from the vehicle and check for leakage. If the shock absorber is in good condition, compress and expand the unit several times to expel any trapped air prior to reinstallation.

5. Position the inner washer and insulator on the upper attaching stud. Place the shock absorber in such a position that the upper attaching stud enters the hole in the spring upper seat. While maintaining the shock absorber in this position, install the outer insulator, washer, and new nut on the stud from the top side of the spring upper seat. Torque the attaching nut to 14–26 ft. lbs.

6. Extend the shock absorber. Locate the lower stud in the mounting bracket hole on the axle housing. Install and torque the locknut to 50–85 ft. lbs.

STEERING
Steering Wheel
REMOVAL AND INSTALLATION
1971–74

1. Open the hood and disconnect the negative cable from the battery.

2. On models equipped with safety crash pads, remove the crash pad attaching screws from the underside of the steering wheel spoke and remove the pad. Remove the horn button or ring by pressing down evenly and turning it counterclockwise approximately 20 degrees and then lifting it from the steering wheel. Disconnect the shorn wires.

3. Remove the nut at the end of the shaft. Mark the steering shaft and hub prior to removal. Install a steering wheel puller on the end of the shaft and remove the wheel.

CAUTION: *The use of a knock-off type steering wheel puller or the use of a hammer on the steering shaft will damage the column bearing and, on collapsible columns, the column itself may be damaged.*

4. Lubricate the horn switch brush plate and the upper surface of the steering shaft upper bushing with Lubriplate or a similar product. Transfer all serviceable parts to the new steering wheel.

5. Position the steering wheel on the shaft so that the alignment marks made prior to removal line up. Install a new locknut and torque it to 20–30 ft. lbs. Connect the horn wires.

6. Install the horn button or ring by turning it clockwise and install the crash pad.

1975–82

1. Open the hood and disconnect the negative cable from the battery.

2. On models with safety crash pads, remove the crash pad attaching screws from the

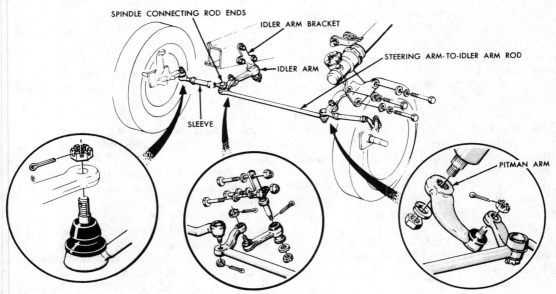

Typical manual steering linkage

underside of the steering wheel spoke and remove the pad. On all models equipped with a horn button, remove the horn button or ring by pressing down evenly and turning it counterclockwise approximately 20° and then lifting it from the steering wheel. On 1981–82 Cougar, XR-7, Thunderbird, pull straight out on the hub cover. Disconnect the horn wires from the crash pad on models so equipped.

3. Remove and discard the nut from the end of the shaft. Install a steering wheel puller on the end of the shaft and remove the wheel.

CAUTION: *The use of a knock-off type steering wheel puller or the use of a hammer on the steering shaft will damage the collapsible column.*

4. Lubricate the upper surface of the steering shaft upper bushing with white grease. Transfer all serviceable parts to the new steering wheel.

5. Position the steering wheel on the shaft so that the alignment marks line up. Install a locknut and torque it to 30–40 ft. lbs. Connect the horn wires.

6. Install the horn button or ring by turning it clockwise or install the crash pad.

TURN SIGNAL SWITCH REPLACEMENT

1971–74

1. Open the hood and disconnect the negative battery cable.

2. Remove the retaining screw from the underside of each steering wheel spoke and remove the crash pad and horn switch cover as an assembly.

3. Remove the steering wheel retaining nut. Remove the steering wheel as outlined in the steering wheel "Removal and Installation" section.

4. Remove the turn signal handle from the side of the column. Remove the emergency flasher retainer and knob, if so equipped.

5. Remove the wire assembly cover and disconnect the wire connector plugs. Record the location and color code of each wire and tape the wires together. Make sure that the horn wires are disconnected. Remove the plastic cover from the wiring harness. Attach a piece of heavy cord to the switch wires to pull them through the column during installation.

6. Remove the retaining clips and attaching screws from the turn signal switch and lift the switch and wire assembly from the top of the column.

7. Tape the ends of the new switch wires

together and transfer the pull cord to these wires.

8. Pull the wires down through the column with the cord and attach the new switch to the column hub.

9. Connect the wiring plugs to their matting plugs at the lower end of the column and install the plastic cover at the harness.

10. Install all retaining clips and wire assembly covers that were removed and install the turn signal handle. Install the emergency flasher retainer and knob, if so equipped.

11. Install the steering wheel and retaining nut as outlined in the "Steering Wheel Removal and Installation" section.

12. Install the horn ring or button. Install the crash pad with the retaining screws at the underside of each steering wheel spoke.

13. Connect the negative battery cable and test the operation of the turn signals, horn, and emergency flashers, if so equipped.

LTD II, Montego, Torino, Versailles, 1975–79 Cougar, 1977–79 Thunderbird

1. Open the hood and disconnect the negative battery cable.

2. Remove the steering wheel.

3. Unscrew the turn signal handle from the side of the column. Remove the emergency flasher retainer and knob, if so equipped.

4. Remove the wire assembly cover and disconnect the wire connector plugs. Record the location and color code of each wire and tape the wires together. Make sure that the horn wires are disconnected. Remove the plastic cover from the wiring harness. Attach a piece of heavy cord to the switch wires to pull them through the column during installation.

5. Remove the retaining clips and attaching screws from the turn signal switch and pull the switch and wire assembly from the top of the column.

6. Tape the ends of the new switch wires together and transfer the pull cord to these wires.

7. Pull the wires down through the column with the cord and attach the new switch to the column hub.

8. Connect the wiring plugs to their matting plugs at the lower end of the column and install the plastic cover at the harness.

9. Install all retaining clips and wire assembly covers that were removed and install the turn signal handle. Install the emergency flasher retainer and knob, if so equipped.

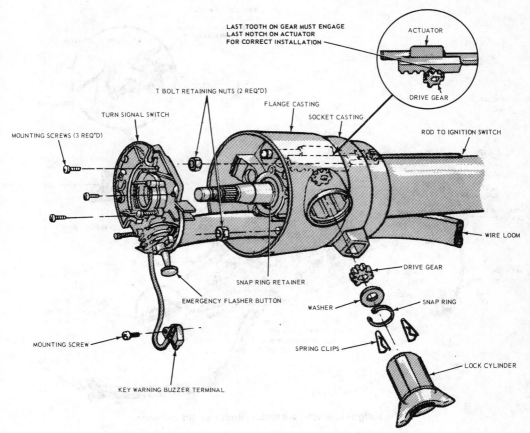

LAST TOOTH ON GEAR MUST ENGAGE
LAST NOTCH ON ACTUATOR
FOR CORRECT INSTALLATION

ACTUATOR

DRIVE GEAR

T BOLT RETAINING NUTS (2 REQ'D)

TURN SIGNAL SWITCH

FLANGE CASTING

SOCKET CASTING

ROD TO IGNITION SWITCH

MOUNTING SCREWS (3 REQ'D)

WIRE LOOM

DRIVE GEAR

SNAP RING RETAINER

EMERGENCY FLASHER BUTTON

WASHER

SNAP RING

MOUNTING SCREW

SPRING CLIPS

LOCK CYLINDER

KEY WARNING BUZZER TERMINAL

Turn signal switch and lock cylinder on fixed columns

10. Install the steering wheel and retaining nut.

11. Connect the negative battery cable.

1980–82 Thunderbird and Cougar XR-7, 1981–82 Cougar, 1982 Continental

1. Remove the four screws retaining the steering column shroud.

2. Remove the turn signal lever by pulling and twisting straight out.

3. Peel back the foam shield. Disconnect the two electrical connectors.

4. Remove the two attaching screws and disengage the switch from the housing.

5. To install, position the switch to the housing and install the screws. Stick the foam to the switch.

6. Install the lever by aligning the key and pushing the lever fully home.

7. Install the two electrical connectors, test the switch, and install the shroud.

Manual Steering, Except Rack and Pinion

STEERING GEAR INSPECTION

Before any steering gear adjustments are made, it is recommended that the front end of the car be raised and a thorough inspection be made for stiffness or lost motion in the steering gear, steering linkage, and front suspension. Worn or damaged parts should be replaced, since a satisfactory adjustment of the steering gear cannot be obtained if bent or badly worn parts exist.

It is also very important that the steering gear be properly aligned in the car. Misalignment of the gear places a stress on the steering worm shaft, therefore a proper adjustment is impossible. To align the steering gear, loosen the mounting bolts to permit the gear to align itself. Check the steering gear mounting seat and if there is a gap at any of the mounting bolts, proper alignment may be

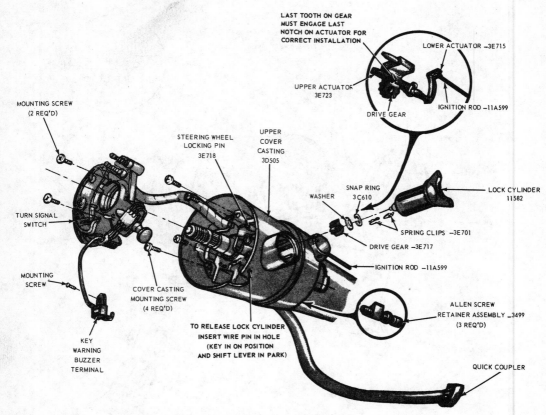

LAST TOOTH ON GEAR MUST ENGAGE LAST NOTCH ON ACTUATOR FOR CORRECT INSTALLATION

LOWER ACTUATOR –3E715

UPPER ACTUATOR 3E723

IGNITION ROD –11A599

DRIVE GEAR

MOUNTING SCREW (2 REQ'D)

STEERING WHEEL LOCKING PIN 3E718

UPPER COVER CASTING 3D505

SNAP RING 3C610

WASHER

LOCK CYLINDER 11582

TURN SIGNAL SWITCH

SPRING CLIPS –3E701

DRIVE GEAR –3E717

IGNITION ROD –11A599

MOUNTING SCREW

COVER CASTING MOUNTING SCREW (4 REQ'D)

ALLEN SCREW RETAINER ASSEMBLY –3499 (3 REQ'D)

KEY WARNING BUZZER TERMINAL

TO RELEASE LOCK CYLINDER INSERT WIRE PIN IN HOLE (KEY IN ON POSITION AND SHIFT LEVER IN PARK)

QUICK COUPLER

Turn signal switch and lock cylinder on tilt columns

obtained by placing shims where excessive gap appears. Tighten the steering gear bolts. Alignment of the gear in the car is very important and should be done carefully so that a satisfactory, trouble-free gear adjustment may be obtained.

STEERING WORM AND SECTOR GEAR ADJUSTMENT

The ball nut assembly and the sector gear must be adjusted properly to maintain a minimum amount of steering shaft end-play and a minimum amount of back-lash between the sector gear and the ball nut. There are only two adjustments that may be done on this steering gear and they should be done as given below:

1. Disconnect the pitman arm from the steering pitman-to-idler arm rod.

2. Loosen the locknut on the sector shaft adjustment screw and turn the adjusting screw counterclockwise.

3. Measure the worm bearing preload by attaching an in. lbs. torque wrench to the steering wheel nut. With the steering wheel off center, note the reading required to ro-

tate the input shaft about 1½ turns to either side of center. If the torque reading is not about 4–5 in. lbs., adjust the gear as given in the next step.

4. Loosen the steering shaft bearing adjuster locknut and tighten or back off the bearing adjusting screw until the preload is within the specified limits.

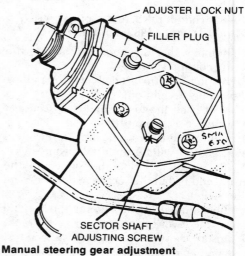

ADJUSTER LOCK NUT

FILLER PLUG

SECTOR SHAFT ADJUSTING SCREW

Manual steering gear adjustment

5. Tighten the steering shaft bearing adjuster locknut and recheck the preload torque.

6. Turn the steering wheel slowly to either stop. Turn *gently* against the stop to avoid possible damage to the ball return guides. Then rotate the wheel 2¾ turns to center the ball nut.

7. Turn the sector adjusting screw clockwise until the proper torque (9–10 in. lbs.) is obtained that is necessary to rotate the worm gear past its center (high spot).

8. While holding the sector adjusting screw, tighten the sector screw adjusting locknut to 32–40 ft. lbs. and recheck the backlash adjustment.

9. Connect the pitman arm to the steering arm-to-idler arm rod.

STEERING GEAR REMOVAL AND INSTALLATION

1. Remove the bolt(s) that retains the flex coupling to the steering shaft.

2. Remove the nut and lock washer that secures the Pitman arm to the sector shaft. Using a puller, remove the Pitman arm from the sector shaft. Do not hammer on the end of the puller as this can damage the steering gear.

3. On vehicles with standard transmissions it may be necessary to disconnect the clutch linkage to obtain clearance. On 8-cylinder models, it may be necessary to lower the exhaust system.

4. Remove the bolts that attach the steering gear to the side rail. Remove the gear.

5. Position the steering gear and flex coupling on the steering shaft. Install steering gear-to-side rail bolts and torque to 50 to 65 ft. lb.

6. Install the clutch linkage if disconnected. Reposition the exhaust system if it was lowered.

7. Place the Pitman arm on the sector shaft and install the attaching nut and lock washer. Torque the nut to 150 to 225 ft. lb.

8. Install the flex coupling attaching nut(s) and torque to 18–23 ft. lb.

Manual Steering, Rack and Pinion Type

ADJUSTMENTS

The rack and pinion gear provides two means of service adjustment. The gear must be removed from the vehicle to perform both adjustments.

Support Yoke to Rack

1. Clean the exterior of the steering gear thoroughly and mount the gear by installing two long bolts and washers through the mounting boss bushings and attaching to Bench Mounted Holding Fixture, Tool T57L-500-B or equivalent.

2. Remove the yoke cover, gasket, shims, and yoke spring.

3. Clean the cover and housing flange areas thoroughly.

4. Reinstall the yoke and cover, omitting the gasket, shims, and the spring.

5. Tighten the cover bolts lightly until the cover just touches the yoke.

6. Measure the gap between the cover and the housing flange. With the gasket, add selected shims to give a combined pack thickness 0.13–0.15mm (.005–.006 inch) greater than the measured gap.

7. Remove the cover.

8. Assemble the gasket next to the housing flange, then the selected shims, spring, and cover.

9. Install cover bolts, sealing the threads with ESW-M46-132A or equivalent, and tighten.

10. Check to see that the gear operates smoothly without binding or slackness.

Pinion Bearing Preload

1. Clean the exterior of the steering gear thoroughly and place the gear in the bench mounted holding fixture as outlined under Support Yoke to Rack Adjustment.

2. Loosen the bolts of the yoke cover to relieve spring pressure on the rack.

3. Remove the pinion cover and gasket. Clean the cover flange area thoroughly.

4. Remove the spacer and shims.

5. Install a new gasket, and fit shims between the upper bearing and the spacer until the top of the spacer is flush with the gasket. Check with a straightedge, using light pressure.

6. Add one 0.13mm (.005 inch) shim to the pack in order to preload the bearings. The spacer must be assembled next to the pinion cover.

7. Install the cover and bolts.

Tie Rod Articulation Effort

1. Install hook end of pull scale through the hole in the tie rod end stud. Effort to move the tire rod should be 1–5 pounds. Do not damage tie rod neck.

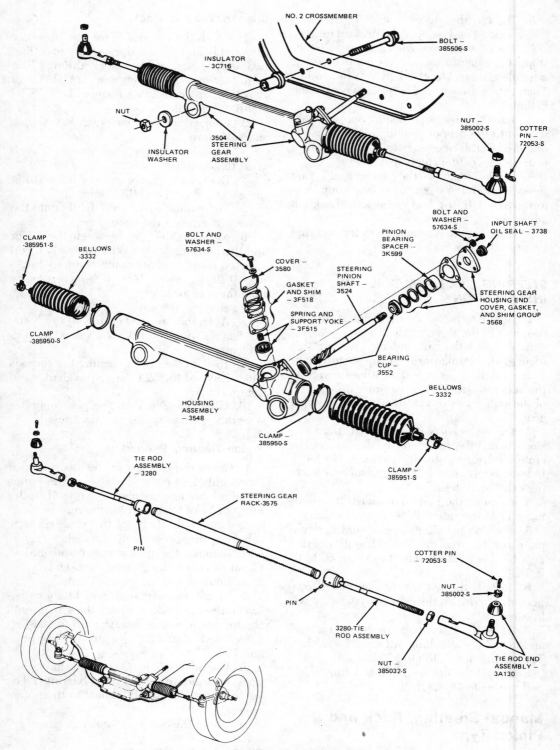

Typical rack and pinion steering gear linkage

2. Replace ball joint/tie rod assembly if effort falls outside this range. Save the tie rod end for use on the new tie rod assembly.

REMOVAL AND INSTALLATION

1. Disconnect the negative battery cable from the battery.

2. Remove the one bolt retaining the flexible coupling to the input shaft.

3. Leave the ignition key in the ON position, and raise the vehicle on a hoist.

4. Remove the two tie rod end retaining cotter pins and nuts. Separate the studs from the spindle arms, using the ball joint separator tool. Do not use a hammer or similar tool as this may damage spindle arms or rod studs.

5. Support the steering gear, and remove the two nuts, insulator washers, and bolts retaining the steering gear to the No. 2 crossmember.

6. Remove the steering gear assembly from the vehicle.

7. Insert the input shaft into the flexible coupling aligning the flats and position the steering gear to the No. 2 crossmember. Install the two bolts.

8. Connect the tie rod ends to the spindle arms, and install the two retaining nuts. Tighten the nuts to specifications, and install the two cotter pins.

9. Lower the vehicle, and install the one bolt retaining the flexible coupling to the input shaft. Tighten the bolt to specifications.

10. Turn the ignition key to the OFF position.

11. Connect the negative battery cable to the battery.

12. Check the toe, and reset if necessary.

Power Steering

Four Different power steering systems have been used:

Bendix Non-Integral System
• 1971 All
• All Versailles

Ford Integral System
• 1972–79 All except Versailles, 1974 Torino and Montego with the 8-302 engine, and 1975–76 models with the 8-351 engine and without air conditioning

Saginaw Integral System
• 1974 Torino and Montego with the 8-302 engine

• 1975–76 models with the 8-351 engine and without air conditioning

Ford Integral Rack and Pinion System
• 1980–82 All

ADJUSTMENTS

Bendix Non-Integral System

WORM AND SECTOR

The ball nut assembly and sector gear must be properly adjusted to steering shaft end play (a factor of preload adjustment) and backlash between the sector gear and ball nut. Only two adjustments can be made. Perform these operations in the following order to avoid damage to the gear.

1. Disconnect the linkage from the gear by removing the Pitman arm from the sector shaft.

2. Loosen the nut that locks the sector adjusting screw and turn the screw counterclockwise. Remove the horn pad from the steering wheel.

3. Measure worm bearing preload by attaching an in. lb. torque wrench to the steering wheel nut. With the steering wheel off center, measure the pull required to rotate the input shaft approximately one and one-half turns to either side of center.

4. If preload is 3–8 in. lb., loosen the worm shaft bearing adjuster lock nut and tighten or loosen the bearing adjuster (as required) to bring the preload within the specified limits.

5. Tighten the worm shaft bearing adjuster lock nut to 60–80 ft. lb. and recheck preload.

6. Turn the steering wheel slowly to one stop. Turn gently against the stop to avoid damage to the ball return guides. Rotate the wheel to center the ball nut. 6½ turns should be needed to rotate the steering wheel lock-to-lock. Divide by two to determine the center position. The blind tooth on the gear input shaft should be at the 12 o'clock position when centered.

7. Torque the sector adjusting screw clockwise until resistance is felt. Using an in. lb. torque wrench, recheck the center mesh load by rotating the steering shaft approximately 90 degrees either way across center. If the meshload is not within 10–16 in. lb., turn sector shaft adjusting screw until meshload is within specification. Hold the sector shaft adjusting screw and torque the locknut to 32–40 ft. lb.

8. Re-check preload adjustment by turn-

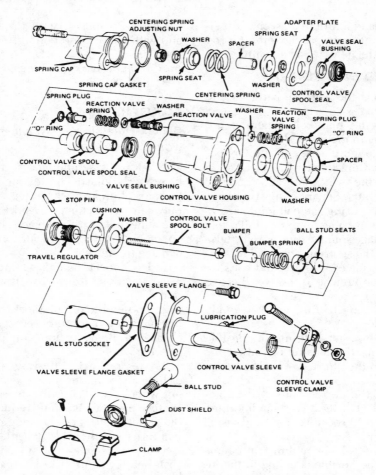

Exploded view of the Bendix linkage system control valve

ing the steering wheel one and one-half turns from center.

9. Connect the Pitman arm to the sector shaft.

CONTROL VALVE CENTERING

1. Raise the vehicle and remove two spring cap attaching screws and lock washer assemblies. Remove the spring cap and discard the spring cap gasket. Never start the engine with the spring cap removed.

2. Torque the centering spring adjusting nut to 90–100 in. lb. Do not tighten beyond specification. Loosen the same spring adjusting nut ¼ turn.

NOTE: *Because the control valve spool bolt and nut may turn together slightly, be sure that only the nut-relative-to-bolt movement is counted.*

3. Lubricate spring cap and gasket and position on valve housing. Lubricate and install

the two screw and washer assemblies. Torque to 72–100 in. lb.

4. Lower the vehicle.

Ford Integral System

MESH LOAD

During the vehicle breaking-in period, some factory adjustments may change. These changes will not necessarily affect operation of the steering gear assembly, and need not be adjusted unless there is excessive lash or other malfunctioning. Adjust the total-over-center position load to eliminate excessive lash between the sector and rack teeth as follows:

1. Disconnect the Pitman arm from the sector shaft.

2. Disconnect the fluid return line at the reservoir and cap the reservoir return line pipe.

3. Place the end of the return line in a clean container and turn the steering wheel from

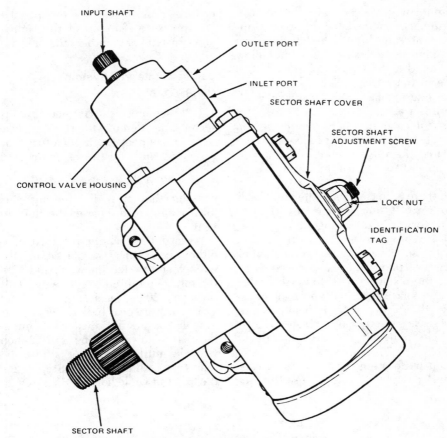

INPUT SHAFT

OUTLET PORT

INLET PORT

SECTOR SHAFT COVER

SECTOR SHAFT
ADJUSTMENT SCREW

CONTROL VALVE HOUSING

LOCK NUT

IDENTIFICATION
TAG

SECTOR SHAFT

Ford integral power steering gear

left to right to discharge the fluid from the gear.

4. Turn the steering wheel to 45 degrees from the left stop.

5. Using an in. lb. torque wrench on the steering wheel nut, determine the torque required to rotate the shaft slowly approximately ⅛ turn from the 45 degree position.

6. Turn the steering wheel back to center, and determine the torque required to rotate the shaft back and forth across the center position. Loosen the nut, and turn the adjuster screw until the reading is 11 to 12 in. lb. greater than the torque measured at 45 degrees from the stop. Tighten the nut while holding the screw in place.

7. Recheck the readings and replace the Pitman arm and steering wheel hub cover.

8. Connect the fluid return line to the reservoir and fill the reservoir. Do not pry against the reservoir to obtain proper belt load. Pressure may deform the reservoir causing it to leak.

9. Recheck belt tension and adjust, if nec-

essary. Torque the bolts and nut to 30 to 40 ft. lb.

VALVE SPOOL CENTERING CHECK

1. Install a 0–2000 psi pressure gauge in the pressure line between the power steering pump outlet port and the integral steering gear inlet port. Be sure the valve on the gauge is fully open.

2. Check the fluid level and add fluid, if necessary.

3. Start the engine and turn the steering wheel from stop-to-stop to bring the steering lubricant to normal operating temperature. Turn off the engine and recheck fluid level. Add fluid, if necessary.

4. With the engine running at approximately 1000 rpm and the steering wheel centered, attach an in. lb. torque wrench to the steering wheel nut. Apply sufficient torque in each direction to get a gauge reading of 250 psi.

5. The reading should be the same in both directions at 250 psi. If the difference be-

tween the readings exceeds 4 in. lb., remove the steering gear and install a thicker or thinner valve centering shim in the housing. Use as many shims as necessary, but do not allow thickness of the shim pack to exceed .030 inch. The piston must be able to bottom on the valve housing face. No clearance is allowed in this area.

6. Test for clearance between the piston end and valve housing face as follows:

    a. Hold the valve assembly so the piston is up and try to turn the input shaft to the right.

    b. If there is no clearance, the input shaft will not turn. If there is clearance, the piston and worm will rotate together.

    c. If two or more shims must be used to center the spool valve, and a restriction or interference condition is experienced when turning the piston to its stop on the valve housing, replace the shaft and control assembly. If steering effort is heavy to the left, increase shim thickness. If steering effort is light to the left, decrease shim thickness.

7. When performing the valve spool centering check outside the vehicle, use the procedures described above except take torque and pressure readings at the right and left stops instead of at either side of center.

Saginaw Integral System
MESH LOAD

1. Disconnect the Pitman arm from the sector shaft. Remove the steering wheel hub.

2. Disconnect the fluid return line at the reservoir, and cap the reservoir return line pipe.

3. Place the end of the return line in a clean container and turn the steering wheel from left to right to discharge the fluid from the gear.

4. Turn the gear one-half turn off center in either direction. Using a 24 in. lb torque wrench on the steering wheel nut, determine the torque required to rotate the shaft slowly through a 20 degree arc.

5. Turn the gear back to center and repeat Step 4. Loosen the adjuster lock nut and turn the screw inward using a 7/32-inch Allen wrench, until the reading is 6 in. lb greater than the reading taken in Step 4. Retighten the lock nut while holding the screw in place.

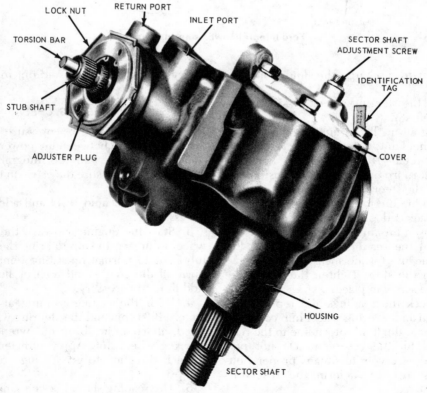

LOCK NUT   RETURN PORT

INLET PORT

TORSION BAR

SECTOR SHAFT ADJUSTMENT SCREW

IDENTIFICATION TAG

STUB SHAFT

ADJUSTER PLUG

COVER

HOUSING

SECTOR SHAFT

Saginaw integral steering gear

6. Recheck the readings and replace the Pitman arm and steering wheel hub.

7. Connect the fluid return line to the reservoir and fill the reservoir.

Ford Integral Rack and Pinion System

The power rack and pinion steering gear provides for only one service adjustment. The gear must be removed from the vehicle to perform this adjustment.

RACK YOKE PLUG PRELOAD

1. Clean the exterior of the steering gear thoroughly.

2. Install two long bolts and washers through the bushings, and attach to the bench mounted holding fixture, Tool T57L-500-B or equivalent.

3. Do not remove the external pressure lines, unless they are leaking or damaged. If these lines are removed, they must be replaced with new lines.

4. Drain the power steering fluid by rotating the input shaft lock-to-lock twice using Tool T74P-3504-R or equivalent. Cover ports on valve housing with shop cloth while draining gear.

5. Insert an lb-in torque wrench with maximum capacity of 30–60 in. lb. into the input shaft torque adapter, Tool T74P-3504-R.or equivalent. Position the adapter and wrench on the input shaft splines.

6. Loosen the yoke plug locknut with wrench, Tool T78P-3504-H or equivalent.

7. Loosen yoke plug with a ¾ inch socket wrench.

8. With the rack at the center of travel,

tighten the yoke plug to 45–50 in. lb. Clean the threads of the yoke plug prior to tightening to prevent a false reading.

9. Back off the yoke plug approximately ⅛ turn (44 degrees min. to 54 degrees max.) until the torque required to initiate and sustain rotation of the input shaft is 7–18 in. lb.

10. Place Tool T78P-3504-H or equivalent on the yoke plug locknut. While holding the yoke plug, tighten the locknut to 44–66 ft. lb. Do not allow the yoke plug to move while tightening or the preload will be affected. Recheck input shaft torque after tightening locknut.

11. If the external pressure lines were removed, they must be replaced with new service line. Remove the copper seals from the housing ports prior to installation of new lines.

STEERING GEAR REMOVAL AND INSTALLATION

Bendix Non-Integral System

1. Remove the bolt(s) that retains the flex coupling to the steering shaft.

2. Remove the nut and lock washer that secures the Pitman arm to the sector shaft.

3. Raise the vehicle and disconnect the two fluid lines from the power cylinder and drain the lines.

4. Remove the pal nut, attaching nut, washer, and the insulator from the end of the power cylinder rod.

5. Remove the cotter pin and castellated nut that secures the power cylinder stud to the centerlink.

6. Disconnect the power cylinder stud

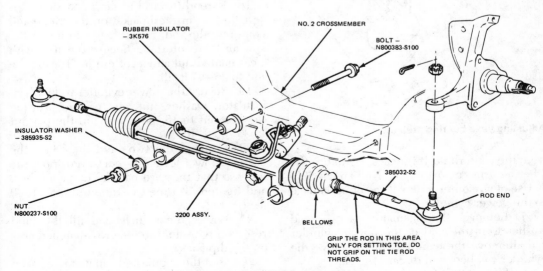

RUBBER INSULATOR – 3K576

NO. 2 CROSSMEMBER

BOLT – N800383-S100

INSULATOR WASHER – 385935-S2

385032-S2

ROD END

NUT N800237-S100

3200 ASSY.

BELLOWS

GRIP THE ROD IN THIS AREA ONLY FOR SETTING TOE. DO NOT GRIP ON THE TIE ROD THREADS.

Ford power rack and pinion steering gear

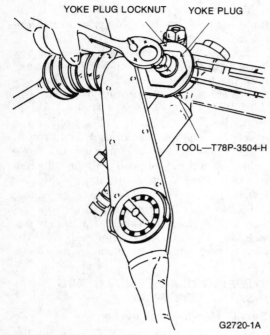

YOKE PLUG LOCKNUT   YOKE PLUG

TOOL—T78P-3504-H

G2720-1A

Tightening yoke plug locknut

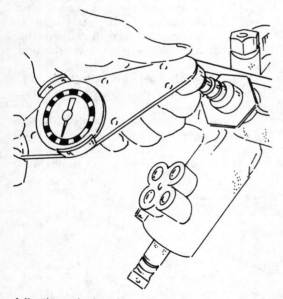

Adjusting yoke bearing preload

from the centerlink. It is necessary to use the steering arm remover tool, No. T64P-3590-F. Use of any other tool will result in damage to the power cylinder.

7. Remove the insulator sleeve and washer from the end of the power cylinder rod. Remove the cylinder rod. Remove the cylinder rod boot and discard the clamp.

8. Inspect the tube fittings and seats in the power cylinder for damage. Replace the seats in the cylinder or the tubes as required. If any tube seat is removed, a new seat must be used.

9. Using Tool T64P-3590-F remove the Pitman arm from the sector shaft. Do not hammer on the end of the puller as this can damage the steering gear.

10. On vehicles with standard transmissions it may be necessary to disconnect the clutch linkage to obtain clearance. On 8 cylinder models, it may be necessary to lower the exhaust system.

11. Remove the bolts that attach the steering gear to the side rail. Remove the gear.

12. Position the steering gear and flex coupling on the steering shaft. Be sure that the missing tooth on the spline of the gear input shaft is pointing straight up and aligns with the blind tooth on the flex coupling. Install steering gear-to-side rail bolts and torque to 50–60 ft. lb.

13. Install the clutch linkage if disconnected. Reposition the exhaust system if it was lowered.

14. Place the Pitman arm on the sector shaft and install the attaching nut and lock washer. Align the blind tooth on the Pitman arm with the blind tooth on the steering sector shaft. Torque the nut to specification 200–225 ft. lb.

15. Install the flex coupling attaching nut(s) and torque to 18–23 ft. lb.

16. Install the cylinder rod boot with a new clamp.

17. Install the washer, sleeve, and the insulator on the end of the power cylinder rod.

18. Extend the rod as far as possible. Insert the rod in the bracket on the frame and compress the rod, if necessary, to insert the stud in the centerlink. Secure the stud with a castellated nut and a cotter pin. Torque the nut to 35–47 ft. lb.

19. Secure the power cylinder rod with an insulator, washer, nut, and pal nut. Torque the hex nut to 18–34 ft. lb. and the pal nut to 36–60 ft. lb.

20. Connect the two fluid lines into the correct power cylinder ports. Position the lines so that they are parallel to each other, and tighten. Torque the tube nuts to 21–30 ft. lb.

21. Lower the vehicle and fill the fluid reservoir with fluid to the cross-hatched area on the dip stick.

22. Start the engine and run it at idle speed for about two minutes to warm the fluid, then

turn the steering wheel all the way to the left and right several times and check the system for leaks.

23. Increase the engine speed to about 1,000 RPM and turn the steering wheel all the way to the left and right several times.

24. Stop the engine and check the control valve and hose connections; repair any leaks.

25. Check the fluid level and refill, if necessary.

Ford Integral System

1. Tag the pressure and return lines for future identification.

2. Disconnect the pressure and return lines from the steering gear. Plug the lines and ports in the gear to prevent entry of dirt.

3. Remove the bolts that secure the flexible coupling to the steering gear and column.

4. Raise the vehicle and remove the sector shaft attaching nut.

5. Remove the Pitman arm from the sector shaft with Tool T64P-3590-F. Remove the tool from the Pitman arm. Do not damage the seals.

6. On vehicles with standard transmissions, remove the clutch release lever retracting spring to provide clearance for removing the steering gear.

7. Support the steering gear. Remove the steering gear attaching bolts.

8. Remove the clamp bolt that holds the flexible coupling to the steering gear. Work the gear free of the flex coupling and remove.

9. If the flex coupling did not come off with the gear, lift it off the shaft.

10. Slide the flex coupling into place on steering shaft assembly. Turn the steering wheel so the spokes are in the normal position.

11. Center the steering gear input shaft.

12. Slide the steering gear input shaft into the flex coupling and into place on the frame side rail. Install the attaching bolts and torque to 35–40 ft. lb.

13. Be sure the wheels are in the straight ahead position. Then install the Pitman arm on the sector shaft. Install and tighten the sector shaft and attaching bolts. Torque the bolts to 55–70 ft. lb.

14. Move the flex coupling into place on the input and steering column shaft. Install the attaching bolts and torque to 18–22 ft. lb.

15. Connect the pressure and the return lines to the steering gear. Tighten the lines.

16. Disconnect the coil wire.

17. Fill the reservoir. Turn on the ignition and turn the steering wheel from stop-to-stop to distribute the fluid.

18. Recheck the fluid level and add fluid, if necessary.

19. Install the coil wire. Start the engine and turn the steering wheel from left to right. Inspect for fluid leaks.

Saginaw Integral System

1. Disconnect the pressure and return lines from the steering gear. Plug the lines and ports in the gear to prevent entry of dirt.

2. Remove the bolts that secure the flex coupling to the steering gear and column.

3. Raise the vehicle and remove the Pitman arm attaching nut and lock washer.

4. Using Tool T64P-3590-F, remove the Pitman arm from the sector shaft. Do not hammer on the end of the tool when pulling the Pitman arm from the shaft. Damage to the gear or cover could result. Remove the tool from the Pitman arm.

5. On vehicles with standard transmissions, remove the clutch release lever retracting spring to provide clearance for removing the steering gear.

6. Support the steering gear. Remove the steering gear attaching bolts.

7. Work the steering gear free of the flex coupling and remove.

8. Lift the flex coupling off the shaft if it did not come off with the gear.

9. Slide the flex coupling into place on the steering shaft. Turn the steering wheel so that the spokes are in their normal position.

10. Center the steering gear input shaft.

11. Slide the steering gear input shaft into the flex coupling and into place on the frame side rail. Install the attaching bolts and torque to 45–50 ft. lb.

12. Be sure that the wheels are in the straight-ahead position. Then install the Pitman arm on the sector shaft. Install the sector shaft attaching nut and torque to 200 ft. lb.

13. Move the flex coupling into place on the input shaft and steering column shaft. Install the attaching bolts and torque to 18–23 ft. lb.

14. Connect the pressure and the return lines to the steering gear. Tighten the lines.

15. Disconnect the coil wire. Fill the pump reservoir. Crank the engine with the starter and continue adding fluid until the level remains constant. Turn the steering wheel from side to side without hitting the stops. Turn

off the ignition and recheck the fluid level. Add fluid, if necessary.

16. Reconnect the coil wire. Start the engine and allow it to run for several minutes. Turn the steering wheel from stop to stop.

17. Turn off the engine and recheck the fluid level. Add fluid, if necessary.

Ford Integral Rack and Pinion System

1. Disconnect the negative battery cable from the battery.

2. Remove the one bolt retaining the flexible coupling to the input shaft.

3. Leave the ignition key in the On position, and raise the vehicle on a hoist.

4. Remove the two tie rod end retaining cotter pins and nuts. Separate the studs from the spindle arms, using the ball joint separator tool.

5. Support the steering gear, and remove the two nuts, insulator, washers, and bolts retaining the steering gear to the No. 2 crossmember. Lower the gear slightly to permit access to the pressure and return line fittings.

6. Disconnect the pressure and return lines from the steering gear valve housing. Plug the lines and parts in the valve housing to prevent entry of dirt.

7. Remove the steering gear assembly from the vehicle.

8. Support and position the steering gear, so that the pressure and return line fittings can be connected to the valve housing. Tighten the fittings to 15–20 ft. lb. The design allows the hoses to swivel when tightened properly. Do not attempt to eliminate looseness by overtightening, since this can cause damage to the fittings.

NOTE: *The rubber insulators must be pushed completely inside the gear housing before the installation of the gear housing on the No. 2 crossmember.*

9. No gap is allowed between the insulator and the face of the gear boss. A rubber lubricant should be used to facilitate proper installation of the insulators in the gear housing. Insert the input shaft into the flexible coupling, and position the steering gear to the No. 2 crossmember. Install the two bolts, insulator washers, and nuts. Tighten the two nuts to 80–100 ft. lb.

10. Connect the tie rod ends to the spindle arms, and install the two retaining nuts. Tighten the nuts to 35–45 ft. lb., then, after tightening to specification, tighten the nuts

to their nearest cotter pin castellation, and install two new cotter pins.

11. Lower the vehicle, and install the one bolt retaining the flexible coupling to the input shaft. Tighten the bolt to 18–23 ft. lb.

12. Turn the ignition key to the Off position.

13. Connect the negative battery cable to the battery.

14. Remove the coil wire.

15. Fill the power steering pump reservoir.

16. Engage the starter, and cycle the steering wheel to distribute the fluid. Check the fluid level and add as required.

17. Install the coil wire, start the engine, and cycle the steering wheel. Check for fluid leaks.

18. If the tie rod ends were loosened, check the wheel alignment.

Power Steering Pump
REMOVAL AND INSTALLATION

1. Drain the fluid from the pump reservoir by disconnecting the fluid return hose at the pump. Disconnect the pressure hose from the pump.

2. Remove the mounting bolts from the front of the pump. On eight cylinder engines through 1977, there is a nut on the rear of the pump that must be removed. After removal, move the pump inward to loosen the belt tension and remove the belt from the pulley. Remove the pump from the car.

3. To install the pump, position on mounting bracket and loosely install the mounting bolts and nuts. Put the drive belt over the pulley and move the pump outward against the belt until the proper belt tension is obtained. Do not pry against the pump body. Measure the belt tension with a belt tension gauge for the proper adjustment. Only in cases where a belt tension gauge is not available should the belt deflection method be used.

4. Tighten the mounting bolts and nuts.

Tie Rod End Replacement
TORINO, MONTEGO, ELITE, LTD II, 1975–79 COUGAR, 1977–79 THUNDERBIRD

1. Raise and support the front end.

2. Remove the cotter pin and nut from the rod end ball stud.

3. Loosen the sleeve and clamp bolts and

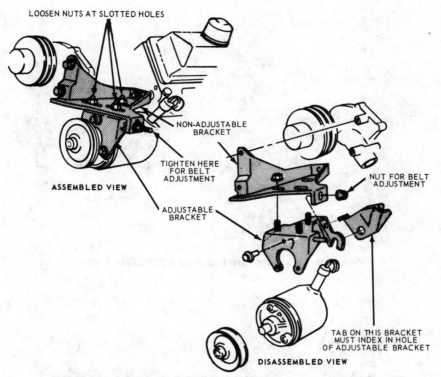

Power steering pump installation on 429 and 460 engines

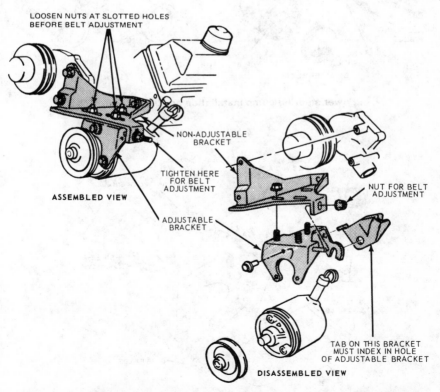

Power steering pump installation on 351C, 351W and 400 engines through 1977

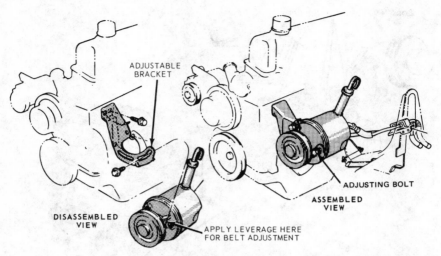

Power steering pump installation on 6-250 through 1977

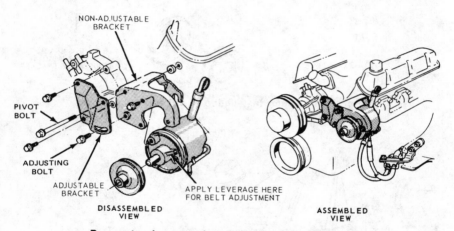

Power steering pump installation on 302 through 1977

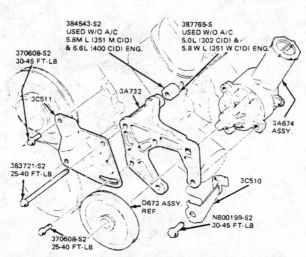

Power steering pump installation on all 1978–79 models except Versailles

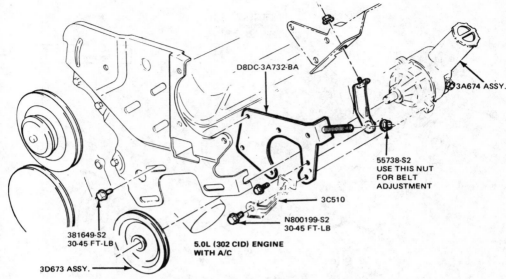

D8DC-3A732-BA

3A674 ASSY.

55738-S2
USE THIS NUT
FOR BELT
ADJUSTMENT

3C510

N800199-S2
30-45 FT-LB

381649-S2
30-45 FT-LB

5.0L (302 CID) ENGINE
WITH A/C

3D673 ASSY.

Power steering pump installation on Versailles

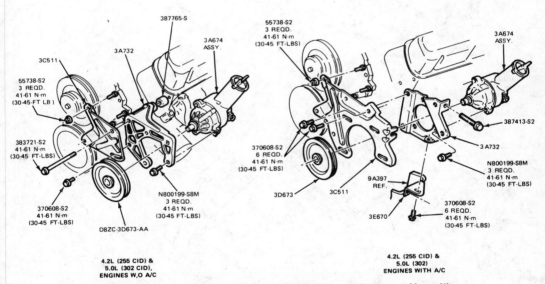

387765-S

3A674
ASSY.

3A732

3C511

55738-S2
3 REQD.
41-61 N·m
(30-45 FT LB)

383721-S2
41-61 N·m
(30-45 FT-LBS)

370608-S2
41-61 N·m
(30-45 FT-LBS)

D8ZC-3D673-AA

N800199-S8M
3 REQD.
41-61 N·m
(30-45 FT-LBS)

4.2L (255 CID) &
5.0L (302 CID),
ENGINES W,O A/C

55738-S2
3 REQD.
41-61 N·m
(30-45 FT-LBS)

3A674
ASSY.

387413-S2

3 A732

N800199-S8M
3 REQD.
41-61 N·m
(30-45 FT-LBS)

370608-S2
6 REQD.
41-61 N·m
(30-45 FT-LBS)

9A397
REF.

3D673

3C511

3E670

370608-S2
6 REQD.
41-61 N·m
(30-45 FT-LBS)

4.2L (255 CID) &
5.0L (302)
ENGINES WITH A/C

Power steering pump installation on all 1980–81 models except Versailles

remove the rod end from the spindle arm center link using a ball joint separator.

4. Remove the rod end from the sleeve, counting the exact number of turns required.

5. Install the new end using the exact number of turns it took to remove the old one.

6. Install all parts. Torque the stud to 40–43 ft. lbs. and the clamp to 20–22 ft. lbs.

7. Check the toe-in.

MAVERICK, COMET, 1975–80 GRANADA, MONARCH, VERSAILLES

1. Raise and support the front end.

2. Remove and discard the cotter pin and nut from the rod end ball stud.

3. Disconnect the rod end from the spindle arm or center link.

4. Loosen the rod sleeve clamp bolts and

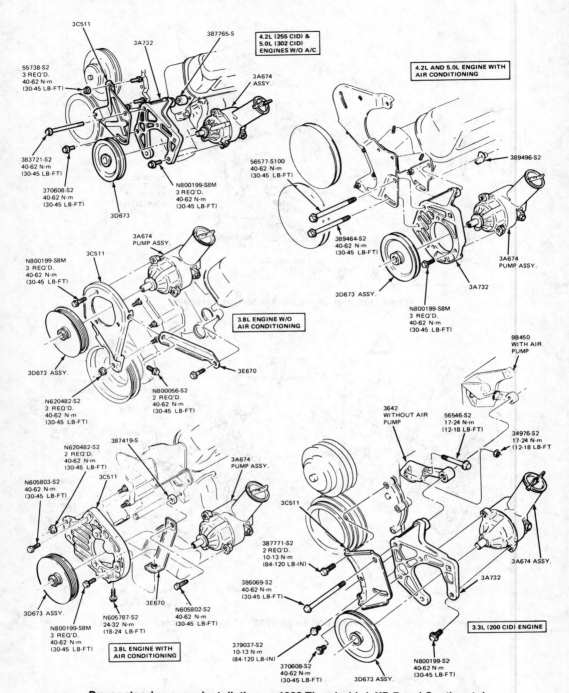

Power steering pump installation on 1982 Thunderbird, XR-7 and Continental

turn the rod to remove. Count the exact number of turns required.

5. Install a new rod end using the exact number of turns it took to remove the old one.

6. Install all parts in reverse of removal. Torque stud to 40–43 ft. lbs. and clamp to 20–22 ft. lbs.

7. Check the toe-in.

RACK AND PINION MODELS

1. Remove the cotter pin and nut at the spindle. Separate the tie rod end stud from the spindle with a puller.

2. Matchmark the position of the locknut with paint on the tie rod. Unscrew the lock-

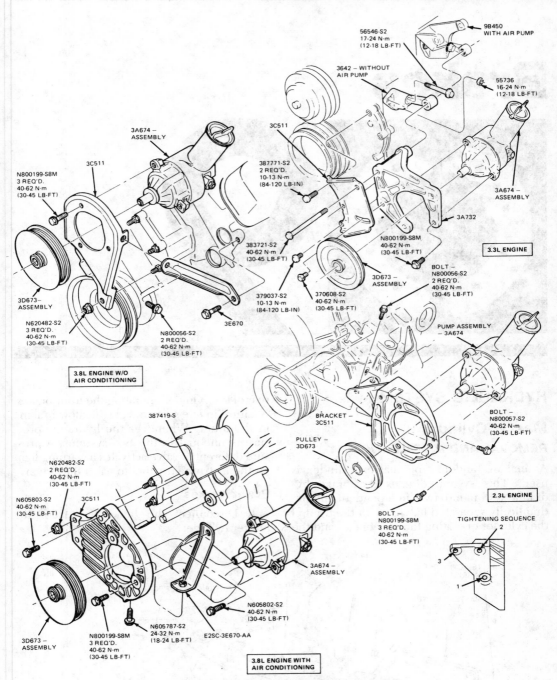

Power steering pump installation on 1982 Cougar

nut. Unscrew the tie rod end, counting the number of turns required to remove.

3. Install the new end the same number of turns. Attach the tie rod end stud to the spindle. Install the nut and torque to 35 ft. lbs., then continue to tighten until the cotter pin holes align. Install a new cotter pin. Check the toe and adjust if necessary, then torque the tie rod end locknut to 35 ft. lbs.

Brakes

HYDRAULIC SYSTEM

Master Cylinder

REMOVAL AND INSTALLATION

A dual or tandem-type master cylinder is used. This system divides the brake hydraulic system into two, independent and hydraulically separated halves, with the front of the cylinder operating the rear brakes and the rear of the cylinder operating the front brakes. A failure in one system will still allow braking in the other. Whenever the hydraulic pressure is unequal in the two systems, a pressure differential valve activates a warning light on the instrument panel to warn the driver.

Power Brakes

1. Disconnect the brake line from the master cylinder.

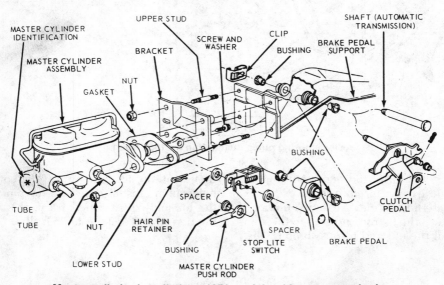

Master cylinder installation—1971 models with non-power brakes

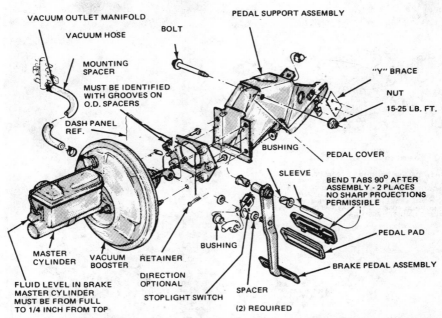

VACUUM OUTLET MANIFOLD

VACUUM HOSE

BOLT

PEDAL SUPPORT ASSEMBLY

MOUNTING SPACER

MUST BE IDENTIFIED WITH GROOVES ON O.D. SPACERS

DASH PANEL REF.

"Y" BRACE

NUT

15-25 LB. FT.

BUSHING

PEDAL COVER

SLEEVE

BEND TABS 90° AFTER ASSEMBLY - 2 PLACES NO SHARP PROJECTIONS PERMISSIBLE

PEDAL PAD

MASTER CYLINDER

VACUUM BOOSTER

RETAINER

BUSHING

DIRECTION OPTIONAL

STOPLIGHT SWITCH

SPACER

(2) REQUIRED

BRAKE PEDAL ASSEMBLY

FLUID LEVEL IN BRAKE MASTER CYLINDER MUST BE FROM FULL TO 1/4 INCH FROM TOP

Master cylinder installation on 1972–79 models with power assist, except Versailles

2. Remove the two nuts and lockwashers that attach the master cylinder to the brake booster.

3. Remove the master cylinder from the booster.

4. Reverse the above procedure to install. Torque the master cylinder attaching nuts to 13–25 ft. lb.

5. Fill the master cylinder and bleed the entire brake system.

6. Refill the master cylinder.

Standard Brakes

1. Working under the dash, disconnect the master cylinder pushrod from the brake

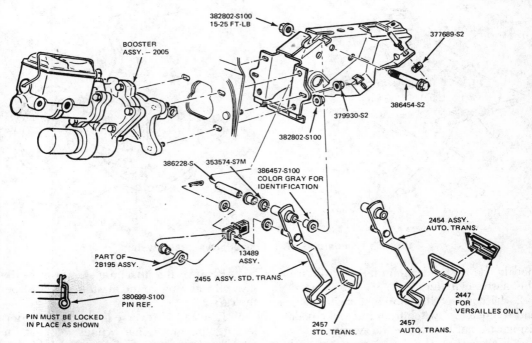

382802-S100 15-25 FT-LB

BOOSTER ASSY. – 2005

377689-S2

386454-S2

379930-S2

382802-S100

386228-S

353574-S7M

386457-S100 COLOR GRAY FOR IDENTIFICATION

PART OF 2B195 ASSY.

13489 ASSY.

2455 ASSY. STD. TRANS.

2454 ASSY. AUTO. TRANS.

2447 FOR VERSAILLES ONLY

380699-S100 PIN REF.

PIN MUST BE LOCKED IN PLACE AS SHOWN

2457 STD. TRANS.

2457 AUTO. TRANS.

Hydro-Boost power brake system, Versailles

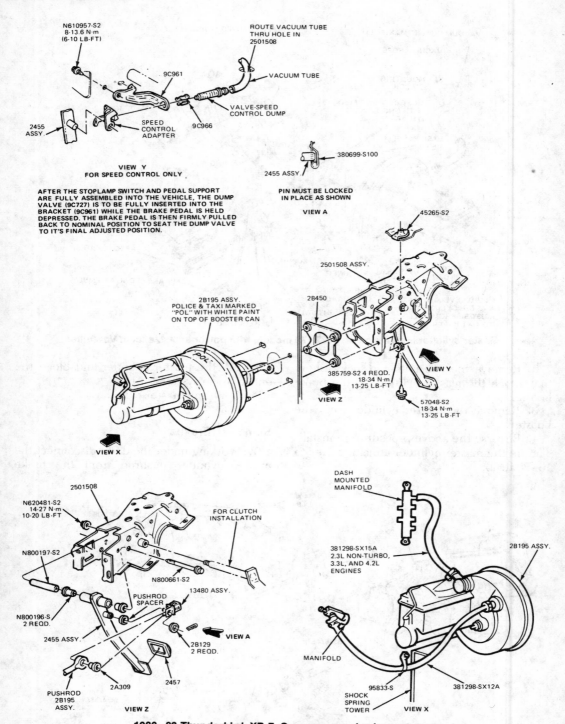

N610957-S2
8-13.6 N·m
(6-10 LB-FT)

9C961

ROUTE VACUUM TUBE
THRU HOLE IN
2501508

VACUUM TUBE

VALVE-SPEED
CONTROL DUMP

2455
ASSY.

SPEED
CONTROL
ADAPTER

9C966

VIEW Y
FOR SPEED CONTROL ONLY

380699-S100

2455 ASSY.

AFTER THE STOPLAMP SWITCH AND PEDAL SUPPORT
ARE FULLY ASSEMBLED INTO THE VEHICLE, THE DUMP
VALVE (9C727) IS TO BE FULLY INSERTED INTO THE
BRACKET (9C961) WHILE THE BRAKE PEDAL IS HELD
DEPRESSED. THE BRAKE PEDAL IS THEN FIRMLY PULLED
BACK TO NOMINAL POSITION TO SEAT THE DUMP VALVE
TO IT'S FINAL ADJUSTED POSITION.

PIN MUST BE LOCKED
IN PLACE AS SHOWN

VIEW A

45265-S2

2501508 ASSY.

2B450

2B195 ASSY.
POLICE & TAXI MARKED
"POL" WITH WHITE PAINT
ON TOP OF BOOSTER CAN

VIEW Y

385759-S2 4 REQD.
18-34 N·m
13-25 LB-FT

VIEW Z

57048-S2
18-34 N·m
13-25 LB-FT

VIEW X

2501508

N620481-S2
14-27 N·m
10-20 LB-FT

FOR CLUTCH
INSTALLATION

N800197-S2

N800661-S2

13480 ASSY.

PUSHROD
SPACER

N800196-S
2 REQD.

VIEW A

2455 ASSY.

2B129
2 REQD.

PUSHROD
2B195
ASSY.

2A309

2457

VIEW Z

DASH
MOUNTED
MANIFOLD

381298-SX15A
2.3L NON-TURBO,
3.3L, AND 4.2L
ENGINES

2B195 ASSY.

MANIFOLD

95833-S

SHOCK
SPRING
TOWER

381298-SX12A

VIEW X

1980–82 Thunderbird, XR-7, Cougar power brake system

pedal. The pushrod cannot be removed from the master cylinder.

2. Disconnect the stoplight switch wires and remove the switch from the brake pedal, using care not to damage the switch.

3. Disconnect the brake lines from the master cylinder.

4. Remove the attaching screws from the firewall and remove the master cylinder from the car.

5. Reinstall in reverse of the above order, leaving the brake line fittings loose at the master cylinder. Torque the master cylinder nuts to 13–25 ft. lb.

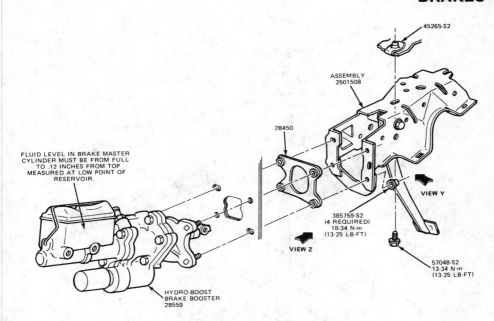

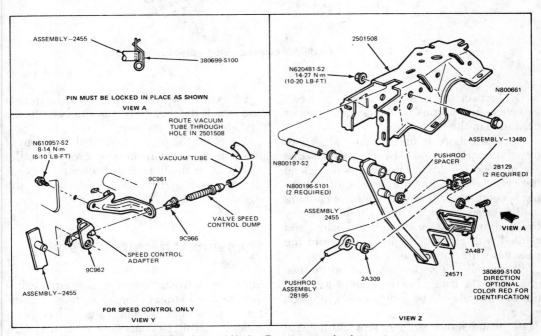

1982 Continental Hydro-Boost power brake system

6. Fill the master cylinder and, with the brake lines loose, slowly bleed the air from the master cylinder using the foot pedal.

OVERHAUL—ALL TYPES

1. Remove the cylinder from the car and drain the brake fluid.

2. Mount the cylinder in a vise so that the outlets are up then remove the seal from the hub.

3. Remove the stopscrew from the bottom of the front reservoir.

4. Remove the snap-ring from the front of the bore and remove the rear piston assembly.

5. Remove the front piston assembly using compressed air. Cover the bore opening with a cloth to prevent damage to the piston.

6. Clean metal parts in brake fluid and discard the rubber parts.

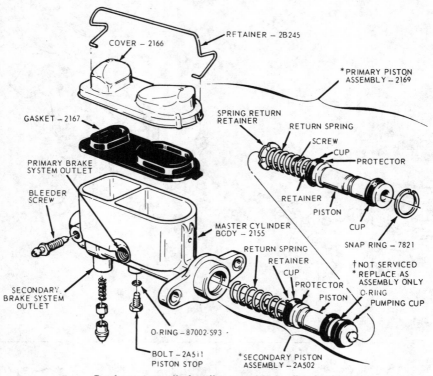

Dual master cylinder disassembled—disc brakes

7. Inspect the bore for damage or wear, and check the pistons for damage and proper clearance in the bore.

8. If the bore is only slightly scored or pitted it may be honed. Always use hones that are in good condition and completely clean the cylinder with brake fluid when the honing is completed. If any evidence of contamination exists in the master cylinder, the entire hydraulic system should be flushed and refilled with clean brake fluid. Blow out the passages with compressed air.

9. Install new secondary seals in the two grooves in the flat end of the front piston. The lips of the seals will be facing away from each other.

10. Install a new primary seal and the seal protector on the opposite end of the front piston with the lips of the seal facing outward.

11. Coat the seals with brake fluid. Install the spring on the front piston with the spring retainer in the primary seal.

12. Insert the piston assembly, spring end first, into the bore and use a wooden rod to seat it.

13. Coat the rear piston seals with brake fluid and install them into the piston grooves with the lips facing the spring end.

14. Assemble the spring onto the piston and install the assembly into the bore spring first. Install the snap-ring.

15. Hold the piston train at the bottom of the bore and install the stopscrew. Install a new seal on the hub. Bench-bleed the cylinder or install and bleed the cylinder on the car.

Pressure Differential Warning Valve

Since the introduction of dual master cylinders to the hydraulic brake system, a pressure differential warning signal has been added. This signal consists of a warning light on the dashboard activated by a differential pressure switch located below the master cylinder. The signal indicates a hydraulic pressure differential between the front and rear brakes of 80–150 psi, and should warn the driver that a hydraulic failure has occurred.

After repairing and bleeding any part of the hydraulic system the warning light may remain on due to the pressure differential valve remaining in the off-center position. To centralize the valve a pressure difference must

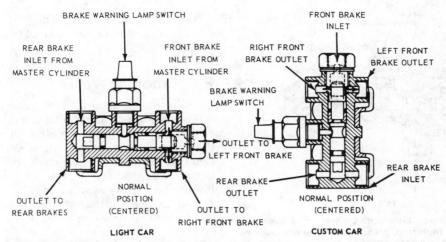

Pressure differential valve and brake light warning switch on models with front drum brakes

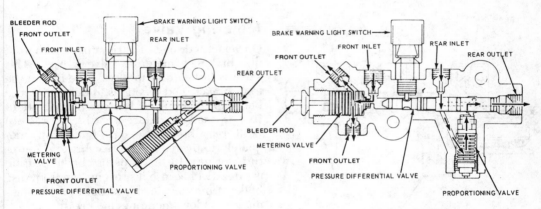

Control valve assembly on front disc brake models through 1979

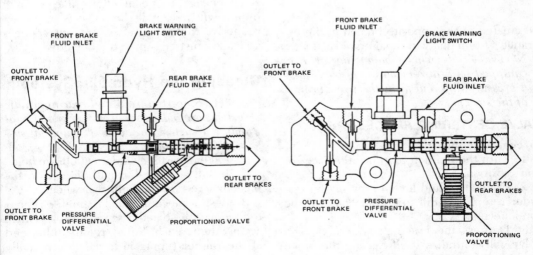

Control valve assembly on models with 4-wheel disc brakes

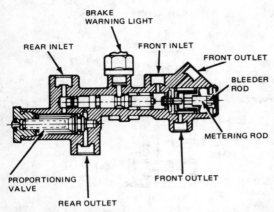

1980–82 3-way aluminum control valve assembly (contains metering, pressure differential and proportioning valves)

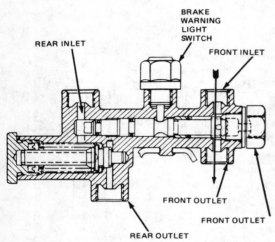

1980–82 2-way aluminum control valve assembly (contains pressure differential and proportioning valves)

be created in the opposite branch of the hydraulic system that was repaired or bled last.

NOTE: *Front wheel balancing of cars equipped with disc brakes may also cause a pressure differential in the front branch of the system.*

VALVE CENTERING PROCEDURE

To centralize the valve:

1. Turn the ignition to either the "acc" or "on" position.

2. Check the fluid level in the master cylinder reservoirs. Fill to within ¼ in. of the top if necessary.

3. Depress the brake pedal firmly. The valve will centralize itself causing the brake warning light to go out.

4. Turn the ignition off.

5. Prior to driving the vehicle, check the operation of the brakes and obtain a firm pedal.

Proportioning Valve

On vehicles equipped with front disc and rear drum brakes, a proportioning valve is an important part of the system. It is installed in the hydraulic line to the rear brakes. Its function is to maintain the correct proportion between line pressures to the front and rear brakes. *No attempt at adjustment of this valve should be made, as adjustment is preset and tampering will result in uneven braking action.*

To assure correct installation when replacing the valve, the outlet to the rear brakes is stamped with the letter "R."

Metering Valve

On vehicles through 1980 equipped with front disc brakes, a metering valve is used. This valve is installed in the hydraulic line to the front brakes, and functions to delay pressure build-up to the front brakes on application. Its purpose is to reduce front brake pressure until rear brake pressure builds up adequately to overcome the rear brake shoe return springs. In this way disc brake pad life is extended because it prevents the front disc brakes from carrying all or most of the braking load at low operating line pressures.

The metering valve can be checked very simply. With the car stopped, gently apply the brakes. At about 1 in. of travel, a very small change in pedal effort (like a small bump) will be felt if the valve is operating properly. Metering valves are not serviceable and must be replaced if defective.

Bleeding the Hydraulic System

NOTE: *Since the front and rear hydraulic systems are independent, if it is known that only one system has air in it, only that system has to be bled.*

1. Fill the master cylinder with brake fluid.

2. Install a ⅜ in. box-end wrench to the bleeder screw on the right rear wheel.

3. Push a piece of small-diameter rubber tubing over the bleeder screw until it is flush against the wrench. Submerge the other end of the rubber tubing in a glass jar partially filled with clean brake fluid. Make sure the rubber tube fits on the bleeder screw snugly.

4. Have a friend apply pressure to the brake pedal. Open the bleeder screw and observe the bottle of brake fluid. If bubbles appear in the glass jar; there is air in the system. When your friend has pushed the pedal to the floor, immediately close the bleeder screw before he releases the pedal.

5. Repeat this procedure until no bubbles appear in the jar. Refill the master cylinder right front and left front wheels, in that order. Periodically refill the master cylinder so it does not run dry.

7. Center the pressure differential warning valve as outlined in the "Pressure Differential Warning Valve" section.

Hydraulic Brake Line Check

The hydraulic brake lines and brake linings are to be inspected at the recommended intervals in the maintenance schedule. Follow the steel tubing from the master cylinder to the flexible hose fitting at each wheel. If a section of the tubing is found to be damaged, replace the entire section with tubing of the same type (steel, not copper), size, shape, and length. When installing a new section of brake tubing, flush clean brake fluid or denatured alcohol through to remove any dirt or foreign material from the line. Be sure to flare both ends to provide sound, leak-proof connections. When bending the tubing to fit the underbody contours, be careful not to kink or crack the line. Torque all hydraulic connections to 10–15 lbs.

Check the flexible brake hoses that connect the steel tubing to each wheel cylinder. Replace the hose if it shows any signs of softening, cracking, or other damage. When installing a new front brake hose, position the hose to avoid contact with other chassis parts. Place a new copper gasket over the hose fitting and thread the hose assembly into the front wheel cylinder. A new rear brake hose must be positioned clear of the exhaust pipe or shock absorber. Thread the hose into the rear brake tube connector. When installing either a new front or rear brake hose, engage the opposite end of the hose to the bracket on the frame. Install the horseshoe-type retaining clip and connect the tube to the hose with the tube fitting nut.

Always bleed the system after hose or line replacement. Before bleeding, make sure that the master cylinder is topped up with high-temperature, extra-heavy-duty fluid of at least SAE 70R3 quality.

Power Assist

VACUUM BOOSTER REMOVAL AND INSTALLATION

All Except Versailles and 1982 Continental

1. Working inside the car below the instrument panel, disconnect the booster valve operating rod from the brake pedal assembly.

2. Open the hood and disconnect the wires from the stop light switch at the brake master cylinder.

3. Disconnect the brake line at the master cylinder outlet fitting.

4. Disconnect the manifold vacuum hose from the booster unit.

5. Remove the four bracket-to-dash panel attaching bolts.

6. Remove the booster and bracket assembly from the dash panel, sliding the valve operating rod out from the engine side of the dash panel.

7. Mount the booster and bracket assembly to the dash panel by sliding the valve operating rod in through the hole in the dash panel, and installing the attaching bolts.

8. Connect the manifold vacuum hose to the booster.

9. Connect the brake line to the master cylinder outlet fitting.

10. Connect the stop light switch wires.

11. Working inside the car below the instrument panel, install the rubber boot on the valve operating rod at the passenger side of the dash panel.

12. Connect the valve operating rod to the brake pedal with the bushings, eccentric shoulder bolt, and nut.

HYDRO-BOOST HYDRAULIC BOOSTER REMOVAL AND INSTALLATION

Versailles and 1982 Continental

A hydraulically powered brake booster was used on these models. The power steering pump provides the fluid pressure to operate both the brake booster and the power steering gear.

The hydro-boost assembly contains a valve which controls pump pressure while braking, a lever to control the position of the valve and a boost piston to provide the force to operate a conventional master cylinder attached to the front of the booster. The hydro-boost also has a reserve system, designed to store sufficient pressurized fluid to provide at least 2 brake applications in the event of insufficient fluid flow from the power steering pump. The brakes can also be applied unassisted if the reserve system is depleted.

Before removing the hydro-boost, discharge the accumulator by making several brake applications until a hard pedal is felt.

1. Working from inside the vehicle, below the instrument panel, disconnect the pushrod from the brake pedal. Disconnect the stoplight switch wires at the connector. Remove the hairpin retainer. Slide the stoplight switch off the brake pedal far enough for the switch outer hole to clear the pin. Remove the switch from the pin. Slide the pushrod, nylon washers and bushing off the brake pedal pin.

2. Open the hood and remove the nuts attaching the master cylinder to the hydro-boost. Remove the master cylinder. Secure it to one side without disturbing the hydraulic lines.

3. Disconnect the pressure, steering gear and return lines from the booster. Plug the lines to prevent the entry of dirt.

4. Remove the nuts attaching the hydro-boost. Remove the booster from the firewall, sliding the pushrod link out of the engine side of the firewall.

5. Install the hydro-boost on the firewall and install the attaching nuts.

6. Install the master cylinder on the booster.

7. Connect the pressure, steering gear and return lines to the booster.

8. Working below the instrument panel, install the nylon washer, booster pushrod and bushing on the brake pedal pin. Install the switch so that it straddles the pushrod with the switch slot on the pedal pin and the switch outer hole just clearing the pin. Slide the switch completely onto the pin and install the nylon washer. Attach these parts with the hairpin retainer. Connect the stoplight switch wires and install the wires in the retaining clip.

9. Remove the coil wire so that the engine will not start. Fill the power steering pump and engage the starter. Apply the brakes with a pumping action. Do not turn the steering wheel until air has been bled from the booster.

10. Check the fluid level and add as required. Start the engine and apply the brakes, checking for leaks. Cycle the steering wheel.

11. If a whine type noise is heard, suspect fluid aeration.

DRUM BRAKES

1971 was the last year that drum brakes were standard equipment on the front of the Ford mid-size cars. Starting in 1972, sliding caliper disc brakes are standard equipment on the front, with drum brakes on the rear. Front discs were an option in 1971. While Ford has had an optional four-wheel disc system since 1977, it has yet to be offered on the mid-size cars.

Bendix Duo-Servo Self-Adjusting Drum Brakes

Drum brakes on all Ford Mid-Size cars employ single-anchor, internal-expanding, and self-adjusting brake assemblies. The automatic adjuster continuously maintains correct operating clearance between the linings and the drums by adjusting the brake in small increments in direct proportion to lining wear. When applying the brakes while backing up, the linings tend to follow the rotating drum counterclockwise, thus forcing the upper end of the primary shoe against the anchor pin. Simultaneously, the wheel cylinder pushes the upper end of the secondary shoe and cable guide outward, away from the anchor pin. This movement of the secondary shoe causes the cable to pull the adjusting lever upward and against the end of the tooth on the adjusting screw star wheel. As lining wear increases, the upward travel of the adjusting lever also increases. When the linings have worn sufficiently to allow the lever to move upward far enough, it passes over the end of the tooth and engages it. Upon release of the brakes, the adjusting spring pulls the adjuster level downward, turning the star wheel and expanding the brakes.

INSPECTION

1. Raise the front or rear of the car and support the car with safety stands. Make sure the parking brake is not on.

2. If you are going to check the rear brakes, remove the lug nuts that attach the wheels to the axle shaft and remove the tires and wheels from the car. Using a pair of pliers, remove the tinnerman nuts from the wheel studs. Pull the brake drum off the axle shaft. If the brakes are adjusted too tightly to remove the drum, see Step 4. If you can remove the drum, see Step 5.

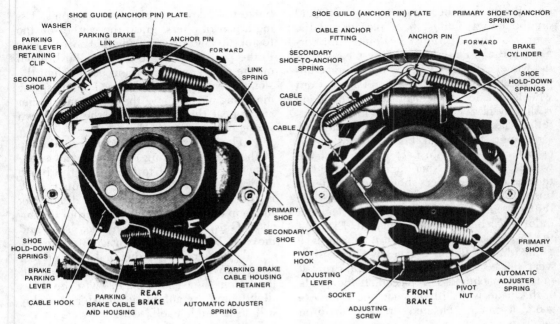

Self-adjusting drum brake assemblies

3. If you are going to check the front brakes, then the front tire, wheel and brake drum can be removed as an assembly. Remove the hub cap, then either pry the dust cover off the spindle with a screwdriver or pull it off with a pair of channel-lock pliers. Remove the cotter pin from the spindle. Slide the nut lock off the adjusting nut, then loosen the adjusting nut until it reaches the end of the spindle. Do not remove the adjusting nut yet. Grab the tire and pull it out toward yourself, then push it back into position. This will free the outer wheel bearing from the drum

hub. If the brakes are adjusted up too tightly to allow the drum to be pulled off them, go to step four and loosen up the brakes, then return here. Remove the adjusting nut, washer and outer bearing from the spindle. Pull the tire, wheel, and brake drum off the spindle.

4. If the brakes are too tight to remove the drum, get under the car (make sure you have safety stands under the car to support it) and remove the rubber plug from the bottom of the brake backing plate. Shine a flashlight into the slot in the plate. You will see the top of the adjusting screw star wheel and the adjusting lever for the automatic brake adjusting mechanism. To back off on the adjusting screw, you must first insert a small, thin screwdriver or a piece of firm wire (coat-hanger wire) into the adjusting slot and push the adjusting lever away from the adjusting screw. Then, insert a brake adjusting spoon into the slot and engage the top of the star wheel. Lift up on the bottom of the adjusting spoon to force the adjusting screw star wheel downward. Repeat this operation until the brake drum is free of the brake shoes and can be pulled off.

5. Clean the brake shoes and the inside of the brake drum. There must be at least $1/16$ in. of brake lining above the heads of the brake shoe attaching rivets. The lining should not be cracked or contaminated with grease

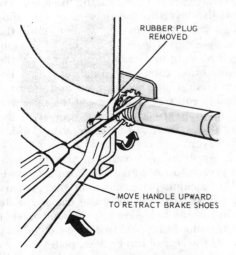

Backing off brake adjusting starwheel

or brake fluid. If there is grease or brake fluid on the lining it must be replaced and the source of the leak must be found and corrected. Brake fluid on the lining means leaking wheel cylinders. Grease on the brake lining means a leaking grease retainer (front wheels) or axle seal (rear brakes). If the lining is slightly glazed but otherwise in good condition, it can be cleaned up with medium sandpaper. Lift up the bottom of the wheel cylinder boots and inspect the ends of the wheel cylinders. A small amount of fluid in the end of the cylinders should be considered normal. If fluid runs out of the cylinder when the boots are lifted, however, the wheel cylinder must be rebuilt or replaced. Examine the inside of the brake drum; it should have a smooth, dull finish. If excessive brake shoe wear caused grooves to wear in the drum it must be machined or replaced. If the inside of the drum is slightly glazed, but otherwise good, it can be cleaned up with medium sandpaper.

6. If no repairs are required, install the drum and wheel. If the brake adjustment was changed to remove the drum, adjust the brakes until the drum will just fit over the brakes. After the wheel is installed it will be necessary to complete the adjustment. See "Brake Adjustment" later in this chapter. If a front wheel was removed, tighten the wheel bearing adjusting nut to 17–25 ft. lbs. while rotating the wheel. This will seat the bearing. Loosen the adjusting nut ½ turn, then retighten it to 10–15 lbs.

Brake Shoe
REMOVAL

NOTE: *If you are not thoroughly familiar with the procedures involved in brake replacement, only disassemble and assemble one side at a time, leaving the other wheel intact as a reference.*

1. Remove the brake drum. See the inspection procedure.

2. Place the hollow end of a brake spring service tool (available at auto parts stores) on the brake shoe anchor pin and twist it to disengage one of the brake retracting springs. Repeat this operation to remove the other spring.

CAUTION: *Be careful that the springs do not slip off the tool during removal, as they could cause personal injury.*

3. Reach behind the brake backing plate and place a finger on the end of one of the brake hold-down spring mounting pins. Using a pair of pliers, grasp the washer on the top of the hold-down spring that corresponds to the pin that you are holding. Push down on the pliers and turn them 90° to align the slot in the washer with the head on the spring mounting pin. Remove the spring and washer and repeat this operation on the hold-down spring on the other brake shoe.

4. Place the tip of a screwdriver on the top of the brake adjusting screw and move the screwdriver upward to lift up on the brake adjusting lever. When there is enough slack in the automatic adjuster cable, disconnect the loop on the top of the cable from the anchor. Grasp the top of each brake shoe and move it outward to disengage it from the wheel cylinder (and parking brake link on rear wheels). When the brake shoes are clear, lift them from the backing plate. Twist the shoes slightly and the automatic adjuster assembly will disassemble itself.

5. If you are working on rear brakes, grasp the end of the brake cable spring with a pair of pliers and, using the brake lever as a fulcrum, pull the end of the spring away from the lever. Disengage the cable from the brake lever.

INSTALLATION

1. If you are working on the rear brakes, the brake cable must be connected to the secondary brake shoe before the shoe is installed on the backing plate. To do this, first transfer the parking brake lever from the old secondary shoe to the new one. This is accomplished by spreading the bottom of the horseshoe clip and disengaging the lever. Position the lever on the new secondary shoe and install the spring washer and the horseshoe clip. Close the bottom of the clip after installing it. Grasp the metal tip of the parking brake cable with a pair of pliers. Position a pair of side cutter pliers on the end of the cable coil spring and, using the plier as a fulcrum, pull the coil spring back with the side cutters. Position the cable in the parking brake lever.

2. Apply a *light* coating of high-temperature grease to the brake shoe contact points on the backing plate. Position the primary brake shoe on the front of the backing plate and install the hold-down spring and washer over the mounting pin. Install the secondary shoe on the rear of the backing plate.

3. If working on the rear brakes, install the parking brake link between the notch in

the primary brake shoe and the notch in the parking brake lever.

4. Install the automatic adjuster cable loop end on the anchor pin. Make sure the crimped side of the loop faces the backing plate.

5. Install the return spring in the primary brake shoe and, using the tapered end of a brake spring service tool, slide the top of the spring onto the anchor pin.

CAUTION: *Be careful to make sure that the spring does not slip off the tool during installation, as it could cause injury.*

6. Install the automatic adjuster cable guide in the secondary brake shoe, making sure the flared hole in the cable guide is inside the hole in the brake shoe. Fit the cable into the groove in the top of the cable guide.

7. Install the secondary shoe return spring through the hole in the cable guide and the brake shoe. Using the brake spring tool, slide the top of the spring onto the anchor pin.

8. Clean the threads on the adjusting screw and apply a light coating of high-temperature grease to the threads. Screw the adjuster closed, then open it one-half turn.

9. Install the adjusting screw between the brake shoes with the star wheel nearest to the secondary shoe. Make sure the star wheel is in a position that is accessible from the adjusting slot in the backing plate.

10. Install the short hooked end of the automatic adjuster spring in the proper hole in the primary brake shoe.

11. Connect the hooked end of the automatic adjuster cable and the free end of the automatic adjuster spring in the slot in the top of the automatic adjuster lever.

12. Pull the automatic adjuster lever (the lever will pull the cable and spring with it) downward and to the left and engage the pivot hook of the lever in the hole in the secondary brake shoe.

13. Check the entire brake assembly to make sure that everything is installed properly. Make sure that the shoes engage the wheel cylinder properly and are flush on the anchor pin. Make sure that the automatic adjuster cable is flush on the anchor pin and in the slot on the back of the cable guide. Make sure that the adjusting lever rests on the adjusting screw star wheel. Pull upward on the adjusting cable until the adjusting lever is free of the star wheel, then release the cable. The adjusting lever should snap back into place on the adjusting screw star wheel and turn the wheel one tooth.

14. Expand the brake adjusting screw until the brake drum will just fit over the brake shoes.

15. Install the wheel and drum and adjust the brakes. See "Brake Adjustment."

DRUM BRAKE ADJUSTMENT

1. Raise the car and support it with safety stands.

2. Remove the rubber plug from the adjusting slot on the backing plate (if so equipped).

3. Insert a brake adjusting spoon into the slot and engage the lowest possible tooth on the star wheel. Move the end of the brake spoon downward to move the star wheel upward and expand the adjusting screw. Repeat this operation until the brakes lock the wheel.

4. Insert a small screwdriver or piece of firm wire (coat-hanger wire) into the adjusting slot and push the automatic adjuster lever out and free of the star wheel on the adjusting screw.

5. Holding the adjusting lever out of the way, engage the topmost tooth possible on the star wheel with a brake adjusting spoon. Move the end of the adjusting spoon upward to move the adjusting screw star wheel downward and contract the adjusting screw. Back off the adjusting screw star wheel until the wheel spins freely with a minimum of drag. Keep track of the number of turns the star wheel is backed off.

6. Repeat this operation for the other side. When backing off the brakes on the other side, the adjusting lever must be backed off the same number of turns to prevent side-to-side brake pull.

7. Repeat this operation on the other set of brakes (front or rear).

8. When all four brakes are adjusted, make several stops, while backing the car, to equalize all of the wheels.

9. Road-test the car.

Wheel Cylinders
OVERHAUL

Since the travel of the pistons in the wheel cylinder changes when new brake shoes are installed, it is possible for previously good wheel cylinders to start leaking after new brakes are installed. Therefore, to save yourself the expense of having to replace new brakes that become saturated with brake fluid and the aggravation of having to take everything apart again, it is strongly recommended

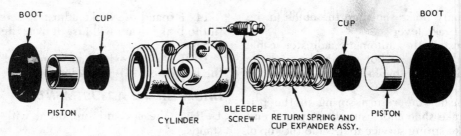

BOOT   CUP   BOOT

PISTON   CYLINDER   BLEEDER SCREW   RETURN SPRING AND CUP EXPANDER ASSY.   PISTON

Wheel cylinder disassembled

that wheel cylinders be rebuilt every time new brake shoes are installed. This is especially true on high-mileage cars.

1. Remove the brakes.

2. Place a bucket or old newspapers under the brake backing plate to catch the brake fluid that will run out of the wheel cylinder.

3. Remove the boots from the ends of the wheel cylinders.

4. Push one piston toward the center of the cylinder to force the opposite piston and cup out the other end of the cylinder. Reach in the open end of the cylinder and push the spring, cup, and piston out of the cylinder.

5. Remove the bleeder screw from the rear of the cylinder, on the back of the backing plate.

6. Inspect the inside of the wheel cylinder. If it is scored in any way, the cylinder must be honed with a wheel cylinder hone or fine emery paper, and finished with crocus cloth if emery paper is used. If the inside of the cylinder is excessively worn, the cylinder will have to be replaced, as only 0.003 in. of material can be removed from the cylinder walls. When honing or cleaning the wheel cylinders, keep a small amount of brake fluid in the cylinder to serve as a lubricant.

7. Clean any foreign matter from the pistons. The sides of the pistons must be smooth for the wheel cylinders to operate properly.

8. Clean the cylinder bore with alcohol and a lint-free rag. Pull the rag through the bore several times to remove all foreign matter and dry the cylinder.

9. Install the bleeder screw and the return spring in the cylinder.

10. Coat new cylinder cups with new brake fluid and install them in the cylinder. Make sure that they are square in the bore or they will leak.

11. Install the pistons in the cylinder after coating them with new brake fluid.

12. Coat the insides of the boots with new brake fluid and install them on the cylinder. Install the brakes.

REPLACEMENT

1. Remove the brake shoes.

2. On rear brakes, loosen the brake line on the rear of the cylinder but do not pull the line away from the cylinder or it may bend.

3. On front brakes, disconnect the metal brake line from the rubber brake hose where they join in the wheel well. Pull off the horseshoe clip that attaches the rubber brake hose to the underbody of the car. Loosen the hose at the cylinder, then turn the whole brake hose to remove it from the wheel cylinder.

4. Remove the bolts and lockwashers that attach the wheel cylinder to the backing plate and remove the cylinder.

5. Position the new wheel cylinder on the backing plate and install the cylinder attacking bolts and lockwashers.

6. Attach the metal brake line or rubber hose by reversing the procedure given in Steps 2 or 3.

7. Install the brakes.

FRONT DISC BRAKES

INSPECTION

1. Raise the vehicle until the wheel and tire clear the floor. Place safety stands under the vehicle.

2. Remove the wheel cover. Remove the wheel and tire from the hub and disc.

3. Visually inspect the shoe and lining assemblies. If the lining material has worn to a thickness of 0.030 in. or less, or if the lining is contaminated with brake fluid, replace all pad assemblies on both front wheels. Make all thickness measurements across the thinnest section of the pad assembly. A slight taper on a used lining should be considered normal.

4. To check disc run-out, tighten the wheel bearing adjusting nut to eliminate end-play. Check to make sure the disc can still be rotated.

5. Hand-spin the disc and visually check for run-out. If the disc appears to be out of round or if it wobbles, it needs to be machined or replaced. When the run-out check is finished, loosen the wheel bearing adjusting nut and retighten to specifications, in order to prevent bearing damage.

6. Visually check the disc for scoring. Minor scores can be removed with a fine emery cloth. If it is excessively scored, it must be machined or replaced.

7. The caliper should be visually checked. If excess leakage is evident, the caliper should be replaced.

8. Install the wheel and hub assembly.

Hub and Disc
REMOVAL

1. Raise the vehicle on a hoist and remove the wheel.

2. Remove the caliper mounting bolts. Slide the caliper assembly away from the disc and suspend it with a wire loop. It is not necessary to disconnect the brake line. Insert a clean cardboard spacer between the linings to prevent the piston(s) from coming out of the cylinder bores while the caliper is removed.

3. Remove the grease cap from the hub. Remove the cotter pin, nut lock, adjusting nut, and flat washer from the spindle.

4. Remove the outer wheel bearing cone and roller assembly from the hub.

5. Remove the hub and disc assembly from the spindle.

INSTALLATION

NOTE: *If a new disc is being installed, remove the protective coating with carburetor degreaser. If the original disc is being installed, make sure that the grease in the hub is clean and adequate, that the inner bearing and grease retainer are lubricated and in good condition, and that the disc breaking surfaces are clean.*

1. Install the hub and disc assembly on the spindle.

2. Lubricate the outer bearing and install the thrust washer and adjusting nut.

3. Adjust the wheel bearing as outlined in the "Wheel Bearing Adjustment" section.

4. Install the nut lock, cotter pin, and grease cap.

5. Install the caliper assembly with the attaching bolts finger-tight. Torque first the upper, then the lower bolt to 45–60 ft. lbs.

Safety-wire both bolts, making sure that any sharp wire ends are turned away from the brake hose.

6. Install the wheel and tire assembly and torque the nuts to 75–110 ft. lbs.

7. Lower the vehicle and road-test it.

Kelsey-Hayes Single-Piston, Floating-Caliper Disc Brakes— 1971 Models
PAD REPLACEMENT

1. Raise the vehicle on a hoist and remove the front wheel.

2. Remove the lockwires from the two mounting bolts and lift the caliper away from the disc.

3. Remove the retaining clips with a screwdriver and slide the outboard pad and retaining pins out of the caliper. Remove the inboard pad.

4. Slide the new inboard pad into the caliper so that the tabs are between the retaining clips and anchor plate and the backing plate lies flush against the piston.

5. Insert the outboard pad retaining pins into the outboard pad and position them in the caliper.

NOTE: *Stabilizer, insulators, pad clips, and pins should always be replaced when the disc pads are replaced.*

6. Hold the retaining pins in place (one at a time) with a short drift pin or dowel and install the retaining clips.

7. Slide the caliper assembly over the disc and align the mounting bolt holes.

8. Install the lower bolt finger-tight. Install the upper bolt and torque to specification. Torque the lower bolt to specification. Safety-wire both bolts.

CAUTION: *Do not deviate from this procedure. The alignment of the anchor plate depends on the proper sequence of bolt installation.*

9. Check the brake fluid level and pump the brake pedal to seat the linings against the disc. Replace the wheels and road-test the car.

CALIPER ASSEMBLY SERVICE

1. Raise the vehicle on a hoist and remove the front wheels.

2. Disconnect and plug the brake line.

3. Remove the lockwires from the two caliper mounting bolts and remove the bolt. Lift the caliper off the disc.

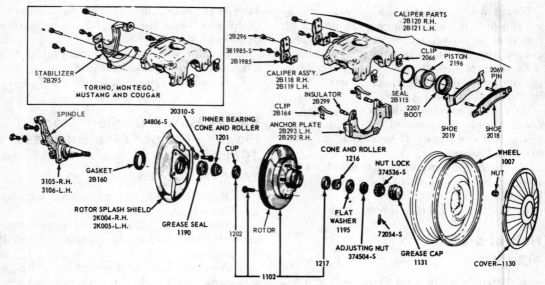

1971 floating caliper front disc brake

4. Remove and discard the locating pin insulators. Replace all rubber parts at reassembly.

5. Remove the retaining clips with a screwdriver and slide the outboard pad and retaining pins out of the caliper. Remove the inboard pad. Loosen the bleed screw and drain the brake fluid.

6. Remove the two small bolts and caliper stabilizers.

7. Remove the inboard pad retaining clips and bolts.

8. Clean and inspect all parts, and reinstall on the anchor plate. Do not tighten the stabilizer bolts at this time.

9. Remove the piston by applying compressed air to the fluid inlet hole. Use care to prevent the piston from popping out of control.

CAUTION: *Do not attempt to catch the piston with the hand. Use folded towels to cushion it.*

10. Remove the piston boot. Inspect the piston for scoring, pitting, or corrosion. The piston must be replaced if there is any visible damage or wear.

11. Remove the piston seal from the cylinder bore. *Do not use any metal tools for this operation.*

12. Clean the caliper with fresh brake fluid. Inspect the cylinder bore for damage or wear. Light defects can be removed by rotating crocus cloth around the bore. (Do not use any other type of abrasive.)

13. Lubricate all new rubber parts in brake

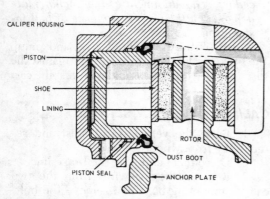

Floating caliper—sectional view

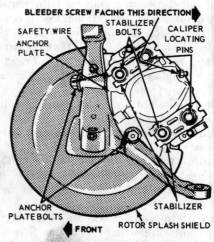

Floating caliper installed—inboard view

fluid. Install the piston seal in the cylinder groove. Install the boot into its piston groove.

14. Install the piston, open end out, into the bore while working the boot around the outside of the piston. Make sure that the boot lip is seated in the piston groove.

15. Slide the anchor plate assembly onto the caliper housing and reinstall the locating pins. Tighten the pins to specification. Tighten the stabilizer anchor plate bolts.

16. Slide the inboard pad into the caliper so that the tabs are between the retaining clips and anchor plate and the backing plate lies flush against the piston.

17. Insert the outboard pad retaining pins into the outboard pad and position them in the caliper.

18. Hold the retaining pins in place (one at a time) with a short drift pin or dowel and install the retaining clips.

19. Slide the caliper assembly over the disc and align the mounting bolt holes.

20. Install the lower bolt finger-tight. Install the upper bolt and torque to specification. Torque the lower bolt to specification. Safety-wire both bolts.

CAUTION: *Do not deviate from this procedure. The alignment of the anchor plate depends on the proper sequence of bolt installation.*

21. Connect the brake line and bleed the brakes (see "Brake Bleeding").

22. Install the front wheels, recheck the brake fluid level, and road-test the car.

Ford Single-Piston Sliding-Caliper Disc Brakes 1972–79 Models
PAD REPLACEMENT

1. Remove approximately ⅔ of the fluid from the rear reservoir of the tandem master cylinder. Raise the vehicle, taking proper safety precautions.

2. Remove the wheel and tire assembly.

3. Remove the key retaining screw from the caliper retaining key.

4. Slide the retaining key and support spring either inward or outward from the anchor plate. To remove the key and spring, a hammer and drift may be used, taking care not to damage the key in the process.

5. Lift the caliper assembly away from the anchor plate by pushing the caliper downward against the anchor plate and rotating the upper end upward out of the anchor plate. Be careful not to stretch or twist the flexible brake hose.

6. Remove the inner shoe and lining assembly from the anchor plate. The inner shoe antirattle clip may become displaced at this time and should be repositioned on the anchor plate. Lightly tap on the outer shoe and lining assembly to free it from the caliper.

7. Clean the caliper, anchor plate, and disc assemblies, and inspect them for brake fluid leakage, excessive wear or signs of damage. Replace the pads if either of them are worn to within $1/32$ in. of the rivet heads.

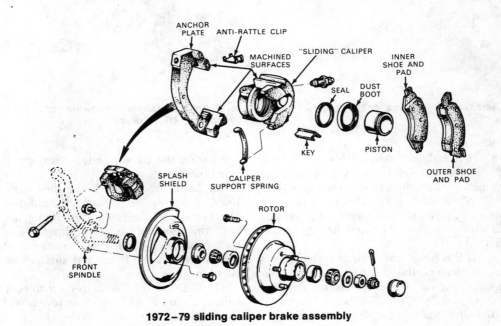

1972–79 sliding caliper brake assembly

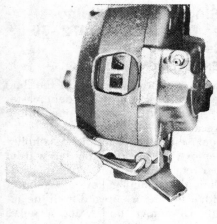

1. Front caliper removal

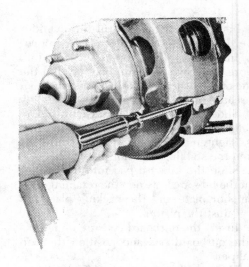

2. Remove the caliper retaining screw. Drive the caliper screw and support spring inward or outward.

3. Remove the key and caliper support spring.

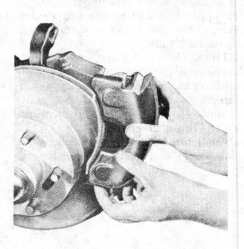

4. Push the caliper downward and work the upper end off the disc.

8. To install new pads, use a 4 in. C-clamp and a block of wood 1¾ in. x 1 in. and approximately ¾ in. thick to seat the caliper hydraulic piston in its bore. This must be done in order to provide clearance for the caliper to fit over the rotor when new linings are installed.

9. At this point, the antirattle clip should be in its place on the lower inner brake shoe support of the anchor plate with the pigtail of the clip toward the inside of the anchor plate. Position the inner brake shoe and lining assembly on the anchor plate with the pad toward the disc.

10. Install the outer brake shoe with the lower flange ends against the caliper leg abutments and the brake shoe upper flanges over the shoulders on the caliper legs. The shoe is installed correctly when its flanges fit snugly against the machined surfaces of the shoulders.

11. Remove the C-clamp used to seat the caliper piston in its bore. The piston will remain seated.

12. Position the caliper housing lower V-groove on the anchor plate lower abutment surface.

13. Pivot the caliper housing upward toward the disc until the outer edge of the piston dust boot is about ¼ in. from the upper edge of the inboard pad.

14. In order to prevent pinching of the dust boot between the piston and the inboard pad during installation of the caliper, place a clean piece of thin cardboard between the inboard pad and the lower half of the piston dust boot.

15. Rotate the caliper housing toward the disc until a slight resistance is felt. At this point, pull the cardboard downward toward the disc centerline while rotating the caliper over the disc. Then remove the cardboard and complete the rotation of the caliper down over the disc.

16. Slide the caliper up against the upper abutment surfaces of the anchor plate and center the caliper over the lower anchor plate abutment.

17. Position the caliper support spring and key in the key slot and slide them into the opening between the lower end of the caliper and the lower anchor plate abutment until the key semicircular slot is centered over the retaining screw threaded hole in the anchor plate.

18. Install the key retaining screw and torque to 12–16 ft. lbs.

19. Check the fluid level in the master cylinder and fill as necessary. Install the reservoir cover. Depress the brake pedal several times to properly seat the caliper and pads. Check for leakage around the caliper and flexible brake hose.

20. Install the wheel and tire assembly and torque the nuts to 70–115 ft. lbs. Install the wheel cover.

21. Lower the car. Make sure that you obtain a firm brake pedal and then road-test the car for proper brake operation.

CALIPER ASSEMBLY SERVICE

1. Raise the vehicle and place jackstands underneath.

2. Remove the wheel and tire assembly.

3. Disconnect the flexible brake hose from the caliper. To disconnect the hose, loosen the tube fitting which connects the end of the hose to the brake tube at its bracket on the frame. Remove the horseshoe clip from the hose and bracket, disengage the hose, and plug the end. Then unscrew the entire hose assembly from the caliper.

4. Remove the key retaining screw from the caliper retaining key.

5. Slide the retaining key and support spring either inward or outward from the anchor plate. To remove the key and spring, a hammer and drift may be used, taking care not to damage the key in the process.

6. Lift the caliper assembly away from the anchor plate by pushing the caliper downward against the anchor plate and rotating the upper end upward out of the anchor plate.

7. Remove the piston by applying compressed air to the fluid inlet port with a rubber-tipped nozzle. Place a towel or thick cloth over the piston before applying air pressure to prevent damage to the piston. If the piston is seized in the bore and cannot be forced from the caliper, lightly tap around the outside of the caliper while applying air pressure.

CAUTION: *Do not attempt to catch the piston with your hand.*

8. Remove the dust boot from the caliper assembly.

9. Remove the piston seal from the cylinder and discard it.

10. Clean all metal parts with isopropyl alcohol or a suitable non-petroleum solvent and dry them with compressed air. Be sure there is no foreign material in the bore or component parts. Inspect the piston and bore for excessive wear or damage. Replace the piston if it is pitted, scored, or if the chrome plating is wearing off.

11. Lubricate all new rubber parts in brake fluid. Install the piston seal in the cylinder groove, being careful not to twist it. Install the dust boot by setting the flange squarely in the outer groove of the bore.

12. Coat the piston with brake fluid and install it in the bore. Work the dust boot around the outside of the piston, making sure that the boot lip is seated in the piston groove.

13. Install the caliper as outlined in Steps 12–18 in the sliding caliper "Shoe and Lining Replacement" procedure.

14. Thread the flexible brake hose and gasket onto the caliper fitting. Torque the fitting to 12–20 ft. lbs. Place the upper end of the flexible brake hose in its bracket and install the horseshoe clip. Remove the plug from the brake tube and connect the tube to the hose. Torque the tube fitting nut to 10–15 ft. lbs.

15. Bleed the brake system as outlined in the "Brake Bleeding" section.

16. Check the fluid level in the master cylinder and fill as necessary. Install the reser-

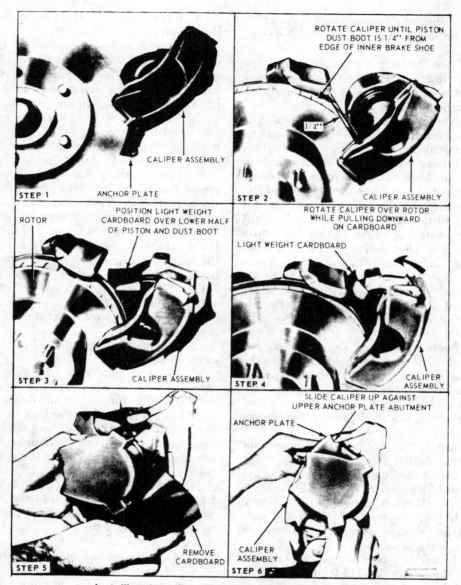

STEP 1   CALIPER ASSEMBLY   ANCHOR PLATE

ROTATE CALIPER UNTIL PISTON DUST BOOT IS 1/4'' FROM EDGE OF INNER BRAKE SHOE

1/4''

STEP 2   CALIPER ASSEMBLY

ROTOR   POSITION LIGHT WEIGHT CARDBOARD OVER LOWER HALF OF PISTON AND DUST BOOT

STEP 3   CALIPER ASSEMBLY

ROTATE CALIPER OVER ROTOR WHILE PULLING DOWNWARD ON CARDBOARD

LIGHT WEIGHT CARDBOARD

STEP 4   CALIPER ASSEMBLY

STEP 5   REMOVE CARDBOARD

SLIDE CALIPER UP AGAINST UPPER ANCHOR PLATE ABUTMENT

ANCHOR PLATE

CALIPER ASSEMBLY   STEP 6

Installing the caliper assembly on 1972–79 models

voir cover. Depress the brake pedal several times to properly seat the caliper and shoes. Check for leakage around the caliper and the flexible brake hose.

17. Install the wheel and tire assembly and torque the nuts to 70–115 ft. lbs. Install the wheel cover.

18. Lower the car. Make sure that you obtain a firm brake pedal and then roadtest the car for proper brake operation.

Ford Single Piston Sliding Caliper Disc Brakes—1980–82
PAD REPLACEMENT

1. Remove the master cylinder cap, and check the fluid level in the primary (large) reservoir. Remove brake fluid until the reservoir is half full. Discard this fluid.

2. Remove the wheel and tire assembly from the hub. Be careful to avoid damage to

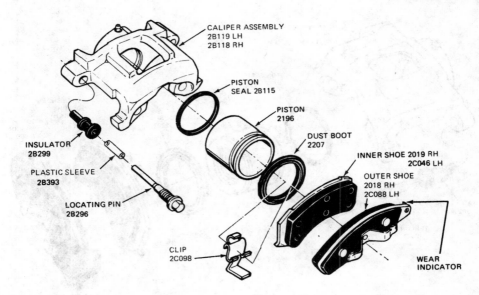

PIN SLIDER CALIPER ASSEMBLY—DISASSEMBLED
RH SIDE SHOWN

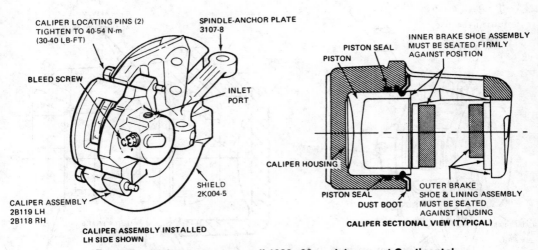

Front disc brake components, all 1980–82 models except Continental

or interference with the caliper splash shield or bleeder screw fitting.

3. Remove the caliper locating pins.

4. Lift the caliper assembly from the integral spindle/anchor plate and rotor. Remove the outer shoe from the caliper assembly on Lincoln Continental slip shoe down the caliper leg until clip is disengaged.

5. Remove the inner shoe and lining assembly. On Lincoln Continental, pull shoe straight out of piston. This could require a force as high as 20–30 lbs. Inspect both rotor braking surfaces. Minor scoring or build-up of lining material does not require machining or replacement of the rotor.

6. Suspend the caliper inside the fender housing with a wire hooked through the outer leg hole of the caliper. Be careful not to damage the caliper or stretch the brake hose.

7. Remove and discard the plastic sleeves that are located inside the caliper locating pin insulators. These parts must not be reused.

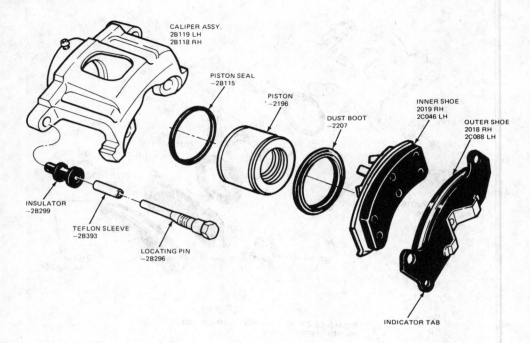

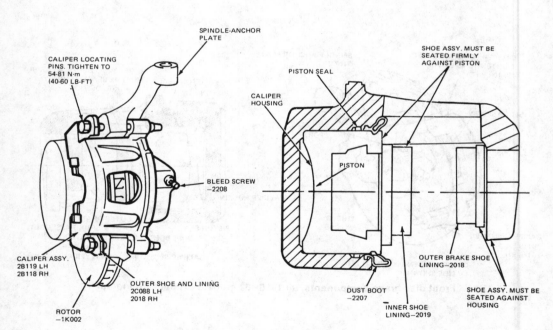

1982 Continental front disc brake components

8. Remove and discard the caliper locating insulators. These parts must not be reused.

9. Use a 4 inch C-clamp and a block of wood 2¾ inch x 1 inch and approximately [6] inch thick to seat the caliper hydraulic piston in its bore. This must be done to provide clearance for the caliper assembly to fit over the rotor when installed. Remove the C-clamp

from the caliper (the caliper piston will remain seated in its bore).

CAUTION: *On Lincoln Continental, the piston is made of phenolic material and must not be seated in bore by applying C-clamp directly to the piston.*

10. Install new locating pin insulators and plastic sleeves in the caliper housing. Do not use sharp-edged tool to insert insulators in

the caliper housing. Check to see if both insulator flanges straddle the housing holes and if the plastic sleeves are bottomed in the insulators as well as slipped under the upper lip.

11. Install the correct inner shoe and lining assembly in the caliper piston. All vehicles, except Lincoln Continental, have a separate anti-rattle clip and insulator that must be installed to the inner shoe and lining prior to their assembly to the caliper. The inner shoes are marked LH or RH and must be installed in the proper caliper. Also, care should be taken not to bend the anti-rattle clips too far in the piston or distortion and rattles can result.

Inner shoe installation on Lincoln Continental is accomplished by holding each end of the shoe, making sure it is square with the piston, and pushing the shoe in firmly until

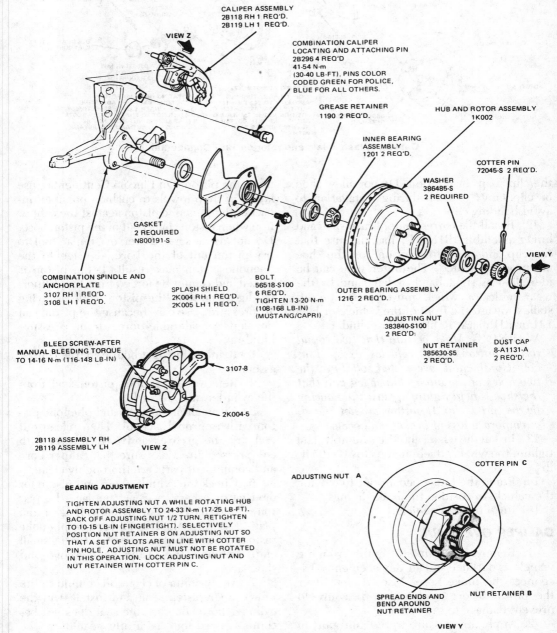

Caliper, splash shield and rotor on all 1980–82 models except Continental

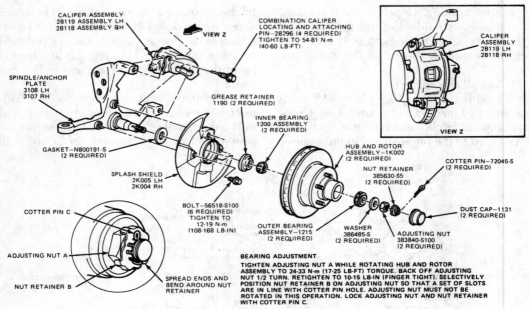

Caliper, splash shield and rotor on 1982 Continental

the clip snaps in position. Do not allow shoe or clip tangs to cock during installation to avoid bending clip.

12. Install the correct outer brake shoe and lining assembly (RH/LH), making sure that the clip and/or buttons located on the shoe are properly seated. The outer shoe can be identified as right hand or left hand by the wear indicator which must always be installed toward the front of the vehicle or by a LH or RH mark. Refill master cylinder.

WARNING: *Make certain that two round torque buttons on all vehicles, except Lincoln Continental, are seated solidly in the two holes of the outer caliper leg and that the shoe is held tightly against the housing by the spring clip. If buttons are not seated, a temporary loss of brakes may occur.*

13. Install the wheel and tire assembly, and tighten the wheel attaching nuts to 80–105 ft. lbs.

14. Pump the brake pedal prior to moving the vehicle to position the brake linings.

15. Road test the vehicle.

CALIPER OVERHAUL

1. Remove the caliper assembly from the vehicle as outlined in Pad Replacement. Disconnect the brake hose. Place a cloth over the piston before applying air pressure to prevent damage to the piston.

2. Apply air pressure to the fluid port in the caliper with a rubber-tipped nozzle to re-

move the piston. On Lincoln Continental, use layers of shop towels to cushion possible impact of the phenolic piston against the caliper iron when piston comes out of the piston bore. Do not use a screwdriver or similar tool to pry piston out of the bore, damage to the phenolic piston may result. If the piston is seized and cannot be forced from the caliper, tap lightly around the piston while applying air pressure. Use care because the piston can develop considerable force from pressure build-up.

3. Remove the dust boot from the caliper assembly.

4. Remove the rubber piston seal from the cylinder, and discard it.

5. Clean all metal parts and phenolic piston with isopropyl alcohol. Then, clean out and dry the grooves and passageways with compressed air. Make sure that caliper bore and component parts are thoroughly clean.

6. Check the cylinder bore and piston for damage or excessive wear. Replace the piston if it is pitted, scored, corroded, or the plating is worn off. Do not replace phenolic piston cosmetic surface irregularities or small chips between the piston boot groove and shoe face.

7. Apply a film of clean brake fluid to the new caliper piston seal, and install it in the cylinder bore. Be sure the seal does not become twisted but is firmly seated in the groove.

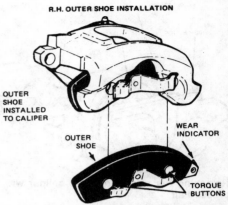

R.H. OUTER SHOE INSTALLATION

OUTER SHOE INSTALLED TO CALIPER

OUTER SHOE

WEAR INDICATOR

TORQUE BUTTONS

WARNING: OUTER SHOE TORQUE BUTTONS MUST BE SOLIDLY SEATED IN CALIPER HOLES OR TEMPORARY LOSS OF BRAKES MAY OCCUR.

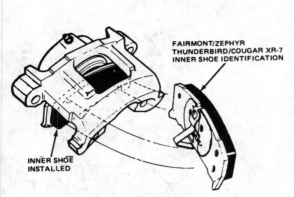

FAIRMONT/ZEPHYR THUNDERBIRD/COUGAR XR-7 INNER SHOE IDENTIFICATION

INNER SHOE INSTALLED

R.H. INNER SHOE INSTALLATION

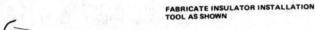
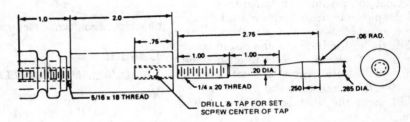

1.0 2.0 .75 2.75 .06 RAD.

1.00 1.00 .20 DIA.

5/16 x 18 THREAD 1/4 x 20 THREAD .250 .265 DIA.

DRILL & TAP FOR SET SCREW CENTER OF TAP

FABRICATE INSULATOR INSTALLATION TOOL AS SHOWN

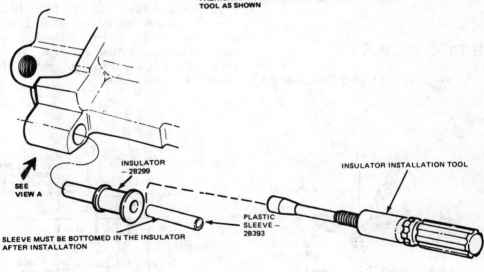

SEE VIEW A

INSULATOR – 2B299

INSULATOR INSTALLATION TOOL

PLASTIC SLEEVE – 2B393

SLEEVE MUST BE BOTTOMED IN THE INSULATOR AFTER INSTALLATION

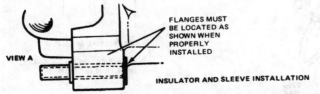

VIEW A

FLANGES MUST BE LOCATED AS SHOWN WHEN PROPERLY INSTALLED

INSULATOR AND SLEEVE INSTALLATION

Servicing the pin-slider caliper

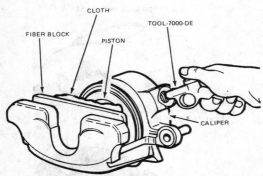

Removing the piston from the caliper with compressed air

8. Install a new dust boot by setting the flange squarely in the outer groove of the caliper bore.

9. Coat the piston with brake fluid, and install the piston in the cylinder bore. Be sure to use a wood block or other flat stock when installing the piston back into the piston bore. Never apply C-clamp directly to a phenolic piston, and be sure pistons are not cocked. Spread the dust boot over the piston as it is installed. Seat the dust boot in the piston groove.

10. Install the caliper over the rotor as outlined.

REAR DISC BRAKES

Applies to Versailles and 1982 Continental.

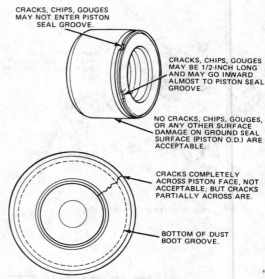

Checking piston surface for irregularities

Caliper

REMOVAL AND INSTALLATION

Versailles

1. Raise the car and install jackstands. Remove the rear wheels.

2. Remove the brake line from the caliper. Disconnect the hose bracket from the axle spring seat and remove the hollow retaining bolt used for connecting the hose fitting to the caliper, if so equipped. Unhook the parking brake cable.

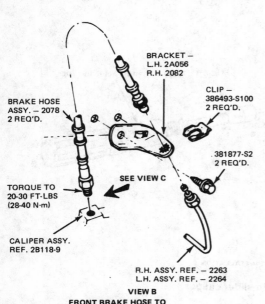

VIEW B
FRONT BRAKE HOSE TO CALIPER CONNECTION

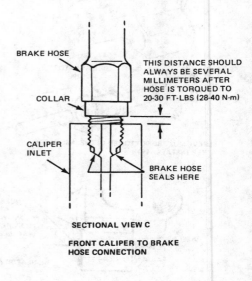

SECTIONAL VIEW C

FRONT CALIPER TO BRAKE HOSE CONNECTION

Hydraulic connections on all except Continental

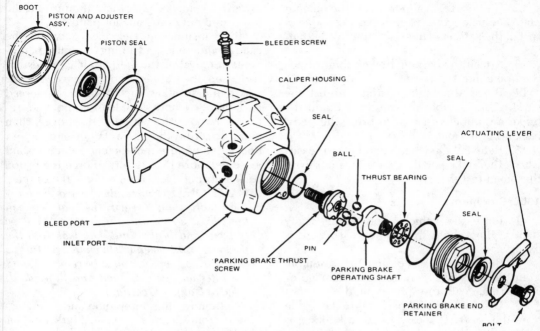

Versailles rear disc brake caliper

3. Remove the retaining screw from the caliper retaining key.

4. Tap the retaining key and support spring from the caliper, using a hammer and a drift pin of some sort. Don't use excessive force. The key should slide out easily.

5. Rotate the caliper assembly up and away from the anchor plate and the rotor. It may be necessary to scrape away the rust buildup on the rotor edge in order to gain enough clearance to remove the caliper. Remove the caliper. If the caliper still cannot be removed, loosen the caliper end retainer one-half turn, after removing the retaining screw and caliper parking brake lever.

NOTE: *Turning the retainer more than one-half turn could cause internal fluid leaks in the caliper, which would make caliper rebuilding necessary.*

6. If the end retainer was loosened in order to remove the caliper, perform the following:

  a. Install the caliper on the anchor plate and secure it with the key, but do not install the pads.

  b. Torque the end retainer to 75–95 ft. lb.

  c. Install the caliper parking brake lever with the arm pointing rearward and down. Tighten the lever retaining screw to 16–22 ft. lb. Check for free rotation of the lever.

  d. Remove the caliper from the anchor plate.

7. Make sure that the antirattle clip is correctly positioned in the lower inner brake pad support and that the clip loop is facing the inside of the anchor plate.

8. Place the inner brake pad on the anchor plate. Install the outer brake pad in the caliper.

9. Position the bottom of the caliper against the anchor plate lower abutment surface. Rotate the caliper housing until it is completely over the disc. Be careful not to damage the dust boot.

10. Slide the caliper outward until the inner pad is seated firmly against the disc. Measure the outer pad-to-disc clearance. It should be $1/16$ inch or less. If it is more, you will need a special tool (available from your Ford dealer) which is used to adjust the piston outward until the correct clearance is obtained.

11. Using the special tool, adjust the caliper piston outward if this needs to be done.

NOTE: *See the pad replacement section for instructions on how to use the special tool. Because of the parking brake assembly, pad-to-rotor clearance is critical. If piston clearance is more than $1/16$ inch, the adjuster may pull out of the piston when the brakes are applied, causing adjuster failure.*

12. Center the caliper over the anchor plate and install the retaining spring and key. Install the setscrew and tighten it to 12–16 ft. lb.

13. Attach the parking brake cable. Attach the brake line.

14. Bleed the brake system. Adjust the parking brake cable if necessary. Pump the brake a number of times to bring the pedal back up to normal.

15. Reinstall the wheels and lower the car. Check the brake pedal to make sure it is firm, then road test the car.

1982 Continental

1. Raise the vehicle, and install safety stands. Block both front wheels if a jack is used.

2. Remove the wheel and tire assembly from the axle. Use care to avoid damage or interference with the splash shield.

3. Disconnect the parking brake cable from the lever. Use care to avoid kinking or cutting the cable or return spring.

4. Remove the caliper locating pins.

5. Lift the caliper assembly away from the anchor plate by pushing the caliper upward toward the anchor plate, and then rotate the lower end out of the anchor plate.

6. If insufficient clearance between the caliper and shoe and lining assemblies prevents removal of the caliper, it is necessary to loosen the caliper end retainer ½ turn, maximum, to allow the piston to be forced back into its bore. To loosen the end retainer, remove the parking brake lever, then mark or scribe the end retainer and caliper housing to be sure that the end retainer is not loosened more than ½ turn. Force the piston back in its bore, and then remove the caliper.

CAUTION: *If the retainer must be loosened more than ½ turn, the seal between the thrust screw and the housing may be broken, and brake fluid may leak into the parking brake mechanism chamber. In this case, the end retainer must be removed, and the internal parts cleaned and lubricated; refer to Caliper Overhaul.*

7. Remove the outer shoe and lining assembly from the anchor plate. Mark shoe for identification if it is to be reinstalled.

8. Remove the two rotor retainer nuts and the rotor from the axle shaft.

9. Remove the inner brake shoe and lin-

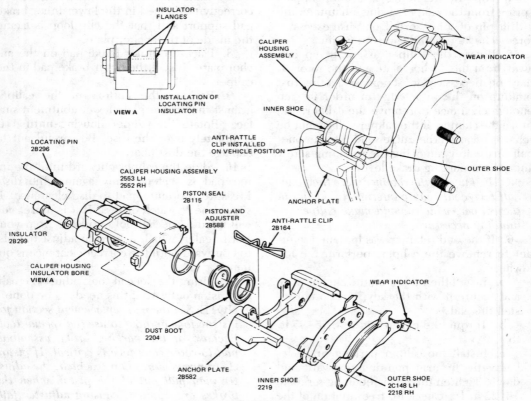

1982 Continental rear disc brake caliper

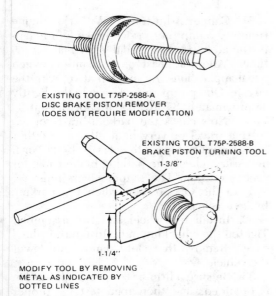

EXISTING TOOL T75P-2588-A
DISC BRAKE PISTON REMOVER
(DOES NOT REQUIRE MODIFICATION)

EXISTING TOOL T75P-2588-B
BRAKE PISTON TURNING TOOL
1-3/8"

1-1/4"

MODIFY TOOL BY REMOVING
METAL AS INDICATED BY
DOTTED LINES

Special tools needed for servicing the rear disc brake caliper

ing assembly from the anchor plate. Mark shoe for identification if it is to be reinstalled.

10. Remove anti-rattle clip from anchor plate.

11. Remove the flexible hose from the caliper by removing the hollow retaining bolt that connects the hose fitting to the caliper.

12. Clean the caliper, anchor plate, and rotor assemblies and inspect for signs of brake fluid leakage, excessive wear, or damage. The caliper must be inspected for leakage both in the piston boot area and at the operating shaft seal area. Lightly sand or wire brush any rust or corrosion from the caliper and anchor plate sliding surfaces as well as the outer and inner brake shoe abutment surfaces. Inspect the brake shoes for wear. If either lining is worn to within ⅛ inch of the shoe surface, both shoe and lining assemblies must be replaced using the shoe and lining removal procedures.

13. If the end retainer has been loosened only ½ turn, reinstall the caliper in the anchor plate without shoe and lining assemblies. Tighten the end retainer to 75–96 ft. lb. Install the parking brake lever on its keyed spline. The lever arm must point down and rearward. The parking brake cable will then pass freely under the axle. Tighten the retainer screw to 16–22 ft. lb. The parking brake lever must rotate freely after tightening the retainer screw. Remove the caliper from the anchor plate.

14. If new shoe and lining assemblies are to be installed, the piston must be screwed

back into the caliper bore, using Tool T75P-2588-B or equivalent to provide installation clearance. This tool requires a slight modification for use on Continental rear disc brakes. This modification will not prevent using the tool on prior year applications. New tools purchased from the Special Service Tool catalog under the T75P-2588-B number will already be modified. Remove the rotor, and install the caliper, less shoe and lining assemblies, in the anchor plate. While holding the shaft, rotate the tool handle counterclockwise until the tool is seated firmly against the piston. Now, loosen the handle about ¼ turn. While holding the handle, rotate the tool shaft clockwise until the piston is fully bottomed in its bore; the piston will continue to turn even after it becomes bottomed. When there is no further inward movement of the piston and the tool handle is rotated until there is firm seating force, the piston is bottomed. Remove the tool and the caliper from the anchor plate.

15. Lubricate anchor plate sliding ways with lithium or silicone grease. Use only specified grease because a lower temperature type of lubricant may melt and contaminate the brake pads. Use care to prevent any lubricant from getting on the braking surface.

16. Install the anti-rattle clip on the lower rail of the anchor plate.

17. Install inner brake shoe and lining assembly on the anchor plate with the lining toward the rotor.

18. Be sure shoes are installed in their original positions as marked for identification before removal.

19. Install rotor and two retainer nuts.

20. Install the correct hand outer brake shoe and lining assembly on the anchor plate with the lining toward the rotor and wear indicator toward the upper portion of the brake.

21. Install the flexible hose by placing a new washer on each side of the fitting outlet

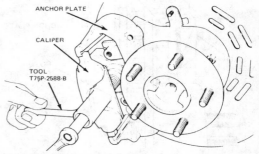

ANCHOR PLATE

CALIPER

TOOL
T75P-2588-B

Adjusting the piston depth

and inserting the attaching bolt through the washers and fitting. Tighten to 20–30 ft. lb.

22. Position the upper tab of the caliper housing on the anchor plate upper abutment surface.

23. Rotate the caliper housing until it is completely over the rotor. Use care so that the piston dust boot is not damaged.

24. Piston Position Adjustment: Pull the caliper outboard until the inner shoe and lining is firmly seated against the rotor, and measure the clearance between the outer shoe and caliper. The clearance must be $^1/_{32}$ inch to $^3/_{32}$ inch. If it is not, remove the caliper, then readjust the piston to obtain required gap. Follow the procedure given in Step 13, and rotate the shaft counterclockwise to narrow gap and clockwise to widen gap ($^1/_4$ turn of the piston moves it approximately $^1/_{16}$-inch).

CAUTION: *A clearance greater than $^3/_{32}$-inch may allow the adjuster to be pulled out of the piston when the service brake is applied. This will cause the parking brake mechanism to fail to adjust. It is then necessary to replace the piston/adjuster assembly following the procedures under Overhaul.*

25. Lubricate locating pins and inside of insulator with silicone grease.

26. Add one drop of Loctite® E0AC-19554-A or equivalent to locating pin threads.

27. Install the locating pins through caliper insulators and into the anchor plate; the pins must be hand inserted and hand started. Tighten to 29–37 ft. lb.

28. Connect the parking brake cable to the lever on the caliper.

29. Bleed the brake system. Replace rubber bleed screw cap after bleeding.

30. Fill the master cylinder as required to within $^1/_8$ inch of the top of the reservoir.

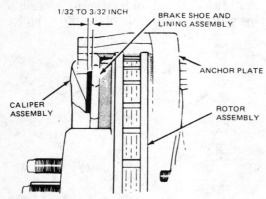

Checking lining clearance

31. Caliper Adjustment: With the engine running, pump the service brake lightly (approximately 14 lbs. pedal effort) about 40 times. Allow at least one second between pedal applications. As an alternative, with the engine Off, pump the service brake lightly (approximately 87 lbs. pedal effort) about 30 times. Now check the parking brake for excessive travel or very light effort. In either case, repeat pumping the service brake, or if necessary, check the parking brake cable for proper tension. The caliper levers must return to the Off position when the parking brake is released.

32. Install the wheel and tire assembly. Tighten the wheel lug nuts. Install the wheel cover. Remove the safety stands, and lower the vehicle.

33. Be sure a firm brake pedal application is obtained, and then road test for proper brake operation, including parking brakes.

OVERHAUL

All Models

1. Remove the caliper assembly from the vehicle as outlined.

2. Remove the caliper and retainer.

3. Lift out the operating shaft, thrust bearing, and balls.

4. Remove the thrust screw anti-rotation pin with a magnet or tweezers.

NOTE: *Some anti-rotation pins may be difficult to remove with a magnet or tweezers. In that case, use the following procedure.*

a. Adjust the piston out from the caliper bore using the modified piston adjusting tool. The piston should protrude from the housing at least one inch.

b. Push the piston back into the caliper housing with the adjusting tool. With the tool in position on the caliper, hold the tool shaft in place, and rotate the handle counterclockwise until the thrust screw clears the anti-rotation pin. Remove the thrust screw and the anti-rotation pin.

5. Remove the thrust screw by rotating it counterclockwise with a $^1/_4$ inch allen wrench.

6. Remove the piston adjuster assembly by installing Tool T75P-2588-A or equivalent through the back of the caliper housing and pushing the piston out.

CAUTION: *Use care not to damage the polished surface in the thrust screw bore, and do not press or attempt to move the adjuster can. It is a press fit in the piston.*

SILICONE LUBE
D7AZ-19A331-A

END RETAINED REMOVED

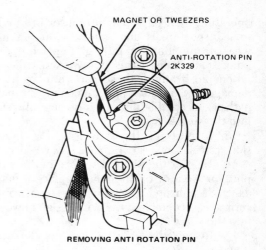

MAGNET OR TWEEZERS

ANTI-ROTATION PIN
2K329

REMOVING ANTI ROTATION PIN

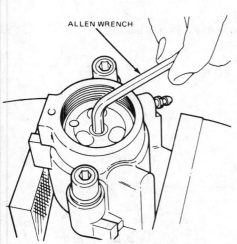

ALLEN WRENCH

REMOVING THRUST SCREW

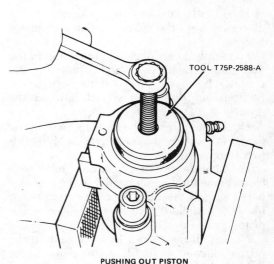

TOOL T75P-2588-A

PUSHING OUT PISTON

Servicing the caliper assembly

7. Remove and discard the piston seal, boot, thrust screw C-ring seal, end retainer O-ring seal, end retainer lip seal, and pin insulators.

8. Clean all metal parts with isopropyl alcohol. Use clean, dry, compressed air to clean out and dry the grooves and passages. Be sure the caliper bore and component parts are completely free of any foreign material.

9. Inspect the caliper bores for damage or excessive wear. The thrust screw bore must be smooth and free of pits. If the piston is pitted, scored, or the chrome plating is worn off, replace the piston/adjuster assembly.

10. The adjuster can must be bottomed in the piston to be properly seated and provide consistent brake function. If the adjuster can is loose in the piston, appears high in the piston, or is damaged, or if brake adjustment is regularly too tight, too loose, or nonfunctioning, replace the piston/adjuster assembly.

NOTE: *Do not attempt to service the adjuster at any time. When service is necessary, replace the piston/adjuster assembly.*

11. Check adjuster operation by first assembling the thrust screw into the piston/adjuster assembly, pulling the two pieces apart by hand approximately ¼ inch, and then releasing them. When pulling on the two pieces, the brass drive ring must remain stationary, causing the nut to rotate. When releasing the two parts, the nut must remain stationary, and the drive ring must rotate. If the action of the components does not follow this pattern, replace the piston/adjuster assembly.

12. Inspect ball pockets, threads, grooves, and bearing surfaces of the thrust screw and

operating shaft for wear, pitting, or brinnell-ing. Inspect balls and anti-rotation pin for wear, brinnelling, or pitting. Replace oper-ating shaft, balls, thrust screw, and anti-ro-tation pin if any of these parts are worn or damaged. A polished appearance on the ball paths is acceptable if there is no sign of wear into the surface.

13. Inspect the thrust bearing for corro-sion, pitting, or wear. Replace if necessary.

14. Inspect the bearing surface of the end plug for wear or brinnelling. Replace if nec-essary. A polished appearance on the bearing surface is acceptable if there is no sign of wear into the surface.

15. Inspect the lever for damage. Replace if necessary.

16. Lightly sand or wire brush any rust or corrosion from the caliper housing insulator bores.

17. Apply a coat of clean brake fluid to the new caliper piston seal, and install it in the cylinder bore. Be sure that the seal is not twisted and that it is seated fully in the groove.

18. Install a new dust boot by seating the flange squarely in the outer groove of the cal-iper bore.

19. Coat the piston/adjuster assembly with clean brake fluid, and install it in the cylinder bore. Spread the dust boot over the piston, like it is installed. Seat the dust boot in the piston groove.

20. Install the caliper in a vise and fill the piston/adjuster assembly with clean brake fluid to the bottom edge of the thrust screw bore.

21. Coat a new thrust screw O-ring seal with clean brake fluid, and install it in the groove in the thrust screw.

22. Install the thrust screw by turning it into the piston/adjuster assembly with a ¼ inch allen wrench until the top surface of the thrust screw is flush with the bottom of the threaded bore. Use care to avoid cutting the O-ring seal. Index the thrust screw, so that the notches on the thrust screw and caliper housing are aligned. Then install the anti-ro-tation pin.

NOTE: *The thrust screw and operating shaft are not interchangeable from side to side because of the ramp direction in the ball pockets. The pocket surface of the op-erating shaft and the thrust screw are stamped with the proper letter (R or L), in-dicating part usage.*

23. Place a ball in each of three pockets of

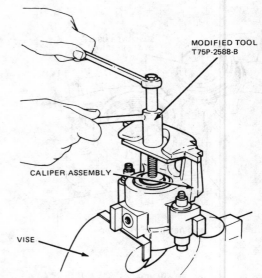

Bottoming the piston in the caliper

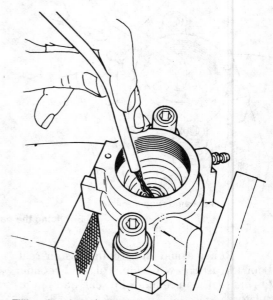

Filling the piston/adjuster assembly with clean fluid

the thrust screw, and apply a liberal amount of silicone grease on all components in the parking brake mechanism.

24. Install the operating shaft on the balls.

25. Coat the thrust bearing with silicone grease and install it on the operating shaft.

26. Install a new lip seal and O-ring on the end retainer.

27. Coat the O-ring seal and lip seal with a light film of silicone grease, and install the end retainer in the caliper. Hold the operat-ing shaft firmly seated against the internal mechanism while installing the end retainer

to prevent mislocation of the balls. If the lip seal is pushed out of position, reseat the seal. Tighten the end retainer to 75–95 ft. lb.

28. Install the parking brake lever on its keyed spline. The lever arm must point down and rearward. The parking brake cable will then pass freely under the axle. Tighten the lever retaining screw to 16–22 ft. lb. The parking brake lever must rotate freely after tightening.

29. Arrange the caliper in a vise and bottom the piston with modified Tool T75P-2588-B.

30. Install new pin insulators in the caliper housing. Check to see if both insulator flanges straddle the housing holes.

31. Install the caliper on the vehicle.

Disc Brake Pads
REMOVAL AND INSTALLATION
All Models

1. Remove the caliper as outlined earlier. In this case, however, it is not necessary to disconnect the brake line. Simply wire the caliper to the frame to prevent the brake line from breaking.

2. Remove the pads and inspect them. If they are worn to within ⅛ inch of the shoe surface, they must be replaced. Do not replace pads on just one side of the car. Uneven braking will result.

3. To install new pads, remove the disc and install the caliper without the pads. Use only the key to retain the caliper.

4. Seat the special tool firmly against the piston by holding the shaft and rotating the tool handle.

5. Loosen the handle one-quarter turn. Hold the handle and rotate the tool shaft clockwise until the caliper piston bottoms in the bore. It will continue to turn after it bottoms.

6. Rotate the handle until the piston is firmly seated.

7. Remove the caliper and install the disc.

8. Place the new inner brake pad on the anchor plate. Place the new outer pad in the caliper.

9. Reinstall the caliper according to the directions given earlier.

Brake Discs
REMOVAL AND INSTALLATION

1. Raise the car and support it. Remove the wheels.

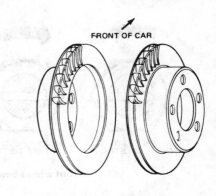

LEFT REAR ROTOR   RIGHT REAR ROTOR
Versailles rear rotor

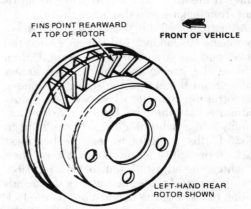

FINS POINT REARWARD AT TOP OF ROTOR   FRONT OF VEHICLE

LEFT-HAND REAR ROTOR SHOWN
1982 Continental rear rotor

2. Remove the caliper, as outlined earlier.

3. Remove the retaining bolts and remove the disc from the axle.

4. Inspect the disc for excessive rust, scoring or pitting. A certain amount of rust on the edge of the disc is normal. Refer to the specifications chart and measure the thickness of the disc, using a micrometer. If the disc is below specifications, replace it.

5. Reinstall the discs, keeping in mind that the two sides are not interchangeable. The words "left" and "right" are cast into the inner surface of the raised section of the disc. Proper reinstallation of the discs is important, since the cooling vanes cast into the disc must face in the direction of forward rotation on versailles, and opposite forward rotation on 1982 Continental.

6. Reinstall the caliper.

7. Install the wheels and lower the car.

Front Wheel Bearings
ADJUSTMENT

The front wheels each rotate on a set of opposed, tapered roller bearings as shown in the

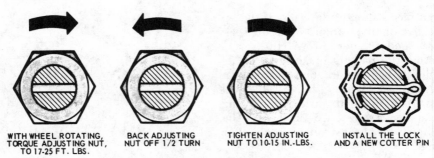

| WITH WHEEL ROTATING, TORQUE ADJUSTING NUT, TO 17-25 FT. LBS. | BACK ADJUSTING NUT OFF 1/2 TURN | TIGHTEN ADJUSTING NUT TO 10-15 IN.-LBS. | INSTALL THE LOCK AND A NEW COTTER PIN |

Front wheel bearing adjusting sequence

accompanying illustration. The grease retainer at the inside of the hub prevents lubricant from leaking into the brake drum.

Adjustment of the wheel bearings is accomplished as follows: Lift the car so that the wheel and tire are clear of the ground, then remove the grease cap and remove excess grease from the end of the spindle. Remove the cotter pin and nut lock shown in the illustration. Rotate the wheel, hub and drum assembly while tightening the adjusting nut to 17–25 ft. lbs. in order to seat the bearings. Back off the adjusting nut one half turn, then retighten the adjusting nut to 10–15 in. lbs. (*inch-pounds*). Locate the nut lock on the adjusting nut so that the castellations on the lock are lined up with the cotter pin hole in the spindle. Install a new cotter pin, bending the ends of the cotter pin around the castellated flange of the nut lock. Check the front wheel for proper rotation, then install the grease cap. If the wheel still does not rotate properly, inspect and clean or replace the wheel bearings and cups.

REMOVAL, REPACKING, AND INSTALLATION

Drum Brakes

The procedure for cleaning, replacing and adjusting front wheel bearings on vehicles equipped with self-adjusting drum brakes is as follows:

1. Taking proper safety precautions, raise the car until the wheel and tire clear the floor. Install jackstands under the lower control arms.

2. Remove the wheel cover. Remove the grease cap from the hub. Then remove the cotter pin, nut lock, adjusting nut, and flat washer from the spindle. Remove the outer bearing cone and roller assembly.

3. Pull the wheel, hub and drum assembly off the spindle. When encountering a brake drum that will not come off, disengage the adjusting lever from the adjusting screw by inserting a narrow screwdriver through the adjusting hole in the carrier plate. While the lever is disengaged, back off the adjusting screw with a brake adjusting tool. The self-adjusting mechanism will not function properly if the adjusting screw is burred, chipped, or otherwise damaged in the process, so exercise extreme care.

4. Remove the grease retainer and the inner bearing cone and roller assembly from the hub.

5. Clean all grease off from the inner and outer bearing cups with solvent. Inspect the cups for pits, scratches, or excessive wear. If the cups are damaged, remove them with a drift.

6. Clean the inner and outer cone and roller assemblies with solvent and shake them dry. If the cone and roller assemblies show excessive wear or damage, replace them with the bearing cups as a unit.

7. If the new grease retainer is of leather, soak it in light engine oil for 30 minutes, prior to installation. Wipe any excess from the metal portion of the retainer. Clean the spindle and the inside of the hub with solvent to thoroughly remove all old grease.

8. Covering the spindle with a clean cloth, brush all loose dirt and dust from the brake assembly. Remove the cloth carefully so as to not get dirt on the spindle.

9. If the inner and/or outer bearing cups were removed, install the replacement cups on the hub. Be sure that the cups seat properly in the hub.

10. It is imperative that all old grease be removed from the bearings and surrounding surfaces before repacking. The new lithium-base grease is not compatible with the sodium base grease used in the past.

11. Pack the inside of the hub with wheel bearing grease. Add grease to the hub until

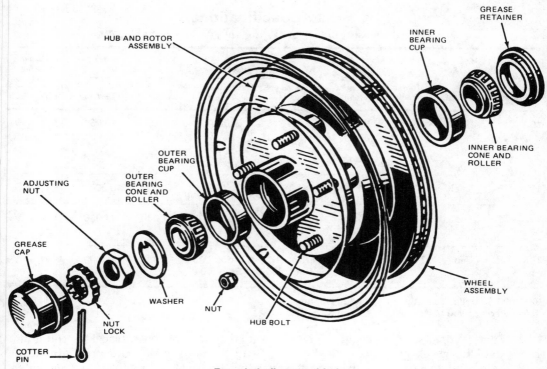

HUB AND ROTOR
ASSEMBLY

INNER
BEARING
CUP

GREASE
RETAINER

INNER BEARING
CONE AND
ROLLER

OUTER
BEARING
CUP

OUTER
BEARING
CONE AND
ROLLER

ADJUSTING
NUT

GREASE
CAP

NUT
LOCK

WASHER

NUT

HUB BOLT

WHEEL
ASSEMBLY

COTTER
PIN

Front hub disassembled

it is flush with the inside diameter of both bearing cups. Work as much grease as possible between the rollers and cages in the cone and roller assemblies. Lubricate the cone surfaces with grease.

12. Position the inner bearing cone and roller assembly in the inner cup. If a leather grease retainer has soaked for 30 minutes, wipe all excess from the metal portion of the retainer and install. Other grease retainers require a light film of grease on the lips before installation. Make sure that the retainer is properly seated.

13. Install the wheel, hub, and drum assembly on the wheel spindle. To prevent damage to the grease retainer and spindle threads, keep the hub centered on the spindle.

14. Install the outer bearing cone and roller assembly and the flat washer on the spindle. Install the adjusting nut.

15. Adjust the wheel bearings by tightening the adjusting nut to 17–25 ft. lbs. with the wheel rotating to seat the bearing. Then back off the adjusting nut ½ turn. Retighten the adjusting nut to 10–15 in. lbs. Install the locknut so that the castellations are aligned with the cotter pin hole. Install the cotter pin. Bend the ends of the cotter pin around the

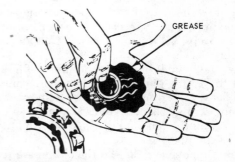

GREASE

Packing bearings

castellations of the locknut to prevent interference with the radio static collector in the grease cap. Install the grease cap.

16. Remove the adjusting hole cover from the carrier plate and, from the carrier plate side, turn the adjusting screw star wheel upward with a brake adjusting tool. Expand the brake shoes until a slight drag is felt with the drum rotating. Replace the adjusting hole cover.

17. Install the wheel cover.

Disc Brakes

The procedure for cleaning, repacking, and adjusting front wheel bearings on vehicles equipped with disc brakes is as follows:

Brake Specifications

All measurements given are (in.) unless noted

Year	Model	Lug Nut Torque (ft. lbs.)	Master Cylinder Bore	Brake Disc		Brake Drum		Minimum Lining Thickness	
				Minimum Thickness	Maximum Run-Out	Diameter	Max. Wear Limit	Front	Rear
1971	all	70–115	0.9375 (disc) 1.0 (drum)	.875	.0007	10.0	10.060	2/32	2/32
1972–75	all	70–115	1.00	1.180	.003	10.0①	10.060 ②	1/32	2/32
1976–78	all	70–115	1.00	Front 1.100 Rear .895	Front .003 Rear .004	11.030	11.090	1/32	2/32
1979–82	all	70–115	1.00	Front .972 Rear .895	Front .003 Rear .004	11.030	11.090	1/8	2/32

① 11.030 on police package cars, and all wagons
② 11.090 on police package cars, and all wagons

1. Taking proper safety precautions, raise the car until the wheel and tire clear the floor.

2. Remove the wheel cover. Remove the wheel and tire from the hub.

3. Remove the caliper from the disc and wire it to the underbody to prevent damage to the brake hose. For floating-caliper brakes, follow Steps 3, 4, 5, and 6 under "Caliper Assembly Service."

4. Remove the grease cap from the hub, and the cotter pin, nut lock, adjusting nut, and flat washer from the spindle. Remove the outer bearing cone and roller assembly.

5. Pull the hub and disc assembly off the wheel spindle.

6. Remove and discard the old grease retainer. Remove the inner bearing cone and roller assembly from the hub.

7. Follow Steps 5–10 of the "Removal, Repacking, and Installation" procedure for "Drum Brakes" as previously outlined.

8. Install the hub and disc on the wheel spindle. To prevent damage to the grease retainer and spindle threads, keep the hub centered on the spindle.

9. Install the outer bearing cone and roller assembly and the flat washer on the spindle. Install the adjusting nut.

10. Adjust the wheel bearings by torquing the adjusting nut to 17–25 ft. lbs. with the wheel rotating to seat the bearing. Then back off the adjusting nut ½ turn. Retighten the adjusting nut to 10–15 in. lbs. Install the locknut so that the castellations are aligned with the cotter pin hole. Install the cotter pin. Bend the ends of the cotter pin around the castellations of the locknut to prevent interference with the radio static collector in the grease cap. Install the grease cap.

NOTE: *New bolts must be used when servicing. The upper bolt must be tightened first. For floating-caliper units, follow Steps 19, 20, and 21 under "Caliper Assembly Service." For sliding-caliper units, follow Steps 12–19 under "Shoe and Lining Replacement."*

11. Install the wheel and tire on the hub.

12. Install the wheel cover.

PARKING BRAKE

Checking and Adjusting
REAR DRUM BRAKES

The parking brake should be checked for proper operation every 12 months or 12,000 miles and adjusted whenever there is slack in the cables. A cable with too much slack will not hold a vehicle on an incline which presents a serious safety hazard. Usually, a rear brake adjustment will restore parking brake efficiency, but if the cables appear loose or stretched when the parking brake is released, adjust as necessary.

The procedure for adjusting the parking brake on all pedal-actuated systems is as follows:

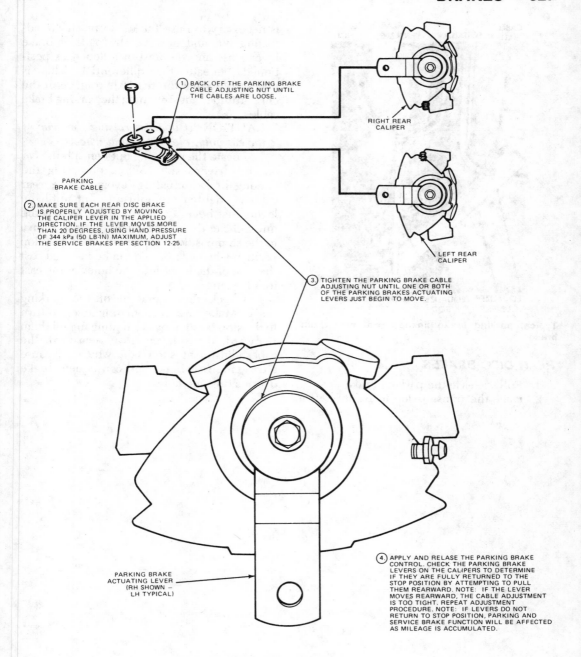

① BACK OFF THE PARKING BRAKE CABLE ADJUSTING NUT UNTIL THE CABLES ARE LOOSE.

RIGHT REAR CALIPER

PARKING BRAKE CABLE

② MAKE SURE EACH REAR DISC BRAKE IS PROPERLY ADJUSTED BY MOVING THE CALIPER LEVER IN THE APPLIED DIRECTION. IF THE LEVER MOVES MORE THAN 20 DEGREES, USING HAND PRESSURE OF 344 kPa (50 LB-IN) MAXIMUM, ADJUST THE SERVICE BRAKES PER SECTION 12-25.

LEFT REAR CALIPER

③ TIGHTEN THE PARKING BRAKE CABLE ADJUSTING NUT UNTIL ONE OR BOTH OF THE PARKING BRAKES ACTUATING LEVERS JUST BEGIN TO MOVE.

④ APPLY AND RELEASE THE PARKING BRAKE CONTROL. CHECK THE PARKING BRAKE LEVERS ON THE CALIPERS TO DETERMINE IF THEY ARE FULLY RETURNED TO THE STOP POSITION BY ATTEMPTING TO PULL THEM REARWARD. NOTE: IF THE LEVER MOVES REARWARD, THE CABLE ADJUSTMENT IS TOO TIGHT. REPEAT ADJUSTMENT PROCEDURE. NOTE: IF LEVERS DO NOT RETURN TO STOP POSITION, PARKING AND SERVICE BRAKE FUNCTION WILL BE AFFECTED AS MILEAGE IS ACCUMULATED.

PARKING BRAKE ACTUATING LEVER (RH SHOWN – LH TYPICAL)

PARKING BRAKE ADJUSTMENT - REAR DISC BRAKE

Parking brake adjustment on models with rear disc brakes

1. Fully release the parking brake.

2. Depress the parking brake pedal one notch from its normal released position. On vacuum release brakes, the first notch is approximately 2 in. of travel.

3. Taking proper safety precautions, raise the car and place the transmission in Neutral.

4. Loosen the equalizer locknut and turn the adjusting nut forward against the equalizer until moderate drag is felt when turning the rear wheels. Tighten the locknut.

5. Release the parking brake, making sure that the brake shoes return to the fully released position.

6. Lower the car and apply the parking brake. Under normal conditions, the third notch will hold the car if the brake is adjusted properly.

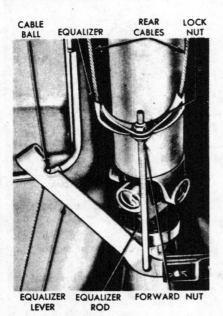

CABLE   EQUALIZER   REAR   LOCK
BALL   CABLES   NUT

EQUALIZER   EQUALIZER   FORWARD NUT
LEVER   ROD

**Typical parking brake linkage with rear drum
brakes**

REAR DISC BRAKES

1. Fully release the parking brake.
2. Place the transmission in Neutral. If it

is necessary to raise the car to reach the adjusting nut and observe the parking brake levers, use an axle hoist or a floor jack positioned beneath the differential. This is necessary so that the rear axle remains at the curb attitude, not stretching the parking brake cables.

CAUTION: *If you are raising the rear of the car only, block the front wheels.*

3. Locate the adjusting nut beneath the car on the driver's side. While observing the parking brake actuating levers on the rear calipers, tighten the adjusting nut until the levers just begin to move. Then, loosen the nut sufficiently for the levers to fully return to the stop position. The levers are in the stop position when a ¼ in. pin can be inserted past the side of the lever into the holes in the cast iron housing.

4. Check the operation of the parking brake. Make sure the actuating levers return to the stop position by attempting to pull them rearward. If the lever moves rearward, the cable adjustment is too tight, which will cause a dragging rear brake and consequent brake overheating and fade.

Body

10

You can repair most minor auto body damage yourself. Minor damage usually falls into one of several categories: (1) small scratches and dings in the paint that can be repaired without the use of body filler, (2) deep scratches and dents that require body filler, but do not require pulling, or hammering metal back into shape and (3) rust-out repairs. The repair sequences illustrated in this chapter are typical of these types of repairs. If you want to get involved in more complicated repairs including pulling or hammering sheet metal back into shape, you will probably need more detailed instructions. Chilton's *Minor Auto Body Repair, 2nd Edition* is a comprehensive guide to repairing auto body damage yourself.

TOOLS AND SUPPLIES

The list of tools and equipment you may need to fix minor body damage ranges from very basic hand tools to a wide assortment of specialized body tools. Most minor scratches, dings and rust holes can be fixed using an electric drill, wire wheel or grinder attachment, half-round plastic file, sanding block, various grades of sandpaper (#36, which is coarse through #600, which is fine) in both wet and dry types, auto body plastic,

primer, touch-up paint, spreaders, newspaper and masking tape.

Most manufacturers of auto body repair products began supplying materials to professionals. Their knowledge of the best, most-used products has been translated into body repair kits for the do-it-yourselfer. Kits are available from a number of manufacturers and contain the necessary materials in the required amounts for the repair identified on the package.

Kits are available for a wide variety of uses, including:

- Rusted out metal
- All purpose kit for dents and holes
- Dents and deep scratches
- Fiberglass repair kit
- Epoxy kit for restyling.

Kits offer the advantage of buying what you need for the job. There is little waste and little chance of materials going bad from not being used. The same manufacturers also merchandise all of the individual products used—spreaders, dent pullers, fiberglass cloth, polyester resin, cream hardener, body filler, body files, sandpaper, sanding discs and holders, primer, spray paint, etc.

CAUTION: *Most of the products you will be using contain harmful chemicals, so be extremely careful. Always read the complete label before opening the containers. When* *you put them away for future use, be sure they are out of children's reach!*

Most auto body repair kits contain all the materials you need to do the job right in the kit. So, if you have a small rust spot or dent you want to fix, check the contents of the kit before you run out and buy any additional tools.

ALIGNING BODY PANELS

Doors

There are several methods of adjusting doors. Your vehicle will probably use one of those illustrated.

Whenever a door is removed and is to be reinstalled, you should matchmark the position of the hinges on the door pillars. The holes of the hinges and/or the hinge attaching points are usually oversize to permit alignment of doors. The striker plate is also moveable, through oversize holes, permitting up-and-down, in-and-out and fore-and-aft movement. Fore-and-aft movement is made by adding or subtracting shims from behind the striker and pillar post. The striker should be adjusted so that the door closes fully and remains closed, yet enters the lock freely.

DOOR HINGES

Don't try to cover up poor door adjustment with a striker plate adjustment. The gap on each side of the door should be equal and uniform and there should be no metal-to-metal contact as the door is opened or closed.

1. Determine which hinge bolts must be loosened to move the door in the desired direction.

2. Loosen the hinge bolt(s) just enough to allow the door to be moved with a padded pry bar.

3. Move the door a small amount and check the fit, after tightening the bolts. Be sure that there is no bind or interference with adjacent panels.

4. Repeat this until the door is properly positioned, and tighten all the bolts securely.

Hood, Trunk or Tailgate

As with doors, the outline of hinges should be scribed before removal. The hood and trunk can be aligned by loosening the hinge bolts in their slotted mounting holes and moving the hood or trunk lid as necessary.

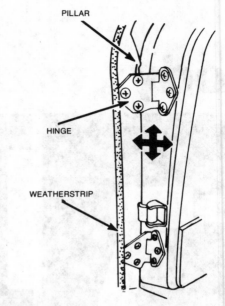

Door hinge adjustment

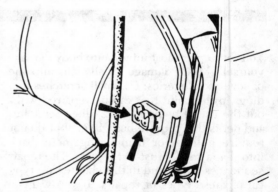

Move the door striker as indicated by arrows

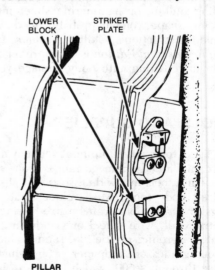

Striker plate and lower block

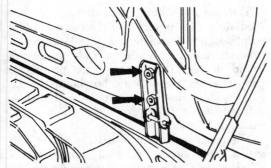

Loosen the hinge boots to permit fore-and-aft and horizontal adjustment

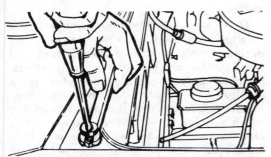

The hood is adjusted vertically by stop-screws at the front and/or rear

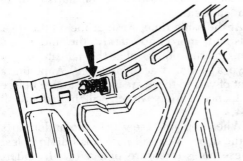

The hood pin can be adjusted for proper lock engagement

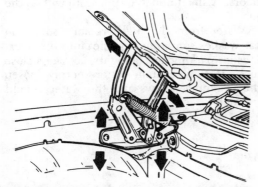

The height of the hood at the rear is adjusted by loosening the bolts that attach the hinge to the body and moving the hood up or down

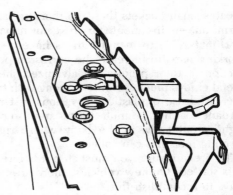

The base of the hood lock can also be repositioned slightly to give more positive lock engagement

The hood and trunk have adjustable catch locations to regulate lock engagement. Bumpers at the front and/or rear of the hood provide a vertical adjustment and the hood lockpin can be adjusted for proper engagement.

The tailgate on the station wagon can be adjusted by loosening the hinge bolts in their slotted mounting holes and moving the tailgate on its hinges. The latchplate and latch striker at the bottom of the tailgate opening can be adjusted to stop rattle. An adjustable bumper is located on each side.

RUST, UNDERCOATING, AND RUSTPROOFING

Rust

Rust is an electrochemical process. It works on ferrous metals (iron and steel) from the inside out due to exposure of unprotected surfaces to air and moisture. The possibility of rust exists practically nationwide—anywhere humidity, industrial pollution or chemical salts are present, rust can form. In coastal areas, the problem is high humidity and salt air; in snowy areas, the problem is chemical salt (de-icer) used to keep the roads clear, and in industrial areas, sulphur dioxide is present in the air from industrial pollution and is changed to sulphuric acid when it rains. The rusting process is accelerated by high temperatures, especially in snowy areas, when vehicles are driven over slushy roads and then left overnight in a heated garage.

Automotive styling also can be a contributor to rust formation. Spot welding of panels creates small pockets that trap moisture and form an environment for rust formation. Fortunately, auto manufacturers have been working hard to increase the corrosion protection of their products. Galvanized sheet metal enjoys much wider use, along with the increased use of plastic and various rust retardant coatings. Manufacturers are also designing out areas in the body where rust-forming moisture can collect.

To prevent rust, you must stop it before it gets started. On new vehicles, there are two ways to accomplish this.

First, the car or truck should be treated with a commercial rustproofing compound. There are many different brands of franchised rustproofers, but most processes involve spraying a waxy "self-healing" compound under the chassis, inside rocker panels, inside doors and fender liners and similar places where rust is likely to form. Prices for a quality rustproofing job range from $100–$250, depending on the area, the brand name and the size of the vehicle.

Ideally, the vehicle should be rustproofed as soon as possible following the purchase. The surfaces of the car or truck have begun to oxidize and deteriorate during shipping. In addition, the car may have sat on a dealer's lot or on a lot at the factory, and once the rust has progressed past the stage of light, powdery surface oxidation rustproofing is not likely to be worthwhile. Professional rustproofers feel that once rust has formed, rustproofing will simply seal in moisture already present. Most franchised rustproofing operations offer a 3–5 year warranty against rust-through, but will not support that warranty if the rustproofing is not applied within three months of the date of manufacture.

Undercoating should not be mistaken for rustproofing. Undercoating is a black, tarlike substance that is applied to the underside of a vehicle. Its basic function is to deaden noises that are transmitted from under the car. It simply cannot get into the crevices and seams where moisture tends to collect. In fact, it may clog up drainage holes and ventilation passages. Some undercoatings also tend to crack or peel with age and only create more moisture and corrosion attracting pockets.

The second thing you should do immediately after purchasing the car is apply a paint sealant. A sealant is a petroleum based product marketed under a wide variety of brand names. It has the same protective properties as a good wax, but bonds to the paint with a chemically inert layer that seals it from the air. If air can't get at the surface, oxidation cannot start.

The paint sealant kit consists of a base coat and a conditioning coat that should be applied every 6–8 months, depending on the manufacturer. The base coat must be applied before waxing, or the wax must first be removed.

Third, keep a garden hose handy for your car in winter. Use it a few times on nice days during the winter for underneath areas, and it will pay big dividends when spring arrives. Spraying under the fenders and other areas which even car washes don't reach will help remove road salt, dirt and other build-ups which help breed rust. Adjust the nozzle to a high-force spray. An old brush will help break up residue, permitting it to be washed away more easily.

It's a somewhat messy job, but worth it in the long run because rust often starts in those hidden areas.

At the same time, wash grime off the door sills and, more importantly, the under portions of the doors, plus the tailgate if you have a station wagon or truck. Applying a coat of wax to those areas at least once before and once during winter will help fend off rust.

When applying the wax to the under parts of the doors, you will note small drain holes. These holes often are plugged with undercoating or dirt. Make sure they are cleaned out to prevent water build-up inside the doors. A small punch or penknife will do the job.

Water from the high-pressure sprays in car washes sometimes can get into the housings for parking and taillights, so take a close look. If they contain water merely loosen the retaining screws and the water should run out.

Repairing Scratches and Small Dents

Step 1. This dent (arrow) is typical of a deep scratch or minor dent. If deep enough, the dent or scratch can be pulled out or hammered out from behind. In this case no straightening is necessary

Step 2. Using an 80-grit grinding disc on an electric drill grind the paint from the surrounding area down to bare metal. This will provide a rough surface for the body filler to grab

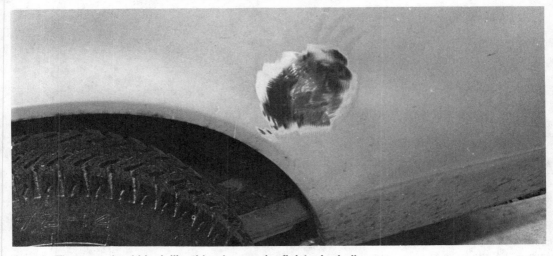

Step 3. The area should look like this when you're finished grinding

Step 4. Mix the body filler and cream hardener according to the directions

Step 5. Spread the body filler evenly over the entire area. Be sure to cover the area completely

Step 6. Let the body filler dry until the surface can just be scratched with your fingernail

Step 7. Knock the high spots from the body filler with a body file

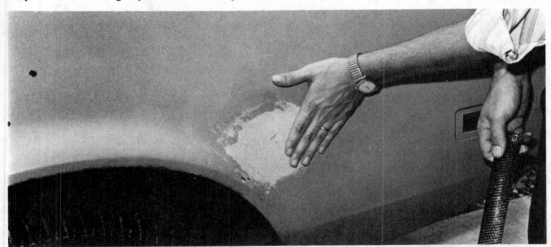

Step 8. Check frequently with the palm of your hand for high and low spots. If you wind up with low spots, you may have to apply another layer of filler

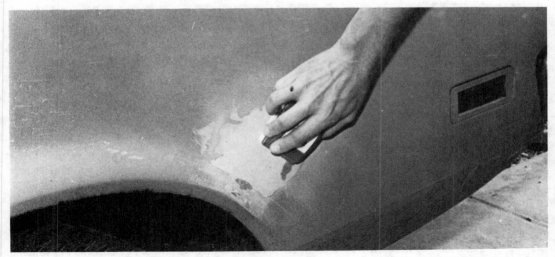

Step 9. Block sand the entire area with 320 grit paper

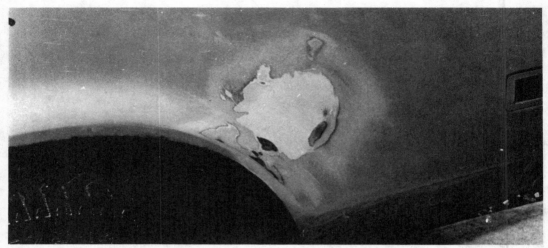

Step 10. When you're finished, the repair should look like this. Note the sand marks extending 2—3 inches out from the repaired area

Step 11. Prime the entire area with automotive primer

Step 12. The finished repair ready for the final paint coat. Note that the primer has covered the sanding marks (see Step 10). A repair of this size should be able to be spotpainted with good results

REPAIRING RUST HOLES

One thing you have to remember about rust: even if you grind away all the rusted metal in a panel, and repair the area with any of the kits available, *eventually* the rust will return. There are two reasons for this. One, rust is a chemical reaction that causes pressure under the repair from the inside out. That's how the blisters form. Two, the back side of the panel (and the repair) is wide open to moisture, and unpainted body filler acts like a sponge. That's why the best solution to rust problems is to remove the rusted panel and install a new one or have the rusted area cut out and a new piece of sheet metal welded in its place. The trouble with welding is the expense; sometimes it will cost more than the car or truck is worth.

One of the better solutions to do-it-yourself rust repair is the process using a fiberglass cloth repair kit (shown here). This will give a strong repair that resists cracking and moisture and is relatively easy to use. It can be used on large or small holes and also can be applied over contoured surfaces.

Step 1. Rust areas such as this are common and are easily fixed

Step 2. Grind away all traces of rust with a 24-grit grinding disc. Be sure to grind back 3—4 inches from the edge of the hole down to bare metal and be sure all traces of rust are removed

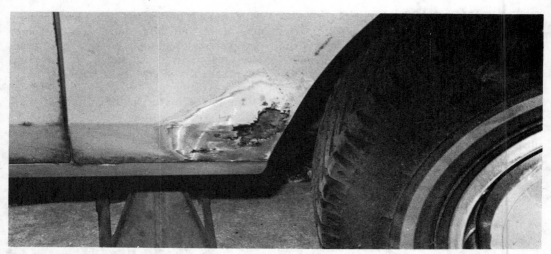

Step 3. Be sure all rust is removed from the edges of the metal. The edges must be ground back to un-rusted metal

Step 4. If you are going to use release film, cut a piece about 2″ larger than the area you have sanded. Place the film over the repair and mark the sanded area on the film. Avoid any unnecessary wrinkling of the film

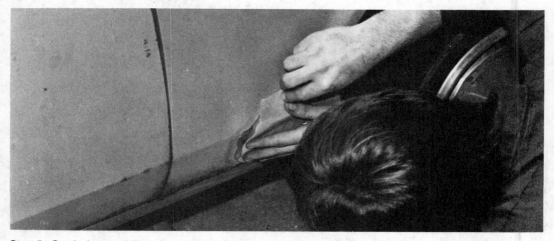

Step 5. Cut 2 pieces of fiberglass matte. One piece should be about 1″ smaller than the sanded area and the second piece should be 1″ smaller than the first. Use sharp scissors to avoid loose ends

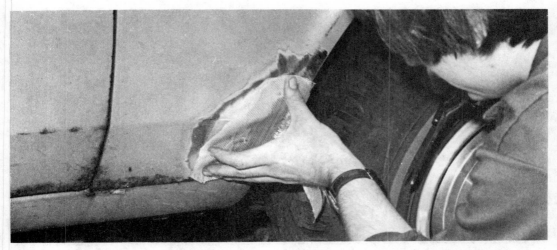

Step 6. Check the dimensions of the release film and cloth by holding them up to the repair area

Step 7. Mix enough repair jelly and cream hardener in the mixing tray to saturate the fiberglass material or fill the repair area. Follow the directions on the container

Step 8. Lay the release sheet on a flat surface and spread an even layer of filler, large enough to cover the repair. Lay the smaller piece of fiberglass cloth in the center of the sheet and spread another layer of repair jelly over the fiberglass cloth. Repeat the operation for the larger piece of cloth. If the fiberglass cloth is not used, spread the repair jelly on the release film, concentrated in the middle of the repair

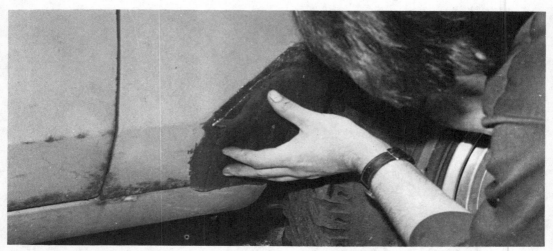

Step 9. Place the repair material over the repair area, with the release film facing outward

Step 10. Use a spreader and work from the center outward to smooth the material, following the body contours. Be sure to remove all air bubbles

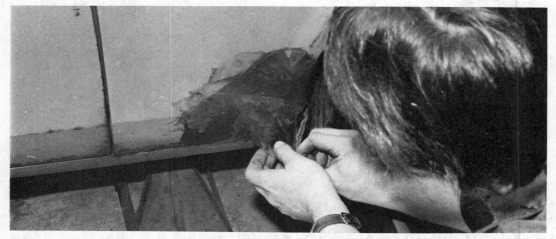

Step 11. Wait until the repair has dried tack-free and peel off the release sheet. The ideal working temperature is 65—90° F. Cooler or warmer temperatures or high humidity may require additional curing time

Step 12. Sand and feather-edge the entire area. The initial sanding can be done with a sanding disc on an electric drill if care is used. Finish the sanding with a block sander

Step 13. When the area is sanded smooth, mix some topcoat and hardener and apply it directly with a spreader. This will give a smooth finish and prevent the glass matte from showing through the paint

Step 14. Block sand the topcoat with finishing sandpaper

Step 15. To finish this repair, grind out the surface rust along the top edge of the rocker panel

Step 16. Mix some more repair jelly and cream hardener and apply it directly over the surface

Step 17. When it dries tack-free, block sand the surface smooth

Step 18. If necessary, mask off adjacent panels and spray the entire repair with primer. You are now ready for a color coat

AUTO BODY CARE

There are hundreds—maybe thousands—of products on the market, all designed to protect or aid your car's finish in some manner. There are as many different products as there are ways to use them, but they all have one thing in common—the surface must be clean.

Washing

The primary ingredient for washing your car is water, preferably "soft" water. In many areas of the country, the local water supply is "hard" containing many minerals. The little rings or film that is left on your car's surface after it has dried is the result of "hard" water.

Since you usually can't change the local water supply, the next best thing is to dry the surface before it has a chance to dry itself.

Into the water you usually add soap. Don't use detergents or common, coarse soaps. Your car's paint never truly dries out, but is always evaporating residual oils into the air. Harsh detergents will remove these oils, causing the paint to dry faster than normal. Instead use warm water and a non-detergent soap made especially for waxed surfaces or a liquid soap made for waxed surfaces or a liquid soap made for washing dishes by hand.

Other products that can be used on painted surfaces include baking soda or plain soda water for stubborn dirt.

Wash the car completely, starting at the top, and rinse it completely clean. Abrasive grit should be loaded off under water pressure; scrubbing grit off will scratch the finish. The best washing tool is a sponge, cleaning mitt or soft towel. Whichever you choose, replace it often as each tends to absorb grease and dirt.

Other ways to get a better wash include:

• Don't wash your car in the sun or when the finish is hot.

• Use water pressure to remove caked-on dirt.

• Remove tree-sap and bird effluence immediately. Such substances will eat through wax, polish and paint.

One of the best implements to dry your car is a turkish towel or an old, soft bath towel. Anything with a deep nap will hold any dirt in suspension and not grind it into the paint.

Harder cloths will only grind the grit into the paint making more scratches. Always start drying at the top, followed by the hood and trunk and sides. You'll find there's always more dirt near the rocker panels and wheelwells which will wind up on the rest of the car if you dry these areas first.

Cleaners, Waxes and Polishes

Before going any farther you should know the function of various products.

Cleaners—remove the top layer of dead pigment or paint.

Rubbing or polishing compounds—used to remove stubborn dirt, get rid of minor scratches, smooth away imperfections and partially restore badly weathered paint.

Polishes—contain no abrasives or waxes; they shine the paint by adding oils to the paint.

Waxes—are a protective coating for the polish.

CLEANERS AND COMPOUNDS

Before you apply any wax, you'll have to remove oxidation, road film and other types of pollutants that washing alone will not remove.

The paint on your car never dries completely. There are always residual oils evaporating from the paint into the air. When enough oils are present in the paint, it has a healthy shine (gloss). When too many oils evaporate the paint takes on a whitish cast known as oxidation. The idea of polishing and waxing is to keep enough oil present in the painted surface to prevent oxidation; but when it occurs, the only recourse is to remove the top layer of "dead" paint, exposing the healthy paint underneath.

Products to remove oxidation and road film are sold under a variety of generic names—polishes, cleaner, rubbing compound, cleaner/polish, polish/cleaner, self-polishing wax, pre-wax cleaner, finish restorer and many more. Regardless of name there are two types of cleaners—abrasive cleaners (sometimes called polishing or rubbing compounds) that remove oxidation by grinding away the top layer of "dead" paint, or chemical cleaners that dissolve the "dead" pigment, allowing it to be wiped away.

Abrasive cleaners, by their nature, leave thousands of minute scratches in the finish, which must be polished out later. These should only be used in extreme cases, but are usually the only thing to use on badly oxidized paint finishes. Chemical cleaners are much milder but are not strong enough for severe cases of oxidation or weathered paint.

The most popular cleaners are liquid or paste abrasive polishing and rubbing compounds. Polishing compounds have a finer abrasive grit for medium duty work. Rubbing compounds are a coarser abrasive and for heavy duty work. Unless you are familiar with how to use compounds, be very careful. Excessive rubbing with any type of compound or cleaner can grind right through the paint to primer or bare metal. Follow the directions on the container—depending on type, the cleaner may or may not be OK for your paint. For example, some cleaners are not formulated for acrylic lacquer finishes.

When a small area needs compounding or heavy polishing, it's best to do the job by hand. Some people prefer a powered buffer for large areas. Avoid cutting through the paint along styling edges on the body. Small, hand operations where the compound is applied and rubbed using cloth folded into a thick ball allow you to work in straight lines along such edges.

To avoid cutting through on the edges when using a power buffer, try masking tape. Just cover the edge with tape while using power. Then finish the job by hand with the tape removed. Even then work carefully. The paint tends to be a lot thinner along the sharp ridges stamped into the panels.

Whether compounding by machine or by hand, only work on a small area and apply the compound sparingly. If the materials are spread too thin, or allowed to sit too long, they dry out. Once dry they lose the ability to deliver a smooth, clean finish. Also, dried out polish tends to cause the buffer to stick in one spot. This in turn can burn or cut through the finish.

WAXES AND POLISHES

Your car's finish can be protected in a number of ways. A cleaner/wax or polish/cleaner followed by wax or variations of each all provide good results. The two-step approach (polish followed by wax) is probably slightly better but consumes more time and effort. Properly fed with oils, your paint should never need cleaning, but despite the best polishing job, it won't last unless it's protected with wax. Without wax, polish must be renewed at least once a month to prevent oxidation. Years ago (some still swear by it today), the best wax was made from the Brazilian palm, the Carnuba, favored for its vegetable base and high melting point. However, modern synthetic waxes are harder, which means they protect against moisture better, and chemically inert silicone is used for a long lasting protection. The only problem with silicone wax is that it penetrates all layers of paint. To repaint or touch up a panel or car protected by silicone wax, you have to completely strip the finish to avoid "fish-eyes."

Under normal conditions, silicone waxes will last 4–6 months, but you have to be careful of wax build-up from too much waxing. Too thick a coat of wax is just as bad as no wax at all; it stops the paint from breathing.

Combination cleaners/waxes have become popular lately because they remove the old layer of wax plus light oxidation, while putting on a fresh coat of wax at the same time. Some cleaners/waxes contain abrasive cleaners which require caution, although many cleaner/waxes use a chemical cleaner.

Applying Wax or Polish

You may view polishing and waxing your car as a pleasant way to spend an afternoon, or as a boring chore, but it has to be done to keep the paint on your car. Caring for the paint doesn't require special tools, but you should follow a few rules.

1. Use a good quality wax.

2. Before applying any wax or polish, be sure the surface is completely clean. Just because the car looks clean, doesn't mean it's ready for polish or wax.

3. If the finish on your car is weathered, dull, or oxidized, it will probably have to be compounded to remove the old or oxidized paint. If the paint is simply dulled from lack of care, one of the non-abrasive cleaners known as polishing compounds will do the trick. If the paint is severely scratched or really dull, you'll probably have to use a rubbing compound to prepare the finish for waxing. If you're not sure which one to use, use the polishing compound, since you can easily ruin the finish by using too strong a compound.

4. Don't apply wax, polish or compound in direct sunlight, even if the directions on the can say you can. Most waxes will not cure properly in bright sunlight and you'll probably end up with a blotchy looking finish.

5. Don't rub the wax off too soon. The result will be a wet, dull looking finish. Let the wax dry thoroughly before buffing it off.

6. A constant debate among car enthusiasts is how wax should be applied. Some maintain pastes or liquids should be applied in a circular motion, but body shop experts have long thought that this approach results in barely detectable circular abrasions, especially on cars that are waxed frequently. They advise rubbing in straight lines, especially if any kind of cleaner is involved.

7. If an applicator is not supplied with the wax, use a piece of soft cheesecloth or very soft lint-free material. The same applies to buffing the surface.

SPECIAL SURFACES

One-step combination cleaner and wax formulas shouldn't be used on many of the special surfaces which abound on cars. The one-step materials contain abrasives to achieve a clean surface under the wax top coat. The abrasives are so mild that you could clean a car every week for a couple of years without fear of rubbing through the paint. But this same level of abrasiveness might, through repeated use, damage decals used for special trim effects. This includes wide stripes, wood-grain trim and other appliques.

Painted plastics must be cleaned with care. If a cleaner is too aggressive it will cut through the paint and expose the primer. If bright trim such as polished aluminum or chrome is painted, cleaning must be performed with even greater care. If rubbing compound is being used, it will cut faster than polish.

Abrasive cleaners will dull an acrylic finish. The best way to clean these newer finishes is with a non-abrasive liquid polish. Only dirt and oxidation, not paint, will be removed.

Taking a few minutes to read the instructions on the can of polish or wax will help prevent making serious mistakes. Not all preparations will work on all surfaces. And some are intended for power application while others will only work when applied by hand.

Don't get the idea that just pouring on some polish and then hitting it with a buffer will suffice. Power equipment speeds the operation. But it also adds a measure of risk. It's very easy to damage the finish if you use the wrong methods or materials.

Caring for Chrome

Read the label on the container. Many products are formulated specifically for chrome, but others contain abrasives that will scratch the chrome finish. If it isn't recommended for chrome, don't use it.

Never use steel wool or kitchen soap pads to clean chrome. Be careful not to get chrome cleaner on paint or interior vinyl surfaces. If you do, get it off immediately.

Troubleshooting

This section is designed to aid in the quick, accurate diagnosis of automotive problems. While automotive repairs can be made by many people, accurate troubleshooting is a rare skill for the amateur and professional alike.

In its simplest state, troubleshooting is an exercise in logic. It is essential to realize that an automobile is really composed of a series of systems. Some of these systems are interrelated; others are not. Automobiles operate within a framework of logical rules and physical laws, and the key to troubleshooting is a good understanding of all the automotive systems.

This section breaks the car or truck down into its component systems, allowing the problem to be isolated. The charts and diagnostic road maps list the most common problems and the most probable causes of trouble. Obviously it would be impossible to list every possible problem that could happen along with every possible cause, but it will locate MOST problems and eliminate a lot of unnecessary guesswork. The systematic format will locate problems within a given system, but, because many automotive systems are interrelated, the solution to your particular problem may be found in a number of systems on the car or truck.

USING THE TROUBLESHOOTING CHARTS

This book contains all of the specific information that the average do-it-yourself mechanic needs to repair and maintain his or her car or truck. The troubleshooting charts are designed to be used in conjunction with the specific procedures and information in the text. For instance, troubleshooting a point-type ignition system is fairly standard for all models, but you may be directed to the text to find procedures for troubleshooting an individual type of electronic ignition. You will also have to refer to the specification charts throughout the book for specifications applicable to your car or truck.

TOOLS AND EQUIPMENT

The tools illustrated in Chapter 1 (plus two more diagnostic pieces) will be adequate to troubleshoot most problems. The two other tools needed are a voltmeter and an ohmmeter. These can be purchased separately or in combination, known as a VOM meter.

In the event that other tools are required, they will be noted in the procedures.

Troubleshooting Engine Problems

See Chapters 2, 3, 4 for more information and service procedures.

Index to Systems

System	To Test	Group
Battery	Engine need not be running	1
Starting system	Engine need not be running	2
Primary electrical system	Engine need not be running	3
Secondary electrical system	Engine need not be running	4
Fuel system	Engine need not be running	5
Engine compression	Engine need not be running	6
Engine vacuum	Engine must be running	7
Secondary electrical system	Engine must be running	8
Valve train	Engine must be running	9
Exhaust system	Engine must be running	10
Cooling system	Engine must be running	11
Engine lubrication	Engine must be running	12

Index to Problems

Problem: Symptom	Begin at Specific Diagnosis, Number
Engine Won't Start:	
Starter doesn't turn	1.1, 2.1
Starter turns, engine doesn't	2.1
Starter turns engine very slowly	1.1, 2.4
Starter turns engine normally	3.1, 4.1
Starter turns engine very quickly	6.1
Engine fires intermittently	4.1
Engine fires consistently	5.1, 6.1
Engine Runs Poorly:	
Hard starting	3.1, 4.1, 5.1, 8.1
Rough idle	4.1, 5.1, 8.1
Stalling	3.1, 4.1, 5.1, 8.1
Engine dies at high speeds	4.1, 5.1
Hesitation (on acceleration from standing stop)	5.1, 8.1
Poor pickup	4.1, 5.1, 8.1
Lack of power	3.1, 4.1, 5.1, 8.1
Backfire through the carburetor	4.1, 8.1, 9.1
Backfire through the exhaust	4.1, 8.1, 9.1
Blue exhaust gases	6.1, 7.1
Black exhaust gases	5.1
Running on (after the ignition is shut off)	3.1, 8.1
Susceptible to moisture	4.1
Engine misfires under load	4.1, 7.1, 8.4, 9.1
Engine misfires at speed	4.1, 8.4
Engine misfires at idle	3.1, 4.1, 5.1, 7.1, 8.4

Sample Section

Test and Procedure	Results and Indications	Proceed to
4.1—Check for spark: Hold each spark plug wire approximately ¼" from ground with gloves or a heavy, dry rag. Crank the engine and observe the spark.	→ If no spark is evident:	4.2
	→ If spark is good in some cases:	4.3
	→ If spark is good in all cases:	4.6

Specific Diagnosis

This section is arranged so that following each test, instructions are given to proceed to another, until a problem is diagnosed.

Section 1—Battery

Test and Procedure	Results and Indications	Proceed to
1.1—Inspect the battery visually for case condition (corrosion, cracks) and water level.	If case is cracked, replace battery:	**1.4**
	If the case is intact, remove corrosion with a solution of baking soda and water (**CAUTION:** *do not get the solution into the battery*), and fill with water:	**1.2**

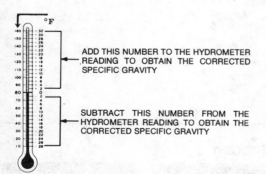

DIRT ON TOP OF BATTERY
PLUGGED VENT
CORROSION
LOOSE CABLE OR POSTS
CRACKS
LOW WATER LEVEL

Inspect the battery case

Test and Procedure	Results and Indications	Proceed to
1.2—Check the battery cable connections: Insert a screwdriver between the battery post and the cable clamp. Turn the headlights on high beam, and observe them as the screwdriver is gently twisted to ensure good metal to metal contact.	If the lights brighten, remove and clean the clamp and post; coat the post with petroleum jelly, install and tighten the clamp:	**1.4**
	If no improvement is noted:	**1.3**

TESTING BATTERY CABLE CONNECTIONS USING A SCREWDRIVER

Test and Procedure	Results and Indications	Proceed to
1.3—Test the state of charge of the battery using an individual cell tester or hydrometer.	If indicated, charge the battery. **NOTE:** *If no obvious reason exists for the low state of charge (i.e., battery age, prolonged storage), proceed to:*	**1.4**

°F

ADD THIS NUMBER TO THE HYDROMETER READING TO OBTAIN THE CORRECTED SPECIFIC GRAVITY

SUBTRACT THIS NUMBER FROM THE HYDROMETER READING TO OBTAIN THE CORRECTED SPECIFIC GRAVITY

Specific Gravity (@ 80° F.)

Minimum	Battery Charge
1.260	. . . . 100% Charged
1.230	. . . . 75% Charged
1.200	. . . . 50% Charged
1.170	. . . . 25% Charged
1.140	. . . . Very Little Power Left
1.110	. . . . Completely Discharged

The effects of temperature on battery specific gravity (left) and amount of battery charge in relation to specific gravity (right)

Test and Procedure	Results and Indications	Proceed to
1.4—Visually inspect battery cables for cracking, bad connection to ground, or bad connection to starter.	If necessary, tighten connections or replace the cables:	**2.1**

Section 2—Starting System
See Chapter 3 for service procedures

Test and Procedure	Results and Indications	Proceed to

Note: Tests in Group 2 are performed with coil high tension lead disconnected to prevent accidental starting.

Test and Procedure	Results and Indications	Proceed to
2.1—Test the starter motor and solenoid: Connect a jumper from the battery post of the solenoid (or relay) to the starter post of the solenoid (or relay).	If starter turns the engine normally:	**2.2**
	If the starter buzzes, or turns the engine very slowly:	**2.4**
	If no response, replace the solenoid (or relay).	**3.1**
	If the starter turns, but the engine doesn't, ensure that the flywheel ring gear is intact. If the gear is undamaged, replace the starter drive.	**3.1**
2.2—Determine whether ignition override switches are functioning properly (clutch start switch, neutral safety switch), by connecting a jumper across the switch(es), and turning the ignition switch to "start".	If starter operates, adjust or replace switch:	**3.1**
	If the starter doesn't operate:	**2.3**
2.3—Check the ignition switch "start" position: Connect a 12V test lamp or voltmeter between the starter post of the solenoid (or relay) and ground. Turn the ignition switch to the "start" position, and jiggle the key.	If the lamp doesn't light or the meter needle doesn't move when the switch is turned, check the ignition switch for loose connections, cracked insulation, or broken wires. Repair or replace as necessary:	**3.1**
	If the lamp flickers or needle moves when the key is jiggled, replace the ignition switch.	**3.3**

Checking the ignition switch "start" position

STARTER RELAY (IF EQUIPPED)

Test and Procedure	Results and Indications	Proceed to
2.4—Remove and bench test the starter, according to specifications in the engine electrical section.	If the starter does not meet specifications, repair or replace as needed:	**3.1**
	If the starter is operating properly:	**2.5**
2.5—Determine whether the engine can turn freely: Remove the spark plugs, and check for water in the cylinders. Check for water on the dipstick, or oil in the radiator. Attempt to turn the engine using an 18″ flex drive and socket on the crankshaft pulley nut or bolt.	If the engine will turn freely only with the spark plugs out, and hydrostatic lock (water in the cylinders) is ruled out, check valve timing:	**9.2**
	If engine will not turn freely, and it is known that the clutch and transmission are free, the engine must be disassembled for further evaluation:	**Chapter 3**

Section 3—Primary Electrical System

Test and Procedure	Results and Indications	Proceed to
3.1—Check the ignition switch "on" position: Connect a jumper wire between the distributor side of the coil and ground, and a 12V test lamp between the switch side of the coil and ground. Remove the high tension lead from the coil. Turn the ignition switch on and jiggle the key.	If the lamp lights:	3.2
	If the lamp flickers when the key is jiggled, replace the ignition switch:	3.3
	If the lamp doesn't light, check for loose or open connections. If none are found, remove the ignition switch and check for continuity. If the switch is faulty, replace it:	3.3

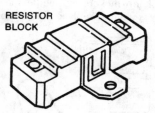

COIL   BATTERY

Checking the ignition switch "on" position

3.2—Check the ballast resistor or resistance wire for an open circuit, using an ohmmeter. See Chapter 3 for specific tests.	Replace the resistor or resistance wire if the resistance is zero. **NOTE:** *Some ignition systems have no ballast resistor.*	3.3

RESISTOR BLOCK

CALIBRATED RESISTANCE LEAD

Two types of resistors

3.3—On point-type ignition systems, visually inspect the breaker points for burning, pitting or excessive wear. Gray coloring of the point contact surfaces is normal. Rotate the crankshaft until the contact heel rests on a high point of the distributor cam and adjust the point gap to specifications. On electronic ignition models, remove the distributor cap and visually inspect the armature. Ensure that the armature pin is in place, and that the armature is on tight and rotates when the engine is cranked. Make sure there are no cracks, chips or rounded edges on the armature.	If the breaker points are intact, clean the contact surfaces with fine emery cloth, and adjust the point gap to specifications. If the points are worn, replace them. On electronic systems, replace any parts which appear defective. If condition persists:	3.4

Test and Procedure	Results and Indications	Proceed to
3.4—On point-type ignition systems, connect a dwell-meter between the distributor primary lead and ground. Crank the engine and observe the point dwell angle. On electronic ignition systems, conduct a stator (magnetic pickup assembly) test. See Chapter 3.	On point-type systems, adjust the dwell angle if necessary. **NOTE:** *Increasing the point gap decreases the dwell angle and vice-versa.*	**3.6**
	If the dwell meter shows little or no reading;	**3.5**
	On electronic ignition systems, if the stator is bad, replace the stator. If the stator is good, proceed to the other tests in Chapter 3.	

CLOSE OPEN

NORMAL DWELL

WIDE GAP

SMALL DWELL

INSUFFICIENT DWELL

NARROW GAP

LARGE DWELL

EXCESSIVE DWELL

Dwell is a function of point gap

Test and Procedure	Results and Indications	Proceed to
3.5—On the point-type ignition systems, check the condenser for short: connect an ohmeter across the condenser body and the pigtail lead.	If any reading other than infinite is noted, replace the condenser	**3.6**

OHMMETER

Checking the condenser for short

Test and Procedure	Results and Indications	Proceed to
3.6—Test the coil primary resistance: On point-type ignition systems, connect an ohmmeter across the coil primary terminals, and read the resistance on the low scale. Note whether an external ballast resistor or resistance wire is used. On electronic ignition systems, test the coil primary resistance as in Chapter 3.	Point-type ignition coils utilizing ballast resistors or resistance wires should have approximately 1.0 ohms resistance. Coils with internal resistors should have approximately 4.0 ohms resistance. If values far from the above are noted, replace the coil.	**4.1**

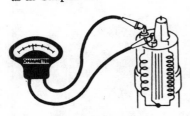

Check the coil primary resistance

Section 4—Secondary Electrical System
See Chapters 2–3 for service procedures

Test and Procedure	Results and Indications	Proceed to
4.1—Check for spark: Hold each spark plug wire approximately ¼″ from ground with gloves or a heavy, dry rag. Crank the engine, and observe the spark.	If no spark is evident:	**4.2**
	If spark is good in some cylinders:	**4.3**
	If spark is good in all cylinders:	**4.6**

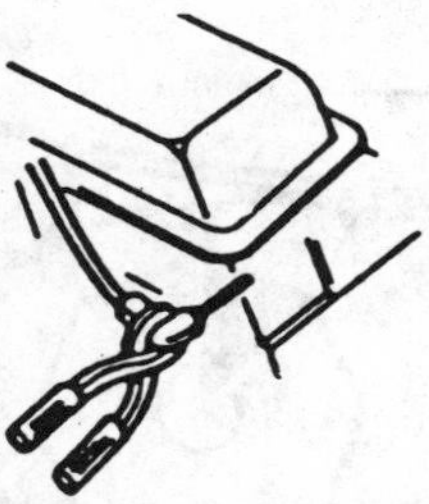

Check for spark at the plugs

Test and Procedure	Results and Indications	Proceed to
4.2—Check for spark at the coil high tension lead: Remove the coil high tension lead from the distributor and position it approximately ¼″ from ground. Crank the engine and observe spark. **CAUTION:** *This test should not be performed on engines equipped with electronic ignition.*	If the spark is good and consistent:	**4.3**
	If the spark is good but intermittent, test the primary electrical system starting at 3.3:	**3.3**
	If the spark is weak or non-existent, replace the coil high tension lead, clean and tighten all connections and retest. If no improvement is noted:	**4.4**
4.3—Visually inspect the distributor cap and rotor for burned or corroded contacts, cracks, carbon tracks, or moisture. Also check the fit of the rotor on the distributor shaft (where applicable).	If moisture is present, dry thoroughly, and retest per 4.1:	**4.1**
	If burned or excessively corroded contacts, cracks, or carbon tracks are noted, replace the defective part(s) and retest per 4.1:	**4.1**
	If the rotor and cap appear intact, or are only slightly corroded, clean the contacts thoroughly (including the cap towers and spark plug wire ends) and retest per 4.1: If the spark is good in all cases:	**4.6**
	If the spark is poor in all cases:	**4.5**

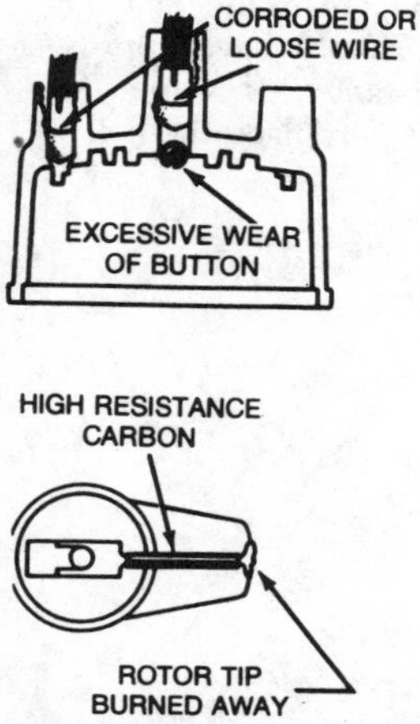

CORRODED OR LOOSE WIRE

EXCESSIVE WEAR OF BUTTON

HIGH RESISTANCE CARBON

ROTOR TIP BURNED AWAY

Inspect the distributor cap and rotor

Test and Procedure	Results and Indications	Proceed to

4.4—Check the coil secondary resistance: On point-type systems connect an ohmmeter across the distributor side of the coil and the coil tower. Read the resistance on the high scale of the ohmmeter. On electronic ignition systems, see Chapter 3 for specific tests.

The resistance of a satisfactory coil should be between 4,000 and 10,000 ohms. If resistance is considerably higher (i.e., 40,000 ohms) replace the coil and retest per 4.1. **NOTE:** *This does not apply to high performance coils.*

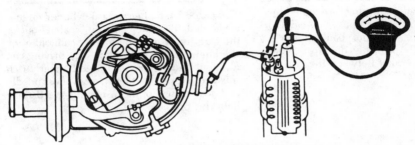

Testing the coil secondary resistance

4.5—Visually inspect the spark plug wires for cracking or brittleness. Ensure that no two wires are positioned so as to cause induction firing (adjacent and parallel). Remove each wire, one by one, and check resistance with an ohmmeter.

Replace any cracked or brittle wires. If any of the wires are defective, replace the entire set. Replace any wires with excessive resistance (over $8000\,\Omega$ per foot for suppression wire), and separate any wires that might cause induction firing.

4.6

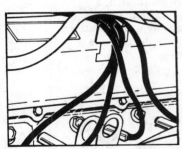

Misfiring can be the result of spark plug leads to adjacent, consecutively firing cylinders running parallel and too close together

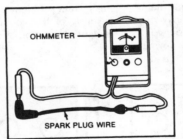

On point-type ignition systems, check the spark plug wires as shown. On electronic ignitions, do not remove the wire from the distributor cap terminal; instead, test through the cap

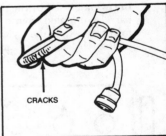

Spark plug wires can be checked visually by bending them in a loop over your finger. This will reveal any cracks, burned or broken insulation. Any wire with cracked insulation should be replaced

---

4.6—Remove the spark plugs, noting the cylinders from which they were removed, and evaluate according to the color photos in the middle of this book.

See following.

See following.

Test and Procedure	Results and Indications	Proceed to
4.7—Examine the location of all the plugs.	The following diagrams illustrate some of the conditions that the location of plugs will reveal.	4.8

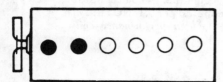

Two adjacent plugs are fouled in a 6-cylinder engine, 4-cylinder engine or either bank of a V-8. This is probably due to a blown head gasket between the two cylinders

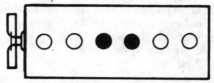

The two center plugs in a 6-cylinder engine are fouled. Raw fuel may be "boiled" out of the carburetor into the intake manifold after the engine is shut-off. Stop-start driving can also foul the center plugs, due to overly rich mixture. Proper float level, a new float needle and seat or use of an insulating spacer may help this problem

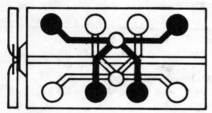

An unbalanced carburetor is indicated. Following the fuel flow on this particular design shows that the cylinders fed by the right-hand barrel are fouled from overly rich mixture, while the cylinders fed by the left-hand barrel are normal

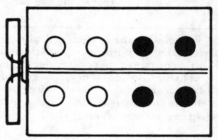

If the four rear plugs are overheated, a cooling system problem is suggested. A thorough cleaning of the cooling system may restore coolant circulation and cure the problem

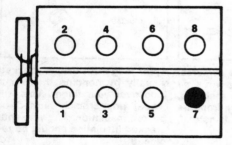

Finding one plug overheated may indicate an intake manifold leak near the affected cylinder. If the overheated plug is the second of two adjacent, consecutively firing plugs, it could be the result of ignition cross-firing. Separating the leads to these two plugs will eliminate cross-fire

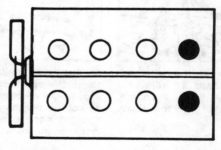

Occasionally, the two rear plugs in large, lightly used V-8's will become oil fouled. High oil consumption and smoky exhaust may also be noticed. It is probably due to plugged oil drain holes in the rear of the cylinder head, causing oil to be sucked in around the valve stems. This usually occurs in the rear cylinders first, because the engine slants that way

Test and Procedure	Results and Indications	Proceed to
4.8—Determine the static ignition timing. Using the crankshaft pulley timing marks as a guide, locate top dead center on the compression stroke of the number one cylinder.	The rotor should be pointing toward the No. 1 tower in the distributor cap, and, on electronic ignitions, the armature spoke for that cylinder should be lined up with the stator.	4.8
4.9—Check coil polarity: Connect a voltmeter negative lead to the coil high tension lead, and the positive lead to ground (**NOTE:** *Reverse the hook-up for positive ground systems*). Crank the engine momentarily.	If the voltmeter reads up-scale, the polarity is correct: If the voltmeter reads down-scale, reverse the coil polarity (switch the primary leads): **Checking coil polarity**	5.1 5.1

Section 5—Fuel System
See Chapter 4 for service procedures

Test and Procedure	Results and Indications	Proceed to
5.1—Determine that the air filter is functioning efficiently: Hold paper elements up to a strong light, and attempt to see light through the filter.	Clean permanent air filters in solvent (or manufacturer's recommendation), and allow to dry. Replace paper elements through which light cannot be seen:	5.2
5.2—Determine whether a flooding condition exists: Flooding is identified by a strong gasoline odor, and excessive gasoline present in the throttle bore(s) of the carburetor.	If flooding is not evident: If flooding is evident, permit the gasoline to dry for a few moments and restart. If flooding doesn't recur: If flooding is persistent: **If the engine floods repeatedly, check the choke butterfly flap**	5.3 5.7 5.5
5.3—Check that fuel is reaching the carburetor: Detach the fuel line at the carburetor inlet. Hold the end of the line in a cup (not styrofoam), and crank the engine.	If fuel flows smoothly: If fuel doesn't flow (**NOTE:** *Make sure that there is fuel in the tank*), or flows erratically: **Check the fuel pump by disconnecting the output line (fuel pump-to-carburetor) at the carburetor and operating the starter briefly**	5.7 5.4

Test and Procedure	Results and Indications	Proceed to
5.4—Test the fuel pump: Disconnect all fuel lines from the fuel pump. Hold a finger over the input fitting, crank the engine (with electric pump, turn the ignition or pump on); and feel for suction.	If suction is evident, blow out the fuel line to the tank with low pressure compressed air until bubbling is heard from the fuel filler neck. Also blow out the carburetor fuel line (both ends disconnected):	5.7
	If no suction is evident, replace or repair the fuel pump: NOTE: *Repeated oil fouling of the spark plugs, or a no-start condition, could be the result of a ruptured vacuum booster pump diaphragm, through which oil or gasoline is being drawn into the intake manifold (where applicable).*	5.7
5.5—Occasionally, small specks of dirt will clog the small jets and orifices in the carburetor. With the engine cold, hold a flat piece of wood or similar material over the carburetor, where possible, and crank the engine.	If the engine starts, but runs roughly the engine is probably not run enough. If the engine won't start:	5.9
5.6—Check the needle and seat: Tap the carburetor in the area of the needle and seat.	If flooding stops, a gasoline additive (e.g., Gumout) will often cure the problem:	5.7
	If flooding continues, check the fuel pump for excessive pressure at the carburetor (according to specifications). If the pressure is normal, the needle and seat must be removed and checked, and/or the float level adjusted:	5.7
5.7—Test the accelerator pump by looking into the throttle bores while operating the throttle.	If the accelerator pump appears to be operating normally:	5.8
	If the accelerator pump is not operating, the pump must be reconditioned. Where possible, service the pump with the carburetor(s) installed on the engine. If necessary, remove the carburetor. Prior to removal:	5.8

Check for gas at the carburetor by looking down the carburetor throat while someone moves the accelerator

5.8—Determine whether the carburetor main fuel system is functioning: Spray a commercial starting fluid into the carburetor while attempting to start the engine.	If the engine starts, runs for a few seconds, and dies:	5.9
	If the engine doesn't start:	6.1

Test and Procedure	Results and Indications	Proceed to
5.9—Uncommon fuel system malfunctions: See below:	If the problem is solved:	6.1
	If the problem remains, remove and recondition the carburetor.	

Condition	Indication	Test	Prevailing Weather Conditions	Remedy
Vapor lock	Engine will not restart shortly after running.	Cool the components of the fuel system until the engine starts. Vapor lock can be cured faster by draping a wet cloth over a mechanical fuel pump.	Hot to very hot	Ensure that the exhaust manifold heat control valve is operating. Check with the vehicle manufacturer for the recommended solution to vapor lock on the model in question.
Carburetor icing	Engine will not idle, stalls at low speeds.	Visually inspect the throttle plate area of the throttle bores for frost.	High humidity, 32–40° F.	Ensure that the exhaust manifold heat control valve is operating, and that the intake manifold heat riser is not blocked.
Water in the fuel	Engine sputters and stalls; may not start.	Pump a small amount of fuel into a glass jar. Allow to stand, and inspect for droplets or a layer of water.	High humidity, extreme temperature changes.	For droplets, use one or two cans of commercial gas line anti-freeze. For a layer of water, the tank must be drained, and the fuel lines blown out with compressed air.

Section 6—Engine Compression
See Chapter 3 for service procedures

6.1—Test engine compression: Remove all spark plugs. Block the throttle wide open. Insert a compression gauge into a spark plug port, crank the engine to obtain the maximum reading, and record.	If compression is within limits on all cylinders:	7.1
	If gauge reading is extremely low on all cylinders:	6.2
	If gauge reading is low on one or two cylinders: (If gauge readings are identical and low on two or more adjacent cylinders, the head gasket must be replaced.)	6.2

Checking compression

6.2—Test engine compression (wet): Squirt approximately 30 cc. of engine oil into each cylinder, and retest per 6.1.	If the readings improve, worn or cracked rings or broken pistons are indicated:	See Chapter 3
	If the readings do not improve, burned or excessively carboned valves or a jumped timing chain are indicated:	
	NOTE: *A jumped timing chain is often indicated by difficult cranking.*	7.1

Section 7—Engine Vacuum
See Chapter 3 for service procedures

Test and Procedure	Results and Indications	Proceed to
7.1—Attach a vacuum gauge to the intake manifold beyond the throttle plate. Start the engine, and observe the action of the needle over the range of engine speeds.	See below.	**See below**

INDICATION: normal engine in good condition

Proceed to: 8.1

Normal engine
Gauge reading: steady, from 17–22 in./Hg.

INDICATION: sticking valves or ignition miss

Proceed to: 9.1, 8.3

Sticking valves
Gauge reading: intermittent fluctuation at idle

INDICATION: late ignition or valve timing, low compression, stuck throttle valve, leaking carburetor or manifold gasket

Proceed to: 6.1

Incorrect valve timing
Gauge reading: low (10–15 in./Hg) but steady

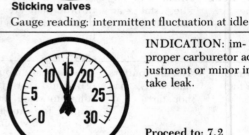

INDICATION: improper carburetor adjustment or minor intake leak.

Proceed to: 7.2

Carburetor requires adjustment
Gauge reading: drifting needle

INDICATION: ignition miss, blown cylinder head gasket, leaking valve or weak valve spring

Proceed to: 8.3, 6.1

Blown head gasket
Gauge reading: needle fluctuates as engine speed increases

INDICATION: burnt valve or faulty valve clearance. Needle will fall when defective valve operates

Proceed to: 9.1

Burnt or leaking valves
Gauge reading: steady needle, but drops regularly

INDICATION: choked muffler, excessive back pressure in system

Proceed to: 10.1

Clogged exhaust system
Gauge reading: gradual drop in reading at idle

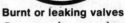

INDICATION: worn valve guides

Proceed to: 9.1

Worn valve guides
Gauge reading: needle vibrates excessively at idle, but steadies as engine speed increases

White pointer = steady gauge hand

Black pointer = fluctuating gauge hand

Test and Procedure	Results and Indications	Proceed to
7.2—Attach a vacuum gauge per 7.1, and test for an intake manifold leak. Squirt a small amount of oil around the intake manifold gaskets, carburetor gaskets, plugs and fittings. Observe the action of the vacuum gauge.	If the reading improves, replace the indicated gasket, or seal the indicated fitting or plug: If the reading remains low:	**8.1** **7.3**
7.3—Test all vacuum hoses and accessories for leaks as described in 7.2. Also check the carburetor body (dashpots, automatic choke mechanism, throttle shafts) for leaks in the same manner.	If the reading improves, service or replace the offending part(s): If the reading remains low:	**8.1** **6.1**

Section 8—Secondary Electrical System
See Chapter 2 for service procedures

Test and Procedure	Results and Indications	Proceed to
8.1—Remove the distributor cap and check to make sure that the rotor turns when the engine is cranked. Visually inspect the distributor components.	Clean, tighten or replace any components which appear defective.	**8.2**
8.2—Connect a timing light (per manufacturer's recommendation) and check the dynamic ignition timing. Disconnect and plug the vacuum hose(s) to the distributor if specified, start the engine, and observe the timing marks at the specified engine speed.	If the timing is not correct, adjust to specifications by rotating the distributor in the engine: (Advance timing by rotating distributor opposite normal direction of rotor rotation, retard timing by rotating distributor in same direction as rotor rotation.)	**8.3**
8.3—Check the operation of the distributor advance mechanism(s): To test the mechanical advance, disconnect the vacuum lines from the distributor advance unit and observe the timing marks with a timing light as the engine speed is increased from idle. If the mark moves smoothly, without hesitation, it may be assumed that the mechanical advance is functioning properly. To test vacuum advance and/or retard systems, alternately crimp and release the vacuum line, and observe the timing mark for movement. If movement is noted, the system is operating.	If the systems are functioning: If the systems are not functioning, remove the distributor, and test on a distributor tester:	**8.4** **8.4**
8.4—Locate an ignition miss: With the engine running, remove each spark plug wire, one at a time, until one is found that doesn't cause the engine to roughen and slow down.	When the missing cylinder is identified:	**4.1**

Section 9—Valve Train
See Chapter 3 for service procedures

Test and Procedure	Results and Indications	Proceed to
9.1—Evaluate the valve train: Remove the valve cover, and ensure that the valves are adjusted to specifications. A mechanic's stethoscope may be used to aid in the diagnosis of the valve train. By pushing the probe on or near push rods or rockers, valve noise often can be isolated. A timing light also may be used to diagnose valve problems. Connect the light according to manufacturer's recommendations, and start the engine. Vary the firing moment of the light by increasing the engine speed (and therefore the ignition advance), and moving the trigger from cylinder to cylinder. Observe the movement of each valve.	Sticking valves or erratic valve train motion can be observed with the timing light. The cylinder head must be disassembled for repairs.	**See Chapter 3**
9.2—Check the valve timing: Locate top dead center of the No. 1 piston, and install a degree wheel or tape on the crankshaft pulley or damper with zero corresponding to an index mark on the engine. Rotate the crankshaft in its direction of rotation, and observe the opening of the No. 1 cylinder intake valve. The opening should correspond with the correct mark on the degree wheel according to specifications.	If the timing is not correct, the timing cover must be removed for further investigation.	**See Chapter 3**

Section 10—Exhaust System

Test and Procedure	Results and Indications	Proceed to
10.1—Determine whether the exhaust manifold heat control valve is operating: Operate the valve by hand to determine whether it is free to move. If the valve is free, run the engine to operating temperature and observe the action of the valve, to ensure that it is opening.	If the valve sticks, spray it with a suitable solvent, open and close the valve to free it, and retest. If the valve functions properly: If the valve does not free, or does not operate, replace the valve:	10.2 10.2
10.2—Ensure that there are no exhaust restrictions: Visually inspect the exhaust system for kinks, dents, or crushing. Also note that gases are flowing freely from the tailpipe at all engine speeds, indicating no restriction in the muffler or resonator.	Replace any damaged portion of the system:	11.1

Section 11—Cooling System
See Chapter 3 for service procedures

Test and Procedure	Results and Indications	Proceed to
11.1—Visually inspect the fan belt for glazing, cracks, and fraying, and replace if necessary. Tighten the belt so that the longest span has approximately ½″ play at its midpoint under thumb pressure (see Chapter 1).	Replace or tighten the fan belt as necessary:	**11.2**

Checking belt tension

Test and Procedure	Results and Indications	Proceed to
11.2—Check the fluid level of the cooling system.	If full or slightly low, fill as necessary:	**11.5**
	If extremely low:	**11.3**
11.3—Visually inspect the external portions of the cooling system (radiator, radiator hoses, thermostat elbow, water pump seals, heater hoses, etc.) for leaks. If none are found, pressurize the cooling system to 14–15 psi.	If cooling system holds the pressure:	**11.5**
	If cooling system loses pressure rapidly, reinspect external parts of the system for leaks under pressure. If none are found, check dipstick for coolant in crankcase. If no coolant is present, but pressure loss continues:	**11.4**
	If coolant is evident in crankcase, remove cylinder head(s), and check gasket(s). If gaskets are intact, block and cylinder head(s) should be checked for cracks or holes. If the gasket(s) is blown, replace, and purge the crankcase of coolant:	**12.6**
	NOTE: *Occasionally, due to atmospheric and driving conditions, condensation of water can occur in the crankcase. This causes the oil to appear milky white. To remedy, run the engine until hot, and change the oil and oil filter.*	
11.4—Check for combustion leaks into the cooling system: Pressurize the cooling system as above. Start the engine, and observe the pressure gauge. If the needle fluctuates, remove each spark plug wire, one at a time, noting which cylinder(s) reduce or eliminate the fluctuation.	Cylinders which reduce or eliminate the fluctuation, when the spark plug wire is removed, are leaking into the cooling system. Replace the head gasket on the affected cylinder bank(s).	

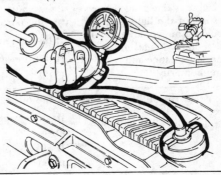

Pressurizing the cooling system

Test and Procedure	Results and Indications	Proceed to
11.5—Check the radiator pressure cap: Attach a radiator pressure tester to the radiator cap (wet the seal prior to installation). Quickly pump up the pressure, noting the point at which the cap releases.	If the cap releases within ± 1 psi of the specified rating, it is operating properly:	**11.6**
	If the cap releases at more than ± 1 psi of the specified rating, it should be replaced:	**11.6**

Checking radiator pressure cap

Test and Procedure	Results and Indications	Proceed to
11.6—Test the thermostat: Start the engine cold, remove the radiator cap, and insert a thermometer into the radiator. Allow the engine to idle. After a short while, there will be a sudden, rapid increase in coolant temperature. The temperature at which this sharp rise stops is the thermostat opening temperature.	If the thermostat opens at or about the specified temperature:	**11.7**
	If the temperature doesn't increase: (If the temperature increases slowly and gradually, replace the thermostat.)	**11.7**
11.7—Check the water pump: Remove the thermostat elbow and the thermostat, disconnect the coil high tension lead (to prevent starting), and crank the engine momentarily.	If coolant flows, replace the thermostat and retest per 11.6:	**11.6**
	If coolant doesn't flow, reverse flush the cooling system to alleviate any blockage that might exist. If system is not blocked, and coolant will not flow, replace the water pump.	

Section 12—Lubrication
See Chapter 3 for service procedures

Test and Procedure	Results and Indications	Proceed to
12.1—Check the oil pressure gauge or warning light: If the gauge shows low pressure, or the light is on for no obvious reason, remove the oil pressure sender. Install an accurate oil pressure gauge and run the engine momentarily.	If oil pressure builds normally, run engine for a few moments to determine that it is functioning normally, and replace the sender.	—
	If the pressure remains low:	**12.2**
	If the pressure surges:	**12.3**
	If the oil pressure is zero:	**12.3**
12.2—Visually inspect the oil: If the oil is watery or very thin, milky, or foamy, replace the oil and oil filter.	If the oil is normal:	**12.3**
	If after replacing oil the pressure remains low:	**12.3**
	If after replacing oil the pressure becomes normal:	—

Test and Procedure	Results and Indications	Proceed to
12.3—Inspect the oil pressure relief valve and spring, to ensure that it is not sticking or stuck. Remove and thoroughly clean the valve, spring, and the valve body.	If the oil pressure improves: If no improvement is noted:	— **12.4**
12.4—Check to ensure that the oil pump is not cavitating (sucking air instead of oil): See that the crankcase is neither over nor underfull, and that the pickup in the sump is in the proper position and free from sludge.	Fill or drain the crankcase to the proper capacity, and clean the pickup screen in solvent if necessary. If no improvement is noted:	**12.5**
12.5—Inspect the oil pump drive and the oil pump:	If the pump drive or the oil pump appear to be defective, service as necessary and retest per 12.1: If the pump drive and pump appear to be operating normally, the engine should be disassembled to determine where blockage exists:	**12.1** **See Chapter 3**
12.6—Purge the engine of ethylene glycol coolant: Completely drain the crankcase and the oil filter. Obtain a commercial butyl cellosolve base solvent, designated for this purpose, and follow the instructions precisely. Following this, install a new oil filter and refill the crankcase with the proper weight oil. The next oil and filter change should follow shortly thereafter (1000 miles).		

TROUBLESHOOTING EMISSION CONTROL SYSTEMS

See Chapter 4 for procedures applicable to individual emission control systems used on specific combinations of engine/transmission/model.

TROUBLESHOOTING THE CARBURETOR

See Chapter 4 for service procedures

Carburetor problems cannot be effectively isolated unless all other engine systems (particularly ignition and emission) are functioning properly and the engine is properly tuned.

Condition	Possible Cause
Engine cranks, but does not start	1. Improper starting procedure 2. No fuel in tank 3. Clogged fuel line or filter 4. Defective fuel pump 5. Choke valve not closing properly 6. Engine flooded 7. Choke valve not unloading 8. Throttle linkage not making full travel 9. Stuck needle or float 10. Leaking float needle or seat 11. Improper float adjustment
Engine stalls	1. Improperly adjusted idle speed or mixture **Engine hot** 2. Improperly adjusted dashpot 3. Defective or improperly adjusted solenoid 4. Incorrect fuel level in fuel bowl 5. Fuel pump pressure too high 6. Leaking float needle seat 7. Secondary throttle valve stuck open 8. Air or fuel leaks 9. Idle air bleeds plugged or missing 10. Idle passages plugged **Engine Cold** 11. Incorrectly adjusted choke 12. Improperly adjusted fast idle speed 13. Air leaks 14. Plugged idle or idle air passages 15. Stuck choke valve or binding linkage 16. Stuck secondary throttle valves 17. Engine flooding—high fuel level 18. Leaking or misaligned float
Engine hesitates on acceleration	1. Clogged fuel filter 2. Leaking fuel pump diaphragm 3. Low fuel pump pressure 4. Secondary throttle valves stuck, bent or misadjusted 5. Sticking or binding air valve 6. Defective accelerator pump 7. Vacuum leaks 8. Clogged air filter 9. Incorrect choke adjustment (engine cold)
Engine feels sluggish or flat on acceleration	1. Improperly adjusted idle speed or mixture 2. Clogged fuel filter 3. Defective accelerator pump 4. Dirty, plugged or incorrect main metering jets 5. Bent or sticking main metering rods 6. Sticking throttle valves 7. Stuck heat riser 8. Binding or stuck air valve 9. Dirty, plugged or incorrect secondary jets 10. Bent or sticking secondary metering rods. 11. Throttle body or manifold heat passages plugged 12. Improperly adjusted choke or choke vacuum break.
Carburetor floods	1. Defective fuel pump. Pressure too high. 2. Stuck choke valve 3. Dirty, worn or damaged float or needle valve/seat 4. Incorrect float/fuel level 5. Leaking float bowl

Condition	Possible Cause
Engine idles roughly and stalls	1. Incorrect idle speed 2. Clogged fuel filter 3. Dirt in fuel system or carburetor 4. Loose carburetor screws or attaching bolts 5. Broken carburetor gaskets 6. Air leaks 7. Dirty carburetor 8. Worn idle mixture needles 9. Throttle valves stuck open 10. Incorrectly adjusted float or fuel level 11. Clogged air filter
Engine runs unevenly or surges	1. Defective fuel pump 2. Dirty or clogged fuel filter 3. Plugged, loose or incorrect main metering jets or rods 4. Air leaks 5. Bent or sticking main metering rods 6. Stuck power piston 7. Incorrect float adjustment 8. Incorrect idle speed or mixture 9. Dirty or plugged idle system passages 10. Hard, brittle or broken gaskets 11. Loose attaching or mounting screws 12. Stuck or misaligned secondary throttle valves
Poor fuel economy	1. Poor driving habits 2. Stuck choke valve 3. Binding choke linkage 4. Stuck heat riser 5. Incorrect idle mixture 6. Defective accelerator pump 7. Air leaks 8. Plugged, loose or incorrect main metering jets 9. Improperly adjusted float or fuel level 10. Bent, misaligned or fuel-clogged float 11. Leaking float needle seat 12. Fuel leak 13. Accelerator pump discharge ball not seating properly 14. Incorrect main jets
Engine lacks high speed performance or power	1. Incorrect throttle linkage adjustment 2. Stuck or binding power piston 3. Defective accelerator pump 4. Air leaks 5. Incorrect float setting or fuel level 6. Dirty, plugged, worn or incorrect main metering jets or rods 7. Binding or sticking air valve 8. Brittle or cracked gaskets 9. Bent, incorrect or improperly adjusted secondary metering rods 10. Clogged fuel filter 11. Clogged air filter 12. Defective fuel pump

TROUBLESHOOTING FUEL INJECTION PROBLEMS

Each fuel injection system has its own unique components and test procedures, for which it is impossible to generalize. Refer to Chapter 4 of this Repair & Tune-Up Guide for specific test and repair procedures, if the vehicle is equipped with fuel injection.

TROUBLESHOOTING ELECTRICAL PROBLEMS

See Chapter 5 for service procedures

For any electrical system to operate, it must make a complete circuit. This simply means that the power flow from the battery must make a complete circle. When an electrical component is operating, power flows from the battery to the component, passes through the component causing it to perform its function (lighting a light bulb), and then returns to the battery through the ground of the circuit. This ground is usually (but not always) the metal part of the car or truck on which the electrical component is mounted.

Perhaps the easiest way to visualize this is to think of connecting a light bulb with two wires attached to it to the battery. If one of the two wires attached to the light bulb were attached to the negative post of the battery and the other were attached to the positive post of the battery, you would have a complete circuit. Current from the battery would flow to the light bulb, causing it to light, and return to the negative post of the battery.

The normal automotive circuit differs from this simple example in two ways. First, instead of having a return wire from the bulb to the battery, the light bulb returns the current to the battery through the chassis of the vehicle. Since the negative battery cable is attached to the chassis and the chassis is made of electrically conductive metal, the chassis of the vehicle can serve as a ground wire to complete the circuit. Secondly, most automotive circuits contain switches to turn components on and off as required.

Every complete circuit from a power source must include a component which is using the power from the power source. If you were to disconnect the light bulb from the wires and touch the two wires together (don't do this) the power supply wire to the component would be grounded before the normal ground connection for the circuit.

Because grounding a wire from a power source makes a complete circuit—less the required component to use the power—this phenomenon is called a short circuit. Common causes are: broken insulation (exposing the metal wire to a metal part of the car or truck), or a shorted switch.

Some electrical components which require a large amount of current to operate also have a relay in their circuit. Since these circuits carry a large amount of current, the thickness of the wire in the circuit (gauge size) is also greater. If this large wire were connected from the component to the control switch on the instrument panel, and then back to the component, a voltage drop would occur in the circuit. To prevent this potential drop in voltage, an electromagnetic switch (relay) is used. The large wires in the circuit are connected from the battery to one side of the relay, and from the opposite side of the relay to the component. The relay is normally open, preventing current from passing through the circuit. An additional, smaller, wire is connected from the relay to the control switch for the circuit. When the control switch is turned on, it grounds the smaller wire from the relay and completes the circuit. This closes the relay and allows current to flow from the battery to the component. The horn, headlight, and starter circuits are three which use relays.

It is possible for larger surges of current to pass through the electrical system of your car or truck. If this surge of current were to reach an electrical component, it could burn it out. To prevent this, fuses, circuit breakers or fusible links are connected into the current supply wires of most of the major electrical systems. When an electrical current of excessive power passes through the component's fuse, the fuse blows out and breaks the circuit, saving the component from destruction.

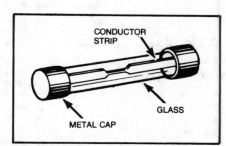

Typical automotive fuse

A circuit breaker is basically a self-repairing fuse. The circuit breaker opens the circuit the same way a fuse does. However, when either the short is removed from the circuit or the surge subsides, the circuit breaker resets itself and does not have to be replaced as a fuse does.

A fuse link is a wire that acts as a fuse. It is normally connected between the starter relay and the main wiring harness. This connection is usually under the hood. The fuse link (if installed) protects all the

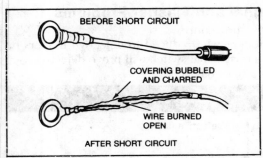

Most fusible links show a charred, melted insulation when they burn out

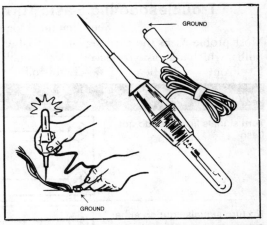

The test light will show the presence of current when touched to a hot wire and grounded at the other end

chassis electrical components, and is the probable cause of trouble when none of the electrical components function, unless the battery is disconnected or dead.

Electrical problems generally fall into one of three areas:

1. The component that is not functioning is not receiving current.

2. The component itself is not functioning.

3. The component is not properly grounded.

The electrical system can be checked with a test light and a jumper wire. A test light is a device that looks like a pointed screwdriver with a wire attached to it and has a light bulb in its handle. A jumper wire is a piece of insulated wire with an alligator clip attached to each end.

If a component is not working, you must follow a systematic plan to determine which of the three causes is the villain.

1. Turn on the switch that controls the inoperable component.

2. Disconnect the power supply wire from the component.

3. Attach the ground wire on the test light to a good metal ground.

4. Touch the probe end of the test light to the end of the power supply wire that was disconnected from the component. If the component is receiving current, the test light will go on.

NOTE: *Some components work only when the ignition switch is turned on.*

If the test light does not go on, then the problem is in the circuit between the battery and the component. This includes all the switches, fuses, and relays in the system. Follow the wire that runs back to the battery. The problem is an open circuit between the

battery and the component. If the fuse is blown and, when replaced, immediately blows again, there is a short circuit in the system which must be located and repaired. If there is a switch in the system, bypass it with a jumper wire. This is done by connecting one end of the jumper wire to the power supply wire into the switch and the other end of the jumper wire to the wire coming out of the switch. If the test light lights with jumper wire installed, the switch or whatever was bypassed is defective.

NOTE: *Never substitute the jumper wire for the component, since it is required to use the power from the power source.*

5. If the bulb in the test light goes on, then the current is getting to the component that is not working. This eliminates the first of the three possible causes. Connect the power supply wire and connect a jumper wire from the component to a good metal ground. Do this with the switch which controls the component turned on, and also the ignition switch turned on if it is required for the component to work. If the component works with the jumper wire installed, then it has a bad ground. This is usually caused by the metal area on which the component mounts to the chassis being coated with some type of foreign matter.

6. If neither test located the source of the trouble, then the component itself is defective. Remember that for any electrical system to work, all connections must be clean and tight.

Troubleshooting Basic Turn Signal and Flasher Problems
See Chapter 5 for service procedures

Most problems in the turn signals or flasher system can be reduced to defective flashers or bulbs, which are easily replaced. Occasionally, the turn signal switch will prove defective.

F = Front   R = Rear   ● = Lights off   ○ = Lights on

Condition		Possible Cause
Turn signals light, but do not flash	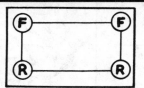	Defective flasher
No turn signals light on either side	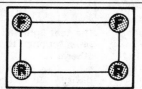	Blown fuse. Replace if defective. Defective flasher. Check by substitution. Open circuit, short circuit or poor ground.
Both turn signals on one side don't work	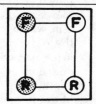	Bad bulbs. Bad ground in both (or either) housings.
One turn signal light on one side doesn't work	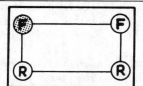	Defective bulb. Corrosion in socket. Clean contacts. Poor ground at socket.
Turn signal flashes too fast or too slowly	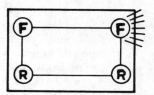	Check any bulb on the side flashing too fast. A heavy-duty bulb is probably installed in place of a regular bulb. Check the bulb flashing too slowly. A standard bulb was probably installed in place of a heavy-duty bulb. Loose connections or corrosion at the bulb socket.
Indicator lights don't work in either direction		Check if the turn signals are working. Check the dash indicator lights. Check the flasher by substitution.
One indicator light doesn't light		On systems with one dash indicator: See if the lights work on the same side. Often the filaments have been reversed in systems combining stoplights with taillights and turn signals. Check the flasher by substitution. On systems with two indicators: Check the bulbs on the same side. Check the indicator light bulb. Check the flasher by substitution.

Troubleshooting Lighting Problems

See Chapter 5 for service procedures

Condition	Possible Cause
One or more lights don't work, but others do	1. Defective bulb(s) 2. Blown fuse(s) 3. Dirty fuse clips or light sockets 4. Poor ground circuit
Lights burn out quickly	1. Incorrect voltage regulator setting or defective regulator 2. Poor battery/alternator connections
Lights go dim	1. Low/discharged battery 2. Alternator not charging 3. Corroded sockets or connections 4. Low voltage output
Lights flicker	1. Loose connection 2. Poor ground. (Run ground wire from light housing to frame) 3. Circuit breaker operating (short circuit)
Lights "flare"—Some flare is normal on acceleration—If excessive, see "Lights Burn Out Quickly"	High voltage setting
Lights glare—approaching drivers are blinded	1. Lights adjusted too high 2. Rear springs or shocks sagging 3. Rear tires soft

Troubleshooting Dash Gauge Problems

Most problems can be traced to a defective sending unit or faulty wiring. Occasionally, the gauge itself is at fault. See Chapter 5 for service procedures.

Condition	Possible Cause

COOLANT TEMPERATURE GAUGE

Gauge reads erratically or not at all	1. Loose or dirty connections 2. Defective sending unit. 3. Defective gauge. To test a bi-metal gauge, remove the wire from the sending unit. Ground the wire for an instant. If the gauge registers, replace the sending unit. To test a magnetic gauge, disconnect the wire at the sending unit. With ignition ON gauge should register COLD. Ground the wire; gauge should register HOT.

AMMETER GAUGE—TURN HEADLIGHTS ON (DO NOT START ENGINE). NOTE REACTION

Ammeter shows charge Ammeter shows discharge Ammeter does not move	1. Connections reversed on gauge 2. Ammeter is OK 3. Loose connections or faulty wiring 4. Defective gauge

Condition	Possible Cause

OIL PRESSURE GAUGE

Gauge does not register or is inaccurate	1. On mechanical gauge, Bourdon tube may be bent or kinked.
	2. Low oil pressure. Remove sending unit. Idle the engine briefly. If no oil flows from sending unit hole, problem is in engine.
	3. Defective gauge. Remove the wire from the sending unit and ground it for an instant with the ignition ON. A good gauge will go to the top of the scale.
	4. Defective wiring. Check the wiring to the gauge. If it's OK and the gauge doesn't register when grounded, replace the gauge.
	5. Defective sending unit.

ALL GAUGES

All gauges do not operate	1. Blown fuse
	2. Defective instrument regulator
All gauges read low or erratically	3. Defective or dirty instrument voltage regulator
All gauges pegged	4. Loss of ground between instrument voltage regulator and frame
	5. Defective instrument regulator

WARNING LIGHTS

Light(s) do not come on when ignition is ON, but engine is not started	1. Defective bulb
	2. Defective wire
	3. Defective sending unit. Disconnect the wire from the sending unit and ground it. Replace the sending unit if the light comes on with the ignition ON.
Light comes on with engine running	4. Problem in individual system
	5. Defective sending unit

Troubleshooting Clutch Problems

It is false economy to replace individual clutch components. The pressure plate, clutch plate and throwout bearing should be replaced as a set, and the flywheel face inspected, whenever the clutch is overhauled. See Chapter 6 for service procedures.

Condition	Possible Cause
Clutch chatter	1. Grease on driven plate (disc) facing
	2. Binding clutch linkage or cable
	3. Loose, damaged facings on driven plate (disc)
	4. Engine mounts loose
	5. Incorrect height adjustment of pressure plate release levers
	6. Clutch housing or housing to transmission adapter misalignment
	7. Loose driven plate hub
Clutch grabbing	1. Oil, grease on driven plate (disc) facing
	2. Broken pressure plate
	3. Warped or binding driven plate. Driven plate binding on clutch shaft
Clutch slips	1. Lack of lubrication in clutch linkage or cable (linkage or cable binds, causes incomplete engagement)
	2. Incorrect pedal, or linkage adjustment
	3. Broken pressure plate springs
	4. Weak pressure plate springs
	5. Grease on driven plate facings (disc)

Troubleshooting Clutch Problems (cont.)

Condition	Possible Cause
Incomplete clutch release	1. Incorrect pedal or linkage adjustment or linkage or cable binding 2. Incorrect height adjustment on pressure plate release levers 3. Loose, broken facings on driven plate (disc) 4. Bent, dished, warped driven plate caused by overheating
Grinding, whirring grating noise when pedal is depressed	1. Worn or defective throwout bearing 2. Starter drive teeth contacting flywheel ring gear teeth. Look for milled or polished teeth on ring gear.
Squeal, howl, trumpeting noise when pedal is being released (occurs during first inch to inch and one-half of pedal travel)	Pilot bushing worn or lack of lubricant. If bushing appears OK, polish bushing with emery cloth, soak lube wick in oil, lube bushing with oil, apply film of chassis grease to clutch shaft pilot hub, reassemble. NOTE: Bushing wear may be due to misalignment of clutch housing or housing to transmission adapter
Vibration or clutch pedal pulsation with clutch disengaged (pedal fully depressed)	1. Worn or defective engine transmission mounts 2. Flywheel run out. (Flywheel run out at face not to exceed 0.005") 3. Damaged or defective clutch components

Troubleshooting Manual Transmission Problems
See Chapter 6 for service procedures

Condition	Possible Cause
Transmission jumps out of gear	1. Misalignment of transmission case or clutch housing. 2. Worn pilot bearing in crankshaft. 3. Bent transmission shaft. 4. Worn high speed sliding gear. 5. Worn teeth or end-play in clutch shaft. 6. Insufficient spring tension on shifter rail plunger. 7. Bent or loose shifter fork. 8. Gears not engaging completely. 9. Loose or worn bearings on clutch shaft or mainshaft. 10. Worn gear teeth. 11. Worn or damaged detent balls.
Transmission sticks in gear	1. Clutch not releasing fully. 2. Burred or battered teeth on clutch shaft, or sliding sleeve. 3. Burred or battered transmission mainshaft. 4. Frozen synchronizing clutch. 5. Stuck shifter rail plunger. 6. Gearshift lever twisting and binding shifter rail. 7. Battered teeth on high speed sliding gear or on sleeve. 8. Improper lubrication, or lack of lubrication. 9. Corroded transmission parts. 10. Defective mainshaft pilot bearing. 11. Locked gear bearings will give same effect as stuck in gear.
Transmission gears will not synchronize	1. Binding pilot bearing on mainshaft, will synchronize in high gear only. 2. Clutch not releasing fully. 3. Detent spring weak or broken. 4. Weak or broken springs under balls in sliding gear sleeve. 5. Binding bearing on clutch shaft, or binding countershaft. 6. Binding pilot bearing in crankshaft. 7. Badly worn gear teeth. 8. Improper lubrication. 9. Constant mesh gear not turning freely on transmission mainshaft. Will synchronize in that gear only.

Condition	Possible Cause
Gears spinning when shifting into gear from neutral	1. Clutch not releasing fully. 2. In some cases an extremely light lubricant in transmission will cause gears to continue to spin for a short time after clutch is released. 3. Binding pilot bearing in crankshaft.
Transmission noisy in all gears	1. Insufficient lubricant, or improper lubricant. 2. Worn countergear bearings. 3. Worn or damaged main drive gear or countergear. 4. Damaged main drive gear or mainshaft bearings. 5. Worn or damaged countergear anti-lash plate.
Transmission noisy in neutral only	1. Damaged main drive gear bearing. 2. Damaged or loose mainshaft pilot bearing. 3. Worn or damaged countergear anti-lash plate. 4. Worn countergear bearings.
Transmission noisy in one gear only	1. Damaged or worn constant mesh gears. 2. Worn or damaged countergear bearings. 3. Damaged or worn synchronizer.
Transmission noisy in reverse only	1. Worn or damaged reverse idler gear or idler bushing. 2. Worn or damaged mainshaft reverse gear. 3. Worn or damaged reverse countergear. 4. Damaged shift mechanism.

TROUBLESHOOTING AUTOMATIC TRANSMISSION PROBLEMS

Keeping alert to changes in the operating characteristics of the transmission (changing shift points, noises, etc.) can prevent small problems from becoming large ones. If the problem cannot be traced to loose bolts, fluid level, misadjusted linkage, clogged filters or similar problems, you should probably seek professional service.

Transmission Fluid Indications

The appearance and odor of the transmission fluid can give valuable clues to the overall condition of the transmission. Always note the appearance of the fluid when you check the fluid level or change the fluid. Rub a small amount of fluid between your fingers to feel for grit and smell the fluid on the dipstick.

If the fluid appears:	It indicates:
Clear and red colored	Normal operation
Discolored (extremely dark red or brownish) or smells burned	Band or clutch pack failure, usually caused by an overheated transmission. Hauling very heavy loads with insufficient power or failure to change the fluid often result in overheating. Do not confuse this appearance with newer fluids that have a darker red color and a strong odor (though not a burned odor).
Foamy or aerated (light in color and full of bubbles)	1. The level is too high (gear train is churning oil) 2. An internal air leak (air is mixing with the fluid). Have the transmission checked professionally.
Solid residue in the fluid	Defective bands, clutch pack or bearings. Bits of band material or metal abrasives are clinging to the dipstick. Have the transmission checked professionally.
Varnish coating on the dipstick	The transmission fluid is overheating

TROUBLESHOOTING DRIVE AXLE PROBLEMS

First, determine when the noise is most noticeable.

Drive Noise: Produced under vehicle acceleration.

Coast Noise: Produced while coasting with a closed throttle.

Float Noise: Occurs while maintaining constant speed (just enough to keep speed constant) on a level road.

External Noise Elimination

It is advisable to make a thorough road test to determine whether the noise originates in the rear axle or whether it originates from the tires, engine, transmission, wheel bearings or road surface. Noise originating from other places cannot be corrected by servicing the rear axle.

ROAD NOISE

Brick or rough surfaced concrete roads produce noises that seem to come from the rear axle. Road noise is usually identical in Drive or Coast and driving on a different type of road will tell whether the road is the problem.

TIRE NOISE

Tire noise can be mistaken as rear axle noise, even though the tires on the front are at fault. Snow tread and mud tread tires or tires worn unevenly will frequently cause vibrations which seem to originate elsewhere; *temporarily, and for test purposes only,* inflate the tires to 40–50 lbs. This will significantly alter the noise produced by the tires, but will not alter noise from the rear axle. Noises from the rear axle will normally cease at speeds below 30 mph on coast, while tire noise will continue at lower tone as speed is decreased. The rear axle noise will usually change from drive conditions to coast conditions, while tire noise will not. Do not forget to lower the tire pressure to normal after the test is complete.

ENGINE/TRANSMISSION NOISE

Determine at what speed the noise is most pronounced, then stop in a quiet place. With the transmission in Neutral, run the engine through speeds corresponding to road speeds where the noise was noticed. Noises produced with the vehicle standing still are coming from the engine or transmission.

FRONT WHEEL BEARINGS

Front wheel bearing noises, sometimes confused with rear axle noises, will not change when comparing drive and coast conditions. While holding the speed steady, lightly apply the footbrake. This will often cause wheel bearing noise to lessen, as some of the weight is taken off the bearing. Front wheel bearings are easily checked by jacking up the wheels and spinning the wheels. Shaking the wheels will also determine if the wheel bearings are excessively loose.

REAR AXLE NOISES

Eliminating other possible sources can narrow the cause to the rear axle, which normally produces noise from worn gears or bearings. Gear noises tend to peak in a narrow speed range, while bearing noises will usually vary in pitch with engine speeds.

Noise Diagnosis

The Noise Is:	Most Probably Produced By:
1. Identical under Drive or Coast	Road surface, tires or front wheel bearings
2. Different depending on road surface	Road surface or tires
3. Lower as speed is lowered	Tires
4. Similar when standing or moving	Engine or transmission
5. A vibration	Unbalanced tires, rear wheel bearing, unbalanced driveshaft or worn U-joint
6. A knock or click about every two tire revolutions	Rear wheel bearing
7. Most pronounced on turns	Damaged differential gears
8. A steady low-pitched whirring or scraping, starting at low speeds	Damaged or worn pinion bearing
9. A chattering vibration on turns	Wrong differential lubricant or worn clutch plates (limited slip rear axle)
10. Noticed only in Drive, Coast or Float conditions	Worn ring gear and/or pinion gear

Troubleshooting Steering & Suspension Problems

Condition	Possible Cause
Hard steering (wheel is hard to turn)	1. Improper tire pressure 2. Loose or glazed pump drive belt 3. Low or incorrect fluid 4. Loose, bent or poorly lubricated front end parts 5. Improper front end alignment (excessive caster) 6. Bind in steering column or linkage 7. Kinked hydraulic hose 8. Air in hydraulic system 9. Low pump output or leaks in system 10. Obstruction in lines 11. Pump valves sticking or out of adjustment 12. Incorrect wheel alignment
Loose steering (too much play in steering wheel)	1. Loose wheel bearings 2. Faulty shocks 3. Worn linkage or suspension components 4. Loose steering gear mounting or linkage points 5. Steering mechanism worn or improperly adjusted 6. Valve spool improperly adjusted 7. Worn ball joints, tie-rod ends, etc.
Veers or wanders (pulls to one side with hands off steering wheel)	1. Improper tire pressure 2. Improper front end alignment 3. Dragging or improperly adjusted brakes 4. Bent frame 5. Improper rear end alignment 6. Faulty shocks or springs 7. Loose or bent front end components 8. Play in Pitman arm 9. Steering gear mountings loose 10. Loose wheel bearings 11. Binding Pitman arm 12. Spool valve sticking or improperly adjusted 13. Worn ball joints
Wheel oscillation or vibration transmitted through steering wheel	1. Low or uneven tire pressure 2. Loose wheel bearings 3. Improper front end alignment 4. Bent spindle 5. Worn, bent or broken front end components 6. Tires out of round or out of balance 7. Excessive lateral runout in disc brake rotor 8. Loose or bent shock absorber or strut
Noises (see also "Troubleshooting Drive Axle Problems")	1. Loose belts 2. Low fluid, air in system 3. Foreign matter in system 4. Improper lubrication 5. Interference or chafing in linkage 6. Steering gear mountings loose 7. Incorrect adjustment or wear in gear box 8. Faulty valves or wear in pump 9. Kinked hydraulic lines 10. Worn wheel bearings
Poor return of steering	1. Over-inflated tires 2. Improperly aligned front end (excessive caster) 3. Binding in steering column 4. No lubrication in front end 5. Steering gear adjusted too tight
Uneven tire wear (see "How To Read Tire Wear")	1. Incorrect tire pressure 2. Improperly aligned front end 3. Tires out-of-balance 4. Bent or worn suspension parts

HOW TO READ TIRE WEAR

The way your tires wear is a good indicator of other parts of the suspension. Abnormal wear patterns are often caused by the need for simple tire maintenance, or for front end alignment.

Excessive wear at the center of the tread indicates that the air pressure in the tire is consistently too high. The tire is riding on the center of the tread and wearing it prematurely. Occasionally, this wear pattern can result from outrageously wide tires on narrow rims. The cure for this is to replace either the tires or the wheels.

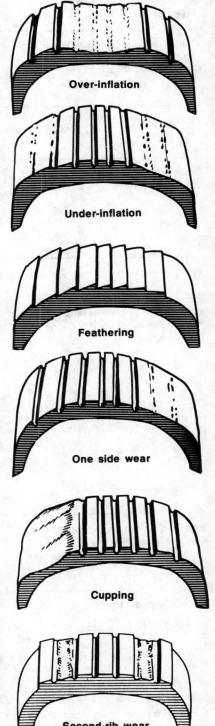

Over-inflation

This type of wear usually results from consistent under-inflation. When a tire is under-inflated, there is too much contact with the road by the outer treads, which wear prematurely. When this type of wear occurs, and the tire pressure is known to be consistently correct, a bent or worn steering component or the need for wheel alignment could be indicated.

Under-inflation

Feathering is a condition when the edge of each tread rib develops a slightly rounded edge on one side and a sharp edge on the other. By running your hand over the tire, you can usually feel the sharper edges before you'll be able to see them. The most common causes of feathering are incorrect toe-in setting or deteriorated bushings in the front suspension.

Feathering

When an inner or outer rib wears faster than the rest of the tire, the need for wheel alignment is indicated. There is excessive camber in the front suspension, causing the wheel to lean too much putting excessive load on one side of the tire. Misalignment could also be due to sagging springs, worn ball joints, or worn control arm bushings. Be sure the vehicle is loaded the way it's normally driven when you have the wheels aligned.

One side wear

Cups or scalloped dips appearing around the edge of the tread almost always indicate worn (sometimes bent) suspension parts. Adjustment of wheel alignment alone will seldom cure the problem. Any worn component that connects the wheel to the suspension can cause this type of wear. Occasionally, wheels that are out of balance will wear like this, but wheel imbalance usually shows up as bald spots between the outside edges and center of the tread.

Cupping

Second-rib wear is usually found only in radial tires, and appears where the steel belts end in relation to the tread. It can be kept to a minimum by paying careful attention to tire pressure and frequently rotating the tires. This is often considered normal wear but excessive amounts indicate that the tires are too wide for the wheels.

Second-rib wear

Troubleshooting Disc Brake Problems

Condition	Possible Cause
Noise—groan—brake noise emanating when slowly releasing brakes (creep-groan)	Not detrimental to function of disc brakes—no corrective action required. (This noise may be eliminated by slightly increasing or decreasing brake pedal efforts.)
Rattle—brake noise or rattle emanating at low speeds on rough roads, (front wheels only).	1. Shoe anti-rattle spring missing or not properly positioned. 2. Excessive clearance between shoe and caliper. 3. Soft or broken caliper seals. 4. Deformed or misaligned disc. 5. Loose caliper.
Scraping	1. Mounting bolts too long. 2. Loose wheel bearings. 3. Bent, loose, or misaligned splash shield.
Front brakes heat up during driving and fail to release	1. Operator riding brake pedal. 2. Stop light switch improperly adjusted. 3. Sticking pedal linkage. 4. Frozen or seized piston. 5. Residual pressure valve in master cylinder. 6. Power brake malfunction. 7. Proportioning valve malfunction.
Leaky brake caliper	1. Damaged or worn caliper piston seal. 2. Scores or corrosion on surface of cylinder bore.
Grabbing or uneven brake action—Brakes pull to one side	1. Causes listed under "Brakes Pull". 2. Power brake malfunction. 3. Low fluid level in master cylinder. 4. Air in hydraulic system. 5. Brake fluid, oil or grease on linings. 6. Unmatched linings. 7. Distorted brake pads. 8. Frozen or seized pistons. 9. Incorrect tire pressure. 10. Front end out of alignment. 11. Broken rear spring. 12. Brake caliper pistons sticking. 13. Restricted hose or line. 14. Caliper not in proper alignment to braking disc. 15. Stuck or malfunctioning metering valve. 16. Soft or broken caliper seals. 17. Loose caliper.
Brake pedal can be depressed without braking effect	1. Air in hydraulic system or improper bleeding procedure. 2. Leak past primary cup in master cylinder. 3. Leak in system. 4. Rear brakes out of adjustment. 5. Bleeder screw open.
Excessive pedal travel	1. Air, leak, or insufficient fluid in system or caliper. 2. Warped or excessively tapered shoe and lining assembly. 3. Excessive disc runout. 4. Rear brake adjustment required. 5. Loose wheel bearing adjustment. 6. Damaged caliper piston seal. 7. Improper brake fluid (boil). 8. Power brake malfunction. 9. Weak or soft hoses.

Troubleshooting Disc Brake Problems (cont.)

Condition	Possible Cause
Brake roughness or chatter (pedal pumping)	1. Excessive thickness variation of braking disc. 2. Excessive lateral runout of braking disc. 3. Rear brake drums out-of-round. 4. Excessive front bearing clearance.
Excessive pedal effort	1. Brake fluid, oil or grease on linings. 2. Incorrect lining. 3. Frozen or seized pistons. 4. Power brake malfunction. 5. Kinked or collapsed hose or line. 6. Stuck metering valve. 7. Scored caliper or master cylinder bore. 8. Seized caliper pistons.
Brake pedal fades (pedal travel increases with foot on brake)	1. Rough master cylinder or caliper bore. 2. Loose or broken hydraulic lines/connections. 3. Air in hydraulic system. 4. Fluid level low. 5. Weak or soft hoses. 6. Inferior quality brake shoes or fluid. 7. Worn master cylinder piston cups or seals.

Troubleshooting Drum Brakes

Condition	Possible Cause
Pedal goes to floor	1. Fluid low in reservoir. 2. Air in hydraulic system. 3. Improperly adjusted brake. 4. Leaking wheel cylinders. 5. Loose or broken brake lines. 6. Leaking or worn master cylinder. 7. Excessively worn brake lining.
Spongy brake pedal	1. Air in hydraulic system. 2. Improper brake fluid (low boiling point). 3. Excessively worn or cracked brake drums. 4. Broken pedal pivot bushing.
Brakes pulling	1. Contaminated lining. 2. Front end out of alignment. 3. Incorrect brake adjustment. 4. Unmatched brake lining. 5. Brake drums out of round. 6. Brake shoes distorted. 7. Restricted brake hose or line. 8. Broken rear spring. 9. Worn brake linings. 10. Uneven lining wear. 11. Glazed brake lining. 12. Excessive brake lining dust. 13. Heat spotted brake drums. 14. Weak brake return springs. 15. Faulty automatic adjusters. 16. Low or incorrect tire pressure.

Condition	Possible Cause
Squealing brakes	1. Glazed brake lining. 2. Saturated brake lining. 3. Weak or broken brake shoe retaining spring. 4. Broken or weak brake shoe return spring. 5. Incorrect brake lining. 6. Distorted brake shoes. 7. Bent support plate. 8. Dust in brakes or scored brake drums. 9. Linings worn below limit. 10. Uneven brake lining wear. 11. Heat spotted brake drums.
Chirping brakes	1. Out of round drum or eccentric axle flange pilot.
Dragging brakes	1. Incorrect wheel or parking brake adjustment. 2. Parking brakes engaged or improperly adjusted. 3. Weak or broken brake shoe return spring. 4. Brake pedal binding. 5. Master cylinder cup sticking. 6. Obstructed master cylinder relief port. 7. Saturated brake lining. 8. Bent or out of round brake drum. 9. Contaminated or improper brake fluid. 10. Sticking wheel cylinder pistons. 11. Driver riding brake pedal. 12. Defective proportioning valve. 13. Insufficient brake shoe lubricant.
Hard pedal	1. Brake booster inoperative. 2. Incorrect brake lining. 3. Restricted brake line or hose. 4. Frozen brake pedal linkage. 5. Stuck wheel cylinder. 6. Binding pedal linkage. 7. Faulty proportioning valve.
Wheel locks	1. Contaminated brake lining. 2. Loose or torn brake lining. 3. Wheel cylinder cups sticking. 4. Incorrect wheel bearing adjustment. 5. Faulty proportioning valve.
Brakes fade (high speed)	1. Incorrect lining. 2. Overheated brake drums. 3. Incorrect brake fluid (low boiling temperature). 4. Saturated brake lining. 5. Leak in hydraulic system. 6. Faulty automatic adjusters.
Pedal pulsates	1. Bent or out of round brake drum.
Brake chatter and shoe knock	1. Out of round brake drum. 2. Loose support plate. 3. Bent support plate. 4. Distorted brake shoes. 5. Machine grooves in contact face of brake drum (Shoe Knock). 6. Contaminated brake lining. 7. Missing or loose components. 8. Incorrect lining material. 9. Out-of-round brake drums. 10. Heat spotted or scored brake drums. 11. Out-of-balance wheels.

Troubleshooting Drum Brakes (cont.)

Condition	Possible Cause
Brakes do not self adjust	1. Adjuster screw frozen in thread. 2. Adjuster screw corroded at thrust washer. 3. Adjuster lever does not engage star wheel. 4. Adjuster installed on wrong wheel.
Brake light glows	1. Leak in the hydraulic system. 2. Air in the system. 3. Improperly adjusted master cylinder pushrod. 4. Uneven lining wear. 5. Failure to center combination valve or proportioning valve.

Appendix

General Conversion Table

Multiply by	To convert	To	
2.54	Inches	Centimeters	.3937
30.48	Feet	Centimeters	.0328
.914	Yards	Meters	1.094
1.609	Miles	Kilometers	.621
6.45	Square inches	Square cm.	.155
.836	Square yards	Square meters	1.196
16.39	Cubic inches	Cubic cm.	.061
28.3	Cubic feet	Liters	.0353
.4536	Pounds	Kilograms	2.2045
3.785	Gallons	Liters	.264
.068	Lbs./sq. in. (psi)	Atmospheres	14.7
.138	Foot pounds	Kg. m.	7.23
1.014	H.P. (DIN)	H.P. (SAE)	.9861
—	To obtain	From	Multiply by

Note: 1 cm. equals 10 mm.; 1 mm. equals .0394".

Conversion—Common Fractions to Decimals and Millimeters

Common Fractions	Decimal Fractions	Millimeters (approx.)	Common Fractions	Decimal Fractions	Millimeters (approx.)	Common Fractions	Decimal Fractions	Millimeters (approx.)
1/128	.008	0.20	11/32	.344	8.73	43/64	.672	17.07
1/64	.016	0.40	23/64	.359	9.13	11/16	.688	17.46
1/32	.031	0.79	3/8	.375	9.53	45/64	.703	17.86
3/64	.047	1.19	25/64	.391	9.92	23/32	.719	18.26
1/16	.063	1.59	13/32	.406	10.32	47/64	.734	18.65
5/64	.078	1.98	27/64	.422	10.72	3/4	.750	19.05
3/32	.094	2.38	7/16	.438	11.11	49/64	.766	19.45
7/64	.109	2.78	29/64	.453	11.51	25/32	.781	19.84
1/8	.125	3.18	15/32	.469	11.91	51/64	.797	20.24
9/64	.141	3.57	31/64	.484	12.30	13/16	.813	20.64
5/32	.156	3.97	1/2	.500	12.70	53/64	.828	21.03
11/64	.172	4.37	33/64	.516	13.10	27/32	.844	21.43
3/16	.188	4.76	17/32	.531	13.49	55/64	.859	21.83
13/64	.203	5.16	35/64	.547	13.89	7/8	.875	22.23
7/32	.219	5.56	9/16	.563	14.29	57/64	.891	22.62
15/64	.234	5.95	37/64	.578	14.68	29/32	.906	23.02
1/4	.250	6.35	19/32	.594	15.08	59/64	.922	23.42
17/64	.266	6.75	39/64	.609	15.48	15/16	.938	23.81
9/32	.281	7.14	5/8	.625	15.88	61/64	.953	24.21
19/64	.297	7.54	41/64	.641	16.27	31/32	.969	24.61
5/16	.313	7.94	21/32	.656	16.67	63/64	.984	25.00
21/64	.328	8.33						

Conversion—Millimeters to Decimal Inches

mm	inches	mm	inches	mm	inches	mm	inches	mm	inches
1	.039 370	31	1.220 470	61	2.401 570	91	3.582 670	210	8.267 700
2	.078 740	32	1.259 840	62	2.440 940	92	3.622 040	220	8.661 400
3	.118 110	33	1.299 210	63	2.480 310	93	3.661 410	230	9.055 100
4	.157 480	34	1.338 580	64	2.519 680	94	3.700 780	240	9.448 800
5	.196 850	35	1.377 949	65	2.559 050	95	3.740 150	250	9.842 500
6	.236 220	36	1.417 319	66	2.598 420	96	3.779 520	260	10.236 200
7	.275 590	37	1.456 689	67	2.637 790	97	3.818 890	270	10.629 900
8	.314 960	38	1.496 050	68	2.677 160	98	3.858 260	280	11.032 600
9	.354 330	39	1.535 430	69	2.716 530	99	3.897 630	290	11.417 300
10	.393 700	40	1.574 800	70	2.755 900	100	3.937 000	300	11.811 000
11	.433 070	41	1.614 170	71	2.795 270	105	4.133 848	310	12.204 700
12	.472 440	42	1.653 540	72	2.834 640	110	4.330 700	320	12.598 400
13	.511 810	43	1.692 910	73	2.874 010	115	4.527 550	330	12.992 100
14	.551 180	44	1.732 280	74	2.913 380	120	4.724 400	340	13.385 800
15	.590 550	45	1.771 650	75	2.952 750	125	4.921 250	350	13.779 500
16	.629 920	46	1.811 020	76	2.992 120	130	5.118 100	360	14.173 200
17	.669 290	47	1.850 390	77	3.031 490	135	5.314 950	370	14.566 900
18	.708 660	48	1.889 760	78	3.070 860	140	5.511 800	380	14.960 600
19	.748 030	49	1.929 130	79	3.110 230	145	5.708 650	390	15.354 300
20	.787 400	50	1.968 500	80	3.149 600	150	5.905 500	400	15.748 000
21	.826 770	51	2.007 870	81	3.188 970	155	6.102 350	500	19.685 000
22	.866 140	52	2.047 240	82	3.228 340	160	6.299 200	600	23.622 000
23	.905 510	53	2.086 610	83	3.267 710	165	6.496 050	700	27.559 000
24	.944 880	54	2.125 980	84	3.307 080	170	6.692 900	800	31.496 000
25	.984 250	55	2.165 350	85	3.346 450	175	6.889 750	900	35.433 000
26	1.023 620	56	2.204 720	86	3.385 820	180	7.086 600	1000	39.370 000
27	1.062 990	57	2.244 090	87	3.425 190	185	7.283 450	2000	78.740 000
28	1.102 360	58	2.283 460	88	3.464 560	190	7.480 300	3000	118.110 000
29	1.141 730	59	2.322 830	89	3.503 903	195	7.677 150	4000	157.480 000
30	1.181 100	60	2.362 200	90	3.543 300	200	7.874 000	5000	196.850 000

To change decimal millimeters to decimal inches, position the decimal point where desired on either side of the millimeter measurement shown and reset the inches decimal by the same number of digits in the same direction. For example, to convert 0.001 mm to decimal inches, reset the decimal behind the 1 mm (shown on the chart) to 0.001; change the decimal inch equivalent (0.039″ shown) to 0.000039″.

Tap Drill Sizes

Screw & Tap Size	National Fine or S.A.E. Threads Per Inch	Use Drill Number
No. 5	44	37
No. 6	40	33
No. 8	36	29
No. 10	32	21
No. 12	28	15
1/4	28	3
5/16	24	1
3/8	24	Q
7/16	20	W
1/2	20	29/64
9/16	18	33/64
5/8	18	37/64
3/4	16	11/16
7/8	14	13/16
1 1/8	12	1 3/64
1 1/4	12	1 11/64
1 1/2	12	1 27/64

Tap Drill Sizes

Screw & Tap Size	National Coarse or U.S.S. Threads Per Inch	Use Drill Number
No. 5	40	39
No. 6	32	36
No. 8	32	29
No. 10	24	25
No. 12	24	17
1/4	20	8
5/16	18	F
3/8	16	5/16
7/16	14	U
1/2	13	27/64
9/16	12	31/64
5/8	11	17/32
3/4	10	21/32
7/8	9	49/64
1	8	7/8
1 1/8	7	63/64
1 1/4	7	1 7/64
1 1/2	6	1 11/32

Decimal Equivalent Size of the Number Drills

Drill No.	Decimal Equivalent	Drill No.	Decimal Equivalent	Drill No.	Decimal Equivalent
80	.0135	53	.0595	26	.1470
79	.0145	52	.0635	25	.1495
78	.0160	51	.0670	24	.1520
77	.0180	50	.0700	23	.1540
76	.0200	49	.0730	22	.1570
75	.0210	48	.0760	21	.1590
74	.0225	47	.0785	20	.1610
73	.0240	46	.0810	19	.1660
72	.0250	45	.0820	18	.1695
71	.0260	44	.0860	17	.1730
70	.0280	43	.0890	16	.1770
69	.0292	42	.0935	15	.1800
68	.0310	41	.0960	14	.1820
67	.0320	40	.0980	13	.1850
66	.0330	39	.0995	12	.1890
65	.0350	38	.1015	11	.1910
64	.0360	37	.1040	10	.1935
63	.0370	36	.1065	9	.1960
62	.0380	35	.1100	8	.1990
61	.0390	34	.1110	7	.2010
60	.0400	33	.1130	6	.2040
59	.0410	32	.1160	5	.2055
58	.0420	31	.1200	4	.2090
57	.0430	30	.1285	3	.2130
56	.0465	29	.1360	2	.2210
55	.0520	28	.1405	1	.2280
54	.0550	27	.1440		

Decimal Equivalent Size of the Letter Drills

Letter Drill	Decimal Equivalent	Letter Drill	Decimal Equivalent	Letter Drill	Decimal Equivalent
A	.234	J	.277	S	.348
B	.238	K	.281	T	.358
C	.242	L	.290	U	.368
D	.246	M	.295	V	.377
E	.250	N	.302	W	.386
F	.257	O	.316	X	.397
G	.261	P	.323	Y	.404
H	.266	Q	.332	Z	.413
I	.272	R	.339		

Anti-Freeze Chart

Temperatures Shown in Degrees Fahrenheit +32 is Freezing

Cooling System Capacity Quarts	Quarts of ETHYLENE GLYCOL Needed for Protection to Temperatures Shown Below													
	1	2	3	4	5	6	7	8	9	10	11	12	13	14
10	+24°	+16°	+ 4°	−12°	−34°	−62°								
11	+25	+18	+ 8	− 6	−23	−47								
12	+26	+19	+10	0	−15	−34	−57°							
13	+27	+21	+13	+ 3	− 9	−25	−45							
14			+15	+ 6	− 5	−18	−34							
15			+16	+ 8	0	−12	−26							
16			+17	+10	+ 2	− 8	−19	−34	−52°					
17			+18	+12	+ 5	− 4	−14	−27	−42					
18			+19	+14	+ 7	0	−10	−21	−34	−50°				
19			+20	+15	+ 9	+ 2	− 7	−16	−28	−42				
20				+16	+10	+ 4	− 3	−12	−22	−34	−48°			
21				+17	+12	+ 6	0	− 9	−17	−28	−41			
22				+18	+13	+ 8	+ 2	− 6	−14	−23	−34	−47°		
23				+19	+14	+ 9	+ 4	− 3	−10	−19	−29	−40		
24				+19	+15	+10	+ 5	0	− 8	−15	−23	−34	−46°	
25				+20	+16	+12	+ 7	+ 1	− 5	−12	−20	−29	−40	−50°
26					+17	+13	+ 8	+ 3	− 3	− 9	−16	−25	−34	−44
27					+18	+14	+ 9	+ 5	− 1	− 7	−13	−21	−29	−39
28					+18	+15	+10	+ 6	+ 1	− 5	−11	−18	−25	−34
29					+19	+16	+12	+ 7	+ 2	− 3	− 8	−15	−22	−29
30					+20	+17	+13	+ 8	+ 4	− 1	− 6	−12	−18	−25

For capacities over 30 quarts divide true capacity by 3. Find quarts Anti-Freeze for the ⅓ and multiply by 3 for quarts to add.

For capacities under 10 quarts multiply true capacity by 3. Find quarts Anti-Freeze for the tripled volume and divide by 3 for quarts to add.

To Increase the Freezing Protection of Anti-Freeze Solutions Already Installed

Cooling System Capacity Quarts	Number of Quarts of ETHYLENE GLYCOL Anti-Freeze Required to Increase Protection												
	From +20° F. to					From +10° F. to					From 0° F. to			
	0°	−10°	−20°	−30°	−40°	0°	−10°	−20°	−30°	−40°	−10°	−20°	−30°	−40°
10	1¾	2¼	3	3½	3¾	¾	1½	2¼	2¾	3¼	¾	1½	2	2½
12	2	2¾	3½	4	4½	1	1¾	2½	3¼	3¾	1	1¾	2½	3¼
14	2¼	3¼	4	4¾	5½	1¼	2	3	3¾	4½	1	2	3	3½
16	2½	3½	4½	5¼	6	1¼	2½	3½	4¼	5¼	1¼	2¼	3¼	4
18	3	4	5	6	7	1½	2¾	4	5	5¾	1½	2½	3¾	4¾
20	3¼	4½	5¾	6¾	7½	1¾	3	4¼	5½	6½	1½	2¾	4¼	5¼
22	3½	5	6¼	7¼	8¼	1¾	3¼	4¾	6	7¼	1¾	3¼	4½	5½
24	4	5½	7	8	9	2	3½	5	6½	7½	1¾	3½	5	6
26	4¼	6	7½	8¾	10	2	4	5½	7	8¼	2	3¾	5½	6¾
28	4½	6¼	8	9½	10½	2¼	4¼	6	7½	9	2	4	5¾	7¼
30	5	6¾	8½	10	11½	2½	4½	6½	8	9½	2¼	4¼	6¼	7¾

Test radiator solution with proper hydrometer. Determine from the table the number of quarts of solution to be drawn off from a full cooling system and replace with undiluted anti-freeze, to give the desired increased protection. For example, to increase protection of a 22-quart cooling system containing Ethylene Glycol (permanent type) anti-freeze, from +20° F. to −20° F. will require the replacement of 6¼ quarts of solution with undiluted anti-freeze.

Index